S0-AJD-086

International Mergers and Acquisitions

In memory of my mother

International Mergers and Acquisitions

TERENCE E. COOKE

in association with
Arthur Young International

Basil Blackwell

First published 1988

Basil Blackwell Ltd
108 Cowley Road, Oxford, OX4 1JF, UK

Basil Blackwell Inc.
432 Park Avenue South, Suite 1503
New York, NY 10016, USA

British Library Cataloguing in Publication Data
Cooke, Terence E.
International mergers and acquisitions.
1. International business enterprises
2. Consolidation and merger of corporations
I. Title II. Arthur Young International
338.8′81 HD2755.5

ISBN 0-631-14748-9

Library of Congress Cataloging in Publication Data
International mergers and acquisitions/(Edited by) Terence E. Cooke in association with Arthur Young International.
p. cm.
Includes bibliographies and index.
ISBN 0-631-14748-9
1. Consolidation and merger of corporations. 2. International business enterprises—Deregulation. I. Cooke, Terrence E., 1952–
II. Arthur Young International.
HD2746.5.157 1988 87-29364
338.8′81—dc19 CIP

Typeset in 10 on 11 pt Times
by Photo·graphics, Honiton, Devon, England
Printed in Great Britain by TJ Press, Padstow

Contents

List of Contributors

The following member firms and individuals of Arthur Young International have assisted with the review and provision of information for various chapters of the book:

Argentina	Arthur Young
Australia	Arthur Young
Brazil	Arthur Young Clarkson Gordon & Co.
Canada	Arthur Young Clarkson Gordon & Co.
France	HSD
Germany	Schitag Schwabische Treuhand AG
Hong Kong	Arthur Young
Italy	Arthur Young
Japan	Arthur Young
Malaya	Arthur Young
Netherlands	Moret & Limperg
Nigeria	Arthur Young, Osindero & Moret
Sweden	Hagstrom & Sillen
South Africa	Arthur Young
U.K.	Arthur Young
U.S.A.	Arthur Young

Arthur Young International

Preface

This is a technical book on major issues affecting mergers and acquisitions in different countries and is a follow-up to *Mergers and Acquisitions* (Basil Blackwell, 1986). It would be impossible to cover the major issues exhaustively in the 16 countries covered in this international book. Rather the book is a first reference source to highlight key issues: it should not be relied on for investment purposes, nor is it a substitute for professional advice.

The text deals with mergers and acquisitions, including business organizations and types of business combinations; trends in takeover activity; merger control; significant taxation implications; accounting implications of business combinations, and a comparison between national accounting practices and international accounting standards; and exchange control and foreign investment regulations. Not all the issues are equally important for all countries; each contributor has made a judgement as to their importance.

I hope that the book will prove useful to practitioners, corporate executives, and students and academics interested in extending their knowledge on mergers and acquisitions and gaining from the international nature of this book. In particular, since the issues are dealt with on a country-by-country basis it will enable comparative analysis to be undertaken.

My role in this project was to initiate the idea, edit the whole book, write chapters 1–5, 12 and 13, and prepare the appendix and index. I would like to thank Professor M. Kikuya, Dr. R. Wallace and Mr. G.B. Enriga for their substantial contributions to the material on Japan, Nigeria and Hong Kong respectively. I am grateful to members of Arthur Young International for their contributions to the rest of the book and for their comments on the manuscript. I would also like to thank others who supplied information for this book and Tony Sweeney of Basil Blackwell for his sound advice. Last, but not least, I am grateful to my wife and children who have borne the brunt of my involvement in a number of research projects.

T. E. Cooke
Department of Economics
University of Exeter

Part I

BACKGROUND

1

Introduction

This book is concerned with the international aspects of mergers and acquisitions. In this introductory chapter an explanation is given for the choice of countries included in this study, the features which distinguish national from cross-border transactions are described and a review of the motives for international investment is provided.

Part I sets the scene by providing an outline of the theoretical and practical considerations involved in direct foreign investment and considers deregulation in capital markets, the growth of multinational enterprises (MNEs) and country risk analysis. Part I also contains a summary of the country studies that are included in Part II. The aim of the summary chapter is not to foreshadow the text contained in the country studies but rather to highlight important areas of interest and their background, and to emphasize particular differences in treatment. In addition, the chapter provides some detail on areas which are common to many of the countries included in this study such as EEC merger control and international accounting standards.

CHOICE OF COUNTRY STUDIES

In choosing which countries should be included here the main requirement was that merger and acquisition activity should be of some economic significance. Since activity tends to predominate in countries with significant stock exchanges, it is not surprising that the top eleven 'countries' (Hong Kong is not a country but a British Crown Colony which is currently administered by Britain although, from 1 July 1997, its status changes to become a Special Administrative Region of China). with major stock exchanges all met the economic significance criterion. Table 1.1 lists the top fifteen major stock exchanges in the world in terms of turnover. It shows that total value of turnover has increased by over 1442 per cent between 1974 and 1986.

Each of the top eleven 'countries', with the exception of Hong Kong, has a separate chapter. Changes in Hong Kong's status may make foreign

Table 1.1 Turnover on major stock exchanges

			Total value of turnover in US $ billion			*% of total*	
			1986	*1984*	*1974*	*1986*	*1974*
1.	USA	New York S.E.	1373.8	755.9	99.2	47.8	53.2
2.	Japan	Tokyo 1st section	954.2	267.1	41.6	33.2	22.3
3.	UK	London	133.3	48.4	14.8	4.6	7.9
4.	FRG	All exchanges	136.1	29.7	5.1	4.7	2.8
5.	Canada	All exchanges	57.3	25.3	6.3	2.0	3.4
6.	Netherlands	Amsterdam	29.8	11.9	1.9	1.0	1.0
7.	Australia	All exchanges	26.8	10.8	0.8	0.9	0.4
8.	France	Paris	56.1	10.2	5.3	1.9	2.8
9.	Sweden	Stockholm	20.0	8.5	0.5	0.7	0.3
10.	Hong Kong	All exchanges	14.5	6.2	2.2	0.5	1.2
11.	Italy	Milan	44.9	3.8	3.3	1.6	1.8
12.	Singapore/Malaysia	All exchanges	5.0	6.5	0.5	0.2	0.3[b]
13.	Spain	Main exchanges[b]	15.9	2.7	3.7	0.6	2.0
14.	Belgium	Brussels	6.6	2.7	1.2	0.2	0.6
15.	Denmark	Copenhagen	1.9	0.2	0.1	0.1	–
	Total major stock market		2876.2	1189.9	186.5	100	100

[a] Singapore only.
[b] Prior to 1983 the turnover includes the shares traded in *corredores de commercio*.

investors somewhat wary of taking over local businesses but it was considered to be of sufficient importance to be included in chapter 14 on 'other countries'. This chapter provides a flavour of the important issues affecting merger activity in a number of other countries. Two were selected from South America (Argentina and Brazil), two from Africa (Nigeria and South Africa), and two from South-East Asia (Malaysia and Hong Kong). The criterion here was that foreign direct investment in each country should be of some economic significance.

DIFFERENCES BETWEEN NATIONAL TRANSACTIONS AND CROSS-BORDER TRANSACTIONS

Foreign direct investment may take a number of different forms including:

1. The establishment of a new enterprise in an overseas country (either a branch or subsidiary).
2. The expansion of an existing branch or subsidiary.
3. The acquisition of a business enterprise or its assets.

Whatever type of foreign direct investment is contemplated a whole new range of decisions must be made which do not have a domestic counterpart, including:

1. The raising of funds in one market for investment in another country. For instance, in the financial accounts of Electrolux in 1984 the company highlights the raising of funds in London to be used primarily for investment in the US.
2. Additional complexities of exchange rate changes on the value of assets.
3. The dangers that even if the project is successful, a foreign government may not have sufficient foreign exchange to permit the remittance of capital, dividends, interest, fees or royalties.
4. The complexities of assessing the economic and political framework of the host country and the probability of changes in that environment.
5. The danger of expropriation of assets by a foreign government.
6. Managing businesses which are a considerable distance away from head office. This involves a consideration of whether local management should be left to its own devices or whether the parent company should send a senior executive to control the organization. Such problems are not uncommon for multinational enterprises investing in the US. For example, in the summer of 1986 BP despatched a senior executive to the US after the parent company had become concerned about its US subsidiary, Standard Oil Company.
7. Tax complications, including discrimination against cross-border transactions. Discrimination may include designating a transaction as not 'tax-free' – a status sometimes afforded to domestic transactions.

The parent company will need to assess the taxation affects of transactions on a global basis since what may be tax-efficient for the subsidiary may be tax-inefficient for the parent company.

8. The problems of assessing financial information on a global basis which involves understanding many different accounting practices which may lead to integration and reporting problems.
9. The problem of investing in a country which has substantial government control over foreign investment. Other regulatory problems may occur involving the anti-trust and monopoly authorities.
10. Specific exchange control regulations constraining cross-border transactions.
11. Problems generated by operating in an overseas country such as language, customs and communications.
12. Legal barriers between countries which make it difficult to integrate an overseas investment successfully.
13. A consideration of which capital markets to raise funds from.
14. A consideration of debt/equity ratios (thin capitalization) which may be imposed by foreign governments.

These fourteen points are a summary of some of the factors which must be borne in mind when contemplating foreign direct investment. The list is not exhaustive but helps to outline the importance of a full and detailed analysis of not only the target company but also the host country.

If so many additional complexities arise from foreign direct investment why do domestic companies bother to become multinational?

MOTIVES FOR FOREIGN DIRECT INVESTMENT

Cooke (1986) gives a summary of motives for domestic acquisitions. Even at the domestic level motives are complex and multivariate, and this is all the greater in cross-border transactions. Here we give a brief review of some of the motives and theories that have been put forward to explain foreign direct investment decisions of MNEs. Motives for direct foreign investment may be classified as strategic, behavioural or economic. Whilst this classification is useful, some of the factors may not be readily allocated since motives are often interrelated.

Strategic motives

Imperfections and locational factors

One of the motives for foreign direct investment may be explained by the product life-cycle hypothesis. This hypothesis is based on the concept that most products go through a number of clearly defined stages from introduction into the market, to their eventual withdrawal as they are replaced by new, improved products.

Vernon's early theory (1966) suggested that expensive research to develop new products is undertaken in the most advanced countries whose citizens have sufficient income to be able to demand the new product. Once developed, the product is introduced into the home market and, as demand increases, it enters the growth stage in which the product is improved and standardized, and economies of scale gained. As production increases, new export markets are opened. The success of exports encourages domestic companies in host countries to enter the market, with the consequence that the corporation from the advanced country needs to set up local production facilities to gain any advantages that an indigenous producer may possess. The motive for foreign direct investment at this stage is defensive. However, the product will eventually move into the maturity stage in which the growth rate begins to decline as there is a diminishing number of potential customers. Competition from new products occurs and competition for market share takes place with the consequence that margins are squeezed. Price competition is often severe so that the labour-intensive stages of production are undertaken, via foreign direct investment, in less well-developed countries where labour is cheapest.

The simple model first proposed by Vernon tried to explain US investment in other advanced countries with production located in low labour cost countries. However, the simple model failed to explain the growth of European and Japanese multinationals. As a result, the model was refined in 1977 and emphasis was placed on the necessity for an oligopolistic market structure. Different methods are used by MNEs to create and maintain oligopoly which were classified by Vernon into three different competitive devices:

Innovation-based oligopoly

Companies classified into this category normally spend considerable sums on research to develop new products and differentiate existing ones. Products are developed initially for the home market but local needs often exist overseas as well. An example of a company in this category is Matsushita Electric, Japan's largest electronic company. Due to trade friction, demands for protectionism in overseas markets and the problem of providing a good after-sales service in high-technology products, the company is aiming to reduce its export ratio and raise its overseas production ratio. The aim of the company is for 50 per cent domestic sales, 25 per cent exports and 25 per cent overseas production. The last will be achieved by 'greenfield investments' but perhaps also by acquisition.

Mature oligopoly

Mature MNEs obtain cost advantages from economies of large-scale production including a considerable decrease in costs as a result of learning effects. To ensure that the company remains internationally competitive it may be necessary to attack potential rivals in their local markets as well as in other potential markets. Examples include televisions and video recorders. The product need not be the most technically advanced but must be reliable and affordable. For instance, when video recorders were being developed, Japanese manufacturers concentrated their efforts on developing the VHS system, whereas in Europe, Grundig and Philips developed the 2000 series. The VHS system was a more reliable product but the European system produced better picture quality. Japanese manufacturers swamped the European market with VHS recorders so much so that it did not seem commercially viable to record films on the 2000 series. Eventually Grundig and Philips were forced to cease production of the 2000 series and move to the VHS system.

In order to prevent instability by price-cutting and promotional activity when demand slackens, MNEs develop strategies aimed at encouraging co-operation. Such strategies include follow-the-leader behaviour in entering new countries or developing new product lines; joint ventures amongst the oligopolists; tacit price collusion; and cross investment. An example of joint ventures amongst oligopolists can be seen from manufacturers of telecommunications equipment. Table 1.2 shows the leading manufacturers of telecommunications equipment based on sales in 1984. Fujitsu has a long history of joint ventures which started in 1935 when the company was formed. At the inception of the company technical assistance was given to Siemens. Co-operation has continued and now extends to supplying large-scale computers for distribution by the German company. In 1981, Fujitsu signed an agreement with International Computers Limited (ICL) of the UK to supply LSI technology and very large-scale computers to the European market through ICL's sales network. Since then ICL has been using Fujitsu technology to develop new ICL mainframes.

Table 1.2 Leading manufacturers of telecommunications equipment

Rank	*Company*	*Sales 1984 £ billion*
1	AT & T (US)	7.59
2	ITT (US)	3.50
3	Siemens (FRG)	2.53
4	N. Telecom (Canada)	2.46
5	L.M. Ericsson (Sweden)	2.38
6	NEC (Japan)	2.01
7	Alcatel-Thomson (France)	1.93
8	GTE (US)	1.71
9	Philips (Netherlands)	0.89
10	GEC (UK)	0.75
11	Fujitsu (Japan)	0.74
12	Plessey (UK)	0.68

Source: GEC evidence to the Monopolies and Mergers Commission

Tacit price collusion is another way of avoiding destabilization in a market but problems can be encountered from the regulatory authorities. For instance, in April 1986 the European Commission imposed fines totalling Ecu 58 million on the top fifteen European manufacturers of polypropylene although all but one has appealed to the European Court of Justice in Luxembourg. The Commission claimed that twice-monthly meetings were held, to set target prices, to attempt to raise prices and to implement a mandatory system of annual quotas.

Senescent oligopoly

Due to standardization of the product and widespread dissemination of the technological base barriers to entry become eroded. New geographical markets are entered and product differentiation and the formation of cartels may occur. Old products are dropped and new products are developed.

To a large extent Vernon's work has been superseded because of the growth in global competition between experienced firms. Vernon's model proved a very useful attempt at explaining corporate strategies and its weaknesses serve to demonstrate the dynamic focus of the growth of MNEs. The hypothesis also proved to be an interesting alternative to the simple notion that MNEs are able to invest abroad and compete with domestic enterprises because all possess advantages over domestic companies. Such an approach was associated with Hymer (1976) and Kindleberger (1969). The fact that an overseas company can successfully invest in other countries was tantamount to saying that imperfections exist between national and international markets for products and factors of production.

In an article entitled 'The Demise of the Product Cycle Model in International Business Theory', Ian Giddy (1978) again lays emphasis on the fact that most, if not all, MNEs are oligopolists. A national oligopolist can only become a global oligopolist by transferring the source of their domestic advantage to overseas markets. Whatever advantage the company has it must be unique to itself if national firms are not to take advantage of better knowledge of their domestic market. Giddy describes this process as 'internalizing markets across national boundaries'.

This process of internalization has been further refined by Buckley and Casson (1976) and Dunning (1977). The basis of the thory is that MNEs have firm-specific competitive advantages in the form of intangible capital such as goodwill, patents, trademarks, marketing and distribution skills or organizational abilities. Dunning (1981) has proposed an eclectic theory of international production which attempts to link firm-specific advantages with host country characteristics. These locational factors include the cost and availability of key factors of production, particularly labour; the size and character of the domestic market; and government policy with respect to innovation, protection of property rights and competition. An interesting example of the importance of locational factors is the Iberian peninsula. Foreign investment in Portugal in 1985 was approximately $250 million

– a 30 per cent increase on the 1984 level. A locational advantage is that labour is cheap, certainly one of the cheapest in the EEC and possibly below rates in some Asian manufacturing countries. It has been estimated that labour costs in Portugal are about 40 per cent of those of Spain and yet investment in Spain in 1985 was over $3 billion. What locational disadvantages might Portugal have compared with Spain? A number of reasons have been put forward which include: a small domestic market with low consumer purchasing power; short-lived and inconsistent governments; and bureaucratic delays. It seems fairly clear that not only must an MNE have firm-specific advantages which it can translate to other markets, but that its foreign direct investment is also determined by locational factors.

Diversification

An alternative theory of the MNE is based on diversification in order to smooth earnings. Products are diversified geographically and income is thereby earned in a variety of different currencies. As a result of restrictions in capital markets a company can undertake international diversification that cannot be replicated by shareholders. Whether an MNE can achieve superior results is an empirical question which has not been finally resolved although there is some evidence that this is indeed the case (Rugman, 1981). If it is correct a question relevant to the future is that, if capital market imperfections decline (a process which will be outlined in chapter 2), will MNEs be able to continue to earn superior returns? Whatever the evidence it is clear that MNEs diversify by product and by region, and that the objective of stabilizing earnings is an international rather than national motive. For example, in the late 1970s the Board of Management Report for Volkswagen stated that one of its objects was the assurance of continued profitability through involvement in growth areas whose business cycle is anticyclical to that of the automobile industry. It is not difficult to cite many other MNEs who pursue a policy of diversification in an attempt to reduce risks.

Other strategic motives

Other strategic reasons have been classified by Hogue (1967) into the following four areas:

1. market seekers
2. raw material seekers
3. knowledge seekers
4. production efficiency seekers

Market seekers produce abroad because a local market exists for their products. There are many examples of this in the automobile industry for instance, and the strategies of Ford, General Motors, Volkswagen and Volvo can all be included. An example of this being achieved by acquisition is VW's acquisition of Seat, the Spanish automobile manufacturer, from the government in 1986. Prior to 1980 Fiat had provided technical assistance to Seat to fill a technological gap, but the agreement was terminated after industrial differences arose. VW moved in and sees Spain as one of the last substantially closed markets in Western Europe with the protection of transitional arrangements as Spain moves to become a fully integrated member of the EEC.

The market selling objective is one of the key advantages of investing in the US with its large homogeneous market with high consumer orientation. In comparison, markets in Europe are small, saturated and highly competitive and suffer from differences in language, culture and the vagaries of differing governments. These reasons are often cited as impediments to further investment in Europe by US MNEs.

Raw material seekers operate in any part of the world where minerals can be found. For instance, there is a considerable presence of UK and US firms in Australia, Canada and South Africa. Such activities may be reciprocal. Witness, for instance, the considerable presence of US firms in the exploration of North Sea oil, and BP in exploring for oil in Alaska.

Knowledge seekers operate to gain access to technology or managerial ability. For example, in 1985 the Italian MNE, Pirelli, acquired several companies in the UK and US which specialize in fibre optic communications.

Production efficiency seekers produce in countries where a vital production factor is cheap relative to its productivity. For example, in response to the rapidly appreciating yen, Aiwa, the Japanese consumer electronics group, has moved most of its productive capacity to Singapore.

Behavioural motives

Aharoni (1966) studied the investment strategy of US MNEs in considering whether to locate in Israel. The study emphasizes the interaction between the motives of management and the external environment. The motives of a corporate organization is a reflection of the motives of management and represents the interaction of their needs, goals, fears and commitments. Crucial to the investment decision appears to be the sequence of the investigation process. Important external factors include encouragement to invest by foreign governments, the fear of losing a market, strong competition from foreigners in the domestic market, and the bandwagon effect of success by an overseas competitor.

Economic motives

Synergy. When two firms combine and increase their value the process is known as synergy. The basis of synergy is that operating economies of scale can be achieved because existing firms are operating at a level below optimum.

A company can take advantage of economies of scale by exploiting overseas markets to secure a cost advantage over its competitors, and can include research and development, marketing, finance and transportation. For example, a number of countries, including the UK, have liberalized certain aspects of their capital markets to permit the development of commercial paper markets. In the US the market is estimated to be worth over $300 billion (1985) and offers cheaper finance by linking borrowers and lenders and bypassing the banking system and conventional securities exchanges. In the UK pressure for development of the commercial paper market came from UK MNEs which felt that they could obtain financial economies of scale by raising money on lower rates of interest. The process is described as 'disintermediation' as the commercial banks do not act as mediators.

Growth. Another motive for a company to invest abroad is that the home market has become so saturated that growth can only be made in overseas markets. Growth can be pursued either by setting up new foreign subsidiaries or by acquisition. Which alternative is decided by the relationship between the value of a firm's shares and the replacement cost of its assets. Where assets stand at a discount it will be cheaper to make an overseas acquisition rather than make 'greenfield investments'.

The growth motive may be part of a defensive strategy just as much as an aggressive expansionary policy. For example, Boots, the UK pharmaceutical company, was suffering from such slow growth in sales in the first half of the 1980s that in 1986 the company became vulnerable to a takeover bid. Recognizing this it embarked on a growth policy by acquiring Flint, a US drug company, for $600 million (£400 million). In order to pay for the acquisition, Boots embarked on a vendor placing in August 1986 to raise nearly £370 million. The market reaction to these transactions was less than favourable. Criticism of the acquisition included its high cost because of the purchase P/E ratio of 25; the fact that only 2.3 per cent of the cost of the acquisition was covered by tangible assets; that Flint was a one-product company with no patent protection; and that Flint had no research facilities.

Boots defended the acquisition on the grounds that it would provide direct access of its products to the US market rather than the less lucrative licensing arrangements it had previously used. The company cited the case of Ibuprofen, an anti-rheumatic drug, which was licensed to Upjohn, a US drug company in 1974. The product became the biggest selling drug in the US in 1980 which provided a return to Upjohn of $38 million in 1981 against royalties of only $13 million to Boots.

Acquiring assets at a discount

The aim of acquiring assets at a discount is to exploit the full potential of the assets by retention or to sell off the assets piecemeal. An example of the former is the willingness of European MNEs to acquire companies in unglamorous industries, such as the building sector, in the US. The US facilities are then modernized providing a technological lead over its US counterpart. An example of selling off assets piecemeal is the UK

MNE, Hanson Trust. In January 1986 Hanson Trust completed a $920 million battle to acquire SCM, the US typewriters and chemical group. Three months later it succeeded in taking over the Imperial Group, the UK tobacco and brewing group for £2.6 billion. By August 1986 Hanson had sold nearly half of the SCM group and had already recouped its purchase price and was still left with the profitable businesses involving titanium dioxide and also Smith Corona typewriter and Allied Business Forms. Sales were made with some UK MNEs, including Durkell Famous Foods to Reckitt & Colman for $120 million, and Glidden to ICI for $580 million. By July 1986 Hanson was ready to sell Imperial's hotels and restaurants to Trusthouse Forte for some £190 million and was preparing to sell Golden Wonder, the crisp and snacks company, and Courage, the brewing company. On 18 September 1986 Elders IXL, the Australian brewing group, agreed to pay £1.4 billion for Courage. The acquisition by Elders is believed to be the largest foreign acquisition by an Australian company and makes Elders the eighth largest brewing company in the world.

Multiple Sourcing

In order to avoid disruption in the supply of raw materials or components MNEs often seek to diversify their sources. Disruption can occur due to strikes or political changes, and multiple sourcing has the advantage of exerting leverage over national governments. An example of a recent economic change is the appreciation of the Japanese yen which has had the effect of encouraging overseas expansion and obtaining intermediate goods and components from foreign suppliers rather than local ones.

Follow-the-customer

In order to retain a domestic customer it is common for service industries to follow their customers overseas. Examples of this are common in accountancy, law and advertising. Growth in MNEs has led to the formation of MNEs in accountancy as the partnerships seek to fulfil the needs of their international clients.

Taxation advantages

Taxation is sometimes a motive for investing abroad. Profits may be subject to lower rates of tax in some countries than in others and MNEs can try to move profits to low-tax countries by their intercompany pricing policies. Certain other areas of profitable tax planning may arise such as dual-resident companies. However, the advantages of such measures may quickly change; for example, it appears that recent changes in tax legislation in the US will mean the end to the advantages attributable to dual-resident companies.

Defensive reasons

In highly competitive markets that are sometimes contracting it may be necessary to merge to defend positions. For example, in order to defend market share and try to cut costs Ovako of Finland and SKF Steel of Sweden merged in 1986 to become Europe's biggest special steel producer. In 1985 SKF Steel had made a loss of SEK65 million, primarily as a result of heavy research and development costs in pioneering its plasma technology-based metal recovery plant. It is estimated that the new group will have sales of SEK5.5 billion, a workforce of 7000, and an annual production of about 1.2 million tonnes of steel.

Foreign direct investment as an alternative to exporting or licensing

Caves (1971) proposed a classification of firm-specific advantages and their appropriate strategies. For example, if a corporation had a product that did not need adapting for local markets then exporting would be the appropriate strategy (e.g. Boeing). Where the firm-specific advantage is knowledge of a particular product or process, then the knowledge can be transmitted by licensing. Where, however, the advantage is principally organizational then the appropriate strategy would be to invest directly in the country.

The simple classification advocated by Caves needs refining to include other factors. For example, as previously mentioned in this chapter, Boots had a firm-specific advantage in knowledge of a particular product which it transmitted by licensing. However, the distribution of returns between the licenser and Boots meant a change in strategy for the UK drugs company.

Political safety

For economic reasons an MNE may wish to locate its operations in politically safe countries and to divest its activities that become politically unsafe. In chapter 2 consideration is given to country risk analysis, an important element of any foreign investment decision.

Synthesis of motives

For many years economists have attempted to synthesize the various strands of theories of MNEs in an attempt to provide a general theory. The eclectic theory of production which relies on firm-specific advantages, locational factors and internalization advantages has so far proved the most promising but remains difficult to test empirically. Even if the theory could be tested, many examples could be found which fall outside it. This serves to underline the fact that motives are complex and multivariate.

Attempts at explaining the investment behaviour of MNEs seems to start with the implicit assumption that MNEs are homogeneous and whose chief common characteristic is investment abroad. An alternative approach might be to accept the heterogeneity of MNEs, to classify them by common features and develop different strands of theory for different classifications. For example, an accountant might classify companies according to their underlying strategic objectives based either on a proprietary approach or an entity approach. The characteristics of companies classified like this are shown in table 1.3. This approach may prove useful in advancing the eclectic approach. Empirical research, at present, suggests that MNEs are large, undertake considerable research and development, and operate in oligopolistic markets at home and abroad. Yet the classification in table 1.3 suggests that proprietary companies do not invest heavily in research and development, and indeed restrict capital expenditures of all types. Furthermore, size may not be of paramount importance either. On the one hand profitability is positively correlated with market share and yet the UK, which probably has the highest industrial concentration in Europe, has lost the largest share of its markets when compared with other EEC countries.

SUMMARY

The evaluation of acquisitions within a country is a complex process which involves assessing a company's own strengths and weaknesses, evaluating promising candidates and selecting the most suitable and integrating the new company. The essential difference between internal mergers and cross-border transactions is that the evaluation process is even more complex and requires a detailed analysis of the industry in another country as well as an evaluation of the economic and political situation in the host country. Furthermore, foreign direct investment requires familiarity with new procedures and frameworks involving regulatory bodies, tax authorities and new accounting practices.

Despite the complexity of investing in foreign countries the growth in multinational enterprises continues rather than abates. Competition in many products is now conducted on a global basis rather than on a national one, and this trend will continue as tastes become increasingly homogeneous. At the same time there are not many national, homogeneous markets as large as the US which permit firms to obtain economies of scale and to undertake vast expenditure on research and development which is now required in many industries. For non-US companies to compete with their US counterparts it has become essential that foreign direct investment is undertaken to obtain the advantages of size and market power.

Economists have tried to synthesize the various strands of theories on the development of multinational enterprises in an attempt to provide a general theory. The theories have moved from a simple approach of firm-specific advantages which may be transferred to other countries, to an eclectic theory which involves firm-specific advantages, imperfections in

Table 1.3 Proprietary *v.* entity views

	Proprietary	*Entity*
Top management		
Characteristics	strong in finance, accountancy, and tax	strong in the core area of the business
Goals	maximize returns on assets with great emphasis on short-term performance	emphasis on long-term performance
	attaches great importance to earnings per share (EPS) figures	no great emphasis on EPS
	will adopt accounting policies commensurate with increasing EPS such as merger accounting to increase distributable profits. Will allocate costs to extraordinary items wherever possible	may deliberately avoid using merger accounting as it may lead to increased pressure to pay higher dividends as a result of increased distributable profits
Main objective	to make money as quickly as possible	to make or provide good quality, and profitable, goods and services
Features		
Growth	organically but particularly by acquisitions	mainly organically but will adopt a bandwagon approach when market share issues are raised or when appropriate as part of its defensive policy
	not market share-oriented	
	not particularly research and development-oriented	tries to innovate with new products and invest in research and development
Strategy	willing to move into any profitable sector where a business is considered undervalued	stays close to the core business

– *Continued*

Table 1.3 Continued

	Proprietary	*Entity*
Acquisition strategy	issues highly priced securities for opportunistic acquisitions	puts together what it considers to be an appropriate financial package at the appropriate time
	needs to repeat acquisitions	no necessity to repeat acquisitions
	develops into an MNE by acquisition and does not shirk a contested bid	sets up its own subsidiaries abroad but may acquire when considered essential. Prefers agreed bids
Post-acquisition strategy	eliminate head office expenditure and staff	leads from the top. Replaces members of management it feels it can replace with better quality staff
	delegate to line management as essential to run the business	it knows its business and how to run it
	introduces high-performance-related bonuses	
	exerts very tight control over capital expenditure	
Other characteristics	adopts a portfolio approach to business like many of its investors. Its investors are often institutions with short-term horizons	does not normally adopt a portfolio approach. Sticks near its core business
	good relations with institutional investors	often not unduly concerned with its institutional investors as it is too busy running its business. Can normally rely on its small investors to vote with management

– *Continued*

Table 1.3 Continued

	Proprietary	*Entity*
	recognizes the importance of financiers, accountants and lawyers to its business and is willing to use their services. Good 'City' image	not particularly active in this field and therefore less well known
	earnings and assets are reflected in a high share price because it dispenses with any of its difficult problems	may not be fully reflected in high share price. Would rather invest and reorganize to try to overcome problems. Divestment is viewed as tantamount to failure
Public perception	admired by financiers as both have common characteristics	neutral attitude of financiers
	some suspicion because a bad image can be created by asset-stripping	
	the public often has little perception of what the company does	the public often do know what the company does and it is often admired, e.g. Rolls Royce aero-engines

product markets and for factors of production but also includes locational factors such as the cost and availability of key factors of production. The motives for foreign direct investment are certainly complex and multivariate and theories have been developed which seem to assume that multinational enterprises are homogeneous. The complexity of foreign direct investment is such that it may be necessary to classify companies and to develop alternative strands of theory which help explain behaviour within each classification. One such classification might be based on the accounting concepts of proprietary and entity companies. The characteristics of these types of companies are summarized in table 1.3.

2

Deregulation, the Growth of Multinational Enterprises and Country Risk Analysis

DEREGULATION

History shows that global deregulation in the world's capital markets was inspired mainly by political ideologies and regulatory authorities in the UK and US. Its first origins can be traced back to 1975 when the US abolished fixed rate commissions on securities dealing. Concern was expressed in the UK over the following years that trading securities in the US was cheaper than in the UK. It is not clear that this was indeed the case but the London Stock Exchange was concerned about the possibility that it might lose some of its business to the US.

A second major factor was the election of a Conservative government in the UK in 1979. The UK was becoming, at this stage, almost totally self-sufficient for energy sources and a perceived danger was an appreciation in the value of sterling. In order to counteract this possibility, the government decided to abolish exchange controls in 1979 and allow capital to flow freely abroad. The abolition of exchange controls was coupled with a very tight monetary policy which precipitated an economic recession. It may prove somewhat ironic that one of the effects of deregulation of the world's capital markets may be to reduce the effectiveness of traditional monetary policy by national governments.

A third factor was the role of the Office of Fair Trading in the UK with respect to fixed rate commissions on the London Stock Exchange. The Director General started proceedings against this practice in the Restrictive Practices Court in 1983, although the action was withdrawn by Mr Cecil Parkinson, then Trade Secretary, on condition that the

Exchange put its own house in order. As a result, fixed rate commissions on international securities dealing were abolished in 1984. On 27 October 1986 the same occurred on the domestic market.

A fourth factor was undoubtedly the growth of international markets such as Euromarkets which thrived during the 1970s. Advantages of such markets include flexibility, competitiveness and a dearth of controls.

A fifth and very important factor was the growth in advanced communications and computer technology which permits worldwide dealing in securities to the exclusion of exchanges which do not conform to international trading practices.

A sixth factor has been increasing pressure, particularly by the US, on Japan to become more internationally minded. The process began in 1980 with the lifting of exchange controls. By 1985 Japan had overtaken Saudi Arabia as the world's biggest creditor nation and had also become the highest investor in that year in the US. However, the process of opening up markets in Japan is a slow and somewhat painful process although some progress is being achieved.

The seeds of deregulation were sown by the UK and US and this had a bandwagon effect on many other countries. With relatively high rates of unemployment in many of the industrialized nations a number of countries did not wish to be left out of the possibility of attracting foreign investment. This required two things – first, deregulation of their own capital markets; and secondly, deregulation of many of the controls on foreign investment. For example, in both Australia and Canada deregulation in the banking sector was coupled with a major dismantling of investment controls applicable to foreigners. Table 2.1 shows some of the deregulation measures that have been implemented worldwide.

Deregulation in the industrialized countries has been followed by deregulation in developing countries as they seek to remain competitive and attract foreign investment. For example, in 1969 Malaysia introduced a New Economic Policy (NEP) which reflects a more liberal attitude towards foreign investors and allows a majority shareholding to be held by overseas investors. Examples of companies taking immediate advantage of these new rules include Rothmans Malaysia, Nestlé and ICI. Other developing countries that have become increasingly open to foreign investors include Indonesia, Taiwan, Singapore and China.

China may appear to be an unlikely country to be subjected to deregulation and as such is worthy of further consideration. The process began on 1 July 1979 with the enactment of the Law of the People's Republic of China Concerning Joint Ventures Using Chinese and Foreign Investment which permitted joint ventures with the Chinese. By the end of 1985, 2300 sino-foreign joint ventures had been undertaken and 3700 co-operative enterprises had been set up. From 1980 foreign investors were allowed to set up enterprises operated by themselves and by the end of 1985 120 undertakings had been started with a total value of US $570 million. Of the total investment made, US $150 million had been invested in industrial projects, US $170 million in real estate projects and the rest in commercial projects, construction, agriculture, education, culture, sports and scientific research and finance. The main investors so far originate from Hong Kong and Singapore but other investors include the US, Japan, Thailand, the Netherlands and Macao.

On 12 April 1986 the Fourth Session of the Sixth National People's Congress, adopted the Law on Enterprises Operated Exclusively with Foreign Capital. Article 1 of the Act states:

> With a view to expanding economic co-operation and technological exchange with other countries and promoting the development of its national economy, the People's Republic of China permits foreign firms, other economic entities or individuals to set up enterprises exclusively with foreign capital in China and protects the lawful rights and interests of the enterprises so established.

Article 2 specifies that the Act is not applicable to branches set up in China by foreign investors. Whatever enterprise is envisaged the investment must be '. . . conducive to the development of China's national economy. Such enterprises shall use advanced technology and equipment or market all or most of their products outside China.' Article 5 tries to allay fears of expropriation of assets or enterprises although '. . . should it prove necessary to do so in the public interest, legal procedures will be followed and reasonable compensation will be made.'

What are the implications of deregulation? It will permit capital to flow more freely throughout the world in pursuit of the highest return. For the protagonists of deregulation this should mean greater financial efficiency as resources become allocated on a global scale. For investors on capital markets benefits may be derived from cheaper transaction costs as fixed-rate commissions are abolished. However, a fall in transaction costs is not likely to be uniform and it seems likely that in the UK, institutional investors will enjoy reduced costs whereas smaller investors may actually suffer from higher costs.

Another consequence of deregulation is the increased innovation in financial instruments. With, for example, increased use of floating rate notes, zero coupon bonds, currency swaps and certificates of deposit additional challenges must be faced. Some of the financial instruments such as Euroequity paper do not confer any voting rights and Euronotes involve considerable off-balance sheet risks. Supervisors over financial statements will need to consider carefully the implications of the proliferation of such instruments if the investing public is to be adequately informed in order to make judgements on the inherent risks of the investment. Such risks have not gone unnoticed and the Bank for International Settlements has openly stated that some of the new instruments are underpriced in relation to their risk.

From a national point of view deregulation may mean a loss of some of its options in controlling its own destiny as individual markets can be circumvented. The reimposition of regulations by any one state may not have the consequences that had previously applied. Furthermore, a major financial crisis in one country may be more readily transmitted to other

Table 2.1 Some deregulation measures that have been implemented worldwide

Date	*Exchange and investment controls*	*Tax barriers*	*New instruments*	*Restrictive dealing*
US				
1974	Employee Retirement Security Act (ERISA) permits pension funds to diversify overseas			
1975				Fixed commission securities dealing abolished
1984		Withholding tax on interest payments to non-residents withdrawn		
UK				
1979	Exchange controls abolished			
1984		Withholding tax on interest payments to non-residents withdrawn.		Abolished fixed commissions on international securities
1986	Permits foreigners to acquire gilt-edged stocks subject to reciprocity in the case of Japan	Stamp duty on securities reduced	Commercial paper market started	Abolished fixed commissions on domestic securities

Norway				
1981	Non-residents may purchase shares in Norwegian companies			
1985	Liberalization of currency legislation. Eurobonds may be traded freely in the secondary market. Currency licence on direct investment in Norway abolished		Creates a certificate market for the government, private companies and banks. Eliminates compulsory investments in bonds by insurance companies which helps to create a functioning bond market	Seven foreign banks allowed to establish premises
Greece				
1984	Further liberalization of foreign exchange controls		Commercial banks are allowed to accept deposits in convertible drachmas by foreign residents and can use these funds to extend loans to banks abroad	
Sweden				
1980			Introduction of bank certificates of deposit	

– *Continued*

Table 2.1 Continued

Date	*Exchange and investment controls*	*Tax barriers*	*New instruments*	*Restrictive dealing*
1982	Lifting of liquidity requirements for banks. Removal of the obligation for insurance companies to hold bonds. Abolition of liquidity requirements for banks		Treasury discount note introduced. Development of a secondary market for bonds	
1984				Foreign banks allowed to undertake normal banking activities in Sweden
FRG				
1981	Lifts controls on capital inflows			
1984		Withholding tax on interest payments to non-residents withdrawn		
1985	Foreign-owned banks allowed to be lead managers of D-mark Euro-bond issues (except Japan)		Allows use of floating rate notes, zero coupon bonds and dual currency issues	Relaxes formal procedures for foreign issues. Bill introduced to create a newly regulated market sector with less strict disclosure requirements

1986	Minimum reserve requirements for banks relaxed		Certificates of deposit denominated in D-marks may be issued	
Denmark				
1983	Relaxes foreign exchange controls. Firms allowed to obtain loans abroad. Residents can invest in bonds with an initial maturity greater than two years			Lifts ban on foreign investments in government bonds
1985	Further liberalization of exchange controls			
Switzerland				
1985	Liberalization of capital markets – no ceiling on foreign borrowers on public sector loans			
1986				Revision of commission structure. Negotiated commissions on larger deals Major banks reduce commissions on Swiss franc bond issues

– *Continued*

Table 2.1 Continued

Date	*Exchange and investment controls*	*Tax barriers*	*New instruments*	*Restrictive dealing*
Italy				
1984	Liberalization of financial investment abroad			
1985	Liberalization of borrowing on foreign financial markets. Liberalization for residents in acquiring shares in overseas mutual funds. The ceiling on foreign borrowing by the banking sector is lifted			
1986	Further liberalization of currency flows			
Finland				
1986	Some liberalization on short-term import credits, foreign exchange and securities brokers			

Australia				
1983	Floating of the Australian dollar			
1984	Changes in rules regarding foreign ownership of stockbroking firms allowing up to 50 per cent foreign ownership. Regulation of banks relaxed			Brokerage rates may be negotiated
New Zealand				
1983				Minister of Finance ready to accept applications from financial institutions for foreign exchange dealing licences
1984	Foreign-owned companies would generally have unrestricted access to capital markets. Financial institutions free to borrow abroad			
1985	N.Z. dollar floated		A future exchange began operating with a US dollar contract	

– *Continued*

Table 2.1 Continued

Date	*Exchange and investment controls*	*Tax barriers*	*New instruments*	*Restrictive dealing*
1986	Restrictions on foreign ownership of financial institutions, advertising agencies and fish processors were abolished			
Canada				
1984	Ceiling on foreign banks share ownership of domestic assets increased from 8 to 16 per cent			
France				
1984	Measures to ease exchange controls. Easing of controls on direct investment inward and outward	Tax on foreign investment in bonds abolished		
1985			New market in short-term commercial paper and certificate of deposit	

countries as a result of the globalization of commodities and financial markets. Indeed, the crisis with the US balance of payments deficit in October–November 1987 led to dramatic falls in stock prices on Wall Street which precipitated falls on all the world's stock markets. One danger of such a crash is that the collapse of one large securities house could endanger the health of the world financial system as a whole. Such crises suggest, *inter alia*, that the world's regulatory bodies should co-operate more closely to ensure that securities firms have an adequate capital base.

At the corporate level there are, potentially, advantages and disadvantages to deregulation. The opportunity may arise, for the first time, to have genuine multinational enterprises rather than national enterprises with multinational operations. For a genuine MNE, control and ownership would need to be on a global basis and management would need to be appointed on the basis of the distribution of the corporation's worldwide assets. Some movement in the raising of capital on an international basis has already begun. For example, in May 1986 Electrolux announced that it would issue 2 million shares to raise approximately SEK 26 million in the UK, the US, FRG, Switzerland, France, Italy, Canada, the Far East and the Netherlands. Whilst the world's biggest household appliance manufacturer is internationalizing its financing and trading operations, control remains very much in Sweden.

The international placement of corporate securities will permit and enhance the growth in MNEs and much of the money raised will find its way into takeover activity. For example, Electrolux became the world's biggest household appliance manufacturer by the acquisition of Zanussi at the end of 1984 and the takeover of White Consolidated Industries, the third largest white goods manufacturer in the US, in March 1986. Another factor which will lead to further growth in MNEs is the realization in Europe and elsewhere, that to compete effectively with MNEs in the US and Japan, partnerships and mergers will need to be developed to gain similar economies of scale. Realization of this factor led Sir Hector Laing, Chairman of the UK food manufacturer, United Biscuits, to make a takeover bid for the Imperial group even though it raised market share issues in the national market. Similarly, in the Federal Republic of Germany (FRG) Daimler-Benz enhanced its position as the country's biggest industrial group by the acquisitions of MTU, the engine builder, 65.6 per cent of Dornier, the aerospace company, and 56 per cent in AEG over the period 1985–6. The acquisition of the controlling interest in AEG proved very controversial with the opposition political party, the Social Democrats, insisting that the takeover should be prevented.

In order to undertake acquisitions at an international level funds must be readily available. There is no apparent shortage of funds, with banks in many countries of the world recording record profits and with liquidity good after a period of enhancing reserves between 1982 and 1986. Reserves have improved after concern in the early 1980s about the threat of Third World default on debt interest and capital repayments. Whilst the threat of immediate default has declined somewhat, Mr Antonio Ortiz Mena, President of the Inter-American Development Bank, has stated that he expects most of the largest debtor nations in Latin America will still be experiencing payment problems at the end of this century. Economic events can change this somewhat, for example, the fall in the price of oil has enhanced the problems of Mexico but temporarily alleviated immediate difficulties for Brazil, Chile and Uruguay.

Threats of default by developing countries has led to a massive reduction and even termination of new loans to some countries. With lending by commercial banks to developing countries reduced in 1985–6, funds are finding their way to other markets. A characteristic of an increase in takeover activity in many parts of the world has been the ability of a relatively small company to finance a bid in an attempt to acquire a large company. For example, the largest company in Australia, Broken Hill Proprietary (BHP), suffered the indignity of receiving a takeover bid from the Bell Group, a company with net assets in 1985 of about a thirtieth of BHP's. The Bell Group was able to finance its bid with a reported A$2 billion line of credit from the Standard Chartered Bank and an additional A$625 million from a rights issue.

Another feature of deregulation is that demands for deregulation in one area of the national or international economy are often met by demands for additional regulation in other areas as a counterbalancing effect. For example, deregulation in the banking sector has permitted banks to indulge in off-balance sheet financing. As a result, demands are already being made for additional regulations or improved regulation of commercial banks by central bank monitoring units In the UK, for example, deregulation in the securities sector has led to the formation of six self-regulatory organizations under the auspices of the Securities and Investments Board. The self-regulatory organizations and their roles are shown on the next page.

Demands are likely to arise for additional controls to be introduced in two other key areas – trading using price-sensitive information and accounting standards. The US seems to be more active than any other country in trying to reduce insider dealing. For example, in April 1986 the Securities and Exchange Commission (SEC) successfully completed what was dubbed 'The Sante Fe Insider Trading Scandal'. The SEC started to investigate the case in October 1981 when the government-owned Kuwait Petroleum Corporation purchased Sante Fe International, an oil and gas engineering and services company based in California. The pre-bid price per share was $24.95 but the bid price was $51 per share. What interested the SEC was that certain large purchases of shares were made during the weeks before the bid. The network of international investors unravelled by the SEC included not only investors in the US but also from the UK, France, Switzerland and the Middle East.

In May 1986, the SEC accused Mr Dennis Levine, a Wall Street investment banker, of making profits of more than $12.6 million by using inside information. In June 1986 the SEC won another case involving insider dealing, this time involving profits of $3.5 million made on the purchase of shares in St Joe Minerals in March 1981 prior to the company's takeover by Seagrain.

Self-regulatory organizations and their roles in the UK

Name	*Regulatory role*
1. Association of futures brokers and dealers	Firms dealing and broking in futures and options, incidental investment management and business advice
2. The Stock Exchange	Firms dealing and broking in securities and related options and futures, incidental investment management and business advice
3. Life Assurance and Unit Trust regulatory organization	Life companies and unit trust managers and trustees
4. International securities regulatory organization	Firms dealing and broking in securities, international money-market instruments, forward agreements and related futures and options
5. Financial intermediaries managers and brokers regulatory association	Will regulate the markets formerly covered by the National Association of Dealers in Securities and Investment Managers and the life and unit trust intermediaries regulatory organization
6. Investment managers regulatory organization	Will regulate investment managers and advisers, including managers and trustees of collective investment schemes and, in-house pension fund managers

Countries already reacting to the new threat of insider dealing include the UK, Sweden and New Zealand. In June 1986 the House of Commons in the UK approved an amendment to the Financial Services Bill which provides additional powers to fight insider dealing. On 12 June 1986 the Corporate and Consumer Affairs Minister, Mr Michael Howard, said, in the House of Commons, that inspectors would be able to apply to the Trade and Industry Secretary to withdraw authority to trade from a company suspected of withholding information, or to prohibit other businesses from trading in investments on its behalf. The effect of this would be that access to the UK market would be cut off to overseas intermediaries if information is withheld without reasonable cause.

In October 1985 Sweden introduced a new law which made insider dealing illegal and in June 1986 the Banking Inspectorate reported the group chief executive of Fermenta, Mr Refaat El-Sayed, to the Public Prosecutor in Stockholm for an alleged breach of the new law.

In June 1986 the New Zealand government ordered an enquiry into allegations of widespread insider dealing over the previous two years. The Securities Commission prepared a report for the government which was critical of interlocking directorships in many companies. After receiving the report, the Minister of Justice ordered a full review as there are, at present, no regulations to prevent insider trading.

As a result of the internationalizing of securities markets the SEC has taken a more global outlook to controlling abuses of the capital markets. For instance in 1986, the International Association of Securities Commission (IASC) decided to set up a permanent secretariat headquarters in Quebec and regional committees will be formed to monitor developments in Europe. The IASC is an organization which brings together stock exchange regulatory bodies in North and South America. In practice, however, the organization has been dominated by the SEC. In 1983 the IASC agreed to allow non-American members and as a result representatives joined from Australia, France, Hong Kong, Indonesia, Nigeria, South Korea, Tunisia and the UK. Following a meeting in July 1986, the IASC has agreed to liberalize its statutes to permit more European countries to join. The impetus for change has come from the SEC as it seeks to introduce mechanisms for exchanging information between the regulatory authorities. The SEC view such a move as a necessary requirement for controlling international fraud and insider trading.

A second challenge that the growth in international capital markets will produce is the need for global standards of accounting. A lack of global accounting is likely to inhibit the growth of an international equities market as figures will need to be restated according to different generally accepted accounting principles. Some international companies already do this – for example, Volvo and British Telecom – but there is a cost to reporting under different principles in different languages. Another important point is that as direct and indirect investment becomes more international the demands on users to be familiar with many different sets of accounts is extremely onerous. Accounting standards bodies should continue to move in the direction of adherence to international standards if the demands for accounts which show a true and fair view on a global scale are to be met.

David Cairns, secretary to the International Accounting Standards Committee, points to the following developments which have already led to an increase in the acceptance of international accounting standards:

1. The growth in the number of companies raising finance abroad, particularly from Scandinavian countries, has led to the presentation of financial statements which reflect best international practice.
2. Many companies are being encouraged by their auditors to disclose compliance with international standards.
3. More regulatory bodies are recognizing international standards. For example, the Toronto stock exchange requires adherence to international standards, and CONSOB in Italy also advocates their use

where there is no relevant Italian accounting standard.
4. Pressure is being exerted on the SEC to recognize international standards as a way of reducing reporting costs to foreign companies.

The second aspect of this theme on accounting standards is that there is a need for more effective control over national accounting standards. This challenge must be met by all countries interested in ensuring that corporate reporting is of the highest standard. The problem is that as companies extend their shareholding base by obtaining quotations on listed markets, unlisted markets and even third-tier markets, there is an increasing tendency to present results in their most favourable perspective. The object of the exercise is often to smooth results to demonstrate to shareholders that earnings and profitability are growing at a steady rate. This is sometimes achieved by circumventing national accounting standards and indulging in off-balance sheet financing. More sinister is the deliberate attempt made by some companies and merchant banks to undermine the whole process of regulating corporate reporting by accounting standards.

The Accounting Standards Committee (ASC) in the UK, one of the most influential in the world, has produced accounting standards since 1971. Many of the issues dealt with have not been unduly controversial but where an issue proves problematic the ASC has often taken the easy path by allowing options. In 1981, however, the ASC faced its greatest challenge by producing SSAP 16 on current cost accounts. Opposition to the standard, from both companies and shareholders, became so prevalent that in 1986 the standard was withdrawn. Opposition came from management because current cost accounts showed lower profit levels to historical cost accounts and made it more difficult to show a steady growth rate which, in reality, often comes as a result of inflation. Shareholders also seemed opposed to the disclosure of such information which may, on first consideration, seem surprising. However, shareholders are united in protecting their own interests and dislike information that may have a harmful effect on their investments, at least the disclosure of such information before they can disinvest. With securities markets in the UK and indeed in the rest of the world being dominated by institutions perhaps it is not surprising the UK institutions should encourage management to oppose and eventually undermine the standard.

The withdrawal of SSAP 16 in the UK has had subsequent knock-on effects. In an endeavour to avoid conflict of a similar nature subsequent pronouncements have been characterized by their weakness e.g. SSAP 22 on goodwill and SSAP 23 on business combination. The Institute of Chartered Accountants in England and Wales is undertaking some work on the problems of compliance with accounting standards but it is clear that the profession will need the support of other groups, such as the stock exchange, and in particular the government if the needs of society for adequate accounting are to be met. In the increasingly competitive world that international accounting firms trade in, it is essential that legislative support for accounting standards is provided.

MULTINATIONAL ENTERPRISES

Realization that European companies must be large to compete effectively with MNEs in the US and Japan will lead to an increase in the propensity to acquire competitors at home and aboard. National governments have not stepped in to stop this process. However, US and Japanese MNEs will not passively watch their markets eradicated. Rather there will be a tendency for them to expand and obtain even greater advantages of economies of scale.

Deregulation in the capital markets has paralleled increasing restrictions on the physical movement of goods and services. This has led to a number of trade disputes involving the US, Europe and Japan. One radical change in the world economy may result from the Group of Five (G5) agreement made at the Plaza Hotel in New York in September 1985. The agreement was marked by increasing intervention in the foreign exchange markets to force down the US dollar and force up the value of the yen. Some commentators feel that the G5 agreement may herald the end of the post-war era for Japan as the yen continues to strengthen. Such agreements and disputes are likely to lead to two changes in the Japanese economy. First, a movement away from the export economy to develop its domestic economy. This may be characterized by increasing takeover activity as some of the major corporations have massive cash surpluses. Secondly, Japanese corporations are likely to continue their investment abroad. One way of avoiding import quotas and 'forced' agreements is to invest in the host country. Over recent years Japanese companies have made considerable 'greenfield' investments in the US and have now turned to Europe.

Such developments pose challenges to host governments. As MNEs continue to develop, their market share in the domestic economy is likely to increase, posing new problems of concentration. There will be a lag between this development and changes in national control institutions. Secondly, host governments will need to examine carefully the distribution of the costs and benefits of investment by MNEs. Whilst the host country will welcome increased employment prospects, new technologies and new managerial and entrepreneurial skills, disadvantages can accrue. For example, economies can suffer an imbalance between manufacturing and resources or be forced into 'truncated' enterprises whose activities are essentially assembly of overseas components. Furthermore, MNEs are likely to continue to strengthen their positions *vis-à-vis* governments. However, foreign direct investment should not be viewed as an unbridled threat to the national economy as the investment is usually long-term, made for strategic reasons and not with a view to short-term gains.

As part of the distribution of gains between the host government, the home government and MNEs, taxation is likely to pose increasing problems. The importance of unitary taxation in the US has led to a major dispute between the UK and US with Japan supporting the UK case. In addition, many developing countries are looking carefully at the potential of imposing unitary taxation. Unitary taxation is a method of assessment which originated in Hollywood in the 1930s as a way of countering tax avoidance by the film industry. This system of taxation ignores the separate legal entity status of subsidiaries and associates forming part of a group and also ignores state and national boundaries. Instead the group's aggregate worldwide earnings are allocated on a *pro rata* basis to an area, be it a state or country, on the basis of a criterion such as payroll or sales. The actual earnings of the company in a particular area are thereby ignored in favour of the pro-rated earnings which are then taxed in that area.

On 5 September 1986 the state governor of California signed a bill which permits MNEs in California to elect not to be taxed on a unitary basis but to be taxed by the 'water's-edge' method which means that tax will only be levied on its US earnings. The bill is effective from 1 January 1988 and leaves only Alaska, Montana and North Dakota raising tax on a unitary basis. However, objections to the Californian bill have already been made by MNEs, as companies choosing the water's-edge method may do so only on payment of a levy. This election levy is equivalent to 0.03 per cent of a company's sales, payroll and property in California and once the election is made it must remain in force for at least ten years.

As a general rule national governments, other than the US, have not imposed unitary taxation but instead stipulate that transactions should be on an arm's length basis. The aim of this is to stop international companies from transferring profits to low-tax countries. However, the Franchise Tax Board of California has consistently argued that arm's length pricing is an outdated concept because of the spread of specialist components for which there is no external market.

To ensure that transactions are undertaken on an arm's length basis the OECD has been developing new controls to police international tax evasion and avoidance. The OECD has been working with the Council of Europe to produce a convention on mutual administrative assistance in tax matters. The scheme permits tax authorities from one country to exchange information with another country where tax evasion is suspected.

The growth in MNEs is not likely to lead to optimism for the poorest nations of the world. Whilst they have the advantage of cheap labour, political and economic risks are often too great for the MNEs to make major investments. The prospects of such economies ever producing their own competitors to such enterprises is virtually non-existent. Their prospects are that they will never be able to compete at the industrial level and their only hope is to supply industrialized countries with agricultural products. However, a feature of advanced economies is that national governments, such as the US, and organizations such as the EEC, subsidize agriculture to such an extent that large surpluses are produced. If advanced economies are unwilling to allow the poor countries to exist even at a subsistence level then poor countries are likely to increase their demands to export people to compensate for their failure to export goods.

Whilst economic and political risks are extremely high in the poorest countries of the world such risks do, to some extent, pervade every foreign investment. Careful analysis of what is known as 'country risk' is needed before any investment is made. The next section discusses what risks exist and how some organizations offer a service providing country risk ratings.

COUNTRY RISK ANALYSIS

Investing in the domestic economy by takeovers involves considerable analysis of the industry and the firm in which a proposed investment is to be made. Investing overseas poses additional risks which may be classified as transfer risk and generalized country risk (Calverley, 1985). Transfer risk is the risk that, despite an overseas project generating cash flows, the foreign government does not have sufficient foreign exchange to permit the remittance of capital, dividends, interest, fees or royalties. Whilst this element of risk is very real it is not usually catastrophic for an MNE because investments are normally long-term so that MNEs would then have to wait until the restrictions were terminated for remittances to resume. Generalized country risk is of paramount importance to MNEs since economic and political risks can fundamentally change the basis upon which the investment was made.

The above elements of risk are interrelated. For example, careful analysis of a company and the industry in which it operates, such as the extractive industries, may lead the analyst to conclude that a viable investment exists. However, this is one industry which has been subjected to expropriation of assets with and without compensation. Country risk analysis is therefore vital in assessing the 'rules of the game' and to establish the probability that the 'goal posts' might be moved during the game.

Firm risk and industry risk are integral parts of analysis regardless of whether the investment is in the home country or abroad. Appendix A, pp. 490–7, provides an information checklist on salient considerations of this element of the analysis. Further analysis is provided in Cooke (1986). The rest of this section deals mainly with generalized country risk analysis which should be of great importance in MNEs investment appraisal. Initial sources of information for preliminary investigation includes publications by the following organizations:

1. International Monetary Fund (IMF)
2. Organisation for Economic Co-operation and Development (OECD)
3. Asian Development Banks
4. Inter-American Development Bank
5. United Nations Economic Commission for Latin America (CEPAL)
6. Bank for International Settlements.

Much of the available information and many of the articles and books written in this area are biased towards bank lending. This is naturally of primary importance to multinational banks but the analysis concentrates on assessing the probability that a country will be unable to meet their debts as they fall due whereas analysis for non-financial MNEs is somewhat different.

Assessment of country risk concerns economic and political factors. An economic downturn in an overseas economy can lead to a major change in the variables used to evaluate the investment. Such changes may lead to a transfer risk problem and in extreme cases the expropriation of assets by the government. Furthermore, specific regulations imposed on an industry or major changes in taxes etc. may also affect the viability of the investment. This may include changes in the rules of the game. A number of approaches can be adopted to the problem of analysing generalized country risk:

1. Checklists can be prepared and reviewed regularly. An example is incorporated into the checklist contained in Appendix A.
2. Scoring systems which aim to provide one figure which incorporates economic and political risk.
3. Econometric and statistical analysis. Econometric models aim to provide a model of an overseas economy whereas some statistical approaches have been undertaken in an attempt to predict whether a country is likely to meet its debts as they fall due.

With respect to scoring systems a number of institutions have developed to provide such information and include

1. BERI SA
2. Euromoney
3. International Reports Group
4. Institutional Investor

All the above institutions provide country risk assessments appropriate for bank lending decisions. Those may be useful to non-financial MNEs in assessing transfer risk but they will not be particularly useful in assessing generalized country risk. One exception is the BERI index. The Beri organization offers three services – a business risk service, Forelend, and Force. The business risk service offers qualitative and quantitative analyses and forecasts on 48 countries. The quantitative risk ratings consist of a political risk index, an operations risk index, a remittance and a repatriation factor which are incorporated into a profit opportunity recommendation. Forelend provides a rating system on 50 countries on the outlook for interest and principal repayments by foreign governments. The Force service is a country-by-country study of socio-political and economic forecasts and operating conditions including financial and monetary conditions for 31 countries.

The business risk service is the most appropriate one for assessing generalized country risk. First, a political risk index is drawn up based upon the views of political scientists for the present, the next five years, and the next ten years. Each expert assigns a score of 0–7 to each factor per country where a score of seven denotes no problems for investment by an international corporation. The eight factors which are considered are:

1. Fractionalization of the political spectrum and the power of these factions.
2. Fractionalization by language, ethnic and/or religious groups and the power of these factions.
3. Restrictive (coercive) measures required to retain power.
4. Mentality, including xenophobia, nationalism, corruption, nepotism, willingness to compromise.
5. Social conditions, including population density and wealth distribution.
6. Organization and strength of forces for a radical left government.
7. Dependence on and/or importance to a hostile major power.
8. Negative influences of regional political forces.

In addition to these factors, the following two symptoms are also assigned a similar range of scores:

1. societal conflict involving demonstrations, strikes, and street violence;
2. instability as perceived by nonconstitutional changes, assassinations, and guerrilla wars.

With these ten points, a maximum score of 70 can be achieved by a 'perfect country'.

The second step is for the experts to allocate up to 30 discretionary points, with typically 20 points being attributed to a low-risk country and 10 points for a country with moderate risk. The first two steps are repeated for not only the current period but also for a five- and ten-year period. The scores are interpreted as follows:

1. 70–100 Low risk. Political changes will not lead to conditions seriously adverse to business. No major socio-political disturbances are expected.
2. 55– 69 Moderate risk. Political changes seriously adverse to business have occurred, but governments in power during the forecast period have a low probability of introducing such changes. Some disturbances will take place.
3. 40– 54 High risk. Political developments seriously adverse to business exist or could occur in the near future. Major socio-political disturbances are occurring periodically.
4. 0– 39 Prohibitive risk. Political conditions severely restrict business operations. Loss of assets is possible. Disturbances are part of daily life.

The second index assesses operations risk for the business operations environment. This is done by making an assessment of the extent to which nationals are given preferential treatment and the general quality of the business climate, including the political environment for day-to-day business. A permanent panel of 105 experts around the world is used to assess the conditions for 15 criteria on the country's business climate. Each criterion is given a weight by BERI ranging from 1 to 3 and each expert has to give a score for each element of between 0, where conditions are unacceptable, to 4, where conditions are considered to be very good. The criteria and weights are given below:

	Criteria	*Weighting*
1.	Political continuity	3.0
2.	Attitude: foreign investors and profits	1.5
3.	Nationalization	1.5
4.	Monetary inflation	1.5
5.	Balance of payments	1.5
6.	Bureaucratic delays	1.0
7.	Economic growth	2.5
8.	Currency convertibility	2.5
9.	Enforceability of contracts	1.5
10.	Labour cost/productivity	2.0
11.	Professional services and contractors	0.5
12.	Communications and transportation	1.0
13.	Local management and partners	1.0
14.	Short-term credit	2.0
15.	Long-term loans and venture capital	2.0
		25.0

With each criterion being assigned a maximum of 4 points and with weights totalling 25.0 the maximum achievable score is 100. In addition to the current ratings, experts are asked to make an assessment for the five-year period so that a forecast operations risk index can be established. The scores allocated are as follows:

70–100 Stable environment typical of an advanced industrialized economy. Problems for foreign businesses are offset by the country's efficiency, market opportunities, financial infrastructure, etc.

55– 69 Moderate-risk countries with complications in day-to-day operations. Usually the political structure is sufficiently stable to permit consistent operations without serious disruption.

40– 54 High risk for foreign-owned businesses. Only special situations should be considered, e.g. scarce raw materials or high profits.

0– 39 Unacceptable business conditions for foreign-owned businesses.

The third index is called 'factor R', which concentrates on remittances and repatriation of capital. 'Factor R' reflects the ability of foreign companies to convert and transfer local currency into 'hard' currency. A computer program is used to process a considerable amount of data to produce four sub-indices:

1. Legal framework subindex (20 per cent of R) the following factors are given weights and assigned scores ranging from 0 in the worst case, to 5 in the best case.

Law as written	*Weighting*
Profit and dividend remittances	4
Royalties, fees and remuneration for non-dividend cash flow services	3
Repatriation of capital	3
	10

Actual practices	
Practices on dividends, royalties, and other periodic compensation	4
Practices on repatriation of capital	3
Hedging opportunities against a devaluing currency	3
	10

2. Foreign exchange generation subindex (30 per cent of R). This sub-index is based on IMF statistics and 50 points to current account performance and 50 points for capital flows.
3. Accumulated international reserves sub-index (3 per cent of R). The first part of this sub-index is to assess requirements for hard currency by looking at the months of coverage for imports of merchandise and services. A range of points are allocated with 50 being awarded to a country with the most coverage and those with the fewest months coverage are awarded zero. A second aspect is to add the international reserve total to the London valuation for gold holdings to give a complete total on reserves. A ratio is then calculated using total public foreign debt as the numerator.
4. Foreign debt assessment sub-index (20 per cent of R). The basic source of information on public foreign debt for developing countries is that published by the World Bank whereas several sources are used for industrialized countries. In order to put debt into perspective with the economy a ratio is calculated using gross domestic product converted to US $ as the denominator. Forty points are allocated to creditor nations. A second aspect of this sub-index is the capacity to service debt and this is measured by a ratio of annual public foreign loan obligations (numerator) to foreign exchange earned (denominator). Again 40 points are allocated to creditor nations. A third aspect is to calculate a 'saturation factor' which occurs when debt service plus

imports of petroleum equal foreign exchange earned. Where saturation occurs no points are allocated but 5 points or less is critical. A maximum of 20 points is allocated to this theoretical calculation.

The three indices – political risk index, operations risk index and 'factor R' – are then combined to produce a profit opportunity recommendation (POR). PORs are assigned based on five-year forecasts since many projects involve considerable lead time between the feasibility study and actual operation. Table 2.2 shows the combined scores for 1985 and combined scores and ranking for 1986. In addition, the table shows the five-year forecast for the combined score and its POR.

The PORs are rated by the forecast combined scores and after taking into consideration any special conditions. The ratings may be interpreted as follows:

Investment quality – combined scores 180+

Scores greater than 180 reflect conditions worthy of equity investment and the incurrence of debt to be serviced from operations in that country. Expectations concerning currency convertibility and dividend remittances are considered to be good.

POR	*Score*		*Comment*
1A	210+	Increasing need for high early remittable profits ↓	Decreasing level of capital to be committed
1B	200–209		
1C	190–199		
1D	180–189		

Non-dividend cash flow – combined scores 160+

Minimum commitment of resources but frees can be earned for management of operations, the sharing of technology, training of nationals, and sales of other services.

POR	*Score*		*Comment*
2A	180+	Investment not recommended due to special conditions	Increasing problems with payments, resulting competition, etc. ↓
2B	160–179	All three measures	
2C	160–179	Receiver has potential to penetrate markets traditionally held by the supplier	

Trade only – combined scores 120+

POR	*Score*	*Comment*
3A	160–179 140–159	Non-dividend cashflow is restricted legally or effectively
3B	120–139	Caution is required about obtaining payment.

Table 2.2 Profit opportunity recommendation (POR) ranked by combined score

	Present conditions			*Five-year forecast*			
	300=Perfect country	*Present combined score*	*1985-III combined score*	*300=Perfect country*	*Combined score*	*POR*	
	1. Switzerland	242	242	1. Switzerland	243	1A	
	2. Japan	238	238	2. Japan	233	1A	
	3. Singapore	225	229	3. Germany	224	1A	
	4. United States	220	223	4. Singapore	223	1A	
	5. Germany	219	223	5. United States	212	1A	
	6. Netherlands	211	212	6. Netherlands	210	1A	
	7. Norway	209	211	7. Taiwan (R.O.C.)	208	1B	
	8. Taiwan (R.O.C.)	206	201	8. Norway	201	1B	
	9. Canada	191	200	9. Belgium	190	1C	
	10. Belgium	189	188	10. Canada	186	1D	
	United Kingdom	189	195	11. Sweden	185	2A	
	12. Australia	188	190	12. United Kingdom	184	1D	
	13. Denmark	186	175	13. France	181	1D	
180	Sweden	186	189	14. Australia	180	1D	
	15. Ireland	174	169	Denmark	180	1D	180
	16. France	167	167	16. Ireland	174	2C	
	17. Malaysia	166	168	17. Saudi Arabia	168	2B	
	18. Korea (South)	165	171	18. Korea (South)	166	2C	
160	19. Saudi Arabia	163	162	19. Malaysia	163	2B	160
	20. Spain	154	149	20. Spain	159	3A	
	21. Italy	148	145	21. Italy	148	3A	

	22.	Thailand	146	142	22. Thailand	145	3A	
	23.	Greece	141	145	Turkey	145	3A	
140		Turkey	141	142	24. Portugal	141	3B	
	25.	Portugal	137	136	25. Greece	140	3A	140
		South Africa	137	149	26. South Africa	135	3A	
	27.	Ivory Coast	135	135	27. India	133	3B	
	28.	India	133	123	28. Ivory Coast	126	3B	
		Indonesia	133	124	29. Indonesia	125	3B	
		Kenya	133	123	30. Israel	124	3B	
	31.	Venezuela	131	133	Pakistan	124	3B	
	32.	Colombia	129	129	32. Colombia	123	3B	
		Israel	129	130	33. Venezuela	122	3B	
	34.	Brazil	125	125	34. Kenya	120	3B	
	35.	Egypt	121	125	35. Brazil	118	4A	120
		Pakistan	121	119	36. Egypt	116	4A	
120	37.	Equador	120	127	37. Chile	115	4A	
	38.	Chile	119	123	38. Ecuador	113	4A	
	39.	Nigeria	116	118	39. Iraq	107	4A	
	40.	Argentina	112	111	40. Argentina	106	4A	
	41.	Mexico	111	124	Nigeria	106	4A	
		Morocco	111	105	Philippines	106	4A	
	43.	Peru	109	111	43. Peru	103	4A	
		Philippines	109	108	44. Mexico	101	4A	
	45.	Iraq	106	101	Morocco	101	4A	
	46.	Iran	94	92	46. Iran	92	4A	
	47.	Bolivia	93	89	47. Bolivia	90	4A	
	48.	Zaire	86	74	48. Zaire	82	4A	

No business transactions – combined scores up to 120

POR	*Score*
4A	up to 120

Whilst country risks should be taken very seriously it is also important to consider the type of investment in relation to the country risk. For example, investment in the extractive industries or where major capital investment is required is inherently more risky than investing in an assembly operation using leased assets.

SUMMARY

Deregulation in capital markets has developed on a worldwide basis as countries review their regulations in the light of increased competition. A reduction in restrictions on capital markets has also been matched by increasing freedom for foreign investors. For example, Australia and Canada are two industrialized countries with very high levels of foreign control of their business enterprises. In order to restrict its spread Australia set up the Foreign Investment Review Board in 1974, and in the same year Canada passed a Foreign Investment Review Act. However, in 1985–6 Australia relaxed its regulations, and in 1985 Canada replaced its regulatory body with Investment Canada designed to attract new foreign investment.

Deregulation in the capital markets poses new problems in other areas of the national and international economy as MNEs continue to grow. These problems include off-balance sheet financing, the need for global accounting standards, the need for methods which equitably allocate tax burdens and problems of insider dealing and control of national monopolies.

A parallel movement with the deregulation of capital markets may be the tendency to intervene more in the foreign exchange markets. This change in strategy started in September 1985 with the Group of Five agreement which started the process of reducing the value of the US dollar and increasing the value of the Japanese yen. It is possible that Japan will react to an increase in value of the yen by moving away from export orientation towards developing its domestic economy. Also, trade disputes are likely to lead to increased investment overseas by Japanese MNEs as well as an increase in takeover activity in their domestic markets.

Finally this chapter has considered a prerequisite to all foreign investment – the evaluation of country risk. The evaluation process should consist of an assessment of the political and economic risks of investing in a particular country in the context of the proposed investment. Some investments, such as those in extractive industries, are more prone to political intervention than other sectors such as retailing. In addition, risks need to be assessed in relation to the level of the proposed investment. It is far riskier to invest abroad in projects requiring heavy capital outlays than projects involving assembly using leased assets.

Recognition of some of the concepts mentioned in these two introductory chapters can be gleaned from company accounts, particularly the Chairman's statement or Directors' report. Two examples are shown below. Firstly, A. Johnson & Co, a Swedish international trading company:

> 1985 was marked by strategic moves aimed at further concentrating our efforts on areas where we have unique capabilities. These moves had adverse effects on earnings in the short-term perspective, but increase the strength and competitiveness of A. Johnson & Co in the long-term. The long-term perspective has been a consistent element of the management philosophy in the Company, which is now entering its 114th year of operations.
>
> We have a base in regular business transactions world-wide through our presence – for a period of decades – in a number of product markets. This base forms our equivalent of an industrial company's know-how, contacts and experience on which to build new transactions.
>
> The internationalization – or, rather, the globalization – of raw materials trading within A. Johnson & Co has moved a step forward. Among other measures, I include in this activity Axel Johnson Ore and Metals' establishment in the important US market and Axel Johnson's Petroleum's acquisition of a 50 per cent interest in Oroleum International Ltd, one of the largest trading companies handling oil and oil products in the Far East.
>
> North Coal's purchase of Stora Trading should also be included in this category. The acquisition broadens North Coal's competence and strengthens its competitiveness internationally.

Secondly, the 1985 annual report of Engelhard Corporation, a US company specializing in chemical and metallurgical technologies, provides interesting reading on its global strategy and approach to business. Indeed the front and back covers of the report are devoted to four global shapes which 'symbolize the structure of international trade today, the existing opportunities and challenges being created by rapid communication and travel, and the regions of the world where Engelhard is focusing its efforts'. Here are some extracts from the report:

> 1985 was a year in which the Company achieved many of its key business goals. Among them were increased market shares, new product introductions, acquisitions, manufacturing expansion and improved operating efficiencies.
>
> In fact, we see the evolution of a highly competitive global market place as so significant that the editorial portions of this report are dedicated to the subject.
>
> At the very foundation of our future business plans are the strategic priorities which govern our profitable global expansion. Summarized below, they constitute the theme of this report:
>
> —Sustaining the exceptional technologies which underpin our success in acquiring and keeping customs against global competition;

—Marketing selectively to those global opportunities which are most attractive;
—Maximizing our financial flexibility to fund expansion in the global capital marketplace;
—Managing technological, capital and human resources aggressively, with sensitivity and a view towards being a significant global company now and into the twenty-first century.

Commitment to global expansion

Two decades ago, it took a giant room-sized computer to match the capabilities of today's personal desktop versions. Advanced technology has relentlessly shrunk the artificial computer world of bits and bytes. It is also uniting the real world.

Driven by technology, the business day now runs a full 24 hours all across the globe, spanning the major markets of the world without interruption. Businesses and their customers can track their financial position, their manufacturing capacity and their inventories at any time on a global basis. Information itself has become a global commodity.

The inevitable result has been to tie the world together economically, and to bring Engelhard closer to markets that can greatly benefit from its technologically-based performance products.

Over the past decade, the economies of countries across the world have grown increasingly interdependent. The result is a global business structure which lets us drive cars from other nations, watch television on imported sets, eat foods from around the world and converse with people 8000 miles away.

While the forces for economic change shift throughout the world, the drive towards a global economy remains steadfastly on course. It is creating international businesses as well – not only household names but major industrial firms providing technology and making process-control equipment and components for familiar products of familiar companies.

In the emerging world economy, staying ahead of the competition demands information. Servicing markets demands a broad distribution system. And, expanding market participation demands innovative products.

In approaching and analysing world opportunities, Engelhard is seeking market segments where this differential in product value generates leading market shares. The differential comes from matching Engelhard technology with customer need. To be the number one or two supplier is the goal in every market the Company enters.

In segmenting markets for each product line, Engelhard studies how each product fits the economic needs of the country and region. It also considers the nature of the competition: who is there now and who is likely to come in as the market grows. Other factors influence the decision that a market opportunity is potentially viable over the long term to justify an investment. These include the level of profitability and the rate of return that can be achieved. Generally, rates of return reflect the long-term intent in building a market.

Political, economic and social factors also are weighed: trade incentives and barriers, stability of local governments and their attitudes towards trade, and the basic economic structure of the area – its history, how it is developing and at what pace.

How business is conducted in a given country or region typically determines the marketing approach. The Company is attuned to local cultures and stresses the importance of being a responsible member of each business community.

Engelhard's method of entering a market may be direct, through acquisition, with a joint venture partner, or by employing local sales agents. Substantial market potential often justifies nearby manufacturing, either by Engelhard or a joint venture partnership.

Strategies to meet current challenges and to carve long-term positions focus on preserving and expanding critical North American markets; reaching European market segments where Engelhard's proprietary technologies give customers value-added benefits; participating on the ground floor in the emerging economies of the Pacific Basin; and serving giant international customers operating plants throughout the world.

With major facilities in Japan and Australia, Engelhard is stepping up its marketing of products and technological expertise to participate in the economic growth of South Korea, China, Hong Kong, Singapore and other Pacific Basin countries. These nations are building their infrastructures, creating manufacturing industries, modernizing agriculture, and enthusiastically embracing Western tastes for clothing and consumer electronic goods.

Engelhard also is concentrating on serving companies that have established worldwide manufacturing operations to gain market share and manufacturing efficiency. Leading international companies for each major product line are prime sales targets.

Behind all the effort is a commitment by Engelhard management to the economic reality that the opportunities to optimize shareholder value must be played out on a global landscape.

Some interesting comments are made about the North American market:

As products from the Pacific Basin, Europe and Latin America flow in, manufacturing industries and jobs have been moving out of the US. The decline in manufacturing is partly attributable to imports and partly to American companies shifting production 'offshore' in order to compete with the lower labour rates of foreign firms.

. . . the sheer size of the US market makes it imperative for American corporations to retain their foothold and for foreign companies to seek a share.

Finally, the President explains how the strategy is to be achieved and the Finance and Chief Financial Officer outlines how future business will be financed:

The Company's global strategy is aimed at enhancing market position while protecting and adding to shareholder value. It involves five key elements:

—Segmenting markets where superior technology and product differentiation are important advantages to customers;
—Building up global economies-of-scale in manufacturing;
—Controlling effective distribution channels;

—Fully benefiting from a worldwide network of precious metals management;
—Maintaining economic access to global capital markets.

Engelhard's strategy is to work from its strength-technology, which creates performance products that differentiate the Company from competitors by offering customers advantages in their manufacturing processes. The Company has also made it a top priority to control its own manufacturing costs, with the objective of being the low-cost producer.

In short, Engelhard's ability to compete effectively throughout the world is based on identifying attractive market segments and sustaining a competitive advantage through technological superiority and manufacturing efficiency.

Global expansion requires a long-term outlook, focussed both on the marketing of performance products supported by accelerated research and development, and on the selective acquisition of complementary businesses.

Two principles guide how Engelhard manages international finance.

1. Access to capital markets and sources of liquidity must be international. Financial markets are globalized, with many areas outside the US offering economic opportunity. Engelhard has the global capability to sell commercial paper and long-term debt through rated securities and to secure short-term or medium-term funding from banks around the world for flexibility in liquidity.
2. International businesses are managed in the currency of the owner. A decision to place fixed assets in a foreign country follows the operating premise that Engelhard has made a long-term investment. In most cases, the Company will reinvest earnings to expand its foreign operation.

3

Summary of the Country Studies

The aim of this chapter is to highlight particular differences in treatment of important areas relevant to mergers and acquisitions. Some comparative analysis is undertaken in order to draw attention to special areas of interest. In addition, areas that are common to several countries in this survey are dealt with in this chapter. For example, consideration is given to the Seventh Directive, to the proposed Tenth Directive on International Mergers, to the proposed Eleventh Directive on the Disclosure Requirements of Branches, and to the introduction of the concept of a European Economic Interest Grouping.

In effect this chapter serves as a summary of the country studies that follows in Part II.

BUSINESS ORGANIZATIONS AND COMBINATIONS

In Anglo-Saxon countries businesses of any reasonable size are formed as limited companies, branches of foreign enterprises or joint ventures. However, it is noticeable that in continental countries such as France and the Federal Republic of Germany business of some significance is conducted through partnerships. However, the acquisition of partnership interests is not often considered by foreign investors but is normally used to accommodate domestic or family businesses. Generally, foreign investors may commence business in another country through their own branch but once activity becomes significant a limited liability company is formed. The advantage of this is to restrict liability to the overseas company and to improve a company's image abroad.

In all the countries included in this survey it is possible to acquire either shares or assets of a target company. However, there are a number of complications. For example, whilst the formal takeover offer is most common, in Australia a variety of other approaches is permitted including a scheme of arrangement. Such arrangements owe their origins to legislation in the UK. The concept of a merger or statutory amalgamation is prevalent in a number of countries. For example, a statutory amalgamation in Canada is one in which two or more corporations come together to form one new company whilst accepting the rights and obligations of the predecessor businesses. The merger concept is further refined in France into a merger and a split. The former consists of dissolving part or all of the entities involved, whereas a split refers to the absorption of a whole company by two or more entities simultaneously.

The merger concept is also recognized in the Federal Republic of Germany in which the acquired enterprise is simultaneously liquidated and the shareholders receive shares in the acquiring company in exchange for their former interests. Other factors become important in determining the type of transactions that become prevalent in a country. For example, whilst it is perfectly feasible for the assets of a Swedish company to be acquired it is not common in practice because such transactions are treated unfavourably by the taxation authorities.

The concept of a 'fusion' is also common in Europe, e.g. in the Netherlands and Italy. Another variation, 'absorption', refers to a merger between independent companies, i.e. one company is incorporated into the other. Such transactions tend to be less common than the acquisition of shares or assets.

Whilst the takeover of shares in the capital markets is common in Anglo-Saxon countries it is rare in countries such as Japan where it is avoided because of the steep rise in share price that usually follows. This obviously has implications for the distribution of gains to the merger participants. For example, in the UK the acquiree's shareholders normally make considerable gains from such transactions whereas in Japan a share acquisition through the market is avoided.

TAKEOVER TRENDS

It is difficult to make generalizations on takeover trends from a survey of 16 countries since a number of special factors are important to particular countries and some do not publish any statistics on takeover activity. However, it seems clear that there has been an upsurge in merger and acquisition activity in nearly every country covered. It is not accurate to describe the acquisition boom as an Anglo-Saxon takeover phenomenon (*Financial Times*, 17 February 1987). This increase in activity is in terms of numbers of transactions completed and, more significantly, involves more transactions of high value. Activity is particularly pronounced in advanced economies with highly developed stock exchanges. The trend then is for an increase in immensely powerful business organizations which inevitably pose problems of control.

The trend can be accounted for in a number of ways. First, economic factors have been important. In the late 1970s and early 1980s the world was suffering from recession and this had the effect of depressing stock market values and discouraging foreign investment. As the world economy improved, stock markets boomed and companies that emerged strong were able to acquire companies that had found it more difficult to cope with changes in economic conditions. Furthermore, improved trading conditions encouraged foreign investment and foreign predators.

Special features apply to certain countries. For example, in South Africa there has been a tendency for high-value transactions and for the purchase of some foreign subsidiaries by local businessmen. Management buyouts have become more significant as foreign multinationals, particularly those from the US, have sought to divest from a country that has become increasingly politically sensitive. In contrast, Japan has had to deal with the problem of a rapidly increasing currency which has led to some areas of its economy encountering difficulties. This has led to acquisition activity as conglomerates have sought to protect their margins as the rate of economic growth has declined.

Merger and acquisition activity has also increased for a number of strategic reasons and these can be summarized as follows:

1. to diversify regionally and politically;
2. to protect profit margins by acquiring market share;
3. to protect margins by acquiring competitors;
4. to cope more readily with the shortening of the product life-cycle;
5. to obtain economies of scale to compete internationally;
6. as a countermeasure to trade friction, e.g. Japan;
7. to maintain close business relationships during a period of divestment by some companies, e.g. Japan;
8. to mitigate against legal controls on mergers and acquisitions and foreign investment;
9. to provide access to needed technology;
10. to broaden product lines;
11. to expand markets;
12. to acquire undervalued companies as this is often a cheaper option than building from scratch;
13. to restrict competition;
14. to integrate forwards and backwards;
15. to obtain know-how such as patents, trademarks etc.;
16. to improve a branch network;
17. to acquire management or technical personnel.

Thus, acquisition activity is undertaken in order to gain an advantage over competitors. Of course, the political and economic ambitions of individual directors or boards of directors should also be taken into consideration in explaining motivation.

In order for acquisition activity to take place there must be sufficient currency to complete transactions. Since 1983 corporate profitability has increased and companies have become considerably more liquid thereby permitting more cash transactions. Furthermore, buoyant world stock markets have encouraged share-for-share transactions to be concluded.

Another feature has been the availability of funds as banks have increasingly become reluctant to lend to foreign governments in developing and newly industrialized countries. In addition, there has been a slowdown in loans to countries that do not have debt servicing problems such as South Korea and China. This has also led to an increase in available funds for other ventures, including mergers and acquisitions. Another factor is the current exchange rate between one country and another. For example, an appreciation in the value of the Deutschmark relative to the US dollar has made it more difficult for German companies to export to the US. A fall in export orders has been particularly noticeable in motor vehicles and industrial plant and machinery. To avoid exchange rate difficulties one strategy is to manufacture in the desired market, and indeed many German companies have adopted this approach.

Another feature of acquisition activity has been the tendency for hostile takeovers to occur more frequently. Whilst this is not new in Anglo-Saxon countries it is in some European countries, e.g. France. However, there does not appear to be any immediate prospect of this type of transaction becoming acceptable in Japan. Whilst takeover activity is high in Japan nearly all are negotiated, friendly mergers. Certainly, a hostile foreign takeover would be greeted with considerable concern and would ultimately fail.

The direction of acquisitions is also important. For example, the UK has traditionally acquired in the US rather than invested in European mergers. This has not changed since the UK became a member of the EEC. A simple explanation could be that the UK already has ready access to the European market and does not need to extend its presence by acquisition. Furthermore, some argue that the UK rationally looks to the safer, larger and more homogeneous US market rather than the highly competitive, almost saturated and fragmented European market. However, this explanation represents only a partial exposition. History and Anglo-Saxon culture still remain as important factors. The UK's history is one of close links with the US and vice versa. Their language, culture and business relationships are closer than those between the UK and Europe. For centuries the UK has distrusted a number of significant countries in Europe – this distrust does not change over a few years. Where distrust does not exist, for example between the Netherlands and the UK, business, joint ventures and acquisitions have flourished.

The Anglo-Saxon relationship between the UK and US is not one-way. The US invests more in the UK than in any other overseas country. Furthermore, the Anglo-Saxon relationship extends beyond the UK–US link to Australasia.

In constrast, Continental Europeans do not possess the same degree of distrust between each other. The French and Italians and French and Germans are very willing to invest, acquire and trade with each other. Scandinavian countries, such as Sweden, are willing to accept any profitable investment wherever it is located.

These directional flows are likely to change at a very slow rate although deregulation of stock markets in Europe may make it easier for companies to make acquisitions through the market. The EEC has a part to play in removing barriers to cross-border transactions.

MERGER CONTROL

Twelve of the 16 countries included in this survey have some form of merger control policy and these are summarized in table 3.1. It is possible to classify control, and in particular abuse of a dominant position, into *a priori* control, in which all such activities are forbidden unless the authorities grant permission, and *a posteriori* control, in which such abuses are not forbidden but there is a requirement that experts examine each case to decide if a merger should be allowed.

The *a priori* approach is adopted in Canada, US, Argentina, Brazil, W. Germany, the Netherlands and Japan. The EEC too adopts this approach – if, indeed, one can describe their inadequate set of competition rules as an approach. It is obvious that the US approach of dealing with monopoly, which stems back to the Sherman Act 1890, has been very influential. Indeed the Act has its roofs in the period after the Civil War when the North was afraid of the size and influence of the trusts in the South. A strong case can be made that an approach developed in the mid-nineteenth century is inappropriate to the later stages of the twentieth century and onwards.

In contrast, the *a posteriori* approach is adopted in France, South Africa, Sweden and the UK. South Africa and the UK adopt a public interest approach which is more general than a competition test, whereas France and Sweden adopt abuse of a dominant position as its *modus operandi*.

Australia has a mixed system in which the Trade Practices Act 1974 prohibits some types of anti-competitive arrangements and behaviour and advance authorization is required from the Trade Practices Commission. Like the UK, firms can obtain the guidance of the Commission on a confidential basis, but unlike the UK, it is possible to obtain advance authorization from the Commission. The Commission will consider rationalization and restructuring of industry as one of the public benefit considerations and if the Commission decides not to authorize the merger, the parties concerned can apply to the Trade Practices Tribunal for a review of the case. Authorization is not obligatory so that a merger can proceed without prior consultation and carry the risk of whether a breach of the Act will result.

A fourth category of companies included in this survey are those countries that have no anti-trust legislation. This group includes Italy, where mergers and acquisitions are subject to EEC merger control, Malaysia where control is exercised by exchange regulations, Hong Kong where there are rules based on the UK City Code, and Nigeria where there is extensive monopoly or oligopoly and there is little desire by foreigners to acquire local businesses.

In most countries there are some restrictions on foreigners acquiring companies in host countries. These regulations may range from those which apply equally to the indigeneous population, particularly in areas

Table 3.1 Main features of merger control in 16 countries and in the EEC

	Prior notification		*Ex-post notification*		*Quantitative criteria for notification or investigation*	
Country	*Compulsory*	*Optional*	*Compulsory*	*Optional*	*Market share*	*Absolute size criteria*
Argentina	Yes	No	No	No	No	No
Australia	No except some foreign takeovers	Yes	No	No	No	No
Brazil	No except for certain industries	No	No	No	No	No
Canada	Yes	Yes	No	No	No	Yes
France	No	Yes	No	Yes	No	Yes

Basic criteria for prohibiting mergers	*Criteria for notification of a foreign takeover*	*Appeals procedure*
National Commission of defence of competition. General control over abuse of a dominant position	Foreign investments secretariat. Investments in strategic areas require professional approval	
Trade Practices Commission. Anti-competitive behaviour detrimental to consumers. Abuse of substantial control over the market	Foreign Investment Review Board. Against the national interest. Investigates substantial foreign interests. Notification required for ownership of at least 15 per cent of an Australian company. 40 days notice required	Trade Practices Tribunal Reviews Commission's decisions. Remedies are through the Federal Court
The Administrative Council of Economic Defence. Abuse of economic power	No special control except in sensitive areas. Takeovers must be registered but do not need approval. Control indirectly through exchange and taxation rules	
Competition Tribunal Abuse of dominant position	Investment Canada to encourage investment in Canada. Notification of all foreign investment above certain limits	Appeal to the Federal Court and Minister
Commission for Competition. Criteria. 40 per cent horizontal 25 per cent non-horizontal	Abuse of a dominant position	Appeal to the Highest Administrative Court, The Conseil d'Etat

– *Continued*

Table 3.1 Continued

Country	Prior notification		Ex-post notification		Quantitative criteria for notification or investigation	
	Compulsory	*Optional*	*Compulsory*	*Optional*	*Market share*	*Absolute size criteria*
Federal Republic of Germany	Yes	Yes	Yes	No	Yes	Yes
Hong Kong	Yes	No	No	No	No	Yes
Italy	No	No	No	No	No	No
Japan	Yes	No	Yes	No	No	Yes
Malaysia	Yes	No	No	No	No	Yes
Netherlands	No	No	No	No	No	No
Nigeria	Yes	No	No	No	No	No
South Africa	No	No	No	No	No	No

Basic criteria for prohibiting mergers	*Criteria for notification of a foreign takeover*	*Appeals procedure*
Federal Cartel Office. Abuse of a dominant position	No limitations	Appeal to the Federal Minister of Economics
Committee on takeovers and mergers. Abuse of the rules of the Securities Ordinance		
None	Possible political interference	None
Fair Trade Commission. Prohibits private monopoly and anti-competitive arrangements	Give notice to the Minister of Finance of a proposed purchase of Japanese securities. A licence may be required in some circumstances	Appeal to the Tokyo High Court
There is no monopoly or anti-trust legislation	Foreign Investments Committee. Guidelines that if breached lead to penalties	
Committee on Economic Competition. Abuse of economic power	No restrictions	
There is no monopoly or anti-trust legislation	Federal Ministry of Finance. Approval is required for all foreign investment	
Competition Board. Operating against the public interest	None	

– *Continued*

Table 3.1 Continued

	Prior notification		Ex-post notification		Quantitative criteria for notification or investigation	
Country	*Compulsory*	*Optional*	*Compulsory*	*Optional*	*Market share*	*Absolute size criteria*
Sweden	Yes in certain circumstances	No	No	No	No	Yes in certain circumstance
UK	No	No	No	No	Yes 25 per cent	Yes gross assets
US	Yes	No	No	No	No	Yes shares assets sales
EEC	Yes larger	No	No	No	No	Yes turnover

where there are state monopolies or where the industry is deemed to be sensitive, to those which specifically apply to foreigners. For example, there has been substantial foreign presence in industry in both Canada and Australia which has led to strong control. However, these extensive controls have been relaxed somewhat in order to encourage multinationals to invest because of the employment advantages they offer. For example, whilst a pre-notification condition for large-scale acquisitions was introduced in Canada in 1987, the Foreign Investment Review Act 1974 was replaced by the Investment Canada Act 1986. The purpose of the new Act is to encourage investment in Canada by non-Canadians provided that the investment contributes to economic growth and domestic employment opportunities. The introduction of this Act represents a considerable shift in policy by the Canadian government to encouraging, rather than discouraging, foreign investment in Canada. It has been estimated that approximately 90 per cent of the cases which would have

Basic criteria for probibiting merger	*Criteria for notification of a foreign takeover*	*Appeals procedure*
Competition Act 1982. Prevent a dominant position in the market. Compliance undertaken by the anti-trust secretary	Foreign takeovers of Swedish Enterprises Act. Approval required in certain cases. Designed to protect the public interest	
Office of Fair Trading. Operating against the public interest	None	
Department of Justice and Fair Trade Commission. Reduction in the competitive environment	None	
Abuse of a dominant position		Court of Justice

required Federal approval under the Foreign Investment Review Act will now be exempt. In addition to encouraging foreign investment, there has been a significant relaxation of the takeover regulations.

Australia has also introduced some amendments to the administration of the Foreign Takeovers Act 1975. The aim of modification is to reduce the administrative burden on business in order to simplify the procedures for the screening of foreign investment proposals, to ease the policy criteria for certain types of investment proposals, and to exempt other proposals from examination. One of the important modifications was introduced on 29 October 1985 which changed the requirement that a proposed foreign acquisition must be made public so that Australians were given the opportunity to bid for the business itself – the 'opportunity test'. This practice has now been discontinued mainly because it was rare for an Australian bidder to come forward.

The New Economic Policy introduced in Malaysia has changed perspective actively to encourage foreign investment through equity participation, particularly in the high-technology area. The Industrial Coordination Act was introduced specifically to encourage foreign investment.

Generally, there has been a change in attitude towards multinational investment. Whether a less hostile atmosphere will lead to more harmonization of anti-trust and merger legislation remains to be seen. On the one hand, the UK is undertaking a thorough review of competition policy with the possibility that existing laws will be strengthened. On the other hand, for example, the US is adopting a more liberal approach. The 1984 Guidelines strengthened the international dimension of mergers and acquisitions in considering dominant positions. The level of actions against companies to stop a merger are at a level which is very much lower than that prevailing in the 1970s. The Chicago School has been influential in this change of emphasis, and have challenged the notion that high profits in industries that were concentrated was the result of an abuse of monopoly power. Rather they legitimized the level of profits by suggesting that the high level of profits was the result of greater efficiency. The idea of 'contestable markets' was introduced in the early 1980s which suggested that the optimal properties of perfect competition could be enjoyed in markets where there were few participants. What was emphasized was the ability of enterprises to enter or leave markets.

In addition to the Chicago School, the neo-Austrian school argues that the standard neoclassical theory inadequately reflects modern capitalism where the reality is a world of great business rivalry, innovation and change in the face of uncertainty. High profits result from efficiency and expansion under difficult market conditions.

These two schools have been reinforced by others. For example, Professor Armentano has suggested that price-fixing and collusions can be legitimate business responses. These rationalizations have weakened the arguments against takeovers in the US. In reality they probably reflect no more than active lobbying to legitimize large enterprises and many of their practices in the light of increased international competition particularly from the Japanese. As long as US corporations dominate major sectors of the world economy abuses can be rationalized away.

As well as the US, the FRG is also taking a more relaxed position about merger control. Mergers are being approved more quickly and a lower number are being prohibited. The Chicago School seems to have been influential in convincing the Federal Cartel Office that certain agreements including restrictive practices and mergers may actually be pro-competitive.

As for the EEC, Article 3(f) states that a system be instituted to ensure that competition in the Common Market is not distorted. The specific rules applying to undertakings are laid down in Articles 85 and 86. Barring dispensation, Article 85 of the treaty prohibits agreements, decisions by business associations and mutually agreed effective conduct that adversely affect trade between Member States and restrict competition with the Common Market. Restriction of competition by the agreement must be manifest and must actually or potentially hamper trade between Member States. One of the problems with Article 85 is that it is so wide-ranging that it may affect not only anti-competitive behaviour but also behaviour that might be pro-competitive. Article 85 applies to patents, know-how licensing agreements, distribution agreements and franchising arrangements. Whilst merger control is not covered by this Article it does apply to joint ventures.

The purpose of Article 86 is to combat the abuse of a dominant position. A dominant position must be exercised in the Common Market or in a material part of it. An abuse may arise by:

a. directly or indirectly imposing unfair purchase or selling prices or other unfair trading conditions;
b. limiting production, markets or technical development to the prejudice of consumers;
c. applying dissimilar conditions to equivalent transactions with other trading parties, thereby placing them at a competitive disadvantage;
d. making the conclusion of contracts subject to acceptance by other parties of supplementary obligations which, by their nature or according to commercial usage, have no connection with the subject of such contracts.

The classic case under Article 86 is Continental Can, since it provides the foundation of merger control in the Community. In 1969 Continental Can, a US multinational with a diverse product range which includes the manufacture of metal containers, purchased its largest German competitor. The following year Continental Can also acquired a Dutch company producing metal containers. The Commission opposed these mergers on the grounds of an abuse of a dominant position. In 1973, however, the Court of Justice dismissed the case, but the foundation for merger control had been laid.

Article 86 has some significant limitations. First, it does not appear to be applicable where a dominant market position is achieved by a merger, but rather where an existing dominant position is further strengthened. Secondly, the provisions are not pre-emptive and can only be applied where an abuse has already occurred. Since there are no pre-notification procedures under Article 86, the remedy of an abuse might entail the divestiture of companies or assets.

In addition to Articles 85 and 86, the European Commission can act against national governments that provide assistance to individual businesses by means of subsidies or special tax benefits. Articles 92–4 of the Treaty of Rome deal with this aspect and are part of the rules to ensure that a competitive environment prevails in the Common Market.

In 1973 the Commission adopted a proposal for the control of concentration between undertakings. The main points of this proposal are summarized below:

1. Concentration which prevents effective competition is incompatible with the Common Market. The Commission may order the dissolution of a merger or distribution of some of the assets. However, this Article is not applicable where concentrations 'are dispensable to the attainment of an objective which is given priority treatment in the common interest of the Community'.
2. Larger mergers shall be notified to the Commission before completion where the aggregate turnover is not less than 1000 million units of account. There are detailed rules for calculating turnover and market shares. Where the market share is less than 20 per cent of a market, it is presumed to be compatible with the Common Market. Prior notification is not required when an undertaking has a turnover less than 30 million units of account.
3. Where mergers have been notified in advance of consummation, the Commission shall commence proceedings within three months of the notification date, unless some misleading information has been provided.
4. The Commission may request information from the undertakings associates or advisers. A time-limit can be provided and a fine may be imposed for non-compliance. The Commission may examine the books, business records, and documents and demand oral explanations immediately as well as enter premises, land and means of transport. All such information obtained must be treated in the strictest of confidence.
5. Decisions shall be taken within nine months of the date of commencement of proceedings.

A number of amendments have been introduced to accommodate Member States, but by July 1987 Britain was delaying introduction of the proposals on the grounds that it believes takeover rules should not be directed by the Common Market. This is somewhat ironic in that Britain wishes to reduce the burden of the common agricultural fund, quite rightly, in order to redirect Community resources to reflect its industrial base. Surely one aspect of an industrialized community is that competition, anti-competitive practices and takeovers should in some way be controlled by the Commission if abuses of a dominant position are to be avoided.

One of the amendments already made to the proposals is that mergers with a turnover of more than 750 million ECU (£525 million) will be required to notify the Commission before completion compared with the original of 1000 million ECU. This is part of the strategy of toughening competition rules to prevent an abuse of a dominant position.

If introduced, officials estimate that about forty transactions a year would be involved in the notification process of which fifteen would involve multinationals outside the Community. However, it is estimated that only two to three cases a year will require extensive scrutinization and in such cases the Commission has committed itself to producing a final assessment within six months of notification.

TAXATION

Taxation is an important factor in international mergers and acquisitions which involves a thorough understanding of the tax regime operating in the country of the proposed investment. Not only will it be necessary to establish the tax position of the acquired company but also its impact on the group as a whole and its shareholders in particular. The importance of taxation has implications for the form of the offer to be made.

Tax planning has been a growth area in the 1970s and 1980s and there is no doubt that it will continue to be important. Tax evasion – the avoidance of taxation by illegal means – has also been growing. One way of dealing with this problem has been to reduce nominal rates of tax and to reduce allowances; this has the effect of reducing the profitability of artificial avoidance schemes. Another way of avoiding international tax evasion is for the taxation authorities to co-operate among countries. In 1987 the Council of Europe opened for signature a convention of mutual cooperation – a proposal fiercely opposed by the International Chamber of Commerce. The convention was drafted by the EEC and involves the exchange of information, the enforcement of tax claims and the initiation of prosecutions involving all taxes except customs duties. If accepted, the convention would apply to twenty-one Member States of the Council of Europe as well as Australia, Canada, Finland, Japan, New Zealand and the US. However, it is possible for governments to opt out and it is likely that W. Germany, Luxembourg and Switzerland will do so. Advocates of the convention have argued that there are safeguards for taxpayers and that confidential information will be treated in accordance with a strict code of conduct. It is always interesting to see vested interests, such as the International Chamber of Commerce, defending crime: equally legitimate would be an International Chamber for Football Hooligans or even an Organization for the Protection of Drug Traffickers.

In finalizing the price to be paid for an acquisition, latent and actual tax liabilities must be established and indemnities secured where necessary. Key considerations include the following:

1. review tax charges and the extent of agreement with the authorities;
2. consider any matters in dispute with the authority;
3. establish the extent to which relief has been obtained for leases;
4. to what extent is the company affected by special provisions such as close company status and establish the implications of that status;
5. review potential liabilities, tax planning and tax avoidance;
6. consider group relief provisions in the context of capital gains, dividends and advance corporation tax where appropriate.

Tax grouping

In certain countries it is possible for a group to submit a consolidated tax return. Countries included in this survey operate different levels of control to constitute a tax group and these are shown in table 3.2. In most of the countries included in this survey there is no concept of a consolidated tax return. The UK is the most liberal in this respect where an advance corporation tax group is formed where a parent owns more than 50 per cent of the shares in another company, i.e. a parent/subsidiary relationship. Where this relationship exists a parent may, subject to normal restrictions, surrender advance corporation tax paid by it to its subsidiaries for offsetting against their own corporation tax liabilities. The advantage of such an arrangement is that dividends can be paid without bringing forward tax payment dates. Other group relationships, such as the group relief group and the capital gains group, are formed when 75 per cent of the shares of another company are owned. The group relief group permits trading losses to be surrendered between companies in a group and the capital gains tax group allows companies to transfer assets within the group without incurring capital gains tax. Australia, the FRG, the Netherlands and the US all permit consolidated tax returns provided the subsidiary is wholly owned, except for the US, where the threshold is 80 per cent.

Tax implications for the acquiring company

Generally, when a company acquires the assets of another company, the assets and liabilities are transferred on a tax-free basis. Consequently, assets and liabilities are transferred at book value and there is no step-

Table 3.2 Thresholds for tax groupings

Country	*Percentage threshold*	*Comment*
Argentina	Not permitted	
Australia	100	
Brazil	Not permitted	
Canada	Not permitted	Except in amalgamations
France	Not normally permitted	95 per cent with Ministry of Economy approval
FRG	100	Strict rules. Can include partnerships
Hong Kong	Not permitted	
Italy	Not permitted	Can write down investments
Japan	Not permitted	
Malaysia	Not permitted	
Netherlands	100	Or virtually all for a fiscal unity
Nigeria	Not permitted	
South Africa	Not permitted	
Sweden	Not permitted	Permits some transfer of earnings
UK	75	51 per cent for ACT group
US	80	

up in tax basis for either depreciable or non-depreciable property. For example, in Canada there is no step-up in tax value of assets and the value of the assets is cost to the acquirer provided the transaction is on an arm's length basis. In contrast, if a transaction is designated as a taxable-asset acquisition in the US then the asset value used is its fair market value. This is known as the step-up in tax basis.

In the FRG, it is possible to transfer assets into the new enterprise at tax book value, at current market value or indeed at a value somewhere in between the two. The transfer cost does have tax implications however. If the assests are transferred and introduced into the new business at current market value the 'profits' arising upon the deemed disposal will be subject to tax at half the capital gains tax rate normally applicable, only if the person disposing of the assets is an individual. For corporations, capital gains tax can be avoided provided the interest received in the new or reorganized business is the same or of equal value to the assets introduced into the new entity.

In Italy the purchase of assets results in the imposition of registration tax on the acquirer and any gains are taxable to the seller. The value of assets acquired is reduced proportionately for any liabilities taken on. In contrast, in Japan only the gain derived from the appreciation in the book value of the transferred property should be aggregated with other sources of income and taxed at the ordinary tax rate because it can be regarded as the capital gain earned as a result of the merger. On acquiring land or buildings, real property acquisition tax is levied at the prefectual level.

In Nigeria, cessation and commencement rules normally apply, although the tax authorities may waive them provided that they are satisfied that the transfer is made in order to facilitate better management of the business or to transfer the management to Nigeria.

In Australia there are no major tax consequences for the purchaser provided the transaction is on an arm's length basis. The Commissioner of Taxation can decide upon an alternative value when he considers that the transaction is not at arm's length.

In the UK, the decision as to whether the acquiring company should purchase assets or shares depends to some extent on its own tax position. For example, a taxpaying acquiring company may prefer to purchase assets rather than shares since it is able to obtain writing-down allowances on qualifying assets based on purchase cost rather than original cost. This rule does not apply to industrial or agricultural buildings where the original cost of construction is the relevant cost. This means that by acquiring assets rather than shares writing-down allowances will be higher initially and also reduces the potential liability on capital gains tax. In contrast, a non-taxpaying acquiring company may prefer to purchase shares rather than assets to obtain a reduced purchase price to reflect tax avoided by the seller on balancing charges or chargeable gains.

An advantage of purchasing a company rather than assets is that any prevailing losses may be carried forward and offset against future trading income, provided there is no major change in the nature or conduct of the company's business – the continuity of business test. In the UK there must not be a major change for at least three years, and in certain circumstances it is possible to obtain group relief for the tax losses. A further advantage of a share acquisition rather than an asset purchase is that the latter is normally more complicated from a legal perspective and there is likely to be close scrutiny of such transactions by the Revenue to ensure that the arrangement is not part of a tax avoidance scheme.

The main advantage of an asset purchase is that the acquirer knows exactly what is being purchased and that no hidden liabilities, particularly tax liabilities, are also being acquired.

In Australia, taxable losses may be carried forward for a period of seven years provided that either the continuity of shareholding or continuity of business test is fulfilled.

In the US, the Tax Reform Act has imposed a regulation which would limit deductions for net operating losses, in any year, to the pre-acquisition equity of the corporation.

Another aspect that can lead to problems is the allocation of the purchase consideration. For example, in the US since depreciation is allowed against tax on tangible assets but not on intangible assets the purchaser will wish to allocate as much of the consideration to tangible assets. In contrast, the seller will wish the converse to occur in order to subject his gains to capital gains tax rather than ordinary income tax. Such problems must be addressed at the negotiation stage.

Tax implications for the acquirer's shareholders

There are no significant taxation implications affecting the acquirer's shareholders in most of the countries covered in this survey. This is because shares are received in the new company instead of shares in the old company. No taxation liability arises provided the shares represent capital property.

Tax implications for the acquiree company

Where an acquiree company sells assets rather than shares it is possible that the gain will be subjected to capital gains tax. However, in most countries included in this survey capital gains are treated as ordinary income. However, in the UK gains are subjected to capital gains tax at a maximum rate of 30 per cent. However, gains are index-linked and it is possible to obtain rollover relief on qualifying assets. A number of countries are reviewing or have reviewed the treatment of capital gains. For example, in Sweden the government has set up a Commission to review the position since at present capital gains are treated as ordinary income. In contrast, Australia introduced a separate capital gains tax from 30 September 1985 which involves similar treatment of gains to that in the UK. For assets held for a period of at least 12 months the gains are index-linked. However, in the US the Tax Reform Act 1986 repealed the separate capital gains tax and made them subject to ordinary income tax. Other variations include Canada where half the gain is treated as ordinary income whereas in Japan gains are subject to corporation tax plus a surcharge. In France, a clear distinction is made between short-term and long-term gains and losses.

In the UK assets may be transferred between members of the same group without the penalty of incurring capital gains tax. The requirement for this is that at least 75 per cent of the shares of the subsidiary must be owned by the parent company. Such an arrangement represents a deferral of tax only, since the asset is deemed to be transferred at cost to the group and a gain does not arise until the asset is transferred outside the group. A similar position applies in the US where a transaction may be considered to be a reorganization. An essential feature of a reorganization is that the acquirer either continues the acquired company's historic business or uses a significant part of the acquiree's assets in the business. Where the acquirer and acquiree are in the same business, it is normally presumed that the business continues.

Other implications include the treatment of taxable losses and the ability to carry forward such allowances. These have been discussed in the previous section.

Tax implications for the acquiree's shareholders

One of the major implications for the acquiree's shareholders is the form of consideration as this has an impact on capital gains. For example, in the UK a disposal of shares or debentures by a shareholder, by either a person or a holding company, represents a chargeable event for capital gains purposes, except where the securities are held as a current asset or where the disposal is part of a reorganisation. In the UK, as in many other countries, the price placed on the shares of the acquirer should be on the basis of commercial considerations and not for tax reasons. Where the transaction is solely an exchange of stock it is common for no tax to accrue until the securities are finally realized whereas a cash deal normally represents a realized capital gain. In the US where a capital gain arises 60 per cent of the long-term gain may be excluded. In some countries, for example Canada, the vendor may elect for a tax-free rollover in a share-for-share transaction or to recognize gains or losses as they arise. A condition of such an arrangement is that the transaction should be at arm's length.

Where the transaction involves the liquidation or dissolution of the acquired company it is possible that a liquidation dividend is paid which is often treated as a liability to income tax. For example, in the Netherlands the excess of that received over the average paid up capital is subject to income tax at an individual's marginal rate.

In other countries the type of company acquired becomes important. For example, in Australia there are no direct consequences for shareholders of a public company but there may be if a private company is involved. If a private company makes a profit it may be necessary for a dividend to be made to ensure that the minimum level of distribution is achieved to avoid the undistributed profits tax.

In the FRG any profits arising upon the sale or disposal of shareholdings by a shareholder is subject to income tax, or corporation tax where the shareholder is a corporation. However, the profit is only subject to tax where the shareholder directly or indirectly held more than a 25 per cent interest in the company – a substantial interest. There are anti-avoidance provisions to prevent substantial interests from being gradually depleted on a tax-free basis. Foreign shareholders are not normally liable to such provisions as they are generally excluded by double taxation agreements.

In Japan where shares, money or property are issued or paid to the shareholders of the merged corporation in excess of the sum of paid-up capital and capital surplus (i.e. retained earnings) or the merged corporation, the excess is subject to withholding income tax as a deemed dividend to the shareholders of the merged corporation.

Tax planning

Great care needs to be taken in formulating a business strategy that has taxation implications. Generally, legislation in many countries insists that transactions should be conducted on an arm's length basis and should be for commercial reasons and not for taxation reasons. For example, in Australia there are anti-avoidance provisions which try to ensure that transactions are not undertaken with a view to transferring taxable profits out of the country. The objective of the government is not to penalize foreign investors but rather to ensure that they pay equivalent taxation to indigenous companies. In the UK tax avoidance schemes developed solely with the purpose of avoiding tax will not succeed.

Transactions with countries which are designated as tax havens are carefully scrutinized and if tax avoidance is suspected penalties may be invoked. For example, in Australia exchange approval will not be granted.

Where money is raised in the country in which the investment is to be made, the interest will normally be deductible for tax purposes provided it is used eventually in income-generating activities. In some countries, such as Australia, Canada and the US thin capitalization provisions apply. Provided interest is reasonable no penalties are likely to be incurred. In other countries, for example Japan, there is no concept of thin capitalization.

ACCOUNTING

In chapter 2 there was some discussion of the growth of international capital markets and the need for global standards of accounting. A lack of global accounting standards is likely to be detrimental to international investors, particularly in the light of rapid growth in international diversification by financial institutions, detrimental to the growth of an international equities market and create difficulties for those wishing to gain a greater insight into financial reports. The International Accounting Standards Committee has tried to improve and develop generally accepted accounting principles but it faces many problems, not least a lack of commitment by some major powers, in achieving its objectives. A more fundamental problem is that financial reports are not prepared on a uniform basis within any country of the world. Differences in accounting policies and their implementation produces many distortions.

Problem areas in accounting are many although they may be categorized into the following:

1. a lack of international harmonization;
2. the extent of flexibility in accounting standards offered by some major countries;
3. the enormous scope for subjectivity permitted in complying with accounting standards;
4. a lack of accounting standards in key areas in some major countries;
5. a lack of statutory backing for accounting standards;
6. non-compliance with prevailing accounting standards.

A lack of harmonization is a problem of such importance that it was considered necessary to prepare a summary of significant differences between generally accepted accounting practices in each country and international accounting standards. A summary was not prepared for those countries included in chapter 14 since reliance on international accounting standards is substantial. This results from a lack of guidance offered by both governments and the accounting profession in those countries.

The extent of flexibility provided by a standard makes comparisons between domestic companies difficult, if not impossible, and often makes international comparisons fruitless. This is of great significance when there is considerable flexibility in accounting standards of countries that are significant in accounting influence. For example, I think that it is possible to classify countries into standard-setting countries and standard-taking countries. The former would include the UK and US and the latter would include many European countries, newly industrialized countries and developing nations. Standard-setting countries are those nations to whom the rest of the world look for guidance in accounting, and standard taking countries are those which follow the guidance offered by the standard setting countries. For example, Sweden is an advanced industrialized country with many multinational companies. Its population is only 8.3 million and as such it must be a standard-taking country – it would not make sense for the country to develop standards before the standard-setting countries since the exercise might quickly be superseded by international events. Sweden, therefore, looks for guidance from the International Accounting Standards Committee and the UK and the US in particular, and to a lesser extent the European Community. Flexibility in recommendations issued by standard-setting countries causes problems for standard-taking countries. In Sweden, deferred tax is not usually provided for in financial accounts – this is a significant difference from generally accepted accounting principles prevailing in standard-setting countries. In 1983, Sweden's Business Community's Stock Exchange

Committee (NBK) proposed a new recommendation on the format of financial statements which included a requirement for the provision of deferred taxes using the comprehensive method adopted in the US. However, at that time the UK was moving away from deferred taxes on the bases of the comprehensive method towards a partial approach. As a result, Swedish companies objected vehemently and argued that they should have the flexibility to use the partial approach. This has now been introduced but practice is not yet accommodating either method. This example serves to show that flexibility in approach and a lack of international harmonization amongst standard-setting countries can lead to problems for standard taking countries.

In the area of accounting for mergers and acquisitions there is considerable scope for flexibility in the UK. Not only are the alternatives of acquisition accounting and the pooling of interests approach (merger accounting) provided for but also merger relief which has, in practice, been used in conjunction with merger accounting. Indeed, Britain argued for the inclusion of merger accounting in the Seventh Directive, at a somewhat late stage in its progress. Despite opposition from some quarters, for example the Netherlands, merger accounting was introduced into the Directive provided certain restrictions were attached. Some of these issues will be considered in greater depth later in this section.

In certain key areas there are a lack of accounting standards in some countries. For example, consolidated accounts need only be prepared by listed companies in many countries including France and Japan; and in others, for example Italy, there is no legal requirement at all. Leases cannot be capitalized in France, are rarely capitalized in Sweden, and are capitalized in the UK and US if certain conditions are fulfilled. In Italy there is no accounting standard on mergers and acquisitions and no legal framework either. In many countries, for example the Netherlands, the publication of a funds statement is not required. In some countries tax accounting is prevalent, for example Sweden and the FRG. All of these differences make comparisons exceedingly difficult and make the process of acquiring overseas companies highly complex.

If accounting standards are produced by the appropriate accountancy body it is rare for them to have statutory back-up. Only Canada stipulates that generally accepted accounting principles are those developed and published by the Canadian Institute of Chartered Accountants. In Australia, the government has created an Accounting Standards Review Board (ASRB) to develop approved accounting standards which must be complied with if a true and fair view is to prevail. Such an approach is surely the way forward for most countries if the problem of non-compliance with accounting standards is to be avoided. Furthermore, in my opinion it is essential for standard-setting bodies to liaise more closely with their appropriate stock exchanges and, if possible, to encourage a situation where non-compliance will lead to a suspension of its listed status. In my research on financial reporting in Sweden, I established that the key independent variable in determining disclosure was quotation status. Furthermore, that when high standards of financial reporting are required of listed companies there is a tendency for good practice to be followed by smaller companies.

Consolidations

The purpose of consolidated accounts is to reflect the financial results and financial condition of a parent company and its subsidiaries as if they were a single organization. For some countries included in this survey the preparation of consolidated accounts is relatively new and for others there is an extensive history. In every country included in this survey there is some obligation to prepare consolidated financial statements.

In the UK, the preparation of group accounts has been required since Companies Act 1947 although practice stretches back as far as 1910. The requirement is for group accounts, one form being consolidated accounts, although this will be changed in the near future to comply with the Seventh Directive of the European Community.

In contrast, in Japan there is no legal or tax requirement to publish consolidated financial statements. However, in 1975 the Business Accounting Deliberation Council published 'Accounting Principles for Consolidation Statements'. Consequently, listed companies have been required to prepare consolidated financial statements from 1 April 1977 and they must be audited by a CPA.

Italy is in a similar position to Japan in as much as there is no requirement in the Civil Code to prepare consolidated financial statements. However, the Commissione Nazionale per le Società e le Borsa (CONSOB), the Stock Exchange Authority, has the authority to require listed companies to prepare consolidated accounts and it has done so since 1982. However, there is no internal guidance as to their preparation so it advises that the International Accounting Standard be followed.

In determining what should be consolidated it is noticeable that there are different definitions of a subsidiary. In the UK, it is normal to define a subsidiary as one in which more than 50 per cent of the nominal value of issued equity share capital is owned by the parent. In addition, a company may be consolidated where one company controls the board of another company. These conditions are also followed in Australia.

In Japan, however, control over a board of directors is not a reason for consolidating a company. In contrast, the definition in the FRG is one of unitary of management provided there is an interest in the company.

Generally, the threshold for control is 50 per cent. Note, however, that other organizations such as stock exchanges or takeover codes stipulate other thresholds to gain control. For example, 20 per cent is the threshold for control in Australia and Canada, 25 per cent in the FRG, 30 per cent in South Africa and the UK, and 35 per cent in Hong Kong.

Significant influence seems to be presumed once 20 per cent of the equity capital of a company is acquired. In some countries such as the UK and US, it is possible to exercise significant control at less than 20 per cent provided that this can be adequately demonstrated.

In most countries in this survey there are exceptions to the requirement to prepare consolidated accounts. For example, in the UK the directors of a company may exclude a subsidiary from group accounts if:

1. its activities are so dissimilar that they cannot be considered to be a single undertaking; or
2. it would be harmful to the business of the company or any of its subsidiaries; or
3. it is impracticable; or
4. it would be of no real value to members as the amounts involved are not material; or
5. it would involve undue expense or delay out of proportion to the value of members of the company; or
6. it would be misleading.

In contrast, in Japan a subsidiary may be excluded from consolidation where there is no longer effective control; where it is no longer a going concern; where the investment is only temporary; or where interested parties would be misled.

Accounting for mergers and acquisitions

There are two main methods of accounting for mergers and acquisitions. The most common approach is acquisition (purchase) accounting in which the acquiring company records the cost of the subsidiary at the fair value of the consideration given. Where the purchase consideration is in the form of shares, any excess of fair value over the nominal value of the shares issued is taken to a share premium account. In the consolidated accounts, the fair values are assigned to the assets of the subsidiary and any excess of the purchase consideration over the fair value of assets acquired is shown as goodwill.

An alternative approach is to use merger accounting in which the acquiring company would record the cost of investment in the acquired company at the nominal value of the shares issued in exchange. In the consolidated accounts, the assets of the offeree company continue to be stated at their book value, and any difference between the nominal value of the shares exchanged is taken to reserves.

The mechanics of these two approaches were dealt with in Cooke (1986) and will not be reiterated here. However, the UK position in particular is worthy of further consideration as it demonstrates the difficulties that flexibility engenders, which could lead to problems in other countries if such an approach is imported by overseas companies. Perhaps it will be of value if the benefits and disadvantages of merger accounting are summarized. The advantages are as follows:

1. A share premium account is not required. Under UK law the difference between the nominal value of ordinary shares and fair value is taken to a share premium account when acquisition accounting is used. The

Companies Act 1985 imposes a considerable number of restrictions on the use of the share premium account.
2. Pre-acquisition reserves of the subsidiary are available for distribution by the parent company.
3. The whole of the subsidiaries' profits for the year, regardless of the date of acquisition, are included in the group profits and loss account in the period in which the merger takes place.
4. Future reported profits are higher, as depreciation is based on cost rather than fair value, and goodwill, which needs amortizing, does not arise.
5. On the disposal of acquired assets a holding gain arises which is partly due to the fact that the assets were introduced at their carrying value rather than fair value.

The disadvantages of merger accounting are as follows:

1. Since the assets of the company acquired are included at their carrying value and not their fair value to the parent it is misleading and inconsistent. First, it misleads shareholders about the cost of the assets; and secondly, it is inconsistent with the concept of historical cost which is a fundamental concept adopted by most countries in the world. The concept of historical cost normally requires that it is the cost of purchase to the parent company which is appropriate rather than the carrying value to the subsidiary.
2. Since the pre-acquisition profits of the subsidiary acquired are available for distribution it misleads investors to believe that dividends are a return on the company's investment rather than a return of the investment.
3. Since pre-acquisition profits are available for distribution the method can increase demands for dividend payments.
4. The investment in the subsidiary by the parent would have to be shown in the parent company's accounts at either the nominal value of the shares acquired or the historical cost of the subsidiary at acquisition with a corresponding merger reserve which would probably not be distributable..
5. There are practical difficulties in analysing the current year's profit between pre-merger and post-merger periods where the operations of the companies are combined in the post-merger period.

The rationale for merger accounting is that it represents an exchange of interests between undertakings. Presumably this method might be appropriate where there is continuity of ownership, voting rights and equity interests are merged, and continuity of the existing businesses within the combined undertaking. Thus, it might be appropriate to use this method where two similar-sized organizations come together to form a new entity – a genuine merger. This seems to have been the interpretation adopted by most countries in the world except the UK. For example, stringent conditions were imposed in APBO16 in the US after it was perceived that merger accounting was being abused. Furthermore, in Canada 'Accounting for business combinations' which has statutory back-up, stipulates that merger accounting may only be used in 'those rare transactions where an acquirer cannot be identified'.

In contrast to merger accounting, the rationale underlying acquisition accounting is that one entity acquires another entity and what needs to be accounted for is the cost of the acquisition to the parent company. This method is consistent with the historical cost convention, since it represents cost to the entity, and is prudent in that the investment is capitalized and pre-acquisition profits are not available for distribution. Furthermore, it is normally easier for investors to interpret the results for the year.

Since merger accounting fails to measure the cost to the parent company of giving up the purchase consideration in exchange for shares it fails to reflect the economic substance of the exchange transaction.

Whilst merger accounting is a concept acknowledged by most countries in this survey – there is no such concept in the FRG – its application is rare. Indeed, despite the flexibility in approach of SSAP23 in the UK only 14 cases (at July 1987) of its use have so far been established. This is not because the requirements for its use are stringent since they are not – the standard is more lax than any comparable standard in this area – but rather that SSAP23 has opened up a Pandora's box. The box has produced an abundance of areas for creative accounting using acquisition accounting, particularly when used in conjunction with S131 of Companies Act 1985 which provides for merger relief. The advantages of this combination is that in the parent company's accounts merger relief can be used so that the investment in a subsidiary is stated at a lower value since no share premium account is created. This enhances distributable profits in the entity. In the group accounts, flexibility in the establishment of fair values, the application and creation of provisions, and flexibility in the treatment of goodwill have all been used to throw a smoke-screen over the underlying results. It is virtually impossible for the intelligent user to unravel the charade. Despite these abuses only the provision for future losses is specifically in breach of International Accounting Standard No. 22 (IAS22). Fortunately, the Accounting Standards Committee is undertaking an extensive review of group accounts, goodwill, mergers and acquisitions and accounting for associated companies. To a large extent the review is being undertaken in the light of the adoption by the Council of Ministers of the European Communities of the Seventh Directive on consolidated accounts. Member states must enact the necessary laws by 1 January 1988 although companies will not be required to produce consolidated accounts until 1 January 1990 and in fact some financial institutions can delay implementation until 1993.

Equity Accounting

Where an investment in another entity results in ownership of at least 20 per cent and not more than 50 per cent of the shares, and there is significant influence, it is international practice to account for it using the equity accounting method. Using the equity method, the investing group's share of profits less losses in the investee are incorporated into the investing group's consolidated profit and loss account. The investment in associated companies is usually shown separately in the consolidated balance sheet as the group's share of the associates' net assets. It is important to point out that an investment in an associated company is different to a joint venture. For example Article 32(1) of the Seventh Directive permits the use of proportional consolidation where an undertaking is managed jointly with one or more enterprises which are not included in that consolidation. The proportional method, sometimes called the line-by-line approach, is an approach to consolidation whereby a proportion of an investee's assets, liabilities and profits are incorporated in the accounts of the investing group, thereby eliminating any minority interest. Proportional consolidation is sometimes practised in France.

Whilst it is international accounting practice to use equity accounting in the circumstancs outlined, there are a number of national differences. For example, equity accounting is not used in Italy as it has adverse tax implications, in Brazil all investments over 20 per cent including subsidiaries are accounted for in this way, whereas in Sweden there has been considerable controversy as to whether the method was illegal. In an attempt to clarify the position the Swedish Institute of Authorized Accountants, FAR, issued an exposure draft in February 1986 which states that equity accounting may only be applied in consolidated financial statements and that the equity in an associated company's undistributed earnings must be classified as non-distributable consolidated equity. Equity accounting may not be applied in parent company or single company financial statements.

The Seventh Directive

The Seventh Directive makes it mandatory for all parent undertakings in the European Community to prepare annual consolidated accounts which must include all subsidiaries located anywhere in the world. However, Article 11 provides an exemption to subgroups where the ultimate parent is located outside the European Community, provided that certain conditions are fulfilled.

The Directive aims to accommodate both control over a company by ownership of shares, *de jure* control, and control over a company by control of management, *de facto* control. Thus the Directive allows the concept often applied in the FRG, *de facto* control, and that which is normally applied internationally.

There are a number of exemptions which may be introduced by member states, which limit the scope of the Directive and the major ones are summarized below:

1. exemption for partnerships – in some countries such as the FRG and France partnerships may have a considerable economic impact;

2. exemption for financial holding companies – of particular importance to Luxembourg;
3. exemptions based on size with transitional arrangements – the group must not exceed two of the following criteria:

Balance sheet total	:	4 million ECU
Net turnover	:	8 million ECU
Average number of employees during the year	:	250

4. exemptions for wholly-owned subgroups;
5. exemptions where wholly-owned subsidiaries are prohibited;
6. exemptions where the minorities concur.

The FRG adopted the required legislation in 1985 and France and the Netherlands partly adopted the legislation in 1986. A further discussion of the Seventh Directive and its impact on member states is provided in Cooke (1984) and Cooke (1986).

Accounting for goodwill

Goodwill arises because the value of a business as a whole differs from the value of its separable net assets. As such, this intangible asset cannot be realized except when the business as a whole is sold. Whilst most businesses possess goodwill through the development of relations with suppliers and customers it is unusual for this form of goodwill, called inherent goodwill, to be valued in the accounts. In all countries included in this survey only purchased or acquired goodwill is to be incorporated in the accounts.

Since purchased goodwill is recognized in all countries, the accountant must consider what to do with it. In Hong Kong goodwill may be retained as an asset unless there is a permanent impairment of its value in which case it should be written down through the profit and loss account and treated as an extraordinary item. Thus, goodwill may remain as a permanent asset. However, it is possible for it to be amortized or written off at the time of the acquisition.

In all other countries goodwill is either written off on acquisition or amortized over a period of time. The recommended practice in the UK is SSAP22 which prefers the write-off of goodwill on acquisition, although the 'standard' does permit amortization over its useful life. The Netherlands also permits flexibility in allowing goodwill to be charged to shareholders' equity although it may be capitalized and amortized through the profit-and-loss account over a period not normally exceeding five years. However, the period of amortization may be extended to ten years where there are good reasons to do so.

Goodwill is also amortized over a period not exceeding five years in Japan, Italy, the FRG and France, in most instances. The amortization period can be as long as ten years in Sweden and Italy (though it is generally reduced to five years for tax purposes), twenty years in Australia provided benefits are still arising, whereas in Canada and the US the maximum period is forty years. The other countries look either to the International Accounting Standards Committee or the UK and US for guidance. However, whereas goodwill should be amortized through the profit-and-loss account in the US it may either be written off on acquisition or amortized in the UK.

OTHER EEC DIRECTIVES

Proposed Tenth Directive on International Mergers

As part of its aim of bringing about a homogeneous and enduring Common Market, the European Commission brought forward a proposal, in the form of a Directive in 1985, to deal with cross-border mergers. The history of this proposed Directive extends back to the early 1970s when work began on this subject. In 1973 a draft convention was proposed but negotiations were terminated because of company law and tax problems. Furthermore, the FRG and the Netherlands were concerned that cross-border mergers would enable major companies to avoid its employee participation laws. However, in 1984 a compromise was reached which would permit a Member State to oppose a merger if the undertaking would no longer meet their employee participation laws (Article 1(3)).

The proposed Directive is complementary to the Third Directive which deals with mergers between two companies which are both subject to the laws of the same Member State. Both the Third Directive and proposed Tenth Directive deal with mergers that are not normally encountered in the UK but are encountered on the Continent. The Directives deal with a 'merger by acquisition' whereby one or more companies are wound up without going into liquidation. All the assets and liabilities are transferred in exchange for shares in the acquiring company. If cash forms part of the consideration it must not exceed 10 per cent of the nominal or par value of the shares issued. The second type is the 'merger by the formulation of a new company' in which a number of companies are wound up without going into liquidation. All the assets and liabilities are transferred in exchange for shares in the new company. The cash limit also applies to this type of merger.

The main requirements of the Directive are summarized below in accordance with the Articles of that document:

1. The coordination measures apply to public companies limited by shares or by guarantee (UK) or their equivalent. The Directive therefore applies to *Aktiengesellschaft* in the FRG, *société anonyme* in France, *società par azioni* in Italy, and *naamloze vennootschaap* in the Netherlands.

   Member States need not apply this Directive where an undertaking whether or not it was involved, would no longer meet the conditions for employee representation. Employees rights are to be protected by the Directive on Employees' Rights in Cases of Transfers or Mergers of Businesses.

2. The definition of cross-border mergers is the same as that introduced in the Third Directive.
3. A cross-border merger by acquisition is the same as that introduced in the Third Directive with the exception that two or more of the companies involved must be governed by the laws of different Member States.
4. Article 4 is the same as Article 3 except that it applies to cross-border merger by the formation of a new company.
5. Draft terms of the merger must be prepared by the administration or management bodies of the companies involved. The draft terms of merger shall specify at least:

   a. the type, name and registered office of each of the merging companies;
   b. the share exchange ratio and the amount of any cash payment;
   c. the terms relating to the allotment of shares in the acquiring company;
   d. the date from which the holding of such shares entitles the holders to participate in profits and any special conditions affecting that entitlement;
   e. the date from which the transactions of the company being required shall be treated for accounting purposes as being those of the acquiring company;
   f. the rights conferred by the acquiring company on the holders of shares to which special rights are attached and the holders of securities other than shares, or the measures proposed concerning them;
   g. any special advantage granted to the experts (see below) and members of the merging companies' administrative, management, supervisory or controlling bodies.
   (Whilst the term 'experts' is not defined they should act on behalf of each of the merging companies but be independent of them. They should be appointed or approved by a judicial or administrative authority and be responsible for examining the draft terms of the merger and draw up a written report to the shareholders.)

6. The draft terms for each of the merging companies shall contain the following information:

   a. the type, name and registered office of each of the merging companies;
   b. the register in which a file has been opened in accordance with the 1st Directive for each of the merging companies and the number of the entry in that register;
   c. the conditions which determine the date on which the cross-border merger takes effect.

In addition, disclosure should include the details of the exercise of the right of the creditors.

7. A merger shall require at least the approval of the general meeting of each of the merging company. Approval is by at least two-thirds of the votes attaching either to the shares or to the subscribed capital represented, but Member States may not require a larger majority than they require for a merger in which all the companies involved are governed by their law.
8. The draft terms of the merger shall be examined by experts and a written report prepared for shareholders.
9. The rights of creditors and holders of securities should be protected.
10. Each Member State must ensure that a merger complies with the judicial or administrative preventive supervision in order to ensure its legality.
11. The date a merger takes effect is governed by the laws of Member States.
12. A merger must be publicised in the manner prescribed by the laws of each Member State. However, the publication of a cross-border merger must take place for the company or companies being acquired before publication for the acquiring company.

The above represents a summary of the key elements of the proposed Tenth Directive. In some areas it is vague so it will be left to Member States to be more precise when enacting the legislation. For example, there is some doubt as to whether adequate protection is given to creditors. Furthermore whilst a report on the merger terms should be prepared by experts, the Directive does not define the term. Another example of vagueness is provided by Article 10(3) which states that 'where both the law governing the acquiring company and the law governing the company or companies being acquired provides for judicial or administrative preventive supervision of the legality of the cross-border merger, that supervision shall be carried out first in respect of the acquiring company. It may not be carried out in respect of a company being acquired until proof is furnished that it has already been carried out in respect of the acquiring company.' Some of the phraseology is unclear since terms like 'supervision shall be carried out' are not adequately defined. In some areas the Directive is permissive. For example, Article 7 permits approval in accordance with the requirements of Member States. Since these vary from country to country there appears to be a lack of consistency. Perhaps the two thirds majority should apply to all countries. Another area of inconsistency is in the area of declaring a merger a nullity since it depends on the laws of Member States governing the acquiring company. These laws vary from one country to another so that shareholders in acquired companies might not be treated equally.

Despite these deficiencies the proposed Directive marks a step towards using cross-border mergers. For example, in some Member States cross-border mergers involve complex techniques involving the formation of a group of companies with a financial holding company in order to transfer assets. Another advantage is that the draft merger terms are certified in due legal form by a person or authority competent under the law of one of those Member States.

Regulation on the European Economic Interest Grouping (EEIG)

The EEIG is a new legal form of business activity intended for cross-border co-operation among enterprises. The initiative stems from the popularity of such enterprises in France, particularly for small and medium-sized businesses. Formalities are kept to a minimum and an EEIG is designed to support and strengthen the position of members participating in the association. The organization represents a service entity operating exclusively in a supportive role for the benefit of participating members, which have unlimited and joint and several liability for any debts of the association. The first EEIGs are expected to be formed as from 1 July 1989.

Proposed Eleventh Council Directive on the Disclosure Requirements of Branches

This proposed Directive covers branches of companies exercising their rights of establishment in another Member State. One of the reasons for the proposal is that the lack of coordination of disclosure of information gives rise to disparity in respect of the protection of shareholders and third parties between companies and branches which operate in other Member States. The Directive proposes that branches should disclose the annual accounts of the company or the consolidated accounts in which the company is included. Disclosure should include the following:

1. the address of the branch;
2. the register in which the company file is kept, together with its registration number;
3. the name of the branch if that is different from the name of the company;
4. the appointment, termination of office and particulars of the persons authorised to represent the company in dealings with third parties and in legal proceedings;
5. the annual accounts and report of the company unless it is a subsidiary in which case the consolidated accounts should be disclosed;
6. the closure of the branch.

CONCLUSIONS

Over the period 1985–7 there has been an increase in merger and acquisition activity at both domestic and international levels. This increase in activity is not restricted to Anglo-Saxon economies although there is considerable correlation between the number of transactions and the importance of Stock Exchanges within a country. Since Anglo-Saxon economies often have more developed stock exchanges it might appear that takeover activity is concentrated in those economies. However, countries such as Japan and those in Continental Europe are showing an increase in propensity to acquire.

Globalization of markets will lead to an increase in cross-border transactions as firms compete for international market shares. This development raises problems of control of dominant economic entities. The US Sherman Act of 1890 has been influential in Canada, Argentina, Brazil, the FRG, the Netherlands, Japan, and in the EEC. In contrast, other countries such as France and the UK adopt a case-by-case approach to merger control. In others there is no legislation or there is a mixed system. Thus, there is a lack of harmonization in merger control at present. However, although there is no real desire for harmonization it is possible that the two main systems of control will actually move closer together. On the one hand, the US and the FRG are relaxing their clear prohibitions of dominant positions whereas a likely outcome of the review of competition policy in the UK could be the establishment of a tougher regime. The concept of the 'public interest' has always been a vague notion which requires strengthening. In any new competition environment it will be important to recognize the international dimension and, where necessary, control oligopolies in domestic markets where size is important to compete on a worldwide basis. However, a large domestic market is not necessary for the development of successful multinationals as Sweden has demonstrated with companies such as Volvo, Electrolux, Esselte and Ericsson.

In the mid-1980s attitudes towards foreign investment have changed in many countries of the world from hostile or neutral towards a welcoming approach because of the favourable impact on employment. For example, Canada and Australia have both relaxed their regulations on foreign investment.

The important taxation aspect is that there is now extensive legislation to prevent avoidance schemes from being successful. Whilst close scrutiny is given to transactions with tax haven countries, the aim is not to penalize transactions but rather to ensure that foreign investors pay equivalent tax to that incurred by indigenous companies. In many countries there are thin-capitalization provisions to ensure that a foreign subsidiary in a country with high rates of tax, is not debt-laden. The international exchange of tax information is likely to increase in the future.

Accounting is a very important area as it represents the language of business. It is important that the process of international harmonization of accounting standards is continued to improve comparability and understandability. Each country has a responsibility to develop accounting standards that are generally accepted and complied with as a first stage to ensuring comparability between companies in their own country. Particular responsibility rests with standard-setting countries such as the US and UK. Regrettably the UK has developed accounting standards on goodwill and mergers and acquisitions that are unduly flexible, subject to abuse, and fail to show a lead to other countries. It is essential that 'standards' are indeed standards – not a codification of creative practices.

Exchange control regulations represent an important way of regulating foreign investment. These controls are exercised extensively by emerging nations and other countries where regulation is weak in other areas. Naturally acquisition activity is subject to exchange control regulations.

Finally, it is the responsibility of the EEC to ensure that legal and fiscal barriers are eliminated so that cross-border acquisitions are not penalised. Furthermore it is essential that the EEC increases its influence over merger control and accounting to improve harmonization within the Community.

Part II
COUNTRY STUDIES

4

Australia

1. BUSINESS ORGANIZATIONS AND COMBINATIONS

Business organizations

The principal types of business organization in Australia are companies, branches of foreign companies, unincorporated joint ventures, partnerships, sole traders and trading trusts. Prospective foreign investors will be interested mainly in companies, branches of foreign companies and to a lesser extent joint ventures.

The Companies Act 1981 provides uniform companies legislation for the six states and two territories. The Companies Act is administered by the Corporate Affairs Commissions in each state or territory and the National Companies and Securities Commission. A feature of this uniform system of company law and administration is that a company is required to file all documents with the appropriate office in the state or territory in which it is incorporated but not in the other states or territories.

Whilst there are a number of different types of company the foreign investor will usually form a limited liability company. There are three types of limited liability company – the proprietary limited company (Pty Ltd), the public company (Ltd) and the no-liability company (N/L). The important difference between the proprietary company and the public company is that the former type may not issue securities to the public and naturally may not be listed on the stock exchange. A public company must comply with the requirements of Australian company law and Stock Exchange regulations of the city where it will be listed. In practice, 98 per cent of all registered companies are proprietary companies. There are two types of proprietary companies – exempt and non-exempt. Generally, an exempt proprietary company is one that does not have a public company as a shareholder and such a status permits it not to appoint an auditor. In addition, the exempt proprietary company is excluded from the requirement to file detailed annual financial statements with the Corporate Affairs Commission. A non-exempt proprietary company must appoint an auditor and file detailed financial statements. Note that the form of incorporation does not necessarily mean that the

Commissioner of Taxation will follow the corporate structure when assessing taxes. For example, it is perfectly possible for a company to be incorporated as a proprietary company and yet for tax purposes be treated as a public company and vice versa.

To form a company it is necessary to file its memorandum of association, articles of association and other documents with the Corporate Affairs Commission of the appropriate State or Territory. The memorandum of association normally sets out the objectives of the company, its capital in terms of nominal value, the classification of its share capital, the fact that the company is limited by shares and the names of the subscribers. The above information is required except that the objectives of the company need not necessarily be stated.

The articles of association set out the internal regulations of the company and determine the relationship between management and shareholders. Where the articles of association are not specifically drawn up the model provided in Table A of the Companies Act 1981 applies. A further regulation is that the name of the company to be incorporated must be approved by the Registrar of Companies and may not be similar to an existing corporate name.

To form a proprietary company at least two shareholders are required although they may be nominees of one person or company. In addition, there must be at least two directors and at least one director should be resident. Control over a company is effective by simple majority and a quorum consists of at least two people who may vote on issues in person or by proxy.

In contrast, a limited company requires at least five shareholders and the company must maintain a share register which provides details of shareholders and their sharedealings. Control is exercised by simple majority but companies may vary the voting rights of foreign shareholders. Annual shareholders' meetings are required and a special resolution (75 per cent) is required for changes in the memorandum or articles or when issuing new shares. Minority interests may appeal to the courts where they feel that they are being unduly oppressed.

Once the Commission's approval has been obtained and the memorandum, articles and other documents have been filed and the fees paid, a certificate of incorporation will be issued. The other documents include, *inter alia* and where appropriate, the directors' consents to act, the address of the registered office and a copy of the prospectus.

In practice foreign investors usually form proprietary companies although for tax purposes such companies constitute limited companies. An alternative approach is to trade through a branch in Australia although the registration fees are normally high as they are related to the capital of the parent company. Once the branch commences business it must be registered with the appropriate state Registrar of Companies which consists of submitting information on the parent company including its accounts. As with most branches, liability in Australia extends to the total assets of the company regardless of where located. In contrast the liability of a foreign subsidiary in Australia is limited to that company and does not extend to the overseas parent corporation.

In addition to the normal requirements to form a company, foreign investors may need to obtain approval from the Foreign Investment Review Board (FIRB) and must also comply with exchange control regulations. However, it is important to note that the form of business organization is a matter for foreign corporations to decide and the provisions of the Foreign Takeovers Act and exchange control are not interrelated or even contingent upon company registration requirements.

Types of business combination

An Australian company may be acquired by a foreign company by the purchase of assets or shares but subject to the extensive regulatory framework which is considered in sections 3 and 6. For example, if a foreign investor wishes to acquire the assets of a company, approval must be obtained from the Foreign Investment Review Board (FIRB). The FIRB must be convinced that on balance the increase in foreign investment will be beneficial to the Australian economy.

The Companies (Acquisition of Shares) Act 1980 is relevant for the takeover of most proprietary, public and listed companies. However, the acquisition of proprietary companies is not relevant where the offeree does not have more than 15 shareholders or where it does the members must agree to the takeover in writing. In other circumstances, shares may be purchased up to a limit of 20 per cent of voting securities. There is effective prohibition of all purchases of shares beyond 20 per cent including the situation where a shareholder owns between 20 per cent and 90 per cent and tries to increase his entitlement. However, further shares may be purchased in the following ways:

(1) The formal takeover offer. This is the most common type of acquisition, particularly where the consideration is in the form of shares, whereby the offer is made to the shareholders of the offeree. However, before the offer can be sent, the offeror sends a 'Part A Statement' to the directors of the offeree giving the required information as specified in the Act in order for shareholders to make an informed decision. In return the directors of the offeree must supply a 'Part B Statement', in accordance with the Act, which must be sent to the offeror within 14 days of the receipt of the 'Part A Statement'. The object of the Part B Statement is to keep its shareholders informed and to provide reasons for the directors' recommendation to the offer.

(2) The on-market offer. In this case the offeror appoints a member firm of a stock exchange to buy shares offered to him at a specified price, in cash, for a specified period of time. An offeror who owns more

than 30 per cent in the offeree may not use this method of increasing its shareholding.

As in the formal takeover offer the regulations must be observed and information supplied as before except that the statements are 'Part C' and 'Part D'.

(3) 'Creeping acquisition'. Section 15 of the Companies (Acquisition of Shares) Act 1980 permits a person or company with 19 per cent of the voting shares to increase ownership by not more than 3 per cent of the issued capital in any six-month period. The 19 per cent threshold applies only if the shares are held for a continuous period of six months.

(4) Schemes of arrangement. The restrictions on takeovers, as stated above, were imposed by Section II of the Companies (Acquisition of Shares) Act 1980. However, a compromise or scheme of arrangement may be approved by the Court under Part III of the Act and has been used in a number of larger takeovers in recent years. For example, judicial approval was granted in the Bank of Adelaide case (1980) 22 S.A.S.R. 481, in which the ANZ Bank proposed to issue new shares to holders of shares in the Bank of Adelaide. The existing shares in the Bank of Adelaide would be cancelled and new shares issued to the ANZ Bank. The advantage of such an arrangement was that shareholder approval for the scheme was lowered to 75 per cent rather than the 90 per cent necessary for compulsory acquisition of a minority.

It should be borne in mind, however, that such schemes may not be given judicial approval in the future since it would appear that section 315(21) of the Companies (Acquisition of Shares) Act 1980 effectively prohibits such an arrangement. Takeovers by schemes of arrangement are likely to become less common in the future.

2. TRENDS IN TAKEOVER ACTIVITY

Available merger data are summarized in tables 4.1 to 4.4. Tables 4.1 to 4.3 are those published by the Australian Reserve Bank and are based on a survey of a constant group of public and major proprietary companies operating primarily in Australia, other than those engaged in finance or primary industry. Tables 4.1 and 4.2 provide statistics on all-industrial companies and mining corporations whilst table 4.3 shows the value of assets taken over on a disaggregated basis.

One research study undertaken by Walker (1973) estimated that between 1960 and 1970, 38 per cent of companies quoted on the Sydney Stock Exchange were subject to a bid and that in 80 per cent of the cases the bids were successful. A later study by Walker (1982) estimates that there were 72 takeover bids of Australian listed companies between 1966 and 1972 and the rate of success of those bids was nearly 67 per cent.

Looking at more recent data the number of industrial companies making takeovers fell from 96 in 1981 to 69 in 1983 and the number of companies taken over also fell from 200 in 1981 to 128 in 1983. Whilst the number of transactions fell between 1981 and 1983 the value of assets taken over in the industrial sector rose in all sectors other than manufacturing (table 2.3). The decline in the number of transactions might be due to a decline in industrial profitability coupled with a substantial increase in interest payments. As a result of falling profits and increased debt financing the ratio of debt to equity rose substantially in 1982 and 1983 so that only

Table 4.1 Identified takeovers

	Companies making takeovers, 1976–84		
	All industrials	*Mining*	*Total non-financial*
1976	94	—	94
1977	92	2	94
1978	107	—	107
1979	98	4	102
1980	99	5	104
1981	96	3	99
1982	85	3	88
1983	69	3	72
1984	74	4	78
	814	24	838

Source: Reserve Bank of Australia, Bulletin Supplements: Company Finance March 1985 and August 1986

Table 4.2 Companies taken over, 1976–84

	All industrials	*Mining*	*Total non-financial*
1976	172	—	172
1977	177	3	180
1978	173	—	173
1979	192	7	199
1980	178	10	188
1981	200	6	206
1982	170	4	174
1983	128	4	132
1984	137	5	142
	1527	39	1566

Source: Reserve Bank of Australia, *Bulletin Supplements: Company Finance*, March 1985 and August 1986

Table 4.3 Value of assets taken over by sector ($Am)

Year	Manufacturing	Wholesale trade	Retail trade	Services	All industrials	Mining	Total non-finance
1976	316	51	21	38	426	—	426
1977	389	18	42	84	533	69	602
1978	585	119	24	82	810	—	810
1979	904	114	118	185	1321	199	1520
1980	1778	207	108	144	2237	467	2704
1981	2785	95	59	81	3020	223	3243
1982	1570	242	73	249	2134	74	2208
1983	1719	194	515	270	2698	147	2845
1984	5167	1418	158	742	7485	394	7879
	15,213	2458	1118	1875	20,664	1573	22,237
%	69	11	5	8	—	7	= 100

Source: Reserve Bank of Australia, *Bulletin Supplements: Company Finance*, March 1985 and August 1986

Table 4.4 Companies registered as at 30 June 1985

	Limited by shares					
	Public	*Proprietary*	*Limited by guarantee*	*No liability*	*Unlimited*	*Total*
Australian Capital Territory	555	17,048	226	7	22	17,858
New South Wales	2168	228,555	4382	138	292	235,535
Queensland	637	89,185	817	51	6	90,696
South Australia	442	41,987	48	21	126	42,624
Tasmania	105	9057	223	13	—	9398
Victoria	2351	180,257	818	76	223	183,725
Western Australia[a]	1134	52,780	57	221	13	54,205
	7392	618,869	6571	582	676	634,041

[a] Estimated.
[b] Included in total for proprietary companies.

Source: National Companies and Securities Commission

companies with an adequate financial base could undertake the larger takeover bids. Part of the increase in net assets acquired occurred in the manufacturing sector although the largest increase took place in the retail sector which included one very large bid. However, in 1984 the number of companies making takeovers rose slightly as did the number of companies taken over. The value of assets taken over rose dramatically from $A3845 million to $A7879 million, an increase of 177 per cent. This increase was due mainly to major acquisitions made by BHP which accounted for approximately 45 per cent of the total value of assets acquired in the industrial sector in 1984. Even ignoring the major acquisitions made by BHP it is apparent that there were substantial increases in the value of assets taken over in all categories of takeover.

The average size of takeovers has fluctuated widely in the 1980s after adjusting for the effects of inflation although there was a steady increase in 1983 and a substantial increase in 1984. In order to place the level of takeovers in some context table 4.4 shows the total number of companies registered as at 30 June 1985 analysed by territory.

Table 4.5 shows the number of takeover offers for companies listed on the Australian Associated Stock Exchanges and includes data for 1984 and 1985. According to Irving (in Bruce, McKern and Pollard, 1983) acquisitions became attractive in the 1970s due to the disparity between the aggregate book values and replacement cost of companies assets. This trend increased throughout the 1970s with the exception of 1974 and 1975 when there was a slowing down in economic activity. Compared with the low point for 1983 there has been an upsurge in activity in both 1984 and 1985. However, the success rate was only 26 per cent in 1984 and 21 per cent in 1985 compared with 54 per cent in 1979. Table 4.6 shows that each year during the period 1981–5 between 2.5 per cent and 4.5 per

Table 4.5 Takeover offers for companies listed on the Australian Associated Stock Exchanges

Year ended 30 June	*Number of takeover offers*	*Successful offer*			*Total successful as a % of number of offers*
		by listed companies	*by unlisted companies*	*Total*	
1978	113	28	19	47	42
1979	115	38	23	61	53
1980	133	32	12	44	33
1981	164	24	14	38	23
1982	105	32	13	45	43
1983	84	17	13	30	36
1984	138	22	14	36	26
1985	129	20	7	27	21
1986	126	26	21	47	37
1987	116	8	4	12	10

Source: Sydney Stock Exchange

Table 4.6 Analysis of the official list (excluding public authorities) – year ended 30 June

Year ended 30 June	*Industrial*	*Mining & oil*	*Total*	*Successful offers*	*Percentage of total*
1981	752	283	1035	38	3.7
1982	702	291	993	45	4.5
1983	655	299	954	30	3.1
1984	633	327	960	36	3.8
1985	654	362	1016	27	2.7

Source: Sydney Stock Exchange

cent of companies listed on Australian stock exchanges were taken over. However, the number of new listings on the exchanges exceeded those removed from the Official List in both 1984 and 1985.

Table 4.7 shows the value of assets disposed of by industrial companies through sales of subsidiaries. Divestiture reached record levels in 1983 and again in 1984 reflecting extensive rationalization of activities by many companies due to adverse economic conditions and declining profitability. Whilst the value of assets sold increased in all sectors, significant divestitures in the mining industry only occurred in 1983.

3. MERGER CONTROL

Controls affecting mergers and acquisitions in Australia consist of:

1. The Companies (Acquisition of Shares) Act 1980 which deals with the acquisition of shares.
2. The Trade Practices Commission which administers the antitrust legislation incorporated in the Trade Practices Act 1974.
3. The Securities Industry Act 1980 which provides for national regulation of the securities industry.

The administration of the above legislation is undertaken by the Corporate Affairs Commissions in each State or Territory subject to overall control by the National Companies and Securities Commission (NCSC) which is a federal Government agency. In addition, specific State or Territory statutes may also impinge on takeover activity.

The Companies (Acquisition of Shares) Act 1980 (the Code)

The types of transaction which can be undertaken are outlined in section (1) of this chapter. Sections 59 and 60 of the Code stipulate the overriding

Table 4.7 Sale of subsidiaries: value of assets sold

	Manufacturing	*Wholesale trade*	*Retail trade*	*Services*	*All industrials*	*Mining*	*Total non-financials*
1979	42	9	—	6	57	4	61
1980	124	24	39	35	222	14	236
1981	13	1	26	18	58	8	66
1982	25	—	—	2	27	—	27
1983	159	28	40	68	295	56	351
1984	229	86	79	96	490	—	490

Source: Reserve Bank of Australia, *Bulletin Supplements: Company Finance*, March 1985 and August 1986

principles of the Code which were those recommended by Sir Richard Eggleston and incorporated into Part VIB of the old Companies Acts. The following principles control freedom of action over the acquisition of companies:

1. The identity of the offeror should be known to the directors and shareholders of the company.
2. The directors and shareholders of the offeree should have a reasonable amount of time to consider the proposal.
3. Sufficient information should be given to the offeree by the offeror for a proper evaluation of the proposal. Where shares and debentures are being offered as part or all of the consideration, sufficient information should be provided for the offer to be valued.
4. As far as possible, each shareholder should have an equal opportunity to participate in the benefits offered.

The takeover of companies by share acquisition is more common than the acquisition of business assets. There are a number of reasons for this. First, in order to acquire the assets of a business, approval is required from the directors of the offeree. Secondly, it is normally cheaper to buy a going concern than individual assets. This is because the share price often does not adequately reflect the asset backing of the company. Furthermore, stamp duty on share transfers is lower than for the purchase of assets.

When acquiring public companies listed in Australia there are, in reality, only two possible ways of achieving this – the formal takeover offer and the on-market offer. These methods are not mutually exclusive so that, in practice, it is permissible to use both methods at the same time. The 'creeping acquisition' approach is not a realistic option for an aggressive acquirer, since the acquisition of no more than 3 per cent of the target company shares each six months is too limiting.

The formal takeover offer has two main advantages over the on-market offer. First, the on-market offer must be for cash, whereas the formal takeover offer may be for cash, securities, or a combination of both. Secondly, a formal takeover offer may be conditional upon achieving a certain proportion of the shares whereas the on-market offer cannot be conditional.

When acquiring shares in a listed company the offeror may decide to purchase up to 20 per cent as cheaply and quickly as possible before a formal takeover offer is made. The share acquisition may be undertaken through nominees although once 10 per cent of the shares are obtained the real identity of the purchaser must be disclosed. In addition, a listed company may require the identity of a purchaser to be disclosed within 14 days of a request to do so. However, this may be difficult where overseas nominees are involved and also requires diligent stock monitoring.

In relation to formal takeover offers and on-market offers the Code specifies the following:

1. The offeror may not sell shares to the offeree during the bid period.
2. Profit forecasts of the offeror or offeree may only be given after approval from the Commission.
3. A revaluation of assets must have approval from the Commission.
4. Once an offeror has acquired at least 90 per cent of the shares the residual shareholders can be compulsorily bought out on the same terms.
5. Material inaccuracies in relevant documents or statements are subject to both civil and criminal liability.
6. The Supreme Court may issue variation orders.
7. The Court can set aside unfair service agreements made in anticipation of a bid.
8. It is not permissible to make an announcement of a bid without carrying it through. The aim of this section is to eliminate 'bluffing offers'.
9. The Commission may decide whether an offer is unacceptable even where the Code has been complied with.

Despite the wide-ranging terms of the Code the NCSC became concerned about the use of complex offers which had the effect of placing less sophisticated shareholders at a disadvantage. In order to promote certainty the NCSC introduced the Companies and Securities Legislation Act. The object of the Act is:

1. to protect shareholders from manipulation by sophisticated practitioners;
2. to simplify the takeover process;
3. to reduce business costs.

These aims are to be achieved by providing more effective control of 'prescribed conditions' attached to takeover offers and to establish 'requirements' appropriate to these conditions. The 'prescribed conditions' are those normally approved by the Commission so that where a condition is not fulfilled a takeover scheme will fail and be withdrawn.

The Trade Practices Act 1974

Foreign takeovers in Australia are subject to permission being granted by both the Foreign Investment Review Board (see section 6) as well as the Trade Practices Commission which administers the Trade Practices Act 1974 although their requirements are not interrelated. Applications to both organizations are often submitted simultaneously. In addition, there is a Trade Practices Tribunal which reviews decisions of the Commission on authorization applications and has the power to set aside decisions. However, the Federal Court has exclusive power of granting remedies provided by the Act.

The Trade Practices Act 1974 prohibits some types of anti-competitive arrangements and behaviour and also contains provisions to protect consumers. In addition, section 46 of the Act prevents a corporation which has substantial control over a market from taking advantage of such power so as to:

1. eliminate or substantially damage a competitor;
2. prevent the entry of a person into a market;
3. deter or prevent a person from engaging in competitive conduct.

Unlike US legislation the phrase 'monopolization' is not used but instead the concept of 'substantial control' is introduced but is not defined in terms of percentage of the market. Substantial control is ultimately determined in an individual case in the Federal Court.

A corporation with substantial control includes those which '. . . by reason of its share of the market, or its share of the market combined with the availability to it of technical knowledge, raw materials or capital, the power to determine the prices, or control the production or distribution, of a substantial part of the goods or services in that market' (section 46(3)).

The above provisions apply equally to Australian corporations and overseas corporations trading in Australia as well as to individuals. Certain conduct is exempt from the legislation where specifically authorized by a Federal or State Act or a Territory Law or arises from:

1. industrial relations agreements;
2. sale of goodwill;
3. compliance with standards set by the Standards Association of Australia or with prescribed performance standards;
4. partnership agreements between individuals;
5. export agreements, particulars of which have been disclosed to the Commission within fourteen days of being made;
6. consumer boycotts;
7. certain arrangements relating to the law of copyrights, trade marks or designs;
8. some primary product marketing arrangements.

Section 50 of the Trade Practices Act 1974 is relevant to mergers and acquisitions and states that:

> A corporation shall not acquire, directly or indirectly, any shares in the capital, or any assets, of a body corporate if
>
> (a) As a result of the acquisition, the corporation would be, or be likely to be, in a position to control or dominate a market for goods or services; or
>
> (b) In a case where the corporation is in a position to control or dominate a market for goods or services,
>
> (i) The body corporate or another body corporate that is related to that body, is, or is likely to be, a competitor of the corporation or of a body corporate that is related to the corporation;

and

(ii) The acquisition would, or would be likely to, substantially strengthen the power of the corporation to control or dominate that market.

The purpose of the legislation is to prohibit acquisitions which result in an acquirer controlling or dominating a market. In addition, section 50 reinforces restrictive practice legislation since one possible way of avoiding such legislation is by acquisition.

The 1984–5 Annual Report of the Trade Practices Commission specifies the three courses of action that businesses may take to acquisitions in the context of the Act:

(a) seek guidance from the Commission: in these instances the Commission's decision provides a quick insight as to Commission attitude, although if the approach is on a confidential basis, it is necessarily subject to the qualification that the Commission has not been able to go into the market to learn what others have to say about the proposed merger;
(b) seek authorization: this allows the Commission to consider rationalization and restructuring of industry as public benefit considerations. If the Commission does not authorize the merger, the parties concerned can apply to the Trade Practices Tribunal for a review of the case;
(c) proceed with the merger without prior consultation or authorization and carry the risk of whether a breach of the Act will result.

Most companies make use of courses (a) or (c). Since 1977 the Report states that there have been 17 applications for authorization. The result of these applications has been as follows:

Ten were granted authorization
—six on the basis of public interest benefits.
—one on the basis of ensuring continuance of product supplies and employment
—two on the basis that dominance was unlikely to result
—one was granted for other reasons.

Six were withdrawn
—in five of these cases the Commission indicated that no breach was indicated.

One was rejected
—this case was resubmitted in a modified form and then authorized.

Under existing legislation, acquisitions which involve a 'bare transfer' of monopoly power still fall within section 50 even though there is no effect on competition. The effect of this might be to reduce the threat of a takeover of companies enjoying dominant positions with, perhaps, consequential adverse implications on business efficiency. In practice, however, the Trade Practices Commission has been reluctant to intervene in such cases.

A further criticism of existing legislation is that the test is based not on competition but on 'control or dominate'. Consequently, an acquisition is allowed provided it does not lead to control or domination of a market even though there may be a reduction in competition with no compensating public benefits.

Like the UK, there is no requirement to notify the Commission in advance so that if an acquisition contravenes section 50, action may be taken to enforce a divestiture or pursue damages. The former approach may be very disruptive particularly on the workforce. An example of such an action occurred in 1984 with the Petersville/General Foods frozen food merger.

Another cause for concern has been overseas acquisitions which have an impact on Australian subsidiaries. Whilst such activity may have an impact on competition in the Australian market they are, at present exempt from section 50.

As a result of criticism of some aspects of the legislation the government published a discussion paper (the green paper) in February 1984. Bannerman (1984) categorized the proposals into six groups:

1. provision of a 'housekeeping nature', for example in plugging loopholes, in relation to restrictive trade practices and consumer protection;
2. expansion of the term 'consumer';
3. extension of the resale price maintenance law (section 48);
4. strengthening of monopolization law (section 46);
5. strengthening of price discrimination law (section 49);
6. strengthening of merger law (section 50). This also includes a proposed new section 50A which deals with the above criticism concerning overseas mergers with implications for Australian subsidiaries.

As far as foreign investors are concerned section 46 on monopolization law and section 50 on merger law seem to be of prime importance. However, section 46 has not been important in practice since it requires companies to exercise substantial control to take advantage of market power and also to eliminate or block others. With respect to the 'taking advantage of market power' section, the Commission has brought only one case which it lost. The Trade Practices Amendment Bill introduced in 1985 proposed that there should be a change from a company 'being in a position substantially to control a market' to test whether 'a corporation has a substantial degree of market power'. It is the intention of this revised section to apply to oligopolies as well as monopolies.

The proposals to amend section 50 include several aimed at closing loopholes although the existing 'dominance' test is to remain substantially unchanged. The Bill also makes it specific that section 50 does not apply to the 'bare transfer of monopoly power'. Additional provisions are directed at joint venture acquisitions and to foreign takeovers with implications for Australian takeovers. Other proposed amendments include the speeding-up of authorization procedures in an attempt to encourage such courses of action in restructuring industry.

Some of the proposals in the green paper were promulgated in 1987.

Regulation of the securities industry

The conduct of stock exchanges and their members is regulated by law. A co-operative Commonwealth/State framework was introduced in December 1979 to provide for a system of law and administration which was uniform with respect to company law and regulation in the six States and Australian Capital Territory. In addition, provisions were included to extend the agreement to the Northern Territories and various external Territories.

Under the agreement, general companies and securities legislation was to be introduced by the Australian Capital Territory, with each State enacting the provisions of the new code. The first legislative Act was introduced in 1979, the National Companies and Securities Act, which established the National Companies and Securities Commission (NCSC). The NCSC was given responsibility for companies and securities matters under the directions of the Ministerial Council comprising the Attorney-General of each State and the Federal Attorney-General.

A new securities law was introduced in 1980, the Securities Industry Act, which was based on the Securities Industry Acts of the four States which were parties to the Interstate Corporate Affairs Agreement. The 1980 Act came into force on 1 July 1981.

Administration of the co-operative legislation is undertaken by the Corporate Affairs Commission in each State. In addition, the exchanges continue to evolve and tighten up rules of conduct. Thus the system of control is one of self-regulation within the general framework of NCSC control which is often referred to as a system of co-regulation.

Stock exchange controls

Stock exchanges

There are six stock exchanges in the capital cities of Sydney, Melbourne, Brisbane, Adelaide, Perth and Hobart. Listing requirements are uniform and the stock exchanges are associated through the Australian Associated Stock Exchanges (AASE) Limited which was established in 1937. The aim of the AASE is to protect 'the interests of the investing public and to consider and secure the adoption of uniform regulations governing the operations and practice of Member Exchanges'. The Listing Requirements are stated in the Listing Manual and are of great importance to listed companies since failure to comply with the regulations may lead to removal from the official list and for the securities to lose official quotation.

The purposes of the listing requirements may be summarized as follows:

1. to avoid the establishment of false markets;
2. to ensure adequate disclosure in order to protect potential investors;
3. to ensure fairness between shareholders;
4. to administer the relationship between listed companies and the Exchange.

The minimum requirements for a limited liability industrial company seeking an official quotation include:

1. paid up capital at least $A200,000;
2. paid up capital plus share premium reserve at least $A300,000;
3. at least 300 holders of shares of the one class and paid-up value; and
4. members of the public should hold at least 140,000 shares of the one class and paid-up value.

A foreign company with a listing on a recognized overseas stock exchange may obtain a listing in Australia where at least 200,000 shares, or a lesser amount where approval is obtained, are held by at least 200 Australian residents on an Australian register.

The listing requirements with respect to takeovers (section 3R) are summarized below:

1. Secrecy in discussions should be maintained if an offer is possible.
2. Where a company receives a notice of a takeover that notice should be lodged with its Home Exchange.
3. Where a notice of an offer has been received the company must not, within the period of three months, allot equity securities or other securities with conversion rights unless:

   (a) the issue has been approved in a general meeting; or
   (b) the issue is to all shareholders on a pro-rata basis; or
   (c) details of the issue had been lodged with the Home Exchange prior to the receipt of the notice; or
   (d) the allotment arises as a result of the exercise of conversion rights.

4. Where the time-limit for acceptance is extended the offeror should announce the percentage of acceptances already received.
5. On the closing date the offeror should inform the offeree's Home Exchange the percentage of acceptances received and whether the outstanding shares will be compulsorily acquired as permitted by the Companies (Acquisition of Shares) Act 1980.
6. Where securities are issued as part or all of the consideration, the offer document should state whether an application will be lodged for the securities to be officially quoted. In addition, the offer document must state the date from and extent to which dividends will be paid on the new securities.

In addition to the traditional board, the Australian Associated Stock Exchange has established a Second Board Market to allow companies, other than mining companies, to obtain public company status. The market is similar to the Unlisted Securities Market in the UK and the Over-the-Counter Market in the US. There are two types of companies considered suitable for the market:

1. viable small or medium commercial or industrial businesses owned by families or individuals or divisions of larger companies, and
2. high technology and new venture companies.

A company fulfilling these requirements should have the following additional credentials:

1. a successful track record,
2. sound future prospects,
3. the possibility of an early dividend,
4. a capable board of directors with sound industrial experience, and
5. can be compared favourably with other listed companies.

In the case of high-technology companies no track record is required where the prospects of the company lie in the successful development and application of some invention or process. Mining companies, property trusts and overseas companies are specifically excluded from the market.

4. TAXATION

Background

Taxes in Australia are raised at the Commonwealth government, state and municipal levels. The income tax system which is applicable to companies is a classical system of tax which is administered under the authority of the Commonwealth government. The actual administration is undertaken by the Commissioner of Taxation and Second Commissioners who are appointed by the Federal Parliament. The administration is conducted centrally at the Australian Taxation Office in Canberra, with responsibilities further delegated to regional offices under the auspices of Deputy Commissioners.

The main Act imposing income tax is the Income Tax Assessment Act 1936 which is supplemented by annual Acts which set the rates of taxation for the fiscal year which ends on 30 June. Normally all taxpayers have the same tax year although permission may be granted for an alternative date. Corporate taxes are collected in equal instalments on a quarterly basis based on the income of the preceding year.

In addition to income tax which is levied on companies and individuals the Commonwealth government also levies customs and excise duties and sales taxes. In contrast the seven states raise taxes on oil and minerals in the form of royalties and also impose land, payroll and gift taxes in addition to stamp duties. At the municipal level (local authorities) charges are levied on the owners of the real estate and are called rates.

The tax on corporations applies to all companies which includes all incorporated and unincorporated bodies excluding partnerships. The income to be assessed for income tax purposes is dependent upon whether the company is resident or non-resident. A company is deemed to be resident if it is incorporated in Australia or, where unincorporated in Australia, it is a trading company which has its voting shares controlled by resident shareholders or where central management and control is exercised in Australia. This distinction is important since resident companies are subject to income tax at 46 per cent whereas non-resident companies are currently subject to an additional tax of 5 per cent on certain branch profits. This branch profits tax was eliminated from 1 July 1987. A further difference is that resident companies are currently taxed on their worldwide income, subject to exemption for foreign source income taxed in the country of source, while non-resident companies are taxed only on their Australian income. Resident companies however, are entitled to tax credits and rebates levied overseas. Income earned by resident companies outside Australia is not subject to tax provided it has been taxed in the source country. This general principle is not applicable to dividends, royalties and some interest payments which derive from countries with which Australia has concluded double tax treaties. Tax credits are available to resident taxpayers receiving income from these sources. A foreign tax credit system was introduced on 1 July 1987 which taxes an Australian company on worldwide income and allows a credit of foreign tax paid against Australian tax liability.

A further important distinction for tax purposes is between public and private companies. As previously stated, status for tax purposes does not automatically follow legal status since tax status in Australia is determined by the status of its parent company. A company constitutes a public corporation if it meets two criteria. First, a company must have non-preference shares which are listed on an official stock exchange on the last days of its income year or it is a subsidiary of such a company. Secondly, at any time during the year, 20 or fewer persons must not hold, or have options to hold, 75 per cent or more of:

1. the equity capital of the company,
2. the voting shares,
3. the rights to dividends, or
4. the rights to capital distributions.

A corporation that fulfils the above conditions is classified as a public company. A subsidiary is therefore a public company for tax purposes if it is wholly owned by a public company and where not wholly owned is more than 50 per cent beneficially owned by a listed public company. Companies not fulfilling these conditions are normally deemed to be private companies for tax purposes although the Commissioner of Taxation has some discretion if the conditions are not fully met. For example, the

Commissioner has the discretion to deem a company to be public if the conditions are not quite met and similarly he has the power to deem a company to be private even though the conditions are met. In the latter case the Commissioner only has this power if he considers that the organization of the company is designed with the intention of avoiding taxation by an artificial arrangement.

One of the penalties of being designated a private company is that a minimum level of distributions out of profits must be made each year. If the minimum level is not retrieved the company may be subject to undistributed profits tax of 50 per cent beyond the retention allowance. The retention allowance is the sum of 80 per cent of after-tax trading income and 10 per cent of after-tax property income. Property income includes rents, interest and public company dividends. In contrast, a public company, for tax purposes, is not required to make a minimum distribution out of profits.

Taxation is levied on companies on their taxable income which is based on profits recorded in the financial accounts but subject to certain adjustments. In calculating cost of sales the value for tax purposes should be that used in the financial accounts. In valuing inventory a taxpayer may use FIFO, market selling price, replacement cost or other methods approved by the Commissioner of Taxation. The cost of manufactured goods may include both fixed and variable manufacturing overhead costs. The same method need not be used for all stocks although whatever valuation is arrived at for the year-end must be used as the opening stock for the following year.

Transactions involving the purchase of foreign goods must be made on an arm's length basis to ensure that profits are not transferred overseas. During the 1970s many multinational companies used transfer pricing to shift profits from Australia. Such artificial arrangements were challenged successfully in the courts by the Commissioner of Taxation. Anti-avoidance sections were introduced in 1982 with effect from 27 May 1981 to add to the Income Tax Assessment Act. The arm's length transaction rule applies to the cross-border supply or acquisition of property as well as to the provision of goods and services. The rule applies to branches and head offices as well as to residents and non-residents who are parties to international transactions. However, where transactions are covered by a double tax treaty the rights of the Commissioner of Taxation may not exceed the provisions of that treaty. If the Commissioner finds that a corporation has artificially avoided taxation in Australia, he has the power to increase taxable income and to impose a substantial additional penalty tax.

Income received in the form of company dividends forms part of assessable income. When received from Australian resident companies by non-resident companies not conducting a business in Australia the dividends are subject only to withholding tax. Where a non-resident corporation is conducting a business in Australia the dividends form part of normal income. Dividends received from resident companies are taxable although a section 46 rebate is granted to resident companies.

The effect of this rebate is that dividends received by resident companies are tax-free. With respect to private companies the full rebate may not be received when dividends are paid by another private company.

With effect from 1 July 1987 Australia has a dividend imputation system similar to that in operation in the UK. The main features of the new system include:

1. payment of compensatory tax at the time of dividend distribution at the rate of $49 for every $51 distributed;
2. compensatory tax is a credit against the company's primary tax liability;
3. resident individual shareholders will receive a tax credit equal to the compensatory tax paid which will render dividend income effectively tax-free. The credit will not be available to non-resident shareholders although dividend withholding tax will be eliminated;
4. the company tax rate will increase from 46 per cent to 49 per cent;
5. undistributed profits tax will be abolished for private companies.

The general rule is that expenses are allowable against tax provided they are not of a capital or private nature. Expenditure may be offset against income even where the Commissioner considers it unnecessary, provided the expense is appropriate to the type of business. The expenditure need not necessarily have been incurred in Australia.

In calculating assessable income the following common deductions are permitted.

1. *Depreciation*. As a general rule depreciation on most assets is allowable against tax. Generally a taxpayer may elect to adopt the diminishing value (sometimes referred to as the declining or reducing balance basis) or the prime cost method (straight line basis). Each method has its own series of rates, with the diminishing value method being 50 per cent higher than the prime cost rates. An extensive list of applicable rates for different types of capital expenditure has been produced by the Commissioner for Taxes. The rates were devised on the basis of estimated useful lives of assets which are kept in good order.

   On 19 July 1982 accelerated rates of depreciation were introduced for fixed assets. In most cases the applicable rate is 20 per cent of prime cost except where the plant was eligible for a higher rate in which case the accelerated rate of 33.33 per cent of prime cost applies. The accelerated depreciation rates do not apply to motor vehicles, structural improvements, paintings and assets which already qualify for higher rates.

   Depreciation allowances on buildings are low. For non-residential buildings commenced after 21 August 1984 an annual allowance of 4 per cent is provided for a period of 25 years. After 19 July 1982 and up to 21 August 1984, the applicable rate was 2.5 per cent per annum. Buildings in this context include office blocks, factories and rental properties used for residential accommodation and constructed after 19 July 1985. Where assets are revalued the depreciation allowance for tax purposes remains unaltered and is based on cost which may include installation costs.

A limit is imposed on depreciation of motor vehicles and for 1986–7 is $A29,646. The limit is index-linked.

When assets which have received a depreciation allowance are sold a gain or loss might arise. Where the sale proceeds exceed the tax written-down value a gain is made. The gain in excess of the depreciation allowance received may be brought into the taxable profit in the year of sale. Alternatively the profit may be used to reduce the tax cost of its replacement or other depreciable items of plant and machinery.

2. *Research and development*. Between 1 July 1985 and 30 June 1991 expenditure for research and development purposes qualifies for taxation concessions: revenue expenditure is 150 per cent deductible in the year incurred; expenditure on plant and equipment qualifies for a 150 per cent deduction over three years; expenditure on buildings qualifies for a 100 per cent deduction over three years.

3. *Other industry allowances*. There are also special capital allowance schemes for some industries particularly dealing with mineral exploitation and for investors in the film industry.

As far as mining is concerned the exploration for petroleum, which includes both crude oil and natural gas, is dealt with separately from other mining. Whilst taxable income of a petroleum explorer is calculated as for any other business, deductions for capital expenditure are different. Qualifying capital expenditure, which includes most expenses but not pipelines to customers, may be offset against tax at the lesser of ten years on the life of the field or mine and is calculated on a straight-line basis. Income to be assessed extends to mining and exploration on the continental shelf of Australia.

There are also special provisions for other mining operations. For example, profits derived from gold mining are exempt from income tax although the income from other prospecting and exploration, but not extraction, of minerals is allowable in the year incurred. Where losses are incurred they may be carried forward or deducted from any other class of income. The treatment of capital expenditures is the same as for the petroleum industry. It is important to realize that the taxation provisions relating to extractive industries is a very complex subject and requires expert specialist advice.

Another specific industry allowance introduced to encourage development is for investors in film production. Capital expenditure by an Australian resident in which the resident becomes a part owner in the film qualifies for a deduction at the rate of 133 per cent. In order to qualify for this generous relief the film must generate income within two years of the expenditure incurred. An additional incentive for investment in the industry is that net income is exempt from tax up to an amount equal to 33 per cent of the qualifying capital expenditure.

4. *Interest.* Interest is normally deductible when it becomes due and payable. The concept of thin capitalization is not generally applicable although foreign investors should be aware that companies owned by non-residents are subject to debt/equity restrictions which are imposed by the government under its foreign investment policy. The aim of the government is to ensure that unfair advantages do not accrue to overseas investors investing in Australian companies. The FIRB will scrutinize the capital structure employed to ensure that commercial practices for that particular industry are generally complied with.

   An advantage that could accrue to an overseas investor, if normal commercial practices are not adhered to, might occur in the choice of repatriating interest payments or dividends. Since interest is a deductible expense any expenditure paid to a non-resident is subject to a withholding tax of 10 per cent, whereas dividends are subject to withholding tax of 30 per cent (normally reduced to 15 per cent where a double tax treaty is in force). This was eliminated with the introduction of the dividend imputation system from 1 July 1987.

   As a guide the FIRB expects the debt-to-equity ratio not to exceed 3 : 1. However, commercial practice in a particular industry may dictate an alternative ratio. For example, a ratio of 6 : 1 would not be unreasonable in the banking industry.

5. *Losses.* Where a loss occurs in one of the activities of a company, it may be offset against other income. Any unrelieved losses may be carried forward but may not be carried back. A loss may be carried forward provided certain conditions are fulfilled, for a period up to seven years with the exception of agricultural production. A loss incurred in an agricultural business may be carried forward indefinitely or offset against all other types of income.

   There are two conditions which must be fulfilled for a loss to be carried forward involving the continuity of shareholding or continuity of the same business. The continuity of shareholding test requires that at all times during the year in which the relief is provided, more than 50 per cent of the voting power, dividend rights and rights to the return of capital in the case of a liquidation are beneficially held by the same shareholders as when the loss occurred. If this test is not fulfilled the company may still obtain relief if it can demonstrate that the business remains the same as that before the change in ownership which prevented the company from fulfilling the continuity of shareholding test. Losses may be transferred between resident companies that are members of a common wholly-owned group of companies.

   Loss relief is a complicated area which requires specialist advice and many problems can arise. For example, if a company fulfils the continuity of shareholding test, loss relief may still be denied if the continuity of business test is not met where certain transactions are undertaken for tax avoidance reasons.

Foreign subsidiaries and branches

Period to 30 June 1987

As previously mentioned the only income earned abroad which is currently taxed abroad and is also included in income in Australia is income from dividends, interest and royalties which have been subject to withholding taxes. Income derived from these sources is included in its tax return in Australia at the grossed up amount. A tax credit is given which is the lower of the foreign tax deducted or the Australian tax payable. All other income which is earned is exempt from any further liability.

Interest received by a foreign company from an Australian subsidiary is subject to withholding tax of 10 per cent regardless of whether the interest is paid to a resident of a country with which Australia has a double tax treaty. There are circumstances in which the withholding tax is reduced to nil. Withholding tax is levied on interest where a permanent business is established in Australia by a foreign company so that the tax applies to foreign branches as well as foreign subsidiaries. In contrast, dividends paid to a foreign company are subject to withholding taxes of 30 per cent unless a double tax treaty is in force in which case the rate is 15 per cent.

The branch profits of a foreign company are taxed in the same way as company profits and as such the tax status of the branch is determined by the status of the parent company. The distinction between a public company and a private company is important in determining whether adequate distributions are made. Dividend distributions are assessed in relation to worldwide net income.

Where a non-resident company trades in Australia through a branch, an additional tax of 5 per cent is levied on its reduced income bringing the rate up to 51 per cent. Reduced income is calculated by reducing taxable income by net dividends received, overseas shipping income, film royalties and insurance premiums and profits of non-resident life insurance companies. The additional branch profits tax may be reduced depending on the provision of double taxation treaties.

Period from 1 July 1987

From 1 July 1987 resident companies will be taxed under a Foreign Tax Credit System. Resident companies will pay 49 per cent tax on worldwide income with a credit allowed for foreign taxes paid up to the amount of domestic tax. As mentioned above, the branch profits tax, dividend withholding tax and minimum distribution requirements for private companies will all be eliminated from 1 July 1987.

Capital gains tax

Capital gains tax was introduced in Australia with effect from 20 September 1985. Assets acquired after that date are subject to the new tax which will be payable on the profit made on disposal. Where assets are held for over 12 months the cost base is adjusted for inflation to reduce the taxable amount of profit realized. Individual residences are exempt from capital gains tax. Rollover provisions exist which defer liability to tax where assets are transferred on death or between companies in a wholly-owned group.

Taxation implications of mergers and acquisitions

Implications for the acquiring company

There are basically two approaches a foreign investor can adopt to acquire a business in Australia. The foreign investor may have or set up a branch or subsidiary in Australia with a view to acquiring the business assets of a resident company. Alternatively a foreign subsidiary may be used to acquire the shares of a resident company.

Where an asset acquisition is undertaken it may be possible for any unused tax losses to be carried forward provided the continuity of business test is fulfilled. Provided that transactions are on an arm's-length basis capital assets acquired are subject to the appropriate asset depreciation allowance. Where transactions are not conducted on an arm's length basis the Commissioner of Taxation can decide on a value which he considers to reflect the lower of depreciated cost or market value. This also applies if the Commission decides that an excessive price has been paid for a particular asset. Where the value of depreciable assets is not specified in the contract the Commissioner has the authority to apportion the consideration amongst the assets. Unlike the US it is not possible to step up the cost of the assets in any circumstances.

If the purchase of assets of an Australian company is undertaken by a foreign branch it is important to remember that profits will until 30 June 1987 be liable to branch-profits tax in addition to standard tax. If the foreign company is a private corporation the rules for adequate distributions may also apply (up to 30 June 1987).

In acquiring real estate stamp duty is levied at a rate which increases to 3.5 per cent for purchases at or above $A100,000. The acquisition of plant and machinery does not lead to any major tax consequences for the purchaser. Depreciation is allowed on the purchase consideration for these assets on an arm's-length transaction. In acquiring stock the Commissioner may decide to alter the purchase cost if it is not acquired at market value on the date of sale. Since only assets of value are acquired in this type of transaction it is not possible to transfer any bad debt allowances.

Where the shares of an Australian company are acquired instead of its assets the tax consequences are slightly different. Losses may be carried forward for up to seven years provided that either the continuity of shareholding or continuity of business test is fulfilled. In most other instances the tax position of the acquired company remains unchanged. In acquiring shares the transaction is subject to stamp duty which varies between states and territories. There are anti-avoidance provisions to ensure that the appropriate duty is paid.

There is no step-up basis for taxation purposes and as such the purchase price should reflect the deferred tax liability. This occurs because when acquired assets are eventually sold the base cost is the original cost and not that reflected in the purchase consideration. Where the assets are not subject to capital gains tax this is not a problem unless the assets were acquired with a view to making a profit or were acquired for a period of less than 12 months.

Assets which were acquired by a company before 20 September 1985, and therefore not subject to capital gains tax on disposal, will lose that guaranteed status if more than 50 per cent of the beneficial ownership of the company changes as from that date. The cost base of these assets is then their market value on the date of change in majority beneficial ownership.

When undertaking a share acquisition a foreign investor should take into consideration that profits and losses of resident companies may be offset against each other provided that there is 100 per cent common ownership.

Implications for the acquiree company

Where the assets of a company are sold, capital allowances terminate at the date of sale of those assets and the acquirer is then able to obtain them. Where a gain is made on the sale of an asset the excess over the depreciation allowance received may be brought into the profit and loss account in the year of sale. The taxpayer has the option to use the profit to reduce the cost of its replacement or other depreciable items of plant and machinery. Where a loss arises it may be treated as a deductible loss.

The sale of inventories will be treated as being realized at its market value and is taxable. Any losses that have arisen to the date of sale may be used by the seller to offset against other income. This aspect must be agreed between the seller and buyer as it affects the consideration. Since assets of value may only be transferred a loss on the sale of debtors is not deductible.

Where the shares of a company are sold a capital gains tax liability will not accrue unless the shares were originally acquired with the intention of making a profit or if the shares have been held for a period less than 12 months or if the shares were acquired after 19 September 1985.

Implications for the acquiree's shareholders

If the acquirer merges with an Australian company the tax consequences are similar to a transfer of a business. There are no direct consequences for the shareholders of a public company but there may be if a private company is involved. If a private company makes a profit it may be necessary for a distribution to be made to ensure that the minimum level of distributions is achieved to avoid the undistributed profits tax (in force until 30 June 1987). Note that considerable legislation now exists to prevent the avoidance of taxation by asset-stripping. We have already noted that legislation was introduced in 1982 to ensure that transactions are at arm's length in order to avoid the transfer of taxable profits out of Australia. In addition, the Crimes (Taxation Offences) Act 1980 made asset-stripping a criminal offence so that evaders may suffer imprisonment as well as be charged for the tax evaded. In certain situations the Commissioner of Taxation has the authority to raise a tax assessment on shareholders for tax not paid by a company.

Where the shares of a target company are acquired the shareholders of the acquiree will not normally be taxed on their gain. However, if the shares were acquired with a view to making a profit or if the shares were held for a period of less than 12 months before the takeover or where acquired after 19 September 1985 the profit will form part of their assessable income.

Tax planning

Extreme care needs to be exercised in planning transactions for tax purposes. There are many anti-avoidance provisions which try to ensure that transactions are not undertaken with a view to transferring taxable profits out of Australia. The objective of the government is not to penalize foreign investment but rather to ensure that they pay equivalent taxation as indigenous companies. Transactions with countries which are designated as tax havens are carefully scrutinized and if tax avoidance is suspected exchange control approval will not be granted. Provided that transactions are undertaken on an arm's length basis problems should not ensue even where one of the parties to a transaction is resident in a tax haven country. However, there are double taxation treaties between most of its major trading partners and as such it is important to scrutinize the specific treaty.

Where money is raised in Australia the interest will be deductible for tax purposes provided that it is used eventually in income-generating activities. Where offshore finance is used to acquire a company withholding tax of 10 per cent is levied on the interest regardless of the destination of the interest payments. However, where the borrowing is made in a tax haven country the Commissioner for Taxation may ask for no interest payments to be met or that tax relief will not be granted for the loan. When raising debt it is important to remember that the FIRB will scrutinize the proposed capital structure to ensure that thin capitalization does not occur.

Due to the disadvantages outlined above it will often be advantageous to raise funds in Australia by establishing an Australian holding company. First, an Australian subsidiary provides a better presence than a foreign branch; and secondly, there are advantages to be gained from a group structure since 30 June 1985. However, in order to gain group tax concessions it is necessary for there to be 100 per cent common ownership between the companies.

A final word of warning should be made about tax avoidance. On 28 April 1983, the Minister of Finance announced that the government would

> as necessary employ retrospective legislation to ensure that tax sought to be avoided under any blatant tax avoidance scheme that comes to light during our term of office will be collected, irrespective of when the scheme was entered into. Any legislation that it becomes necessary to introduce in pursuance of that policy will be made to operate from the date of first known use of the particular scheme.

5. ACCOUNTING

Background

Company disclosure in Australia is influenced by:

1. professional accounting bodies in Australia;
2. Companies Act 1981 and subsequent amendments;
3. approved accounting standards:
4. the listing requirements of the AASE; and
5. international recommendations such as those issued by the International Accounting Standards Committee (IASC) and to a lesser extent the Organization for Economic Co-operation and Development (OECD).

There are two professional accounting bodies in Australia, the Australian Society of Accountants, and the Institute of Chartered Accountants in Australia. The two organizations are independent of each other although they both sponsor the Australian Accounting Research Foundation (AARF), the organization responsible for formulating Statements of Accounting Standards and Statements of Standard Auditing Practice. Members of the two professional bodies are obliged to comply with the statements issued by AARF although the standards did not have legal force until 1985.

Companies Act 1981 is a federal Act which is implemented in each State and Territory under a Code. The Code requires accounting records to be kept and section 269 stipulates that a profit and loss account, balance sheet, and a set of group accounts where there is a holding company, must be prepared from these records. In addition, section 269 requires a statement by directors, section 270 requires that a directors' report be attached to the accounts and the accounts generally must be audited (section 285). Amendments to the 1981 Act were introduced in 1984 which has the effect of providing legislative backing to accounting standards. An Accounting Standards Review Board (ASRB) has been formed which is responsible to the Ministerial Council for company law. Directors are required to ensure that financial statements comply with approved accounting standards and that the records show a true and fair view. In general it is intended that 'approved accounting standards' issued by the ASRB will become the same as 'Australian accounting standards' issued by AARF.

The listing requirements of the AASE, which apply to public companies with listed securities, attempt to improve the disclosure of information to investors. The requirements include the preparation of a half-yearly report which need not be audited (section B(1)), the preparation of a preliminary final statement (section 3B(2)), and further disclosures in the annual report (section 3C) and for mining exploration companies (section 3B(5)–(10)). The further disclosures required in the annual report include a statement of sources and application of funds and information about major shareholders.

Whilst the number of standards issued in Australia has lagged behind the US and to a lesser extent the UK, there has been increasing recognition of the role of the International Accounting Standards Committee (IASC). Australia is a full voting member of the IASC and as such undertakes to support the standards promulgated by the International Committee. Paragraph 3 APS1, issued by the Institute of Chartered Accountants in Australia, states that each future Australian Accounting Standard will be drafted only after a detailed consideration of the relevant International Accounting Standard (if in existence) and the Australian Standard will refer to any unavoidable divergence between the two. Consequently, conformity with Australian Accounting Standards should normally result in conformity also with International Accounting Standards! However, there are some significant differences between Australian accounting standards and International accounting standards and these are dealt with later in this section (table 4.8).

When foreign investors set up business in Australia it is normal to form a subsidiary rather than to form a branch. This is because a local company provides a better profile and can obtain commercial advantages, for example, when borrowing funds. Furthermore, since 1984/5 losses can be transferred between companies which are wholly-owned subsidiaries within a group common for foreign investors to set up a holding company in Australia which acquires subsidiaries on behalf of the ultimate parent company. Such a corporate formation necessitates the preparation of consolidated accounts.

Accounting for groups, acquisitions and mergers

Historically, the two major influences on group accounts are the Listing Requirements of the AASE and Companies Act 1981 including Schedule 7 to the Companies Regulations. In the future, recently issued standards on equity accounting, goodwill and business combinations are likely to become increasingly influential.

Section 3C of the Listing Requirements states that the annual audited accounts shall be prepared in consolidated form. In the first financial year in which a company adopts equity accounting there shall be stated by way of note to the accounts, the principles adopted, the amount of any increase or decrease in profits or losses and the amount of assets or reserves resulting from the adoption of equity accounting.

Legislation requiring the preparation of group accounts in Australia has been influenced considerably by the UK. Consolidated accounts began to appear in the UK in the 1920s and in 1938 the State of Victoria in Australia introduced group accounts as a disclosure requirement for certain companies.

The Companies Act 1981 in Australia adopts the UK approach to defining a subsidiary. Section 7 stipulates that a corporation is a subsidiary of another company if it:

1. controls the composition of the board of directors; or
2. controls more than 50 per cent of the votes; or
3. holds more than 50 per cent of the issued share capital excluding any part that carries no right to participate beyond a specified amount in a distribution of either profits or capital.

Control over the composition of a corporation's board of directors is defined as the exercise of power by another company to appoint or remove all or a majority of the directors. It is noticeable from the above definition that a holding company–subsidiary relationship may exist even where more than 50 per cent of the issued share capital is not owned.

Section 269(3) of Companies Act 1981 require the directors of a holding company to prepare group accounts dealing with the profit or loss of the company and its subsidiaries and the state of affairs of the company and its subsidiaries. Like the UK, the requirement is to produce group accounts rather than consolidated accounts which may take four alternative forms of presentation. Section 266 states that group accounts, in relation to a holding company means:

1. a set of consolidated accounts for the group of companies of that holding company;
2. two or more sets of consolidated accounts together covering that group;
3. separate accounts for each corporation in that group; or
4. a combination of one or more sets of consolidated accounts and one or more separate accounts together covering that group.

Like the UK, majority practice is to prepare one set of consolidated statements. An accounting research study published in 1980 by the Australian Accounting Research Foundation (Ryan et al.) found that over the period 1976–9, 97–8 per cent of companies included in a survey prepared a single set of consolidated accounts.

The directors are required to prepare a profit and loss account for the holding company (section 269(1)) and a balance sheet (section 269(2)) which give a true and fair view of the profit or loss for the year and the state of affairs at the end of that financial year. In addition, section

269(3) requires group accounts to be prepared which deal with the profit or loss of the company and its subsidiaries for their respective last financial years and the state of affairs of the company and its subsidiaries as at the end of their respective last financial year. The group profit or loss and state of affairs should show a true and fair view as far as the members of the holding company are concerned.

Clause 5 of Schedule 7 requires the group accounts to show the net amount of consolidated profit or loss of the group for the financial year after provision for income tax. The contribution to consolidated profit or loss of each member of the group should also be stated after minority interests have been excluded.

In preparing group accounts a holding company is required (section 269(8)) to ensure that the accounts comply with Schedule 7 of the Companies Regulations. Where the accounts do not give a true and fair view the directors are obliged to disclose additional information and explanations which will give a true and fair view.

Schedule 7 of the Companies Regulations provided additional requirements concerning group accounts. All intercompany transactions must be eliminated from the consolidated accounts and the form of the accounts of a subsidiary should be in the same form as the accounts of the holding company.

There is also a requirement that where group accounts are prepared in a form other than one set of consolidated accounts the directors must certify that the preparation of one set is impracticable or that another format is beneficial to the interests of shareholders. In addition, the directors must state that intercompany transactions do not materially affect the accounts.

Schedule 7 also contains disclosure requirements for group accounts of a holding company. The following information should be stated by way of note or otherwise:

1. the name and place of incorporation of each subsidiary and where the business of a subsidiary is conducted overseas the name of that country;
2. the amount of the holding company's investment in each class of the share capital of each subsidiary;
3. the percentage of each class of the shares in each subsidiary held by the holding company;
4. where the year ends of a subsidiary and the holding company are not coterminous the date on which the financial year of the subsidiary ends.

AAS14 – Equity method of accounting

Where an investor exercises significant influence over an investee, but is not a subsidiary the investment should be accounted for using the equity method, but only in supplementary financial statements. Consequently equity accounting should not be used in preparing an investor's own accounts or in the consolidated financial statements. The reason for this is that the Attorney-General of Victoria stated that the method, if incorporated into the financial statements, may well be illegal under the Companies Act 1981. The Victorian Corporate Affairs Commission argued that the definition of group accounts did not allow the possibility of incorporating information into consolidated accounts which did not already exist in the accounts of those companies comprising the group. The AARF and its legal advisers disagreed with this view but did not wish to protract the debate pending the outcome of an investigation by the NCSC.

Significant influence is normally presumed where the investment represents 20 per cent or more of the voting power but not more than 50 per cent. The concept of 'significant influence' refers to the ability to exercise influence rather than actually display influence over the financial and operating policies of the investee.

Whilst voting power is the normal criterion for determining significant influence, the following may also indicate an ability substantially to affect policies of an investee:

1. board representation,
2. participation in dividend decisions,
3. participation, in other ways, in policy-making decisions of the investee,
4. significant intercompany transactions,
5. significant interchange of managerial personnel, and
6. dependence on technical information.

In most instances significant control is determined by voting power which is dependent upon the size of its shareholding. However, there are cases where more than 20 per cent of the voting shares are owned by the investor but equity accounting would not be appropriate. For example, the investor may fail to obtain board representation, there may be a legal impediment such as in a regulated company or other investors may act in concert to prevent participation.

In contrast, equity accounting might be appropriate where the investment is less than 20 per cent, for example, where the remaining voting shares are widely distributed among a large number of shareholders, so that significant influence can be exercised at lower levels of shareholding.

The discussion to AAS14 implicitly makes a distinction between the UK standard which was based solely on the cost method of accounting for investments, prior to 1982, and the Australian approach based the equity method of accounting for investments. Prior to the revision of SSAP1, Accounting for Associated Companies, in the UK, the investment was recorded at cost plus proportionate share of retained profits since the date of acquisition without regard to goodwill. Since 1982 the UK requires the disclosure of the share of the net assets of the associate excluding goodwill, and the separate disclosure of the share of goodwill in the associates own financial statements.

In contrast to the cost-based equity method, the Australian standard is based on a pure equity approach. The approaches are different to the extent that under the cost-based equity method there is no recognition of any goodwill or premium on acquisition, and there is no adjustment for any increase in reserves. The pure equity method adopts both of these adjustments to the carrying value of the investment.

AAS14 stipulates that the equity supplementary profit and loss account should show the investor's share of associated companies:

1. operating profits and losses before income tax,
2. income tax expense, and
3. extraordinary items (net of income tax).

Each of the above items should be disclosed separately and, in addition, the extent to which retained earnings and other reserves are attributable to associated companies should also be published. The notes to the accounts should disclose the following information for each associate company:

1. the name and principal activities,
2. the investor's ownership interest,
3. any change in balance sheet dates,
4. any material post-balance sheet events, and
5. any significant differences in accounting policies as compared with the investor.

AAS18 – Accounting for goodwill

In the discussion of the standard it is made explicit that there is no difference between internally generated goodwill and purchased goodwill other than the former cannot be objectively valued. Recognizing this difficulty the standard specifies that internally generated goodwill should not be brought to account.

On the acquisition of assets or shares in a subsidiary or associated company it is appropriate to value the net assets at fair value. Any excess of the purchase consideration over the fair value of the net assets acquired is deemed to be goodwill and should be recognized as a non-current asset except where the investment is in an associated company.

Purchased goodwill should be amortized on a systematic basis against income over its useful life which should not exceed 20 years. Where no future benefits are likely to arise from the purchased goodwill it is appropriate to write down the unamortized balance in the profit and loss account.

Where the net assets acquired are purchased at a discount the fair values of the non-monetary costs should be reduced proportionately to eliminate it. However, if a discount still remains it should be taken to the profit and loss account as a gain.

The following should be disclosed in the financial statements.

1. the unamortized balance of goodwill;
2. the amount of goodwill amortized during the period; and
3. the policy adopted in amortizing goodwill.

The standard is operative for accounting periods ending on or after 31 March 1985.

AAS21 – Accounting for the acquisition of assets (including business entities)

This statement applies to all reporting entities both in the private and public sectors and is operative for accounting periods ending on or after 31 March 1986. In order to reflect the economic substance of transactions all acquisitions should be accounted for using the purchase method. The assets acquired should be the cost to the acquirer being the fair value of shares or other assets given up in making the acquisition.

The pooling of interests method, merger accounting, should not be used on the grounds that the method fails to reflect the economic substance of the exchange transaction. More specifically merger accounting fails to reflect the negotiation process between parties as it does not measure the cost to the acquiring company of giving up the purchase consideration in exchange for shares or costs. Furthermore the recording of shares at par value leads to a misstatement of cost for most transactions.

Where cash dividends are paid out of pre-acquisition reserves the carrying amount of the investment should be reduced as it represents a return by the investee of part of the original entity acquired rather than a return on the investment.

International accounting standards

A summary of the more important differences between Australian standards and international accounting standards is provided in table 4.8.

6. EXCHANGE CONTROL/FOREIGN INVESTMENT REGULATIONS

Foreign investment in Australia is tightly controlled by the state primarily through the FIRB rather than through exchange controls. Exchange and currency controls have been operated by the government since 1939 with the administration being undertaken by the Reserve Bank of Australia, the Central Bank under the authority of the Banking (Foreign Exchange) Regulations of the Banking Act 1959. On 12 December 1983 the Australian dollar was floated and many of the exchange control regulations were abandoned. For exchange control purposes companies incorporated in Australia and branches of foreign corporations are deemed to be resident. The remaining regulations are consistent with the policy of controlling foreign investment via the Foreign Takeovers Act 1975.

As part of the exchange control regulations, certain countries have been designated as tax havens so that contracts and agreements with residents in the designated countries must have prior approval. Other than dealings with tax haven countries there are now no exchange control

Table 4.8 Comparison of Australian accounting practices with international standards

International accounting standards	*Australian accounting standards*
IAS 2 – Valuation and presentation of inventories in the context of the historical cost system	
Last in, first out is permissible as an approach to assigning costs to inventories	Last in, first out base stock and latest purchase price are not permissible (AAS2)
IAS 3 – Consolidated financial statements Uniform accounting policies should be followed, but where not, the proportion of assets and liabilities involved in each balance sheet classification should be disclosed	No equivalent requirement
Requires disclosure of exceptional risks for overseas operations including foreign-exchange rate fluctuations	Uncommon in practice and not required
The equity method of accounting for investments should be used	Equity supplementary financial statements must be prepared (AAS14)
IAS 4 – Depreciation accounting Requires disclosure including useful lives or depreciation rates for each major class of depreciable assets	There is no equivalent requirement (AAS4)
IAS 5 – Information to be disclosed in financial statements	
Requires disclosure of:	
pension and retirement plans	No equivalent requirement
intercompany transactions	No equivalent requirement
sales or other operating revenues	Listed companies only
IAS 9 – Accounting for research and development activities	
Requires research costs to be charged in the year in which incurred but development costs may be deferred in exceptional circumstances	Research and development costs may be deferred in exceptional circumstances
Requires disclosure of the expense incurred	Not required (AAS13)

– *Continued*

Table 4.8 Continued

International accounting standards	*Australian accounting standards*
IAS 11 – Accounting for construction contracts	
The amount of construction work-in-progress should be disclosed and where the percentage-of-completion and the completed-contract methods are simultaneously used, the amount should be analysed accordingly	There is no equivalent requirement (AAS11)
IAS 12 – Accounting for taxes on income	
Full deferred tax should be provided normally although the partial approach may be permitted under certain circumstances	Full provision for deferred tax is required
Either the deferral or liability method may be used	The liability method is required (AAS3)
IAS 14 – Reporting financial information by segment	
Requires disclosure for each reported industry and geographical segment: sales or other operating revenues segment result segment assets employed basis of inter-segment pricing	There is no equivalent requirement (AAS16)
IAS 15 – Information reflecting the effects of changing prices	
Requires disclosure, where material, of adjustments for changing prices on depreciation, cost of sales, monetary items and on overall effects of such adjustments. Such information is regarded as supplementary	No equivalent standard although a statement of accounting practice (SAP1 – Current Cost Accounting) was issued for guidance only
IAS 17 – Accounting for leases	The lessee can choose whether to capitalize finance leases or whether to disclose the information in a note to the accounts (AAS17)

– *Continued*

Table 4.8 Continued

International accounting standards	*Australian accounting standards*
IAS 19 – Accounting for retirement benefits in the financial statements of employers Requires entities to charge past and prior service costs to expenses over a period which does not exceed the expected remaining working lives of the participating employees	There is no equivalent
IAS 20 – Accounting for government grants requires (a) an enterprise should recognize government grants in income only when there is reasonable assurance that the grant will be received and comply with the conditions attached to it (b) grants should be included in income in the same period as the relevant costs accrue (c) grants related to assets should be accounted for either as deferred income or as deductions from related assets	There is no equivalent
IAS 22 – Accounting for business combinations Negative goodwill may not be allocated to non-depreciable assets or to monetary assets	The fair values of the non-monetary assets should be reduced proportionately (AAS18)
Permits immediate write-off of goodwill against shareholders' equity	Not permitted. Write-off on a systematic basis to the profit and loss account over its useful life not exceeding 20 years (AAS18)
IAS 24 – Related party disclosures	
Disclose the nature and type of related party transactions	There is no equivalent

requirements in relation to arrangements and agreements with non-residents, capital raising in Australia by non-residents, capital repatriation by non-residents, exports and imports, and direct investment in Australia by non-residents but subject to approval by the FIRB.

The FIRB scrutinizes takeovers by foreigners under the Foreign Takeovers Act 1974. In addition, policy statements may be issued by the administration in pursuant of powers under the above Act, the Banking (Foreign Exchange) Regulations and also in accordance with exchange control regulations. The FIRB is a non-statutory body with its members chosen from business other than the head of the Foreign Investment Division of the Department of the Treasury who acts as Executive Member. Confidential advice can be given by the FIRB for any investment proposal. The acquisition of a substantial foreign interest in an Australian company may be prohibited by the Commonwealth Treasurer if it is thought to be against the national interest. A substantial foreign interest is defined as ownership of voting shares of at least 15 per cent by foreigners and their associates or 40 per cent by two or more foreigners and their associates. An important test is whether control is a reality. For example, if one foreign interest owns 20 per cent of the voting shares control may be exercised if there are thousands of very small shareholdings. However, if there are two Australian investors each with 40 per cent then the 20 per cent of the voting shares will not probably be sufficient to exercise substantial control.

In a speech to the Business Council of Australia on 29 October 1985, the Prime Minister announced that changes were to be implemented in the government's foreign investment policy. The detailed modifications were announced on that date by the Acting Treasurer. The modifications reflect the government's desire to reduce the administrative burden on business and:

1. simplify the procedures for the screening of foreign investment proposals;
2. ease the policy criteria for certain types of investment proposals;
3. exempt other proposals from examination.

The modifications announced on 29 October 1985 were effective from that date with the exception of two changes which require amendments to the Foreign Takeovers Act. The first amendment will exempt from notification any acquisitions of existing mining exploration rights. A second amendment will be required to exempt from the Act offshore takeovers where both the purchaser and target are located offshore but where Australian assets are involved. The exemption applies where the Australian assets involved exceed $A20 million compared with the previous threshold of $A3 million.

The following constitute examinable proposals by the FIRB and incorporate the modifications introduced on 29 October 1985.

Examinable proposals under the Foreign Takeovers Act

The FIRB will usually investigate the following proposals:

1. An acquisition or issue of shares (including an option to acquire shares) with a substantial foreign interest. Definition of 'foreign person' and 'substantial foreign interest' are the same as those stipulated by the Commonwealth Treasurer for investment policy.
2. The acquisition of the assets (including rural properties) of an Australian business.
3. An arrangement or a termination of an arrangement relating to the leasing or granting of other rights to use the assets of an Australian business or to participate in the profits or management of an Australian business.
4. An agreement to alter the articles of association which would provide foreign investors, already owning at least 15 per cent of the voting shares, representation on the board of an Australian business.

Section 26 of the Foreign Takeovers Act 1975 requires that where an acquisition would involve ownership of at least 15 per cent, or would extend ownership beyond that threshold, the FIRB should be given 40 days' notice of the proposal. In practice nearly all transactions by foreigners are notified even though it is unusual for the government to intervene where total business assets do not exceed $A5 million except in what are designated as sensitive industries. These industries were identified in section 1.

The Foreign Takeovers Act applies equally to the acquisition by foreign investors of an interest in an Australian business or a foreign interest already established in Australia.

Examinable proposals other than those under the Foreign Takeovers Act

The following projects fall within the scope of examination by the FIRB even though they are not included in the Foreign Takeovers Act.

1. Proposals to undertake a project or establish a new business, regardless of size in the media and civil aviation sectors.
2. Proposals to acquire real estate exceeding $A600,000 or proposals to acquire a number of estates even though the total value does not exceed that threshold.
3. Direct investments by foreign governments or their agencies, regardless of their size, excluding portfolio investments.
4. Proposals to establish new businesses in other sectors of the economy where the aggregate investment is at least $A10m. This includes diversification into new areas in Australia, new projects in mining or

other natural resource industries, or new businesses involving real estate development such as hotels. 'Diversification' is defined as activity not listed by the foreign investor under its Australian Standard Industrial Classification grouping.

Criteria for assessing investment proposals

Examination of investment proposals is by the FIRB and is based on a confidential case-by-case approach. The basis of the review, which may involve consultation with a number of government departments and agencies, is that there should be net benefits to the Australian economy of any interest by foreigners.

The Department of Treasury has laid down criteria which should be used to establish whether net benefits accrue to the Australian economy in relation to the following:

1. competition, price levels and efficiency;
2. improvement of the industrial or commercial structure of the economy, or the quality and variety of goods and services available in Australia;
3. development of or access to new export markets.

If an investment proposal appears satisfactory, with respect to the above criteria, the following additional criteria become relevant:

1. Whether the investment is in the best interests of Australia with respect to:
   (a) local processing of materials and the utilization of Australian components and services;
   (b) involvement of Australians or policy-making boards;
   (c) research and development;
   (d) royalties, licensing and patent arrangements;
   (e) industrial relations and employment opportunities.
2. Whether the investment would conform with the government's economic and industrial policies in relation to defence, Aboriginal interests, decentralization, the environment, and international treaty obligations.
3. The extent to which Australian equity participation has been sought and the degree of post-acquisition control and involvement in management by Australians.
4. The extent to which the investment will contribute to taxation income and the financing proposals of the acquisition. In order to avoid penalties from 'thin capitalization' a foreign debt to equity ratio of 3 : 1 should not be exceeded.
5. The interests of Australian shareholders, employees, creditors, and policyholders affected by the proposal.
6. The extent to which commercial opportunities are provided for Australian contracts and consultants to participate in any construction work.

7. Whether there are any benefits and costs to Australia of any export franchise limitations.
8. The contribution of a proposal would make to the improved utilization of resources, or the expansion of productive capacity arising from the introduction and diffusion of new technology and other skills, including managerial and workforce skills new to Australia.

Not all the above criteria are considered in each proposal but rather those that appear applicable to the investment in question. Where foreign investment in a particular sector is significant or might become significant as a result of the proposal the FIRB will expect substantial economic benefits to be generated for the Australian economy before approval is granted.

Prior to the modifications introduced on 29 October 1985 the overriding objective of the above criteria was to ensure that Australians should be able to participate in the development of industries and natural resources in Australia. This requirement normally meant that a foreign acquisition must be made public so that Australians were given the opportunity to express an interest in, or to bid for, the business itself. This was known as the 'opportunities test'.

One of the modifications introduced in 1985 was to discontinue this practice because it was rare for an Australian bidder to come forward. The government estimates that the test applied to about 30 per cent of proposals and its discontinuance represents significant deregulation. An additional advantage of deregulation is the examination period will be shortened and less harm might arise from the detrimental effects on business as a result of the Australian company selling out to a foreign investor.

However, public knowledge of takeovers of publicly listed companies will still continue since proposed acquisitions must be announced to comply with the Companies/Acquisition of Shares Act 1980.

SUMMARY

If a foreign investor wishes to acquire an Australian company it may be necessary to obtain permission from the Foreign Investment Review Board (FIRB). Normally the FIRB will make a decision as to whether the proposed investment will, on balance, benefit the Australian economy. Examination of proposals is on a confidential case-by-case approach. In order to make the decision-making process reasonably certain the Department of Treasury has laid down criteria which should be used to establish whether net benefits accrue to the economy. Not all the criteria are considered in each proposal but rather those that appear applicable to the investment in question.

Before 1985 the overriding objective of the criteria laid down by the Department of Treasury was to ensure that Australians should be able to express an interest in, or bid for, the business itself. This practice has now been discontinued which represents significant deregulation. In addition, the examination period has been shortened and other administrative measures have been taken to simplify the procedures for the screening of foreign investment proposals and to exempt some proposals altogether.

With effect from 1 July 1987, Australia has an imputation tax system similar to that in operation in the UK. This represents a major change in taxation. From the date of its implementation resident companies will be taxed under a foreign tax credit system. Resident companies will pay 49 per cent tax on worldwide income with a credit allowed for foreign taxes paid up to the amount of domestic tax. From that date, the branch profits tax, dividend withholding tax and minimum distribution requirements for private companies will all be eliminated. Another recent change in the taxation system was the introduction of capital gains tax with effect from 20 September 1985. Assets acquired after that date are subject to the new tax which will be payable on the profit made on realization.

Amendments to the 1981 Companies Act were introduced in 1984 have the effect of providing legislative backing to accounting standards. An Accounting Standards Review Board has been formed which is responsible to the Ministerial Council for company law. Directors are required to ensure that financial statements comply with approved accounting standards and that the records show a true and fair view. Such an initiative represents an important development which, hopefully, will improve the comparability of financial statements in Australia.

5

Canada

1. BUSINESS ORGANIZATIONS AND COMBINATIONS

Business organizations

The principal types of business organization in Canada are corporations, branches of foreign corporations, partnerships (limited or general), joint ventures (incorporated or unincorporated) and sole proprietorships. Often an overseas investor will begin trading as a branch in Canada, but once business becomes profitable it is preferable to form a corporation.

A corporation may be formed under any of the ten provincial Acts or under the federal Canada Business Corporations Act. The requirements for provincial incorporation vary from province to province although the difference between provincial incorporation and federal incorporation is not significant. Incorporation at the federal level requires that there is a majority of Canadian residents on the board of directors. This requirement is reduced to one-third for holding companies where the operations in Canada contribute less than 5 per cent to gross revenues. The number of companies incorporated federally was 149,372 as of 31 March 1986.

The choice between federal and provincial incorporation depends upon the trading activities of the corporation. If the corporation intends to trade in more than one province it is usually appropriate for incorporations to be at the federal level. If a foreign corporation intends to trade primarily in one province, and will own substantial property in that province then provincial registration may be appropriate.

Regardless of the locus of incorporation, the corporation is still subject to the laws and requirements administered in each province. Generally, a corporation must be registered and/or licensed in each province in which it conducts business.

Business enterprises incorporated in Canada may be either public or private companies. A public company has the freedom to transfer shares and issue securities to the public within the confines of provincial securities regulation, whereas significant limitations are placed on private corporations. An advantage of a private corporation is that only larger companies need publish their accounts, although disclosure is becoming increasingly prevalent.

In practice, an overseas investor will usually have a wholly-owned private company as its subsidiary although no specific tax advantages accrue to this form of business entity. If a foreign investor decides to operate in Canada through a branch, however, it must be registered and/or licenced in each province in which it will conduct business.

Types of business combination

There are four main ways in which combinations occur in Canada. First, there is recognition of the legal concept of a 'statutory amalgamation' in provincial Companies Acts and in the Canada Business Corporations Act. The concept is one in which two or more corporations come together to form one new company whilst accepting the rights and obligations of the predecessor businesses. The definition of an amalgamation under company law may or may not be the same as for income tax purposes. The rules applicable to statutory amalgamations also depend upon the provincial or federal regulations under which it is incorporated.

A second type of business combination is when an acquirer obtains some or all of the assets of another corporation either for cash or other valuable consideration. In these circumstances, the target company may be wound up and the remaining assets distributed to shareholders.

A third type of transaction involves the acquisition of shares of a private company through a privately negotiated agreement with shareholders of the target corporation.

A fourth type involves the purchase of the shares of a public company by private negotiation with shareholders of the target company, by the acquisition of shares on a stock exchange, by a takeover bid or by a combination of these methods. Such transactions are regulated by the rules and regulations of provincial and federal statutes and also by the appropriate stock exchanges.

2. TRENDS IN TAKEOVER ACTIVITY

Despite a steady increase in merger and acquisition activity in Canada, there are few sources which reliably monitor the volume of transactions. The Director of Investigation and Research has maintained a merger register since 1960 which attempts to record mergers in industries subject to the Combines Investigation Act (1923). Since there is no statutory reporting requirement the data are collected from newspapers, trade journals, business magazines and other publications not only in Canada but also in the UK and US. The data are not entirely comprehensive since they cover only those sectors subject to the Act and its amendments. For example, the service sector was not included in the statistics until 1976. Furthermore, information under the Corporations and Labour Unions Returns Act (1962) suggests that many smaller acquisitions are not reported in the press. A further disadvantage of the data is that the value of firms taken over is not shown nor the way in which transactions are financed. Whilst the data do have shortcomings, the information provides an initial review of merger activity.

Table 5.1 shows the trend in acquisition activity since 1960. Looking somewhat further back to 1950, there were only nine mergers involving a foreign-owned or controlled acquiring company. Since 1950, the number of acquisitions has increased substantially, particularly in the last decade. The proportion of acquisitions involving a foreign owned or foreign

Table 5.1 Acquisition activity since 1960

Year	*Foreign*[a]		*Domestic*[b]		*Total*
	Number	%	*Number*	%	
1960	93	46	110	54	203
1961	86	36	152	64	238
1962	79	43	106	57	185
1963	41	32	88	68	129
1964	80	39	124	61	204
1965	78	38	157	67	235
1966	80	39	123	61	203
1967	85	37	143	63	228
1971	143	37	245	63	388
1972	127	30	302	70	429
1973	100	28	252	72	352
1974	78	26	218	74	296
1975	109	41	155	59	264
1976	124	40	189	60	313
1977	192	49	203	51	395
1978	271	60	178	40	449
1979	307	60	204	40	511
1980	234	57	180	43	414
1981	200	41	291	59	491
1982	371	64	205	36	576
1983	395	63	234	37	629
1984	410	64	231	310	641
1985	466	65	246	35	712
1986	641	68	297	32	938

[a] Acquisitions involving a foreign-owned or foreign-controlled acquiring company (the nationality of the controlling interest in the acquired company prior to the merger could have been foreign or Canadian).

[b] Acquisitions involving an acquiring company not known to be foreign-owned or foreign-controlled (the nationality of the controlling interest in the acquired company prior to the merger could have been foreign or Canadian).

Source: Annual Report, Director of Investigation and Research, Combines Investigation Act, year ended 31 March 1986.

controlled acquiring company has also increased. In 1986, a record high 68 per cent of total merger activity involved foreign owned or foreign controlled acquiring companies.

Acquisition activity has been classified over different periods of time. For example, the Royal Commission on Corporate Concentration (1978) classified activity between 1972 and 1977 into horizontal, vertical and conglomerate. Over this period, horizontal acquisitions accounted for between 52 and 69 per cent of total activity with approximately 66 per cent of residual activity being attributable to conglomerate mergers.

The Bureau of Competition Policy prepared an analysis of acquisitions of Canadian firms by foreign-owned firms for the period 1980 to 1983 (table 5.2). The horizontal axis of the matrix represents the industrial sector of acquired firms and the vertical axis represents the industrial sector of acquiring firms. An aggregation of the figures on the diagonal from left to right reveals 537 acquisitions in the same industrial sector and represents 47 per cent of total activity. In certain sectors of industry, virtually all of the acquisitions were by companies in the same sector. For example, in the industrial classification of mines, quarrying and oil drilling activity, more than 85 per cent of acquisitions were by companies in the same sector. A similar situation also occurred in metal fabricating, machinery, wood, electrical products, chemicals, finance and other services and probably represents an increase in concentration in these sectors.

The total activity column shows that acquisitions were prevalent in the mining, food, trade and finance sectors. The finance, insurance and real estate sector (no. 28), in particular, accounted for over 30 per cent of the total acquiring firms, although it is interesting to note a wide variety of industrial sectors of acquired firms.

The Annual Report of the Director of Investigation and Research provides another insight into merger activity by grouping the sectors into resources, manufacturing, and services. For the period 1976–7, 36 per cent were within manufacturing, 38 per cent within the service sector and 9 per cent within the resource sector. Eighty-three per cent of mergers occurred between firms within the same broad industrial sector.

Merger and acquisition activity in Canada has increased significantly in the past decade. According to Government of Canada statistics, the total number of transactions in Canada was 938 in 1986, three times the number recorded in 1975.

3. MERGER CONTROL

Controls affecting mergers and acquisitions in Canada consist of:

1. anti-trust legislation embodied in the Competition Tribunal Act and the Competition Act which in 1986 significantly revised the Combines Investigation Act;
2. review of foreign investment under the Investment Canada Act which

replaced the Foreign Investment Review Agency in 1986;
3. securities regulations imposed and enforced by provincial securities commissions and appropriate stock exchanges;
4. other provincial and/or federal legislation governing specific industries, e.g. banking, broadcasting and others.

Anti-trust legislation and securities regulation are considered in this section and Investment Canada and industry limitations are considered in section 6.

Anti-trust legislation

In June 1986, Parliament passed amendments to existing anti-trust legislation. These amendments were contained in Bill C–91 which introduced a Competition Tribunal Act and significantly revised the Combines Investigation Act, which was renamed the Competition Act.

The Competition Act provides for general regulation of trade and commerce in respect of conspiracies, trade practices and mergers affecting competition. The purpose of the Act is to maintain and encourage competition in Canada and to promote the efficiency and adaptability of the Canadian economy. The goals of the legislated changes are: (1) to expand opportunities for Canadian participation in world markets while at the same time recognizing the role of foreign competition in Canada, (2) to ensure that small and medium-sized enterprises have an equitable opportunity to participate in the Canadian economy, and (3) to provide consumers with competitive prices and product choices.

The Competition Tribunal Act establishes a Competition Tribunal of four judges and eight other members and replaces the Restrictive Trade Practices Commission which consisted of not more than four members appointed by the Governor in Council. Questions of law shall be determined only by judicial members whereas questions of fact or mixed law shall be determined by all members. The Tribunal has jurisdiction to hear and determine applications under Part VII of the Competition Act. Part VII deals with restrictive trade practices such as refusal to deal, consignment selling, exclusive dealing, tied selling, market restrictions, delivered pricing and abuses of a dominant position. Any decision by the Tribunal is subject to appeal to the Federal Court of Appeal regardless of whether the decision is interim or final.

The Competition Act gives the Tribunal the power to prohibit practices that are considered to be an abuse of a dominant position. An abuse of a dominant position results from an anti-competitive act which includes:

1. squeezing, by a vertically integrated supplier, of the margin available to an unintegrated customer who competes with the supplier, for the purpose of impeding or preventing the customer's entry into, or expansion in a market;

Industry group of acquiring firm	Industry group of acquired firm 1	2	3	4	5	6	7	8	9	10	11	12	13	14	15	16	17	18	19	20	21	22	23	24	25	26	27	28	29	Total (acquiring)
1.	2																										1			3
2		1																												1
3			1																											1
4				24			1											2		3			4							34
5					37	1												1		1			3				5		4	52
6						2																				2	1			5
7							3																2	1						6
8								1																			1			2
9									6																					6
10									1	1																				2
11											9																1			10
12												9																		9
13									1				3											1			1		1	7
14												3		8										1		1	2		1	16
15															8												3			11
16																3											4			7
17												1	1			1	45	2	2	3				1			6	1	1	64
18				1									1				4	23		4				2	2		29		2	68
19							1										3	3	13	1							10	1	1	33
20				1													4	2		44		1		5	1		27	1	3	89
21							1														16		1				1		2	21
22																				2							7			9
23							2										1			1	3		43	1	1		18	2	7	79
24							1				1					1	2	1		1			3	16	1		20	3	2	52
25																	1	1			1				11				2	16
26					1												1			3			1	1		28	3	1	1	40
27		1			3				1		2		2				1	3		1	1		3	2		1	42		1	64
28	2	1	3	2	7		11				1	1	1	2	9		15	20	6	15	9		7	14		2	67	55	93	343
29																											2		83	85
Total (acquired)	4	3	4	28	48	3	20	1	9	1	13	14	8	10	17	5	77	58	21	79	30	1	67	45	16	34	251	64	204	1135

Schedule

1. Agriculture
2. Forestry
3. Fishing and Trapping
4. Mines, quarrying, oil wells
5. Food and Beverage
6. Tobacco Products
7. Rubber
8. Leather
9. Textile
10. Knitting Mills
11. Clothing
12. Wood
13. Furniture and fixtures
14. Paper
15. Printing, publishing
16. Primary metal
17. Metal Fabricating
18. Machinery
19. Transportation equipment
20. Electrical Products
21. Non-Metallic Mineral producers
22. Petroleum and Coal products
23. Chemical and chemical products
24. Miscellaneous manufacturing
25. Construction
26. Transportation, communication, utilities
27. Trade
28. Finance, Insurance, real estate
29. Community, business or personal services

2. acquisitions with the purpose of impeding or preventing the competitor's entry into, or eliminating him from, a market;
3. use of fighting brands introduced selectively on a temporary basis to discipline or eliminate a competitor;
4. pre-emption of scarce facilities or resources required by a competitor for the operation of a business, with the object of withholding the facilities or resources from a market;
5. buying up of products to prevent the erosion of existing price levels;
6. adoption of product specifications that are incompatible with products produced by any other person and are designed to prevent his entry into, or to eliminate him from, a market;
7. requiring or inducing a supplier to sell only or primarily to certain customers, or to refrain from selling to a competitor, with the object of preventing a competitor's entry into, or expansion in, a market;
8. selling articles at a price lower than the acquisition cost for the purpose of disciplining or eliminating the competition; and
9. freight equalization on the plant of a competitor for the purpose of impeding or preventing his entry into, or eliminating him from, a market.

Sections 63–75 of the Competition Act deal specifically with mergers. A merger means the acquisition or establishment, direct or indirect, by one or more persons, whether by purchase or lease of shares or assets, by amalgamation or by combination or otherwise, of control over or significant interest in the whole or a part of a business of a competitor, supplier, customer or other person.

Where the Tribunal finds that a merger is likely to reduce competition it may dissolve the merger or dispose of the assets or shares concerned where the merger has already been completed. For proposed mergers, the Tribunal may make an order for the transaction not to be proceeded with or to prohibit the person against whom the order is directed from doing any act or thing prohibited by the Tribunal. The authority of the Tribunal is granted under section 64 of the proposed Competition Act and substitutes section 33 of the previous Combines Investigation Act in which 'every person who is a party or privy to or knowingly assists in, or in the formation of, a merger or monopoly is guilty of an indictable offence and is liable to imprisonment for two years'.

The Tribunal will consider the following factors in deciding whether competition is prevented or lessened by any merger:

1. the extent to which foreign products and foreign competitors provide effective competition;
2. whether any party to a merger may fail;
3. the extent to which there are acceptable substitutes available to those products supplied by the merger participants;
4. whether there are any barriers to entry in the market such as tariff and non-tariff barriers, interprovincial barriers to trade, or regulatory control over entry;

5. the extent to which effective competition would remain after the merger;
6. the nature and extent of change and innovation in a relevant market;
7. any likelihood that a vigorous and effective competitor would be removed;
8. any other factors relevant to competition that might be affected by a merger.

There are limitations to the authority of the Tribunal with respect to banks and joint ventures. In addition, the Tribunal will not use its powers where efficiency gains are likely to exceed the effects on competition. In assessing market efficiency the Tribunal will consider any possible effects on exports or substitution of domestic products for imported products.

For the first time in Canada there are pre-notification conditions for large-scale acquisitions. The pre-notification requirements were not proclaimed in force concurrent with the passing of the Act in 1986 but were proclaimed later in 1987.

The salient points of the rules and procedures governing pre-notification are that prior notice must be given if (1) the parties to the transaction and their affiliates have consolidated assets or gross revenues in Canada in excess of $400 million; (2) the value of the shares or assets of the target company, or its gross revenues, exceed $35 million (in an amalgamation, the target threshold for the assets or shares outstanding is doubled to $70 million); and (3) if the shares are publicly traded and the acquisition results in a holding of 20 per cent, or 50 per cent if a 20 per cent interest has already been obtained; or, if the shares are not publicly traded, the acquisition results in a holding of 35 per cent of such securities, or 50 per cent if a 35 per cent interest has already been obtained.

Notwithstanding the above requirements, Section 83 of the proposed Act details the classes of transaction which are exempt from pre-notification:

1. an acquisition of real propety or goods in the ordinary course of business if the person or persons who propose to acquire the assets would not, as a result of the acquisition, hold all or substantially all of the assets of a business or of an operating segment of a business;
2. acquisitions for underwriting purposes, gifts or resulting from a foreclosure or default;
3. an acquisition of a Canadian resource property where the acquiring company agrees to incur expenses to carry out exploration or development activities with respect to the property.

If a transaction meets the requirements for pre-notification the parties involved shall notify the Director that the transaction is proposed and supply information in accordance with either sections 93 or 94. Where section 93 information has been provided, the Director may notify those concerned within seven days of receiving the requested material, informing them that the requirements of section 94 must also be met for transaction approval. The following information is required under section 93:

1. a description of the proposed transaction;
2. the business objectives to be achieved;
3. copies of the legal documents;
4. details of names and addresses of participants;
5. a list of affiliates;
6. principal businesses undertaken by those involved including their affiliates;
7. a statement of gross and net assets and gross revenues from sales for the most recent fiscal year;
8. copies of documents such as proxy solicitation circulars, prospectuses and other information filed with a securities commission, stock exchange or other similar authority;
9. the financial statements, where available, of the acquiring party, the continuing corporation, and the combination prepared on a pro forma basis as if the proposed transaction had already occurred.

The information required above is also prescribed in section 94 together with the following information on participants and each of their wholly-owned affiliates in Canada or significant sales in, from or into Canada:

1. the addresses of their principal offices and jurisdiction under which it was incorporated;
2. the names and business addresses of their directors and officers;
3. principal categories and sales of products supplied, distributed or produced for the most recent fiscal year;
4. principal categories and purchases of products for the most recent fiscal year;
5. the number of votes attached to voting shares held, directly or indirectly;
6. financial or statistical information prepared to assist the board of directors in analysing the proposed transaction;
7. if any of the parties have taken a decision or entered into a commitment or undertaking to make significant changes in any business to which the proposed transaction relates, a summary description of that decision, commitment or undertaking.

Once the required information has been filed with the Director a transaction shall not be completed unless otherwise directed before the expiration of:

1. seven days where section 93 information has been given and the Director has not required information set out in section 94;
2. twenty-one days after section 94 information is supplied or is required to be supplied;
3. ten trading days and not exceeding 21 days where the acquisition of voting shares is to be effected through a stock exchange in Canada.

Regulation of the securities industry

The two largest stock exchanges in Canada are located in Toronto and Montreal. The majority of trading is undertaken in Toronto, which has about four times the trading value of the Montreal Exchange. In addition, there are three small provincial stock exchanges which are located in Vancouver, Winnipeg and Calgary. Vancouver is the leading regional exchange, specializes in junior natural resource corporations, and has grown largely because its regulations are less onerous than the two larger exchanges.

The Toronto Stock Exchange is the largest Canadian exchange because of its rigorous listing requirements and improved trading liquidity. Its presence in the US market was increased in June 1986 when a computer-based international trading link was established between the Midwest Stock Exchange of Chicago and the Toronto Stock Exchange. The link allows member brokerage firms in both exchanges to trade in Canadian-based and US-based issues. Initially, the link was established with 19 stocks; dual listings represented by 12 corporations from Canada and seven from the US. The objective of the link is to establish an international market that is well regulated and has the advantage of reduced brokerage costs and quicker execution of orders. A growing problem for the Toronto Stock Exchange, however, is increased trade execution in Canada's ten largest stocks on the New York Stock Exchange, where the securities are interlisted.

Regulation of the securities industry is embodied in the ten provincial securities Acts and two territorial Ordinances. In most instances, takeover bids are regulated by the appropriate Provincial Securities Act although where the target company is federally incorporated the bid must comply with the Federal Act. In addition to the Securities Acts, the regulation of public offerings and trading of securities is supervised by self-regulating organizations. These organizations include the Investment Dealer's Association, the Broker–Dealer Association and others such as the Investment Funds Institute which deals with mutual funds.

Whilst the disclosure and registration requirements are similar in all jurisdictions, national policy statements are issued to provide for uniformity when issuing prospectuses. Where a takeover is to be by the issuance of securities in Canada, a corporation must comply with the minimum listing requirements of the appropriate provincial stock exchange. Typical of the requirements are those of the Toronto Stock Exchange shown below which refer to industrial companies:

1. Financial requirements:
   - (a) net tangible assets of C$1 million. In certain circumstances the exchange may allow intangible assets to be included;
   - (b) adequate working capital and capitalization to carry on the business; or

(c) evidence, satisfactory to the Exchange, indicating a reasonable likelihood of future profitability. As a general guideline, such applicants should file a complete forecast which should be accompanied by an independent auditor's comments. Forecast revenue assumptions should be substantiated, to a significant extent, by purchase orders, contracts or similar documentation, and/or should be logically derived from historic revenues and operations of the applicant. Financing assumptions should be similarly substantiated by independent third-party evidence;
(d) pre-tax profitability in the fiscal year immediately preceding the filing of the listing application;
(e) pre-tax cash flow of $200,000 in the fiscal year immediately preceding the filing of the listing application and an average annual pre-tax cash flow of C$150,000 for the two fiscal years immediately preceding the filing of the listing application; and
(f) adequate working capital and capitalization to carry on the business.

Consideration will also be given to the listing of applicant companies with:

(a) adequate working capital and capitalization to carry on the business, with a minimum working capital of C$350,000; and
(b) evidence, satisfactory to the Exchange, indicating a reasonable likelihood of future profitability. The general guidelines in (1c) above are relevant for this purpose provided that in reviewing such an application, the Exchange will attach considerable weight to the company's management and sponsorship.

2. Public distribution requirement: 200 shareholders each holding one board lot or more, and either
   (a) 200,000 publicly held shares; or
   (b) 100,000 publicly held shares, provided that the product obtained by multiplying the number of publicly held shares by the number of public shareholders each holding one board lot or more is not less than 40 million.
3. Market value of publicly held shares: a minimum of C$350,000.
4. Management: the management of an applicant company shall be an important factor in the consideration of a listing application.
5. Sponsorship or affiliation: while not mandatory, sponsorship of an applicant company by a member firm of the Exchange, or an affiliation with an established enterprise, can be a significant factor in the determination of the suitability of the company for listing, particularly where the company only narrowly meets the prescribed minimum listing requirements. Consideration will be given to the nature, as well as the existence, of the sponsorship or affiliation.
6. Other factors: the Exchange may, in its discretion, take into account any factors it considers relevant in assessing the merits of a listing application and may refuse to grant an application notwithstanding that the prescribed minimum listing requirements are met.

In addition to the above conditions, foreign industrial companies are subject to special listing requirements. A foreign industrial company is one which is organized under the laws of countries other than Canada, the Provinces or Territories of Canada, or the US. The special requirements are a guide and the Exchange has the power to waive certain conditions or impose other conditions if considered to be in the interests of the public. The requirements are as follows:

1. net tangible assets of at least C$10 million;
2. average pre-tax earnings for the last three fiscal years of C$2 million;
3. a minimum of one million issued shares shall be held by a minimum of 3000 public shareholders;
4. the number of issued shares held by the public shall have a market value of a minimum of C$10 million;
5. if listed on a recognized US Exchange there shall be a minimum of 500 public security holders each holding a board lot or more who are residents of the US or Canada;
6. if not listed on a recognized US Exchange there shall be 300 public security holders each holding a board lot or more who are residents of Canada, in which event, the security shall have had a satisfactory over-the-counter market experience in Canada or in the US for a period of at least one year;
7. voting securities of the applicant company shall be issued in registered form;
8. all reports to shareholders, notices of meetings and information circulars shall be issued to Canadian security holders in English and the financial information shall be expressed in Canadian or US funds;
9. the applicant company shall make satisfactory arrangements with the Exchange regarding the expediting of releases in compliance with timely disclosure requirements.

As a general rule, the issuance of any securities to the public requires the preparation of a preliminary prospectus, which must be cleared in advance with the securities commissions of each province or territory in which the securities are offered. Various exemptions are available in special circumstances, which include, for example, a 'seed money' exemption for first time issues made to a small number of investors, issues placed privately with exempt purchasers (general institutions), and issues in which each investor subscribes $150,000 or more. Even in the case of these exempt offerings, the governing principle is that the investor should be provided with prospectus-equivalent disclosure. The prospectus requirements include intricate rules providing for legal and financial disclosure.

Documentation to be filed on application for listing securities of an industrial or investment company on the Toronto Stock Exchange includes one copy of each of the annual reports for the past three years. If the company was formed as a result of an amalgamation, one copy of the annual reports of each of the amalgamating companies for the past three years should be filed. In addition, two copies of the company's most recent audited financial statements should be filed. The most recent financial statements should be signed by two directors of the company on behalf of the Board. Where the most recent audited financial statements are not dated within 120 days of the application date it is permissible for unaudited financial statements to be filed provided that they are dated within 90 days of the application date. Unaudited financial statements must be accompanied by a comfort letter signed by the company's auditors in compliance with section 7100 of the Canadian Institute of Chartered Accountants Handbook. In this case the financial statements shall include the following:

1. a balance sheet,
2. an income statement,
3. a statement of retained earnings,
4. a statement of changes in financial position, and
5. notes to the accounts.

In addition, unaudited financial statements must be signed by two directors of the company on behalf of the Board.

In the case of an application for listing securities of a resource company the above conditions are applicable except that condition (3) refers to an income statement and/or statement of deferred expenditures. In general, listing requirements for mining and oil and gas companies are less onerous than industrial companies.

Once a company has a listing there is an ongoing requirement to file audited annual and unaudited interim financial statements, within specified periods following the end of the reporting period, which differ from one jurisdiction to another.

4. TAXATION

Background

Taxes in Canada are raised at federal, municipal and provincial levels. Income taxes, sales taxes and customs and excise duties are levied at the federal level whereas municipal governments raise property taxes, business taxes and licence fees. Provincial governments raise revenues through income and capital taxes, retail sales taxes, and other taxes and royalties levied on the natural resource industries.

The collection and administration of the federal tax system is the responsibility of the Minister of National Revenue, through Revenue Canada, Taxation. These responsibilities are delegated to local districts although there is an arrangement whereby the federal government collects and administers provincial corporate incomes taxes. This arrangement applies to all provinces except for Alberta, Ontario and Quebec. In order for such a system to operate it necessitates a considerable degree of uniformity in the federal and provincial tax structures.

The Minister of National Revenue applies the tax legislation introduced, normally by the government, in the House of Commons. For convenience some of the detailed tax rules are subject to periodic review and may be altered by the Cabinet by the issuance of new regulations. These regulations must be published in the Canada Gazette before becoming law.

Federal income tax is levied under the Income Tax Act (1970 and subsequently amended) on resident corporations. A corporation may be resident in Canada based on the common law or be deemed to be resident. It is deemed to be resident if it was incorporated in Canada after 26 April 1965. If incorporated before that date and in any tax year carried on a business in Canada or became resident, under common law, the corporation is also deemed to be resident.

Companies resident in Canada pay tax on their worldwide income with appropriate relief for foreign taxes paid or payable overseas. Non-residents are subject to tax on their income derived in Canada and on capital gains on the sale of taxable Canadian property.

The rate of federal income tax depends upon the type of company and the type of income earned. For tax purposes, a distinction is made between public and private, and Canadian-controlled private corporations. A public corporation is a resident company with a listing on a prescribed Canadian stock exchange. A prescribed stock exchange constitutes those at Alberta, Montreal, Toronto, Vancouver and Winnipeg. A corporation may elect or be designated by the Minister of National Revenue to be a public corporation. In order for this to occur a corporation must comply with the following conditions:

1. The company must have a class of shares 'qualified' for distribution to the public.
2. The corporation must have at least 150 external shareholders each of whom holds sufficient to constitute a block of shares with an aggregate fair market value of at least $500.
3. The company must have external shareholders owning at least 20 per cent of outstanding shares of that class.

The combined federal and provincial rate of tax applicable to public and private corporations varies between 32 per cent and 53 per cent on its taxable income including half of any realized capital gains.

A private corporation is one which is not a public company, nor one that is controlled by one or more public corporations. A private corporation therefore includes resident Canadian-controlled private corporations (CCPCs) which are not controlled by one or more non-resident individuals or companies. In order to create a CCPC, however, a non-resident investor must forgo control. The corporation will be a CCPC if 50 per cent or more of the shares are held by Canadian shareholders that are not public corporations. In addition, certain tax advantages accrue to

CPCC. For example, the combined rate of federal and provincial tax on the first $200,000 of active business income varies from 9% to 25%. Income in excess of this amount is taxed at rates from 32% to 53%. Investment income of CPCC is taxed at rates between 46% and 53%. A portion of the federal tax paid on investment income is refundable to the corporation when it pays dividends to its shareholders.

The federal rate of tax is reduced by 10 per cent to reflect the corporation's provincial taxation of such income although provincial rates vary from 10 per cent to 16 per cent of taxable income. It is further reduced by tax credits and abatements available to certain industries including those involved in manufacturing and processing.

A non-resident company also pays tax if it carries on a business in Canada even where the non-resident exports the products directly. This includes a product which is produced, grown, mined, created, manufactured, fabricated, improved, preserved or packed in part or in whole in Canada. In addition, the solicitation of orders or offers either directly or indirectly also constitutes the carrying on of a business. However, some modification of this general rule applies where there is an appropriate treaty such that income derived from carrying on a business in Canada is subject to Canadian tax only if the non-resident has a Canadian 'permanent establishment'.

When calculating taxes, taxable income of a corporation is allocated to provinces and overseas territories on the basis of the average of gross revenues and salaries and wages of one permanent establishment to total gross revenues and salaries and wages. This general rule is modified somewhat for particular industries.

As a general rule transactions should be conducted on an arm's length basis at fair market value. Where this rule is not adhered to penalties such as one-sided adjustment may be imposed. In calculating taxable income, accounts should be prepared using generally accepted accounting principles. The method of valuation of inventory adopted for tax purposes may include cost, market value or the lower of cost or market value. The last-in first-out method, however, is not permitted in Canada for tax purposes. When calculating business income for tax purposes the following deductions are allowed:

1. Business expenses – reasonable expenditures incurred in pursuit of profit are deductible provided that they do not constitute capital payments.
2. Depreciation – depreciation deducted for accounting purposes is not deductible for tax purposes but instead a deduction is permitted for 'capital cost allowances'. Depreciable assets are grouped into classes based on their nature and similarity, and allowances are normally calculated on a declining-balance basis. Revenue Canada prescribes the maximum rates although the company may choose a lower amount if it so wishes and may vary the amount from year to year. The allowances do not in any way relate to the depreciation policy adopted by the company in its financial accounts. The following are typical of the rates and classification of certain depreciable assets:

Class	*% rate*	*Assets*
3	5	Buildings and their component parts.
8	20	Machinery, equipment and furniture not included in another class.
9	25	Aircraft.
10	30	Automotive equipment, computers and films.
29	—	Manufacturing and processing equipment purchased after 8 May 1972 may be written off over three years at the following respective annual rates: 25 per cent, 50 per cent and 25 per cent.

Since 12 November 1981 there has been a reduced capital cost allowance in the year of acquisition of property. The rate in the year of acquisition is normally 50 per cent of the normal rate for most classes. This restriction applies to the amount of excess of cost over the sale proceeds of that class. However, for some classes of purchase such as air or water pollution control equipment, electrical generating equipment and class 29 acquisitions, the property is normally depreciated on a straight line basis of 50 per cent. The effect of the reduction in the first year is shown in the above list for a class 29 asset.

Intangible capital assets with a fixed life such as patents and copyrights may be written off on a straight line basis over the useful life of the asset. Where the asset does not have a fixed life, special tax rules apply which were introduced in 1972. Property included in this definition includes purchased goodwill and some amalgamation and reorganization costs and such assets are restricted to one-half of their cost. These assets are added to a cumulative eligible capital account and are amortized at 10 per cent on a declining balance basis. On disposal only one-half of the proceeds must be credited to the cumulative eligible capital account and where a negative balance appears at the year end that amount must be included in income.

In order to prevent the sheltering of income with rental losses there are special capital cost allowance rules for most rental buildings and leased equipment. These rules aim to ensure that the allowance will not create a tax loss although in certain circumstances, for example where the principal business is the rental or leasing of property, the restriction does not apply.

3. Interest on amount borrowed is deductible provided the funds are applied to purchase property or generate income. There must be a legal obligation to pay interest on the money borrowed and the rate of interest charged must be reasonable. Where interest is paid to non-

residents a withholding tax of 25 per cent (subject to applicable tax treaties) is deductible at source.

Restrictions are imposed on the deductibility of interest where a company is considered to be thinly capitalized. This capitalization is deemed to occur where total debt owing to 'specified' non-residents exceeds three times the non-resident equity in the subsidiary. A 'specified' non-resident also includes one who alone or with other persons not dealing on an arm's length basis, own at least 25 per cent of the issued shares. Equity for these purposes is generally paid-up capital plus retained earnings and the amount of equity is that existing at the start of the year together with any paid up capital introduced by the non-resident during the year.

4. Losses incurred may be carried back three years or carried forward seven years and losses may be allocated to a particular year by the taxpayer.

   Where a change in control of a Canadian corporation occurs, losses may be carried forward provided the business is continued with a reasonable expectation of profit. There is a restriction that such losses may only be offset against income earned from the original or similar business. A corporation's taxation year is also deemed to have ended at the time control changes.
5. Scientific research undertaken in Canada may be fully written off in the year in which the expenses are incurred or deferred where considered desirable.

Other credits and deductions

1. A federal small business deduction applies to the first $200,000 of 'active business income' derived from Canadian sources by a CPCC. The reduction is 21 per cent so that the effective tax rate is approximately halved. A foreign-controlled corporation resident in Canada is not eligible for this benefit.
2. A manufacturing and processing deduction is available which reduces the tax rate by 5 per cent where the income is also available for a small business deduction and 6 per cent where the small business deduction is not available.
3. Investment tax credits of between 5 per cent and 60 per cent against federal income tax are available for the purchase of machinery, equipment and new buildings used for manufacturing or processing. Unused credits may be carried back up to three years and carried forward up to seven years.
4. Foreign tax credits are normally allowable up to the amount of Canadian tax on the foreign income before the credit.
5. Scientific research. Most scientific research is eligible for an investment tax credit which ranges from 20 per cent to 50 per cent.
6. Several provinces also have incentive tax deductions for small businesses and for manufacturing and processing profits.

Foreign subsidiaries and branches

As previously noted, Canada has a system of taxation which taxes a corporation resident in Canada on the basis of its worldwide income with all applicable foreign tax credits applied. In contrast, a Canadian branch of a non-resident corporation is taxed only on the income attributable to Canadian operations. The branch must keep accounting records as if it were an independent organization although reasonable allocations of head office expenses are allowable.

Whilst funds may be readily transferred between the Canadian branch and foreign head office the branch is subject to a special branch tax which is levied at 25 per cent. The tax is levied on Canadian source taxable income after deducting federal and provincial income taxes; taxable capital gains on Canadian non-business property, and investments in fixed and working capital in Canada. The rate of tax may be reduced where a tax treaty exists. Often the rate applicable is limited to the withholding tax rate on dividends specified in a tax treaty.

A non-resident Canadian subsidiary is taxed generally in the same ways as a Canadian branch. Withholding taxes of 25 per cent apply only when the Canadian subsidiary remits after-tax profits in the form of dividends. However, the rate of withholding tax may be reduced to 15 per cent or less where a tax treaty exists. A similar tax treatment is applied to interest paid by a Canadian subsidiary to its non-resident parent company. However, certain statutory exceptions apply to specific loans.

With regard to losses, the parent company of a Canadian subsidiary may not generally make use of them by an offset against its income in the home jurisdiction whereas losses incurred by a branch may be offset against such income.

A disadvantage of having a branch rather than a subsidiary is that the foreign corporation has liability for the obligations of its branch. In addition, the branch, like the subsidiary, will need to file a Canadian tax return for the branch income and it is possible that the foreign corporation will also have to report its income. Revenue Canada may also ask to inspect the books of the head office. Timing differences may also lead to problems. For example, where a Canadian subsidiary exists, the depreciation of fixed assets is calculated at Canadian rates in determining taxable income. The same is true for a branch although foreign rates may apply to the branch in the country of the head office leading to timing differences between paying taxes and obtaining reliefs.

All corporations and branches must be licensed and/or registered in all provincial jurisdictions in which they conduct business. The tax treatment of such costs is that additional licensing fees are allowable against the profits of a branch while incorporation costs are not deductible except as eligible capital expenditures. The incorporation costs of a subsidiary are deductible but no further licensing fees are eligible.

In making a decision between setting up a branch or incorporating a subsidiary the investor should consider carefully general business factors as well as tax implications. In addition, a foreign investor should take into consideration any requirements specified in the Investment Canada Act, Competition Act and other acts of relevance to a specific industry, e.g. banking, broadcasting, etc.

Consolidated tax returns

There is no concept of consolidated tax returns in Canada and as such losses from one company may not be offset against profits from another company. However, special provisions apply to amalgamations (statutory corporate mergers) and on the transfer of a business by a winding-up. In these circumstances the losses flow into the merged company and are available for relief against future income. Rollover provisions also apply to the transfer of most types of property at less than fair market value where the consideration is partly in the form of shares.

Capital gains tax

Tax on the sale of capital property has been levied since 1972 although the definition of capital property has been the subject of a number of legal cases. Generally, half the gain, once realized, is included in income and taxed at normal rates. Similarly where a capital loss arises one-half of the loss may be offset against taxable capital gains. Unrelieved capital losses may be carried back three years or carried forward indefinitely to be applied against capital gains only. On a change in control, unutilized capital losses may not be carried forward. While the whole of the proceeds from the sale of capital property is not received in the year of disposition a capital gain reserve may be claimed. The reserve permits deferral for a period of up to five years.

To the extent that sales proceeds exceed the cost of depreciable property, a capital gain will be realized. The lesser of the cost of the depreciable property sold and the proceeds is credited to the capital cost allowance class. If there is a negative balance in the class at the end of the taxation year, the negative amount is included in income. If there is a positive balance and no assets of that class are owned at the year-end, the balance of the class may be claimed as a deduction.

Taxation implications of mergers and acquisitions

Implications for the acquiring company

As mentioned in section (1) the Canada Business Corporations Act recognizes the concept of a 'statutory amalgamation' by which two companies come together as one company. Provided certain conditions are fulfilled, the assets and liabilities are transferred on a tax-free basis and consequently there is no step-up in tax basis for either depreciable or non-depreciable property. The new corporation must accept the rights and obligations of the old companies and this includes the transfer of losses (other than capital losses if control changes) which may be deductible against future income provided the continuity of business test is fulfilled. It is important to note that amalgamations refer to the merging of Canadian corporations and not a foreign incorporated company with a Canadian company. However, a foreign investor can set up a corporation in Canada with a view to undertaking an amalgamation.

An alternative to an amalgamation is to acquire part of the assets of another corporation for cash or shares. The acquirer will be able to obtain depreciation allowances as previously outlined. The value of the assets acquired is at cost to the acquirer provided the transaction is on an arm's-length basis. However, the rule reducing the capital cost allowance by 50 per cent applies in the year of purchase. Where assets are transferred at a value other than fair market value Revenue Canada may challenge the valuation. As well as obtaining capital cost allowances on depreciable assets, the acquirer may obtain the allowances applicable to intangible assets acquired. Similarly any money borrowed to acquire the assets will normally be subject to interest relief provided there is a legal obligation to pay interest.

Where the acquirer obtains accounts receivable at fair market value an election must be made so that the transaction is not treated on a capital basis. An election may be filed so that any bad debts subsequently arising can be relieved.

When an acquirer obtains the assets of another corporation any losses may not be transferred as the continuity of business test fails. However, where the shares of the target company are acquired non-capital losses may be carried forward and offset against its future income but not against any group income. This arises because, as previously mentioned, there is no concept of a consolidated tax return. Where shares in another corporation are acquired such that control of the corporation changes, it is not possible, under any circumstances, to carry forward any capital losses.

When acquiring the shares of a corporation the actual and contingent tax liabilities of the company remain the same. There are no stamp duties levied on share transfers whereas sales taxes may be payable on the acquisition of assets.

Since there is no step-up in the tax value of assets when a company's shares are acquired the purchase price should reflect the deferred tax liability. This arises because upon the sale of the assets acquired the base cost is the original cost and not the value on acquisition.

Implications for the acquirer's shareholders

Under an amalgamation, shareholders of one company receive shares in the new company without any immediate tax liability provided the shares of the predecessor corporations represent capital property to the transferors. Thus, transfers are at tax value and are deemed to have been rolled over. Where property other than shares is received a capital gain or loss may arise.

Implications for the acquiree company

Where the company is involved in a statutory amalgamation there will not be any tax implications for the acquiree company as there is no disposition of assets. The tax value of the assets are merely transferred to the amalgamated corporation.

Where the assets of the company are sold, there may be a recapture of allowances previously claimed or a terminal loss depending on the sale proceeds, the tax cost and the balance on the class of assets being sold. Where the asset is sold for more than its cost, a capital gain arises.

If non-tangible property is sold, such as goodwill, the rules for that specific asset apply. For example, up to one-half of the sale proceeds are credited against the residual goodwill balance, with any surplus being included as revenue.

The sale of inventories will be realized at market value and will be taxable. The purchaser, on the other hand, may treat the costs as a deductible expense when it disposes of the inventory.

Where accounts receivable are sold the rules outlined under implications for the acquiring company apply. The vendor together with the acquirer should file an election. Where an election is made the transaction is not treated on a capital basis and any discount offered on the receivables may be treated as a deductible expense. However, where an election is not made and a discount is offered, a capital loss arises unless the reduction in value is due to a bad debt.

Where assets are sold in excess of their cost a capital gain arises and is subject to tax. Generally, half the realized gain is included in income and taxed at normal rates. The base for computing the gain is the greater of the cost at the date when originally acquired or on 1 January 1972, the date when capital gains tax was effectively introduced. A non-resident corporation is subject to capital gains tax on the disposition of taxable Canadian properties. This includes real estate, and shareholdings of private companies and certain public companies located in Canada and any other property used to carry on a business in that country. These gains may, however, be exempt from Canadian tax depending on applicable treaties.

Implications for the acquiree's shareholders

If the assets of a vendor corporation are acquired, a tax liability does not accrue to the vendor's shareholders unless the consideration is disbursed. In these circumstances the vendor (other than a wholly-owned subsidiary) is deemed to have paid a dividend. If, however, the vendor corporation is wound up after selling its assets, shareholders will receive a return of funds which constitute a tax-free return of the original paid-up capital, a capital gain and a dividend. The capital gain must be apportioned since only the gain since 1 January 1972 is taxable.

Where the shares of the acquiree are purchased in a share-for-share transaction the vendor shareholders may elect for a tax-free rollover or to recognize any gains or losses arising. If the tax-free rollover arrangements are at arm's length, the purchasing corporation acquires the shares of the target company with a tax basis equal to the lesser of their fair market value and their paid up capital if certain conditions are met.

Where shares are acquired involving consideration other than shares, a capital gains liability accrues to the vendor to the extent that the sale proceeds exceed the tax base.

Tax planning

The Income Tax Act specifies that transactions between companies should be on an arm's length basis for both resident and non-resident corporations. Extra scrutiny is now being given to intercompany transactions and this factor should be taken into consideration in formulating a business strategy for Canada.

As previously mentioned, certain capital gains tax advantages accrue to statutory amalgamations between Canadian corporations. To take advantage of these concessions it would be necessary for a foreign investor to form a corporation in Canada with a view to such an amalgamation.

If an overseas investor decides to acquire the assets of a Canadian corporation by using its Canadian branch then any subsequent Canadian source taxable income will be subject to branch profits tax. For business rather than taxation reasons, it is often preferable for a foreign investor to form a subsidiary in Canada to act as its trading company or to act as a foreign holding company. Note, however, that the majority of directors of a Canadian corporation must be resident in Canada.

Where money is raised in Canada, the interest will normally be deductible for tax purposes provided the funds are used to purchase property or generate income. The interest must be reasonable and the company should not be thinly capitalized. Details of thin capitalization have been previously mentioned in this section.

Loans may be raised in any currency and any foreign gains or losses on the loan principal are generally treated as capital rather than revenue amounts. Where funds are obtained offshore, the interest payments (which should be reasonable on an arm's length basis) are subject to a withholding tax of 25 per cent unless specifically excepted. This is reduced to 15 per cent or less for countries with a tax treaty in Canada.

5. ACCOUNTING

Background

Company disclosure in Canada is influenced by the following:

1. recommendations issued by the Canadian Institute of Chartered Accountants (CICA);
2. Canada Business Corporations Act 1975;
3. securities legislation;
4. US accounting practice;
5. international recommendations such as those issued by the International Accounting Standards Committee (IASC).

The Canadian Institute of Chartered Accountants was established in 1902 and is the main influence on company disclosure although there are two other accountancy bodies in Canada, namely the Certified General Accountants' Association and the Society of Management Accountants of Canada. In 1972 the Board of Governors of CICA stated that the purpose of the Institute was, amongst other things, to discharge 'its responsibility to society in the measurement and communication of information pertaining to the efficient allocation and effective use of resources'.

In 1945 the Institute established the Accounting and Auditing Research Committee and in 1973 the committee was split into the Accounting Research Committee and the Auditing Standards Committee. The main responsibility of these committees is the issuance of 'Accounting Recommendations' and 'Auditing Recommendations' which are included in the CICA Handbook. In order for the recommendations to be incorporated into the handbook, the Committees issue exposure drafts which require approval by two-thirds of the members of the appropriate committee. In addition to auditing and accounting recommendations, the Accounting Standards Committee and the Auditing Standards Committee have the authority to publish Guidelines which are issued to provide guidance and interpretation on existing Recommendations. These Guidelines include the presentation and disclosure of financial forecasts, auditor involvement with supplementary information about the effects of changing prices and full cost accounting in the oil and gas industry.

In addition to the above two committees, there is an Accounting Research Advisory Board which participates in the selection of priorities for the Accounting Standards Committee, the development of new Recommendations, the reconsideration of existing Recommendations and the undertaking of Accounting Research Studies.

The Canada Business Corporations Act 1975 (CBCA) and most of the provincial Companies Acts require that financial statements should be drawn up in accordance with standards as set out in the CICA Handbook. In addition to providing legal back-up for accounting standards, the CBCA requires that adequate accounting records should be maintained including minutes of meetings and resolutions passed. In addition, the Act imposes requirements on public corporations with respect to directors and requirements for all companies on shareholders' meetings, share capital, dividends and the filing of financial statements. Where a corporation is a public company or has assets or revenues in excess of C$5 million or C$10 million respectively, the CBCA requires that accounts are filed with the federal Department of Consumer and Corporate Affairs. In addition to the CBCA, detailed provisions with respect to public companies are contained in the provincial Securities Acts.

CICA standards are specifically mentioned in the CBCA and in the corporation laws of the provinces of Alberta, British Columbia, Manitoba, Ontario and Saskatchewan. The other provinces still retain detailed disclosure requirements although they are often the same as those contained in the CICA Handbook. Furthermore, in 1972 the Canadian Securities Administrators issued a National Policy Statement, which applies to public companies, stating that 'Generally Accepted Accounting Principles' were those contained in the CICA Handbook. Federal and provincial companies' acts require an audit for all companies whose securities are available to the public. In addition, an audit is also required if certain limits, which vary from province to province, are exceeded. For example, the Canada Business Corporations Act specifies that an audit is required for companies whose gross revenues exceed $10 million or whose assets exceed $5 million. If these size criteria are not met, shareholders may pass a resolution which dispenses with the requirement for the accounts to be audited. In practice, many small and medium-sized companies prepare their accounts in accordance with CICA standards but do not have their accounts audited.

The provincial securities commissions specify the required form for filing annual and interim financial statements as well as information to be disclosed in documents such as prospectuses and takeover bids. The general requirements are that financial statements should consist of an income statement, a balance sheet, a statement of retained earnings and a statement of changes in financial position.

The fourth major influence on accounting practice in Canada is the US. This is not surprising for two main reasons. First, the US is a major influence if not the major authority on accounting in the western world and the geographical proximity of the two countries ensures that the US is a substantial influence over Canada. Secondly, the degree of foreign ownership and control in Canada is extraordinarily high with much of this foreign investment coming from the US and, in addition, many Canadian-owned corporations raise capital in the US and thus have to prepare statements for the Securities and Exchange Commission.

Where the CICA Handbook or Canadian literature is silent on a particular topic, accountants would generally look to the US for guidance. Furthermore, in developing accounting standards it would be unusual for the Accounting Standards Committee to make a final decision on an issue without waiting for clarification from the US.

All three accountancy bodies in Canada are members of the International Accounting Standards Committee. When an international accounting standard is issued it is compared with Canadian practice to establish any significant differences. Where there are significant differences, further study is given to the topic to see if there are justifiable reasons for a difference to continue and where there is not, Canadian practice prevails until the Handbook is modified. Where an international standard is issued covering a topic not included in the handbook, the Accounting Standards Committee will consider whether a project should be initiated.

For a number of reasons foreign investors will normally form a subsidiary rather than trade through a branch. Initially some companies do adopt the branch alternative in order for any immediate losses incurring in the branch to be relieved against tax fairly quickly. However, after a short period of time most foreign investors transfer a branch to a corporation as it provides a better profile. Other commercial advantages accrue to a corporate structure such as loss limitation and interest relief on borrowed funds. Sometimes a foreign parent company may set up an overseas holding company in Canada with a view to acquiring subsidiaries on its behalf. Such a corporate formation necessitates the preparation of consolidated accounts.

Accounting for groups, acquisitions and mergers

The major influence on accounting in this area is the CICA Handbook. Section 1580 deals with business combinations including goodwill, section 3050 deals with long-term investments, and section 1600 deals with consolidated financial statements including the equity method of accounting. The following three sections summarize the requirements specified in the Handbook.

Section 1580 Accounting for business combinations

The Handbook makes a distinction between three possible methods of accounting for business combinations. The purchase method by which one company acquires the shares of another company for shares, cash or other consideration. However, where an acquirer cannot be identified because two companies join together through an exchange of stock, a pooling of interests occurs in the sense that resources are combined to carry on the previous businesses in combination. The third type of business combination is the new entity method in which ownership comes together through an exchange of voting shares, a new entity is formed, and an acquirer cannot be identified. Under this method the assets and liabilities are transferred to the new entity at fair value. However, this type of business combination is rejected by CICA and there is no significant precedent for its use in practice.

In making a choice between the purchase method and pooling of interests basis the Handbook states that the former should be used to account for all business combinations, except for those rare transactions where an acquirer cannot be identified. In identifying whether an acquirer exists the type of consideration will be an important factor. For example, where the consideration is in the form of cash or other assets it is reasonable to conclude that they are the acquirer.

Where stock is issued by a company as consideration, the important factor will be the extent of control over the resultant combined company so that a company which owns more than 50 per cent of the voting shares of the combined undertaking will normally be considered to be the acquirer. Other factors such as composition of the board of directors and participation by management are important where the shareholding is only marginally above the 50 per cent threshold. The circumstances surrounding the transaction will determine the appropriate method of accounting, although it is important to note that the methods are not alternatives in accounting for the same business combination. Where the appropriate method is the purchase method the cost of acquisition should be the fair value of the consideration and should be allocated to identifiable assets and liabilities on the basis of fair values at the date of acquisition. Any excess cost over identifiable net assets should be treated as goodwill.

Any goodwill arising on acquisition should be amortized to income using the straight-line method over the estimated useful life of the asset which, like the US, may not exceed 40 years. The period of amortization should be disclosed in the accounts. Unamortized goodwill should appear in the balance sheet as an intangible asset and not as a deduction from shareholders' equity. Where there is a permanent diminution in the value of goodwill the asset should be written down through the income statement.

Where a company has been acquired which has accumulated tax losses the benefit of the losses should be recognized as an asset only if there is reasonable assurance of realization of such benefits. In other circumstances the benefit should be recognized as an extraordinary item on realization.

In the rare circumstances where the pooling of interests method is appropriate, the combined undertaking should reflect the value of the assets and liabilities recorded by the combining corporations and shareholders' equities should be the sum of the equities of the combining entities.

Whichever method is adopted to account for the business combination, it is important to disclose the method of accounting used, the net assets brought into the combination, and details of the consideration.

Section 3050 long-term investments

Section 3050 deals with the circumstances in which the main methods of accounting for long-term investments are appropriate. These methods include consolidation, equity and cost accounting.

Consolidated financial statements are required where one company owns directly or indirectly a majority of the voting shares which control the majority of the members of the board of directors. However, subsidiaries may be excluded from consolidation, provided that the reason for exclusion is stated, under the following circumstances:

1. Increases in the equity of the subsidiary are not likely to accrue to the parent.
2. Control is seriously impaired.
3. Control is temporary because a formal plan exists to dispose of the investment.
4. The subsidiary is a bank or life assurance company with financial statements not prepared in accordance with GAAP.
5. Where consolidation would not provide an informative presentation to the parent company's shareholders.

Under circumstances (1) and (2) the investment should be accounted for using the cost method. Where control is only temporary (3) the investment should be accounted for at the lower of estimated net realizable value and the carrying value of the investment using the equity method.

In circumstances (4) and (5) the investment should be accounted for using the equity method except that in case (4) the earnings will not conform with GAAP. In both these cases the financial statements of the parent should either include the separate financial statements of the subsidiary or the information should be disclosed in condensed form. In addition, there should be a reconciliation of the income of the subsidiary to arrive at the amount included in the income statement of the parent.

Where an investor exercises significant influence over an investee the equity method is required. Significant influence may be indicated by representation on the board of directors, participation in the policy-making processes or an interchange in managerial personnel. Where less than 20 per cent of the voting shares in the investee are held, it should be presumed that significant influence is not exercised unless demonstrated otherwise. Where a holding over 20 per cent of the voting shares is held, significant influence should not automatically be presumed since it depends on other factors.

Where significant influence can be exercised the investment should be accounted for using the equity method. Once significant influence is not able to be exercised the investment should be accounted for using the cost method.

Section 1600 Consolidated financial statements

This section deals with the preparation of consolidated financial statements where the purchase method is used and also the equity method of accounting for investments. This accounting recommendation makes a distinction between consolidated financial statements prepared on a line-by-line basis and combined financial statements which exclude the parent company. Combined financial statements may be useful where an individual owns a controlling interest in several corporations although they are not a substitute for consolidated financial statements. Other situations where combined financial statements may be useful is in presenting the results of a group of unconsolidated subsidiaries or to combine the results of companies under common management.

The accounting recommendation provides considerable technical detail on accounting for consolidated financial statements although the suggestions offered are typical of those generally adopted using the purchase method. In addition, the recommendation deals with the equity method of accounting for an investment. This method results in the net income of the investor being the same as the consolidated net income would have been if the financial statements of the investee had been consolidated with those of the investor. Disclosure of the difference between the cost and the underlying net book value of investee's assets at the date of purchase should be disclosed in the notes to the accounts.

International accounting standards (IASs)

A summary of the more important differences between Canadian recommendations and international accounting standards is provided in table 5.3. In general, compliance with the requirements of Canadian recommendations automatically ensures compliance with IASs.

6. EXCHANGE CONTROL/FOREIGN INVESTMENT REGULATIONS

There are no exchange controls in Canada and there are no restrictions with respect to the repatriation of capital or earnings or on the ability to remit dividends, interest and royalties. There are no restrictions with respect to the sectors available for foreign investment, except for legislation pertaining to the airline, fishing, shipping, banking and finance, uranium mining, and broadcasting industries. For example, under the Broadcasting Act 1936 a licence will only be granted to Canadian citizens or to a Canadian corporation which has Canadian directors and chairman, and at least 80 per cent Canadian ownership.

In a review of foreign direct investment in Canada, a government committee suggested that the degree of foreign ownership and control was greater in Canada than any other industrialized country. The committee suggested that foreign ownership approached 60 per cent in manufacturing, over 90 per cent in petroleum and rubber products and 65 per cent in mining and smelting. Of the foreign-controlled elements of Canadian industries, the US owned approximately 80 per cent. For these reasons, Canada introduced the Foreign Investment Review Act (FIRA) in 1974 in an attempt to control foreign ownership. Control was to be achieved by screening foreign investment and prohibiting overseas ownership in some sectors of the economy where government policies had been adopted to reduce foreign ownership e.g. the National Energy Programme.

FIRA was perceived by foreigners as an impediment to investment, particularly as the review process was lengthy. Attempts had been made to streamline the process but little progress was made until superseded by the Investment Canada Act in 1986. The purpose of the new Act is to encourage investment in Canada by non-Canadians provided that the investments contribute to economic growth and domestic employment opportunities. The introduction of the Investment Canada Act represents a considerable shift in policy by the Canadian government to encouraging, rather than discouraging, foreign investment in Canada. It has been estimated that approximately 90 per cent of the cases which would have required Federal approval under FIRA will now be exempt. In addition to encouraging foreign investment, there has been a significant relaxation of the takeover regulations.

The Investment Canada Act establishes an agency to be known as Investment Canada which will advise and assist the designated minister in the exercising of his powers and duties. Section 5 summarizes the duties of the Minister:

1. to encourage business investment by such means and in such a manner as the Minister deems appropriate;
2. to assist Canadian businesses to exploit opportunities for investment and technological advancement;

Table 5.3 Comparison of Canadian accounting practices with international standards

International accounting standards	*Canadian recommendations*
IAS 1 – Disclosure of accounting policies	
Disclosure of policies and departures	Often Canadian recommendations do not offer alternative methods of accounting
Requires comparative figures in all circumstances	Where meaningful
IAS 2 – Valuation and presentation of inventories in the context of the historical cost system	
Requires valuation at the lower of cost and net realizable value (NRV)	CICA handbook does not cover this point. In practice the lower of the cost and market value is interpreted as NRV, replacement cost, or NRV less normal profit margin
Requires disclosure of the cost method in all cases	Only where the method differs materially from recent cost
IAS 3 – Consolidated financial statements	
Disclose names and descriptions of significant subsidiaries and associated companies	No equivalent requirement but often done in practice
Additional disclosure where accounting policies are not uniform	No equivalent requirement
A subsidiary may be excluded from consolidation where control is temporary	CICA handbook requires that there should be a formal plan to dispose of the subsidiary.
May exclude a subsidiary from consolidation where activities are too dissimilar	Exclude where consolidation would not provide the more informative presentation
IAS 4 – Depreciation accounting	
Disclose depreciation method, useful lives, depreciation rates and charge for the period for each major class of asset	Information is required but not for each major class of asset
IAS 5 – Information to be disclosed in financial statements	
Requires disclosure of the country of incorporation, nature of the activities of the enterprise, methods for providing for pensions and retirement plans and each category of assets	No equivalent requirements

– *Continued*

Table 5.3 Continued

International accounting standards	*Canadian recommendations*
IAS 8 – Unusual and prior period items and changes in accounting policies	
Requires disclosure of the reasons for any change in accounting policy	CICA 1506 requires a description but not necessarily reason for a change.
A change in policy should be quantified and disclosed	Not required but is considered to be desirable
IAS 9 – Accounting for research and development activities	
Permits, but does not require, deferment of development costs when certain conditions are fulfilled	Requires rather than permits deferment
IAS 10 – Contingencies and events occurring after the balance sheet date	
Dividends in respect of the period and which are proposed or declared after the balance sheet date should be either adjusted or disclosed in those statements	No equivalent requirement
IAS 11 – Accounting for construction contracts	
Disclose (a) the amount of construction work-in-progress (b) cash received and receivable as progress payments, advances and retentions on account of contracts included in construction work-in-progress (c) amounts receivable under cost plus contracts not included in construction work-in-progress (d) if both the percentage of completion method and the completed contract methods are used simultaneously by a contractor, the amount of work-in-progress attributable to contracts accounted for under each method	There are no equivalent requirements although the details under (a) are usually given in practice
IAS 12 – Accounting for taxes on income	
Requires disclosure of (a) the tax effects, if any, related to assets that have been revalued to amounts in excess of historical cost or previous revaluation (b) the relationship	No equivalent requirement Required for public companies only

– *Continued*

Table 5.3 Continued

International accounting standards	*Canadian recommendations*
between tax expense and accounting income, if the relationship is not obvious	
IAS 14 – Reporting financial information by segment	
Requires segmented information to be disclosed by enterprises whose securities are publicly traded and other economically significant entities including subsidiaries	Required for publicly traded companies and those which are required to file financial statements annually with a securities commission
IAS 16 – Accounting for property, plant and equipment	
Allows property, plant and equipment to be carried at an amount in excess of cost	Not common in practice
Requires disclosure of the policy on the frequency of valuations	No equivalent requirement
IAS 17 – Accounting for leases	
The fair value of the leased property is after deduction of grants and tax credits receivable by the lessor	The fair value is not reduced by grants and tax credits
Requires immediate recognition of profit or loss on a sale–leaseback transaction when the leaseback is an operating lease and the transaction takes place at fair value	The profit or loss on such a transaction should be deferred and amortized unless the fair value of the property is less than its carrying value
IAS 19 – Accounting for retirement benefits in the financial statements of employers	
Past service costs should either be (a) recognized in income as they arise or (b) amortized	(a) Not normally acceptable (b) In practice amortized over a period less than the international standard
IAS 20 – Accounting for government grants and disclosure of government assistance	
Where a grant, which has been used to reduce the cost of a fixed asset, becomes repayable, the carrying amount of the asset should be increased by the amount repayable	

– *Continued*

Table 5.3 Continued

International accounting standards	*Canadian recommendations*
Additional depreciation should be charged against income in the period the loan becomes payable	The depreciation adjustment may be undertaken in the future
IAS 21 – Accounting for the effects of changes in foreign exchange rates	
Exchange differences on the translation of long-term monetary items may be deferred and amortized on a systematic basis. Losses may be deferred and amortized only when reasonable to expect that recurring exchange losses will not arise	CICA 1650 requires deferral and amortization on translation of monetary items with a fixed or ascertainable life extending beyond the following fixed year. This requirement is more restrictive than IAS 21
Provides provisions on hedging of monetary items by means of forward exchange contracts and of a net investment in a foreign entity by means of foreign currency loans or other foreign currency transactions	CICA 1650 uses a broader definition of what may constitute a hedge
IAS 23 – Capitalization of borrowing costs	
Capitalize or not capitalize borrowing costs on assets that take a substantial time to be made ready for use	New recommendations will require disclosure of policy and amount of interest capitalization
IAS 25 – Accounting for Investments	
Investment properties should either be treated as property in accordance with IAS 16 and depreciated in accordance with IAS 4 or accounted for as long-term investments	No equivalent requirement
Long-term investments, other than marketable securities, should be stated at cost or revalued amounts	Long-term investments should be stated at cost less any provision due to a reduction in value. Revaluations are not normally permitted
On reclassification of investments from current to long-term the transfer should be at the lower of cost or market value or where previously held at market value at that value	No equivalent requirement

3. to carry out research and analysis relating to domestic and international investment;
4. to provide investment information services and other investment services to facilitate economic growth in Canada;
5. to assist in the development of industrial and economic policies that affect investment in Canada;
6. to ensure that the notification and review of investments are carried out in accordance with this Act; and
7. to perform all other duties required by this Act to be performed by the Minister.

The Act makes specific exemptions for certain transactions, for example:

1. dealers in securities acquiring voting shares;
2. in providing venture capital in return for voting interests;
3. in realizing security granted for a loan;
4. acquiring control to facilitate financing provided the investment is divested within two years or other specified time;
5. the acquisition of control leaving direct or indirect control unchanged;
6. the acquisition of control by the Crown under the Financial Administration Act;
7. the acquisition of control of a corporation which is exempt from tax under Part I of the Income Tax Act;
8. transactions under section 307 of the Bank Act;
9. the involuntary acquisition of control say from devolution of an estate;
10. the acquisition of control of insurance companies for which special rules apply;
11. acquisitions of control of farming interests.

Investments by non-Canadians are subject to notification where the investment is to establish a new Canadian business or acquire control of an existing Canadian business. The agency may be notified at any time before the transaction is completed or within 30 days of the investment. The information to be filed is contained in Schedule I of the Investment Canada Regulations. The information required includes details of the investor, the investment, the Canadian business including the number of employees involved and value of the aggregate assets.

Part IV of the Act specifies the investments by non-Canadians which are reviewable by the Agency. All transactions involving an investment to acquire control are receivable where specified limits are exceeded. Control is achieved by acquiring voting shares either directly or indirectly in a Canadian corporation which carries on a business in Canada. Where control is not achieved through voting shares the regulations apply to the acquisition of substantially all the assets used in carrying on a Canadian business. Section 14 (1) sets out the limits for reviewable transactions and provides for a review of all acquisitions by foreigners of Canadian businesses with assets exceeding C$5 million. Where an international transaction involves the acquisition of control, either directly or indirectly, of assets exceeding C$50 million in a Canadian business (including its affiliates) the transaction is subject to review if more than 50 per cent of the value of the total transaction is attributable to the acquisition of Canadian businesses. In addition, the Minister retains the option of reviewing transactions affecting Canada's cultural heritage or national identity where he considers it to be in the public interest.

If the above limits are exceeded, a non-Canadian may not implement the investment unless the review has been completed and the Minister is satisfied that the investment is likely to be of 'net benefit' to Canada. The only exception to this is where a Minister is satisfied that the delay would cause hardship to the non-Canadian or would jeopardize the operations of the Canadian business that is the subject of the investment.

Where a transaction is subject to a review, an application must be filed with the Agency containing the prescribed information in accordance with Schedule II of the Investment Canada Regulations. The regulations require details of:

1. the investor including its financial statements for the three fiscal years immediately preceding the implementation of the investment;
2. the investment including copies of the purchase and sale agreement or the principal terms and conditions of the contract;
3. the Canadian business including its financial statements for the three fiscal years immediately preceeding the implementation of the investment;
4. the assets involved;
5. the investor's plans for the Canadian business with respect to the current operations of the Canadian business and the relevant factors set out in Section 20 of the Act.

The criteria set out in section 20 to be considered in assessing net benefit of the investment are:

1. the effect on the level and nature of economic activity in Canada including the effect on employment, on resource processing, on the utilization of parts, components and services produced in Canada and on exports from Canada;
2. the degree and significance of Canadian participation in the business and industry;
3. the effect on productivity, industrial efficiency, technological development, product innovation and product variety in Canada;
4. the effect on competition in industry;
5. compatibility with national, industrial, economic and cultural policies; and
6. contribution to Canada's international competitive position.

Where the Minister considers that the investment is likely to be of net benefit to Canada, the investor will be informed within 45 days of receipt of the application. If the application cannot be fully considered within this time-scale the Minister may extend the review period a further 30 days or other period agreed on with the applicant. Where the Minister is not satisfied that the investment will be of net benefit to Canada he may order a divestiture where necessary.

The effect of the above provisions, compared with those of FIRA, will be to eliminate the majority of transactions from the review process. In addition, those investments subject to review will be approved by a Minister and not by the federal Cabinet. The reduction in political involvement together with simplified investment guidelines are serving to improve the timeliness of review decisions. A further difference is that the underlying concept of the Investment Canada Act is based on the concept of 'net benefit' to the Canadian economy whereas FIRA policy was based on the premise of 'significant benefit'.

There has also been a change in the way in which control is determined. Under FIRA, control consisted of direct control of voting shares or indirect control through a trust, through another corporation, or as a result of options. Under the Investment Canada Act, control is determined by the acquisition of voting shares either directly or indirectly and specifically excludes contractual rights to acquire voting interests or assets unless the investors require they be considered in the review.

SUMMARY

Statistics on acquisition activity in Canada are somewhat limited since there has not been an obligation for such transactions to be reported. Data collected by the government authorities have been assembled on the basis of media reporting but even then, information has only been collected on sectors subject to the Combines Investigation Act. Up until 1976 services were not covered by this Act.

Acquisition activity has increased dramatically over the past ten years and takeovers by foreign-owned or foreign-controlled acquirers has increased as a proportion of total activity. Sectors where activity has been high include mining, food, trade and the finance fields. It is not possible to comment on the total value or average value of transactions since this information is not published.

There have been significant changes in merger control in Canada in 1986. The Competition Tribunal Act and the Competition Act significantly revised the Combines Investigation Act, and the Investment Canada Act replaced the Foreign Investment Review Agency with Investment Canada.

The aim of the Competition Act is to promote competition and to expand opportunities for Canadian participation in world markets. Abuses of a dominant position may lead to a hearing before the Tribunal which has the power to dissolve a merger or dispose of assets where it considers it necessary. An interesting feature of the Tribunal is that, in considering competition in Canada, it will explicitly consider the extent to which foreign products and foreign competitors provide effective competition.

Furthermore, even where there are adverse effects on competition the Tribunal will not use its powers if efficiency gains are likely to be of greater importance.

For the first time in Canada there is a pre-notification condition for large-scale acquisitions although the requirements were not proclaimed concurrent with the passing of the Act but are expected to be during 1987. Where an acquisition meets the pre-notification requirements, information must be supplied to the Director of Investigation and Research, Competition Act, and the transaction deferred for a specified period of time. However, any delay should not exceed 21 days.

Canada Business Corporation Act recognizes the concept of a 'statutory amalgamation' by which two companies merge to form one company. Provided specified conditions are fulfilled, assets and liabilities may be transferred on a tax-free basis and consequently there is no step-up in tax basis for either depreciable or non-depreciable property. An important point is that a foreign incorporated company cannot undertake such a transaction itself. It is essential therefore, that if such a transaction is contemplated a Canadian corporation should be formed to undertake the amalgamation.

Another important point to note is that transactions should be on an arm's-length basis if a challenge, with respect to the valuation of assets, is to be avoided. Disputes over valuations can lead to problems in obtaining capital cost allowances. Where shares are obtained in another corporation the acquirer may carry forward non-capital losses but may not obtain group relief as there is no such concept in Canada. However, capital losses may not be carried forward under any circumstances. In addition, Revenue Canada Taxation has become increasingly vigilant in analysing intercompany transactions to prevent the transfer of profits to low-tax countries. Furthermore, thin capitalization regulations apply to prevent excessive interest being charged against Canadian source income.

An important feature of accounting in Canada is that accounting standards are given statutory back-up in the Canada Business Corporation Act 1975 and in the corporation laws of the provinces of Alberta, British Columbia, Manitoba, Ontario and Saskatchewan. Furthermore, in 1972 the Canadian Securities Administrators issued a national policy statement for public companies stating that generally accepted accounting principles were those contained in the CICA Handbook.

In accounting for mergers and acquisitions a reasonably clear distinction is made between an acquisition and a merger. In most circumstances a transaction will constitute an acquisition but in certain cases a genuine merger takes place in which case it is compulsory to use the pooling-of-intrests approach.

Whilst a number of differences exist between the technical details of international standards and CICA recommendations they are not of great significance in practice. Anyone familiar with Anglo-Saxon accounting will not find the task of understanding Canadian accounting practices too onerous.

There are no exchange controls in Canada or restrictions on repatriation of capital or earnings. Despite the high level of foreign ownership of its business, Canada is actively encouraging investment from foreigners. To this end the Foreign Investment Review Act has been repealed and Investment Canada set up to encourage investment that contributes to economic growth and domestic employment opportunities. One feature of this shift in policy is a significant relaxation of the takeover regulations. The majority of transactions will be eliminated from the review process and those requiring approval will obtain it from the Minister and not from the federal Cabinet. The reduction in political involvement together with simplified investment guidelines are serving to improve the timeliness of the review process.

All of the above factors are consistent with the BERI appraisal that Canada is worthy of equity investment and the incurrence of debt to be serviced from operations in that country.

6

Federal Republic of Germany

1. BUSINESS ORGANIZATIONS AND COMBINATIONS

Business organizations

Business interests in the Federal Republic of Germany (FRG) can be held, *inter alia*, in either corporations or partnerships. The two most commonly recognized forms of corporate entity are the corporation limited by shares (AG – *Aktiengesellschaft*) and the company with limited liability (GmbH – *Gesellschaft mit beschränkter Haftung*). Partnerships can be formed either as a general partnership (Offene Handelsgesellschaft) or as a limited partnership (*Kommanditgesellschaft*).

Shares, i.e. interests in corporations limited by shares (*Aktiengesellschaften*), can either be quoted on the stock exchange or freely traded. Shares in corporations with limited liability (*Gesellschaften mit beschränkter Haftung* – GmbH), which are commonly referred to as business interests (*Geschäftsanteile*); can only be freely traded and cannot be quoted on any recognized stock exchange. Consequently, without any officially quoted price, business interests and/or shares can change ownership by means of a relatively simple form of agreement between buyer and seller, transferor and transferee. This is the meaning of the term 'freely traded' as it appears in this section covering the FRG.

Shares which are quoted on stock exchanges are, in the main, only those of very large companies. Investments in quoted companies do not usually arise as a result of, or with the intention of, acquiring an entire business or enterprise. The acquisition of partnership interests is not often considered by foreign investors, since this form of business structure is primarily used to accommodate only domestic or family businesses.

The following explanations are, therefore, primarily devoted to interests in corporate bodies which can be freely traded as shares, in particular with shares in companies with limited liability (the GmbH) and with the acquisition of enterprises through the takeover of specific assets and liabilities or through merger, which is a special form of acquisition of business assets.

Types of business combination

The main considerations

The basis of taxation on the takeover of an enterprise can vary considerably in the FRG to that which can arise abroad; there are, for example, particular differences in the depreciation of goodwill, and depreciation following a permanent reduction in value of a holding which, for example, does not even exist in Anglo-Saxon fiscal law. In some instances, there are possibilities available in the tax field, such as, for example, in the US, where shares in a corporation can be acquired and thereafter liquidated with the effect that an increase in the book value of the assets can be achieved (step-up in basis), even though the corporation has not previously suffered any capital gains taxation on those same assets.

Whilst considering the taxation of the transfer of assets it is also important to consider the future taxation of the profits and assets of the business. It is most important to consider which taxes will arise by virtue of the chosen form of transaction and what taxes will be payable thereafter on estimated profits abroad as well as on the subsequent distributions back to the parent company in the home country.

It should also be checked as to whether the costs of financing the acquisition of foreign shareholdings or branches can be deducted from profits in the home country.

At the same time, an investor in Germany must consider whether to establish a subsidiary or whether to trade through a branch. In most cases, the foreign subsidiary is the chosen form of investment in order to limit liability abroad and to provide a better local profile.

The acquisition possibilities

A foreign buyer may acquire the business of a domestic company either by purchasing shares or by acquiring assets. A third form of acquisition is called a merger; this type of transaction is a special form of asset acquisition.

Share acquisition. The acquisition of holdings in a company with limited liability, a GmbH, in the FRG requires to be documented through a Notary Public. This is a relatively simple procedure, which has already been described. It is important to remember that holdings in a GmbH are referred to as business interests (*Geschäftsanteile*) and not as shares, which, on the other hand, are traded without reference to notary documentation. Nevertheless, the acquisition of an interest in a GmbH is the most accessible means of business investment for foreign investors.

Acquisition of assets and liabilities. The acquisition of assets and liabilities in an enterprise does not need to follow any specified legal form or procedure. The transfer of ownership must, however, be agreed in respect of each business asset on a separate basis. The primary condition for this form of acquisition is that an organization is already on hand into which the assets and liabilities can be easily transferred.

Merger. In this case all the assets of the acquired enterprise are transferred to the acquiring enterprise. The acquired enterprise is simultaneously liquidated and the shareholders receive shares in the acquiring company in exchange for their former interests.

2. TRENDS IN TAKEOVER ACTIVITY

General considerations

The development of international business enterprise is obviously affected by the economic events which take place in the respective countries of operations. Changes in the economic climate of any country naturally influence the holdings of foreign investors. Any upward trend in the economy, which opens new perspectives and encourages new investment, similarly provides an incentive to reinvest profits in order to strengthen the equity in the respective foreign location.

After experiencing difficulties in 1982, the economies of most of the countries in the western world have recovered somewhat. This element ot recovery has been reflected in the growing interest shown in foreign investment.

Development of German investment abroad

The value of German business assets in subsidiary companies and branch operations abroad has increased considerably over the last 20 years. During the year ended 31 December 1983, the value of German business interests outside the FRG increased by more than DM10 million to DM106,000 million. Approximately DM2 million of this increase reflected the strength of the US dollar; namely, the value in DM had increased, whilst the value of the investment in dollar terms had remained the same.

The foreign subsidiaries were, themselves, able to contribute to the increase in the investment figures, because improved profits resulted in a higher ratio of retained earnings being reflected in foreign balance sheets.

The reduction in value of foreign currencies would need to be considered as a primary influence in evaluating, in DM terms, the current volume of German investment in foreign assets.

Even though investment incentives, such as state or government grants and start-up assistance, are relatively limited, the current exchange rate of between DM1.60 and DM1.65 against the US dollar is encouraging German manufacturers to consider setting up production in the US. At present, German-produced goods cannot be sold on the US market

Table 6.1 The development of direct investment in industrial and trading enterprises from the end of 1982 until the end of 1983
(DM thousand millions)

Nature of capital, movement in capital	*Direct German investment abroad*		*Direct foreign investment into the Federal Republic of Germany*	
Direct investment as at the end of 1982[a]				
Holdings of nominal share capital[b]	45.8		44.0	
Interests in reserves and retained earnings	35.8		13.6[c]	
less:				
Share of accumulated losses	16.0		9.8	
Total equity share capital		65.6		47.8
Loans and other borrowings[d]		29.8		28.6
Sum total of direct investment as at the end of 1982		95.4		76.4
Changes during the year 1983				
Holdings of nominal share capital[b]	+3.9		+1.1	
Interests in reserves, retained earnings and losses carried forward	+2.9		+2.8	
reinvested profits included therein[e]	(+0.5)		(+0.6)	
Loans and other borrowings	+3.8		+0.3	
distributable profits included therein[3]	(+0.4)		(+0.2)	
Total changes in direct investment		+10.6		+4.2
effected by means of:				
Payments (according to accounting statistics) for new investment in share participation	+9.3		+4.9	
for the liquidation of share participation	−2.0		−3.1	
Changes in value due to the development in currency exchange rates	+0.5		---	
Profits in investment companies[c]	+0.9		+0.8	
Sundry[f]	−1.5		+1.5	

– *Continued*

Table 6.1 Continued

Nature of capital, movement in capital	*Direct German investment abroad*		*Direct foreign investment into the Federal Republic of Germany*	
Granting of borrowed capital[g]	+3.4		+0.1	
Total change in direct investment		+10.6		+4.2
Direct investment as at the end of 1983				
Holdings of nominal share capital[b]	49.7		45.1	
Interests in reserves and retained earnings	40.6		16.4	
less				
Share of accumulated losses	17.9		9.8	
Total equity share capital		72.4		51.7
Loans and other borrowings[d]		33.6		28.9
Sum total of direct investment as at the end of 1983		106.0		80.6

[a] Changed in comparison to already published statistics on the basis of information which became available subsequent to publication.
[b] Less share capital not yet fully paid up.
[c] The figures quoted represent only the global sum of retained earnings after deduction of that part thereof which is intended for distribution; see note d.
[d] Including the part of retained earnings which is intended for dividend distribution (the figures included for foreign investment in the Federal Republic of Germany have been taken from statistics produced for the balance of payments); excluding liabilities owed by banks and financial institutions to the shareholders.
[e] Estimated where necessary.
[f] Partly computed, simply as a balancing figure.
[g] This is not to be compared with the figures given in the balance of payments statistics, which reflect only the the long term financial guarantees of the shareholder which can be directly related to the shareholding concerned as direct investment and where other loans and financial borrowings are included either as borrowed working capital or as short term loan finance.

Source: Deutsche Bundesbank (German Federal Bank)

because the price is too high. German business has noticed a considerable reduction in export orders, especially in motor vehicles and industrial plant and machinery.

Table 6.1 illustrates the trends in investment as at the end of 1983.

The development of foreign business investment into the FRG

Foreign investment in the German economy amounted to DM80,600 million at the end of 1983. The considerable rate of growth since the end of 1982 can, without doubt, be attributed to the upward trend in the German domestic economy, which began in 1983. Investment was, however, almost exclusively attributable to increases in the share capital of already existing German subsidiary companies of foreign enterprises. The formation of new companies and the takeover of existing companies by foreign business during 1983 were virtually non-existent. After several loss-making years, foreign business assets situated in Germany produced a profit of almost one billion DM during 1983. This positive development in the German economy has been maintained so that further growth in business assets and new investments can be anticipated. The incentive to invest may, however, be suppressed by adverse exchange rates. Nevertheless, high rates of profitability in 1985 should be sufficient to compensate for any disadvantageous exchange rate factors.

The situation from the seller's viewpoint

Family companies, particularly those formed since the end of the Second World War, are likely to be sold to larger companies and concerns by any incoming new generation. One easily recognizable factor of this current trend in transactions is the necessity to invest long-term in new technology and many family businesses are either not prepared or are not in a position to finance the required level of investment.

The situation from the point of view of the acquirer

The readiness to sell middle-range enterprises is currently being matched by the growing interest of large companies and concerns to acquire such enterprises because, whereas financial investments are producing low levels of income, trading and industrial activities are reflecting increased profits.

Growth in some companies is exclusively attributable to acquisitions and takeovers, whilst for others acquisitions will only be regarded as complementary to internal growth, for example, to secure markets or suppliers. Acquisitions should enable the acquirer at least to maintain the rate of growth which has been achieved in the past. In many instances, the intention is to cancel out losses and break into profitability in certain areas or at least to ensure the financial stability of the acquiring enterprise. Some acquiring companies simply wish to strengthen existing product groups by acquisition, whilst others acquire in order to diversify into new product areas or other chosen markets; for example, to spread a multinational base into other countries. Acquisitions in enterprises are also effected in order to take over a good existing management team and, for example, to restrict the expansion and activities of any competitors.

Some acquiring companies will adopt an aggressive strategy in order to expand, whilst others adopt a defensive approach by reducing risk in order to maintain market share. Some companies have a clear idea with regard to their acquisition policy and the candidates they wish to take over, whilst others simply have an open mind and will merely be on the lookout for a suitable opportunity.

The motives for the acquisition of an enterprise can, therefore, vary from the desire to expand capacity, to diversify its product range, to improve competitiveness, to improve a branch network, or to integrate its business activities, to acquire management or technical personnel, to the necessity of defending a present market position, or simply the best means of investing surplus liquid funds.

The acquisition of an existing company is of particular interest, since building up a business from scratch is often more expensive than acquiring a going concern.

There is a tendency for large companies to acquire existing factories and plants, and intangible assets such as know-how, management and personnel as operating entities. This has the advantage that the acquiring company does not need to invest time and manpower in the development of manufacturing programmes, the construction of plants, personnel problems and, similarly, the introduction of new products to the market.

Where large companies are concerned, foreign as well as domestic ownership is invariably involved. For example, the Commercial Holding GmbH in Cologne, which is a subsidiary of Lufthansa, acquired an interest in Avis Car Rentals in Frankfurt in 1983, in which Beatrice Companies in Chicago are also shareholders. Many multinational tyre manufacturers operating in the Federal Republic of Germany have secured their long-term future by strengthening their trade and distribution network through the acquisition of small and mid-market trading enterprises.

The German banks have registered a growing interest in the international acquisition market, particularly involving US, UK and Scandinavian concerns. This area of interest has lead to the involvement in the FRG of major US and UK merger and acquisition agents such as Merill Lynch, Citibank and Chase Manhattan. The purely domestic German business has, until now, been dealt with through German banks and brokers, whilst the larger and international mergers and acquisitions have been dealt with through US and UK investment bankers. Transactions of this nature have involved values of more than DM20 million and brokerage fees in excess of US$250,000.

Changes in share ownership in Germany in 1985

The following list illustrates the international entities which have followed a trend of diversification into the German market, or have expanded into related branches of commerce and industry to preserve a market foothold.

Acquiring company or concern/branch	*Acquired enterprise/branch*
BAT/Tobacco	Chr. Andreae/Furnishing materials
Bahlsen/Biscuits	Oker-Mühle/Animal food products
Bayer/Chemicals	Lindauer Zähne/False teeth
Contigummi/Tyres	Semperit/Tyres
Daimler/Cars	MTU/Turbines
Daimler/Cars	AEG/Electricals
Daimler/Cars	Dornier/Space travel
Degussa/Metallic mouldings	Leschuplast/Lagging materials
Electrolux/Electricals	Butenschön/Industrial kitchens
Erste Kulmbacher/Brewery	Tucher Bräu/Brewery
GHH/Plant construction	Fricke/Roof edgings and guttering
Heidelberger Zement/Building materials	Hornbach/Transport of cement
Hoechst/Chemicals	Rosenthal Technik/Technical ceramics
Hussel/Trade	Rüter/Shoes
KHD/Machinery	Motorenwerke Mannheim/Diesel motors
Klöckner/Iron & Steel	Teropharm/Packing materials
Krupp/Iron & Steel	Schmohl/Fire extinguishers
Krupp/Iron & Steel	Hoenig/Fittings
Lingner + Fischer/Pharmaceuticals	Diplona/Body care products
Lohmann/Animal breeding	Geflügelmast Nittenau/ Mast building
Lufthansa/Aviation	Avis/Car leasing
Mannesmann/Piping	HWT/Steam and water and technology
MBB/Space travel and armaments	Krauss-Maffei/Armaments
Melitta/Coffee	Aroma Gold/Coffee filters
Nestlé/Food products	Wilhelm Stubbe/ Wholesale drinks
Oetker/Food products	Brünz Schwarzwald-Torten/Bakery
Oetker/Food products	Meyer & Beck/Sale and manufacture of food products
Otto Beisheim/Trade	Pelikan/Office materials
Otto Wolff/Steel rolling	PHB Weserhütte/Machine construction
Otto Wolff/Steel rolling	Allcons/Plant construction
Otto/Mail order	Alba Moda/Mail order fashions
Pfanni/Noodles	Max Hultsch/Snacks
Quandt/Holding	van Laack/Clothing
Rosenthal/Porcelain	Kühndahl/Porcelain trade
RWE/Energy	Sumatra Oel/Carbon products
Schmalbach-Lubeca/ Packing materials	Niedermeier/Spray cans
Schöller/Ice-cream	Seim/Waffles
Siemens/Electricals	Torus/Aeroplane leasing
Separator/Centrifuges	Stelzer/Mixing techniques
Thyssen/Iron & Steel	Kanzler/Transportation
Unilever/Food products	Grill-Chef/Salads
Veba/Energy	Emstank/Bunkers
Veba/Energy	Lord/Real estate

The allocation of mergers and acquisitions between the various branches of trade and industry

Since the end of 1976, when statistics were first compiled, there has been far more German investment abroad in the chemical industry, motor vehicle production and in electro-technology than the level of foreign investment into the Federal Republic in the same lines of industry. The Federal Republic has, nevertheless, a noticeable deficit in investment in some branches of industry. One such area is the exploration and exploitation of natural resources such as oil which is controlled by a few large foreign enterprises. Similarly, there are no German enterprises engaged abroad in the computer industry or in the sector of food and nutrition which can be compared to the level of foreign investment in the same industries.

Table 6.2 illustrates, in detail, the volume of investment in the various branches and industrial sectors of the economy. It also shows that German outward investment exceeded the volume of inward investment by approximately DM254,000 million at the end of 1983.

Allocation according to countries

The regional allocation of business interests in foreign business assets is highlighted by two main features. German production centres, as well as businesses in the trade and service industry sector can be found in over 120 countries. There are resident investors in at least half of these countries who hold interests in German business enterprises. More than three-quarters of the total German investment abroad can, however, be found in ten important countries and four-fifths of all foreign investment into the Federal Republic of Germany stems from a total of only five countries. The links with the US are, however, the strongest, as illustrated in Table 6.3. German investment into the US, which amounted to DM29,200 million at the end of 1983, has almost caught up with the total American investment into the FRG, which, on the same date, was approximately DM33,700 million.

The increase in the exchange rate on the US dollar over the last few years has obviously had a noticeable impact on the value of German owned assets; e.g. any increase in the actual value of German-owned assets situate abroad is not reflected when converted into DM terms. It remains to be seen how the current German incentive to invest in foreign production will develop, and the impact this will have, if any, on the international merger scene.

Economies of scale

The inclination of German and foreign concerns either to merge or acquire interests in similar markets in order to secure a long-term foothold has, in the trade sector as well as in production, led to a noticeable shift

Table 6.2 The status of West German ownership in foreign assets in various branches of industry

Position as at the end of 1983; DM thousand millions

Branch of the economy	*Direct German investment abroad According to the branches of the*		*Direct investment from abroad into the Federal Republic of Germany*	
	German investors	*Foreign investment*	*following the branch of German investment*	*Remaining branches of the respective investment subjects*[a]
Mining[b]	4.6	5.8	0.2	+5.6
Processing trade	61.5	39.9	44.7	−4.8
Chemical industry	17.5	13.7	7.5	+6.2
Mineral oil processing	1.1	0.1	7.8	−7.7
Manufacture of plastics and rubber products	0.8	0.6	1.8	−1.2
Extraction and processing of stones and minerals, fine ceramics and glass trades	1.6	1.2	1.0	+0.2
Iron and steel manufacture[c]	2.3	1.3	1.0	+0.3
Machinery construction	7.2	3.8	3.5	+0.3

machinery, computers, including installation materials	1.6	0.4	4.7	−4.3
Motor vehicles	11.3	6.7	5.2	+1.5
Electricals	11.5	7.4	4.1	+3.3
Refined mechanics and opticals, manufacture of goods for entertainment purposes[d]	1.6	1.2	2.3	−1.1
Food and nutrition	0.7	0.7	2.7	−2.0
Other processing trades	4.3	2.8	3.1	−0.3
Building trade	2.0	1.3	0.2	+1.1
Trade	4.2	19.3	14.1	+5.2
Transport and communications	1.3	1.3	0.8	+0.5
Financial institutions	8.1	7.4	5.8	+1.6
Investment companies and other investment management enterprises	11.1	20.1	10.5	+9.6
Service industry[e]	6.4	9.8	3.8	+6.0
Other enterprises	1.6	1.1	0.5	+0.6
Private individuals	5.2	—	—	—
Total	106.0	106.0	80.6	+25.4

[a] + = Excess of the German Direct Investment Abroad.
[b] Including mineral oil extraction.
[c] Including cable manufacturing, rolling mills, die-casting, surface processing, hardening and mechanics.
[d] Including the manufacture of musical instruments, sport equipment, toys and jewellery.
[e] Including financial institutions, insurance companies, real estate agents and other real property enterprises.

Table 6.3 The status of German investment in foreign business interests and assets allocated to groups of countries, important countries and areas of investment

Position as at the end of 1983 in DM thousand millions

Groups of countries/Country	*Direct German investment abroad*			*Direct foreign investment into the Federal Republic of Germany*			*Balance*[a]		
	Total	*Divided between*		*Total*	*Divided between*		*Total*	*Divided between*	
		Processing and manufacture	*Trade*		*Processing and manufacture*	*Trade*		*Processing and manufacture*	*Trade*
EEC countries	32.9	10.8	8.9	23.7	9.5	4.7	+9.2	+1.3	+4.2
including:									
Belgium	3.8	2.5	0.6	1.1	0.3	0.4	+2.7	+2.2	+0.2
France	8.4	3.6	3.8	5.3	1.6	1.8	+3.1	+2.0	+2.0
Great Britain	4.4	1.1	1.9	6.8	3.3	0.6	−2.4	−2.2	+1.3
Italy	2.9	1.3	1.2	0.7	0.3	0.2	+2.2	+1.0	+1.0
Luxembourg	5.9	0.1	0.0	0.8	0.1	0.2	+5.1	—	−0.2
Netherlands	5.7	1.3	0.9	8.1	3.5	1.2	−2.4	−2.2	−0.3
Other European countries	16.5	6.0	3.1	15.2	7.8	3.5	+1.3	−1.8	−0.4
including:									
Austria	3.3	1.7	0.9	1.1	0.4	0.3	+2.2	+1.3	+0.6
Switzerland	8.5	1.1	1.4	11.5	6.4	2.3	−3.0	−5.3	−0.9
Spain	3.1	2.4	0.4	0.1	0.0	0.0	+3.0	+2.4	+0.4

Industrial countries outside Europe	39.3	14.1	6.1	38.0	26.3	5.2	+1.3	−12.2	+0.9
including: United States of America	29.2	10.2	4.2	33.7	25.8	3.0	−4.5	−15.6	+1.2
Developing countries	13.8	8.3	1.0	1.3	0.3	0.3	+12.5	+8.0	+0.7
including: Off-shore financial centres[b]	3.0	0.2	0.5	0.9	0.3	0.1	+2.1	−0.1	+0.4
Latin American countries (excluding off-shore financial centres)	8.1	7.1	0.3	0.3	0.0	0.1	+7.8	+7.1	+0.2
including: Brazil	5.8	5.2	0.1	0.1	0.0	0.0	+5.7	+5.2	+0.1
Other developing countries	2.7	1.0	0.2	0.1	0.0	0.1	+2.6	+1.0	+0.1
OPEC countries	3.5	0.7	0.2	0.8	0.2	0.0	+2.7	+0.5	+0.2
Communist countries	0.0	0.0	0.0	0.6	0.0	0.3	−0.6	−0.0	−0.3
Other regions[c]	—	—	—	1.0	0.6	0.1	−0.1	−0.6	−0.1
Total	106.0	39.9	19.3	80.6	44.7	14.1	+25.4	−4.8	+5.2

[a] + = Excess of the direct German Investment Abroad.
[b] Bahamas, Bahrain, Barbados, Bermuda, Hong Kong, Cayman Islands, Lebanon, Liberia, Netherlands, Antilles, Panama, Singapore, Vanuatu, West Indies.
[c] Direct loans from the shareholders of subsidiary companies to their respective subsidiary companies.

Source: Deutsche Bundesbank (German Federal Bank)

in market conditions. The intervention of public bodies, such as Federal Cartel Office, in the activities of business enterprises has noticeably increased. There does not, however, appear to be any tendency to introduce more restrictive legislation into this area at present.

Merger trends

The statistics which have been compiled to date reflect a steady increase in the volume of cross-border business acquisitions, in relation to the total of comparable recorded transactions.

At present, the German inclination to invest abroad is expected to continue, and will, perhaps, even show an increase. If the current trend in foreign exchange rates holds, and the German Mark, thereby, remains a strong currency, investments into the FRG, particularly from the US, are not likely to reflect any growth. A clear trend for the future is not, however, apparent at present.

3. MERGER CONTROL

Introduction

The German law providing the statutory control of mergers and acquisitions is known as *Gesetz gegen Wettbewerbsbeschränkungen* (GWB), the Law against Restraints of Competition, which was passed in 1957. There have been a number of subsequent changes, but the amendment made in 1973 was particularly important, since it introduced, for the first time, specific measures to control mergers.

Essentially, the 1973 amendment makes mergers acceptable if they can be justified on technical or economic grounds, but it is the aim of the law to ensure that markets remain competitive. The law does not, however, prevent the acquisition of a market-controlling position through the internal growth of an enterprise; it simply has the aim to prevent the attainment of a market controlling monopoly through merger or takeover.

The law governing merger control is, in particular, detailed in sections 22–24a of the GWB, which basically splits the elements of control into two parts, namely a formal governmental control, and a material governmental merger control.

The formal government control is contained in sections 23 and 24a of the GWB as statutory registration procedures. The material governmental controls are included in sections 22, 23a and 24 of the GWB as conditions under which the authorities, the Federal Cartel Office (*Bundeskartellamt*) in Berlin, can prevent a merger taking place.

The formal merger controls

Registration procedures under section 23 GWB

A merger must be brought to the attention of the Federal Cartel Office (FCO) in Berlin and will be subject to the controls of this government body provided that the transaction falls within the definition of a merger.

Any of the following constitute a merger as defined by section 23 of the GWB:

1. The acquisition of assets of another enterprise in whole or a substantial part thereof.
2. The acquisition of an interest in another business enterprise, where the acquiring company through the acquisition attains:

   (a) 25 per cent of the voting share capital or
   (b) 50 per cent of the voting share capital or
   (c) a majority holding in accordance with section 16 subparagraph 1 of the German Company Law (*Aktiengesetz*) (a majority of the shares or a majority of the voting rights).

3. Agreements with other enterprises are entered into whereby:

   (a) a single group is formed or expanded or
   (b) profit transfers are in whole or in part agreed upon or
   (c) the business of an enterprise, either in whole or a substantial part thereof, is leased or assigned.

4. An introduction of personnel onto the Board of Directors or other managing body from one or other of the merging companies.
5. Any form of cooperation whereby the control of an enterprise can be influenced.

There is a post-merger notification requirement in the following cases:

1. in the FRG, including the state of West Berlin, or in a substantial part thereof, the merger and/or joint venture will increase or attain a domestic market share of at least 20 per cent;
2. in the same geographical area, a participating company already holds control over at least 20 per cent of the market or, in the last accounting year before the joint venture, the participating companies attained at least DM500 million turnover or had at least 10,000 employees. These figures include any elements of foreign turnover and personnel employed outside the FRG.

The registration or notice of the merger has to include a detailed description of the enterprises involved and their businesses as well as the form and nature of the merger or joint venture, including details of market shares, turnover and the numbers of employees.

Similar details must be supplied in connection with not only the participating companies but also any enterprises which control or are dependent upon the participating enterprises.

The owners of the participating companies must register the merger with the FCO and, once the registration is approved, the merger or joint venture will be announced to the public by means of publication in the *Bundesanzeiger* which is an official Government Gazette.

Failure to comply with the registration procedure does not itself have any effect on the Joint Venture Agreement. However, any such failure constitutes a civil offence, which can result in penalties of up to DM one million under section 39 of the GWB. Penalties in excess of this figure can, given certain circumstances, be imposed and may include the dissolution of the merger. These registration procedures are intended to give the FCO the opportunity to check as to whether or not the material merger controls should be applied, i.e. whether the FCO powers to intervene should be used.

Registration in accordance with section 24a GWB

According to section 24a GWB the mere *intention* to merge or enter into a joint venture must be registered with the authorities. It is not even necessary to enter into any agreement since the mere intention to do so subjects the participating enterprises to compliance with this section of the law.

Pre-merger notification is required in any of the following circumstances:

1. one of the enterprises, which will be party to the intended merger, had, in the last accounting year of its business, a turnover of at least DM2000 million;
2. at least two of the parties involved in the intended merger or joint venture each had turnover of DM1000 million or more in the last completed accounting year;
3. the intended merger or joint venture should be effected through any law or act of sovereignty under the law of the countries involved.

Where it is not necessary for the intended merger to be registered with the authorities, the participating enterprises can, nevertheless, voluntarily register their intentions with the FCO as a precautionary measure. The advantage of doing so is that the FCO is obliged to approve or deny the intended joint venture before the agreements are signed. Under this procedure, the FCO has only four months in which to prevent the merger taking place (i.e. deny approval) whereas the time-limit outside the voluntary registration procedures is 12 months.

The intended merger cannot be carried out within the statutory four month period granted to the FCO under this section of the law. Any actions which bring or attempt to bring the joint venture into being within this four month period will be regarded as invalid and constitute a civil offence, which can be subject to monetary penalties under section 38 GWB.

The prohibition of mergers under section 24 GWB

The FCO can, under certain circumstances, prevent a merger or joint venture where it can be expected that the participating companies, as a result of the merger or joint venture, will attain control of a market or thereby strengthen their market controlling position. The FCO can intervene where market domination occurs provided:

1. (a) the participating companies have attained DM500 million turnover in the last accounting year; or
   (b) the enterprise to be acquired had a DM50 million turnover, or where the enterprise to be acquired had at least a DM4 million turnover and the acquiring company had at least a DM1000 million turnover.

The FCO does not, however, have any power to intervene where the merger affects a market in which business activities have been exercised for at least the last five years and where, during the last calendar year, the turnover amounted to less than DM10 million.

It is important to note that included in the sales figures mentioned above is the foreign turnover of associated enterprises. In addition, foreign mergers can be subject to the intervention of the FCO where, through the activities of associated enterprises, the German domestic market is likely to be affected (see p. 000).

2. A further condition for merger control is where the merger can strengthen or give rise to a market controlling position. The term 'market control' is defined in section 22 GWB and refers to a single enterprise gaining control of a market, or two or more enterprises which dominate a market.

Market control must be clearly recognizable in a specifically defined area of trade or industry. It is not necessary for the merged or joint venture companies to be engaged in the same type of business activities; the so-called horizontal joint venture. Market control is more commonly attained by a so-called vertical merger, for example, between the supplier of raw materials and the product manufacturer using those materials, or in a conglomerate joint venture, where the enterprises involved are actively engaged in different markets.

Goods can only be allocated to one market if such goods are interchangeable. Given the right set of circumstances, the physical locality and the timing of business transactions can be taken into account as factors in determining the existence and relevance of a market.

A market controlling position is to be assumed if an enterprise can operate without competition or where no material competition exists. It is generally recognized that competition does exist where there is still room in the market for enterprises engaged in the same type of business to operate freely and independently of each other.

A market controlling position will also be recognized as in existence where the enterprise, in comparison to competitors, clearly has an advantageous market position. An advantageous, or overriding market position, as well as a market controlling position, will be measured by the criteria of market share (this is by far the most important means of measure), financial power, access to the creation of markets and/or the retention of markets, and the impact on other enterprises such as being able to prevent or limit a competitor's entry into the market. In individual cases the entire picture needs to be examined so that all criteria, taken as a whole, will or will not lead to the assumption that a market controlling position exists.

Sections 22 and 23a GWB set out the various assumptions under which a market controlling position or an unfair market advantage will be deemed to exist. In this instance, the onus of proof is upon the government authorities. According to the law, a market controlling position or an unfair market advantage exists when:

1. one-third or more of a market for goods or services is in the hands of one enterprise and that organization has a turnover of DM250 million or more in the last financial year; or
2. an enterprise with a turnover of at least DM2000 million joins together with another that:

   (a) is actively engaged in a market in which small and medium-sized companies have a market share of at least two-thirds and the enterprises entering into the joint venture or merger together have at least a 5 per cent market share; or
   (b) holds a controlling position in one or several markets, in which a total of at least DM150 million turnover has been attained in the last calendar year; or
   (c) provided that the exceptions in section 23a, paragraph 1 subparagraph 2 GWB do not apply, the companies entering into the joint venture or merger had, in the last accounting year prior to entering into the said joint venture, a total turnover of at least DM12,000 million and at least two of the companies involved each had at least DM1000 million turnover.

Similarly, market control will be assumed to occur where, in a given market

(a) three or less enterprises together hold a market share of 50 per cent or more; or
(b) five or fewer enterprises together hold a market share of two-thirds or more.

The last two assumptions do not apply if the enterprises involved had a turnover of less than DM100 million in the last financial year.

The FCO, in its assessment as to whether or not a market controlling position is either created or strengthened, is not limited to the conditions prevailing at the time the joint venture or merger is effected. In order to determine whether or not market control or any strengthening of a controlling position is achieved, the FCO will be far more interested in taking into account the future development in the market under examination and the companies involved.

3. The FCO cannot intervene in a merger of enterprises or joint venture, regardless of whether a market controlling position or the strengthening thereof is achieved, if the participating enterprises can prove that, by virtue of the joint venture or merger, more opportunities for competition are created and that these opportunities outweigh any disadvantages of market control. In this case, the onus of proof is on the enterprises entering into the merger or joint venture.

   With regard to the question of improving opportunities for competition, one factor to be examined is, for example, the improvement of the offers available to the consumer. For instance, competition would be encouraged if two weak enterprises joined forces to strengthen their mutual position in the face of their competitors. Similarly, structural improvements can also constitute an improvement in the opportunities for competition where, for example, a market controlling enterprise, which is, nevertheless, ripe for liquidation, is, by virtue of a merger, assured of a future and where, without the merger, the liquidation or the enterprise would create a market monopoly for another enterprise in the same business. Market improvements will still be deemed to exist even where a deterioration in conditions in other markets arises as a result of the joint venture.

4. Where a merger or a joint venture falls within the provisions of (1) and (2) above, the approval of the FCO will not be forthcoming. Similarly, any intended merger or joint venture meeting these provisos will be prevented from going ahead.

   Any mergers or joint ventures which have already been entered into can, however, be declared invalid within a period of one year. The one year notice period can only commence upon the date of submission of a complete registration.

   It should be noted that the FCO can only withhold approval of a joint venture or merger once the intention is registered with the authorities provided that within one month from the date of registration of the intention, it is confirmed that an examination of the intended merger is under way and that any prevention thereof is formally announced within a period of four months from the date of the original registration of intent.

5. If the authorities decide to prevent the joint venture taking place, or declare an already effected merger or joint venture invalid, the participating companies have the right of appeal to the Chamber Court in Berlin and any appeals on points of law can be submitted to the

Bundesgerichtshof, the Federal Court, in Karlsruhe.

6. Once approval of a joint venture or merger has been denied, any transactions which would effectively bring the joint venture or merger into being are specifically forbidden by law. Any legal transactions which, therefore, constitute a violation of the law would be invalid and, similarly, any contracts already entered into in order to effect the joint venture or merger will need to be cancelled or otherwise rendered invalid.

Approval procedure

Where the FCO has prevented a merger or joint venture, the Federal Minister for Economic Affairs can, upon application, give special permission for the merger, provided that the restrictions on competitive opportunities are outweighed by the overall economic advantages of the merger, or where the merger can be justified in the general overriding interests of the economy (see section 24, paragraph 3 GWB). This approval can, however, only be granted where any limitation of the competitive opportunities available does not put the economic order of the market in danger.

Approval through the Federal Minister for Economic Affairs has only been granted in the past to secure the supply of national energy resources, to avoid unemployment, to solve crises in the general business structure, to maintain the standards of services in the areas of medicine and health or to maintain an exceptional potential in technical and research fields.

Special provisions for press mergers

Section 23 *et seq.* GWB contain special provisions governing members of the press. Under these provisos, press mergers are subject to stronger controls, since the law applies on substantially reduced figures of turnover.

The limitation of domestic competition through international mergers and joint ventures

Section 98, paragraph 2 GWB still applies to any mergers, which are effected outside of the FRG and West Berlin, but which, nevertheless, bring about a limitation of competitive opportunities on the domestic market.

The compliance rules, namely the registration procedures set out in sections 23 and 24a GWB, are also understood to apply to any mergers or joint ventures entered into abroad which have an impact on domestic conditions. This is because sections 23 *et seq.* GWB apply to all transactions which have an impact on the domestic market and thereby fall under the control of the federal authorities, namely the FCO.

The overriding proviso is, however, that an international merger restricts the freedom of domestic competition. This can only be the case where one of the enterprises participating in the merger or joint venture is actively engaged in the domestic market. Furthermore, there must be a particular impact on the domestic market, as determined by reference to the facts prevailing in the case under examination.

It is highly questionable whether or not the law can apply where none of the parties to the joint venture or merger falls within the ambit of the GWB; it could be argued that at least one party to the merger should, at least, have a registered place of business within the FRG before the GWB can find any application.

The status and role of the Monopolies Commission

A Monopolies Commission exists as a type of 'watchdog' entity to monitor the development of commercial and industrial concentration and the observance of the merger controls provided by law, namely sections 22–24(a) GWB.

In accordance with its statutory responsibilities, the Commission reports on a biannual basis. The report includes details of industrial and commercial density, and the potential development thereof, particularly with regard to the economic and competitive aspects. In addition, the Commission's report also comments on the observance and the application of the statutory merger controls. The Commission reports directly to the government, but the government, in turn, must ensure that the report is made immediately available to the committees and government departments responsible for drafting and introducing any related legislation. At the same time, the report is published by the Monopolies Commission.

When an application for the approval of a merger or joint venture is submitted (see 'Approval procedures'), the Federal Minister for Economic Affairs will request an opinion report from the Monopolies Commission. Furthermore, the Commission can prepare additional opinion reports, which are either directly requested by the Government, or which the Monopolies Commission itself views as necessary, important or of relevance to the economy.

The Monopolies Commission's reports are designed to provide the government and the legislators with complete and detailed information and statistics. The reports include factual information, such as the causes of industrial density or commercial volume in any particular area, and, in addition, the implications thereof, as well as an economic evaluation of the prevailing circumstances and the Commission's assessment of any adjustments or corrective measures which should be considered.

The Commission enjoys an exceptional position of independence, which is specifically provided and protected by statute, and it is only bound in the extent and nature of its activities, which are also laid down by law.

The government and all branches of the Civil Service, including local authorities, are obliged to make information available to the Commission, upon request. The Commission does not, however, have any authority to demand information direct form private enterprise, unions or other associations. Nevertheless, the work of the Monopolies Commission is exceptionally significant and can be of great influence, particularly because of the publication of its reports.

4. TAXATION

General tax aspects

Taxes on income in the FRG are divided between income tax, corporation tax and trade tax. These taxes on income are governed by federal law, but the rate of trade tax varies as the trade tax levy rate is determined on a regional basis by the local authorities. As a general rule, trade tax will amount to approximately 16 per cent of taxable trade income, as determined for income or corporation tax purposes.

Some tax concepts relevant to foreign investors

The ongoing tax position of a corporation

Corporation tax is levied with reference to the Corporation Tax Law (*Körperschaftsteuergesetz*) dating from 10 February 1984 and all subsequent amendments thereto. All corporations, economic societies, mutual insurance companies, and other corporate bodies, as defined in German civil law, as well as bodies corporate which cannot be recognized under civil law, are subject to a so-called unlimited tax liability or unrestricted tax liability if the registered place of business or place of management and control is within the FRG. The same rules apply to any governmental or public service bodies which generate income from any form of economic activity. Corporations are, for the purposes of the corporation tax law, all companies limited by shares (AG), all partnerships limited by shares (KGaA), and the limited liability company (GmbH), but not, however, the limited partnership (a GmbH & Co. KG), i.e. a partnership, in which the partner with unlimited liability for the partnership's debts is a GmbH. In a limited partnership, a GmbH & Co. KG, the partners are personally and respectively liable to tax on their share of the income arising out of the partnership. Therefore, any individuals participating as partners will be subject to income tax and any corporations receiving income as partners will be subject to corporation tax thereon, regardless of whether or not such income is physically distributed out of the partnership to the participating partners.

A limited tax liability applies to all corporations, associations or other corporate bodies who have neither a registered place of business nor their management or control within the FRG. This limited liability to tax can, however, only apply to income arising in Germany.

The corporation tax rate applicable in 1986 to distributed profits is 36 per cent, whereas a rate of 56 per cent is applied to all retained corporate profits. The amount subject to taxation is referred to as taxable income.

Taxable income is the difference between the value of business assets at the close of one year and the value of the same business assets at the close of the preceding year, duly increased by the value of any withdrawals and reduced by the value of any investments of capital into the company.

The primary factors, which are to be taken into account in the computation of taxable income, are:

(1) *Business expenditure*. Business expenses are outgoings which are necessarily incurred in the course of the business. Certain expenditure, such as that incurred by way of gift, or any unreasonable element of entertaining will be limited in its deduction for tax purposes. It is also important to note that any monetary fines are not deductible if such expenses represent a legally imposed penalty rather than a payment of, for example, compensation for damages caused by a punishable offence. Penalties imposed under the law governing mergers and acquisitions are, similarly, not deductible for tax purposes.

(2) *Depreciation*. Business assets with an estimated useful life of more than one year can, in general, be written off for tax purposes over the anticipated period of their useful life by deducting, on an annual basis, an amount equal to a proportion of the manufacturing or acquisition cost. Business assets can be fully written off for tax purposes over the period of their useful life either by means of straight line depreciation or on a declining balance basis. The declining balance method only applies to movable business assets and is computed by reference to the written-down value of the asset at the beginning of the tax year in question. On a declining balance basis, it is possible to apply a higher rate of depreciation than that used in a straight line computation, and it is important to note that special rules exist for buildings, capital expenditure in the so-called *Zonenrandgebiet* (the east of Western Germany which borders onto the German Democratic Republic (East Germany)) and for business assets which serve to protect the environment. Acquired goodwill can be depreciated on a straight line basis over a period of 15 years.

The basic principles for the depreciation of business assets do not, however, apply to shareholdings and the ownership of land. Such assets must generally be included by reference to the cost of acquisition. The market value, namely the amount which a fully informed acquirer would pay for the individual assets as part of the whole business and, therefore, as part of a total purchase price, can be substituted if this amount is lower than the original cost of acquisition or manufacture.

(3) *Interest*. Interest paid is generally considered to be a deductible expense, provided that the loan capital attributable thereto is applied in the acquisition of, or in the course of the business.

(4) *Valuation of inventory*. Generally speaking, inventory must be valued on an item for item basis. In some instances, valuations can be carried out on a group basis or average values can be applied to assets

of a similar nature for tax purposes. Instead of using average valuation factors, inventory values can be determined by reference to the actual order of consequence in which the goods are sold or are otherwise disposed of. Other methods of valuation commonly used for trade account purposes, such as 'last in, first out' (LIFO), first in, first out' (FIFO), 'highest in, first out' (HIFO) are not recognized for tax purposes.

(5) *Loss carry-back and carry forwards.* Once a loss has been agreed for tax purposes, this must first be carried back over the two preceding business years. Where the loss cannot be fully utilized under the carry-back procedure, the remaining balance thereof can be carried forward for a period of five business years. It is important to note that corporate losses cannot, however, be set against the positive income of the company's shareholders.

(6) *Expenditure on research and development.* The costs of research and development – as with all other intangible business assets – can only be capitalized where the results arising out of the research have been acquired for monetary consideration.

(7) *Deductible taxes.* All business taxes are considered deductible; these are, for example, the trade tax, tax on business vehicles, and any property taxes levied on buildings used and owned by the business. Corporation tax, dividend withholding taxes and federal wealth tax cannot be deducted in the computation of taxable income.

The tax position of the shareholders

As mentioned in the introduction of this section, a corporation must subject its distributed profits to corporation tax at a rate of 36 per cent. In addition, a dividend withholding tax of 25 per cent must be deducted from the amount being distributed to the shareholder. The shareholder must report as his taxable income the amount of the net dividend actually distributed to him plus the 25 per cent dividend withholding tax and the underlying 36 per cent corporation tax as the gross amount of the dividend. His personal tax liability will be computed by reference to the gross dividend and he will receive a credit for the underlying corporation tax and the dividend withholding tax suffered. By taxing dividends in this manner, distributed corporate profits are, therefore, effectively subjected to only one tax rate, that being the tax rate applicable to the shareholder's personal income, i.e. an imputation tax system.

Foreign shareholders of corporations with neither a registered place of business nor management or control in Germany are not subject to German tax on any dividends paid by German corporations to the foreign-held corporation. A repayment of the corporation tax suffered by the German subsidiary and the dividend withholding tax paid on distribution will not be available unless this is specifically provided for within the terms of a Double Taxation Agreement. As a result, the domestic profits of German subsidiary companies which are owned by persons resident abroad are generally subject to taxation at a rate of 52 per cent. Foreign shareholders can avoid this comparatively high tax rate by financing the business capital requirement with shareholder loans rather than equity. The interest paid by the subsidiary company in Germany to the foreign shareholder serves to reduce the taxable German profits, and the interest, upon payment, is not subjected to any dividend withholding tax. It is, however, important to note that the element of loan capital should always be reasonable in proportion to the equity in the company. It is, at present, unclear whether a general fixed loan-to-equity quota will be established, or whether statutory guidelines will be introduced on an industry-for-industry basis. Whilst Germany is watchful to avoid so-called thin capitalization, shareholder loans are, nevertheless, recognized for tax purposes, provided that the loan capital is not more than ten times the equity attributable to that shareholder's individual interest in the corporation.

As well as reducing business profits by correctly structuring the loan-to-equity ratio, there may also be some degree of flexibility in the determination of inter-company pricing between parent and subsidiary companies. It is, however, important to note that intercompany prices must be reasonable (arm's length), since any payments made for supplies from the subsidiary company to the parent company could give rise to a so-called 'hidden dividend distribution' if the payment for such supplies is below a recognized market price. As a result, the taxable profits of the subsidiary company would be correspondingly increased and dividend withholding tax would apply to the amount deemed to be distributed as a dividend.

Tax implications for the acquiring company, the acquiring company's shareholders and for the acquired company

Tax points to be watched in mergers and joint ventures

One of the most important points to bear in mind is that losses arising within a corporation cannot be set against the shareholder's taxable profits or income for tax purposes. It is, however, possible to set off partnership losses, including a GmbH & Co. KG, against other positive items of income personally attributable to the partners, although there are certain restrictions on the extent to which partnership losses can be set off for tax purposes by the individual partners. The disadvantage of a corporate structure as opposed to a partnership can, however, be avoided by the formation of a so-called '*Organschaft*' (a group for taxation purposes) whereby the companies within the group agree to transfer all profits to the holding entity and, similarly, the holding entity agrees to carry all losses arising within the subsidiaries. The structure under which group taxation can apply is, however, very formal in comparison to that often seen in other countries such as the UK or the US. One noticeable difference is that the holding entity can be a partnership of individuals and does not necessarily need to be a corporation. The subsidiaries within the group must be corporations and must be integrated as members of the group in such a way so that they are dependent upon the holding entity in three primary respects, namely economically, from an organizational point of view and financially, i.e. ownership. The agreement or contract between the holding entity and the subsidiaries, under which profits and losses are immediately transferred to the holding entity, must be for a minimum period of five years. Provided all conditions, under which group taxation can apply are met, the subsidiary company's profits will, in effect, never be charged to corporation tax where the holding entity is a partnership of individuals. The profits arising will be directly charged to income tax in the hands of the individual partners to whom such profits are allocated under the terms of the partnership agreement. Losses will, similarly, be allocated directly to the partners according to their respective shares.

The method in which reorganizations, mergers or joint ventures are undertaken in the Federal Republic of Germany can also be of significance where a business, a part of a business (*Teilbetrieb*) or an interest in a trading partnership, or even shares in a corporation are exchanged for shares or a similar interest in the new or reorganized enterprise. The term '*Teilbetrieb*' has a special meaning for German tax purposes. A *Teilbetrieb* can be basically described as a part of a business which can be hived off and identified distinctly from other parts of the enterprise. This could be a manufacturing division which could be clearly separated from other lines of production or, for example, a marketing or distribution section, which could exist and operate independently of other parts of the business. The main point to remember is that mergers and reorganizations can take place without realization of capital gains, provided that the interest received in the new or reorganized business is the same or of equal value to the assets introduced into the new entity. The transfer of the assets of the business can, therefore, be dealt with in the same way as the transfer of 100 per cent of the shares of a corporation. Realization of capital gains will, however, occur on the ultimate sale or disposal of the assets brought into the new business, or when the shares or interest in the new business are ultimately sold. In order for a tax-free share-for-share or interest for interest exchange to apply, the taxable person must have an unlimited liability to German taxation. Consequently, corporations registered in the Federal Republic of Germany can be merged without realization of capital gains provided that the assets within the corporations remain within the ambit of German taxation, and the German government can, therefore, be assured that the capital gains will be taxed at some later date. It is not, however, possible to reorganize a corporation into a partnership without the crystallization of capital gains for tax purposes.

If it is possible to introduce assets into the new enterprise or joint venture at tax book value, namely without crystallizing capital gains, then it is also possible to transfer assets at current market value or indeed at a value somewhere in between the two. If the assets are transferred and introduced into the new business at current market value the 'profits' arising upon the deemed disposal will be subject to tax at half the applicable tax rate normally charged, provided that the person 'disposing' of the assets is an individual. The introduction of the assets at current market value effectively increases the tax base for depreciation in the new enterprise and, thereby, correspondingly reduces the profits chargeable to tax in subsequent years in the new enterprise. It is, therefore, advisable to check in every case as to whether the half-tax rate should be applied in order to obtain the benefit of higher depreciation on current market values or whether it is more advantageous to transfer assets at the tax written down value applicable upon the date of the joint venture or merger. Capital gains realized at a later date, following the transfer at tax book value, do not attract the half-tax rate. Unless profit forecasts can be made on a fairly secure basis, many enterprises prefer to avoid paying tax up front even though higher rates of depreciation follow. This method of up front taxation can, however, be particularly useful where the individuals introducing assets into the new entity or joint venture have losses available to carry forward, which could otherwise remain unutilized. It is important to remember that losses can only be carried forward for a period of five years.

Capital contributions tax and property acquisition tax

Investments of equity capital into a corporation give rise to a capital contributions tax of 1 per cent of the value of the investment. Unlike the provisions applying for income tax and corporation tax purposes, a GmbH & Co. KG is regarded as a corporation for the purposes of the law covering taxes on capital transactions. There had been considerable hope and a relatively strong lobby for the abolition of the capital contributions tax, which can be deducted as a business expense for the purposes of income tax and/or corporation tax. It is, however, unlikely that this charge on business investment will be abolished in the foreseeable future.

The transfer of real estate similarly gives rise to a charge to property acquisition tax at a rate of 2 per cent of the value of the property involved. This tax cannot be avoided by dropping real estate into corporations since transferring 100 per cent ownership of shares in a corporation equally gives rise to the property acquisition tax where the corporation owns real estate. This has particular application where the shares in a corporation are transferred into sole ownership; for example, where five members of a family, each owning 20 per cent of a family corporation, transfer their shares to one member of the family. Similarly, property acquisition tax would be charged under the sole ownership provisions where the shares in a corporation owning real estate are partly acquired by a subsidiary company and the remainder by an intermediary company since ultimately it is the parent or holding company which indirectly owns the property involved. Where shares are transferred into effective sole ownership, the property acquisition tax is levied by reference to a unitary value (*Einheitswert*), which is simply a value determined for tax purposes, and which is usually considerably less than the actual market value.

Property acquisition tax cannot be deducted as a business expense for the purposes of income tax or corporation tax; it can, however, be included as a capital cost of the acquisition of the land.

Tax implications for the acquired company's shareholders

Any profits arising upon the sale or disposal of shareholdings by a shareholder is subject to income tax, or corporation tax where the shareholder is a corporation. The profit will, however, only be subject to tax where the shareholder directly or indirectly held more than a 25 per cent interest in the company (a so-called 'substantial' interest). Needless to say, there are anti-avoidance provisions which prevent substantial interests from being gradually depleted on a tax free basis.

Foreign shareholders are usually not subject to German tax on such profits, since these gains are generally excluded from taxation under the terms of the existing double taxation agreements with Germany.

Where, however, the profit arising from the sale of shares can be attributed to the German permanent establishment of a foreign enterprise, the profits will be taxable in the FRG as branch profits, regardless of the size of the holding.

5. ACCOUNTING

Background

As in most other countries, the financial statements in the FRG consist primarily of a balance sheet and a profit and loss account. In contrast to many other countries, where accounting methods and principles are based on guidelines or other non-statutory recommendations, most German accounting principles are provided by law.

As well as German Trade Law (HGB) and Company Law, in which many accounting rules are contained, reference must be made to tax law, which can substantially influence financial accounting.

There is a separate law governing valuation (*Bewertungsgesetz*), and there are statutory obligations with regard to bookkeeping and accounting, contained in what is commonly referred to as the A0 (*Abgabenordnung*) the administrative rules and regulations which, in some ways, can be compared to the UK Taxes Management Act 1970. In addition, accounting principles are often put into statute under the general heading of *Bilanzrecht* (Accounting Law).

German law has recently been brought into line with the fourth and seventh EEC Directives; the introduction of these Directives into German law has, in comparison to the law which has applied to date, brought about considerable change. A new *Bilanzrichtliniengesetz* (Accounting Regulations Law) which was enacted in 1986, but first became effective in 1987, finally brought the majority of the International Accounting Standards (IAS) into use under German law; this measure will also cause considerable change in German accounting practice. Even though Germany was a founding member of the International Accounting Standards Committee (IASC) and the standards were, with some exceptions, generally accepted accounting principles in the FRG, there have, to date, been a number of differences between German practice and the published international standards.

German accounting practice differs in several material areas, particularly in comparison to the principles applied in most countries where practice is derived from Anglo-Saxon law. One such area is that of *Geschäftswert* (goodwill) which will be discussed in detail later in this section.

You will often hear the term 'silent reserves' used in German accounting jargon. Indeed it is not only jargon, since the accounts usually include a provision for '*Stille Reserven*' or '*Rücklage*'. The 'silent' or 'hidden' reserves represent the difference between the actual market value of the business assets and the written-down book value for trade accounts and tax accounts purposes. Since the tax book values, and the tax written-down values, invariably differ from the book values in the trade accounts there are two sets of corresponding figures, namely the hidden tax reserves and the hidden or silent trade reserves. Whilst the trade reserves, when taken into account, reflect the actual market value of the assets, the tax reserves represent the capital gains, which would be subject to tax if the assets were sold or otherwise disposed of by means of a taxable transaction.

Reserves are also made for pension purposes. Although pension funds exist in Germany, they are not really apparent in German business because there are no real tax incentives to compare with those attached to, say, Individual Retirement Annuities (IRA accounts) in the US or Retirement Annuity Plans in the UK. Most German pension plans are operated by the employers and are non-contributory. There are very few employee pension schemes which are linked to insurance or pension companies, which are outside of the employer's control. The employer can build a tax deductible pension reserve which will later cover the pensions payable to retired employees. If the employee dies or leaves the company before pensionable age, the pension reserve has to be reduced accordingly and the amount of that reduction is added back into taxable income.

Certain employment agreements provide for a payment to the widow or the deceased's family, if an employee dies in service, so that the amount in reserve would be applied against that liability. Similarly, most employment agreements provide for a pension to be paid at pensionable age only when the employee has completed ten years service. This is one of the disadvantages of the German system because, in most cases, an employer pension is only secure after the employee has been in the same employment for ten years. If the employee leaves after more than ten years' service, his pension rights remain, but are simply frozen as there are no general means of transferability. If the employee leaves before completion of ten years' service, he will not have any pension rights and will simply have to start afresh with a new employer.

In a merger or joint venture situation any pension rights would, of course, be preserved and the liability and reserves attached thereto would be transferred to the acquiring company; see employee rights as mentioned in section 7.

The acquisition of freely traded shares in corporations (GmbH, AG)

If a domestic company acquires shares in a corporation or limited liability company and its is assumed that such shares will be held for some time, this holding is to be regarded as a 'participation'. In cases of doubt, a 'participation' (*Beteiligung*) will also be assumed if direct or indirect ownership of at least 20 per cent of the nominal capital of a corporation can be demonstrated (section 271, I HGB *Handelsgesetzbuch* – German Trade Law). All interests and shareholdings are included as one entry in the balance sheet under the heading 'financial assets'. Corporations are, however, obliged to detail any shareholdings in an appendix to the accounts including, *inter alia*, the name, registered office, the equity interest and the trading results of the last financial year for each 'participation' (section 285 No. 11 HGB – German Trade Law).

The acquisition cost is generally regarded as the value of each individual shareholding and any higher value is not permitted. An extraordinary rate of depreciation can be applied where the value of the holding on the balance sheet date is lower than acquisition cost. Where a reduction in the value of the holding is likely to be permanent, this must be reflected in the balance sheet. The extent of any depreciation, whether optional or obligatory, is generally computed by reference to income and profits. The restoration of value under section 280 HGB also applies to shareholdings. Foreign shareholdings are, in general, subject to the same provisions but, in this instance, it is generally advisable to be conservative in any assessment for valuation purposes. Any devaluation in foreign shareholdings, which arises by virtue of an upward valuation of the German Mark, is only possible if the duly exchanged value of the shareholding falls below the book value. Any reduction in the value of foreign shareholdings can only be recognized for tax purposes with due reference, where necessary, to any relevant Double Taxation Agreement.

As a general rule, goodwill can never be treated separately for accounting purposes since this is always included in the cost of acquisition or acquisition value of the holding.

Acquisition of interests in partnerships

In accordance with the HFA* report of March 1976, holdings in partnerships (OHG, KG), in so far as they are intended to serve the

* HFA = *Hauptfachausschuß* – a committee set up by the Institut der Wirtschaftsprüfer (Germany's professional body of accountants) to issue statements of practice and opinion.

business interests of an AG, are to be included in the balance sheet as 'financial assets'. It is not necessary to highlight any unlimited commercial liability, which is linked to the interest or holding in the partnership, as a separate note in the balance sheet, but mention does need to be made in an appendix to the accounts. The value of the interest or holding can never exceed the acquisition cost. In cases where there is a difference between the capitalized investment and what has actually been paid, then the balance remaining unpaid must be reflected in the accounts as a liability.

Special rules apply to profit shares in partnerships, which, of course, cannot be treated in the same way as corporate dividends. Since the partners are directly entitled to their respective shares of profits, such interests can, therefore, be used as collateral, and are transferrable, and must be duly 'recognized' in the balance sheet of any corporate partner. There is no requirement to have a vote on the distribution of profits on an annual basis; this automatically follows the allocation specified by the Partnership Agreement. Any corporate partner must, therefore, reflect its share of profit in its own financial statements, even where such profit remains within the partnership itself.

Any such profit share is, in the first instance, shown in the corporate balance sheet as a receivable. Any profit shares which are used to satisfy investment obligations, or to replenish equity (which has, for example, been reduced by trading losses or by transfers to partnership reserves) are to be included as additions or supplements to the capital value of the interest. In general, the equity method is applied in the valuation of such holdings or interests. Where partnership profits are left in the partnership in order to offset losses from earlier years the partner, under the acquisition value principle, is obliged to reflect the profit share in his own balance sheet only where such trading losses have previously been used to reduce the book value of the holding or interest.

Takeover of itemized assets and liabilities

In this form of merger or joint venture, an already existing enterprise buys up another enterprise and thereby acquires the assets and debts of that other business. The transferred assets and liabilities are to be taken into the balance sheet of the acquiring company at the value applicable on the takeover date. The value would be the actual market value, which is usually established by an independent assessor. The company disposing of the assets would, therefore, generally realize any capital gains. The treatment of acquired goodwill is mentioned below (p. 196).

Merger

The merger of corporations (*Aktiengesellschaften* – companies limited by shares) without liquidation is provided for in Sections 339–53 of the *Aktiengesetz* (German Company Law). The merger of companies with limited liability (GmbH) with a company limited by shares (AG), or with a partnership limited by shares (KG a A) is similarly governed by sections

355 and 356 Aktiengesetz.

In accordance with section 348 *Aktiengesetz* the acquisition costs for the acquiring company must be equal to the values specified in the closing balance sheet of the transferring company. Since these final balance sheet values are to be computed by reference to the general provisions of Company Law and German Trade Law, the merger will not give rise to the realization or crystallization of any 'built-in' capital gains. On the other hand, the assets and liabilities of the transferring GmbH can be introduced into the balance sheet of the acquiring company at market value and, in such instances, the transferring company must realize any built-in gains for tax purposes.

Where the base capital of the acquiring company has been increased and the amount paid for the transferred assets or shares plus any cash payments exceed the value of the assets as shown in the final balance sheet of the disposing company, the acquiring company has an option to include the excess amount as business or firm value (goodwill) (also described in the past as excess merger value) as a separate item. The value of goodwill on merger is subject to the same valuation principles as those which apply in cases of takeover or reorganization.

Goodwill

General

The terms '*Geschäftswert*' (business value) or '*Firmenwert*' (firm value) are synonymously used in the Federal Republic of Germany to describe the English expression 'goodwill'. The German terms, however, differentiate between original and derivative, namely acquired (for money or money's worth) goodwill.

Definitions

Goodwill is legally defined in section 153 IV of the German Company Law dating back to 1965. This legal definition has been introduced virtually unchanged in the new German Trade Law, section 255, IV HGB. In accordance therewith, the goodwill value is defined as the difference between 'the amount paid or rendered in money or money's worth and the value of the individual assets acquired by virtue of the takeover less any debts attributable thereto at the point in time of takeover'.

No corresponding definition of goodwill is found in German tax law, although, in principle, the definition has, in the judgement of the *Bundesfinanzhof* (Federal Tax Court), followed the trade law definition. It is, however, important to note that goodwill can only be acquired in the takeover of a going concern or in the acquisition of a '*Teilbetrieb*' – a part of a business which can operate independently as a separate entity. Where a going concern is acquired, but the intention is to close the business upon takeover, goodwill cannot be capitalized in the acquiring company's balance sheet. In such circumstances, the expense is basically viewed as costs incurred for the improvement of one's own goodwill, and such costs cannot be capitalized. German tax law differentiates between the terms '*Geschäftswert*' (business value), intangible assets and other similar 'goodwill'-type of assets. The allocation of values between such assets was, in the past, relevant from a tax point of view because of the varying types of capital allowance, i.e. depreciation available. The factors which are taken into account in determining the goodwill element of the business are, in accordance with previous court judgments, primarily the business name of the firm, the customers, the organization, the value of its advertising, and the firm's employees. Other 'goodwill'-type assets include, in particular, the rights to operate public transport, a freight business, i.e. rights to the transportation of goods or, for example, the right to operate as a chemist and, similarly, publishing rights and acquired account customers, i.e. 'regular' customers with standing agreements. The following expenses for non-tangible assets, which can normally be computed as a separate item, are not included as goodwill:

1. the acquisition of potential profits on or arising from uncompleted contracts, both as purchaser or seller;
2. the acquisition of sole distribution rights;
3. payments for the introduction to customers and other business contacts through the seller of the business;
4. expenses in connection with trade marks, patents, protective rights, unpatented inventions, know-how, ownership rights such as copyrights, and other non-personal concessions.

Is there a choice or an option to capitalize?

The treatment of acquired goodwill in the trading accounts differs considerably from the treatment applied thereto for tax purposes. In both instances, however, it is only possible to include acquired goodwill, so-called derivative goodwill, as a separate item in the balance sheet (section 248, II HGB in connection with section 5, II EStG Income Tax Law). An option to capitalize exists under section 255 IV HGB; once the option is exercised, the capitalized goodwill must be depreciated.

From a tax point of view, acquired goodwill must be capitalized. This obligation, based on sections 5 and 6 EStG *Income Tax Law* has been consequently substantiated by tax court judgments.

Depreciation

In the trade accounts (financial statements). In accordance with section 255, IV, sentence 2 HGB, the depreciation of goodwill is normally at least 25 per cent, so that, in general, the value is fully written off after a period of four years. One alternative is, however, to split the depreciation over the business years in which it is expected to be used or to be of use section 255, IV, sentence 3 HGB). This alternative has recently been introduced into the HGB (German Trade Law) and effectively provides the businessman with more flexibility in the depreciation of goodwill. These provisions apply equally to partnerships and corporations.

In the tax accounts. In the past, goodwill has not been treated as a depreciable asset for tax purposes (section 6 I and section 7 EStG). The German Federal Tax Court has, similarly, in tax case decisions, always upheld the view that goodwill must be regarded as a non-depreciable asset.

In amendments to the Income Tax Law, as introduced on 12 June 1985, goodwill has been listed as a depreciable asset for the first time. With effect from 1987, taxable persons will have the opportunity to depreciate goodwill over a period of 15 years (section 52, VI(a) EStG and section 7 I EStG).

The taxpayer also has the opportunity to depreciate goodwill by reference to the so-called '*Teilwert*'. As previously explained in a foregoing section, German tax law provides a specific definition for the term '*Teilwert*'. This is an amount equal to the price an acquirer would pay for the entire business, having computed the total purchase price by reference to the individual business assets, and under the assumption that the acquirer would continue to operate the business as a going concern (section 6, I EStG). In practice, it has always been difficult to substantiate this lower 'Teilwert' value. Consequently, later profits which are less than normal interest rates on the capital allocated to the business can be used to justify a tax write-off. Similarly, a tax depreciation will be allowed if the tax payer can prove that profits could generally be expected to be higher than those attained, or where it can be proven that the business has partly failed. Any subsequent reduction in the profitability of the enterprise can also necessitate a write-off.

Group or consolidated accounts

Is there an obligation to produce consolidated accounts?

Where one or more enterprises are under the unitary management of a domestic corporation and that the same corporation holds an interest in those enterprises (subsidiary companies), that holding corporate entity is obliged to draw up consolidated accounts consisting of a balance sheet, a profit and loss account with appendix, and an Annual Report (section 290, HGB). Where a foreign holding company prepares consolidated accounts and an Annual Report for the group, any intermediary domestic holding company will, under section 291, HGB, be exempt from the consolidation requirements and, similarly, the need for a consolidated audit. The results of subsidiary companies cannot be included in consolidated accounts if the activities of those companies differentiate to a large extent from the general group activities and the inclusion thereof would give a false or misleading picture of the assets, the financial position and the earnings capacity of the group.

There are basically two methods of consolidation available to those enterprises which are obliged to comply with the regulations. The options available to companies with associated enterprises, namely holdings of 20–50 per cent, are contained in sections 311 and 312 HGB. Shareholdings can be valued in accordance with the equity method, or can be included at book value.

Capital consolidation is governed by section 301, HGB. The shareholder's interest (share of equity) is to be consolidated by reference to either:

1. the book value; that is to say the book value of the business assets, debts, accruals and sundry items which are to be included in the consolidated accounts; or
2. a value equal to the acquisition cost or value of the above mentioned items at the date of acquisition (the new valuation method).

In the second alternative, the equity interest value cannot exceed the acquisition cost of the shares or interest involved.

The difference computed by reference to either of these methods should be included in the consolidated accounts under 'assets' as goodwill or, if necessary, amongst the liabilities as the difference arising in the capital consolidation.

In accordance with section 313, HGB, details of interests and shareholdings must be included in an appendix to the consolidated accounts. Unlike the consolidated accounts, the appendix detailing the ownership of shares does not need to be published in the *Bundesanzeiger* (Federal Business Gazette) but must be submitted to the Handelsregister.

International accounting standards (IASs)

A summary of the more important differences between German recommendations and international accounting standards is provided in Table 6.4.

Table 6.4 Comparison of German accounting practices with international accounting standards

International accounting standards	*Accounting recommendations in the FRG*
IAS 1 – Disclosure of accounting policies	
Requires comparative figures in all circumstances	Corporations are obliged to include the previous year's results in the balance sheet and

– *Continued*

Table 6.4 Continued

International accounting standards	*Accounting recommendations in the FRG*
	in the profit and loss statement. In certain circumstances, further details are to be included in an appendix (section 265, HGB)
IAS 2 – Valuation and presentation of inventories in the context of the historical cost system Requires valuation at the lower cost and net realizable value (NRV)	The cost of acquisition principle in conjunction with the so-called imparity principle applies equally for partnerships and corporations under section 253, HGB. Scheduled as well as extraordinary depreciation is statutory or optional. In principle, only corporations have the opportunity to carry out an upward revaluation, i.e. a restoration of value (sections 253 and 280, HGB). In consolidated accounting, the values of associated shareholdings can be determined by reference to the equity method
IAS 3 – Consolidated accounts Disclose names and description of significant subsidiaries and associated companies Additional disclosure where accounting policies are not uniform	Domestic corporations, which, in accordance with section 290, HGB, are to be regarded as a parent company, must prepare consolidated accounts and include in those accounts all domestic and foreign subsidiaries which are under common control and management. Subsidiaries are *inter alia* those enterprises in which the parent company holds a majority of the voting rights or where that parent company can exercise a controlling influence. The assets and liabilities of the subsidiary companies are, in principle, to be valued by reference to the same methods as those applied to the parent company as at the balance sheet date. Any variance in valuation methods must be reported and explained in the appendix to the accounts in accordance with section 308, HGB
IAS 4 – Depreciation accounting Disclose depreciation method, useful lives, depreciation rates and charge for the period for each major class of asset	Corporations are obliged to include, either in the balance sheet or in an appendix to the accounts, the developments reflected in the individual items of fixed assets and items covering 'expenses attributable to the expansion of the business and those of bringing a business into operation'; the so-called review of investment. In accordance with section 268, II HGB, all additions, disposals, adjustments and advances or write-ups within the trading year, as well as all amounts of depreciation, must be shown in detail, together with the entire acquisition costs and costs of manufacture
IAS 7 – Statement of changes in financial position Required statement	Prepared on a voluntary basis only

– *Continued*

Table 6.4 Continued

International accounting standards	*Accounting recommendations in the FRG*
IAS 9 – Accounting for research and development activities	
Permits, but does not require deferment of development costs when certain conditions are fulfilled	Whether or not the costs of research and development can be capitalized is a question for debate. At least, the costs for basic research cannot be capitalized. Expenses for new developments and the costs of further development can be included as current assets. The area of research and development of the group as a whole must be discussed in the company's annual report (section 315, HGB)
IAS 12 — Deferred and potential taxes	
Requires disclosure of (a) the tax effects, if any, related to assets that have been revalued to amounts in excess of historical cost or previous revaluation (b) the relationship betwen tax expense and accounting income, if the relationship is not obvious	Timing differences are usually not significant due to the similarity between the valuation of assets and liabilities for tax accounting purposes and their valuation for financial statement purposes. Corporations are obliged to include all deferred and potential taxes as a provision in liabilities; there is, however, an option rather than an obligation to capitalize any potential tax repayments
IAS 14 – Reporting financial information by segment	
Requires segmented information to be disclosed by enterprises whose securities are publicly traded and other economically significant entities including subsidiaries	In accordance with section 285 No. 4, HGB, corporations are obliged to show in an appendix to the accounts turnover as divided between the various trading activities in which they are engaged and an analysis of turnover according to geographically determined market areas, wherever there are large differences in the trading results of the markets in question. In accordance with section 315, HGB, groups are subject to the same provisions, so that similar details must be included in the appendix to consolidated accounts
IAS 15 – Information reflecting the effects of changing prices	
Requires disclosure, where material, of adjustments for changing prices on depreciation, cost of sales, monetary items and on overall effects of such adjustments. Such information is regarded as supplementary	There is no equivalent requirement
IAS 19 – Accounting for retirement benefits in the financial statements of employers	
Requires entities to charge past and prior service costs to expenses over a period which does not exceed the expected remaining working lives of the participating employees	Section 249, HGB, which became effective on 1 January 1986, provides a statutory obligation to itemize pension reserves as a liability; there are transitional provisions which must be observed with regard to existing pension obligations and liabilities

– Continued

Table 6.4 Continued

International accounting standards	*Accounting recommendations in the FRG*
IAS 20 – Accounting for government grants requires that (a) an enterprise should recognize government grants in income only when there is reasonable assurance that the grant will be received and comply with the conditions attached to it, (b) grants should be included in income in the same period as the relevant costs accrue, (c) grants related to assets should be accounted for either as deferred income or as deductions from related assets	The method of accounting for grants and other forms of public or state assistance is strongly influenced by the differing tax implications of the various forms of assistance available (HFA 1/1984) The accounting treatment which, therefore, varies considerably from case to case, is dependent upon the tax impact and similarly the effect the contribution will have on future profits demonstrating any potential impact the same may or is likely to have on future profits, can also be governed or influenced by the treatment of the assistance for tax purposes
IAS 21 – Accounting for the effects of changes in foreign exchange rates Transactions in foreign currency should be translated and recorded at the transaction rate or at the rate contracted to be settled in the future	There are no specific statutory provisions but, in general, the acquisition value principle and the so-called imparity principle are to be observed. A Statement of Practice discussing currency exchange is expected from the Institute of Accountants (*Institut der Wirtschaftsprüfer*) in the near future
IAS 23 – Capitalization of borrowing costs A consistent policy towards capitalization should be adopted	Liabilities are to be included as an amount equal to the anticipated capital repayment required. Pension obligations, in respect to which no further contributions are anticipated, are to be included at their cash value

Audit and publication

Medium-sized and large corporations are, under section 316 HGB, subject to a statutory audit. Consolidated accounts, including the corporate annual report, are subject to the same provisions. The audit must include a review of the bookkeeping and internal accounting procedures to ensure that all statutory requirements have been complied with, and to ensure that the Directors' Report accurately comments upon the duly audited financial statements. The auditors must also satisfy themselves that the Annual Report does not in any way present a false or misleading picture of the factual state of the business or enterprise (section 317, HGB).

The auditors must issue a statement confirming the accuracy of the final results, as shown in the accounts (Auditor's Report).

Corporations are obliged to submit the audited financial statements together with the Annual Report and the Directors' Report, including their suggested application of profits, to the *Handelsregister* (Commercial

Register). The corporation must, without delay, publish the *Handelsregister* address and reference number under which the accounts have been submitted in the *Bundesanzeiger* – the official Federal Gazette. Large corporations must, however, publish the accounts in the *Bundesanzeiger*, and submit notice of the publication to the Handelsregister. Similarly, consolidated and group accounts, together with the auditor's report, are to be published in the *Bundesanzeiger* (section 325, HGB).

Small and medium-sized corporations are, under sections 326 and 327 HGB, spared some of these rather far-reaching reporting requirements, some of which have been only recently introduced so that German domestic law corresponds to existing EEC directives.

6. EXCHANGE CONTROL AND FOREIGN INVESTMENT REGULATIONS

Introduction

The existing control regulations for cross-border capital transactions can be of great importance, particularly in the light of the noticeable increase in foreign business investment. These regulations should be regarded as an important factor to consider in any planned investment into the FRG.

General foreign investment regulations

The rules and regulations for the cross-border transfer of capital, monies, goods and services are contained in the *Außenwirtschaftsgesetz* (AWG) (Exchange Control Law) and the *Außenwirtschaftsverordnung* (AWV) (Exchange Control Regulations). The AWG was enacted in October 1961 and effectively repealed the very restrictive exchange control laws of the 1930s and the post-war years.

The FRG is included amongst the countries which enjoy a totally free money and capital market. The AWG, coupled with the AWV, is only intended to provide the scope for limitation or the regulation of money and capital transactions which would have a noticeable impact on the domestic economy. Up until now, the powers to regulate financial transactions have only been used in the period between 1970 and 1974.

The Exchange Control and Foreign Investment Regulations which are of significance for foreign investors wishing to invest in the FRG

Foreign investment into the FRG is not subject to any form of limitation. There is, however, an extensive system under which foreign investment must be registered, and it is extremely important to ensure that these regulations are complied with in every respect. Any non-compliance with the registration procedures will be dealt with accordingly, usually by the imposition of monetary fines. The transactions subject to registration include:

1. investment by foreign residents in assets situate within the domestic economy;
2. the formation or acquisition of business enterprises;
3. the establishment or acquisition of branch operations;
4. the establishment or acquisition of permanent establishments or places of business;
5. the acquisition of shares or interests in business enterprises;
6. supplying business enterprises, branches or places of business with investment funds or working capital or any other form of monetary advance;
7. guaranteeing loans to business enterprises which belong to the foreign lender or in which the same has a direct or indirect interest or where that same foreign lender, by virtue of guaranteeing the loan, can exercise a substantial influence on the management of the domestic business;
8. the sale of business enterprises, branches, permanent establishments or shares;
9. the liquidation of business enterprises, including the closure of branches, permanent establishments and other places of business;
10. the repayment of loan capital, when this has an impact on the domestic investment owned by foreign residents.

All capital investments in the FRG must be registered where the services or value provided in exchange for the consideration exceed DM20,000 in any one calendar year.

The registration requirements mentioned above must be complied with, within four weeks from the date of investment, through the Deutsche Bundesbank (German Federal Bank).

Foreign exchange payments

In addition to the registration procedures mentioned above, any investment by non-residents into the German domestic economy must be registered as a 'monetary transaction' with the Deutsche Bundesbank within four weeks from the date upon which the consideration in money or money's worth is received.

Submission of accounts

Foreign investors are also required to submit financial statements where the balance sheet of the enterprise in which the foreign investor holds an interest shows a value in excess of DM500,000 or where the foreign investor holds a minimum of 25 per cent of the voting rights or where several associated foreign investors together hold at least 25 per cent of the shares or voting rights in the domestic business. Details of the balance sheet must be submitted annually, on or before 30 June to the Deutsche Bundesbank.

Receivables and liabilities involving non-residents

Domestic businesses owned wholly or partly by foreign residents are also subject to exchange control procedures. The Bundesbank issues printed forms which can be used for the monthly reports businesses under foreign ownership are obliged to submit. The details required include the receivables from and accounts payable to foreign residents, as a result of transactions in goods or services with businesses outside of the FRG, where the amounts involved exceed, in total, DM500,000 at the end of each month.

7. OTHER FACTORS

Foreign investment into the FRG does not meet any local hostility. On the contrary, foreign investment is actively encouraged, particularly if such investment can create jobs or otherwise have a positive impact on the domestic economy.

The rights of employees, which exist under either domestic law or tariff agreements, remain unchanged in the event of share acquisition, merger or reorganization. Where only the assets and liabilities of an enterprise are acquired, the employee's rights remain protected since, under civil law, the employer's responsibilities are automatically transferred to the person acquiring the business (section 613a, *Bürgerlichen Gesetzbuch* – German Civil Law). Employees can, within a limited time period, object or appeal against a transfer of their rights and responsibilities, but this is, in practice, of little significance. On the other hand, the transfer of employee rights under the terms of existing contracts of employment may need to be avoided, particularly if the person acquiring the business needs to move the enterprise to another locality or where rationalization is needed. In these cases, it is necessary to structure agreements so that the cost of acquisition of the business effectively reflects the cost of reducing the workforce; that is to say, the cost of redundancy payments is duly taken into consideration at the time of acquisition. In some cases, the acquiring enterprise could arrange for the seller to bear the costs of any necessary rationalization, such as a reduction in the workforce, prior to or in the pursuance of the transfer of the business.

Similarly, the acquisition of shares or a participating interest in an enterprise does not bring about any change in agreements already in force with regard to employee benefits. This can often give rise to practical problems, particularly where the company under acquisition is being merged into a group or concern which operates a different employee benefit structure.

Where assets and liabilities are acquired it is usually necessary to change existing agreements on employee benefits and it may also be necessary to make changes to such items as pension provisions, paying due consideration to the legal aspects which will need attention as a result of the acquisition, and the tax implications involved.

In general it is important to note that employee rights and benefits already in existence prior to a change in ownership cannot be restricted in any extensive way and, in principle, existing rights and benefits must continue to be offered and must be seen to be protected.

The above-mentioned provisions do, of course, equally apply to German investors and, therefore, do not in any way represent any form of discrimination towards the foreign investor.

SUMMARY

In many respects, German business could be viewed as extremely conservative, because the personnel and the owners of business enterprise, who are primarily responsible for making any political or economic business decision, generally ensure that they are personally involved in the necessary preliminary research in order to be fully informed before coming to any conclusion. On the other hand, German business contains a spirit of adventure which dates back not only to the early days of emigration of German nationals to the US and Canada, but even further back to the middle ages, when Germany was regarded as one of the foremost international trading nations.

Although this book will certainly be of interest to those involved in German business at a domestic level, but with an interest in international expansion, perhaps this section, covering the FRG, will be of particular interest to those wishing to invest into Germany.

The FRG should not be viewed simply as one of the markets within the EEC. By virtue of the FRG's special connections to the German Democratic Republic (East Germany), Germany is the only country which offers tax and other incentives to enterprises doing business with the GDR and via the GDR into other eastern bloc, iron curtain countries. The FRG could, therefore, be used as a base or inroad into these markets. The Federal Government and the local authorities, namely the governments of the German States (Länder), are actively encouraging such trade links, particularly through the medium of a joint venture.

In addition, it should not be forgotten that Germany is geographically central in Europe and has excellent road, air and rail connections to other countries. English has long since been recognized as the internationally accepted business language, and, indeed, it is now a compulsory subject for schoolchildren from the age of 11 onwards.

In considering investment into the FRG even multinational corporations should not overlook the medium of a partnership as the possible choice of business structure. Partnerships form part of the discussion, particularly in sections 4 and 5 on taxation and accounting, since most German business, apart from that of the very large corporations, is conducted through the medium of a partnership. In certain circumstances, a limited partnership structure could be of benefit, particularly from a tax standpoint, in comparison to the establishment or formation of a local subsidiary corporation.

7
France

1. BUSINESS ORGANIZATIONS AND COMBINATIONS

Business organizations

SA/SARL

The most important and most commonly used form of business organization is the corporation (*société anonyme*, or SA). However, smaller companies, particularly sales subsidiaries, often take the form of a limited liability company (*société à responsabilité limitée*, or SARL). SARLs may not issue securities to the public, and transfers of their shares are restricted. Table 7.1 summarizes the requirements of SAs and SARLs.

Branch operations

Foreign companies often use the branch form for headquarters operations in France but seldom for sizeable sales operations and almost never for manufacturing operations.

To establish a branch in France, copies of the articles of incorporation and the by-laws of the foreign company must be submitted to the commercial court in whose jurisdiction the branch is to be located. Before it can do business, the company must enter its name in the Commercial Register and make a declaration to the tax authorities. If the branch is managed by a non-EEC national, the necessary business card must be secured.

Branches are governed by almost the same tax and accounting rules as corporations, as described above. For more specific tax considerations see section (4).

Partnerships and joint ventures

This category includes general partnerships (*Sociétés en Nom Collectif*) limited partnerships (*Sociétés en Commandite simple*), joint ventures

Table 7.1 Requirements of SAs and SARLs in France

	SA	*SARL*
Capital	Minimum is FF1.5 million if publicly owned: otherwise, FF250,000	Minimum is FF50,000
	If the capital is reduced to an amount less than the required minimum and the company is not changed into another form of organization, the capital must be increased to at least the minimum amount within one year. Otherwise, any interested party may demand that the company be dissolved	Same rules in the event that capital falls below the required minimum
	If, because of losses recorded in the company's accounts, the net assets of an SA fall below one-half the amount of its capital, a shareholder meeting must decide either to dissolve the company, or, no later than the close of the second financial year following that in which the recording of the losses took place, to reduce the amount of its capital accordingly. Otherwise, any interested party may demand that the company be dissolved	Same rules in the event of losses
	Capital contributions in kind: for publicly listed companies, they must be evaluated by an official court-appointed appraiser and approved by a founders' assembly: for non-public companies, court-appointed appraiser's evaluation must be approved by signature of each founder. Five per cent of annual distributable profits must be set aside in a legal reserve until such a reserve equals 10 per cent of capital	Capital contributions in kind are approved by a court-appointed appraiser or by an appraiser appointed unanimously by founders (who may question the evaluation and appoint a new appraiser). Founders are responsible for evaluation for five years. Reserve requirements are the same as for SAs

Founders, shareholders	Minimum is seven. No restrictions as to nationality or residency	Minimum is two, maximum 50. No nationality or residency requirements
Board of directors, management	Either (1) a single board consisting of elected shareholders (*conseil d'administration*) whose chairman (*président director général*) is chosen by the board and has complete management responsibility – although he may delegate authority to one executive (or two if capital is at least FF500,000) who need not be a board member – or (2) a dual management system consisting of a board (*conseil de surveillance*) and an executive committee (*directoire*) or two to five executives for, alternatively, one general manager and a board in a company with capital of less than FF250,000). These executives are nominated by the board, are not board members, and administer and direct the company's operations under the control of the board. The executive committee votes by majority and is represented by its president in dealings with outsiders (unless the board rules otherwise). Individual members have four-year terms, which can be revoked by shareholders. Boards of directors under both systems must have three to twelve members (may be more after merger), who must own shares but who need not be French citizens or residents. Under a single-board system, one-third of the board may be salaried employees, whereas under dual system, board members may not be employees (though they can be compensated for special *ad hoc* assignments). There are no nationality or residency requirements. No person may be a member of more than eight boards. (This does not apply to insurance companies or banks.)	One or several managers (*gérants*) who must be persons, not entities. They need not be shareholders. They are elected by majority of capital, or as provided for in the articles of association

– Continued

Table 7.1 Continued

	SA	*SARL*
	If any of the following executives of an SA are foreigners, they must obtain a business card (*carte de commerçant étranger*) unless they are nationals of another EEC member country: president/general manager, president of the executive committee (*directoire*): or general manager(s) of an SA with a dual management system	Any SARL manager who is a foreigner must obtain a *carte de commerçant étranger* unless he is a national of another EEC member country
	Special procedures involving notification and authorization apply to all transactions or agreements (other than those relating to current operations and concluded under normal conditions: 1. between the company and a member of its board of directors, a member of its *directoire* or supervisory council, or one of its general managers; or 2. in which one of the above-mentioned persons is indirectly interested or by which one of them deals with the company through a nominee; or 3. between the company and another enterprise in which a member of its board of directors, a member of its *directoire* or one of its general managers is an owner, partner, manager, member of the *directoire* or supervisory council, or general manager	Special procedures involving notification and approval of shareholders, either directly or through a nominee, apply to all transactions or agreements: 1. between the company and one of its managers or shareholders, either directly or through a nominee; or 2. with another company in which one of the managers or shareholders of the SARL is a partner, manager, director, general manager, or member of the *directoire* or supervisory council
	A company cannot in any way whatsoever make loans to or guarantee undertakings of physical persons who are members of its board of directors, members of the *directoire* or supervisory council, or its general managers	A company cannot in any way whatsoever make loans to or guarantee undertakings of its managers or shareholders (or of their spouses, ascendants, descendants or nominees)

Labour	In companies with more than 50 employees, workers-elect every two years a *Comité d'Entreprise* (works council). It is compulsory to inform and take the opinion of this council on any important decision involving the organization, the employment, the management, or the administration of the company More particularly, the *Comité d'Entreprise* writes the annual report on the development of employment during the previous year and the year to come, and this report is transmitted to the competent Administration In order to allow the *Comité* to hold its office, the members are provided a monthly time credit, premises, and basic equipment	Same
Disclosure	All SAs appoint auditors at annual shareholder meetings. Non-public SAs need not publish annual statements, but must deposit their balance sheet and P&L statement with the local commercial court; anyone may consult these records. Publicly owned SAs must publish an annual balance sheet, a P&L statement, quarterly sales figures for each line of business and semiannual provisional balance sheet. Subsidiaries of such companies with assets of FF10 million or more, or portfolios of FF1 million or more, must publish the same information	All SARLs with capital of more than FF300,000 must have a registered auditor. Manager is obliged to reveal all relevant business at an annual meeting to which all shareholders must be invited

– *Continued*

Table 7.1 Continued

	SA	*SARL*
Taxes and fees on incorporation	One per cent on capital in cash and value of capital contributions in kind (and 11.4 per cent transfer tax if such contribution consists of real estate or goodwill), plus, in both cases, local tax on real estate varying, according to the region, from 1 to 1.6 per cent. FF350 fee for registration, plus possible notary fees based on amount of capital (at same rates as for SARLs, shown at right)	Same as for SA, with possible notary fees (based on capital) as follows: *Capital* (FF) — *Fees* (%) 0– 250,000 — 0.75 250,001– 750,000 — 0.25 750,001– 3,600,000 — 0.15 3,600,001– 7,250,000 — 0.06 7,250,001–36,000,000 — 0.03 36,000,000–72,500,000 — 0.015 More than 72,500,000
Types of shares	Both registered and bearer shares permissible. However, shares of non-public companies were required to be placed in their bearer's name by October 1982 All shares and stocks issued in the French territory must be recorded in the accounts maintained by the issuing entity or by an authorized agent Nonvoting shares may be issued only if they are preferred stock, subject to certain limitations under the law. However, registered shares with double voting rights are permitted if they are entirely paid up and have been held for more than two years. (The holding of such shares may be limited to shareholders who are nationals of EEC member countries.) Minimum nominal share value is FF100	No certificates are issued to shareholders of SARLs. Shareholders' rights are described in the company's by-laws

	The articles of incorporation may require that the company's consent be obtained for any transfer of shares to a third party	A shareholder who wishes to sell out his interest is limited by law and the company's by-laws. Generally, he must give other shareholders three months' notice, in which time the latter must indicate if they want to purchase the interest (which must be done in another three months)
Control	Shareholders who represent more than 50 per cent of the company's capital may dismiss the president/general manager at will Shareholders who represent 10 per cent of the company's capital may sue in the commercial court to have the registered auditor replaced or to engage an independent expert to study certain operations of the company. Shareholders representing 5 per cent of capital (or less in large companies) may propose company board resolutions	Same rules as for SAs

(*Sociétés en Participation*), civil companies (*Sociétés civiles*) and joint ventures 'with a common economic interest' (*Groupements d'Intérêt Economique*).

General partnerships. The most important partnership is the general partnership which has two main features. First, a general partnership is always considered to be a commercial entity, whatever its aim; and secondly, the name of each partner must be known (principle of *Intuitus Personae*) as liability is joint and several.

One of the main advantages of a general partnership in comparison to SAs or SARLs is that the partnership may consist of only two individuals. Furthermore, the establishment and management rules are less onerous and less expensive. From a taxation point of view it may be advantageous for a group to have its subsidiaries incorporated as general partnerships in order to be able to consider profits or losses at the parent company's level. The aim of this form of organization is, therefore, to achieve a form of 'tax consolidation' since there are no group taxation provisions similar to those of the UK.

One of the disadvantages of a general partnership is that for certain major decisions, such as the sale of shares (even between partners), the departure of a partner or the dismissal of a manager, unanimous agreement between the partners is required.

Joint ventures 'with a common economic interest'. Joint ventures with a common economic interest (*Groupements d'Intérêt Economique*, or GIE) aim to allow their members to co-operate in developing a particular activity. There are no limitations on the scope of activities of a GIE and its fundamental objective will be the continuation of the economic activity of its members. The main feature of a GIE is that almost all administration rules are defined by founder members in the by-laws. A GIE may be created with or without a capital, or even with an open-ended capital but the interests of the members may, in no circumstances, correspond to negotiable stocks. GIEs are created for a limited period and their members (two at least) are liable without limitation and jointly for the debts of the entity.

The process of allocating expenses is defined in the by-laws; it may be according to each member's share in the joint venture, or according to sales volume. The taxation environment is the same as for general partnerships which have not elected for a corporate income tax assessment.

A joint venture ('Société en participation'). A *société en participation* is a silent partnership and is not a legal entity. It has, therefore, no share capital, no legal commitment towards a third person, it is not allowed to bring an action, and cannot be subject to a legal recovery plan.

It may either be a trade or a civil company, depending on its aim. In fact, the joint venture is mainly founded on the personality of each partner.

A key feature of a joint venture is that it enables partners to keep their association unknown, and avoids all formalities related to legal entities: partners are only responsible for a simple contract.

From a tax standpoint, joint ventures are taxed at the partners' level, except if they elect for a corporate income taxation assessment.

As far as the registration tax and value added tax are concerned, the rules are the same as for other companies.

The *de facto* company (*Société créée de fait*). Where parties behave towards a third person as if they were partners, it is possible to consider that they have formed a *de facto* company. In determining the existence of a société créée de fait the following three criteria are taken into account: the existence of a contribution, the sharing of the benefits, and the following of a common activity.

This concept is mostly used in case of a legal claim. A creditor may, for instance, bring an action against all the partners for a liability contracted by one of them, even if such a company is not a legal entity.

A *de facto* company, identified as such by the tax authorities, is assessed to corporation tax.

Business reorganizations

When reorganizing a business, many companies may have social or fiscal advantages in changing the type of legal structure of their business organization, or in combining such changes with other acquisitions or disposals.

From a legal standpoint, the transformation of the legal structure of a company does not result in the creation of a new entity; it is a bare modification of the by-laws. It is, therefore, subject to the same announcement requirements. The transformation of the legal structure brings the powers of the board of directors to an end but it does not imply a settlement of account, and the prior creditors retain their rights unchanged.

From a tax standpoint, the transformation is subject to a lump-sum tax of FF410 but the tax may be heavier if a company, not subject to corporate income tax, is changed into a company subject to this tax. In the case where an SA or SARL becomes a partnership, the transformation will be taxed to the extent of profits for the period except if the partnership elects for a corporate income tax assessment as soon as it is created.

Where an SARL is transferred into an SA a general report of the state of the SARL must be prepared by an auditor. It is submitted on the condition that the two previous balance sheets of the SARL have been approved by the shareholders. If the SARL is less than two years old, two balance sheets can be established for shorter accounting periods. An audit of the assets is required in order to certify that the amount of equity is at least equal to the amount of share capital. The specific rules governing SAs have to be met (seven shareholders at least, minimum capital of FF250,000, minimum nominal share value of FF100). The transformation is then decided by a majority representing 75 per cent of the shares during a general shareholders meeting.

Unless otherwise stated in the by-laws, a transformation of a general partnership into an SARL requires unanimous agreement of the partners.

After the transformation, the share capital has to amount to FF50,000 and be wholly paid up.

The transformation of an SARL into any other form of corporate organization requires a prior report on the state of the SARL by an auditor. If the SARL is to be changed into a partnership, unanimous agreement of the partners is required.

In order to transform an SA into any other form of corporate organization it is required that the SA is at least two years old, and that the balance sheets of its two first periods have been approved by the shareholders. Auditors must be appointed to certify that the amount of equity is at least equal to the amount of the share capital.

In the case where an SA is to be transformed into a partnership, unanimous agreement of the shareholders is required.

If the SA is to be changed into an SARL, the decision will be taken by a majority representing 75 per cent of the shares. The specific rules governing SARLs must be respected: minimum share capital of FF50,000, wholly paid up; no more than 50 shareholders; and the scope of activity has to meet the SARL requirements.

The transformation of a corporate entity into a GIE is possible under the condition that the aim of the corporate entity meets the requirements mentioned in the paragraph above. This transformation does not result in the winding-up of the corporate entity, nor in the creation of a new entity. Nevertheless, from a tax point of view, the transformation of a share company into a GIE is taxed as a winding-up. The transformation of a GIE into a company results in the winding-up of the GIE and the creation of a new entity. It is therefore heavily taxed.

Types of business combinations

The most common forms used in business combinations are on-going business transfers, acquisition of shares, mergers and joint ventures.

On-going business transfers

On-going businesses (going concerns) include intangible assets (mainly clientele and patents), tangible assets, such as equipment and fixtures, and products themselves. The transfer may concern only some of these elements, but should at least include the clientele. Where an on-going business is purchased or deemed to be purchased it is subject to a registration tax at the rate of 16.60 per cent, less an allowance of FF50,000 on the price if it does not exceed FF200,000. The tax is raised on the fair market value of the assets transferred.

From a legal point of view, it should be noted that when acquiring an on-going business the purchaser assumes all the liabilities that may be contingent to the net assets acquired.

A partial business transfer is an operation by which a company transfers a part of its assets representing the element of an activity as a whole to another company, in return for shares or cash from the recipient company.

The recipient company may exist before the operation or be created simultaneously with the operation. Partial business transfers may, under certain conditions, take advantage of the same tax treatment as mergers themselves.

Acquisition of shares

The purchase of shares of a company in order to take control or to influence its management and to draw a benefit is a common process. The expected benefit is often an economic one such as improved reliability of supply, or an enlargement of the market. The shares may be purchased either when the target company is incorporated, or by subscribing to a capital increase, or during the normal activity with the agreement of the main shareholders, or through a takeover bid. When the acquiring entity is a foreign company, the operation has to meet the rules governing foreign investment in France.

An efficient and speedy process to achieve such business combinations consists of takeover bids. Typically an entity informs the shareholders of a company that it is ready to buy their securities for a determined price, either for cash (*Offre Publique d'Achat*, OPA) or for securities (*Offre Publique d'Exchange*, OPE). The offer must be for at least 10 per cent of the share capital of the target company, or 5 per cent if it amounts to more than FF10 million.

The documents relative to the takeover bid are submitted first to the Stock Exchange Committee, then to the Ministry of Economy. The delay for the Ministry to censure the operation is three days. When the takeover bid is accepted, it has to be notified to the Stock Exchange and the respective companies inform their shareholders.

The operation is under the control of the Stock Exchange Committee. The purchasing company may increase the number of shares or the price of the offer, under the condition that the modification represents at least 5 per cent of the previous offer and occurs at least twenty days before the deadline. Rival offers must comply with the same rules; they must represent at least 5 per cent more than the initial offer, and occur at least 20 days before its deadline.

Mergers and splits

A merger is an operation which results either in the absorption of one or several companies by another one, or in the winding-up of two (or more) companies and the creation of a new entity. In the former case, the absorbed companies are dissolved, while the assets of the acquiring company increase. In the latter case, all the companies are dissolved and they transfer their assets to the newly created entity. Both processes have the same tax effects, but the former is far more commonly used.

A split consists in the absorption of a whole company by two or more entities simultaneously. The integrating entities may exist before the split or be newly created companies. The absorbed company is dissolved and its assets and liabilities are totally transferred to the integrating entities. From a tax standpoint, splits may, under agreement, take advantage of the same treatment as mergers.

From a legal standpoint all these processes involve a universal transfer of patrimony of the old entities to the new one(s) which will assume all their rights and obligations.

Social aspects of changes resulting from business combinations

Under French legislation, all the labour contracts remain unchanged between the new employer and the staff regardless of the type of change in corporate structure. Unchanged means the same terms and same conditions with respect to qualifications, wages and all rights connected with seniority.

2. TRENDS IN TAKEOVER ACTIVITY

The number of takeovers and mergers has considerably increased in France since the late 1970s especially those which involve foreign companies. In 1985, 244,850 businesses were either created or purchased and of the total 29 per cent involved trading firms, 48.5 per cent involved service industries and the remaining 22.5 per cent in the primary sector.

The two major reasons for a company to integrate with another company are to increase its market share (42 per cent) and to achieve diversification (39 per cent). As for the acquirer, it is noticeable that in 61 per cent of the cases declining firms are purchased. The number of bankrupt firms is also increasing, even if in smaller proportions: 26,425 bankruptcies in 1985 consisting of 27 per cent in trading activities, 35 per cent in the service sector and 38 per cent in primary industries.

The special tax incentives for the recovery of declining firms are described in section (4).

A main feature of mergers and acquisitions in France is the large size of the companies in search of takeovers in comparison with the small size of the companies to be acquired. The small firm sector probably accounts for about 45 per cent of the French Gross National Product with some six million employees in approximately 15,000 entities. Whilst there is a lack of a market for takeovers in this area the significance of transfers might be considerable. If 1500 entities were transferred each year the sector would be extinguished in ten years which may have a considerable impact on employers and especially managers where 50 per cent are 50 years or older.

Although new possibilities do arise (Over-the-Counter Market for instance), these operations remain limited because of the administration and tax burden of the changes implied.

In 1986, the number and, more importantly, the size of takeover bids in France has considerably increased. Major takeovers included a battle with the Compagnie du Midi to take over La Providence, and the purchase of General Biscuit by BSN. Furthermore there have been hostile takeovers including foreign companies. For instance, in a battle to acquire Presses de la Cite, a leading French publisher, the parties involved included Goldsmith's La Général Occidentale. Sir James Goldsmith eventually completed the acquisition successfully.

Italian companies have been particularly active in the French takeover market and also in setting up joint centres, for example Fiat. French companies have been increasingly aware of their vulnerability and may have strengthened their defensive armoury. For example, Moët Hennessy, the cognac group, recently made a Eurofranc bond issue of FF800 million aimed at strengthening its financial position and to gather resources for future acquisitions.

French companies have also been active in acquiring companies abroad, particularly in the US. For instance, L'Air Liquide made by largest acquisition in the US by a French company by acquiring Big Three Industries for US$1.066 million. In the past most takeover bids were exchange offers and were not particularly attractive to shareholders as the exchanged securities often fell when the transaction was completed. Furthermore, hostile takeovers were not common. However, the French takeover market is becoming more aggressive with hostile bids and increasing interest in such transactions by the shareholder community. Deregulation in the capital markets and increasing interest in global markets has meant that acquisitions are becoming more popular, hostile takeovers acceptable, and international acquisitions more common. The increasing interest in the Paris stock exchange has meant realignment of some securities to reflect more accurately the actual value of those companies.

3. MERGER CONTROL

Merger control consists of domestic curbs and EEC supervision. EEC merger controls are dealt with in chapter 3.

Until 1977, France had adopted an encouraging attitude to industrial concentration in the belief that large firms are better able to compete in international markets. Previously, controls were only placed on some restrictive practices whose object was to control a market.

Act No. 7-806 of 19 July 1977 on the control of economic concentration and prevention of unlawful cartels and abuses of dominant positions imposed some control on mergers. The Act aims to ensure that arm's-length competition exists rather than to try to restrain mergers themselves. The only operations that may be controlled are ones which meet the following three conditions:

1. They must arise from a legal deed between independent companies and result in either a transfer of property or rights of a part or whole of an enterprise, for example by a merger, partial business transfer,

acquisition of shares or by the creation of common subsidiaries. Alternatively, there must be a legal deed between independent companies which results in the possibility that a company can influence the management of another company such as by exercising an element of direction over financial policy.
2. The integration has to exceed two criteria. First, if the integrated companies have the same scope of activities (same type of products or services-horizontal acquisition) and the parties involved would have annual sales volume of at least 40 per cent of the national market. Secondly, where the integrated companies are not in the same market the limit is 25 per cent each of a national market. All companies financially connected to the integrating enterprises are to be taken into consideration.
3. The economic operation is pursuant to a restraint in normal competition. However, where the integration may bring economic or social gains then these should be weighed against the adverse impact on competition. If the gains exceed the costs the company would not be penalized.

The law of 19 July 1977 directed the Commission for Competition to participate and offer advice, and also to give opinions on all competitive matters laid before it by the government; to perform the functions defined by the present law concerning control of concentration; and to repress illegal cartels and abuses of dominant positions. With regard to the last point, fines may be imposed for an abuse of a dominant position. Section 4 of Title II of the Act contains the definition:

> A concentration for the purposes of the present title shall be the result of any legal act or transaction whatever the form adopted, involving transfer of ownership or tenure of all or part of the goods, rights and obligations of an enterprise or having the object or effect, of enabling one enterprise or a group of enterprises to exercise an influence, directly or indirectly, on one or more other enterprises which is of such a nature as to direct or even orientate the management of working of the latter.

The Commission consists of a chairman, who is chosen from members of the Council of State, and the Magistrates of the administrative or judicial order. The chairman is assisted by a General Reporter and both positions are full time. In addition, there are a number of part-time reporters.

A case can be put to the Commission in four different ways:

1. by the minister in charge of the economy;
2. on its own initiative;
3. by plaintiffs;
4. by jurisdictions: the courts can ask the Commission for advice on cases involving anti-competitive practices.

Unlawful concentration on its own is not a criminal offence, and where sanctions are applied they are purely administrative. If the Minister for the Economy makes a decision on concentration, an appeal may be made to the highest administrative court, the Conseil d'Etat.

Where the level of concentration is unacceptable, the Minister for the Economy must adopt one of five injunctions which seek to:

1. prevent the merger from being completed;
2. re-establish the legal position existing before the merger;
3. change the value of the merger;
4. take measures to ensure that an adequate degree of competition exists;
5. make a contribution to social or economic welfare if competition has been reduced.

However, the Minister cannot exceed the advice of the Commission but can be less strict. If the companies involved do not comply with the decision of the Minister a financial sanction can be imposed of up to 5 per cent of turnover.

There are two elements of control. First, control may be exercised before a merger takes place, if the participants inform the authorities of their proposal. The companies implicated in an integration may elect to notify the operatives within three months of the deed although notification is only required in the case of takeover bids or Exchange Offers. Where notification occurs, the Minister has three months within which to make a decision. The Minister may say nothing (in which case he implicitly approves); he may say that he has no objection; or he may refer the case to the Commission. Where a reference is made to the Commission, a decision must be made within eight months of notification. In contrast, if a reference is made by the state, there is no time limit for a decision.

The second element is that a reference may be made at the initiative of ministers. There are two types of inquiry: *ad hoc* inquiry and the inquiries of observation. The latter type is conducted continuously in areas of high concentration based on the percentage control thresholds already outlined.

Stock exchange control

In addition to legal control over abuses of economic concentration, there are general rules issued by the Stock Exchange Brokers Association, Compagnie des Agents de Change. These rules are designed to protect minority shareholders, although where a bid is acceptable to 90 per cent of the victim's shareholders, the minority are obliged to sell at a fair price.

An essential feature of the code is that secrecy must be observed until the public is made aware of the offer. Once the offer is made public, the acquirer must state how he intends to finance the acquisition and both parties must provide financial statements and prudent forecasts. Partial bids may be made, provided that the offer is for at least 10 per cent of share capital, or at least 5 per cent where the bid exceeds FF10 million.

During the period up to ten days before the bid is completed, it is possible for a counter-offer to be made, provided it is for the same number of shares and is at least 5 per cent above the first offer price.

Where shares are purchased on the Stock Exchange, notification of purchases greater than 10 per cent of the share capital must be provided within five working days to comply with regulations of the Stock Exchange supervisory body, the Commission des Opérations de Bourse (COB).

4. TAXATION

Background

The French tax system is largely codified in the General Tax Code (Code Général des Impôts). French taxes may be divided into three main types: direct taxes (on income and assets), indirect taxes (on transactions) and registration taxes (fees or duties).

Direct taxes include the following:

1. corporate income tax (including capital gains tax)
2. individual income tax (including capital gains tax)
3. professional tax, levied on all nonagricultural business enterprises
4. payroll and other taxes on business enterprises
5. various other municipal and local taxes.

Indirect taxes include value-added tax (VAT), a tax on financial transactions, and taxes levied on sales of certain products (alcoholic beverages, petroleum products, tobacco, etc.). VAT is the single most important source of revenue in the French tax system.

Registration taxes are levied on transfers of certain assets or rights for value received, on the formation or reorganization of companies, and on transfers by deed or gift.

The income tax system

Individual income tax is levied on a worldwide basis, while corporate income tax follows the principle of territoriality. Both the corporate and individual income taxes include special provisions for the taxation of capital gains.

The French income tax system differs from the 'classic' model mainly in its use of the 'avoir fiscal' approach, through which a company's shareholders receive a credit against their individual income tax liability for their proportionate share of corporate income taxes paid. Companies are subject primarily to corporate income tax and to VAT, as well as to the business tax. If dividends are distributed, an equalization tax (*précompte mobilier*) may be payable under certain circumstances.

Payments to foreign recipients are generally subject to withholding tax at source.

Income taxation – companies

French corporations (*sociétés anonymes*, or SAs), private limited liability companies (*sociétés à responsabilité limitée*, or SARLs) and limited parnerships with shares (*sociétés en commandite par actions*) that are organized under French law are subject to the full scope of French taxation. Because the French tax laws embrace the principle of territoriality, however, as described below, the income of foreign branches or other permanent establishments of French corporations and other legal entities are generally not subject to French income tax when earned.

General partnerships (*sociétés en nom collectif*), ordinary limited partnerships (*sociétés en commandite simple*), and joint ventures (*sociétés en participation*) may choose either to have their income to be subject to corporate income tax or to have each partner be personally liable to individual income tax on his proportionate share of their income. Under certain circumstances, SARLs owned by members of a single family can elect to be taxed as partnerships.

Principle of territoriality

As indicated above, the French corporate income tax is levied on the net taxable income derived from all of a company's commercial and industrial activities conducted in French territory, including capital gains as well as income from operations. Income realized or losses incurred by French companies that are attributable to foreign operations conducted through permanent establishments abroad are not normally subject to the French corporate income tax, nor may they be offset against income realized in France. Because of the principle of territoriality, France does not allow any tax credit for foreign income taxes paid on the business income of a foreign permanent establishment. Thus, French companies may retain and invest income from their foreign branches or subsidiaries without the incidence of French income tax. If such untaxed foreign earnings are distributed to shareholders, however, the French company must pay a special levy, the précompte mobilier (discussed later), which may be recoverable by certain shareholders who reside in a country that has an income tax treaty with France. The précompte mobilier due when the distribution of foreign earnings is made is reduced by the amount of the withholding tax paid in the country of origin.

The principle of territoriality applies only to the business income of a foreign permanent establishment. It does not apply to dividends or interest from foreign sources, which are subject to French income tax when earned. In addition, the principle of territoriality does not apply under the following circumstances:

1. If the company has received authorization to consolidate the accounts of its foreign branches, foreign subsidiaries and/or other overseas entities.
2. If application has been made, and approval received, to deduct the start-up losses of a foreign branch or subsidiary.

Start-up losses of foreign branches or subsidiaries

A French company may apply to the Ministry of Economy for authorization to deduct the start-up losses of certain foreign branches or foreign subsidiaries for the first five years of their operation. The deduction for these losses, if approved, must be added back to the company's income over the succeeding five-year period. In practice, such permission is never granted, however, to foreign-controlled companies.

Rates of tax

The normal rate of the French corporate income tax is 45 per cent of a company's net taxable income, whether or not distributed. The former rate for periods beginning before 1 January 1986 was 50 per cent. Preferential rates are applicable to certain long-term capital gains (15 per cent in general, 25 per cent on development land) and special tax reserves.

An important feature is that all entities subject to corporate income tax must pay a minimum tax (IFA: *Imposition Forfaitaire Annuelle*) which varies according to the company's annual turnover, from FF4000 to FF17,000.

Period of limitations

The period of limitations provides, as a general rule, that the delay for the Tax Administration to propose adjustments expires at the end of the third calendar year following the year income tax relates to. This rule applies to income taxes, payroll taxes, VAT, registration and stamp duties (for registration and stamp duties, the normal period can be extended to ten years in the event of failure to report). The period of limitations may be extended an additional two years in the case of fraud.

Determination of taxable income

Taxable income is defined as the total amount of income (less appropriate deductions) derived from the taxpayer's normal business activities in France, including fixed-asset disposals, receipts of rents and interest, and foreign-exchange gains. Deductions are usually normal business expenses, including interest, royalties, reasonable management fees paid to a foreign parent, wages, salaries, repairs and maintenance, and most taxes. Taxable income must be stated in French francs.

Although French accounting principles are the basis for determining taxable income, there are instances in which taxable income and accounting income will differ as a result of the autonomy of the French tax laws. The more significant differences are noted below.

Inventories (stock)

Acceptable methods of inventory valuation are limited to the average-weighted-price method or any comparable method, such as FIFO, that will produce similar results. The LIFO method is not acceptable.

Inventories must appear on the balance sheet at cost. If current market value is lower than cost, a reserve for inventory depreciation may be shown separately as a deduction from cost. Depreciated inventories may also be shown at market value, provided that the depreciation is disclosed in a special reserve schedule in the tax return.

Securities

A distinction is made between short-term investments or marketable securities (*titres de placement*) and long-term investments (*titres de participation*). Securities are shown on the balance sheet at the lower of cost or market value and unrealized profits are ignored. The provision for unrealized depreciation of securities (of both kinds) is not deductible in arriving at current taxable income. The provision is considered a long-term capital loss that can be offset only against long-term capital gains.

Fixed assets

Fixed assets are stated at cost unless they have been revalued in compliance with the law, in which case they are recorded at the revalued amount. A revaluation may have the effect of reducing otherwise expiring loss carryovers because the amount by which the assets have been revalued may be used to offset the losses.

Depreciation must be charged on all tangible assets, immoveable or moveable, that are owned by and used in the business, when the useful life of such assets exceeds one year. Land is the only exception to this rule.

Intangible assets may also be depreciated if their useful lives are known in advance (e.g. patents) or if the value of the business as a whole has been reduced and a substantial decrease in profits can be demonstrated (goodwill, trademarks). Organization expenses are depreciable over three years for tax purposes.

The minimum straight-line depreciation allowance which is mandatory for all depreciable assets (except organization expenses), may be lost for tax purposes if it is not computed and shown as such in a company's tax return. Either the straight-line or the declining balance depreciation method may be used for fixed assets and companies may choose between the two methods on an asset-by-asset basis. It is possible to change methods for tax purposes, but companies contemplating such a change should consider the accounting as well as the tax consequences.

Only the straight-line depreciation method may be applied to use assets. The types of assets (which must have been purchased new, not second-hand) to which the declining-balance method may be applied are identified in the tax law and include machinery and equipment used in manufacturing, handling, storage and warehousing operations.

Doubtful accounts

To be deductible for tax purposes, a provision for doubtful accounts must be based on a debt-by-debt assessment of the probability of payment. Such a deduction will be accepted only if it is demonstrated that every effort has been made to collect the amounts concerned. A reserve for doubtful accounts must be stated net of VAT. The VAT can be recovered by the company if the customer does not ultimately pay. Provisions for doubtful accounts based on a percentage of turnover or of outstanding receivables are not allowed.

Receivables and payables in foreign currencies

For tax purposes, all short-term or long-term receivables and payables in foreign currencies shown in the balance sheet must be expressed in French currency at the year-end exchange rate. Any foreign exchange gains or losses are to be included in taxable income.

Interest expense

Interest expense is fully deductible if paid to banks or other third parties, provided that the debt was incurred for *bona fide* business purposes and at normal rates.

Interest payments to shareholders are allowed as a deductible expense if the amount paid is not more than 80 per cent of the official average annual interest rate, at date of issuance, on debentures of private companies. In addition, the deductibility of interest attributable to loans from foreign controlling shareholders is limited to the interest on that portion of loan principal that does not exceed 150 per cent of the borrowing company's share capital.

Interest expense is deductible only if the company's capital shares are fully paid up. Any non-deductible interest is treated as a deemed dividend distribution to shareholders, but without *avoir fiscal* (see p. 228).

Treatment of capital gains and losses

The rules governing the treatment of capital gains and losses for corporate income tax purposes relate mainly to dispositions of fixed assets and investment assets. The tax treatment is based on the distinction between short-term and long-term gains and losses. The following illustrates the various cases.

At the end of the period, there is a compensation between short-term gains and losses, and long-term gains and losses relating to the same period. Net short-term gains and losses are taken into account without limitation in determining the amount of taxable income that is subject to the normal corporate income tax rate of 45 per cent.

However, short-term capital gains may be carried forward, provided an election is made, so that the tax is paid in equal instalments over a three year period. One-third is therefore taxed in the year in which the gain arises and a further one-third is taxed in each of the following two years. In contrast, net long-term gains are taxable at the preferential rate of 15 per cent (25 per cent for capital gains on development land). After-tax net long-term capital gains income must be credited to a special reserve. If funds from such a capital gains reserve are distributed to shareholders, tax is imposed on the company at an amount equal to the difference between the normal corporate income tax (45 per cent) and the capital gains tax initially imposed (25 or 15 per cent) on that portion of the 'gross capital gain' distributed. However, if such a distribution is made in the course of the company's liquidation, no additional tax is imposed.

Net long-term losses may be carried forward for ten years, and may be offset only against long-term capital gains. In case of suspension of trading, a part equal to 15/45 of their amount (25/45 if they refer to development land) may be offset against the profit of the period of suspension.

Tax incentives

Dividends deduction

Companies that are incorporated or that effected an increase in their capital through a contribution in cash between 1 January 1977 and 31 December 1987 are allowed to deduct from their taxable income, the dividends allocated to shares that represent contributions to capital in cash. For operations effected between 1 January 1977 and 31 December 1982 a dividends deduction is allowed for the first seven years following the operation, although such deductions are limited to 7.5 per cent of that portion of the company's capital. For operations effected between 1 January 1983 and 31 December 1987 the dividends deduction for the first ten years following the operation but without the 7.5 per cent limit.

The dividends deduction for new capital increases is no longer available for dividends paid to foreign companies that hold 10 per cent for more of the shares of the payor company. When the dividends are paid to a French parent company, the deduction is available only if the parent company waives the benefit of the participation exemption.

Reduced tax rate on interest paid to shareholders

To encourage the expansion of permanent capital, interest paid to shareholders or partners on funds loaned to the company for conversion to capital under a shareholder deposit account scheme is taxable at a reduced rate of 25 per cent instead of the ordinary withholding rate of 45 per cent. Such a reduction is subject to the following conditions:

1. The loan cannot be repaid and should be capitalized within five years.
2. The amount of such a loan is limited to FF200,000 per shareholder. For loans of more than that amount, the reduced tax rate applies to interest relating to the first FF200,000 and the normal rate applies to the excess.

For the purposes of this law and for the treatment of interest expense in the payor entity (effective 1 January 1983) indexation proceeds are treated the same as interest. This applies to ordinary cash contributions as well as to loans made through a shareholder deposit account scheme.

Tax aspects of dividend distributions

Avoir fiscal

Although companies resident in France deduct no withholding tax from their dividend distributions to shareholders resident in France, such dividends paid carry with them a tax credit called *avoir fiscal*. (The *avoir fiscal* does not, however, apply to constructive dividend distributions to shareholders.)

Such *avoir fiscal* is designed as a partial credit to the shareholder (corporation or individual) equal to 50 per cent of the corporate income tax paid by the company on such distributed income. The amount of dividend income to be included in the shareholder's taxable income is the actual dividend received plus the *avoir fiscal* of 50 per cent ('grossed up'). Thus, for example, a dividend payment of FF110, representing a pre-tax income of FF200, is regarded as amounting to FF165 in the hands of the shareholder.

For the distributing company:	
Gross income to be distributed	200
Corporate income tax	90
Net income distributed	110
For the shareholder:	
Received	110
Avoir fiscal 50 per cent	55
Taxable income	165
Tax credit	(55)

Précompte mobilier

The *avoir fiscal* represents a partial reimbursement of the 45 per cent corporate tax paid by the distributing company. However, since in some cases a portion or all of the distributing company's income is exempted or partially exempted (e.g. income arising from foreign branches or dividends from a subsidiary enjoying the 95 per cent participation exemption, discussed below) or is taxed at a lower rate (e.g. long-term capital gains, which are taxed at 15 per cent), it is necessary to levy an 'equalization tax' (*précompte mobilier*) on such company's distributed income to compensate for the unpaid corporate tax, for which a 50 per cent refund will still be granted. Companies are required, therefore, to make an equalization tax payment equal to the corporate income tax applicable to that portion of their distributed income that is not fully taxed. This tax payment does not constitute a cost to the company but reduces the amount distributable to shareholders. The rate of such précompte mobilier is 33.33 per cent of that portion of the company's gross distributable income which should bear such tax. The resulting tax will therefore equal the *avoir fiscal* at 50 per cent which applies to the net income distributed. The précompte mobilier also applies to dividend distributions from fully taxed income earned more than five years prior to such a distribution.

In the absence of a double taxation treaty, non-resident shareholders are not entitled to the *avoir fiscal*, even when a *précompte mobilier* has been levied. In addition, dividends paid to non-resident shareholders are subject to a 25 per cent withholding tax. Under the provisions of many of France's tax treaties, foreign residents may, under certain circumstances, claim for a refund of the avoir fiscal.

Loss carryovers

Loss carryforwards

Losses may be carried forward and offset against future income under the following conditions:

1. Trading losses may be offset against income taxable at 45 per cent in the following five years. However, to the extent that such losses result from depreciation charges, they may be carried forward indefinitely.
2. Long-term capital losses may be carried forward for ten years and may be offset only against long-term capital gains.
3. It is possible to offset trading losses against long-term capital gains taxable at 15 per cent (or 25 per cent) instead of against future income taxable at 45 per cent. It must be emphasized, however, that this approach will not always be favourable to the company.
4. In all cases, losses may be carried forward and offset against future income (or long-term capital gains) only if the company is carrying on the same business as when the loss was incurred.

Loss carrybacks

The Finance Act 1985 allows companies, under certain conditions of investment in depreciable assets, to carry back their losses incurred since

1 January 1984 to the undistributed income of the three preceding fiscal years.

The reduction in corporate income tax resulting from this carryback is a credit against future tax liability which is not refundable unless it remains unused at the end of five years, in which case it is refunded. In the meantime, it can be discounted with credit establishments.

The amount of the credit is 50 per cent of the losses carried back to periods beginning before 31 December 1985; and 45 per cent of the losses carried back to periods beginning after 1 January 1986.

Tax credits

Tax credits may be offset against French corporate income tax computed at 45 per cent (or at the lower long-term capital gains rate of 15 or 25 per cent). Credits are available for:

1. dividends paid by French resident companies (with *avoir fiscal* if such dividends have not already enjoyed the 95 per cent participation exemption);
2. 10 per cent withholding tax paid on French bond interest;
3. foreign taxes (generally, withholding taxes) paid on dividends, interest or royalties originating in treaty countries + the amount of such foreign tax credits may not, however, exceed the amount of French tax payable on such foreign income;
4. increased expenditures, between 1983 and 1987, by certain industrial and commercial companies for qualified scientific and technical research operations. This tax credit, amounting to 25 per cent of the increase in research expenses from one year to the next (adjusted for inflation) is credited against the tax otherwise payable (or refundable, to the extent that the credit exceeds the tax otherwise payable), up to a maximum of FF3 million.

These various tax credits may be offset only against actual income tax payable. If no tax is payable in the year in which such credits are available (i.e. if the taxpayer incurs a loss), the credits are lost; they cannot be either reimbursed or carried forward. However, such otherwise 'lost' tax credits may be offset against the *précompte mobilier* over a five-year period.

Liquidations

Upon the liquidation of a company, corporate income tax, at the rate of 45 per cent for reduced rates where applicable, is payable on the income of the final accounting period. The liquidation surplus (i.e. net assets less the amount of capital contributions not yet reimbursed), is taxable to the shareholders and is regarded as a dividend distribution, with all the attendant tax characteristics and consequences: *avoir fiscal, précompte mobilier*, and withholding tax on payments to non-residents.

Tax treatment of loans without interest and forgiveness of debts

Loans without interest

The French Supreme Court ruled in 1982 that a transfer of profits to a foreign country results when a French parent company grants a loan without interest to its foreign subsidiary and derives no compensatory benefit from that arrangement. The subsidiary's financial difficulties might justify deferring the payment of interest, the Court ruled, but not waiving it.

The Finance Act 1983 stipulates the tax treatment when a parent company forgives debt of a subsidiary. Where the parent forgives the loan for financial reasons, income tax is deductible by the parent company if the net assets of the subsidiary are negative. It is not deductible by the parent if the net assets are positive except for the portion representing minority interest (in which case the forgiveness may be viewed as an additional investment).

If the parent forgives the debt of a subsidiary for commercial reasons income tax is deductible by the parent company if the forgiveness is an act of good business practice.

Anti-avoidance legislation

Under Article 57 of the General Tax Code, intercompany transactions must be conducted on an arm's-length basis. Such transactions include, for example, sales, purchases, royalty and interest payments, and head office expense allocations. Article 57 also applies to transactions with unrelated parties in countries that enjoy a privileged tax system.

A French branch or other permanent establishment of a foreign company may be charged both with direct expenses incurred by the foreign company on its behalf and with an appropriate share of head office expenses. Although there are guidelines, there are no definitive rules as to how head office expenses should be allocated. The French tax authorities have the right to require the foreign head office of the French branch or other permanent establishment to submit its books for their inspection in order to determine the reasonableness of the expense allocation. A French subsidiary of a foreign company is allowed to deduct as administrative expense, in so far as they represent arm's-length remuneration, charges for administrative services rendered by the foreign company. The French tax authorities are paying increased attention to all payments to foreign parents or affiliated companies, with a view to identifying possible indirect transfers of income abroad.

Under Article 155.A of the General Tax Code, any payment made to a non-resident person or company for services rendered in France by a person domiciled in France is taxable to the person rendering such services if that person controls, directly or indirectly, the foreign recipient of the payments, or if it cannot be demonstrated that the main business of the recipient is industrial or commercial in nature, or if the recipient is located in a country or territory with a privileged tax system.

Under Article 209.A of the General Tax Code, if a legal entity (other than a non-profit organization) whose head office is outside France has at its disposal one or more parcels of real estate in France and allows them to be used rent-free or for a rent that is less than the actual rental value of the property, such an entity is subject to corporate income tax on three times the actual rental value of the property.

Under Article 209.B of the General Tax Code, if an equity subject to French corporate income tax owns directly or indirectly more than 25 per cent of a subsidiary located in a country or territory with a privileged tax system, such an entity becomes subject to corporate income tax in France on its portion of the subsidiary's income in the year in which such income is realized by the subsidiary, whether or not it is distributed.

Under Article 238.A of the General Tax Code, payments relating to interest, royalties or services (salaries, fees, commissions, etc.) made to a resident of a country or territory with a privileged tax system as defined above) are not deductible unless the French payer can demonstrate that such payments are normal and appropriate in relation to the rights or services received.

Miscellaneous

Income taxation – partnerships

Partnerships, for French income tax purposes, include general partnerships (*sociétés en nom collectif*), limited parnerships (*sociétés en commandites simple*), joint ventures (*sociétés en participation*), civil companies (*sociétés civiles*), and joint ventures 'with a common economic interest' (*groupement d'intérêt économique* or GIE). Except for GIEs, partnerships may elect to be subject to the normal corporate income tax and, in certain circumstances, such treatment is compulsory for some civil companies. Also, in certain very limited cases, SARLs may be taxed as partnerships and for this reason partnerships are briefly mentioned here.

The main feature of the income taxation of partnerships in France is that a partnership's taxable income, even if not distributed, becomes immediately taxable at the partner's level in proportion to each partner's share in the partnership's earnings. This is obviously quite different than the corporate income tax system, under which only distributed income becomes taxable at the shareholders' level.

The worldwide income of a partnership is determined at the partnership's level according to the various categories of income (e.g. rental income, income from professional activities, investment income) and is subject at the partners' level to individual income tax in such categories. If a partner is a corporation, however, that partner's proportionate share of the partnership's income is determined according to the corporate income tax rules and subject to corporate income tax in the hands of the partner.

(The same rule applies to individual entrepreneurs who are members of a partnership engaged in commercial, industrial or agricultural activities whose turnover exceeds a specified limit.)

Partnership losses may be carried forward according to the corporate or individual income tax rules to which the related income is subject. Losses resulting from depreciation charges may be carried forward indefinitely but may be offset only against future income from that same partnership, not against other income of the partners.

Value-added tax

The value-added tax, or VAT (*taxe sur la valeur ajoutée*, or TVA) is a general tax on consumption expenditures within France. The tax is levied on the delivery of goods and the performance of services within France by entrepreneurs, and on the importation of goods and certain services into France.

Under the VAT system, tax is levied at each stage of the manufacturing and distribution process on a non-cumulative basis. The cumulation of tax is avoided through the deduction of VAT on input, the entrepreneur pays VAT on the total amount invoiced by him each month, but he is entitled to recover the 'input' VAT that was invoiced to him during that period one month later, except for input VAT on fixed assets, which is recovered in the same month. If, in any one month, the credit for input VAT is higher than the amount of VAT due on output, the entrepreneur is, under certain conditions, entitled to a refund.

There are four official VAT rates. The standard rate of 18.6 per cent, a 5.5 per cent rate, which applies mainly to water supplies and to most foods, a 7 per cent rate, which applies to most hotel accommodations, personal transportation services, books, medicines, and public performances, and an increased rate of 33.33 per cent, which applies to so-called 'luxury' items such as jewellery, photographic equipment, radios, motor cars, record players and tape recorders, video equipment, and furs. The increased rate now applies to the leasing or rental, as well as to the sale, of motor cars, video recorders, prerecorded video cassettes, etc.

Certain transactions relating to exports are included in the scope of VAT but are exempt from such tax – i.e. they are treated as zero-rated transactions. Such transactions have mainly to do with export sales and deliveries, related commissions and brokerage fees, and deliveries to exporters.

Various special provisions apply to the importation or exportation of services.

If a fixed asset is sold within four years (for buildings, nine years) after the date of its acquisition, the VAT recovered in respect thereof must be repaid to the tax authorities less one-fifth (for buildings, one-tenth) for each year (or part of a year) that the asset has been held. (Such VAT repayments constitute a cost to the seller in computing a capital gain or loss for corporate income tax purposes.)

Local taxes

There are four major local taxes: the so-called 'professional' tax, a tax on improved land, a tax on unimproved land, and a residence or habitation tax.

Under a 1983 law, newly established companies that meet certain criteria may, at the option of the local taxing authorities, be exempted from a number of these local taxes for up to three years. Where such exemptions are granted, they apply to all companies that meet the specified criteria and are not provided on a case-by-case basis.

The *taxe professionnelle*, or business tax, must be paid by all individuals or entities with a business other than farming, except for: employees, persons who work at home, commercial travellers (salesmen), artists, authors and newspaper editors.

The rate of professional tax is determined locally (ranging, in general, between 15 and 25 per cent) and is applied to a basis determined by adding together the following three amounts for the second year prior to the year of taxation (e.g. for 1982 in computing the tax payable in 1984):

1. Rental value of immoveable property (less the land tax thereon) that is used in the taxpayer's gainful activities.
2. 18 per cent of all remunerations paid, (or 10 per cent of receipts in some particular cases).

Some adjustments apply to the professional tax computed on this basis to limit the effective tax rate.

The *taxe foncière sur les propriétés bâties*, or tax on improved land, is levied on owners of all buildings and other structures except for agricultural and religious buildings and certain buildings constructed before 1973. The tax is calculated by applying the local rate to the net annual rental value of the property. The annual rental value of a personal residence is determined by the tax authorities by reference to other, similar properties. The annual rental value of business or industrial property is determined by reference to its cost.

The *taxe foncière sur les propriétés non bâties* (or tax on unimproved land) is levied on owners of unimproved land. The tax is calculated by applying the local rate to the net annual rental value of such land, determined by reference to the most recent assessed valuation.

Payroll-based taxes and social contributions

There are, essentially, two kinds of taxes based on employee compensation in France: (1) payroll-based taxes that are payable by employers only; and (2) social contributions (i.e. for social security, supplementary retirement benefits and unemployment insurance) that are payable partly by the employer and partly by the employee. The overall burden of these payroll-based taxes and social contributions varies between 35 per cent and 45 per cent of total salaries and wages for employers and between 9 per cent and 14 per cent of each employee's compensation, depending on the applicable social security ceilings and the rates of pension contributions.

Taxes payable by employers only include a payroll tax paid when employers are not liable to VAT; an apprenticeship tax; a training tax; a housing schemes tax; and social contributions: sickness allowances; compensation for work-related accidents or illness; disability and death benefits; family benefits; and retirement (pension) benefits.

Registration and stamp duties

Registration duties – General

Certain documents must be registered, including contracts, notarized deeds, deeds on the sale of a business, and documents relating to transfers of goodwill or leasehold rights, transfers of shares, the transformation or dissolution of a company, or an increase or reduction in the company's capital. Certain transactions, such as 'sales' of clientele, must be registered even though no written document has been prepared. Registration, when mandatory, must usually take place within one month of the execution date of the document or the effective date of the transaction. Registration duties are based on the higher of the amount paid and the market value of the property or rights involved.

Registration duties – Companies subject to corporate income tax

Companies or businesses that are not subject to corporate income tax may be subject to different registration duties than those described below:

1. Contributions to capital in cash – 1 per cent rate.
2. Contributions to capital in kind – 1 per cent rate. However, for contributions in kind represented by goodwill, clientele, leasehold rights or immoveable property that are made to a company subject to corporate income tax, the rate of registration duty is 11.4 per cent (plus various local taxes). For contributions to capital of assets that bear a charge (e.g. property on which there is a mortgage) or that are contributed partly for shares and partly for cash, the rate of duty is 16.6 per cent.
3. Capital increases resulting from undistributed earnings – 12 per cent rate. This rate is reduced to 1 per cent for capital increases registered between 1 January 1985 and 31 December 1985 if a contribution to capital of an equal amount in cash is made at the same time or within the preceding or following 12 months.
4. Transfers of shares of French partnerships or of SARLs – 4.8 per cent rate. Such transfers are subject to French registration duty even if they occur outside France.
5. Liquidations – subject to a fixed fee of FF1160 on the act of dissolution

and a 1 per cent duty rate on the total net assets distributed (including shareholder contributions).

Real estate transfer duty

A real estate transfer duty is levied on acquisitions of real estate located in France. The rate of the duty is 16.6 per cent of the market value of such real estate. For new buildings, the initial sale (and, under certain conditions, one subsequent sale within five years) will be subject to VAT and, accordingly, the real estate transfer duty is reduced to 0.6 per cent.

Local taxes, at rates of 0.5 to 1.6 per cent, are also levied on transfers of real estate.

Other taxes

Tax on certain business expenses

Since 1982, a tax has been levied on certain business expenses deducted from taxable income in the preceding year by companies subject to the corporate income tax and most individual businesses as well. The tax is not deductible for either corporate or individual income tax purposes. Its rate will be of 15 per cent in 1987, 10 per cent in 1988, and the tax will be cancelled from 1 January 1989.

Social contribution tax

A social contribution tax (contribution sociale de solidarité) is imposed on companies' turnover (before VAT) at a rate of 0.1 per cent. Such tax becomes deductible for income tax purposes only when it has actually been paid.

Tax on company cars

The amount of this tax currently ranges from FF4800 p.a. for cars of up to 7 hp to FF10,500 p.a. for cars of more than 7 hp. The tax is not deductible for corporate or individual income tax purposes.

Taxation implications of mergers and acquisitions

A special incentive tax rule in case of mergers

Mergers and reorganizations, including splits and partial business transfers are considered to be desirable for the French economy and are encouraged by the government through special incentives. The basic condition to take advantage of these rules is that all the companies involved in the operation must be subject to the corporate income tax. They may be either French or foreign companies; but in case of transfer from French companies to foreign companies, the application of the incentive rules is subject to a prior authorization from the French Treasury.

Mergers

These special rules concern corporate income tax, the taxation of distributed shares, and registration fees.

Corporate income tax. The only taxation of the absorbed company as a result of the merger is computed on the following basis:

1. profits from the beginning of the period to the date of merger;
2. reserves that are no longer justified;
3. long-term capital gains referring to depreciable assets.

But for these long-term capital gains, the law provides the possibility to elect for an immediate preferential taxation rate at 15 per cent.

Rules applying to the absorbing company. In order to qualify for reduced taxation the absorbing company should agree:

1. to reintegrate, over the next five years' results, the untaxed capital gains realized by the target company on depreciable assets, and treat them as ordinary income and pay corporate income tax at the rate of 45 per cent;
2. to incorporate into its balance sheet the untaxed reserves and provisions of the absorbed company;
3. to calculate the capital gains that may occur on any subsequent sale of the non depreciable assets acquired, by using the book value of such assets as stated by the absorbed company.

If the absorbing company commits itself to the foregoing, it is subject to no other tax, including capital gains tax, that would otherwise be imposed on the capital gains it would realize as an initial shareholder of the integrated company. In addition, the absorbing company will depreciate, by either straight line or accelerated method, the depreciable assets transferred on the value assigned to them in the merger agreement and by reference to the date of the merger. It will determine whether its future capital gains on transferred assets are short term or long term gains by reference to the date of purchase by the absorbed company. Furthermore, it will be allowed to take account of the profits of the absorbed company during the five periods prior to a distribution of dividends, in order to lower the amount subject to equalization tax. Under agreement of the French administration it will be allowed to carry forward the losses of the absorbed company on its future profits.

Taxation of distributed shares. Shareholders of the merged entity are not taxed on the shares they received as pursuant to the transfer, except in the case of a significant shareholding (over 25 per cent of total shares), or if the absorbed company was mainly a real estate company. Should the absorbing company hold shares of the integrated company before the merger, the gains that may result from the cancellation of these shares simultaneously with the merger are exempted from corporate income tax.

Registration tax. If the merger is registered before 1 January 1988 a special registration tax at the rate of 1.2 per cent is imposed on the difference between the net assets and the capital of the target company, with a minimum taxation of FF1200. For mergers to be registered after 1 January 1988, the fees will be 1 per cent of the amount of capital increase, not exceeding the capital of the absorbed entity, and 12 per cent beyond this amount. A significant advantage is given here compared to the general 16.6 per cent registration fees applied on transfers of going businesses.

Splits

Under agreement, a split may be regarded as a merger and advantage taken of the same incentives as for corporate income tax and taxation of distributed shares. Otherwise, it is regarded as a winding-up. As far as registration fees are concerned, splits occurring after 1 January 1988 will be regarded as mergers, should they have the agreement or not. Before 1 January 1988, the 1.2 per cent taxation is imposed only in the case of agreement required for the whole operation.

Partial business transfers

To qualify for the same incentive rules as mergers, partial business transfers need an agreement from the Ministry of Economy, except if the transferred business is a complete branch of activity, and if the transferee undertakes to keep the shares for five years and to compute its future gains on these shares by reference to the value of the transferred assets; in this case, no agreement is required.

Taxation of company groups

French tax law does not provide for the computation of taxable income on a consolidated basis. However, under certain conditions, parent companies may take advantage of a participation exemption for the dividends from their subsidiaries; this is the so-called *Regime mère-filiale*. However, French companies may request authorization from the Ministry of Economy to have the corporate income tax apply to either their worldwide profits or losses, or their consolidated profits or losses, or the profits or losses of the French company and its 95 per cent or more controlled subsidiaries.

The 'Régime Mère-Filial'

Aim. The aim of this system is to avoid the double taxation of the profits distributed by the subsidiary to the parent company, and to allow the shareholders of the parent company to take advantage of the tax credit for the re-distributed profits of the subsidiary, without the parent company having to pay the equalization tax (*précompte mobilier*).

Requirements. The application of this system is subject to the following conditions, to be met at the date the dividends are paid by the subsidiary:

1. the parent company and subsidiary must be subject to the corporate tax rate of 45 per cent;
2. the parent company has to be a French corporation, while the subsidiary may be either French or foreign;
3. the interest of the parent company has to represent 10 per cent or more of the capital shares of the subsidiary (or 150MF from 1 January 1988). There is no minimum percentage in the case of securities received as payment for partial business transfers;
4. the shares must have been subscribed when issued, or the parent company must have contracted to keep them for at least two years.

Treatment of the dividends from the subsidiary. The parent company is exempted from corporate income tax for 95 per cent of the global income (dividends plus tax credits) from the subsidiary. The residual 5 per cent represent a lump sum for costs, which cannot be offset against the taxable income. When the parent company distributes these exempted profits to its own shareholders, the corresponding tax credits are offset against the *précompte mobilier*, which is consequently not paid by the parent company. As for the shareholders, they take advantage of the whole tax credit corresponding to the dividends they receive.

Worldwide and consolidated profits or losses

The principal of territoriality may be waived provided special authorization is obtained from the Ministry of Economy. French companies may be allowed to have their corporate income tax apply either to all their activities in France and abroad, i.e. their worldwide profits or losses; or their profits or losses including the part of profits or losses corresponding to their interest in the subsidiaries from which they own 50 per cent or more of the votes: i.e. their consolidated profits or losses. In these cases, they may deduct the foreign corporate income tax paid by the foreign subsidiaries.

95 per cent or more controlled subsidiaries

With authorization from the Ministry of Economy, and in the case of a merger or a reorganization of a group, a French company which is (directly or indirectly) 95 per cent or more controlled by another French company may be regarded as a branch of the parent company for tax purposes. In this case,

1. the profits or losses of the subsidiary are included in the profits or losses of the parent company;
2. the dividends distributed by the subsidiary to the parent company are not regarded as distributed income, and are consequently not subject to the equalization tax (*précompte mobilier*);
3. the dividends redistributed by the parent company are also not subject to the *précompte*.

To date, only a few major French companies have obtained one of the above-mentioned authorizations from the Ministry of Economy.

Special tax considerations for foreign companies

Under the concept of territoriality, French branches and other permanent establishments of non-resident companies are subject to corporate income tax (and to other French taxes) as if they were French companies. Such branches and permanent establishments may, however, deduct a reasonable amount of head office expenses.

The definition of a 'permanent establishment' is included in all of the tax treaties to which France is a party and is largely consistent with the OECD draft Double-Taxation Convention on Income and Capital. The major differences in the French tax treatment of non-resident companies are as follows:

Distribution tax on non-resident companies

The after-tax income of a non-resident company is deemed to be distributed for French tax purposes and, accordingly, a distribution tax (or branch profits tax) is assessed by withholding tax at the rate of 25 per cent (reduced by tax treaties), at the time such income is earned, not when it is distributed.

There are three exceptions to this rule:

1. if the non-resident company does not distribute a dividend in its own country in the fiscal year in which the French income is earned;
2. if the French income is distributed to French residents;
3. or if the worldwide income distributed by the non-resident company in the fiscal year in question is less than the income of its branch or permanent establishment in France.

In any of these circumstances, the income that is still subject to the French distribution tax is that amount which corresponds to a distribution of dividends by the non-resident company to its non-resident shareholders.

Taxation of real estate in France held by a non-resident company

The General Tax Code requires foreign companies owning real estate in France to pay a 3 per cent annual tax on the value of such property.

This tax will not be due, however, if the real property represents less than 50 per cent of the foreign company's French assets or the company's country of residence has a treaty with France.

Taxation of headquarters companies

There are no special provisions for headquarters companies in France. Usually, however, a ruling can be obtained from the French tax authorities to have a headquarters operation taxed on a 'cost-plus' basis, at a rate ranging between 7 and 12 per cent (most commonly, at the present time 8 per cent).

Tax treaties

France has entered into treaties for the avoidance of double taxation with a lot of countries. The provisions of such treaties override any conflicting provisions in France's domestic tax laws and regulations. The treaties provide essentially for a definition of permanent establishment, for a reduction in the rate of withholding tax on dividends, interest, royalties and fees, and for the granting of foreign tax credits for comparable taxes withheld or otherwise paid abroad.

5. ACCOUNTING

Legislative background

There are four principal documents governing accounting and reporting practices in France:

1. The French Commercial Code (as amended by the so-called Accounting Act of 1983).
2. The Companies Act of 1966 and related Decree of 1967.
3. The General Tax Code.
4. The New Accounting System ('Nouveau Plan Comptable', or NPC) established by the Accounting Act of 30 April 1983 and related decree of November 1983.

Each of these sources is described briefly below.

Commercial Code

The French Commercial Code includes the following requirements (Article 8):

1. Every company is obliged to record all of its transactions on a daily basis, in a ledger (*livre journal*), and to summarize these transactions

in a general ledger (*grand livre*) which is maintained according to the company's chart of accounts.

2. Once each year, every company must close its books and prepare a detailed accounting of its operations, its assets and its liabilities (*livre d'inventaire*), including an annual balance sheet, an income statement, and explanatory notes to the financial statements.

Companies Act

The principal statutes governing company law in France are the Companies Act of 24 July 1966 and the related decree of 23 March 1967. These statutes have been amended by the Accounting Act to incorporate the requirements of the EEC's Fourth Directive.

Under the provisions of the Companies Act (and related Decree), a company's annual financial statements and a report of its management must be presented at a general meeting of the shareholders within six months after the end of its accounting year. The same methods of valuation and the same system of classification are expected to be followed each year. Should there be any change in those methods or that system, such change must be explained to and approved by the shareholders.

For SAs and certain SARLs, an individual or a firm with appropriate professional qualifications must examine the financial statements and attest to their completeness, their correctness, and the fairness of their presentation. This obligation has been extended to other types of companies by the 1 March 1984 Act relating to distressed corporations.

General Tax Code

A Decree of 29 October 1965, subsequently incorporated in the General Tax Code, sets forth the definitions and rules of valuation, estimation and presentation to be observed by companies subject to the French corporate income tax. To a great extent, these definitions and rules are also followed in preparing companies' financial statements.

The Decree prescribes standard formats to be followed in preparing the financial statements and various supporting schedules to accompany a company's annual income tax return. The main purpose of these standard formats is to identify clearly the amount of the company's taxable income for the year and to assure the appropriateness of depreciation charges, reserves, etc.

Le Nouveau Plan Comptable

The Nouveau Plan Comptable (NPC), or 'New Accounting System', replaces the 1957 *Plan Comptable* to comply with the requirements of the EEC's Fourth Directive and to provide for more useful financial information: established by the 30 April 1983 Act and the 29 November 1983 Decree, the NPC is effective for financial years beginning on or after 1 January 1984 and is compulsory. A doctrinal work, and not merely a chart of accounts, the NPC introduces standard definitions and rules in the following areas:

1. terminology;
2. methods of valuing assets and liabilities and measuring operating results;
3. the functioning of the accounts and the presentation of financial statements; and
4. cost accounting systems.

The major changes introduced by the *Nouveau Plan Comptable* are as follows:

1. The NPC introduces for the first time to French accounting the concept of a 'true and fair view'. A company's financial statements must present a true and fair view of its financial position and results of operations.
2. The former 'general trading account' and 'profit and loss account' are combined in a single income statement.
3. Supplementary information and notes to the financial statements are compulsory. The amount of detail required varies according to the size of the company.
4. The concepts of 'gross margin' and 'extraordinary items' have been introduced to the income statement.
5. No distinction is made between 'long-term' and 'short-term' (e.g. gains and losses).

Sources of accounting principles

The accounting principles observed by companies in France are generally promulgated by the government, with the advice and assistance of the following institutions:

1. The National Council of Accountancy (CNC), which provides the government with research and counsel on accounting matters. The CNC's members include representatives of management, labour unions, and the accounting profession. Official statements of accounting principles and rules are either prepared by the Council or reviewed by the Council prior to their issuance.
2. The Stock Exchange Commission (*Commission des Opérations de Bourse*, or COB), which controls the financial information provided by companies listed on the French stock exchanges as well as the operations of the exchanges.
3. The appellate courts, which are frequently called upon to give their interpretations of accounting matters and thus exercise considerable influence on French accounting principles and techniques.
4. The Certified Accountants Association (*Ordre des Experts Comptables et Comptables Agréés*), which regularly issues recommendations on accounting principles and information to be provided to shareholders.

Stock Exchange requirements

The Stock Exchange Commission (COB) has two main functions: first, to control the operations of the seven French stock exchanges; and secondly, to supervise the financial reporting and other activities of companies whose shares are listed on the French exchanges. The COB's supervisory function allows it to mandate certain accounting approaches and also to propose modifications to the various laws and rules that govern French accounting and financial reporting. All listed companies are now required to publish, in an official journal, their quarterly turnover figures and, at the end of the second quarter, a schedule detailing the activities and results of their first six months.

Under COB rules, companies that are in the process of selling debt instruments to the public and newly-listed companies are required to issue consolidated financial statements.

Accounting principles and practices

Financial statement presentation

The Companies Act requires that annual financial statements be prepared by all companies and, in the case of SAs and SARLs, filed with the commercial courts (Tribunaux de Commerce). The required annual financial statements according to the *Nouveau Plan Comptable* are as follows:

1. balance sheet,
2. income statement (which combines the previous 'general trading account' and 'the profit and loss account),
3. notes to the financial statements (newly introduced by the NPC), whose main objective is to complement and to comment on the figures presented in the balance sheet and the income statement, in order to provide information relating to social and legal matters. The financial statements must be so prepared as to give to any third person a 'true and fair view', through explanatory notes, analyses and various other kinds of information of the company's financial position and results of operations.

Accounting convention

The historical-cost convention is used, except for certain fixed assets and investments for which a write-up to appraised values is permitted or required by law.

Goodwill

The nature of the goodwill must be disclosed in the notes. Normally, the kind of goodwill that benefits from the protection of the law cannot be amortized but may be written down for book purposes to reflect a depreciation of its underlying value. The kind of goodwill that does not benefit from the protection of the law may be amortized over a period of (generally) five years. When consolidated financial statements are prepared, goodwill arising from such consolidation is normally amortized, often against equity.

Other accounting practices

Inventories are valued at the lower of cost or market value. Cost is generally determined by the FIFO method or on an average basis. Use of the LIFO method is not permitted.

Fixed assets are systematically depreciated over their estimated useful lives by the straight-line method or an accelerated method.

Deferred income taxes are disclosed in the notes to the financial statements.

Profit on long-term contracts is generally recognized when the contract is completed. However, the percentage-of-completion method can be used if certain requirements are met.

Government grants are recorded as liabilities and amortized over the useful lives of the assets to which they relate.

Leases are not capitalized. The minimum rental payments and other information should be disclosed in the notes.

Accounting for groups: consolidated statements

The aim of the consolidated statements is to present the financial situation and the results of interdependent companies as if they consisted of one entity. The preparation of consolidated accounts does not have any taxation implications although, as previously mentioned, companies may obtain approval for tax to be based on worldwide benefit or on a consolidated benefit basis.

Companies concerned

Under the recent legislation (3 January 1985), most private companies and public corporations are required to establish consolidated statements as soon as they have subsidiaries or shares. Unlisted companies may be exempted from this requirement if they are controlled by an entity which includes them in its consolidated statements, or if the global entity composed by the parent company and the subsidiaries does not exceed a determined size (criteria of turnover, balance sheet and staff).

Consolidations: applicability and methods

The legislation lists three specific cases:

1. companies under exclusive control for which the proper method is global integration;

2. companies under joint control for which the proper method is the pro rata or proportional basis;
3. companies under marked influence for which the proper basis is the equivalence or equity method.

A company is under exclusive control when the majority of its votes is directly or indirectly held by another company or when another company has nominated the majority of the Board of Directors for two consecutive years.

A company is deemed to be under joint control if it is controlled by a limited number of partners or shareholders, so that the decisions result from that agreement.

A company is under marked influence if 20 per cent or more of its votes are held by another company.

In some particular cases, controlled companies may not be consolidated especially when serious and durable restrictions question that control or influence, or when there is the possibility of transfers of funds from the subsidiary to the parent company.

The three consolidation methods are as follows:

1. Within the global integration system, the accountable value of the controlled companies shares is replaced by the equity of these companies.
2. Within the *pro rata* system, the accountable value of the controlled companies shares is replaced by the percentage of the equity of these companies corresponding to the interest of the consolidating company.
3. Within the equivalence system, the accountable value of the controlled companies shares is replaced by the portion of the equity each share represents.

SAs that are required to publish consolidated financial statements must have a joint statutory audit performed by two different auditors (individuals or firms). For companies that are listed on the French stock exchange, the appointment of auditors must be approved by the COB.

The statutory auditor is invited to attend the board meeting at which the directors decide upon the closing of the company's accounts for the year. At the annual general meeting at which the shareholders approve the accounts, two kinds of reports are presented by the auditor. A general report which attests that the financial statements examined are complete, correct and present a true and fair view of the company's financial position and results of operations, and that the information provided in the report of the company's management is sincere. Secondly, a special report, which deals with any related-party transactions, such as agreements between the company and any member of its board or any of its general managers. Such agreements or transactions must be approved by the company's board of directors. Other special reports may also be submitted by the statutory auditor e.g. in connection with a reduction of capital or a merger.

International accounting standards

France was one of the founder members of the International Accounting Standards Committee and uses its 'best endeavours' towards harmonizing accounting standards. Prior to the *Nouveau Plan Comptable* substantial differences existed between French generally accepted accounting principles and International Accounting Standards. Whilst the *Nouveau Plan Comptable* has eliminated many of the differences there are still areas in which French practice differs from IASC standards or presents special characteristics, and these are summarized in table 7.2.

The acquisition of declining firms

The creation of a company in order to acquire a declining business may benefit from some tax incentives.

Exemption from some local taxes

If a company acquires a declining firm it may be exempt from local taxes provided the following conditions are fulfilled:

1. the acquisition must consist of the purchase of the business;
2. the exclusive aim of the newly created company has to be the pursuit of the activity of the declining business;
3. the suspension of the 'declining business' has to be inescapable.

The exemption concerns basically real estate and business taxes and may apply on a 2–4 years delay.

Loss carryovers

The acquiring company of a declining business may under agreement carry forward for five years the losses of the purchased entity, provided the following conditions are fulfilled:

1. the acquiring company must hold at least 25 per cent of the purchased entity;
2. the purchased and purchasing companies must be subject to the corporate income tax;
3. the acquiring company has to subscribe capital within five years of at least 150 per cent of the corporate income tax gain;
4. it has to keep the shares of the new company, and the new company must not distribute any dividend for five years, or four years if the above mentioned subscription is achieved.

Table 7.2 Comparison of French accounting practices with International Standards

IAS 3 – Consolidated financial statements	In the past, the presentation of consolidated financial statements has been recommended for companies listed on the French stock exchanges but required only for companies selling debt instruments to the public and companies in the process of being introduced on the Stock Exchange. For financial years ending after 31 December 1984, all listed companies are now required, under the NPC, to present consolidated statements in addition to their statutory financial statements. Where consolidation is not required, investments are carried at cost (less, if necessary, a reserve to reflect a permanent decline in the investment's value)
IAS 4 – Depreciation accounting	That portion of the allowance for depreciation which is booked for corporate tax purposes (accelerated method) and is not economically justified is recorded in an equity account that is subsequently adjusted
IAS 7 – Statement of changes in financial position	Presently, such a statement is recommended by the national organizations of the French accounting profession and by the French Stock Exchange Commission. Under the law of 1 March 1984 relating to troubled corporations, such a statement will have to be prepared (but not published) by all companies of a certain size
IAS 9 – Accounting for research and development activities	Under the NPC, those research and development costs that meet the defined criteria for deferral are to be amortized over a period not exceeding five years
IAS 12 – Accounting for taxes on income	Financial statements reflect only the taxes payable for the fiscal year, the advance payments made, and any tax liabilities remaining from prior years. The tax effect of timing differences is not recognized in the balance sheet and in the income statement, but it must be disclosed in a note to the financial statements. (This standard applies only to companies that present consolidated financial statements.)
IAS 13 – Presentation of current assets and current liabilities	Under the NPC, balance sheet items are no longer classified according to the criteria 'long-term' and 'short-term', but according to their place in the company's economic cycle. As a result, short-term and long-term receivables or payables are presented under the same caption in the balance sheet, with a breakdown in the footnotes

– *Continued*

Table 7.2 Continued

IAS 14 – Reporting financial information by segment	The NPC provides only for disclosure in the notes of turnover by line of business and by geographic market segments, and such disclosure is required only of capital companies
IAS 15 – Information reflecting the effects of changing prices	Information reflecting the effects of changing prices is not required in France, although various experimental approaches have been encouraged by both the Stock Exchange Commission and the Certified Accountants Association. The existing 'inflation accounting' practices are periodic compulsory revaluations of assets for companies of a certain size and various tax provisions on inventories (for price increases and for fluctuations in the quotations of certain raw materials on the international market)
IAS 17 – Accounting for leases	Leases cannot be capitalized in France. The NPC requires that certain data on leases be disclosed in the notes: value of leased equipment or buildings, lease payments made during the period, commitments for future lease payments, etc.
IAS 19 – Accounting for retirement benefits in the financial statements of employers	It is not permitted in France to accrue for the cost of retirement benefits before the retirement of the employees, and therefore French accounting practice does not reflect the international standard
IAS 21 – Accounting for the effects of changes in foreign-exchange rates	Foreign currency receivables and payables are translated at the exchange rate prevailing at the balance sheet date. Unrealized gains and losses are recorded in interim balance sheet accounts, and unrealized losses are charged to the income statement through a provision Accordingly, except in special circumstances, all translation losses are recognized immediately and all translation gains are deferred until realized There are no formal requirements for the translation of foreign-currency financial statements, but current practice favours the monetary/non-monetary method
IAS 22 – Accounting for business combinations	Only the purchase method is used to account for business combinations in France
IAS 23 – Capitalization of borrowing costs	Under French practice, capitalization of borrowing costs is possible only for those fixed assets that are produced or constructed by the company

– *Continued*

Table 7.2 Continued

IAS 24 – Related party disclosures	The notes to the financial statements should disclose certain data (e.g. amount of the investment, receivables and payables at the closing date, interest charges, and revenues booked during the period) relating to any transactions with majority-controlled subsidiaries (whether directly or indirectly controlled). In addition, the company's statutory auditor is required to present, in his special report, information about all agreements or transactions between the company and any members of its board or between the company and other companies with which its board members are associated. This requirement does not apply, however, to normal arm's-length transactions in an SA

Incentives

Currently, the main thrust of France's incentives programme is to encourage job creation or maintenance, especially in declining industrial sectors and underdeveloped regions. The government has tried to balance the commercial and industrial activity in the Paris and Lyons regions by attracting new investors to other parts of France.

The incentives programme for industrial investment in the less-developed areas of France was overhauled and streamlined at the end of 1981. It offers grants based on the number of jobs created by a new investment or expansion as well as decentralization from the Paris region. There are two types of aid given: the regional employment aid programme and the regional restructuring programme. The incentives currently available consist of cash grants. In granting incentives, the government assumes that companies are planning a permanent establishment. Companies that shut down operations within a short time after receiving incentive aid are likely to incur the authorities' ill will, and some have been compelled to repay their regional development grants.

The PRE and PAT incentive programmes

Incentives are available for new investments, expansion of existing facilities, acquisitions of declining manufacturing businesses, research and development activities, and headquarters and administrative facilities in most of France.

Incentives consist of the subsidy for regional employment, or *prime regionale e l'employe*: (PRE), and the subsidy for territory development, *prime d'amenagement du territoire* (PAT). PRE is regionally financed, and is worth a maximum of FF20,000 per job created depending on the area, up to a maximum of 30 jobs. Regional councils award and distribute these grants according to eligibility criteria (including size) which they establish. PRE is exclusive of PAT.

PAT is nationally financed from the Délégation à l'Aménagement du Territoire et l'Action Régionale (DATAR) budget. PAT grants, which were created by a decree dated 6 May 1982, are aimed primarily at industrial conversions in areas severely affected by declining activity, large new industrial investment on the part of major companies that are desirous of aiding a particular locality to overcome unemployment, certain projects in areas experiencing temporary difficulties, projects in service industries, and research and development facilities or other projects of national interest. Except when the government itself elects to make a grant of this type through DATAR, the regional councils award and distribute the PAT grants upon consultation with local government officials. PAT grants are limited to certain eligible areas (the most disadvantaged or weak). Paris and Lyons areas are not eligible for such subsidies.

PAT grants can be made to the following kinds of companies:

1. Those industrial enterprises that, through their investments, create or maintain jobs.
2. Enterprises that create, expand or maintain research activities or certain service activities (such as management, planning, engineering or communications).
3. Under certain conditions, companies that construct new premises or acquire new equipment to be leased to such enterprises as those described above.
4. As for acquisitions of declining businesses in view of their recovery, they may be granted PAT under the condition that the recovery plan have been examined by the CODEFI, CORRI or CIRI.

6. EXCHANGE CONTROL/FOREIGN INVESTMENT REGULATIONS

Exchange controls

The exchange control regulations currently (1987) in force in France were reinstituted in 1968 to prevent a heavy drain on French currency as a result of the political crisis. The banks are responsible for implementing these regulations, and no transaction can take place between residents and non-residents without presentation of the appropriate documents.

The main features of exchange controls are as follows:

1. Any international financial transaction has to be made through an *Intermédiaire agréé.*
2. French residents cannot without prior authorization *settle assets abroad*, and they must *repatriate the income* of all their properties abroad.
3. The France Area includes the metropolitan territory, Monaco, the DOMTOM (overseas Departments and Territories), and 14 African states.

Within the French Franc Area, bilateral agreements with France set the principle of the free transferability of money.

Intermédiaire agréé

An *Intermédiaire agréé* is a bank or a financial institution officially approved by the Ministry of Finance to make the payments connected with international transactions of any kind (goods and services). The legislation put the industrialist under the obligation, when importing or exporting, to make any foreign exchange transaction or capital transaction through an *Intermédiaire agréé*.

Resident/Non-resident

This is a basic customs concept. A company will be regarded as a resident as soon as it is located in France. It may be a branch of a foreign company located in France, or a French company even though foreign-controlled.

As far as capital transactions are concerned a distinction is made between control within the EEC and control of the EEC. A corporation acquires EEC status as soon as 50 per cent or more of its assets and the majority of its votes belong to shareholders or partners who have the status of EEC investors. In contrast, a non-EEC corporation is distinguished on the basis of the percentage of the enterprises share capital. A foreign company is considered as being under French control as soon as 20 per cent of its capital is held by French residents, either directly or through foreign companies under French control. Similarly, a French company is under foreign control when more than 20 per cent of its share capital is held by non-residents or by French companies under foreign control.

Concept of 'foreign direct investment'

The following activities are considered, under the exchange control regulations, to constitute 'foreign direct investment' in France:

1. the purchase, creation or expansion of a business enterprise in France, whether in the form of a corporation, a partnership or a sole proprietorship;
2. all other activities, on one or several occasions, simultaneous or successive, which permit one or several individuals or legal entities to obtain or increase control of a French enterprise or to effect the expansion or extension of a French enterprise already under its or their control.

The determination of whether a particular investment is in fact a foreign direct investment includes consideration of the percentage of any French enterprise's capital which, upon completion of the investment, will be held by non-residents or by legal entities under foreign control when more than 20 per cent of its share capital is held by non-residents. Consideration is also given to other factors – e.g. loans, guarantees, patents, licences or commercial contracts, or the existence of a lease management agreement – that could significantly strengthen or enhance the degree of control that such participation confers upon its holders.

Control of foreign investments

The treatment of foreign investments in France has been substantially liberalized since late 1984. The rules applying to direct investments are different whether the investor is an EEC member or not; the rules applying to indirect investments are the same in both cases.

The essential features of the new rules are shown in table 7.3.

Securing approval for foreign investments

When a Prior Authorization is required, the application must be made to the Treasury and include comprehensive information on the investing company. This includes full financial and legal information on the nature of the investment, information on the investment's scope and intended results (including location, size, number and types of employees, expected impact on foreign trade, etc.).

The liquidation and the capital repatriation of a foreign direct investment in France is free provided the following conditions are fulfilled:

1. In case of transfer to a non-resident or a foreign-controlled company, the transferee is regarded as a direct investor in France and must fulfil the required formalities.
2. The transfer of funds abroad has to go through an *Intermédiaire agré*.
3. If the income resulting from the selling of shares is higher than one million francs, the transfer abroad of this income is subject to prior declaration.
4. A report called *a posteriori* declaration has to be referred within twenty days after the realization of the liquidation.

Licensing arrangements

Licensing is employed extensively in France, and foreign companies commonly use it as a substitute for, or a preliminary to, direct investment. Licensing also represents an effective way of penetrating the French market in key high-technology sectors in which the government wishes to reserve the predominant role for French companies.

The 1968 patent law introduced the preliminary examination, which consists of a 'novelty search' resulting in an *'avis documentaire'*. French patents can still be challenged in the courts: they become fully validated only if successfully defended. On the whole, French courts tend to be conservative in disposing of industrial property rights.

France adheres to the Paris Convention, and a patent applicant may benefit from priority for up to one year if an application has previously been made in another country. France also joined other countries in the

Table 7.3 Control of foreign investments, post-1984

	EEC	*non-EEC*
Creation of a new company in France	D (1 month)	D (1 month)
Less than FF10 million share in a French company	D (1 month)	D (2 months)
More than FF10 million share in a French company	D (2 months)	PA
Acquisition of shares of a foreign-controlled company	D	PA
Additional investments of foreigners in French companies that they control:		
capital increases if more than 75 per cent of the company is held by the same foreign investors	—	—
loans at the market rate, with a set bills-payable book, and copy of the contract by an 'Intermédiaire agréé'	—	—
subsidies	—	—
Loans to a French company (indirect investment)		
at the market rate, with a set bills -payable book, for a length of time > 1 year, and in foreign currencies	—	—
if one of these conditions is not fulfilled	PA	PA
Redemption before due date		
after more than 1 year	—	—
after less than 1 year	PA	PA
Purchase or creation of a business < FF10 million, to be exploited by the investors	—	—
Guarantee granted by non-resident to resident	—	—
Purchase of securities as an indirect investment	—	—

D: Declaration requirement
PA: Prior Authorization requirement.

European Patent Convention and the Patent Co-operation Treaty, both of which went into effect in 1978. In 1976 France signed the Common Market Patent Convention.

France is also a member of the Madrid Arrangement, and trademarks registered in France must be deposited at the International Bureau for the Protection of Industrial Property in Geneva, for protection in other member countries. Conversely, trademarks registered in Geneva will be transmitted to France for registration. France has the right, however, to refuse to provide such protection in accordance with its own laws.

French companies may enter into any sort of licensing arrangement with foreigners. Licensing agreements usually run for periods of between five years with the maximum being ten years, although automatic renewals are frequently built into agreements. A licensing agreement may not outlast the patent right for which it was granted. Know-how is also licensable.

The French party to a licensing or technical assistance agreement, or to the renewal of an existing agreement, must notify the *Institut National de la Propriété Industrielle* (INPI), an agency of the Ministry of Industry, within one month after the execution of such agreement. Licences and technical assistance agreements reported to the INPI are not made public. Having notified the INPI, the licensee receives a registration number, which is required by the central bank for royalty transfers. Without such a number, the licensee is not permitted to sue for patent infringement.

If royalties are too high (particularly if payment is made from a French subsidiary to a foreign parent), the Ministry of Economy may rule that the amount deemed to be excessive may not be deducted for tax purposes. The tax authorities, however, are not bound by the INPI's opinions, and they may permit a licensee to deduct royalty payments that the INPI deems excessive.

SUMMARY

The legal and fiscal provisions that apply specifically to mergers and acquisitions of existing companies in France reflect the economic environment. Investors do not face any major problems in establishing or extending their business provided that standard legal requirements are complied with and, in fact, there are a number of specific incentives and arrangements that make such transactions attractive.

Under French corporate law commercial entities can operate in a variety of forms. The most commonly used forms are the SA and the SARL, their intitial incorporation is rather simple and the transformation or combination of these existing businesses is a common process. French law provides several methods of acquisition and reorganization of the acquired business to achieve the most desirable operational structure.

Rules governing competition aim to protect normal trade. They have been less extensively developed in France than in other countries such as the United States. The French price control regulation was removed in 1986 so that prices can be freely set in all areas of economic activity. However, rules governing illicit trade or anti-trust practices, and unfair competition are still in force. These laws apply as complements to the rules of law adopted by the EEC.

The French tax system is made up of three main branches: direct taxes, indirect taxes and registration taxes. Recent legislation has reduced the tax burden. The corporate tax rate has been reduced to 45 per cent and will be 42 per cent in 1988 whilst the tax credit granted to shareholders remains equal to 50 per cent of the distributed profits. The marginal tax rate for individuals has been reduced to 58 per cent. French law also provides favourable tax rules that apply in cases of merger and business transfers; it also provides a corporate tax exemption for new companies set up to take over bankrupt businesses.

French accounting principles have been legislatively enacted and codified and consequently have the force of law. Although no general legislative rules apply to group companies, principles of consolidated accounts have been established by a law of 1985 and a Decree of 1986 which effectively means that France is now consistent with international accounting principles in this area.

Exchange control and foreign investment regulations are now very liberal and most of the restrictions concerning investments, payments, deposits and transfers have been abolished. Few restrictions relating to foreign investments in France still remain.

In conclusion, the legal and fiscal environment provides different means and technical solutions facilitating business combinations in France. It appears obvious that the general trend in France is to assist business and to reduce the tax burden. The law of July 1984 relating to employee buy-outs provides specific dispositions to initiate this trend, and the stock-option plan constitutes another legal arrangement which offers the opportunity to take control. Moreover, a Bill of Law is being proposed in order to encourage investments in France whereby the French LMBO will be extended to the legal representatives of companies and stock-options plans will be further encouraged.

Takeover activity, including hostile bids, became more common in 1986 and many French companies are becoming acquisitive on an international basis. For example, L'Air Liguide paid $1.06 billion in cash to acquire Three Industries of Houston and Yves Saint Laurent purchased Charles of the Ritz in the US for $630 million. Such acquisitions may represent the start of France becoming strong internationally as well as domestically.

8

Italy

1. BUSINESS ORGANIZATIONS AND COMBINATIONS

Business organizations

The Italian form of business organization which most closely resembles a US corporation is the joint stock company or *Società per Azioni* (SpA). This type of corporate entity must have a minimum capital of 200 million lire and, in order to maintain its limited liability status, it must have more than one shareholder. The capital may be in kind, in which case it is subject to various valuation and appraisal procedures. Should the capital stock be greater than 10,000 million lire, its issuance is subject to approval by the Treasury Department.

Other types of Italian entities with corporate attributes are:

1. *Società in accomandita per Azioni*, or SapA, is a special form of partnership whose general partners are shareholders and directors and are liable for the partnership's obligations jointly and severally but whose sleeping partners have limited liability. This type of business organization is not as commonly encountered as it once was.
2. *Società a responsabilità limitata*, or Srl, is similar to a limited liability company in which the liability to third parties is limited to the extent of the company's assets. The capital cannot be represented by shares but is divided into quotas or parts. The required minimum capital is 20 million lire.

Branches of foreign companies

Foreign companies with one or more branches permanently established in Italy are subject to the provisions of the Italian law regarding the filing and registration of the company's governing statutes, submission of the company's financial statements to the courts as though the branch were a separate legal entity, publication of the names of persons representing the branch on a permanent basis in Italy, etc. Although considered an independent entity for the fulfilment of certain tax and other official requirements, the branch is not in fact a legal entity in itself, so that foreign corporations establishing branches in Italy are liable for the acts and obligations of such branches.

Types of business combination

The types of business combinations in Italy are similar to those in other countries, i.e.:

1. Business transfers whereby the net assets of a division or a whole company are sold to an acquirer. As is discussed in sections 4 and 7, this has certain advantages for the buyer but may be disadvantageous to the seller from a tax standpoint.
2. Sale of shares in exchange for either cash or shares or other form of asset, although the tendency in Italy is generally by cash. Often a business's assets will be transferred to a new corporation in exchange for shares, and the shares would then be sold to the acquirer.
3. Merger of a wholly owned subsidiary into its parent (*fusione per incorporazione*) is very common in Italy but less common with a separate company to form a new company (*fusione propria*), as discussed below.

Takeovers are rare in Italy as the majority of companies are closely owned, or in a number of cases controlled by a syndicate.

There are no barriers to foreign companies acquiring or being acquired by Italian companies, but cross-border transactions must satisfy exchange control as discussed in section 6. Consequently, although possible, an acquisition of shares by a share issue involves certain formalities which may be troublesome, particularly if the foreign shares, in either a buy or sell situation, are not publicly traded.

2. TRENDS IN TAKEOVER ACTIVITY

There are no official statistics available in Italy on activity in mergers and acquisitions but there have been some quite clear trends. After a number of large acquisitions in the 1960s, many by foreign – principally American – companies, the difficult years of the 1970s were characterized by disposal of investments, not only by foreign investors but also by Italians in their family-owned businesses. The reasons for this were not just the economic difficulties arising from the oil crises and the worldwide economic depression but also due to the disruption caused by the unions in the late 1960s and early 1970s (starting with the famous *autunno caldo* – hot autumn – in 1969); the campaign of violence and terrorism by the Red Brigade; political instability in Italy and the spate of kidnappings.

The 1980s has seen substantial resolution of most of these problems and also a quite new era of acquisitions and takeover activity. This new era is characterized both by the size of some of the acquisitions and the

Table 8.1 Merger and acquisition activity in Italy 1982–1986

	1982	*1983*	*1984*	*1985*	*1986*
Italian acquisitions abroad	13	13	22	31	
Foreign acquisitions in Italy	26	33	56	81	
Acquisitions among Italian companies	129	137	193	184	
Total number of deals	168	183	271	296	
Ratio of Italian acquisitions to the total	8%	7%	8	10%	
Ratio of foreign acquisitions to the total	16%	18%	21%	27%	

Source: M & A International.

incidence of Italian groups as buyers (rather than sellers as occurred in the 1960s) both in Italy and abroad. Table 8.1 shows some unofficial statistics prepared by M & A International.

A major Italian force has been Carlo De Benedetti through the various companies he controls, directly or indirectly – CIR, Olivetti, Sasib. The foundations for a major portion of his group was laid down in the difficult years of the 1970s when he took over companies in difficulty and which are now profitable.

Contested takeovers are rare in Italy, because a large number of Italian companies are closely controlled. The only major recent exception was the Montedison acquisition of Bi Invest. Although there is no formal regulation of mergers and acquisitions, political involvement and intereference is high. This has been evident in recent years in the Electrolux purchase of Zanussi, Ford's bid for Alfa Romeo and the Berlusconi offer for the state-owned food group SME after the offer from De Benedetti's food company, Buitoni, had already been accepted by SME shareholders.

3. MERGER CONTROL

With the exception of political interference and, where applicable, exchange control laws, there is no formal legislation or code of practice relating to mergers and acquisitions. Specifically there is:

1. no monopolies commission or anti-trust agency and
2. no code of practice on takeovers either by legislation or by the stock exchange.

The *Commissione Nazionale per le Società e le Borse* (CONSOB) set up in 1974 is the Italian equivalent of the SEC, and has far-reaching powers under its constitution to lay down regulations that have the equivalent effect of law but has not taken any action in this area. It is likely, however, that some measures will soon be taken.

Until then Italy will continue to suffer all the abuses from their absence including insider dealing and undeclared build-up of significant shareholdings prior to a formal offer. CONSOB suspends shares that have an excessive increase or fall (more than 20 per cent) and investigates the reasons. The only deterrent to malpractice or abuse is the ever-present threat of investigation by the public prosecutor (*magistratura*) whose self-perceived area of intervention is continually expanding into uncharted waters.

The shareholders' resolution approving a merger along with the articles and bye-laws, must be appropriately notified and approved by the court (Tribunale) (Art. 2502 C.C). The notification takes the form of copies of the minutes of the shareholders' meetings approving the merger being lodged with the court within 30 days of the meeting together with the financial statements of the two companies on which the exchange of shares is based. The court's principal function is to review formally the basis of the merger to ensure its conformity with the Civil Code and that minority shareholders and creditors are adequately protected.

Any merger involving a company quoted on the Italian stock exchanges has to be vetted by CONSOB. The companies effecting the merger must file with CONSOB the proposed respective shareholders' resolutions and financial positions of the companies 45 days before the shareholders' meetings. In addition, the auditors of the emerging corporation must issue a report within 30 days of this filing giving an opinion on the reasonableness of the values of the shares exchanged.

4. TAXATION

Principal types of taxes

The present Italian system of income taxation has been in effect since 1 January 1974. It should be noted that the tax rules are undergoing revision and it is expected that new rules will be in force in 1988.

Income taxes are levied on a national basis on individuals (IRPEF) and on business entities of all kinds (IRPEG), and also on a local basis (ILOR). IRPEF is levied progressively at rates that increase with the taxpayer's level of income and range from 12 to 62 per cent. IRPEG is levied at a rate of 36 per cent on business income from all sources. ILOR is a local income tax levied on certain individuals and business entities at a rate of 16.2 per cent. ILOR is deductible from IRPEF or IRPEG taxable income, resulting in an effective income tax rate for companies of 46.37 per cent.

Income tax is withheld, at fixed rates, from most payments of interest, dividends and royalties, and such withholdings may be on account, depending on the situation, but usually represent a final tax for individuals, partnerships and non-resident entities.

Income taxes apply to resident companies, which are subject to tax on their worldwide income, and non-resident companies, which are subject to tax only on Italian-source income (i.e. income deemed to have been 'produced' in Italy).

The foreign tax credit granted under Italian law and the various treaties to which Italy is a party minimizes the incidence of double taxation on foreign companies.

Dividends paid to resident companies, as defined by law, are subject to a withholding tax of 10 per cent. Resident shareholders enjoy a tax credit for the IRPEG tax paid by the company that distributes the dividends, thus eliminating double taxation. Dividends paid to non-resident companies or individuals are subject to a final withholding tax of 32.4 per cent, unless existing tax treaties provide otherwise.

A recent law provides for an equalization tax of 15 per cent on distributions of profits earned by a company up to 31 December 1982. On distributions of income earned after that date, the equalization tax rate is 56.25 per cent of the distributed amount in excess of 64 per cent of the company's taxable income.

The Italian government offers investors in certain areas (principally the south of Italy, or Mezzogiorno) several incentives, including tax holidays, cash grants, long-term loans at low interest rates, and reduced social insurance contributions. With respect to income taxes, the most common incentives are: (a) 100 per cent reduction of national income taxes for a period of ten years for new companies from the date of the company's formation; and (b) total exemption from the local income tax (ILOR) for a period of ten years, beginning with the first year in which business income is produced.

Value-added tax (IVA) is levied at various rates, the most common of which is 18 per cent.

Capital gains are taxed as ordinary income for corporations, but are exempt for individuals if the gain is considered not speculative, otherwise it is added to income and taxed as such. Under the new tax rules, taxation of capital gains may be deferred for up to ten years in certain situations.

Briefly, other taxes having an impact on corporations in a merger or acquisition situation are the following.

1. *INVIM*. A property tax levied, either every ten years for companies, on the indexed increase in value over cost of non-manufacturing land and buildings; or, in the event of sale, on the gain since acquisition or last indexed valuation for all categories of land and buildings. Mergers do not trigger the INVIM tax.
2. *Imposta di Registro*. A registration tax on certain types of transactions including purchase of a business or assets, but not shares. The tax rate varies from 3 per cent for the major portion of asset categories to 10 per cent for land and buildings. Where a transaction involves the purchase of a business represented by assets less liabilities, the tax is due on the net value of the transaction and taxes due on the various asset categories are determined by reducing the taxable value in the proportion that total liabilities bear to total assets.

3. *Stamp duty*. A tax on share transactions is levied at varying minimal rates.

Taxation implications of mergers and acquisitions

Tax implications for the seller (acquiree)

By private individuals. Capital gains are not normally taxable in Italy to individuals. The sale of stock or shares only gives rise to tax liability for an individual if the stock is sold within five years of purchase *and* the holding sold in a 12 month period exceeds 2 per cent of a quoted company, 10 per cent of a non-quoted company or 25 per cent of a partnership, joint venture, quota, etc. Taxation of capital gains has been the subject of much discussion in recent years and it seems likely that there will be some change in the legislation in the near future to tax these gains.

A sale of business assets by either a sole trader owned less than five years, would give rise to a capital gain which would be taxable, net of ILOR, at the average of the previous two years' tax rate or at normal income tax rates, respectively.

By legal entities. Any gain on sale of shares or stock or business assets by a legal entity is taxed as normal business income. Taxation of the capital gains on the sale of a business as opposed to shares can be deferred if, within two years, amounts equivalent to the gain are reinvested in productive assets. The carrying value of the investment in these productive assets is reduced by a depreciation reserve equivalent to the gain and the net amount is then depreciated for tax purposes. Under the new tax rules, the period of taxation could be deferred over ten years. In 1980 legislation commonly called the *Pandolfi*, enabled companies to spin off their businesses into separate legal entities at their market values. The gain so created was not taxable to the existing entity and the new entity could depreciate the assets received at market value. It is therefore very common in Italy to find this group structure of a financial holding company with its only asset a wholly-owned operating company. Disposal of the shares in the operating company not only causes taxation of the gain but also recaptures the original *Pandolfi* gain on spin-off to taxation at current rates.

Tax implications for the acquirer

Purchase of assets. If the acquirer buys a business's net assets either from an individual or a corporation the assets are treated for tax purposes as new assets and are depreciable as such. This also applies to any goodwill purchased, which may be depreciated for tax purposes over five years. Registration taxes are payable on the net value of the transaction at rates changing from 3 per cent for moveable property to 10 per cent for land and buildings or 0.5 per cent for receivables. The value of assets for determining registration taxes due is reduced proportionately for any liabilities taken on. The registration taxes paid can be depreciated for tax purposes over five years.

Purchase of stock. If stock is acquired the acquired company continues its business and depreciation for tax purposes as before, therefore the acquirer does not obtain the tax benefit of depreciation on assets and goodwill as it would have done under a purchase of assets.

This can be partially accomplished by merging the acquired company and acquirer. The assets recorded in the acquired company's books can be written up to their market value on merger up to a maximum of the carrying value of the investment to the acquirer. The write-up is exempt from income taxes and the written-up values form the new tax base. If the net carrying value (purchase price) exceeds the market value the excess is allocated to goodwill, but cannot at present be depreciated for tax purposes. It is expected that the new tax rules will allow deduction for tax purposes. Trademarks and patents can also be written up but only if there is already a value assigned to them in the books and records.

There is, however, often an obstacle to this procedure of merging the companies to obtain the tax benefit and that is the two-tier structure mentioned above deriving from the *Pandolfi*. On the merger between the acquirer and the financial holding company acquired, generally, the only asset that can be written up is the investment in the operating subsidiary.

Normally, the whole of the excess of carrying value (purchase price) over net equity would be allocated to the investment. To obtain the tax benefits a subsequent merger should take place with the operating subsidiary but this would effectively reverse the *Pandolfi* spin-off and recapture the original write-up to taxation. Careful evaluation has to be made as to whether the tax benefits of the additional depreciation would exceed those of the taxes on the recaptured *Pandolfi* gain. Depending on the structure of the acquiring group in Italy there are ways of avoiding recapture of the Pandolfi reserve to taxation. This is achieved by having an Italian corporation issue shares to the merged corporation of the acquirer/acquiree in exchange for the investment in the wholly-owned operating company. In this way the holding company (acquirer) could own the Italian corporation which in turn would merge with its new subsidiary (the operating company) writing up the assets as described above.

The values assigned to business's assets when assets are sold as part of a going concern business are examined by the tax authorities and may result in an assessment to the seller for additional taxable gains, particularly goodwill and fixed assets and additional registration taxes for which both parties are liable. The tax authorities have two years following that in which the transaction takes place to make such an assessment.

Italian tax legislation does not include the possibility of consolidated tax returns, but does permit the write-down of an investment to reflect its impairment since acquisition or incorporation. The write-down must be based on the approved official financial statements and there is no requirement to write up the investment once the company becomes profitable.

Recipients of dividends are given a tax credit at the effective current corporate tax rate which renders dividends tax-free for corporations or even a tax refund if the recipient is in a loss position.

If an acquired company has significant retained earnings it is advantageous to pay dividends to the new parent, and create a larger difference between the carrying value of the investment and its net equity for subsequent allocation to assets in the event of a merger.

The divergent interests of the seller and the acquirer, especially if the former is an individual must be fully addressed in the negotiation and contractual stage to ensure the most effective tax structure.

Mergers between Italian companies to form an effective new corporation (*fusione propria*), although envisaged by the law rarely take place because the tax aspects are rarely advantageous. The overriding tax rule is that such mergers should be 'fiscally neutral', therefore no tax benefit is obtained on written-up assets, but any write-up or 'gain' recorded on merger is narrowly interpreted by the tax authorities as 'other income' and taxed. This form of merger in Italy, similar to a pooling of interests, results in a new corporation issuing stock to acquire the assets in two or more existing corporations. The new corporation would continue with the historical values of the old corporation.

It is, therefore, clear from this that the greatest tax benefit is achieved by one corporation acquiring the other, either for cash or stock, and then subsequently merging to write up, free of tax, the assets of the acquired corporation by the excess of cost over net equity and gain the subsequent deductions through depreciation and amortization for tax purposes. Any write-up of assets on merger other than by merging with a wholly owned subsidiary is taxable.

Legal date of merger. The earliest effective legal date of the merger is three months after the merger is approved by the court. In this time creditors may object to the merger and if so they must be paid in cash or an equivalent amount in cash must be deposited with a bank or by some other guarantee determined by the court. The merger can however be backdated with appropriate guarantees for debts.

5. ACCOUNTING

Background

The Civil Code requires an annual balance sheet and a statement of revenues and costs to be prepared and prescribes certain bases of valuation. The Accounting Principles Board of the Italian professions recommends that these be integrated with supplementary financial statements which reflect, in practice, the US and international presentation of the balance sheet, statements of income, changes in financial position, and stockholders' equity and, in addition, have issued pronouncements on accounting principles. These cannot yet be considered generally accepted as small and medium-sized companies frequently file only the financial statements specifically requested by the Civil Code.

The above proposed statements have not been formally recognized by CONSOB as part of the basic set of financial statements as recommended by the profession. However, CONSOB recommended that the directors' report include the additional statements and the notes to the financial statements as part of their report to shareholders. As a matter of fact, all listed companies and other companies subject to audit requirements normally present the additional statements in their annual reports.

The Civil Code contains no requirement to prepare consolidated statements, but it requires annual accounts to include a supporting schedule listing any holdings in subsidiaries or associated companies, and disclosing the nominal and carrying values of each holding. A subsidiary is defined in terms of ownership of a majority of the voting rights and an associated company in any company in which 10 per cent of the share capital is owned or 5 per cent in the case of a listed company. Complete sets of the most recent annual accounts of each subsidiary company must be attached to the parent company's own accounts. Key financial information, including turnover and results for the period, must also be given for associates.

The 1974 law which established CONSOB gave to that commission powers to require consolidated statements from listed companies. From 1982 CONSOB has requested all listed companies to prepare and submit consolidated financial statements. Prompted by the action of CONSOB, the development of standards relating to the preparation of consolidated statements was given high priority by the profession. Difficulties have been experienced in reaching agreement and the standard, although issued, has not yet been officially approved either by Assirevi, the association of auditing firms, or by CONSOB. In the meantime, companies were instructed by CONSOB to follow International Accounting Standards in the absence of approved official Italian principles.

Neither the Civil Code nor the pronouncements specifically deal with accounting for mergers and acquisitions although the accounting pronouncements do discuss goodwill in its pronouncement on consolidation. This pronouncement is very much in line with US accounting standards.

Tax treatment consequently heavily influences accounting treatment. Equity accounting is not normally applied, unless separate consolidated financial statements are prepared, because this would give rise to additional taxation, as mentioned above. However, it is applied where there has been an impairment since acquisition or incorporation, as this is tax deductible under certain circumstances.

Goodwill on consolidation is determined in Italy, as generally elsewhere, as the excess of purchase price over the fair value of the assets of the business acquired. Where, on the other hand, this is purchased as part of the net assets of a business the value is agreed between the parties. As it can be depreciated for tax purposes normally over five years, this is generally the treatment in the financial statements. Goodwill can also be amortized for tax purposes where the business is spun off to a new corporation for shares.

This is a common method in Italy for isolating the acquirer, who would then purchase the stock, from contingent liabilities which would remain with the vendor, except for certain tax liabilities.

Pooling of interests, although envisaged by legislation, is an approach that is rarely applied because of the adverse tax consequences, whereas the only method allowed for by the pronouncements of the accounting profession – Dottori Commercialisti – is the purchase method.

The treatment in Italian financial statements of foreign subsidiaries does not differ to those for Italian subsidiaries, nor do the tax aspects change.

Other significant Italian accounting practices

Consolidation

The concept of consolidation is not mentioned in the Civil Code and, as a result, it is not common for consolidated accounts to be prepared by unlisted companies in Italy. Instead, the separate accounts of majority-owned subsidiaries are commonly attached to those of the parent company. For other associated companies, at least 20 per cent owned, only certain basic data, such as sales, total assets and net income, are disclosed.

Revenue and expense recognition

As a general rule, revenues should be recognized only when their realization is at least reasonably certain and objectively measurable, while expenses are to be accounted for when they are expected to be incurred. In the past, observance of this rule has caused problems, since expenses are deductible for tax purposes only when they are incurred. Tax rules have had a significant effect on the preparation of the income statement as expenses are deductible only when they are certain and some expenses (for example accelerated depreciation) are only allowed for tax purposes if recorded in the official books and financial statements. Consequently, the concept of statements for statutory purposes separate to the tax return is not yet possible in Italy. However, business practices are gradually moving towards a revision of the tax laws in this regard. The pronouncements of the Dottori Commercialisti clearly indicate that the tax rules are not an acceptable alternative to recognized accounting principles in the preparation of financial statements.

Foreign currency translation

The Civil Code does not specifically deal with accounting for foreign exchange gains and losses, and the general practice followed in Italy, with some exceptions, in the past has been to record assets and liabilities in foreign currencies at historical rates. In recent years, it has become increasingly common practice to record current assets and liabilities at current rates and to credit or charge the income statement for the resulting gain or loss. With respect to long-term assets and liabilities, practice varies, but the general tendency is to use the current rate if translation results in a loss and the historical rate if translation results in a gain.

It should be noted that, for tax purposes, unrealized exchange losses are not deductible but recorded exchange gains are taxable. It is expected that this will change with the new tax laws.

Income taxes

Loss carrybacks are not permitted by law, while losses are allowed to be carried forward and offset against income for the national income tax for five years. The benefits from loss carryforwards are not segregated as extraordinary items and their availability together with their expiration date is not usually disclosed in Italian financial statements.

Other matters

There is a number of issues in the United States not having a corresponding issue or practice in Italy. The most important are indicated below:

1. interim financial reporting (not usually used);
2. financial reporting for segments of a business enterprise;
3. accounting by debtors and creditors for troubled debt restructuring;
4. prior period adjustments;
5. accounting for forward exchange contracts; and
6. financial reporting and changing prices.

International accounting standards (IASs)

A summary of the more important differences between Italian accounting standards and International accounting standards is provided in Table 8.2.

Statutory auditing and reporting requirements

Statutory audit

All corporations whose liabilities are limited by shares (*Società per Azioni* – SpA) must have a board of auditors (*Collegio Sindacale*), referred to as statutory auditors, to monitor management and perform certain verification procedures on the annual financial statements, including procedures to ensure that the financial statements are in compliance with the Civil Code. The board consist of three or five active members (*sindaci*) plus two substitute members and is appointed by the shareholders for a three-year term but can be elected for further terms. Limited liability partnerships (*Società a Responsabilità Limitata* – Srl) must also appoint a board of auditors when the partnership capital exceeds 100 million lire. The purpose of the board of auditors is to help safeguard the interests of shareholders and creditors.

Table 8.2 Comparison of Italian accounting standards issued by the professional bodies with international standards

International accounting standards	*Italian accounting standard*
IAS 5 – Information to be disclosed Requires comparative figures	No such requirement, but often shown
IAS 6 – Accounting responses to changing prices	No equivalent requirement
IAS 7 – Statement of changes in financial position	Required by standards but the relative standard has not been ratified by CONSOB
IAS 8 – Unusual and prior period items and changes in accounting policies	No specific standard; it is, however, not possible to make prior period adjustments
IAS 9 – Accounting for research and development activities	No specific standard
IAS 11 – Accounting for construction contracts	No specific standard; practice tends to be percentage of completion.
IAS 12 – Accounting for taxes on income	No specific standard. In practice only deferred tax debits could arise due to the requirements of the tax laws that all deductions from taxable income must be recorded in the financial statements
IAS 13 – Presentation of current assets and current liabilities	Required by standards but the relative standard has not been ratified by CONSOB
IAS 14 – Reporting financial information by segment	No specific standard
IAS 15 – Information reflecting the effects of changing prices	No specific standard
IAS 17 – Accounting for leases	No specific standard
IAS 19 – Accounting for retirement benefits in the financial statements of employers	No specific standard
IAS 20 – Accounting for government grants and disclosure of government assistance prohibits crediting such grants directly to shareholders' interests	There is no specific standard but a credit directly to shareholders equity is acceptable
IAS 21 – Accounting for the effects in foreign exchange rates	No specific standard
IAS 22 – Accounting for business combinations permits pooling of interests	No specific standard; accounting treatment is heavily influenced by tax considerations
IAS 24 – Related party disclosures	No specific standard
IAS 25 – Accounting for investments	No specific standard

The statutory auditors must be individuals and they are required to:

1. review the management of the business;
2. determine that the provisions of the Italian laws and the Company's articles of association are being observed;
3. determine that the Company's books and accounts are in order;
4. determine that the Company's annual financial statements agree with its books and other records and that they have been prepared in conformity with the relevant provisions of the Civil Code and other governing legislation.

No standard form of audit report is required by the Civil Code, which merely provides that the statutory auditors must identify, and provide justification for, any deviations from recognized accounting principles. In addition, the statutory auditors are specifically required to report on the following matters:

1. the basis of valuation of shares and bonds;
2. the method used in accounting for prepaid and deferred expenses;
3. accrued liabilities and deferred expenses;
4. the amounts of any provisions for depreciation, depletion and amortization set aside in each asset category.

The statutory auditors are personally liable for the accuracy and truthfulness of their statements and, with the directors, are jointly liable for the directors' actions or omissions whenever it can be shown that a loss could have been avoided if the auditors had performed their duties properly.

The official register of auditing companies (*Albo delle Società di Revisione*), together with the requirement that listed companies be audited by one of these companies, was set up to increase investor confidence in companies listed on the Italian stock exchanges and thereby contribute to the development of a larger and more active market. The audit performed by the registered audit firm does not substitute the examination performed by the board of auditors, even though some procedures are duplicated.

Subsequent to the requirement for listed companies to have their annual financial statements audited, legislation was also introduced for other groups and categories of companies and organizations. These were generally where public interest issues were involved. In this respect, the audit requirement was to provide an attest function on the reliability of the financial information.

Entities required to have their financial statements audited

Those entities that are currently required to be audited by an auditing company selected from the official register are:

1. companies traded on any of the ten Italian stock exchanges;
2. companies controlled directly or indirectly by the Ministry of State Investments;

3. insurance companies underwriting risks other than life;
4. companies taking advantage of certain export schemes;
5. publishing companies with annual revenues exceeding 10,000 million or with more than five journalists;
6. certain municipal and utility companies;
7. certain categories of banks.

Summary of significant auditing standards and comparison with internationally generally accepted auditing standards

In 1980 the existing auditing firms formed the association of Italian auditing firms, Assirevi. In 1981 Assirevi resolved to approve and adopt all the existing auditing standards established by the Dottori Commercialisti. To date, out of 18 established auditing standards, 17 have been approved by Assirevi. Standard no. 18, which deals with the auditors report has not been formally approved by Assirevi since as soon as it was issued the CONSOB issued its own recommendation for the auditors report, the language of which is significantly different from that recommended by the Dottori Commercialisti. It is foreseen that auditing standard no. 18 will gradually become obsolete in practice since, in order to avoid confusion to the public, it is felt that only one form of auditors report should be issued. The CONSOB has also approved, with the exception of no. 18, the auditing standards established by the Dottori Commercialisti.

The following standards are in the process of being issued by the profession:

1. irregularities and illegal acts;
2. related parties;
3. auditing standards for banks and insurance companies;
4. auditing standards for investment companies.

With the exception of these being issued there are no significant differences between Italian and US auditing standards and procedures.

From time to time Assirevi publishes recommendations to its members to promote uniformity among accounting firms for certain aspects of acceptable auditing procedures in the absence of a particular auditing standard issued by the profession.

6. EXCHANGE CONTROL/FOREIGN INVESTMENT REGULATIONS

Acquisitions either into or out of Italy are subject to valuation by a stockbroker and payment should be through an Italian commercial bank.

To avoid both the additional time and costs connected with this procedure often the acquisitions are effected by incorporating a holding company in Italy as the vehicle for the acquisition through its capital stock or loans.

Foreign investments in Italy are regulated by law 43 of 1956 which places restrictions on disinvestment and dividends. These restrictions are rarely, if ever, applied.

Italy is part of the OECD and as such respects the agreements relating to loans and their repayment and also those of the EEC.

Transactions with foreign companies, particularly subsidiaries, parents or affiliates are frequently scrutinized by both the tax and exchange control authorities, who require that these transactions take place at 'normal value'. Although 'normal value' is rarely easy to establish the authorities may allege violations and assess income taxes and penalties.

7. OTHER FACTORS

The purchase of a company's net business assets as opposed to stock is a favoured method for the acquirer in Italy as this gives a number of advantages:

1. purchase of assets at current market value provides full benefit of depreciation for tax purposes
2. the amortization of goodwill for financial accounts and for tax purposes
3. the identification of specific liabilities to be taken on
4. all contingencies are left with the seller.

Under Italian law, however, if a business is sold as a going concern the buyer is jointly liable with the seller for any liabilities recorded in the books (not contingencies) not transferred to the new entity. Furthermore in certain circumstances tax contingencies both direct and indirect can be pursued and satisfied out of real estate and moveable assets. Also, when transferring going concerns, employees continue to accrue right (seniority pay, severance pay, notice, etc.) based on their original hiring date.

In general, Italians do not have any prejudices against foreigners and are very receptive towards new ideas and methods of working that have a foreign basis.

Political interference in industry and business is high in Italy in major transactions and there have been occasions when it has had an impact on acquisitions and ownership. This intereference is not directed solely at foreigners but they are an easier target and on occasions politically more acceptable.

An Italian merger similar to a pooling (*fusione propria*) although rare in practice as mentioned above, when applied has a number of legal requirements which must be fulfilled for the merger to be effective. These are:

1. The proposal to shareholders should be based on the year-end no earlier than four months before the date of the proposed merger (or six months if based on the latest official accounts). There is much discussion and contrasting decisions as to whether the financial position should be based on historical values or whether an attempted appraisal of the business should be made.
2. The shareholders resolution and financial position at the date of the resolution must be filed with the courts to be effective. The resolution can determine a retroactive effective date of the merger so that losses or gains subsequent to that date accrue to both shareholders. Although the effect can be retroactive for tax this is not true for legal purposes.

SUMMARY

Historically the large private sector industrial and financial companies in Italy are controlled by a very small number of families and individuals. However, in 1986 and 1987 there have been significant changes in ownership and, together with the rapid growth of the Milan Bourse has begun to break down the established oligarchy. This has meant that merger and acquisitions activity has become more significant in Italy. In addition, some Italian companies have become more aggressive in the international arena and a number of acquisitions of French companies have been made. For example, Feruzzi took effective control of Beghin-Say, the French sugar company. There are few regulations in Italy controlling mergers and acquisitions and no control over insider dealing.

In the past, taxation has been a significant factor in acquisition activity and also in affecting accounting standards. However, recent developments have meant that those companies that need to be audited produce financial statements of a high standard. This should improve comparability of Italian company accounts.

9
Japan

1. BUSINESS ORGANIZATIONS AND COMBINATIONS

Business organizations

The main types of business organization authorized under the Commercial Code in Japan (the original Code was issued in 1899 and the latest edition was published in 1981) include the sole proprietorship, an unlimited liability company, *Gomei-Kaisha*, a company with limited and unlimited liability, *Goshi-Kaisha*, and the corporation, *Kabushiki Kaisha* (KK). In addition, there are other forms of business organization such as the limited liability company, *Yugen Kaisha* (YK), whose regulation is provided by the *Yugen-Kaisha* Law 1940 which was modelled on the German *Gesellschaft mit beshränketer Haftung Gesetz* (1892), which in turn evolved from the older Private Company Act in the UK. Business can also be conducted by a branch of a foreign enterprise.

Gomei-Kaisha is a general or unlimited partnership and was a popular type of the *zaibatsu*, a financial combine initially governed by several families such as Iwasaki (Mitsubishi), Mitsui, Sumitomo, Yasuda, etc. One of the goals of the occupation forces after World War II was to dissolve the *zaibatsu* as they were considered to be too powerful both politically and economically. *Goshi-Kaisha* is a limited partnership resembling *Gomei-Kaisha* except that it has both unlimited and limited partners.

Kabushiki Kaisha (KK) is a company limited by shares with the liability of each shareholder being his capital contribution. Foreign business enterprises would most likely adopt this type of organization when establishing a subsidiary in Japan. In contrast to the KK, the *Yugen-Kaisha* (YK) is a limited liability company which requires no public financing. The YK is a common type of organization for small enterprises because the formation procedure and other formalities are simplified compared with those of the KK, and the minimum capital is ¥100,000 (£1 ≃ ¥240 as at 25 June 1987). To the surprise of the government a large number of small-sized enterprises have been formed as KKs. The numbers of each type of Kaisha, or company, are shown in table 9.1.

Table 9.1 Number of companies, February 1986

Share capital (¥m)	Total	Operating companies	Liquidated companies
KK			
below 1	288,228	52,170	236,058
1–10	998,764	714,216	284,548
10–50	305,705	275,087	30,618
50–100	28,203	26,864	1,339
100–300	13,476	13,111	365
300–500	3,769	3,690	79
500–1000	1,798	1,771	27
1000–5000	2,374	2,354	20
5000	979	977	2
	1,643,296	1,090,240	553,056
YK	1,289,694	1,132,556	157,138
Goshi-Kaisha	211,311	80,004	131,307
Gomei-Kaisha	56,146	19,633	36,513
Total	3,200,477	2,322,433	878,014

Source: Shoji – Homu, No. 1076

It should be noted that the great majority of KKs are small enterprises, whose share capital is below ¥10 million. On the other hand, large enterprises whose share capital is ¥500 million or more, or whose liabilities as of the latest balance sheet date are ¥20,000 million or more, total around 5100 companies only.

Types of business combination

Mergers can take place between companies formed under the Commercial Code provided that the surviving company is a KK when either or both parties to the merger are themselves KKs (s.56 ②). The Commercial Code specifies that approval for the merger should be obtained at a shareholders' meeting (s.408 ①). A YK may also merge or be merged with another company provided certain conditions are fulfilled. When either company survives after a merger it must issue new shares to the shareholders of the acquired company (s.409).

A feature of mergers in Japan is that they are invariably friendly and brought about as a result of the initiative of a third party, particularly a bank or other institutional shareholder. This results from the fact that shares are lightly held by the institutions. Also, the Ministry of Finance and the Ministry of International Trade and Industries have often suggested the merger in order to adjust some industries.

Where a company transfers a significant part or whole of its business approval must be obtained at a general meeting of shareholders in accordance with section 245 ① of the Commercial Code.

The main restrictions imposed on share acquisitions is provided by the Law Concerning Prohibition of Private Monopoly and Preservation of Fair Trade, usually referred to as the Anti-Monopoly Law, and by the Law Concerning Control of Foreign Exchange and Foreign Trade. Share acquisitions may be undertaken by:

1. a transfer by a private sale agreement by a small number of major shareholders;
2. the allotment of new shares to non-stock holders; and
3. purchasing shares in the market.

In Japan either or both of the first two procedures are normally adopted in practice but purchasing shares through the market is not usual as it leads to steep rises in the share price.

A takeover bid is defined as an offer by one company to acquire all, or a controlling holding, of the shares in another company. Takeovers are regulated by the Securities and Exchange Law. In reality hostile takeovers are considered to be immoral and in fact since regulations in 1971 only two bids have occurred.

2. TRENDS IN TAKEOVER ACTIVITY

The Anti-Monopoly Law is administered by the Fair Trade Commission (FTC). The FTC produces an annual report which includes government statistics on mergers and acquisitions. The Law requires that where there is a merger, acquisition or a transfer of a significant part or the whole of a business the FTC must be informed before it is completed (s15–2 and s16).

Tables 9.2 and 9.4 show respectively incidence of mergers and business transfers in total and the analysis by industry. After reaching a peak in 1972, pure merger activity declined steadily throughout the 1970s, with the exception of 1977. Since 1979 the trend has been upward and is not likely to diminish until economic restructuring, after the rapid rise in the yen, has been largely completed. Figure 9.2 shows the number of business transfers and the trend over the last 25 years has been largely upward.

The amounts of total assets after mergers and after business transfers are summarized respectively in tables 9.2 and 9.3. The majority of mergers and acquisitions involve assets of below ¥1000 million – for example, in 1983 and 1984 the percentage of small transactions was 57 compared with 52 per cent in 1985. Similarly, the majority of business transfers involve assets of below ¥1000 million, representing 73 per cent of transactions in 1983 and 1985 and 71 per cent in 1984.

Table 9.2 The number of cases by the amount of total asset after mergers and acquisitions

	Amount of total asset (¥'000m)						
Financial year	*below 1*	*1–5*	*5–10*	*10–50*	*50–100*	*100+*	*Total*
1983	584	261	78	64	13	20	1020
1984	626	271	88	78	17	16	1096
1985	575	336	89	87	12	14	1113

Table 9.3 The number of cases by the amount of total assets after business transfers

	Amount of total asset (¥'000m)						
Financial year	*below 1*	*1–5*	*5–10*	*10–50*	*50–100*	*100+*	*Total*
1983	511	76	25	60	8	22	702
1984	559	118	27	38	12	36	790
1985	586	92	29	47	18	35	807

For many years Japan has been a hostile environment for mergers and acquisitions as they were considered to be immoral and therefore socially unacceptable. However, this concept has been reviewed recently as a result of changes in the social, political and economic climate. For example, strategic mergers are becoming increasingly acceptable and prevalent. Indeed, the Economic Research Institution of Daiwa Securities Ltd, analysed the causes of these changes in 1986 under six headings.

1. The needs of conglomerates. Conglomerates are becoming more prevalent as a way of protecting margins. As the rate of growth in the Japanese economy has slowed down and the rate of return has declined, many companies have turned to acquisition as a preferred route to new investment.
2. Shortening in the life-cycle of commodities. The product life-cycle has become progessively shorter as the pace of innovation becomes faster. One way of quickly moving into a new market is through mergers and acquisitions rather than through new investment. Thus mergers and acquisitions enable firms to cope more readily with the shortening product life-cycle.

Table 9.4 The number of cases of mergers and business transfers by industry, 1985

Industries	*Mergers and acquisitions*	*Business transfers*	*Total*
Agriculture, Forestry and Fisheries	6	0	6
Mining	3	2	5
Construction	63	11	74
Manufacturing	221	68	289
Food	30	8	38
Fibre	26	7	33
Wood and Timber	10	9	19
Paper and Pulp	11	3	14
Publishing and Printing	14	1	15
Chemicals, Petroleum and coal	15	8	23
Rubber and Leather	4	2	6
Ceramics, Earth & Rocks	15	6	21
Iron and Steel	4	2	6
Nonferrous Metal	1	1	2
Hardware	14	7	21
Machinery	70	13	83
The others	7	1	8
Wholesale and Retail	408	161	569
Estate Properties	104	4	108
Transportation, Communication & Warehouse	66	49	115
Service	130	34	164
Financing and Insurance	30	16	46
Electricity and Gas	2	1	3
Others	80	461	541
Total	1113	807	1920

Each industry is based upon the surviving companies after mergers and business transfers

3. Countermeasure to the friction of foreign trade. Whilst Japanese foreign trade has been expanding rapidly the imbalance in trade has become a political subject. In order to redress some of this imbalance and to avoid the possibility of retaliation, Japanese companies have begun to shift its emphasis from conventional exports to production abroad. One way of achieving this quickly is to acquire overseas companies to obtain a production and marketing foothold. In particular, the sudden rise in the value of the yen against the dollar has necessitated a change in companies' strategy.
4. Ample funds. In order to undertake mergers, acquisitions, takeovers and business transfers it is necessary to be able to secure adequate funding. Japanese companies are very liquid and in fact the average

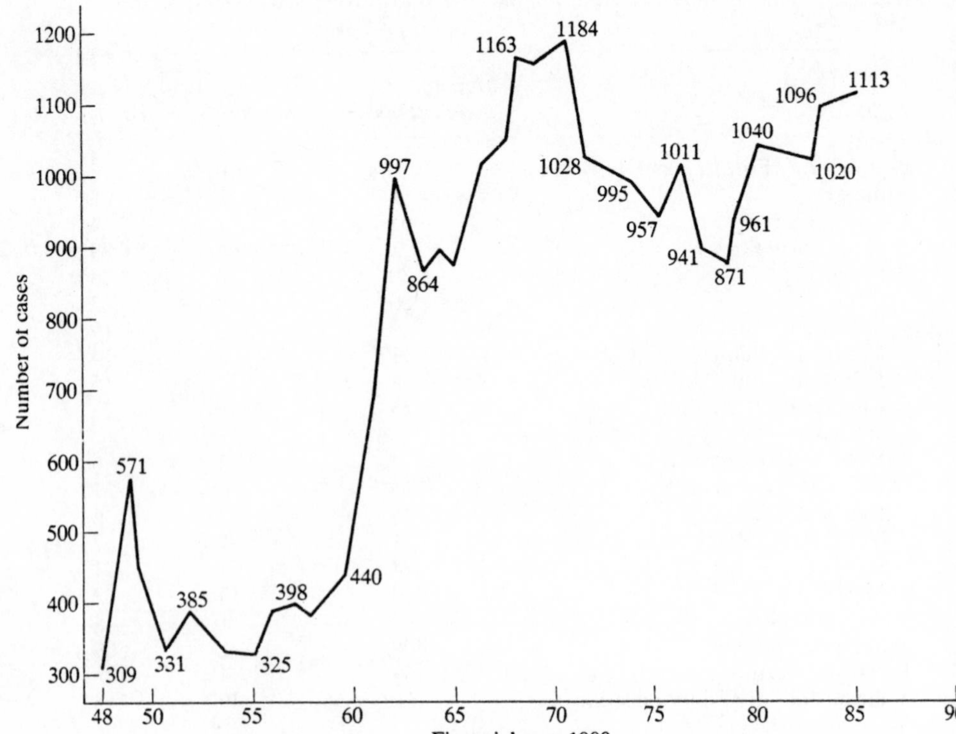

Figure 9.1 Number of cases of mergers and acquisitions

liquidity ratio has increased from 9.8 per cent in 1975 to 11.3 per cent in 1985.

5. Change of management's point of view on shareholdings. In order to maintain a close relationship between one company and another it has been traditional for Japanese companies to own shares in each other. However, there is a growing tendency for divestment of shareholdings without a willingness to discard the old conventions entirely. For example, heavy industrial companies that have fallen into a state of decline are having to sell of their shares in order to cover operating losses.
6. Mitigation of legal controls on mergers, acquisitions and takeovers. The Law concerning Control of Foreign Exchange and Foreign Trade was revised in December 1980 giving effect to a policy of liberalization of its foreign investment policy rather than prohibition.

The *Japan Economic Journal* published the results of a questionnaire on 16 January 1987 which asked the question: Do you think that mergers

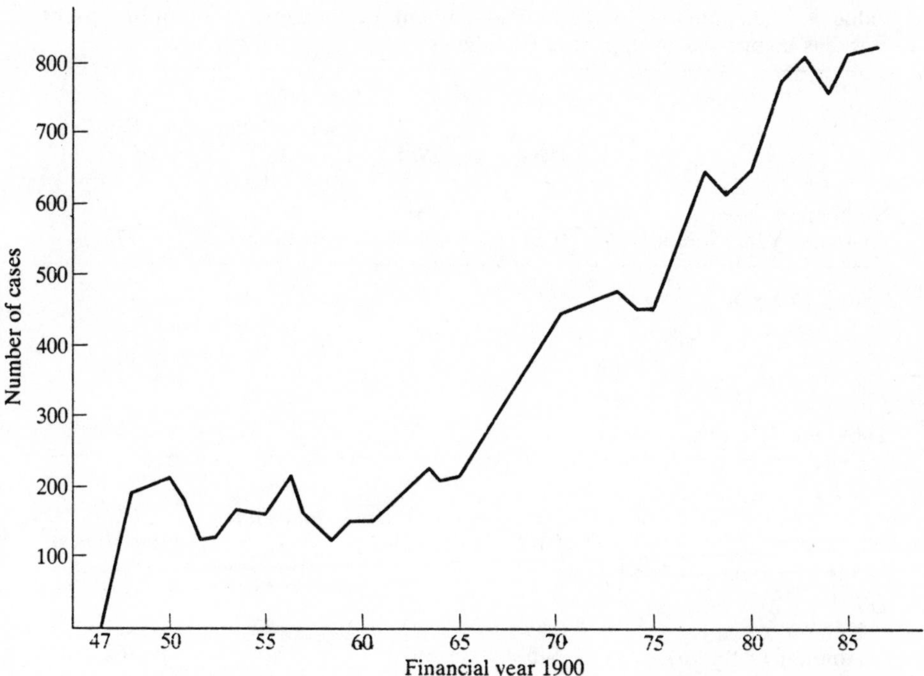

Figure 9.2 Number of cases of business transfers

and acquisitions will be able to take a firm hold on the Japanese business climate within five years? This question was put to top managements in 30 leading companies in Japan. Twenty answered 'yes', eight answered 'yes but subject to certain conditions' and only two answered 'no'. It should be noted that all who answered 'yes' supposed that the merger or acquisition was friendly and no one anticipated hostile takeovers to be established in the near future.

Tables 9.5 to 9.7 show the numbers of mergers and acquisitions of overseas companies by enterprises registered in Japan. By far the majority occurred in the US and the target enterprises are not only large public companies but also small and medium-sized firms.

3. MERGER CONTROL

The main controls that affect mergers and acquisitions in Japan are the Commercial Code, the Anti-Monopoly Law, and the Securities and Exchange Law. The administration of these laws is undertaken respectively

Table 9.5 The number of cases and amount of mergers and acquisitions of overseas companies by Japanese companies

	1984	*1985*	*1986 (Jan.–June) X2*	*1986 (Jan.–June)*
Number of cases	16	31	40	20
Amount (¥100 million)	9.34	1.071	1544	772

Source: Daiwa Securities Ltd

Table 9.6 Regional number

	1984	*1985*	*1986 (Jan.–June) X2*	*1986 (Jan.–June)*
US				
Number of cases	13	22	32	16
Amount (¥100 m)	545	897	1524	762
Other than US				
Number of cases	3	9	8	4
Amount (¥100 m)	389	174	20	10

Source: Daiwa Securities Ltd

Table 9.7 The number of public and private companies

	1984	*1985*	*1986 (Jan.–June) X2*	*1986 (Jan.–June)*
Public companies				
Number of cases	9	20	26	13
Amount (¥100 m)	830	805	1486	743
Private companies				
Number of cases	7	11	14	7
Amount (¥100 m)	104	266	58	29

Source: Daiwa Securities Ltd

by the Ministry of Justice, the Fair Trade Commission and the Ministry of Finance. In addition, the stock exchanges and securities industry provides for self-regulatory controls on takeover bids.

The Commercial Code

The procedure for a merger is laid down in the Commercial Code and consists of the following stages:

1. Conclusion of a contract note for the merger which stipulates the statutory articles (s.408 ②, s. 409 and s.410).
2. Approval must be obtained at a shareholders' meeting provided that there is a quorum of more than 50 per cent of the issued shares and the resolution is accepted by a two-thirds majority vote of the shareholders present (s.408 ① and s.408 ③).
3. An announcement must be made of the period of exception which permits creditors to object to the merger. If the creditors make an objection to the merger, the company must provide collateral security, property or debt for them (s.416 ①).
4. An announcement of the period that the offer remains open (s.416 ③).
5. An extraordinary meeting should be called to report to shareholders that the merger has been completed (s.412).
6. Changes in corporate structure must be registered (s.414 ① and s.414 ②).

With respect to business transfers, approval must be obtained from shareholders when a significant part or whole of a business is transferred (s.245 ① and ③). Any shareholders who objected to the transfer may relinquish their shares for a fair price (s.245–2). The legal procedures for business transfers are simpler than that of mergers because the preparation of the contract notes, announcements of exception to the creditors, and the extraordinary general meeting for report of the business transfer are not required under the Commercial Code.

The acquisition of treasury shares are prohibited although there are exceptions to this general rule (s.210). Furthermore, subsidiary companies may not acquire shares in their parent company (ss.211–2 ②) and this has an indirect influence on the acquisition of a business. This arises because the prohobition on acquisition of treasury shares prevents their use against a hostile acquisition.

The Anti-Monopoly Law

The Anti-Monopoly Law was promulgated in 1947 with the purpose of protecting general consumer interests by facilitating effective enforcement of free and fair competition. The law prohibits private monopolies, unfair trade and anti-competitive arrangements. There are also restrictions on mergers, acquisitions, takeover bids and business transfers. For example, mergers are prohibited when they restrict free competition substantially in an area of trade or when they are achieved by means of unfair trade practices (s.15(1)). If the latter regulation is violated the Fair Trade Commission (FTC) can order the necessary measures to be taken to prevent abuse and may bring a lawsuit against the merger (s.17–2). In order to prevent illegal mergers, any company intending to undertake a merger must report the proposal to the FTC (s.15(2)). There is then a 30-day suspension period during which the merger cannot be completed (s.15(3)). It is up to the FTC to decide whether a merger has been accomplished by unfair means or resulted in a restriction of free competition. The Commission decides whether a further review is required.

The transferee company must report a proposal for a business transfer to the FTC at least 30 days in advance of completion of the transaction. Both the transferee and transferor companies must jointly sign the report (s.16(1)).

Acquisition or ownership of shares which restrict competition or where unfair trade practices exist are illegal. This regulation applies to most businesses including financial institutions (as defined in the Anti-Monopoly Law s.9–2(1) such as banks, insurance companies, etc.), companies with share capital of at least ¥10,000 million, or companies with a net worth of ¥30,000 million or more.

In principle, financial institutions cannot acquire and hold more than 5 per cent (10 per cent in the case of an insurance company) of the issued shares of another domestic company (s.11). Large companies other than financial institutions cannot acquire and hold the shares of another domestic company when the total acquisition costs exceed the higher amount of their share capital or net worth (s.9–2).

Restrictions under the Anti-Monopoly Law described above apply equally to takeover bids as well as to mergers. In addition, with a takeover bid a special registration statement must be submitted to the Ministry of Finance.

The Securities and Exchange Law

In order to protect investors, the rules which the offeror company and the offeree company should obey during a takeover bid are provided in the Securities and Exchange Law 1948 and the related Ministerial Ordinance. When a takeover bid is made, a special registration statement must be completed and sent to the Ministry of Finance, which includes details of the designated takeover period, the takeover price, cancellation of the contract and the settlement amount (s.27–2(1)). A copy of this statement should also be sent to the offeree company (s.27–3(1)). The terms of the takeover offer, the requirements to protect the public interest and any provisions to protect investors must be published in daily newspapers. This information should also be sent to the Stock Exchange or the Securities Dealers Association applicable and an explanatory statement should be sent to the shareholders of the offeree company (s.27–3(2)). The special registration statement submitted to the Ministry of Finance must also be disclosed to the public for a period of one year (s.27–7(1)). The offeree company or its directors must publicly make a statement of their opinion of the offer (s.27–6).

A purchase of shares must be completed within 20–30 days of the public notice of the bid and the bid-price cannot be reduced in that period. However, the bid may be increased provided that the raised price applies to all those prepared to sell. After this period the terms of the transaction cannot be varied. During the bid period the offeror is required to purchase all of the shares offered at the designated price. Within ten days of the public notice, the offeror company can cancel the contract or withdraw the offer (the Ordinance, s.13). In principle, an offeror may only acquire shares in the offeree during the bid period (s.27–4(2)).

In certain industries, such as banking, transportation, electricity and gas, specific business laws apply and it is necessary to seek authorization from the competent ministers for any proposal of a business transfer or merger.

Regulation of the securities industry

In addition to the above regulations the securities industry has its own self-regulatory controls governing takeover bids. There are the resolutions issued by the Council of the Securities Dealers Association and the Articles of the Stock Exchange. The resolutions on takeover bids which the council of the Securities Dealers Association issued on 14 September 1977 are as follows:

1. Resolution 2 provides that all third parties with privileged information to a bid must keep it secret.
2. Third parties should not use privileged information to profit themselves (resolution 3).

Members of the Stock Exchange shall not assist a majority shareholder to acquire further shares in order for him to take advantage of bid proposal. In order to maintain the high reputation of the securities industry the self-regulatory controls on takeover bids and the purchase of shares is undertaken by the Stock Exchange itself.

Stock exchanges

There are eight stock exchanges in Japan located in Tokyo, Osaka, Kyoto, Nagoya, Fukuoka, Sapporo, Hiroshima and Niigata. All of the exchanges have their own listing and delisting regulations although they are, in reality, very similar. Shares of a company may be listed on two or more stock exchanges. Trading volumes and the number of companies listed varies from one exchange to another although the two most important exchanges are those located in Tokyo and Osaka. The Tokyo Stock Exchange, in which 1560 companies (including 55 foreign companies) are listed as at 28 February 1987, is now the largest in the world in terms of volume and its market capitalization exceeded the New York stock exchange at one point in 1987.

The cost of an initial listing is extremely high although subsequent issues are much cheaper. To obtain a listing the appropriate Stock Exchange will consider: the number of shares to be listed; the amount of capital to be raised; the net assets; the record of net income and dividends; the number of marketable shares and the number of potential investors in those shares; the number of years in existence; the transferability of shares; and the handling agents. The Stock Exchange will try to ensure that the issue is done fairly, that potential investors are protected, and that there is a smooth distribution of securities. Consequently there are a considerable number of formalities to be complied with.

In addition to the above administrative formalities a parent company must attach its accounts for the last three years and include consolidated accounts for the last two years. All the financial statements must be audited by either a domestic or foreign CPA or by an audit corporation.

In certain circumstances, such as where the shareholders of a listed company do not receive any dividends; there is a continued deficiency in capital; there is a material falsehood in the financial statements; or there is thin trading in a security the Stock Exchange can order a company to be delisted.

4. TAXATION

Background

Taxes in Japan are raised at the national, prefectual and municipal levels under the provisions of laws enacted by the Japanese Diet, as provided for under article 30 of the Japanese Constitution, 'the people shall be liable to taxation as provided by law'. Japan is divided into 47 prefectures and about 3400 municipalities, all of which are empowered to levy their own taxes within the framework of the Local Tax Law which has been approved by the Diet. There are a variety of taxes imposed on income, property, consumption and the transfer of certain goods. For example, corporation income tax, individual income tax, gifts tax, commodity tax, customs duty, securities transaction tax, registration and licence tax, motor vehicle tonnage tax etc., are collected by the government. Enterprise tax, fixed asset tax, electricity and gas tax, real estate acquisition tax, automobile acquisition tax etc., are imposed mainly by local authorities. Currently there is no value added tax in Japan. The government has been looking for an opportunity to introduce a general consumption tax, which bears a striking resemblance to the value added tax in Western Europe.

The main laws imposing corporation tax are the Corporation Tax Law 1965 which is supplemented by annual laws which, amongst other things, sets the rate of taxation for the fiscal year, and the Special Taxation Measures Law 1957. The above laws are supplemented by the related Ministerial Ordinances, which interpret the tax laws.

The Corporation Tax Law normally divides corporations into domestic and foreign for Japanese tax purposes. A domestic corporation is defined as a corporate entity whose headquarters or main office is located in Japan. A foreign corporation is a corporate entity other than a domestic corporation. Unincorporated associations excluding partnerships may be regarded as taxable entities under certain conditions. According to the Corporation Tax Law, foreign corporations are subject to taxation only on Japanese-source income while domestic corporations are taxed on their worldwide income, including income earned by overseas branches. Double taxation of foreign-source income can be avoided to the extent of taxes paid overseas. In general, income earned by domestic corporations outside Japan is not taxed provided it has been subject to taxation in the source country. Public welfare corporations designated under the specific laws and equivalent foreign corporations are exempt from taxation or income other than that earned from profit-making activities.

A further important distinction for tax purposes is between large corporations with paid-up capital in excess of ¥100 million and small and medium-sized corporations with paid-up capital of ¥100 million or less because the latter has a wide variety of tax advantages. For example, the reduced tax rate of taxable income may be applied.

	Taxable income	
	Distributed income	*Undistributed income*
Large corporation	33.3%	43.3%
Small and medium-sized corporation		
First ¥8 million of annual taxable income	25.0%	31.0%
Remainder of taxable income	33.3%	43.3%

In addition to the national income tax, local income taxes such as the enterprise tax and the inhabitants tax are levied and these depend upon the size of the corporations as well as the area of location. Both are applicable to domestic corporations and branches of foreign corporations. The rates of enterprise tax range from 6 per cent to 13.2 per cent of annual income. The enterprise tax paid can be deducted from annual taxable income when both the corporation tax and the enterprise tax are computed. Although only prefectures are entitled to collect the enterprise tax, the inhabitants tax is levied at both the prefectural and the municipal level. The rates of inhabitants tax apply to the same accounting period as corporation tax payable.

The accounting period for tax purposes can be either a calendar or fiscal year, which may not exceed 12 months. Taxation is levied on taxable income which is based on profits determined in accordance with generally accepted accounting principles in Japan but subject to certain adjustments. As a general rule, the accrual basis may be used for expenses in calculating taxable income, which is based on gross income less cost of goods and allowable expenses. In order to determine the cost of goods sold, corporations may use the identified cost, FIFO, LIFO, weighted-average cost, moving-average cost, straight-average cost, cost of last purchase, retail inventory methods, or cost (applying one of the above) or market which is lower. In the absence of a filed notification to the regional tax authorities, cost of last purchase method shall be adopted.

Intercompany cross-border transactions should be undertaken on an arm's length basis in order to prevent profit manipulation. Until recently many multinational enterprises utilized international transfer prices to shift profits to tax havens. The Japanese tax authorities introduced legislation on transfer pricing with effect from 1 April 1986 to add to the Special Taxation Measures Law and the Special Taxation Law Relating to the Tax Treaty. The arm's length transaction rule applies to property sales or purchases as well as to other transactions, such as loans, consultation and so on. The difference between the arm's-length price (determined by using one third-party comparable price, resale price, cost-plus and other methods approved by law) and the artificial transfer price will not be allowed as a tax deduction.

Dividends received by a domestic corporation from another domestic corporation, less interest payable on borrowings incurred for the acquisition of the shares involved, are fully exempt from taxation as a general rule. However, dividends received from foreign corporations must be fully included in gross income. Dividends received on shares which were purchased within one month before the closing date of an accounting period of the issuing corporation and sold within two months after that date, must also be included in gross income.

The following deductions are mainly allowed in determining the limit of assessible income:

1. Depreciation – the straight-line method, the declining-balance method, the output method or other methods approved by the regional tax authorities may be adopted to depreciate fixed assets. Tangible assets may be depreciated by applying either the straight-line or the declining-balance methods. In the absence of a filed notification, the declining-balance method shall be used. As a general rule, salvage value equals 10 per cent of the acquisition cost of the tangible assets under any of these methods. The statutory useful lives and annual depreciation rates for both straight-line and declining-balance method are determined by the Ministry of Finance. In the period of the acquisition of fixed assets, depreciation must be apportioned on a monthly basis. The half-year convention rule can be adopted as an alternative. Fixed assets purchased at a cost less than ¥100,000 per unit may be deducted in full in the period of acquisition.
2. Accelerated depreciation – the Special Taxation Measures Law provides for accelerated depreciation in certain industries (including branches

of foreign corporations) or for specific types of assets, such as anti-pollution machines, certain equipment to be used in designated development areas, and certain machines purchased by small- and medium-sized corporations. There are two kinds of special accelerated depreciation, the initial allowance which permits a certain percentage of acquisition cost to be deducted in the first period of purchase and an additional deduction which allows a faster rate of depreciation to be applied. Both economic incentives result in the faster write-off of assets and consequently shorter useful lives.

3. Amortization and depletion – intangible fixed assets such as patents and trademarks may be generally amortized within their designated useful life by applying the straight-line method. Goodwill may be written off on a voluntary basis. In practice, goodwill is amortized within five years in accordance with the requirement of the Commercial Code. Deferred charges such as research and development costs, pre-incorporation costs and bond discounts may be currently expensed or amortized within the designated period of years. The disposal value of intangible assets and deferred charges are treated as zero. Wasting assets are written off using the straight line, declining-balance or output methods.
4. Interest – interest is normally deductible on an accrual basis. The concept of thin capitalization is not applicable in Japan. When interest is paid to affiliated companies of domestic or foreign corporations at an excessive rate, the excess must be treated as either a donation or economic benefit, which is not wholly deductible.
5. Provision, reserve and special allowance – under the Corporation Tax Law, the tax-deductible provisions such as provision for bad debts, provision for seasonal employee bonuses, provision for returned unsold goods and provision for warranty costs are allowable against tax to the extent of the applicable statutory rates. Moreover, an additional provision for bad debts is available for small- and medium-sized corporations. Under the Special Tax Measures Law, tax-deductible reserves such as reserves for loss on overseas investment, drought reserves, reserves for improvement of structures of small- and medium-sized corporations and reserves for securities transaction responsibility may be allowed for certain industries or corporations. Further, special allowances such as for mining expenditures and other special allowances are accepted for some other industries or transactions.
6. Losses – generally, corporations and branches of a foreign corporation may be entitled to carry back tax losses for one year or carry forward tax losses for four years. This option is applicable only to corporations which file a 'blue form tax return'.

Foreign subsidiaries and branches

A foreign corporation is generally taxed on all of its Japanese-source income. The determination of Japanese-source income is of particular importance to a foreign corporation because it is subject to taxation, depending on whether the corporation has a permanent establishment to carry on business in Japan. In determining this nature, the tax law may be qualified by provisions of tax treaties with foreign countries. If a foreign corporation takes the form of a branch, the foreign corporation will be taxed on its entire income from all sources within Japan, including dividends, interest, royalties, rents and capital gains unless an applicable tax treaty stipulates otherwise.

Dividends, interest, royalties, technology fees and rents received by a foreign corporation from a Japanese subsidiary or other company are subject to withholding income tax at a flat rate of 20 per cent. This may be reduced to a lower rate as the result of an applicable tax treaty. Under the tax treaty between Japan and UK, for example, the withholding tax rate is reduced to 10 per cent, except certain types of dividends are taxed at 15 per cent. Under the Japan/Zambia treaty, the withholding tax rate is reduced to nil for dividends, while for others it is 10 per cent. The treaty tax rates apply to foreign branches as well as foreign subsidiaries only if the income is not attributable to a permanent establishment in Japan by a foreign company. Otherwise, an ordinary withholding rate of 20 per cent applies as a general rule.

Consolidated tax returns

There are no provisions for the filing of a consolidated tax return by a group of corporations so that each corporation is taxed on its own income as a separate legal entity. However, income earned by a foreign subsidiary located in a tax haven may be required to include that income in the taxable income of the parent company.

Capital gains tax

In general, capital gains must be realized before they are subject to normal rates of taxation. In addition to ordinary corporation tax, a corporation (including a branch of a foreign corporation) is subject to a 20 per cent special additional surtax and the inhabitants tax on the net gain earned by selling or transferring land or rights to land in Japan if the period of the holding is less than ten years as at 1 January in the year in which the sale or transfer is made. However, there are four exceptions to the general rule that capital gains are taxable when they are realized. Capital gains may be deferred where the gain arises from expropriation, an exchange of property, replacement of property or qualified reinvestment.

Taxation implications of mergers and acquisitions

Implications for the acquiring company

There are basically two ways by which a foreign corporation may be able to acquire a business in Japan. A branch or subsidiary may be formed in Japan for the purpose of acquiring the business assets of a domestic corporation. An alternative plan is to let a foreign subsidiary acquire the shares of a Japanese domestic corporation.

On acquiring shares as part of an acquisition of a business, the shares must be purchased at the fair market values. If a corporation acquires the shares at the prices lower than their fair market values, the difference between the acquisition price and 90 per cent of the fair market price will be included in the gross income for that fiscal year. When a corporation acquires other property at a price lower than its fair market price, the difference between actual purchase price and fair market value will be aggregated with other sources of income. On the other hand, the excess over the fair market price may be treated as a deduction in certain circumstances. In addition, 20 per cent of the special additional tax is levied on capital gains on the sale of land as described above.

In the case of a merger, the gain may be computed as the excess of the net assets value acquired by the surviving corporation over the total value of increased shares of the surviving corporation plus cash or property which were delivered to shareholders of the merged corporation. The merger gain is composed of:

1. the capital surplus transferred from the merged corporation;
2. the retained earnings transferred from the merged corporation;
3. the capital reduction gain occurring as a result of a merger, which means capital of the merged corporation as at the date of the merger in excess of the total value of increased shares plus cash or property delivered to shareholders of the merged corporation; and
4. the gain derived from the appreciation in the book value of the transferred property.

1. is the transferred capital surplus, and therefore exempt from taxation and 2. is also not taxed because it was already subject to taxation in the merged corporation. As 3. is regarded as part of paid-up capital by the shareholders of the merged corporation, it should not be included in gross income. Only 4. should be aggregated with other sources of income and taxed at the ordinary tax rate because it can be regarded as the capital gain earned as a result of the merger.

On acquiring land or buildings, real property acquisition tax is levied at the prefectural level. In general, depreciable assets, other than buildings, are not subject to this tax. Furthermore, no tax is imposed on the acquisition of land or buildings as a result of a merger. In the case of a merger or business transfer, registration and licence tax is levied at the national level on registration of the transfer of ownership, on other possessions, on the establishment of a corporation, and on the alternation of directors, etc. Stamp duty, which is levied at the national level, is payable on the relevant documents prepared for a merger or business transfer.

Implications for the acquirer's shareholders

There are no significant taxation implications affecting the acquirer's shareholders.

Implications for the acquiree company

When a corporation is absorbed by a merger, the surviving corporation must file a return and pay tax on the liquidation income of the merged corporation. Liquidation income in the case of a merger is, in general, the excess of the sum of the money, properties and total face value of shares of the surviving corporation delivered to the shareholders of the merged corporation over the capital, capital surplus and retained earnings of the merged corporation at the time of the merger. Accordingly, liquidation income cannot be earned if the surviving corporation accounts for the net assets of the merged corporation at its book value and if new shares issued to shareholders of the merged corporation are for the same amount as the share capital of the merged corporation. However, as the value of shares of the surviving corporation is normally higher than that of the merged corporation, new shares should be issued at a lower price.

It is important to note that 20 per cent of the special surtax is levied in addition to ordinary corporate income tax on the transfer of land whose holding period is less than ten years as described above. In the case of the transfer of securities, a securities transaction tax is levied at the national level.

Implications for the acquiree's shareholders

When shares, money or property are issued or paid to the shareholders of the merged corporation in excess of the sum of paid-up capital and capital surplus (i.e. retained earnings) of the merged corporation, the excess is subject to withholding income tax as a deemed dividend to the shareholders of the merged corporation.

Tax planning

The Special Taxation Measures Law specifies that intercompany cross-border transactions should be made on arm's length basis. Extra scrutiny is now given to transactions with countries which are designated as tax havens. The difference between the taxable incomes calculated by using artificial international transfer prices and an arm's-length price will not be allowed as a tax deduction. This should be taken into consideration in determining an international tax plan.

Where money is raised in Japan the interest will be tax deductible on an accrual basis, unless the company adopts a cash basis. Moreover, there is no regulation on thin capitalization in Japanese tax laws. If foreign corporations utilize loans as a substitute for an investment in a subsidiary, more interest can be treated as tax deductible by the subsidiary. International inter-firm financing may be useful for international tax saving or minimization of tax burdens under certain conditions.

In Japan there are many tax advantages permitted by the Special Taxation Measures Law. Accelerated depreciation, special tax-deductible allowances, etc., can lead to taxable income being reduced somewhat.

5. ACCOUNTING

Background

Two different laws that have a great influence on accounting and reporting in Japan were promulgated in order to protect the interests of investors, creditors, consumers, to maintain a sound advance in the Japanese economy and to equalize taxation. The first of these is the Commercial Code, which requires every KK to prepare a balance sheet, a profit and loss account, a business report, a proposal relating to appropriations of retained earnings and supporting schedules for each financial year. These financial statements, except supporting schedules, must be audited by the statutory auditor(s) appointed by shareholders at a general meeting. The directors must present the financial statements to the statutory auditor(s) at least seven weeks before the date scheduled for any ordinary general meeting of shareholders which must be held within three months after the end of the financial year. The statutory auditor(s) must file the audit report with the directors within four weeks of receiving the financial statements.

In addition to the audit by the statutory auditor, all large KKs whose capital stock is ¥500 million or more, or whose total liabilities are 20,000 million or more are required to provide an audit report by CPA(s) or by an audit corporation independent of the company. The role of the auditors is to assess whether the financial statements show properly the financial condition and results of the company in conformity with the Commercial Code and the Regulation Concerning Balance Sheet, Profit and Loss Account, Business Report and Supporting Schedules for a Limited Stock Company. These regulations were originally promulgated in 1963 by the Ministry of Justice and have been subsequently amended, in 1974, 1975 and 1982.

The financial statements and audit report should be available to investors and creditors at the head office of the company for five years and at the branch(es) for three years. The summarized balance sheet (and profit and loss account in the case of a large company) must be published in newspapers or gazettes.

In addition to the requirements for accounting and reporting under the Commercial Code and the related Regulation, companies that publicly offer shares or bonds amounting to ¥100 million or more, and have their own shares listed on the Stock Exchange or registered over-the-counter, must comply with the requirements under the Securities and Exchange Law and the Regulation Concerning the Terminology, Forms and Preparation Methods of Financial Statements. These regulations were first promulgated in 1963 by the Ministry of Finance and have been subsequently revised. According to the provision of the Securities and Exchange Law, individual financial statements which consist of a balance sheet, a profit and loss account and a statement of appropriations of retained earnings and detailed supporting schedules, must be audited by the independent auditor and filed with the Ministry of Finance. Audited consolidated financial statements must be also presented as supplementary statements. The independent auditor states his opinion as to whether the company has fairly prepared the financial statement in conformity with the generally accepted accounting principles in Japan.

In preparing a full fiscal period or semi-annual financial statements the Statement of Financial Accounting Standards for Business Enterprise published in 1949 (and subsequently amended in 1954, 1963, 1974 and 1982) by the Business Accounting Deliberation Council has served as the authoritative source of accounting principles. The Council is an advisory body to the Ministry of Finance whose members consists of representatives from the Japanese Institute of Certified Public Accountants, academicians, government officials, and business and industry. Consequently, the independent auditor is obliged to comply with the accounting standards for the presentation of opinions. The Business Accounting Deliberation Council has published various statements and opinions, for example, Cost Accounting Standards in 1962, Accounting Principles for Consolidated Statements in 1975, Opinion on Interim Finance Statements Included in Semi-Annual Reports in 1977, Accounting Standards for Foreign Currency Transactions etc. in 1979, in order to establish 'the accounting principles generally accepted as fair and reasonable'.

Furthermore, JICPA which is a founder member of the International Accounting Standard Committee (IASC) founded in 1973, has played a role in preparing International Accounting Standards (IAS). Since then Japan has made an effort to acquire and harmonize its rules and regulations with IAS. However, there are some differences between IAS and Japanese generally accepted accounting principles. Accounting conventions, customs, economic and social climate etc., in Japan hinder the international harmonization of accounting standards. Significant differences between Japanese accounting standards and IAS are dealt with later in this section.

Accounting for consolidations

During the 1960s a number of cases where a large number of investors sustained losses as a result of profit manipulation or window dressing through subsidiary companies, led to considerable criticism of the accounting practices in Japan. The Business Accounting Deliberation Council was asked by the Minister of Finance to consider the matter closely and in 1975 it published the Accounting principles for Consolidated Financial Statements. Consequently, consolidated financial statements became a requirement for listed companies for the financial year beginning on or after 1 April 1977. They must be audited by CPA(s) or an audit corporation and filed with the Ministry of Finance as supplementary information within four months of the end of a financial year. Note that the Commercial Code and the Corporation Tax Law do not require a corporation to prepare or report the consolidated financial statements.

According to the provisions of the Accounting Principles for Consolidated Financial Statements, a parent company is a company that owns more than 50 per cent of the votes in another company. A subsidiary company is a company, in which more than 50 per cent of the votes are owned by a parent company. If 50 per cent of the votes in a company are owned substantially by a parent company and/or by one or more of its subsidiaries, the company involved is also deemed to be a subsidiary company. The criterion of control over the composition of the board of directors cannot be adopted in Japan. Further, the following subsidiary companies are excluded from consolidation:

1. a company which is considered to be no longer within a group of common control, because of a lack of effective control, such as a reorganized company, etc.;
2. a company which is not considered to be a going concern because of bankruptcy, liquidation, etc.;
3. a company in which the parent company owns more than 50 per cent of the votes in the company but the investment is only temporary; or
4. a company which, if included in the consolidation, would mislead interested parties.

As a general rule, investments in unconsolidated subsidiaries or affiliated companies should be shown in the consolidated balance sheet at an amount calculated using the equity method of accounting. The application of the equity method was not mandatory until 1 April 1983. An affiliated company is not a subsidiary, but an investee in which the consolidated group (the parent company and the consolidated subsidiary companies) holds substantially 20 per cent or more of the votes of the investee, and exercises significant influence over the financial and operating policies through board representation or significant interchange of managerial personnel, financing, dependence on technical information or significant intercompany transactions, etc. Under the equity method of accounting, the investment is recorded at cost plus a proportionate share of post-acquisition earnings or losses. Although tax-effect accounting is not generally practised in Japan, the allocation of income taxes may be permitted because unrealized profits result from intercompany transactions and are eliminated on consolidation.

Consolidated financial statements prepared in Japan consist of a consolidated balance sheet, a consolidated profit and loss statement and a consolidated statement of retained earnings, or a combined statement of profit, loss and retained earnings. The notes to the consolidated financial statements should disclose the following information:

1. the consolidation policy;
2. differences in financial year ends;
3. accounting procedures and practices:
   (a) the facts, the reasons for and effects of any change in valuation basis and method of depreciation for significant assets;
   (b) the policy of eliminating inter-group and intra-group unrealized profit when applying the equity method of accounting;

(c) any significant differences in accounting principles and procedures within the group;

4. the appropriation of retained earnings;
5. the method of foreign currency translation used for foreign entities;
6. other significant matters.

Accounting for goodwill

According to the Statement of Financial Accounting Standards for Business Enterprises and the Commercial Code, goodwill should be recognized as an intangible asset in the balance sheet only when purchased or acquired through a business transfer or merger. It should be valued at acquisition price. Internally generated goodwill is not accounted for at all in Japan.

Purchased goodwill should be amortized to income on a systematic basis over its estimated useful life. However, the Commercial Code provides that goodwill shall be amortized by not less than the average amount within five years of the acquisition. In addition, the Corporation Income Tax Law permits voluntary amortization of goodwill. In practice purchased goodwill is amortized within five years in accordance with the requirement of the Commercial Code.

Accounting for mergers

With regard to mergers in Japan there are two main schools of thought. One viewpoint considers an amalgamation to be a unity of juristic persons supported by the Commercial Code and a second viewpoint is that it represents an investment in property (assets), a view suggested by accounting theorists. According to the viewpoint of unity of juristic persons, the essence of a merger is regarded as a union with another juristic person to form a new juristic entity. Therefore, the following characteristics are prevalent:

1. assets and liabilities in the merged companies should be carried forward at their book values;
2. capital surpluses and earned surpluses etc. in the merged companies should remain intact and transferred to the new juristic entity.

On the other hand, the essence of a merger might be recognized as a contribution of capital in the form of an investment in property. Therefore, its characteristics are as follows:

1. valuation of investment by property should be determined on the basis of the fair market value of the related companies;
2. when the amount of net assets valued at fair market value, exceeds the amount of shares issued to shareholders of the merged company

(including consideration delivered) at the time of the merger, the difference should be treated as a capital surplus. This capital surplus is merely an additional paid-in surplus;
3. capital surpluses, earned surpluses, etc. will not remain intact. These capital items disappear at the time of the merger and should be transferred to a capital surplus.

According to section 288–2–①–5 of the Commercial Code, when assets exceed the liabilities and shares of the merged company difference should be set aside as a capital surplus. In such a case the legal earned surplus and other retained earnings may not be treated as a capital surplus under section 288–2–③. Section 288 of the Commercial Code requires that an amount equal to at least 10 per cent of cash dividends paid should be set up as a legal earned surplus which is not available for distribution until the surplus shall have reached a quarter of the stated capital. Accordingly, the Commercial Code permits the succession of the legal earned surplus in the merged company because the retained surplus is discontinued if it is transferred to a capital surplus.

As explained above, the Corporation Tax Law decomposes the merger gain or loss into four elements and permits the assets of the merged company to be valued at their book values. Therefore, the treatment by the Corporation Tax Law is generally said to approximate the viewpoint of unity of juristic persons. However, there is a treatment contradictory to this viewpoint because the assets of the merged company may be valued on the basis of fair market prices.

The Statement of Financial Accounting Standards for Business Enterprise provides that a merger gain or loss should be stated as a capital surplus. The viewpoint of investment by property is clearly suggested. However, when a merger gain or loss occurs, the earned surplus of the merged company may not be treated as a capital surplus. This is consistent with the provisions of the Commercial Code.

In practice, assets of the merged companies are commonly carried forward at their book values. However, some companies value assets on the basis of fair market prices because the Corporation Tax Law and the Commercial Code permit such an accounting procedure. The treatment on a merger gain or loss varies from company to company. Some companies takeover earned surpluses and keep them intact and others retain only the legal earned surplus of the merged companies. Other companies treat the earned surplus of the merged companies as capital surpluses.

International accounting standards

A summary of more important differences between Japanese standards (in particular, the Statement of Financial Accounting Standards for Business Enterprises, and the Regulation Concerning the Terminology, Forms and Preparation Methods of Financial Statements) and international accounting standards is provided in table 9.8.

Table 9.8 Comparison of Japanese accounting practices with international accounting standards

International accounting standards	*Japanese standards*
IAS 1 – Disclosure of accounting policies	
Requires presentation of a two-year statement	No equivalent requirement
Requires disclosure of the facts and reasons if the going concern assumption is not followed	There is no equivalent requirement
IAS 2 – Valuation and presentation of inventories in the context of the historical cost system	
Requires valuation at the lower of cost and net realizable value	Either the cost method or the lower of the cost and market value method may be used. Market value is interpreted as replacement cost or net realizable value
IAS 3 – Consolidated financial statements	
Consolidated financial statements should be issued by a parent company	Consolidated financial statements are prepared only by large companies required by the Securities and Exchange Law and filed as supplementary information.
A company in which a group does not have control, but in which a group owns more than half the equity capital, but less than half the votes may be treated as a subsidiary	A subsidiary is a company, more than 50 per cent of the votes of which is substantially owned by a parent company
IAS 4 – Depreciation accounting	
The useful lives of major depreciable assets or classes of depreciable assets should be reviewed periodically, and depreciable rates should be adjusted for the current and future periods if expectations are significantly different from the previous estimates	The useful lives are not required to review periodically. The useful lives regulated by the Corporation Tax Law are mostly used by Japanese companies
IAS 5–Information to be disclosed in financial statements	
Requires disclosure of various items, including pensions and retirement plans, etc. in financial settlements	Under the Commercial Code, the notes in the financial states are limited to valuation methods for assets, the method for depreciation, the accrual basis for significant allowances, pledged assets, significant assets denominated at foreign currency, liabilities to directors or

– *Continued*

Table 9.8 Continued

International accounting standards	*Japanese standards*
	statutory auditors, contingent liabilities and other significant items. Small companies whose share capital does not exceed ¥100 million may omit these notes
IAS 7 – Statement of changes in financial position	
Required as part of the financial statements	There is no requirement. However, a company whose registration report for subscription or sale of securities is filed with the Minister of Finance, should prepare such a statement. It is commonly prepared as supplementary information
IAS 8 – Unusual and prior period items and changes in accounting policies	
Unusual items should be included in net income	Material losses on assets arising as a result of a natural calamity which can not be covered with the net income in the current year or the current retained earnings less appropriated earnings may be deferred as an asset in the balance sheet provided that it is permitted by any specific laws or regulations.
IAS 9 – Accounting for research and development activities	
Requires research costs to be charged in the year in which incurred but development costs may be deferred in exceptional circumstances	Research and development costs may be deferred in exceptional circumstances
Deferred development costs should be amortized on a systematic basis	The Commercial Code requires that deferred costs should be amortized over a period not exceeding five years
Deferred costs should be reviewed at the end of each year	There is no equivalent requirement
The total of research and development costs should be disclosed	Not required. The amortization method should be disclosed
IAS 10 – Contingencies and events occurring after the balance sheet date	
Requires disclosure in cases where it is probable that a contingent gain will be realized	There is no equivalent requirement

– *Continued*

Table 9.8 Continued

International accounting standards	*Japanese standards*
Any adjustments to assets and liabilities required for events occurring after the balance sheet date must be disclosed	Adjustments to assets and liabilities are not required
Dividends which are proposed or declared after the balance sheet date should be either adjusted or disclosed	Not required
IAS 11 – Accounting for construction contracts	
Where both the percentage of completion and the completed contract methods are simultaneously used, the amount of work in progress should be separately disclosed	There is no equivalent requirement
IAS 12 – Accounting for taxes on income	
Requires tax effect accounting, using either the deferral or the liability method	As the Commercial Code does not permit deferred tax debits, tax effect accounting cannot be used at the individual company level. Tax effect accounting is optional only when the timing differences arise in consolidation. The deferral method is commonly followed rather than the liability method. Disclosure is not required, however
IAS 14 – Reporting financial information by segment	
Requires segment information in financial statements of publicly traded companies and other economically significant entities including subsidiaries	Not common in practice
IAS 15 – Information reflecting the effects of changing prices	
Requires disclosure of the adjusted amount for changing prices on depreciation, cost of sales, monetary items and the overall effects of such adjustments as supplementary information	No equivalent standard although the Opinion on Disclosure of Financial Information for Changing Price Level Accounting was issued in 1980 by the Business Accounting Deliberation Council
IAS 16 – Accounting for property, plant and equipment	

– *Continued*

Table 9.8 Continued

International accounting standards	*Japanese standards*
The gross carrying amount of an asset should be either the historical cost or the revalued amount	In principle historical cost should be used
Requires disclosure of the revaluation method including the policy on the frequency of revaluations	There is no equivalent requirement
IAS 17 – Accounting for leases	There is no equivalent standard. However, the Corporation Tax Law requires that certain types of financing arrangements should be taken into consideration in determining taxable income
IAS 20 – Accounting for government grants and disclosure of government assistance	
Government grants related to assets should be accounted for either as deferred income or as a deduction from related assets	Government grants related to assets may be accounted for as deduction from those assets
IAS 21 – Accounting for the effects of changes in foreign exchange rates	
Long-term monetary items at the balance sheet date should be translated at the closing rate. Exchange differences should be recognized in income in the current period, but may be deferred and amortized on a systematic basis.	Long-term monetary items should be translated at the historical rates. Accordingly, there is no exchange difference
When translating foreign currency financial statements whose activities are relatively self-contained and integrated, the closing rate method should normally be used. The temporal method should be used for a foreign operation whose activities are integral to the operations of the parent	The temporal method should be used for a foreign branch provided that long-term monetary items are translated at the historical rate. A modified temporal method should be used for a foreign subsidiary or affiliate provided that long-term monetary items are translated at the historical rates. Under the modified temporal methods, net income and retained earnings should be translated at the closing rate and exchange differences resulting from the translation of balance sheet items should be charged or credited to assets or liabilities as appropriate

– *Continued*

Table 9.8 Continued

International accounting standards	*Japanese standards*
The restate–translate method should be used for the financial statements of a foreign entity which is affected by high rates of inflation. Alternatively, the temporal method may be used	There is no equivalent requirement
IAS 22–Accounting for business combination	
Permits immediate write-off of goodwill against shareholders' equity	Write-off within five years is commonly applied
IAS 23–Capitalization of borrowing costs	
Borrowing costs includes amortization of discount or premium on the issues of debt securities, amortization of ancillary costs for the arrangement of borrowing, etc.	Borrowing costs are limited only to interest costs incurred from borrowing
Borrowing costs of property, plant and equipment, investments in enterprises, inventory that require a significant period of time to bring to a saleable condition, and real estate and other long-term development projects are capitalized	Capitalization of borrowing costs is limited to only tangible depreciable assets
The capitalization rate should be determined	Borrowing costs for the acquisition of particular assets are capitalized with the assets. Accordingly, the capitalization rate is not required to be calculated
IAS 25 – Accounting for investments	
Long-term investments, should be stated at cost or revalued amounts	Long-term investments should be carried at cost less any reduction in value

6. EXCHANGE CONTROLS/FOREIGN INVESTMENT REGULATIONS

The Law Concerning Control of the Foreign Exchange and Foreign Trade is administered by the Ministry of Finance which has long adhered to the philosophy that all foreign transactions should be restricted in principle. With the advance of Japanese economic power worldwide, such a policy has had to be modified. Since 1 December 1980 a liberalization programme of all exchange controls and foreign investment regulations has been undertaken by revising the appropriate laws. None the less, the Ministry of Finance and the Ministry of International Trade and Industries, with which the ultimate responsibility for exchange control rests, may still restrict foreign investment.

According to section 26 of the Law Concerning Control of the Foreign Exchange and Foreign Trade, direct inward investments by foreign investors (including the subsidiary or affiliated companies of foreign companies in Japan as well as foreign individuals and foreign companies) are defined as:

1. acquisitions of 10 per cent or more of the total shares issued by a Japanese listed company or a company dealt with on the over-the-counter market;
2. acquisitions of shares in Japanese unlisted companies;
3. loans (except by financial institutions) exceeeding a certain amount over one year. These amounts vary for the period of the loans as following:
   ¥100 million: from one year to five years
   ¥500 million: over five years;
4. other investments.

Foreign investors must prepare a report on the proposed direct inward investment which shows the objective of the business and the amount and timing of the investment. At least three months before the scheduled date of the investment the report should be filed with the Ministry of Finance and the competent authorities by way of the Bank of Japan. In principle, the direct inward investment cannot be made within 30 days after the date of the report, during which the government undertakes its investigations. This suspense period can be shortened to two weeks or the same day of the report if the Minister of Finance judges that there is no problem in particular. However, the suspense period may be extended to four months after the date of the report if a special investigation is considered as being required, and to five months in total if the Foreign Exchange Council suggests that this is necessay to make further investigations.

Section 27 of the Law Concerning Control of the Foreign Exchange and Foreign Trade stipulates the criteria investigated by the Minister of Finance. Essentially the main criteria are as follows:

1. investments that would harm the safety of the nation, breach the maintenance of public order or hinder the protection and safety of the public;
2. investments that would remarkably exert a bad influence on the activities of any existing industry related with the proposed investment of where the investment would not enhance the administration of the Japanese economy;
3. investments where there is no reciprocal treaty on direct investments;

4. investments that would hinder the country's balance of payments, the foreign exchange rate of the year or the financial and capital markets in Japan.

Minister of Finance or other parties conclude that if the direct inward investment meets one or more of the above criteria it may issue a recommendation which states that the planned investment should be adjusted or abandoned. The foreign investor has ten days to respond to the recommendation. If the foreign investor does not respond within the appropriate time-period, the Minister of Finance may issue a further order to adjust or abandon the report.

The Law Concerning the Control of Foreign Exchange and Foreign Trade stipulates the regulations for direct outward investment by Japanese companies. The details are similar to those of direct inward investment by foreign companies. The following proposals may be investigated:

1. acquisitions of 10 per cent or more of the share in a foreign company (there is an obligation of a prior report even when the shares in the foreign company to be acquired will be below 10 per cent);
2. loans to a foreign company which extend beyond one year;
3. acquisitions of securities issued by, or loaned to, a foreign company in which a Japanese company has members on the board, sells or buys raw materials or products over a long period of time, or provides significant technology to; and
4. other investments.

A report of the direct outward investment must be prepared and should include, among other things, the details and the timing of the investment. The report should be filed with the Minister of Finance through the Bank of Japan at least two months before the scheduled day of the investment. In principle, the direct outward investment cannot be made within 20 days of the report being acceptable. This suspense period can be reduced to the acceptance day of the report except in special cases. During this suspense period, the Minister of Finance investigates whether the report relates to one or more of the following:

1. an investment that would exert a bad influence on international financial markets or damage international reliance on Japan;
2. investments that would have a bad influence on Japanese financial or capital markets;
3. investments that would have a bad influence on the business activities within a particular industry in Japan or that would be detrimental to Japanese economy; and
4. investments that would be against international agreements, impede international peace or safety, or destroy the maintenance of public order.

If the Minister of Finance concludes that the direct outward investment of Japanese investors comes under one or more of the investments described above, it may recommend that it should be modified or suspended, and, if necessary, abandoned.

SUMMARY

For many years Japan has been a hostile environment for mergers and acquisitions as they were regarded as being immoral. However, this concept has been recently reviewed as a result of changes in the social, economic and political climates. The main factors are the needs of conglomerates, the shortening of the life-cycle of commodities, countermeasures to the friction of foreign trade, and the mitigation of legal controls on mergers, acquisitions and takeovers.

Restrictions on mergers, acquisitions, takeover bids and business transfers are included mainly in the Commercial Code, the Anti-Monopoly Law or the Securities and Exchange Law. Also, the Stock Exchanges and the Securities Dealers Association have their own self-regulatory controls on takeover bids.

In Japan the Special Taxation Measure Law permits many tax advantages for the transactions. For example, there are special tax-deductible allowances, accelerated depreciation, etc. which can reduce assessable income. In planning tax affairs these advantages should be given adequate weight.

Under the Securities and Exchange Law, consolidated accounts for listed companies should be prepared, audited and filed with the Ministry of Finance as supplementary information. It should be noted that the Commercial Code and the Corporation Tax Law do not require consolidated accounts to be prepared. A company, in which more than 50 per cent of the votes are substantially owned by a parent company, may be treated as a subsidiary. The criterion of control over the composition of the board of directors cannot be adopted. The equity method of accounting is appropriate in consolidated accounts where investments of 20 per cent or more of the votes is made in an investee. Although tax-effect accounting cannot be generally used at the individual company level, the allocation of income taxes may be permitted only when timing differences arise on consolidation.

Internally generated goodwill cannot be accounted for but purchased goodwill may be valued at acquisition price. In practice purchased goodwill is amortized within five years in accordance with the requirements of the Commercial Code.

With respect to mergers there are two main schools of thought in Japan. The Commercial Code suggests the viewpoint of unity of juristic persons, which bears a striking resemblance to the pooling of interests method when accounting for a merger. According to this viewpoint, the essence of a merger might be recognized as a union with another juristic person to form a new juristic unity. Alternatively, accounting theorists have suggested the viewpoint that such transactions represent an investment by property, which is similar to the purchase accounting method. The essence of a merger is regarded as a contribution of capital in the form of an investment in property.

Japan has made every effort to acquire and harmonize its rules and regulations with IAS. However, Japanese common practices are often quite different from IAS. Accounting conventions, customs, economic and social climate, etc., in Japan seem to obstruct international harmonization of accounting standards and practices.

With the advance of Japanese economic power worldwide, a liberalization programme of all exchange controls and foreign investment regulations have been undertaken since 1 December 1980. None the less, the Ministry of Finance and the Ministry of International Trade and Industries may still restrict foreign investments, including direct inward investments by foreign investors and direct outward investments by Japanese companies.

10

Netherlands

1. BUSINESS ORGANIZATIONS AND COMBINATIONS

Business organization

Foreign businesses can operate in the Netherlands by establishing a branch office or one or other form of company as provided for in Dutch legislation. Where a foreign business only sells goods in the Netherlands that have been produced abroad and for tax, financial, organizational or other reasons, establishing a branch or subsidiary may not be appropriate. In such a situation, commercial agents, distributors or commission agents could be enlisted who could be either natural persons or legal entities and who need not be residents.

The most common forms of ownership in the Netherlands are the sole proprietorship, the general partnership, the limited partnership and the private (closed) limited liability company. In addition, there are other forms of ownership such as cooperative associations, and public limited liability companies. The limited liability companies will be considered in more detail as these are more relevant to foreign investors.

Since 1971, Dutch law has made provision for two forms of companies with share capital, *Naamloze Vennootschappen* (NVs) (public limited liability companies) and *Besloten Vennootschappen met beperkte aansprakelijkheid* (BVs) (private closed limited companies). These two forms of legal entities are suitable for business purposes because the providers of risk-bearing capital, the shareholders, know that their financial risk is restricted to the nominal value of their capital participation, while on the other hand, they can enforce their entitlement to a portion of the profit from operations by means of their rights as shareholders. In addition, these forms of enterprise help bring about an objective relationship between shareholders and management and to spread or enlarge share ownership over a larger group of providers of risk-bearing capital.

The structure and organization of an NV can be virtually identical to that of a BV. A BV legally has a certain closed structure, one of whose effects is that shares can only be bearer shares, which cannot be sold in the open market or offered on the stock exchange. In practice, a situation has developed in which the BV form is the preferred structure for new companies unless there are clear reasons for opting for the NV form. The latter form has increasingly become the corporate form for public companies, that is to say companies whose shares are held by a large number of people or are negotiable on the unlisted securities market or stock exchange. In mid–1983 the number of registered NVs amounted to around 4000 and the number of BVs to nearly 190,000.

Incorporation formalities for an NV and a BV are relatively simple. The deed of incorporation must be notarially executed and as from 1 October 1986 only one person is required for their formation. There are no provisions as regards the nationality, domicile, natural or legal person status of shareholders. The issued and paid up share capital should amount to at least Dfl.40,000 for BVs and Dfl.100,000 for NVs. The expenses involved in incorporation amount to 1 per cent capital tax, levied on the paid-up share capital; the notary public's fees and minor expenses relating to obtaining a ministerial certificate of non-objection, publication in the *Staats-courant* and registration of the BV at the local Chamber of Commerce. In addition to limited liability companies, foreign enterprises can carry on business in the Netherlands by means of a branch or sales office. These, too, should be registered at the local Chamber of Commerce.

Types of business combination

Companies can unite their economic interests in two ways; namely by entering into business combinations or share mergers. These types of merger are dealt with in more detail and consideration will be given to types of amalgamations and the transfer of shares on the basis of a private agreement.

Business combinations

A business combination takes place when the assets and liabilities of an enterprise are transferred with the object of transferring its economic activities. The transfer is frequently effected by the transferee company issuing its own shares to the transferor company or to a component of the group to which it belongs. There is no objection under law that when an undertaking is acquired, contracts of employment are also transferred, since the employer remains, even though the shareholders have changed.

Share merger

In a share merger, it is not fixed assets but shares that are transferred against the issue of shares by the transferee company. It is essential in a share merger for the company acquiring the shares to obtain control of the company whose shares have been transferred. Such a transaction is often referred to as a takeover if the transferee company's management team and name do not change or change only on minor points, and there is said to be a merger when the equality of both entities involved is evident. One way to put this into effect is to float a new company which acquires the shares of the companies involved and whose management team and name reflect that parity.

Amalgamation

A characteristic of an amalgamation is that the equity of the transferor company is transferred by virtue of general title and the company disappears or the equity of the two or more companies involved disappears owing to its acquisition by a new company formed by the latter two. Except for the transferee company, the companies involved in this transfer cease to exist owing to the shareholders of the disappearing company(ies), through the amalgamation, becoming shareholders of the transferee company or of the new company to be formed by the amalgamating parties.

Share transfer

The transfer of blocks of shares on the basis of a private agreement can be the result of a multitude of considerations. For example, private investment companies may proceed to participate in the risk-bearing capital of enterprises if the share capital is likely to become quoted on the unlisted securities market or stock exchange. Another objective might be to obtain a specific circle of shareholders for the purpose of strengthening shareholders' equity where large capital expenditures are envisaged in a demerger or management buy-out situation.

Takeover

The initiative for such a transaction may lie with either the prospective transferee or the prospective transferor. Should the initiative lie with the former, it will in principle be based on a long-term development plan. This could imply that plans have been developed with the specific purpose of acquiring growth. However, it is also possible for a takeover strategy to be based on plans geared to a change in the company's structure or to the consolidation.

Apart from a development plan, a takeover is based on the philosophy that the envisaged co-operation with the party to be taken over must be complete. In principle, it will be the latter party that will have to adapt unilaterally and in fact be fused into the entity as a whole since such a transaction implies a unilateral surrender of independence.

Also in cases where the initiative lies with the acquiree, it will have to be taken over in the negotiations that follow by the acquirer as this party will ultimately decide in what way the company to be taken over will be incorporated in the overall business structure. The acquirer will, therefore, take the lead in the negotiation process that has to be gone through. Although the concepts of merger and takeover are often used interchangeably to indicate diverging forms of a co-operation process, in their practical execution they differ from one another in virtually all aspects.

For example, the consequences relative to procedures; the duration involved in realizing the transaction; how the exchange ratio or price relative to the business concerned is determined; the new organizational structure; the operations development plan of the new entity; and the description of new objectives.

The underlying contractual arrangement of a takeover can be relatively simple and remain restricted to the description of the object to the takeover, the price and a number of guarantee clauses and payment arrangements. The time needed to realize the transaction, too, differs widely; whereas for a takeover it can take a few weeks to months, a merger will in practice take at least a year.

Split-off

Whenever a business is no longer able to generate sufficient financial resources for all its component parts at least to keep pace with market trends, companies have a tendency to concentrate on its own know-how. This can imply business components or certain interests acquiring autonomous status, followed by their sale. Through specific know-how and more flexibility than used to be possible within the original corporate or group relationships, organizations that have been split-off can expand their sales and consolidate their relative position in the market.

Influenced by the recession of the late 1970s and early 1980s businesses developed new strategic thinking and, helped along by the impact of a number of spectacular failures, of multinational conglomerates, in the Netherlands more social acceptance of the strategic rethink process came about. A significant supporting factor in this process has been the ample liquidity position of financing institutions and the manner in which the capital market became involved in the split-off process, particularly the growing willingness of banks to provide risk-bearing capital subject to certain conditions, the vigorous development of a venture capital market and, encouraged by the Dutch government's guarantee scheme, the formation of (private) venture capital companies are all factors that have made a major contribution to the reorientation process and the stimulation of new initiatives.

The buy-out of split-off entities frequently takes place by the sitting management actively participating in transactions and in the financing arrangements. Since management and staff will only rarely be able to settle the acquisition price fully from private means, funds will have to be borrowed resulting in leverage effects. The original parent company can, as the selling party, also contribute to the financing of business components that have been given independent status. Management buy-outs generally take the following forms:

Share transaction

This method implies that with the transfer of legal title, the risks and benefits of the autonomous business component in question or of the subsidiary are also taken over.

Asset transaction

Besides the acquisition of tangible and intangible assets and certain liabilities, an important role is played under this method by current obligations related to existing labour relationships in terms of the law (Article 1639 of the Dutch Civil Code).

2. TRENDS IN TAKEOVER ACTIVITY

Introduction

In the 1960s and 1970s, trade and industry in the Netherlands moved strongly in the direction of scale increases, growing by vertical integration and by the creation of conglomerates. Cyclical economic downturns revealed that these combinations had reached their outer limits of usefulness. Exceeding these limits rapidly decreases the usefulness of continued combinations; the reverse effect can even occur when top management loses sight of the divergent forms of expertise in the various divisions of the business and its manageability fails.

At present, mergers and takeovers are inspired by purposeful strategy, such as restricting and controlling competition, bringing about an increase in scale in core business or access into a market which is difficult to enter. Since many businesses in the Netherlands have postponed investment decisions in recent years, the resultant more favourable liquidity position constitutes an encouragement to venture into takeovers. This development is being stimulated by relatively low interest rates and ample liquidity of financing institutions.

All who venture into takeovers can enhance their chances of success by careful advance analysis and by planning and guiding the takeover operation well. Empirically, however, it has been established that a mere half of completed takeover operations of listed NVs in Europe and the US have ultimately been successful.

In the Netherlands, mergers and takeovers of any consequence must be reported to the Merger Matters Committee. This Committee was formed by the *Sociaal Economische Raad* (SER), a council which deals with socio-economic matters. The SER also produces the Takeover and Mergers Code (*Besluit Fusiegedragsregels*). The Merger Code of Conduct is not a law in the formal sense; it is a code setting out the manner in which, in the SER's opinion, the persons and institutions involved in a merger ought to behave, on the assumption that the code will be accepted by the public at large as guidelines of decent conduct. Section 4 provides further details on the working and the area of application of this merger code.

The period 1981–3 was characterized by a decline in mergers and takeovers, but in the years after that the number of applications is again significantly higher as shown by the following table.

	Mergers and takeovers reported to the SER
1980	431
1981	373
1982	401
1983	414
1984	525
1985	451
1986 (first 6 months)	197

3. MERGER CONTROL

Economic Competition Act

Since the 1930s, the Dutch government has seen it as part of its task to support economic co-operation where competition is unnecessarily excessive. On the other hand, it has subscribed to the philosophy of preventing positions of economic power. The current Economic Competition Act 1956 (*Wet Economische Mededinging*) is based on the same fundamental idea that both excessive restrictions and excessive freedom in the economy are detrimental to prosperity.

The support of economic co-operation on the one hand and the freedom of competition on the other needs a certain balancing in which price control measures play an active role. The Dutch government promoted in the past and is still supporting co-operation between businesses in the same industries as well as combined economic efforts of related industries. Price control measures, which have been one of the tools to regulate competition apart from macroeconomic objectives, like the levelling-off of inflation, unemployment and general increases in prices and wages, have been enforced over the last 15 years and 1985 was the first year in a long period in which not a single price control measure was in force.

The Ministry of Economic Affairs furthermore plays an active role in the economic process by providing assistance in restoring ailing individual companies and business sectors in general. In this context mergers and/or takeovers of specific businesses have been actively promoted in specific cases, with which instruments like incentive schemes, subsidies and participation in risk capital have been used in the framework of an industry and/or sectoral structuring policy. In principle the Economic Competition Act 1956 is a form of abuse legislation that must guard against creating positions of economic power. In the context of this law, agreements in restraint of trade are not *a priori* prohibited. In principle, these agreements should be reported to the Ministry of Economic Affairs within one month of their conclusion. These reports are internally recorded in the cartel register of which a summary has recently been made public. Although a Bill regulating the publication of the cartel register has been rejected by Parliament, the desirability of publication has been raised as the major point of a new policy of the Dutch Government on Economic Competition.

Competition procedures aimed at regulating the Dutch market can, in addition to Dutch policy on competition, be subject to policies laid down on this point in international treaties to which the Netherlands is a party. Apart from the relevant provision of the ECSC treaty, these would relate above all to the rules for enterprises referred to in article 85 of the EEC treaty.

Other rules

As indicated above, the rules that should be observed in the preparation and issue of a public bid for shares and the preparation and execution of a merger or takeover of a business have been laid down in the SER's 1975 Resolution. The Dutch Takeover and Mergers Code (*Fusiecode*) indicates how persons and institutions involved in a merger should behave. The code is not a law in a substantive sense but does contain sanctions. According to article 32 of the Resolution, the Committee on Merger Matters can, in the event of an infringement, pronounce a public reprimand or make a public announcement. The Committee monitors mergers with the objective of protecting the interests of workers and shareholders.

More important, however, it is an indirect sanction, of which there is no mention in the code itself. The '*Vereniging voor de Effectenhandel*' (Securities Trade Association) has, at the request of the Committee on Merger Matters, compelled its members in the event of a public reprimand not to lend their co-operation to the issue and settlement of a share bid. Since a member of the stock exchange is required to intercede in all stock exchange transactions, a merger involving the takeover of shares transacted on the stock exchange can therefore not be concluded.

The rules of conduct are concerned with the protection of shareholders' interests and those of employees. Additionally, there is enforcement of the reporting duty by the Ministry of Economic Affairs.

As far as the protection of shareholders' interests is concerned, the rules of conduct as laid down in the Code are applicable in particular to takeovers through the issue of a public bid for listed shares or unlisted shares that are regularly traded. The merger code is therefore not applicable in cases of a private bid. Among the provisions included in the rules is one that lays down that no public bid is allowed to be made without prior written notification to the board of management of the company to be taken over. The intention of this provision is above all to frustrate 'dawn raids', i.e. ones planned by means of a publicly issued bid without prior consultation.

As far as the aspect of protection of employees' interests is concerned, it should be noted that the Code applies when at least one business, regardless of its legal form, involved in the merger or takeover is established in the Netherlands which employs more than 100 employees or when the business belongs to a group of enterprises which together employ at least 100 employees. Trade unions are deemed to look after the interests of employees. Prior to furnishing information, secrecy can be imposed on trade unions. Apart from trade unions, works councils should also be informed and given the opportunity to issue an opinion. A number of collective labour agreements additionally contain directives related to consultations with employees' organizations.

Lastly, the Dutch Civil Code contains a number of provisions in labour legislation that are geared to the protection of employees' rights in case of mergers and in particular to ensure that employees' rights remain unaffected.

Furthermore mergers and takeovers in themselves do not constitute a reason for dismissal and the party taking over is bound by the working conditions as laid down in contracts of employment by which the former employer was bound.

4. TAXATION

Background

In Netherlands, the profits of entities/legal persons is subject to corporation tax levied by the government. The tax regime in respect of entities established in the Netherlands is based on the classical system, comparable with the US system. Profits are taxable in the hands of the entity. Distributions are not deductible from profits and are subject to dividend withholding tax. In addition, dividends are subject to income tax in the hands of shareholders/natural persons, a credit being allowed for dividend tax withheld. In certain circumstances, dividends received by shareholders/entities are exempt from corporation tax (participation exemption).

All companies and co-operative societies incorporated under Dutch law are resident taxpayers for the purpose of corporation tax, as are other companies whose capital is either fully or partly divided into shares if they are established in the Netherlands. The status of non-resident taxpayer applies when there is either a permanent establishment or permanent representative or specifically defined income sources (real estate, among others).

An interesting aspect of the Dutch tax system is that a taxpayer can conclude prior arrangements as to the tax consequences of certain transactions or legal acts. In contrast to the US, such rulings are not made public.

Corporation tax is levied at a rate of 42 per cent with no distinction being made between profit from operations and capital gains. However, the effective rates can be considerably lower as a result of tax relief facilities such as:

1. the Investment Account Act (WIR), a 12.5 per cent tax-free investment premium on capital expenditure;
2. the equity deduction, an abatement of 4 per cent of shareholders' equity for tax purposes as at the beginning of the year; and

3. the stock deduction, an abatement of 4 per cent of stocks on hand as at the beginning of the year (in so far as stocks amount to more than shareholders' equity for tax purposes).

When determining profits for tax purposes, the following normal deductions are allowed:

1. *Operating expenses* – ordinary expenses related to the conduct of operations are deductible in the year to which they relate if these expenses are the result of transactions at arm's length except where they have been incurred in respect of foreign participating interests.
2. *Depreciation* – no particular depreciation or amortization system for expenditure on tangible and intangible fixed assets is in force in the Netherlands. Acceptable methods are: straight-line depreciation, based on cost less a residual value, or the diminishing balance method, as well as the unit-of-production method. Depreciation is always based on the historical cost concept. The method used for accounting purposes will frequently be used for tax purposes as well.
3. *Interest* – as a general rule, interest owing is deductible. However, interest owing on loans in respect of foreign participations is not deductible (in connection with the participation exemption).
4. *Stocks* – may be valued either on a FIFO or LIFO basis or on the basis of a substantialistic valuation system (e.g. base stock method). Only stocks valued on a FIFO basis qualify for the 4 per cent deduction.
5. *Losses* – losses from any year can be carried back three years and carried forward eight years. Carryback takes preference over carryforward. In principle, the oldest loss is first carried back to the year furthest removed.
6. *Research and development (R&D)* – R&D expenses may be either charged directly to profits or may be capitalized. Should the taxpayer opt to capitalize these expenses, the asset may be amortized through the profit and loss account in so far as profits allow. Where research results in a tangible or intangible asset, WIR subsidies can be claimed on it and its depreciation or amortization respectively would be in accordance with one of the acceptable methods.
7. *Taxes* – in principle, all taxation by central and local government authorities is deductible except for corporation tax itself. Domestic dividend tax withheld can be set off against corporation tax owing. Foreign withholding tax can be claimed as a credit in certain circumstances.

In principle, all income wherever received in the world is taxable. As a rule, foreign profits from operations are exempted either on the grounds of treaties or on the grounds of the Unilateral Regulation for the Avoidance of Double Taxation. In the latter case, profits are required to be subjected to taxation, comparable to Dutch taxation, by the (local) authorities.

Foreign subsidiaries and permanent establishments

Profits of foreign participating interests are not ordinarily taxable in the Netherlands, even when they are distributed to a Dutch parent company. Distributions to Dutch natural persons are subject to income tax although set-off of Dutch or foreign corporation tax is not possible. In the corporation tax sphere, the Netherlands does not have an arrangement comparable with Subpart F. in the US.

Profits of Dutch permanent establishments of foreign entities are taxable in the Netherlands in so far as they are allocated, and assigned for taxation, to the Netherlands in accordance with Dutch national law or an applicable tax treaty. Profits of permanent establishments are subject to the normal rate of corporation tax. The same applies to interest, dividends and royalties received that are imputed to the permanent establishment. Where there is no permanent establishment or where these items are not imputed to it, only dividends of Dutch entities will be subject to 25 per cent (or the lower Treaty rate of) dividend tax. It follows that interest and royalties paid by a Dutch resident are not subject to a withholding tax.

Profits of foreign permanent establishments of a Dutch head office are in principle taxable in the Netherlands. Double taxation is avoided by means of a *pro rata* exemption of foreign profits.

In principle, all items that qualify for deduction as regards an independent subsidiary, also qualify as regards the determination of the results of a permanent establishment. Head office costs imputed at arm's length also form part of deductible costs.

In the Netherlands, the repatriated profits of permanent establishments are not taxed, nor are there any forms of second dividend tax.

Taxation implications of mergers and acquisitions

In the paragraphs that follow we shall generally restrict ourselves to the most common form of merger: that between entitites whose capital is divided into shares. Furthermore, we will restrict ourselves to the uniting of interests in which the legal autonomy of the participating entities is not lost.

Tax consequences related to enterprises involved in a share merger or takeover

Corporation tax. A share merger or takeover has no consequences for the remittance of corporation tax by the entitites except that, in certain circumstances Article 20, clause 5 of the Corporation Tax Act includes a provision by virtue of which the possibility to carry losses forward is forfeited. This applies when the entity, following discontinuation in full or almost in full of its business operations, undergoes a change in its body of shareholders such that profits to be earned after the discontinuation no longer accrue exclusively to the shareholders/natural persons in that entity at the time of the discontinuation.

Forfeiture of loss carryovers occurs in situations where more than 30 per cent of shareholders/natural persons are replaced in an entity, whose business operations have been discontinued in full or almost in full, subsequent to the moment of discontinuation. As this is generally the case when shares are sold it is therefore relevant to trace whether there has been a (partial) discontinuation of operations in the past.

Article 20, clause 5 of the Corporation Tax Act, which is effective from 1 January 1987, is due to be extended by a provision whereby current losses from new business operations may not be set off against the profits of the three preceding years if these new business operations occur after the transfer of more than 30 per cent of the shares. This extension is relevant where the acquiring company is considering the integration of new or existing operations in the company taken over.

(1) *Participation exemption for Netherlands based transferee companies.* Following a share merger or takeover, the transferee company will have acquired a block of shares which in certain circumstances will constitute a participating interest as defined by Article 13 of the Corporation Tax Act. The participation exemption will in this case apply to all the benefits accruing from that participating interest. The same applies to capital gains, if any, on foreign participating interests which result from exchange rate increases.

Losses on participating interests are not deductible except in the event of liquidation. The acquiring company should hold at least 5 per cent of the nominal paid up capital of the acquired company. Furthermore, for exemption to apply it is required that the participating interests should have existed from the beginning of the parent company's financial year (so-called year-long ownership).

There are two additional requirements for foreign participating interests:

1. the subsidiary must be subject to a profits tax abroad, in any form;
2. in the case of a participating interest of more than 5 per cent of the capital of a company, the participation exemption need not apply if the shares are held as a portfolio investment.

The year-long ownership requirement can be of relevance in the case of the acquisition of shares. Non-compliance with this requirement implies, on the one hand, that gains by virtue of a participating interest are not exempted but that losses, on the other hand, are deductible from the parent company's profit.

Where a participating interest loses value, its downward revaluation in the year of its acquisition can be charged to profits for tax purposes. The same would be achieved by liquidating the participating interest directly after acquiring it, since a liquidation loss is deductible. However, this method can only be put into practice in exceptional cases. The consideration paid to acquire the participating interest is of relevance to determine both what is deductible and the liquidation loss. The consideration is determined by the following elements:

1. the cost price of the participating interest at the time of acquiring it. (if, at the moment that it satisfies the year-long ownership requirement for the first time, the book value for tax purposes of the participating interest is lower than its cost price at the time of its acquisition, the parent company can, in principle, benefit from a double loss carryover);
2. subsequent changes in capital;
3. distribution of dividends included in the acquisition price;
4. other changes, including profit-sharing, share premium and share rights.

In practice, a common problem involves the use of the notion 'interest' in merger contracts, by which is meant a deemed profit and/or compensation based on the purchase price related to the time between the purchase agreement and payment and/or compensation for late payment. In this case, only that which is paid by way of compensation from the time of the purchase agreement will be a business expense, the rest being part of the cost of the participating interest.

Where the acquiring company is not based in the Netherlands, dividends paid by the Dutch company taken over will be subject to 25 per cent dividend tax. Most of the tax treaties concluded by the Netherlands state a considerably reduced rate for dividends as far as participating interests are concerned.

(2) *Intercompany pricing*. The parent/subsidiary relationship brought about by the takeover will be carefully scrutinized by the tax authorities to ensure that transactions are conducted at arm's length and that profits for tax purposes between the two entities, are not being shifted, e.g. profit distributions and syphoning within a group.

Where both the parent and subsidiary company are based in the Netherlands, while neither is entitled to carryover losses, a shift of profits will generally not have any impact in practice on corporation tax. This is different, however, where either the parent or subsidiary company is based abroad and is not a taxpayer in the Netherlands or where the parent or subsidiary company, although liable to tax is entitled to carryover losses. In practice, the tax authorities try to ensure that all goods and services transferred between affiliated enterprises are on an arm's length-basis.

(3) Fiscal unity (consolidated tax return). If the acquiring company holds all or virtually all the shares of the company taken over, which will, as a rule, be the case with a successful takeover, a fiscal unity can be formed. A fiscal unity implies that for the purpose of corporation tax, the subsidiary is no longer a taxpayer but is regarded as having been fully absorbed by the parent company (tax consolidation). The most important benefit of a fiscal unity is that profits within the group may be set off against losses, horizontally as well as vertically, of the parent and subsidiary company. This can be relevant particularly if the purchase of the shares in the subsidiary has been financed by means of borrowings.

Intercompany pricing problems likewise play no part in a fiscal unity. The facility is available provided both the parent and subsidiary company are NVs or BVs incorporated under the laws of the Netherlands and the subsidiary must be at least 99 per cent owned by the parent company.

The creation of fiscal unities is subject to a number of conditions that can have a detrimental effect on the tax position. These include the strict provisions concerning the set-off of pre-merger losses and the shifting of hidden reserves between parent and subsidiary company.

The effective date of a fiscal unity is the starting date of the first complete joint financial year of parent and subsidiary company.

VAT. Share mergers and takeovers are exempt from VAT.

Transfer taxes

(1) *Capital transfer tax*. No capital transfer tax is due on the takeover of shares against cash. However, a merger by means of a share exchange does generate a capital tax liability if the acquiring company is based in the Netherlands (i.e. the higher of 1 per cent of the actual value of the contribution or the nominal value of the issued shares). There is, however, a significant merger facility by virtue of which the 1 per cent is computed on the difference between the nominal value of the (newly) issued shares less the nominal value of the contributed shares. Any share premium consequently does not count. For the purpose of applying this exemption, a transaction will qualify as a merger as soon as the acquiring NV or BV obtains at least 75 per cent of the shares of the target NV or BV.

To be eligible for this exemption the merging parties need not be exclusively Dutch companies; however, all of them do have to be based within the EEC.

The merger facility is also available to real estate companies. It should be borne in mind that in the case of merger by means of shares and cash, the facility will only apply where the payment does not exceed 10 per cent of the nominal value of the issued shares.

(2) *Real estate transfer tax*. Transfer tax is levied only where shares are acquired in an entity whose assets consist of more than 70 per cent of real estate and whose activities are confined to the running of that real estate. Should the acquiring company obtain more than one-third of the outstanding shares, 6 per cent will normally be owing on the value of the real estate. Such a levy is expensive since the transfer tax raises the cost of the participating interest and is therefore not chargeable to profits.

Mergers of real estate companies by a share exchange do not qualify for any special merger facility other than the exemption referred to below in respect of the transfer in full of an enterprise. Should a reorganization be undertaken shortly after the merger, transfer tax could be owing for a second time because of the few transfer tax exemptions.

(3) *Stock exchange tax*. Stock exchange tax (1.2 per cent) is due on mergers by means of the purchase of existing shares, unless an exemption

is obtained in pursuance of the *Beschikking Beursverkeer*, a decree regulating stock exchange transactions and the tax owing thereon.

Tax consequences for enterprises involved in a business combination or takeover

Corporation tax

(1) *Consequences for the transferor company*. The transferor company will, in principle, have to settle its taxes on the basis of the surplus realized on the transfer of assets and liabilities, this being a sequel to the rules of sound business practice. The settlement obligation applies regardless of whether the assets and liabilities are transferred for cash or shares. In addition, the transferor company will have to repay the WIR subsidies received, if any, in the preceding eight years.

Where a merger takes place by means of shares, the transferor company can find itself with a liability for corporation tax and also for disinvestment payments. In that case the Corporation Tax Act makes provision for a (merger) facility which implies that the transferor entity does not, in respect of the transfer owe any corporation tax and any disinvestment payments. The merger facility is granted provided the acquiring company accounts for the assets and liabilities acquired at the same value for tax purposes as the value in the target company's balance sheet for tax purposes, and provided further that it takes over the obligations pursuant to the WIR. This merger facility is, in principle, also available when the transferee company is not based in the Netherlands, provided the enterprise transferred constitutes a permanent establishment in the Netherlands for the transferee company.

Following a business combination by means of shares, the same applies for the purpose of corporation tax as applies to a share merger; as a rule, a participatory relationship is brought about in which Article 13 of the Corporation Tax Act is applicable. Unlike the situation with a share merger, the transferor company becomes a (part-) parent company. Where the merger facility is invoked, the acquired shares are not allowed to be sold for a period of three years following their acquisition. The comments made concerning share mergers as regards transaction between parent and subsidiary company also apply to business combinations.

(2) *Consequences for the transferee company*. No special tax consequences ensue for the transferee company from the purchase, for cash, of the business of the transferor. The assets and liabilities taken over will have to be disclosed in the balance sheet for tax purposes at cost, including goodwill paid. WIR subsidies can be obtained for the assets acquired based on their cost (except for some assets excluded from the subsidies such as land and goodwill), unless the transferee and transferor companies were already affiliated prior to the transfer.

Of relevance in this context is the WIR regime amendment effective 1

May 1986. As from that date, WIR subsidy entitlements can only be enforced if and in so far as any corporation tax is owing. WIR subsidies can be claimed as tax credits against corporation tax owing in respect of the three preceding years and in respect of the eight subsequent years. A 12-year carryforward facility is available to newly formed entities.

In computing its annual profits, the transferee entity is in no way bound by the valuation principles and profit depreciation methods used by the transferor entity. In a share takeover, which has been effected without generating any tax consequences, the transferee entity must account for the assets and liabilities acquired at the value at which they were disclosed in the transferor's balance sheet for tax purposes at the time of the transfer. The transferee company must also adopt the valuation principles and depreciation methods used by the transferor.

VAT. A transfer of a business as a whole or of an autonomous part of a business is exempted from VAT.

Transfer taxes

(1) *Capital transfer tax*. Shares issued in the context of a business combination, in principle, qualify for the same facility as share mergers. However, the transfer is required to involve a business as a whole or an autonomous part of a business. The exemption then applies to a *pro rata* portion of the nominal paid up capital of the transferor company.

(2) *Real estate transfer tax*. Where real estate is transferred in the context of a business combination, 6 per cent transfer tax will, in principle, be owing on the value of the real estate. A share takeover is exempted, however, if the real estate is part of a business taken over as a whole.

An internal reorganization is also subject to a restricted exemption as regards transfer tax. Where the internal reorganization is effected shortly after the merger, the exemption concerning the merger could lapse so that 6 per cent transfer tax would be owing. This is normally the case if, shortly after the merger, the real estate is separated from the rest of the assets of the business and the action had been premeditated.

(3) *Stock exchange tax*. Stock exchange tax is not due on the issue of new shares; it follows that a business combination is not subject to stock exchange tax.

Tax consequences for the shareholders of an entity involved in a share merger or takeover

Shareholder/natural person resident in the Netherlands. Where the transferor-shareholder does not have a substantial interest (less than one-third within a family circle), the transfer of shares (for cash or for shares) does not result in an income taxation liability as it constitutes an ordinary capital gain which is not taxable in the Netherlands. However, a problem could arise where the sale is followed quickly by the liquidation of the company taken over. Depending on the amount of the liquidation profit,

20–45 per cent income tax may be due on the liquidation balance less the average capital paid up on the shares.

It is customary for a provision to be included in the merger contract to the effect that the company taken over may not be liquidated in the first five years. Should the actual situation be devoid of all real meaning, however, the non-liquidation provision will not achieve the envisaged goal.

(1) *Paid up capital with a share exchange.* With a share exchange the question often is how much has been paid for the newly issued shares. This is of relevance to the question whether capital can be repaid in full or in part free of income tax. The Income Tax Act contains a provision which, in the case of a share exchange, restricts the payment on the shares of the company taking over *vis-à-vis all* its shareholders (the new as well as the old shareholders regardless of the fact whether their shareholding is corporately or privately owned or constitutes a substantial interest) to that which was paid on the shares of the company taken over, regardless of the value of these shares at the time of the takeover. Share premium construed at the time of the share exchange is therefore eliminated for the purpose of applying the Income Tax Act.

The part of the capital payment not admitted for tax purposes is referred to as *kapitaalmanco* (capital shortage for tax purposes). This provision serves to secure the tax claim (liquidation claim) on the shares of the company taken over. Through the wording '*vis-à-vis* all its shareholders' of Article 44 of the Income Tax Act, the provision can also have an adverse effect on the old shareholders of the transferee company. The impact of this article is therefore felt in all cases where paid up capital plays a role for income tax purposes at a later stage (such as on the purchase of the company's own shares or on liquidation). Apart from the paid up capital not admitted for tax purposes on the grounds of Article 44 of the Income Tax Act, there can be 'ordinary' share premium from which bonus shares can be issued without any income tax being levied.

The existence of a capital shortage for tax purposes in pursuance of Article 44 of the Income Tax Act consequently does not inhibit the possibility of issuing tax-free bonus shares chargeable to share premium and paid at a different moment in time (either prior or subsequent to the merger). Nor can a subsequent issue with share premium, or existing share premium, therefore make up for share discount for tax purposes.

Where there are foreign shareholders, the question arises whether this provision applies to dividend tax. Although this provision is not found in the Dividend Tax Act, the Ministry of Finance works on the assumption that it does apply. In practice, this will have to be put to the test by means of a lawsuit.

Shareholder/natural person with substantial interest. For shareholders having a substantial interest (equal to or larger than one-third within a family circle) in the company taken over, the alienation of their shares implies that income tax at a rate of 20 per cent must, in principle, be paid on the profit realized. In determining whether somebody has a substantial interest, all shares count, including preference and priority shares which do not confer any rights to liquidation distributions. Profits, if any, achieved on the alienation sale of these special shares are, however, not taxed. In this context the word 'alienation' stands for any obligation under which a shareholder gives up his rights to the shares with the exception of a transfer upon death.

If, in the context of a merger, the transfer of shares takes place in exchange for shares of the acquiring company, the Income Tax Act allows deferral of this tax by shifting the substantial interest claim to the newly acquired shares. Among the conditions attaching to the facility is one requiring both merging companies to be Netherlands-based entities engaged in running a business. A share exchange between investment companies is, therefore, not a merger as meant by this facility. In certain circumstances, the acquired block of shares in the acquiring company is regarded as a so-called fictitious substantial interest.

Except in the case of prior sale alienation, the fictitious substantial interest only disappears at death. Also for shareholders with an actual substantial interest in the acquiring company, a share exchange can have other consequences. For example, the issue can result in their substantial interest disappearing in which case they should retain a terminable substantial interest for five years.

For holders of a substantial interest in the acquiring company a share merger can result in the average capital paid up on the shares changing, so that the minimum acquisition price for the substantial interest also undergoes changes. The minimum acquisition price, which applies as a basis for computing taxable profit, has been set by law at the average capital paid up on the shares. The restriction on paid up capital, described earlier in the context of a share exchange, also applies by way of limit in this context.

It should be borne in mind that the provisions relating to substantial interests do not apply if the transaction is to be regarded either as profit from operations or income from capital.

Thus a sale followed by a liquidation and the purchase of shares are subject to a rate of tax between 20–54 per cent even if the selling party has a substantial interest.

Shareholder/entrepreneur. Where the shares transferred are corporately owned by the transferor-shareholder, profit is taxed at the normal rate. For natural persons this can be as high as 72 per cent. Where the shareholder is an entity and the shares transferred constitute a participating interest as meant by Article 13 of the Corporation Tax Act, the surplus value acquired, in terms of the exchange, is exempted by virtue of the participation exemption.

Tax consequences for shareholders of an entity involved in a business combination or takeover

Shareholders of the transferor company. After a business combination by means of cash, the transferor company's assets consist exclusively of cash. From this cash, corporation tax owing in respect of the transfer will, in the very first place, have to be paid. Should the shareholders/natural persons subsequently dissolve the company, the remaining amount would be distributed to them as a liquidation dividend, and they would be liable to income tax on that which they received in excess of the average paid up capital. The rate of tax amounts to 20–54 per cent. This levy would be in addition to the corporation tax paid shortly before. If the shareholders do not terminate the company's existence by liquidation or by a large dividend payment in cash, other solutions are available.

Shareholders of the transferee company. With business combinations, income tax consequences can also occur at the time of merging for the shareholders of the transferee company. If merging is effected by shares, substantial interest positions, if any, held by the shareholders of the transferee company could be forfeited, as in the case of share mergers discussed earlier. Another consequence for the shareholders of the transferee company could be that the average capital paid up on the shares undergoes changes. This will occur if a different amount is paid up on the shares to be issued for the merger than was paid up on the original shares (at the time of merging, the new shares mostly have a completely different issue price from the original shares). This change in the average paid up capital will play a role in a great many situations. As we saw, for the holders of the substantial interest it also has consequences for the mininum acquisition price.

5. ACCOUNTING

Background

Dutch reporting regulations are laid down in Book 2 of the Civil Code. These regulations, which are primarily geared to the unconsolidated annual accounts of NVs and BVs, require annual accounts to be prepared in accordance with generally acceptable accounting standards and to provide such information as to enable the reader to form a sound opinion on the financial position and profit or loss and, to the extent that the nature of annual accounts permits, on the solvency and liquidity of the company. The Dutch Civil Code lays down principles to be used in stating assets and liabilities and also provides detailed disclosure requirements. The law also lays down that regulations are of corresponding application to consolidate annual accounts. As far as the latter type of accounts is concerned, new rules may be expected within the forseeable future in connection with the implementation of the Seventh EEC Directive dealing with company law, which addresses the problem of consolidation. It should be noted that this new legislation is not expected to cause fundamental changes in Dutch reporting practices.

A special feature of accounting in the Netherlands is that the administration of justice as regards, *inter alia*, annual accounts has been entrusted to a special tribunal, namely the Enterprise Chamber which passes judgement on disputes in first and in last instance. The only body competent to hear appeals against decisions of this Court is the Supreme Court of the Netherlands.

In interpreting the law, frequent reference is made to the pronouncements of the Council for Annual Reporting. This Council is made up of representatives from employees' and employers' organizations and the Institute of Registered Accountants. It regularly publishes guidelines setting out interpretations on the wording of the law and the manner in which specific situations should be, or are being, dealt with in the practice. The guidelines have authoritative value in the Netherlands, and deviations from them should only occur in rare instances.

In drawing up the guidelines the Council also reviews if, and to what extent reporting practices harmonize with the standards laid down by the International Accounting Standards Committee. As regards these standards it should be noted that the Dutch accountants' organization – the Nederlands Instituut van Registeraccountants (NIvRA) – has committed itself to promote adherence to these standards.

Valuation of interests in other companies

If an interest in another company is intended to be long-term and serves the participating entity's own operations, such an interest qualifies as a 'participating interest'. A participating interest is legally presumed to exist if the interest in the share capital amounts to 20 per cent or more.

In pursuance of the law (Article 389, Book 2 of the Civil Code), participating interests should, in principle, be valued on the basis of the equity method of accounting. Where a participating interest is involved over which the participating company exercises control, the net asset value method of accounting is virtually always used as intended by law. This implies that on acquisition, the assets, provisions and liabilities of the participating interest are valued at fair value. This value is accounted for in the balance sheet under fixed asset investments. Where the net asset value, so determined, is lower than the value of the participating interest at cost, the difference is accounted for as goodwill. Where cost is lower, the difference between it and net asset value is added to a revaluation which forms part of shareholders' equity. A revaluation reserve is not available for distribution.

In determining net asset value, the parent company's accounting principles are always used at subsequent stages. Changes in value consist of results and revaluations on the basis of the parent company's principles, less dividend distribution, if any. The parent company should add revaluations to the revaluation reserve and profits to a legal reserve not available for distribution. The statutory reserve is available for distributions.

Treatment of goodwill

As indicated above, goodwill is isolated from cost by determining the net asset value. Goodwill is also disclosed separately when other forms of businesses are taken over. In practice, goodwill is frequently charged to shareholders' equity. The law allows goodwill to be capitalized as an intangible fixed asset and it should be amortized through the profit and loss account over a period not exceeding five years (Article 386, Book 2 of the Civil Code). However, where there are good reasons for doing so, acquired goodwill can be charged to the profit and loss account over a period in excess of five years, but not exceeding ten years. The period of amortization is to be disclosed and explained in the notes.

Whether goodwill is capitalized and taken directly to equity is frequently determined by the choice of accounting method, namely the acquisition method or the pooling of interests method. These will be dealt with in more detail in subsequent paragraphs.

Layout

Dutch legislation on annual reports lays down formats for the balance sheet and profit and loss account. Where it is intended to be long-term an interest in another business should be included in the balance sheet under the heading 'Fixed asset investments'. If it concerns an interest serving the participating entity's own operations, it is classified under the heading 'participating interests in group companies' or 'other participating interests'. Amounts owed by participating interests are split in the same manner.

According to Article 76 of Book 2 of the Civil Code, group companies are those entities which are associated in a group, but at present, the law does not provide a definition of the term 'group'. In practice the term 'group' is interpreted as companies or partnerships forming an economic unit, co-ordinately managed, in which the leading enterprise can exercise control.

Disclosure of information related to participations (Article 379 of Book 2 of the Civil Code)

All legal entities in which the participating legal entity owns at least 20 per cent of the issued capital should be disclosed on a list attached to the annual accounts. The information disclosed should include the name, residence, issued capital and the amount of shareholders' equity and the company's results over the last financial year for which annual accounts are available. The same particulars should be disclosed if the subsidiary of a legal entity, a legal entity jointly with a subsidiary, or group company respectively, provides, or causes to provide, at least 20 per cent of the issued capital.

Should the business so wish, the list need not be included in the annual accounts provided it is deposited for public inspection at the offices of the trade registry and this fact is disclosed in the annual accounts. The particulars may be omitted in so far as their disclosure is not material to the annual accounts. Particulars relating to shareholders' equity and results may be omitted if the participating interest has been stated at net asset value or if the annual accounts in pursuance of legislation applicable to the participating interest do not have to be made public. Where particulars to be made public are restricted, only the balance sheet and the notes thereto need to be disclosed, so that the results may be omitted. Also when particulars concerning the participation have been included in the consolidated annual accounts (see below), data related to shareholders' equity and results may be omitted. When so requested, the Minister of Economic Affairs can grant exemption from disclosure of all the particulars referred to above if there are good reasons for fearing that such disclosure will be seriously detrimental.

If a legal entity provides, or causes to provide, more than 50 per cent of the capital of another legal entity, this latter legal entity constitutes a subsidiary of the former (Articles 76 and 187 of Book 2 of the Civil Code). Even when the capital is provided by, or with, another subsidiary or group company, a parent/subsidiary relationship is still deemed to exist.

Subsidiaries' financial data must be included in group annual accounts drawn up in accordance with the consolidation method of accounting. Where a subsidiary does not form part of the group, its annual accounts are included under 'supplementary information'. Where a subsidiary does form part of a group, but is engaged in wholly different activities, its annual accounts must be included in the notes.

It should be noted that joint ventures, although they cannot, in principle, be classified as group companies and should therefore be included in the parent company's annual accounts under 'Supplementary information', are allowed to be consolidated either in full or in part.

Consolidation method

The law does not provide any terms of reference as regards the method of consolidation. In practice, two methods are in use, namely the acquisition method of accounting, and the pooling of interests method of accounting. The methods differ as regards comparative figures and the manner in which results are accounted for and, in a number of circumstances, as regards the treatment of goodwill. Both methods will be briefly discussed below.

The acquisition method

Under the acquisition method, data of the company taken over (stated at current value; see above) are included as at the takeover date in the consolidated balance sheet. From that time the results of the company are included in the consolidated profit and loss account. As a rule, goodwill (or negative goodwill) is calculated when using this method. This method is applicable to all cases of takeovers for payment in cash.

The pooling of interests method

Under the pooling of interests method, the assets and liabilities as well as the income and expense over the whole year are combined with those of the transferee company. Comparative figures are also adjusted.

Generally, no goodwill is accounted for under this method since it is mostly applicable to cases where the participating interest is acquired in exchange for shares. This implies that the former shareholders of the company taken over acquire an interest in the company taking over and through it in the results of the combined enterprises. Since goodwill can be characterized as compensation for foregoing future profit entitlements, accounting for goodwill would not be appropriate to such a situation.

In general, the difference between the balance of assets and liabilities of the company taken over (valued at current cost) and the nominal value of the shares issued is accounted for under shareholders' equity as share premium.

The choice between the two methods is, however, not exclusively determined by the form of *quid pro quo* used in connection with the alienation. Whether a takeover or a combination of businesses is involved can also be resolved by other circumstances, such as the relative size of the enterprises in question, their market position, management continuity, etc.

International accounting standards

A summary of significant differences between the Tripartite Accounting Standards Committee's Accounting Guidelines with international accounting standards is provided in table 10.1.

6. EXCHANGE CONTROL/FOREIGN INVESTMENT REGULATIONS

The Netherlands has a long-standing tradition of a liberal policy in relation to international trade and foreign investments and of neutrality between domestic and foreign capital. Foreign investments constitute a not inconsiderable share in the total volume of investments in the country.

Residents may generally make payments abroad without a limit through any authorized bank, under a control mechanism operated by the central bank (De Nederlandse Bank). There are no restrictions whatsoever on borrowings by residents from non-residents. Shares may freely be issued by resident corporations to non-residents.

Generally speaking there are no exchange controls and foreign investment regulations that affect normal financial or business transactions or financial participation. The law which governs the financial relations with foreign countries (Wet Financiële Betrekkingen Buitenland 1981) stipulates a freedom in principle of exchange in foreign currency and transfer of funds. The central bank monitors compliance with the administrative procedures and reporting requirements for balance of payments purposes.

The government is authorized by law to prohibit foreign investment in any industry if it is considered necessary in the 'national interest'. This law, however, has not been applied to date. No restrictions on foreign ownership are therefore in effect.

7. OTHER FACTORS AFFECTING MERGERS AND ACQUISITIONS

Industry policy, sectoral restructuring policy and institutional facilities

Following the recession in the late 1970s and early 1980s, the economic recovery in the Netherlands began to take shape clearly after 1983. Policies pursued up to that time, which were mainly geared to provide assistance in restoring ailing businesses and business sectors to health and the nature of which was therefore principally to conserve, have progressed in the direction of policies characterized by three main features:

1. the creation of the right conditions;
2. reindustrialization; and
3. market-oriented technology.

Measures designed to meet the need for risk-bearing capital were also taken in the context of these policies. These measures brought new providers of capital, such as private venture capital companies (PVCC) and since 1982 the *Maatschappij voor Industriële Projecten* (MIP) (an industrial development corporation), on the scene alongside the traditional providers of capital (stock exchange, investment companies, etc.). The corporation's objective is the promotion and stimulation on a commercial basis of projects able to make a substantial contribution to strengthen industrial activity. It views its objectives sufficiently broadly that it actively canvasses the American market by drawing the corporate sector's attention to the possibility that in locating subsidiaries of promising new industries in the Netherlands, the MIP can participate in their share capital.

In this context should also be mentioned the long-term participation in risk capital by the NPM (*Nederlandse Participatie Maatschappij*). This organization pursues a philosophy of supporting the management of expanding corporations by supplying capital funds on a long term basis. The shares of the NPM are quoted on the parallel market.

Lastly, there are a number of arrangements geared to making credits available subject to guarantees from the government, such as the *Kredietregeling voor het midden- en kleinbedrijf 1985* (a credit scheme for medium-sized and small businesses), *Regeling bijzondere financiering* (a special financing scheme), etc. Regionally, development corporations such as the BOM (Brabant Development Corporation), GOM (Gelderland Development Corporation), LIOF (Limburg Investment and Development Corporation), NOM (Northern Development Corporation) and OOM (Overijssel Development Corporation) successfully fulfil a not insignificant role in the area of assistance, participation and guidance of locally established businesses and initiatives in the sphere of participation of foreign companies in locally established corporations.

Table 10.1 Comparison between the Tripartite Accounting Standards Committee's accounting guidelines with international accounting standards

IAS 2 – Valuation and presentation of inventories in the context of the historical-cost system	There is no equivalent guideline in the Netherlands
IAS 3 – Consolidated financial statements	There are no legal provisions or accounting standards which deal with business combinations in the Netherlands. Consolidated financial statements are mandatory for groups of companies and in theory both purchase accounting and merger accounting are acceptable methods of accounting for acquistions. In practice, merger accounting is rarely used but when it is, it refers to the coming together of fairly equal partners where there is continuity of management Proportional consolidation is regarded as an acceptable method of consolidation. There are no disclosure requirements for business combinations and in practice little information is normally supplied. Often disclosure is limited to the terms of the transaction including the consideration paid, and goodwill
IAS 5 – Information to be disclosed in financial statements	The guidelines recommend that intercompany transactions should be disclosed but there are no equivalent guidelines for disclosure of other information as recommended in IAS 5
IAS 7 – Statement of changes in financial position	The international standard requires a statement of changes in financial position to be included as part of the financial statements. In the Netherlands it is recommended but is not mandatory and where it is included it is shown as supplementary information
IAS 8 – Unusual and prior period items and changes in accounting policies	Reserve accounting is practised in the Netherlands and covers adjustments such as changes in deferred tax balances as a result of changes in rates of tax, accounting for uninsured losses as a result of a catastrophe, losses incurred as a result of nationalisation, and the amortization of goodwill
IAS 11 – Accounting for construction contracts	There is no equivalent standard in the Netherlands but in practice profits on long-term contracts are usually recognized on completion

– *Continued*

Table 10.1 Continued

IAS 12 – Accounting for taxes on income	Whilst the partial allocation method is mentioned in the guidelines of the Tripartite Accounting Standards Committee, a decision has not yet been made as to its acceptability. In practice, the comprehensive income tax allocation method is used based on the liability concept. Disclosure is limited to amounts stated in the balance sheet
IAS 14 – Reporting financial information by segment	The guidelines recommend the publication of segmental information but there is only an obligation in the Netherlands to disclose segmented information concerning sales. There is no obligation in the Netherlands to disclose assets employed or inter-segment pricing policies
IAS 15 – Information reflecting the effects of changing prices	The guidelines prescribe the disclosure of supplementary information where there is a material difference between historical cost and current cost
IAS 16 – Accounting for property, plant and equipment	There is no equivalent standard in the Netherlands. However, in practice a considerable number of Dutch public companies revalue their fixed assets to replacement cost. This is often done using general price indexes with periodic adjustments for professional valuations
IAS 17 – Accounting for leases	There is no equivalent standard in the Netherlands
IAS 19 – Accounting for retirement benefits in the financial statements of employers	The guidelines in the Netherlands permit companies to take retirement benefits directly to equity although this is not permitted by the international accounting standard
IAS 20 – Accounting for government grants and disclosure of government assistance	The Tripartite guidelines do not cover all the government grants covered by the international standard
IAS 21 – Accounting for the effects of changes in foreign exchange rates	The guidelines permit gains on forward exchange contracts to be recognized directly as income. There is no limit to exchange differences that are included in the book value of the related assets
IAS 22 – Accounting for business combinations	There is no equivalent in the Netherlands
IAS 23 – Related party disclosures	There is no equivalent in the Netherlands

Sundries

There are no other significant factors which are peculiar to international takeovers or mergers since the Netherlands have adopted a policy of non-discrimination between local and foreign-owned corporations.

SUMMARY

The Netherlands has a long-standing tradition of a liberal approach towards business in general and international trade in particular.

There are few formalities to fulfil in establishing a branch office or a company. The most common incorporated business entities are the private limited liability company (*Besloten Vennootschap* or BV). The incorporation formalities are relatively simple and it usually takes only a few weeks for completion. All commercial enterprises have to be registered at the local Chamber of Commerce.

The takeover of a Dutch enterprise by another company, including a foreign company, is subject to the voluntary Merger Code, drawn up by the Social Economic Council (SER) which has dealt with about 3000 of such cases since 1980. Thus far, the government has not attempted to block any acquisition or merger. No restrictions on foreign ownership are in effect.

The regulation concerning competition is also very liberal and is limited to a form of abuse legislation that must guard against creating positions of economic power.

As a member of the European Communities, competition procedures aimed at regulating the Dutch market are not only subject to the national legislation but also to policies laid down on this point in international treaties to which the Netherlands are a party.

Taxes in the Netherlands are levied primarily by central government. Major exceptions are the real-property taxes imposed by municipalities. The principal kinds of taxes levied by the Dutch government are corporate income tax, individual income tax, dividend withholding tax and value added tax. There is no special tax on capital gains, no withholding tax on interest or royalties and there is no tax on remittances of profits by Dutch branches of foreign corporations.

The Dutch company law is set forth in Book 2 of the Civil Code which is concerned with legal entities. In the Civil Code the EC's company law directives – the second, third and fourth – are incorporated. The annual financial statements must furnish, in accordance with generally acceptable accounting principles, such information as is necessary to form a responsible opinion regarding the company's financial position, its profit or loss for the year, and, to the extent that the nature of annual accounts permits, its solvency and liquidity. Dutch company law does not provide any terms of reference as regards the method of consolidation. In practice, two methods are in use, viz. the acquisition method and the pooling of interests method.

The Netherlands has no exchange controls and foreign investment regulations that affect normal financial or business transactions or financial participation. As to administrative procedures and reporting requirements for balance of payments purposes, the central bank fulfils a monitoring role. In the 1980s, measures have been introduced to bring new providers of risk-capital to the market in an effort to stimulate capital investments in the country.

11

Sweden

1. BUSINESS ORGANIZATIONS AND COMBINATIONS

Business organizations

A foreign enterprise wishing to establish a business organization in Sweden or participate in a Swedish enterprise can choose between establishing a corporation (*aktiebolag,* AB), a trading partnership (*handelsbolag*), a limited partnership (*kommanditbolag*) or a branch (*filial*).

The corporation (limited liability company)

The corporation is the form most frequently used for business establishment in Sweden and is used for enterprises of all sizes. Shareholders' liability is limited to the equity held by them. There is no Swedish equivalent to the French *société à responsabilité limitée* or to the German *Gesellschaft mit beschränkter Haftung*.

A corporation may be formed by one or several founders. A person acting as founder must be a Swedish citizen resident in Sweden or a Swedish legal entity. However, the Government through the Board of Commerce (*Kommerskollegium*) may permit any person other than those mentioned above to act as founder. The corporation must be registered with the Swedish National Patent and Registration Office (*Patent- och Registreringsverket*) to become a legal entity.

After registration foreigners may acquire the shares from the founders if the Articles of Association permit. A corporation does not need to have more than one shareholder. Under new legislation in this field, permission for acquisition must be obtained from the County Administration or, in cases of special importance, from the Government if the foreign proportion of the share capital or of the voting rights of the total number of shares in the company as a result of the acquisition, should exceed 10, 20, 40 or 50 per cent. A foreign legal entity or a person non-resident in Sweden, who intends to buy or subscribe for shares in a Swedish corporation, must also obtain the approval of the Central Bank to transfer the necessary funds.

The authorized share capital must be denominated in Swedish kronor (SEK) and it must not be less than SEK 50,000. Only par value shares are permitted. A corporation may have different classes of shares with varying rights. Voting rights may differ, for instance, with a maximum ratio of 10:1. All subscribed shares must be fully paid. Payment may be in cash or property such as assets in an existing business.

Share certificates are negotiable. Commercial banks, lawyers and other advisers offer special services to customers and clients wishing to acquire a Swedish corporation. The costs involved in the incorporation of a new corporation with a minimum share capital amount to approximately SEK 5000 plus the share capital itself, minimum SEK 50,000. The costs for obtaining a going concern may, however, differ greatly from the amount mentioned above.

A corporation must have a board of directors consisting of at least three persons. Where the share capital or the maximum share capital is less than SEK 1 million, the board may, however, consist of one or two members, provided that at least one deputy director is appointed. In a corporation where the share capital or maximum share capital amounts to at least SEK 1 million, the board of directors must appoint a president (managing director). The president need not necessarily be a member of the board. The directors and the president must be resident Swedish citizens, but exceptions may be granted by the Board of Commerce for one-third of the directors and also for the president. The president, however, must be resident in Sweden. Equal with Swedish citizens are citizens from Denmark, Finland, Iceland and Norway. Citizens of these countries residing in one of these countries may be members of the board as long as at least half of the members of the board are resident in Sweden. In corporations with at least 25 employees the employee organizations are entitled to nominate two members and two deputy members. If the board of such a company consists of only one member, the employee organizations are entitled to nominate only one member and one deputy member.

Swedish laws prohibit foreigners and foreign organizations from acquiring real estate in Sweden either directly or indirectly – for example, through a Swedish corporation – without a special permit. Such permits are generally given if the title to the real estate is deemed necessary for the business. Permits cannot, however, normally be obtained for foreigners to acquire mines, farm land and forest property. Legislation permitting foreign banks to start operations was adopted by the Swedish Government by 1 January 1986.

Swedish corporations must file annual reports with the Swedish National Patent and Registration Office. Each company must appoint at least one auditor, ordinarily a Swedish citizen.

A Swedish corporation is obliged to make annual allocations to the statutory reserve. At least 10 per cent of the annual net profit must be set aside until the statutory reserve equals 20 per cent of the share capital. The statutory reserve is not available for distribution to shareholders but may be used to increase the share capital through a bonus issue.

Dividends from Swedish corporations are at present freely transferable to foreign shareholders.

Amendments and additions to the bylaws may be made by a decision of the shareholders at a general meeting.

The trading partnership

If two or more individuals or legal persons enter into a partnership agreement in order to carry on a trade or other business, this constitutes a trading partnership. The name of the partnership must include the term *handelsbolag*.

A trading partnership is considered a legal person. The partners are jointly and severally responsible for its liabilities. Each one of them has, in principle, the right to act for the partnership, but this right can be restricted through an agreement. The partners are free to agree in respect of the management of the business. A foreign partner needs permission from the County Administration or in cases of special importance from the Government, to join a Swedish partnership as well as the approval of the Central Bank before he invests his part of the partnership's capital. If a trading partnership has one or more foreign partners, it is not allowed to acquire real estate in Sweden without a special permit.

The limited partnership

The main difference between a limited partnership and a trading partnership is that in a limited partnership one or more of the partners but not all may limit their liability to the amount of their investment. The name of the partnership must include the term *kommanditbolag*. The partners with limited liability have no right to act on behalf of the partnership without special procuration.

The branch

The establishment by a foreign enterprise of a Swedish branch with independent administration is governed by a law of 1968. The law contains a considerable number of special requirements: the obtaining of a permit from the Board of Commerce or, in cases of special importance, from the government, the presentation of evidence that the foreign enterprise is 'carrying on business in its home country', documentation, with respect to the foreign enterprise's bylaws, statement of accounts, etc.

The branch must have a president who should be a Swedish resident however, not necessarily a Swedish citizen. Its establishment must be reported for recording in the branch register kept by the Swedish National Patent and Registration Office.

The business of the branch must be carried on under a title incorporating the foreign corporation's name with the word *filial* (branch) added and indicating the corporation's country of domicile. The branch has to keep separate books and accounts.

In general, the taxation rules applying to Swedish corporations also apply to Swedish branches of foreign enterprises. The branch of a foreign enterprise is, however, subject to the annual Swedish tax on net wealth, regardless of the parent company's form of organization. Most of the tax treaties that Sweden has entered into contain provisions which in effect exempt foreign branch companies in Sweden from this tax.

To date very few branches have been established, evidently because the advantages they offer are considered to be few in comparison with those of the long established form of a subsidiary corporation.

The non-trading office

Before deciding to establish a business in Sweden, a foreign corporation may set up a local office to make preliminary market studies. An office of this kind is not considered to be a trading or business office and there is no special registration or other requirement to restrict its establishment.

Types of business combination

The three most common forms used in changing the conditions of ownership or control in industry are acquisition, merger and the co-operation agreement.

Acquisition

A Swedish corporation may be acquired by the purchase of its shares. Purchase of net assets is uncommon because it is unfavourable to the seller in regard to taxation. This fact will be discussed in greater depth under section 4. One way, however, in which the purchase of assets can be achieved is by the acquisition of part of a business enterprise. 'Part of a business' means, for example, a special function of the business (distribution, obtaining raw materials, etc.) or all the functions necessary in the marketing of a certain product (production, sales, service, etc.). In Sweden, an acquisition normally takes place through the purchase of shares. Through this procedure all the assets, debts, rights and liabilities of the company are acquired, with possible exceptions as specifically stated in the documents of purchase.

The purchase price may be paid either in cash or in shares in the acquiring company. The mode of payment has no taxation or other significance for the selling company provided, of course, that the amounts are comparable.

Often a combination of cash and shares constitute the purchase price. A strong negotiation stance is often taken advantage of by the vendor to maximize the cash part of the purchase price and vice versa.

Mergers

The Companies Act 1975 specifies the procedure for complete mergers between corporations. A complete merger means that a corporation (the selling company) is absorbed by another corporation (the acquiring company), by a transfer of the assets and liabilities of the selling company to the acquiring company. In this way the selling company is dissolved without being liquidated. Accordingly, it is not possible to limit the transfer to a certain part of the assets and liabilities of the selling company. A complete merger also means that all the rights and liabilities of the selling company are transferred to the acquiring corporation.

In Sweden, there are three specific forms of merger. One of these is usually called 'absorption', and refers to a merger between independent companies, which means that one company is incorporated into the other company. This procedure is unusual and has only rarely been applied. Normally compensation for the 'absorption' is paid in the form of shares, however other modes of remuneration also occur.

The other form of merger is characterized by two or more selling companies which join to form a new company, which then acquires the assets and liabilities of the endorsing companies, in exchange for shares in the takeover company. This type of merger is called a 'combination'. In order to be valid, a combination must be authorized by the AGM of the endorsing company.

A third form of merger is a special case of the 'absorption method'. An example of this method is when a subsidiary is incorporated into the parent company. This is distinguished from ordinary 'absorption' since this does not require an authorization from the AGM of the selling company. This is the normal procedure for mergers between Swedish companies.

Co-operation agreement (samarbetsavtal)

This type of merger is taken up here since, under certain conditions, it may be an appropriate alternative to an acquisition or merger. This may mean, for example, that two enterprises, together, form a common export, production or sales company. This procedure may be suitable if a foreign enterprise is doubtful about entering a new geographic market and does not want to make any major investments.

2. TRENDS IN TAKEOVER ACTIVITY

The Central Price Board (SPK) continuously supervises the purchase and sales of business enterprises, or parts of enterprises in Swedish industry, commerce and trade. The function of this board, which was founded in 1969, is to give information on changes made in the relationships between the affiliated companies of larger business enterprises, as well as to give information on the concentration of activity in different product and service areas.

From 1969 to 1983, 9025 acquisitions have been registered which affects 804,000 employees in the purchased businesses.

The motive for acquisition may vary from time to time, but some of the most common motives are listed below:

1. vertical acquisition;
2. horizontal acquisition;
3. diversification;
4. an asset buy-out;
5. specialization in mature enterprises;
6. tax purposes, such as loss write-offs;
7. shares with high estimated market value gives an opportunity to purchase at a 'low' price.

Takeover trends

During the 1960s and in the early 1970s there were many acquisitions for the purpose of diversification. Groups of companies, operating in different lines of business, which were differently affected by upswings and recessions in the business cycle, were considered to be best equipped to face an unpredictable future. Such high demands were made on management in diversified organizations many groups of companies have abandoned this strategy. In turn this has led to management buy-outs and diversification.

Acquisitions today are mostly of the horizontal type, with a view to acquiring market share, or to secure a position in the market by integrating forwards and backwards in the specialization process network.

There has recently been a significant increase in the acquisition of companies quoted on the stock exchange. This has come about because there have been many companies with shares of high market value, and it has been profitable for them to purchase companies by a share exchange. Large Swedish companies have more cash assets, fewer debts and liabilities, and higher profits in 1985 than they have had for a very long time. The number of corporate acquisitions on the stock exchange have increased considerably during the eighties. Acquisitions in figure 11.1 are based on the amount of capital stock involved in the acquisitions.

Most acquisitions take place in the wholesale trade, retail trade and in services. Together these three areas represent 45 per cent of all takeovers during this period. The forestry and lumber industries, the chemical and plastic industries, the metal goods and engineering industries each represent approximately 5 per cent of the takeovers during this time.

Of the total number of acquired companies between 1969 and 1983 (9025), the majority (6727) or 74 per cent were companies with fewer than 50 employees. During the same period only 241 large companies or

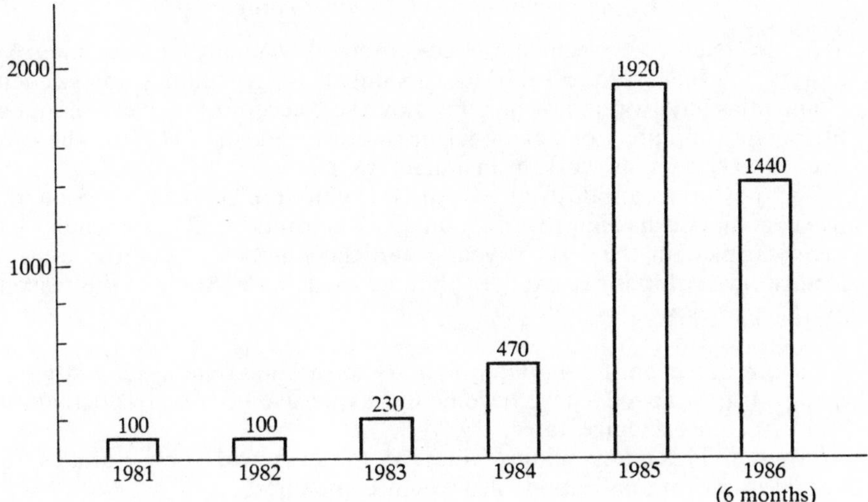

Figure 11.1 Corporate acquisitions on the Stock Exchange

2.7 per cent with a total of approximately 433,000 employees (54 per cent) have been the object of acquisitions. The number of acquired companies during this time with between 50–199 and 200–499 employed amounted to 1666 or 18 per cent and 391 or 4.3 per cent respectively.

Between 1969 and 1983, large companies registered 4750 purchases, representing 53 per cent of the total number of takeovers (9025) during this period. A 'large company', in this case, means companies or corporate groups with at least 500 employees.

Table 11.1 The number of takeovers and mergers, 1976–85

Year	*Manufacturing industry*	*Other industry*	*Total*
1976	203	408	611
1977	173	425	598
1978	195	387	582
1979	215	375	590
1980	236	438	674
1981	216	465	681
1982	284	567	851
1983	346	691	1037
1984	308	467	775
1985	299	471	770
	2475	4694	7169

Foreign ownership in Swedish companies

To date, over 2000 companies have foreign ownership. This is approximately 0.5 per cent of the total number of companies in Sweden. Companies with foreign ownership, however, account for over 7 per cent of the total number of personnel in Swedish industry. Half of these or over 60,000 persons work in manufacturing.

The position of industrial enterprises with foreign ownership on the Swedish market has improved gradually. Their industrial employment has nearly tripled in the last 20 years, and the number of companies with foreign ownership is expected to continue to increase. Some of the reasons are listed below:

1. There has been a continued increase in international specialization.
2. Swedish companies have become less expensive because of fluctuations in foreign exchange rates.
3. Sweden has many mature lines of business with opportunities for structural rationalization for foreign companies.

The majority of companies with foreign ownership are, above all, concentrated in three sectors:

chemicals, including oil;
engineering; and
food processing.

These three branches account for nearly three-quarters of the personnel in industries with foreign ownership. 80 per cent of the companies with

Table 11.2 Companies with foreign ownership divided by country of ownership, 1985

Countries	*Number of companies (%)*
US	26
UK	17
Norway	10
Switzerland	9
The Netherlands	9
Finland	9
Denmark	8
West Germany	6
Other countries	6
	100

foreign ownership have less than 50 personnel, while the larger foreign-owned companies, with more than 200 personnel each, account for 65 per cent of the total personnel of companies with foreign ownership.

The US clearly dominates, with the largest number of foreign-owned businesses in Sweden, followed by the UK. Together, these two countries account for nearly half of all foreign investment in Sweden. An interesting development in this area is the great increase in direct investment from other Scandinavian countries, mainly from Finland, but also from Norway. The Swedish market is an obvious place for Finnish companies interested in foreign investment to begin, and Finland is now in the same phase of development Sweden was in ten or twenty years ago.

In the last few years companies with foreign ownership have taken a substantial lead over Swedish-owned companies in profit making measured by returns on total capital employed. The foreign-owned companies also have the greater proportion of export and import in comparison to total sales.

3. MERGER CONTROL

Takeovers and mergers are legally controlled by the Competition Act of 1982, formerly the Restrictive Trade Practices Act and the Foreign

Table 11.3 The 20 largest foreign-owned companies in Sweden based on gross sales

	Company	*Native country*	*Gross sales, 1984 (SEK m)*	*Personnel*
1.	Svenska BP	Great Britain	10,358	1265
2.	Svenska Shell	Holland	9270	1525
3.	IBM Svenska AB	US	5833	4201
4.	Philips Norden	Holland	4126	4432
5.	Svenska Esso	Norway	4072	1118
6.	Ara-Jet	US	2933	193
7.	Kuwait Petroleum Svenska AB	Kuwait	2669	206
8.	Texaco Oil	US	2495	308
9.	Supra	Norway	2253	1274
10.	Siemensgruppen	West Germany	2113	2882
11.	Unifos Kemi	Finland	1804	788
12.	Unilever	Holland	1668	1367
13.	Flygt	US	1600	30,531
14.	Norsk Hydro Sverige	Norway	1476	831
15.	IKO Kabel	US	1351	1587
16.	Findus	Switzerland	1307	2023
17.	The Ford Group	US	1271	273
18.	Kone	Finland	1152	1402
19.	Luxor	Finland	1134	1478
20.	Svenska Knäcke	Switzerland	1105	1655

Takeovers of Swedish Enterprises Act. The implementation of takeovers and mergers is also effected by the Law on Co-Determination at Work and the Stock Exchange Council's regulations.

The law on Co-Determination at Work stipulates that the trade union(s) involved must be informed of the acquisition plans before an agreement has been signed. The trade union(s) is also entitled to negotiate with the parties involved and present its views. The primary purpose of this law is to safeguard the rights of the employees.

The Stock Exchange Council's regulations apply to cases where at least one party is a company listed on the Stock Exchange. The regulations are contained in the registration contract signed by all listed companies. These regulations mean that companies are required to provide the Stock Exchange Council with certain information. The Council must be informed as soon as an offer has been made or received. In the case of a merger, the contracting parties must place their accounts at the disposal of the Council after which an examination, corresponding to the normal examination made in connection with a company's admission to the stock exchange, is made.

The Foreign Takeovers of Swedish Enterprises Act, which is reproduced in part under the heading 'Exchange control and foreign investment regulations', is primarily designed to ensure that an acquisition does not conflict with any substantial public interest. This law stipulates that permission is required for all acquisitions made by foreign companies. If the company or business to be acquired has had more than 100 employees during its most recent financial year, government approval for the acquisition must be obtained. In other cases, this decision is taken by a County Administration Board.

New regulations are expected to be introduced in 1987 according to which approval will not be required if the company to be acquired has less than ten employees. If the company to be acquired has 10-500 employees, the decision lies with the County Administration, and when more than 500 employees are involved, government approval must be obtained.

Before a decision is made in accordance with the Foreign Takeovers of Swedish Enterprises Act, the trade union which is, or usually is, bound by a union agreement to the company in question shall be given an opportunity to present its views.

The Competition Act 1982 came about partly because its forerunner, the 1953 Restrictive Trade Practices Act, was in need of a general update, but above all the new law was meant to facilitate government surveillance and control, because of the development towards increased concentration of the industrial market at that time. Some of the major prohibitions covered by the present Act are the following:

1. price agreements between companies, or price cartels;
2. the geographical division of the market into sales areas or quotas on the percentage of sales, or market share cartels;

3. discriminating measures, e.g. if a contractor should refuse to deliver goods to a company, or refuse delivery, or if a contractor gives a competing company less favorable conditions of purchase, or price discrimination;
4. a takeover can also lead to limited competition if the acquiring company gains a dominant position on the market. A monopoly is one example, in which only one company is left on the market, or oligopoly, in which only a few companies are left on the market.

An anti-trust secretary (NO), a marketing court (*marknadsdomstolen*) and the Central Price Board (SPK) have been appointed to supervise compliance with the Competition Act. The anti-trust secretary is the first to judge restraints on competition. He can do this at his own initiative or when a company files a complaint of unfair competition, but there is no obligation for the secretary to review cases, e.g. takeovers exceeding certain criteria. Normally, there is no obligation to inform the secretary *before* a takeover. The secretary is, however, entitled by law to order a company to release information prior to a takeover. He may do this if a previous acquisition was approved on condition that the anti-trust secretary would be informed of any additional acquisition plans in a certain branch prior to acquisition. This type of disclosure requirement is, however, only valid for one year at a time. Additional important sources of information for the secretary are the daily press and the public cartel registers kept by the Central Price Board, the Swedish Bank Inspection Board, and the National Swedish Private Insurance Inspectorate. Together, these authorities and the secretary carry out investigations and under the Duty to Report Act (*uppgiftsskyldighetslagen*) they can order a company to release all information necessary to make a correct decision concerning unfair competition, including prices, revenues, costs and profits. The secretary may also order the company in question to release all the information necessary for an inquiry under the Competition Act. If he considers restraints in competition to be harmful, the anti-trust secretary discusses the matter with the company in question. In most cases the company terminates the restraints, or else take steps to eliminate its harmful effects. If the effects are still not eliminated, the Ombudsman then appeals to the marketing court. The marketing court first investigates the effects a takeover or merger may have had on restraints in competition. If the court finds that the effects have been harmful, it usually negotiates with the company (*förhandlingsprincipen*) to eliminate the problem. If the case is considered to be very serious the court is permitted to advise the takeover company to forgo the acquisition and, if necessary, the court can prohibit the takeover. A prohibition of this type must, however, be subect to government approval.

The sections concerned with takeovers in the Competition Act focus, above all, on acquisitions which result in a dominant market position for products or services, or else which reinforce a current dominant position. The effects the takeover may have on restraints in competition are studied to see how the takeover:

1. may influence prices;
2. may have a restrictive influence on the industrial market;
3. may obstruct or prevent other industrial enterprises from carrying out their business.

The anti-trust secretary and the marketing court always use negotiations when dealing with restraints in competition. The aim of negotiations is to define and analyse the market situation where the takeover company may become dominant, and furthermore, to present both the advantages and disadvantages of the acquisition, objectively. For example, an acquisition may be desirable from the public point of view, resulting in improved efficiency, a more rational market, and increased potential for quick technical development and thereby, improved competitive standing for Swedish industry on the international market.

The Competition Act covers all types of acquisitions and mergers, including acquisition of shares, company assets and acquisition through a merger. The acquisition of one or more units of a company is also covered by this Act, while the selling of assets such as machinery not related to the enterprise are not covered. The Act also applies in the case of a takeover company which is part of a corporate group, and which may come to dominate the market through an acquisition.

The negotiations between the marketing court and the takeover company focus, first of all, on methods of preventing harmful effects without having to compel the acquiring company to refrain from making the acquisition. In the preliminary material contained in the Act it is stated that a prohibition can only be issued by the marketing court in the most urgent cases, and the ban must be subject to government approval to be valid. The government is called upon to make the final decision, because of its comprehensive view of the public interest.

Enforcement of the Competition Act

Since the Act took effect in 1982, the marketing court has never needed to prohibit an acquisition. Every case brought before the marketing court has been settled after investigations and negotiations. Examples of justifications for carrying out acquisitions or mergers include:

1. The Swedish market is small, and a concentration of operations would improve the competitive power of Swedish industry, trade and commerce on the international market.
2. Increased structural rationalization in industry, trade and commerce is a prerequisite for long term survival.
3. In some cases the acquisition involved a company in financial crisis, and aspects of employment were taken into consideration.
4. The takeover company pledges to provide a given standard of customer service and information.
5. The takeover company is under obligation to declare any further increase in market shares.

4. TAXATION

Background

In Sweden, as in many other countries, corporations are taxed in the traditional manner. Corporate income tax is first levied on the corporation and subsequently, taxes are levied on the shareholders when dividends are paid. Exceptions are described below.

Dividends paid by a Swedish company to another are not subject to corporate income tax if the recipient owns at least 25 per cent of the payer's voting power. (The percentage is lower if the recipient is engaged in related business activities – e.g. uses raw materials produced by the payer.) If the recipient is an investment company, i.e. a company exclusively or nearly exclusively involved in the administration of marketable securities, then dividends distributed to shareholders the following year are exempt from taxes.

A 'Swedish corporation' is defined as a stock corporation registered in Sweden under Swedish law, and it may also, for example, be a subsidiary to a foreign parent company. A Swedish company is taxable in Sweden for all corporate income, including income earned abroad when actually remitted (i.e. dividends, unless a tax treaty provides otherwise). If a Swedish company markets abroad through a branch office the foreign income thus derived is subject to Swedish tax as earned. Swedish tax treaties effectively eliminate double taxation; usually by means of the ordinary credit method. This method is applied in the new agreements Sweden has entered, and has also applied where a treaty is lacking, which is uncommon. There are a few earlier treaties which still apply exemption with progression; among these is the American Treaty. A new credit agreement was proposed and signed on 15 November 1984. Several points must now be renegotiated to comply, among other things, with the US Tax Reform hence a new credit agreement is not expected to be put into force until 1988, at the earliest.

Foreign corporations are taxed in Sweden for incomes from enterprises run as permanent establishments in Sweden, and for any income from real estate in Sweden. However, it is unusual for a foreign branch office to own real estate abroad, and it is also relatively unusual for a foreign corporation to operate through a branch office in Sweden. Currently, there are only about 70 foreign branch offices registered in Sweden. Branch offices are subject to many of the same regulations applicable to Swedish corporations. For example, the managing director must be a Swedish resident, annual reports must be prepared, and an auditor must be appointed.

Corporate income tax is based on net incomes from both foreign and domestic sources. A deficit from an independently operated foreign enterprise cannot be offset in Sweden, other than the deficit from surplus of such an enterprise, acquired within a six-year period.

Capital (net wealth) tax

No annual capital or net wealth tax is levied on resident joint-stock companies, but foreign companies (branch offices) are subject to tax on the net value of their assets in Sweden at rates ranging from 1 to 3 per cent per annum This tax, however, is waived under most of Sweden's double-tax treaties.

Corporation tax – 52 per cent and profit sharing tax 20 per cent

Since the municipal income tax of legal entities was abolished as of 1 January 1985, they are only subject to a national income tax at a 52 per cent tax rate.

Swedish corporations also pay a 'profit-sharing' tax. As a result of and as a means of financing a national fund to promote employee share ownership a new income tax – *the profit sharing tax* – was introduced from the fiscal year beginning on 1 January 1984. The profit-sharing tax is an income tax. The tax base is the 'true profit' of the company less investment funds. This means that deduction for inventory reserves, profit equalization fund and similar funds will not be granted, nor may prior period losses be deducted. This produces the following computation:

Taxable income for the national assessment
− estimated national and local taxes
+ deductible local taxes
+ current year appropriations to inventory reserves and profit equalization fund
+ losses deducted in the national assessment
+ dividend deductions and similar deductions
= nominal profit

The nominal profit is then adjusted for inflation. The inflation rate times the assets (apart from shares and real property) will be deductible and the inflation rate times the liabilities will be added.

For real property the depreciation times the inflation rate will be deductible. This will result in a 'true profit'. The 'true profit' is reduced by the higher of SEK 1 million or 6 per cent of cash salaries paid during the fiscal year to give the tax base. The tax rate is 20 per cent and the profit sharing tax paid is deductible in the national assessments the following year.

Asssessment and payment

Determination of the tax base, i.e. the base used to calculate the tax levy, is referred to as assessment. Two different kinds of tax bases are determined for companies:

1. assessed income for national income tax, and

2. base for profit sharing tax (this tax is only applicable for companies with an adjusted annual profit over 1 million SEK).

Income taxes are assessed in one year – the assessment year – in which the assessment period goes on from the date returns must be filed, which is either 15 February or 31 March depending when the fiscal year ends, until 31 October. The assessment is based on net income earned in the preceding fiscal year (the income year). The income year is generally the calendar year but may also cover the following periods: 1 May – 30 April, 1 July – 30 June and 1 September – 31 August.

PAYE (pay as you earn)

Companies make preliminary tax payments on their estimated income during the income year. Payments are made six times a year; due dates are 18 March, May, July, September, November and January each year.

Estimating the total taxation basis

Revenue

Business revenue comprises all kinds of receipts. The sale of goods and/or services will naturally be the main source of business revenue. Revenue from the sale of a company's machines and fixtures is also business revenue, as is the utilization of company products for personal use (included at the assets market value when utilized). The sale of business real estate, i.e. property in which a business is conducted, does not give rise to any business revenue. This income is instead listed as income from incidental sources. The same applies to the sale of shares.

Costs

The basic rule is that all costs incurred in acquiring revenue are deductible. There are, however, a number of exceptions to this rule. For example, a salary drawn by a sole trader, partner or member of a close company is not deductible, nor is any deduction due for a salary payable to the trader's spouse or minor children. Similarly no deduction may be made for living expenses (which include membership fees and entertainment). Nor is interest on equity or dividends to shareholders deductible, although numerous, comprehensive exceptions now apply to the latter.

As the calculation of income is always on an accrual basis, major timing problems can arise. Expenditure on a machine cannot be deducted at the time it is incurred but must be deferred over a period of time. Similarly, the inventory of stocks and purchasing costs must also be deferred. The main principles can be summarized as follows:

Depreciation deductions

Deductions for depreciation are permitted for machinery, fittings, intangible rights and real estate. The write-down of machinery is in accordance with the accounts and is governed by two rules, viz. a main rule (or a '30' rule, as it is called) and a supplementary rule (or '20'). The main rule involves reducing balance depreciation by 30 per cent of the opening book value plus purchases less sales during the year. The objective of the supplementary rule is to permit reduction of residual values to zero, which is of course impossible with reducing balance depreciation.

Under the *supplementary rule* straight-line depreciation by 20 per cent of the acquisition cost p.a. is permitted. Businesses which are not obliged to prepare annual accounts in accordance with the Accounting Act may operate *remaining value depreciation* instead of using accounts depreciation. This is the same as the main rule above, except that it only permits 25 per cent annual depreciation and does not require accounts and tax treatment to coincide.

These remarks about machinery also apply to fittings and intangible assets.

The depreciation system for real estate permits annual depreciation by a percentage of the acquisition cost, based on the economic life of the real estate. If the economic life is put at 50 years, depreciation will be at the rate of 2 per cent per annum. For practical reasons, the National Tax Board has issued instructions in which standard percentages are laid down. For the first five years of a property's life this standard percentage can be increased by the 'primary deduction', viz. an extra 2 per cent per annum.

Profit regulating measures

A number of profit-regulating measures are allowed. Among these are the write-down of inventories and appropriations to a profit equalisation fund or to a reserve or investment fund.

Write-offs of inventories are permitted in accordance with the main rule, supplementary rule 1 or supplementary rule 2. The *main rule* lays down that the stocks may not be written down to less than 50 per cent (from the 1984 income year) of the lower of cost or market (LCM) value (in accordance with the FIFO principle) less markdowns due to obsolescence. If no existing markdowns can be demonstrated a 5 per cent deduction is permitted for obsolescence. *Supplementary rule 1* stipulates that depreciation of stocks is permitted by no more than 50 per cent of the mean LCM values for the two preceding years less markdowns for obsolescence. If this results in a negative value for stocks, a negative value may be used provided a special stock regulation account is opened. The objective of supplementary rule 1 is to eliminate the need to dissolve inventory reserves when there is a temporary decline in stock levels.

Supplementary rule 2 can be used by companies which have stocks of raw materials and stores where prices can fluctuate wildly. The stocks may be taken up at no less than 70 per cent of the lowest market price during the tax year and the immediately preceding nine years.

Appropriation to the profit equalization fund is a kind of equivalent to stock markdowns intended mainly for service companies. A sum equal to 20 per cent of the cash salaries paid during the year can be appropriated and treated as a deductible item. It is then written back the following year when a new appropriation will be allowed. This means that only the difference will affect profits. Companies which make appropriations to the profit equalization fund are allowed to write down stock under the main rule and supplementary rule 1, by no more than 35 per cent.

Appropriations to the investment fund and investment reserve fund

Corporations, co-operative economic associations, savings banks and mutual insurance companies are entitled to make tax deductions for transfers to an *investment fund*. For reasons of neutrality, an investment reserve fund was introduced later for private firms and trading/limited partnerships with, in principle, the same functions as an investment fund. Deductions for such appropriations were introduced to encourage businesses to make provisions during good years for use in deferring certain expenses (such as research and development costs, purchase of machinery, costs of new buildings and expenses of export promotion and staff training) in bad years. Appropriations may not exceed half the annual profit. One hundred cent of the investment fund has to be paid into a non-interest-bearing account with the Bank of Sweden. The same rules apply to the investment reserve. When the funds are utilized, depreciation allowed on the assets acquired with the funds is restricted to the net cost of the assets after deduction of the funds appropriated. Thus the investment fund and reserve fund system does not offer permanent tax relief but, through the effective acceleration of depreciation, provides tax deferral. The funds appropriated can only be utilized with official permission.

Capital gains

A government commission is studying the taxation of capital gains, which are currently subject to ordinary income tax. Gains on the sale of real estate are wholly taxable, after deducting improvement costs and post-1951 inflation, irrespective of how long the property has been held. Since 1981, indexation is not allowed during the first four years in which taxable capital gains are realized. Capital gains on shares are 100 per cent taxable if the shares are sold within two years of their purchase. If shares are held for more than two years before they are sold, 40 per cent of the capital gain is taxable, and a general deduction of SEK 2000 p.a. is allowed and for shares held less than two years, SEK 1000. Capital gains on other types of moveable assets (e.g. bonds) are taxed according to a sliding scale, which ranges from 100 per cent (if the asset has been in the seller's possession less than two years) to no tax at all (after five years). The amount of a capital gain is defined as the total proceeds from the disposition of an asset less the related sales expense and less its purchase cost. Deductible losses, which may be offset against capital gains, are determined without indexation.

Companies are allowed to place capital gains from the sale of a business, or part of a business, in special replacement reserves when (1) a parent company liquidates a wholly owned subsidiary and takes up its assets, or (2) shares in an operating company are transferred to another company in the same group, or (3) a sale is made which, in the government's opinion, improves the efficiency and productivity of an industry and may thus be considered structural rationalisation. If such reserves are used within a given period for their stated purpose (i.e. investment in the remaining business or a new business), they are not taxable. Otherwise, they become liable to income tax.

Gains or losses from the sale of depreciable machinery and equipment or of intangibles (e.g. patents) are treated as ordinary gains or losses.

Operating losses for tax purposes

Sweden uses only the carry forward method for the compensation of losses. A corporation is permitted to set off losses against corporate income up to ten years after the loss. In Sweden it has not been considered acceptable to trade in carried forward losses. This was determined as early as 1960 when the right to compensation for losses legislation was passed. However, the legislation was often found to be enforced too strictly, so new regulations were introduced for loss compensation on a change of ownership, and went into effect as of 1 January 1984.

The regulations focus both on closely held companies (*fåmansbolag*), a concept specific to Swedish tax law, and all companies that are not closely held companies and have many shareholders (*flermansbolag*). A closely held company is defined as a company in which more than 50 per cent of the shares are held by less than ten individuals, including closely related persons, or direct or indirect shareholders via another company or companies. Companies quoted on the stock exchange are never closely held companies.

A closely held company (fåmansbolag)

A corporation which is a closely held company at the beginning of the fiscal loss year or at the end of the fiscal year for which the loss carry over is claimed, is not entitled to deduct the loss if:

1. one shareholding person represents more than 50 per cent of the voting power, but who did not hold as many shares or represent as much voting power on the initial day of the fiscal year; or

2. two or more persons hold shares representing more than 50 per cent of the voting power at the end of the fiscal year but not on the initial day.

When determining the ownership structure of a company, any individual who is a shareholder from the day of the inception of the company, and all close relations to the person, are considered to be one owner. Furthermore, shares acquired by a person who was a member of the corporate management of the company both on the opening day and at the time of the acquisition, are considered to be held by this person also from the day of the inception of the company.

A company with many owners (flermansbolag)

The new regulations include a catch for companies planning to acquire another company that is void of assets and operation (*skalbolag*). The regulations are applicable in cases in which a legal person acquires shares in a non-close company and directly or indirectly represents the voting majority in the acquired company. If on that occasion, the takeover company cannot prove that the acquisition was of actual and specific value for the takeover company, then the acquired company loses its right to write off previous losses.

Income from Sweden to foreign countries

The expression a 'permanent establishment' in Swedish tax legislation is considered to be defined in accordance within the definition in the OECD Model Treaty.

Dividends paid to foreign citizens not domiciled in Sweden are subject to a 30 per cent *withholding tax*. The Swedish double taxation treaties, however, usually provide for tax relief of at least 5 per cent of the withholding tax.

Royalties are usually treated as taxable income in Sweden whether or not the recipient otherwise runs an enterprise, or has any form of business operations. In this case, it is not necessary that the person liable to taxation operates the enterprise from a place of operations in Sweden, in order to be liable to taxation. An individual who receives royalities is, instead, considered a party to the profits earned by the enterprise operated here by the payee. Royalties are defined as fees paid out periodically. One lump-sum compensation is not subject to taxation. However, if the royalties are paid partly as a lump sum, for example as an initial or minimum amount, and partly by periodic payments, then the entire amount is subject to taxation, particularly when the initial amount is deductible from the periodic payments. Costs, both in Sweden and abroad associated with the royalties, are also deductible from the taxable amount of the royalties. Deductions are not limited to direct costs, but also include the recipient's administration costs accrued to the royalties. Royalties may be exempt from taxation under double taxation treaties.

'Arm's-length pricing' is regulated by Swedish tax legislation. Compared to the recommendations of the OECD, the Swedish court has taken a generous position and accepts that the financial transactions between a parent company and a subsidiary may be judged, in their entirety, from case to case. A loan with low interest or no interest, granted to a subsidiary company by the parent company, can be balanced by benefits paid to the parent company by the subsidiary, such as higher royalties or higher prices for other products. Transactions of this kind are thus motivated by a financial community of interests. There must, nevertheless, be close financial connections between the companies, for example the subsidiary must be more than a financial investment. The Court has also ruled that the Swedish regulations on arm's-length pricing are not applicable in the assessment of capital gain.

Group taxation

Swedish law defines a 'group' as existing when a parent company represents more than half of the voting power in another company, whether directly or indirectly by means of a subsidiary. Likewise, a group may also be defined as existing when a company both has control and a strong participation right by any means exclusive of shareholding.

It is characteristic of Swedish law that a group is exempt from taxation. However, the group must be taken into consideration in assessing corporate income tax, since the financial situation of each member company is greatly influenced by the group as a whole.

Since the inception of these statutory requirements, it has been the goal of Swedish legislation not to tax groups either more or less than if the enterprise was run as one company. Dividends paid by other companies are now exempt from income tax, which is just one of the consequences of the principle of neutrality.

In Sweden, each company is, however, considered an accounting unit in assessing income tax, while in many other countries like Denmark, Holland and the US there is direct taxation of the joint income of the group. Sweden has achieved a type of neutral taxation which, under certain conditions, permits earnings to be transferred and carried forward from one group company to the other. The most important transfer of profit of this type is the *group contribution*, which must be overtly accounted for. According to current legislation the group contribution given by one Swedish group company to another is tax deductible for the donor and subject to taxation in the hands of the recipient, under certain conditions explained further, below. The regulations are relatively complex, but an extremely basic summary follows below. Group contributions are acceptable between a parent company and a subsidiary if the parent company holds more than 90 per cent of the shares in the subsidiary, and if both are operating companies. Contributions between subsidiaries are also acceptable, on some bases. Furthermore, there is a waiting period of one year from the entry into, or withdrawal from a group, during which a company is not permitted to give or receive group contributions.

In addition, the transfer of assets at book value from one double taxed subject to another is acceptable, as a rule, without being subject to taxation. Recently, however, the Swedish tax authorities have begun to pay strict attention to taxation of donations. If there is not an identity to 100 per cent between the owners of the two companies, then there is the risk that the recipient company will be subject to gift tax, according to previous case law, not the owners as could be expected.

Another possible method for transferring and accounting for profits, through another company, is the 'commission agreement'. The commission agreement proposes that one company runs an enterprise in its own name, but on behalf of another company. The income of the first company may be accounted for in the books of the second company as though the enterprise were actually run by that company. The regulations for commission companies have now been added on to the regulations for group contributions, which is one reason why commission agreements are now generally entered into for reason other than purely taxation.

TAXATION IMPLICATIONS OF MERGERS AND ACQUISITIONS

Mergers

A merger between two corporations means that one corporation is dissolved without entering into liquidation and that its assets and debts are taken over by another corporation. Swedish legislation covers three different types of mergers. They are covered in civil law in ch. 14 of the Companies Act and described in the business organisations part. The most common form of merger is between a parent company and a wholly-owned subsidiary and is the only form covered by regulations contained in Swedish taxation legislation. Consequently, the account given here will cover only this form of merger.

The basic principle governing the tax regulations is the so-called going concern principle which means that the parent company's taxable initial values of the assets, taken over from the subsidiary as a result of the merger, must be equal to the taxable values applying to the subsidiary when the merger takes place. The subsidiary's hidden, untaxed reserves are transferred to the parent company and treated as if they had accrued in the parent company. Claims, stocks and other such assets that are taken over by the parent company from the subsidiary must be booked at the taxable values that applied to the subsidiary. If the parent company books the assets at a higher value, then the parent company is taxed for the amount equivalent to the write-up. In the case of equipment and other such assets, the parent company must take over the subsidiary's taxable residual value. When the merger takes place, the parent company will be liable to pay tax on any provisions for future costs made in the subsidiary's accounts. The parent company itself may then make provision for future costs if it can be shown that, after the merger, the company incurred, or will incur, such costs.

Merger profits/losses arise when the book value of the shares in the subsidiary, declared by the parent company, are less than or more than the taxed equity in the subsidiary. Merger profits are not subject to taxation, and merger losses are not tax deductible.

Distribution tax as applied to mergers

As a matter of principle, mergers are subject to distribution tax. Distribution tax is assessed at 40 per cent of the accumulated equity of the endorsing company, after deductions for contributed amount. However, if distribution tax must be paid on the selling company's total profits in connection with the merger, the two companies may decide not to go through with it. The merger may, however, be extremely desirable for other reasons. In order to resolve this problem, regulations have been introduced that *either* exempt the subsidiary from paying distribution tax in connection with the merger *or* entitle the parent company to take over the subsidiary's distribution tax liability.

Tax exemption will only be granted if the merged subsidiary is wholly-owned and if the parent company has owned nine-tenths of the shares in the subsidiary since (a) 1 January 1940, or (b) from the date the subsidiary started doing business, if the date was after 1 January 1940.

If a group relationship has arisen as a result of the parent company having acquired nine-tenths of the shares in an existing company after 1 January 1940, the National Tax Board may grant an *exemption* permitting the parent company to take over the subsidiary's distribution tax liability. An exemption may be granted on condition that:

1. The merger is justified from the viewpoint of business economics, i.e. that it will result in organizational benefits. In principle, this constitutes a requirement that the two companies must either carry on business or be engaged in farming or, alternatively, in some cases own real estate that is of importance to the business of one of the companies.
2. Distribution tax would constitute a substantial obstacle to the merger. This means that an exemption will only be granted if the merger has *not* been completed. Consequently, it is, in principle, impossible to obtain an exemption after the completion of the merger, even if all the requirements have been satisifed. As a rule, the tax sum of SEK 4000–5000 is considered sufficient to constitute a substantial obstacle.

   Note that exemptions are not made public and that the decision of the National Tax Board cannot be appealed.
3. The merger is not made with a view to gain undue tax advantages. This means that compensation for distribution tax may not have been paid out at some earlier date. There has been only one single case where this requirement has resulted in the rejection of an application for exemption.

An exemption will not be granted if either of the companies in a merger is a limited banking company, a finance company, an insurance company or a company trading in real estate.

The distribution tax liability taken over as a result of an exemption does not have to be settled until the parent company itself is, perhaps in the far future, dissolved.

Acquisitions

Swedish legislation has no equivalent to the American regulations governing acquisitions of whole companies since, in Swedish law, the group is not accepted as a tax subject.

However, a number of regulations, as well as legal practice, have emerged that cover the consequences of taxation when assets of different types are transferred from one business to another.

Asset acquisitions

From the purchaser's viewpoint, the acquisition of assets from a seller not closely associated with him results in a basis for depreciation that is equal to the acquisition cost.

As has been pointed out under the heading Group Taxation, the transfer of assets at their book values between companies in a group is accepted even if such a transfer is not subject to tax. The above mentioned circumstances – that assets are transferred from one company to another at prices over their book value, e.g. at their market value or the highest value that can be calculated without the seller being liable for capital gains tax – is also accepted in principle but, in accordance with accepted practice, the purchaser in such a case must accept having his basis for depreciation adjusted in such a way that he is allowed the same depreciation as the seller would have been entitled to if he had retained the property.

In the purchase agreement, the purchase price must be specified in such a way that the value assigned to different assets, including goodwill, can be seen. When a whole business is sold, the method of taxation is the same as if the assets had been sold individually during the time the business existed. In such a case, the transfer constitutes the last business transaction effected by the business. If the transfer also includes assets subject to capital gains taxation (e.g. a factory building), the income from the sale must be divided between the business and temporary work of an acquisitive nature. This division should first be based on what falls due to the property subjected to capital gains taxation. The remaining part of the income can be assigned to the business. Income that cannot be assigned to any concrete asset is considered to be compensation for the goodwill value of the business, which means that it is taxable operating income.

In the case of the purchaser, this division is of importance to the initial values of the different types of assets he acquires. The purchaser's interests may often conflict with those of the seller. The seller may prefer to assign as much as possible to property subject to capital gains taxation since this profit is calculated in a more favourable way than is operating income. The purchaser, on the other hand, may wish to write off the purchase price as quickly as possible and will thus prefer to assign as much of the purchase price as possible to stocks, equipment, goodwill, etc. This conflict of interest can constitute a self-regulating factor that normally results in the division being made strictly along business lines. An uneven division may well be questioned by the tax authorities.

From the abovementioned, it can be seen that the sale of assets – including goodwill – is taxed as operating income with the exception of real estate which is taxed in accordance with capital gains regulations. See p. 349. Only the company is subject to taxation since the distribution principle as regards shareholders, which is applied in other countries, does not exist in Swedish law. It should be noted, however, that Swedish law contains special regulations governing close companies. These regulations stipulate very heavy taxation of company managers who have the company acquire chattels intended for private consumption or who sell property to the company at a higher price, or acquire property from the company at a lower price, than the market price of the property.

Share acquisition

According to Swedish law, all debt interest is tax-deductible under the heading of income of capital, if it is not tax-deductible under any other income heading. This category includes, for example, interest payments on loans taken up in order to purchase shares. It can be seen here that the regulations are generous since the amount of assessment for a company diminishes which, in turn, results in a lighter, effective tax burden.

As regards goodwill bound to a business, it should be noted that goodwill included in the value of the shares in a corporation does not come under the heading of operating income. The part of the share price relating to goodwill is not treated separately; it is treated in the same way as the purchase price. For the seller, this means that goodwill is taxed according to the regulations governing capital gains while, for the purchaser, it means that the goodwill included in a share purchase is not tax-deductible.

In Swedish law, the write-down of shares is not normally tax-deductible.

It would appear that the following conditions must be satisifed for a deduction to be admitted:

1. The shareholding must have a more direct connection with the company's own business. One example of this is that the shares are held for industry-related purposes, i.e. the shares are owned as part of the organization of an enterprise that does *not* manage property, securities or other chattels of a similar nature. Furthermore, the

shareholding can be the result of a customer or supplier relationship with the company that originally issued the shares, or have been received as payment for goods.

2. It should have been established that a loss has been incurred as a result of either the shares having been sold or the company, which issued the shares, having entered into liquidation. It should be emphasized that the tax authorities are very strict when assessing whether the loss can be expected to be definite. It is thus not sufficient to show that the company has been operating at a loss for a couple of years or that the share capital is depleted.

   It must be a question of an actual loss resulting from the sale or liquidation. This can mean that a liquidation in itself is not sufficient to constitute a tax-deductible loss. If liquidation has only resulted in a book loss, e.g. as a result of goodwill or other assets having been transferred to the company owning the shares, a tax deduction for the loss can be refused. In such a case, in order that a tax deduction for the loss on the shares may be permitted, the company must be able to show that the value of the assets taken over have depreciated to the point where the shareholding has caused an actual loss in the business.

Special regulations of interest in connection with the sale of shares

In Swedish law, certain regulations governing the sale of shares have been introduced. According to these regulations, the whole purchase price obtained from a sale of shares is subject to taxation and not only 40 per cent as is normally the case with shares that have been owned for more than two years. These regulations are applied when an owner of shares in a closely held company sells his shares to another closely held company in which he, or a person closely associated with him, is a partner, or will become a partner within a two-year period, and when shares are sold after the company has been cleared of its material assets. In both these cases, the regulations are complicated and it is possible to obtain exemption. Consequently, expert advice is recommended in cases where these regulations may be applicable.

Miscellaneous

Deductions for dividends

To facilitate the procurement of equity for companies, there are two sets of regulations for deductions, and in some cases for payment of dividends. One set of regulations refers to deductions for dividends on the issuance of new capital shares. This permits a 10 per cent deduction per year for the sum paid for the shares. The Swedish authorities have adopted the other set of regulations to encourage investment in small unlisted companies, by permitting a 70 per cent deduction of the dividend payout from corporate income tax, with a minimum of SEK 700,000. However, the deduction is limited to 15 per cent of the capital shares.

Exchange gains and losses

Exchange gains, according to the prudence principle, are not to be included in the accounts or taxed until they are realized. In contrast, exchange losses are tax-deductible if they are in the form of overhead costs in operation. The tax deductions for similar costs from other sources of income are not equally generous.

The tax deduction may, at the most, be as high as the amount of the exchange losses, based on the rate of exchange applicable on the closing day. The following year, the amount of deduction conceded must be declared for taxation and the question of deduction must once again be considered in the light of the rate of exchange at the close of that year.

Social security costs

Social security contributions are a major expenditure for Swedish companies, and therefore the regulations are explained in detail.

Social security contributions have now become a major source of government revenue. The contributions are only partially related to services received and can largely be viewed as pure taxes. Of approximately 35 per cent levied, about 15 per cent consists of charges for services and 20 per cent represents a tax.

The contributions are laid down in the Social Security Act and the collection thereof in a separate law. The tax base is generally the same as for all statutory contributions.

Who is liable? In principle, the sum chargeable consists of the salary paid to an employee or contractor. Contractors who are treated as self-employed for income tax purposes pay their own social security contributions. These contributions are referred to as personal contributions. It is therefore essential to define an 'employee' in order to determine who is liable to pay contributions. An 'employee' has an explicit or implicit employment relationship with an employer, and the employer supplies work premises, tools, etc.

The determination of who is and who is not an 'employee' is dependent on the facts and the parties involved must, therefore, decide in advance on the basis of the facts as to whether or not their relationship is one of employer and employee.

Self-employed people are permitted to agree with an employer that the employer assumes responsibility for payment of their contributions.

The employee's entitlement to social security benefits is dependent upon the employer making contributions on behalf of the employee.

Basis of charge Contributions paid by employers are based on the value of cash salaries and fringe benefits such as free food, free housing and free car. Salaries of less than SEK 500 a year or pay to an employee who has passed his 65th birthday are not included.

Table 11.4 Contributions, 1987

Type of charge – employees	*% of tax base*
General supplementary pension (ATP)	10.200
National health insurance	9.300
National basic pension	9.450
Partial pension	0.500
Occupational injury insurance	0.600
Occupational safety	0.350
Adult education	0.270
Labour market charges	2.006
Salary guarantee	0.200
Child care	2.200
General payroll tap	2.000
Total percentage contribution for employees	37.076

The superior tax court has attracted a great deal of attention for a series of cases in which it recently ruled that social security contributions, as a result of the scope of the text of the law, are to be based only on the stated benefits. Benefits for such things as free travel are not to be included in the list of fees. A future alteration in the law is feasible.

Contributions laid down in collective bargaining agreements

In addition to the contributions shown in table 11.4, employers are also liable for certain social security charges laid down in collective bargaining agreements. These charges vary for blue-collar and white-collar workers, since the respective collective bargaining agreements differ. The main difference is to be found in the pension contributions which give white-collar workers much enhanced benefits; employer contributions are accordingly higher for white-collar workers.

Thus, total contributions amount to 43.176 per cent of wages for blue-collar workers and 48.326 per cent of salary for white-collar workers. Holiday contributions must also be added to these figures and may be in the form of paid holiday or holiday compensation. The cost is about 12 per cent of salary. Thus, total social security and fringe benefit costs amount to nearly 55 per cent for blue-collar workers and nearly 60 per cent for white-collar workers.

Employer declaration to National Social Insurance Board Social security contributions are reported by employers in a declaration to the National Social Insurance Board. This declaration, which must be filed by 31 January of the year following the contribution year shall contain an

Table 11.5 Contributions laid down in collective bargaining agreements, 1987

	% Tax Base	
	Blue-collar	*White-collar*
TGL (group life assurance)	0.54	0.30
TFA (labour market no fault liability insurance)	0.42	0.05
FGB (severance pay/redundancy pay)	0.20	—
AGS (health and disability insurance)	1.90	—
STP (special supplementary pension)	2.90	—
ITP (supplementary pension)	—	8.25
Employment Security Fund	0.09	0.65
Lay-off pay facility	0.05	—
	6.10	9.25

account of all payments of more than SEK 500 made to employees during that year.

Contributions are paid over on the basis of a preliminary charge on the 18th of every month.

Value added tax

A value added tax (VAT) applies to sales of almost all goods and services. Although the rate of VAT was reduced in 1981, it was increased on 1 January 1983, to 23.46 per cent – about the same as its former level.

The tax is collected from the seller, who receives credit for VAT that he has paid on his purchases, and is remitted to the local county administration (*Länsstyrelsen*). All companies and persons with VAT-liable turnover in excess of SEK 30,000 must be registered with their local *Länsstyrelsen* and must report and pay taxes every two months. VAT on imports is paid to customs at the same time as the applicable duty, either by the importer or by his forwarding agent.

The sale of buildings, the serving of meals and the renting or leasing of rooms are taxed at 60 per cent of the full VAT rate. Civil engineering construction projects (e.g. roads, airports, harbours) and all services performed by architects, building engineers and consultants are taxed at only 20 per cent of the full VAT rate. Until the end of 1982, 10 per cent of investments in machinery and equipment were deductible from a taxpayer's VAT liability.

Items exempt from VAT include fishing vessels and certain other vessels over 20 net registered tons, certain commercial aircraft and equipment, armaments sold to the government, medicines sold by prescription or to hospitals, water, fuels subject to energy sales tax, assets of a company acquired or merged and land and buildings other than those sold by building contractors.

The principal services exempt from VAT are postal services, transportation directly to and from foreign countries, and personal services, such as those of lawyers, physicians, hairdressers, travel agents, banks and entertainers. Exports of goods and services are also exempt from VAT.

Other taxes

Sales taxes

Special sales taxes are levied (usually on the basis of quantity, volume or size) on energy sources, including electricity, coke, fuel oil and gasoline; automobiles; spirits, wine, beer and soft drinks, and their bottles and cans; tobacco, including cigarettes; and confectionery.

Stamp duties

Stamp duties are levied by the Board of Excise and other bodies on acquisitions of large ships (1 per cent), transfers of real estate and site leasehold rights (1.5 per cent for individuals and 3 per cent for companies), issues of shares (1 per cent) or bonds (0.6 per cent), the granting or suspension of mortgages (0.4 per cent) and transfers or pledges of foreign shares (1 per cent) or bonds (0.6 per cent).

Advertising tax

A tax is levied on purchases of advertising space in daily newspapers (at 4 per cent) and in magazines and other advertising media aimed at the Swedish market (at 11 per cent).

5. ACCOUNTING

Background

Accounting principles and reporting requirements in Sweden derive essentially from three sources:

1. The Companies Act of 1975 (ABL)
2. The Accounting Act of 1976 (BFL)
3. The 1981 Act on Annual Reports of Certain Companies.

In addition, Swedish tax law has considerable influence on financial accounting practices.

The *Companies Act* requires every joint-stock company (*aktiebolag* – AB) to prepare an annual report to be submitted to its shareholders and made available to the public by filing with a governmental agency. Chapter 11 of the Act requires such annual reports to include a report on the company's administration during the period as well as the financial statements (including certain notes).

The report on the company's administration is required by the Act to provide information on any circumstances or events, not disclosed in the company's balance sheet or statement of income, that would be useful in evaluating the financial position and results of operations of the company. It must also disclose events that occurred during the fiscal year or after the end of the year but prior to the issuance of the annual report. The report must also provide information about the number of employees, remuneration paid to members of the board and to employees, and the proposed amounts of the company's earnings to be retained or distributed as dividends to shareholders.

The Accounting Act 1976 is the main source of guidance on financial accounting and reporting requirements in Sweden. The Act applies to all business enterprises, regardless of their legal form. The Act presents general valuation rules for current and non-current assets, prescribes a general format for financial statement presentation, and requires all other matters to be handled in accordance with accounting principles generally accepted in Sweden.

In the past, only financial statements of joint-stock companies (ABs) were required to be made public. (The Accounting Act does not require public disclosure.) Since the introduction in 1981 of the *Act on Annual Reports of Certain Companies*, however,the financial statements of all business enterprises, regardless of their legal form, must be made public if the enterprise exceeds a certain size.

Companies with securities listed on the Stockholm exchange are subject to additional disclosure requirements. Some of the more important areas in which public companies go beyond the minimum requirements of the law are the following disclosures:

1. a report from the company's president reflecting his personal views on the company's development over the past year and its current situation;
2. information dealing with problem areas and with the outlook for the future;
3. comments on the external environment in which the company operates;
4. information on the company's financial goals and strategies.

The Swedish Institute of Authorized Public Accountants (*Föreningen Auktoriserade Revisorer*, FAR) has long contributed to the development of generally accepted accounting principles in Sweden by issuing recommendations on accounting matters. At the present time, the Institute's standard-setting body consists exclusively of authorized public accountants, with no representation from industry, financial analysts or the academic world, but changes in its composition are being considered. FAR's accounting standards committee was set up in 1964.

With the introduction of the Accounting Act 1976, a new governmental body, the *Bokföringsnämnden* (BFN) or Accounting Board, was established to encourage the development of generally accepted accounting principles in Sweden and to assist companies and their accountants in interpreting the requirements of the new Accounting Act. The Swedish Institute of Authorized Public Accountants (FAR) is represented on the Accounting Board.

Accounting for groups

In accordance with chapter 11, sections 10 and 11 of the Companies Act, each parent company shall present a consolidated income statement and a consolidated balance sheet.

Increasing importance is being attached to consolidated financial statements. Until recently, the primary financial statements of a Swedish company with subsidiaries were the parent company statements. Today, both the parent company statements and the consolidated statements receive about equal emphasis, and there is an increasing tendency to regard the consolidated statements as the more significant. This is despite the fact that corporate groups as a whole are *not* subject to taxation according to Swedish legislation, unlike other countries like West Germany and the US. Each company in the group is, however, subject to individual taxation.

Companies are required to consolidate all entities (including partnerships) in which, directly or indirectly, they control more than *50 per cent* of the votes.

New subsidiaries are generally accounted for by the purchase method. The great majority of Swedish group accounts are prepared on this basis, but other methods are occasionally used. Under certain specific circumstances, that are generally described below, the pooling-of-interests method is acceptable.

The purchase method (*förvärvsmetod*) is based on the principle that only the profits earned by the subsidiary after the takeover can be counted as part of the group capital. This, then, has a significant effect on the profits available for distribution in the group and on the presentation of the group balance sheet. Presentation of the balance sheet of the group is according to the same principles applied when the balance sheet of a private enterprise is drawn up. The net assets and liabilities acquired by the parent company through the subsidiary are, thus, itemized on the group balance sheet at acquisition value, in some cases after write-offs. The acquisition value of the subsidiary is based on the price of its shares. By purchasing shares, the parent company indirectly acquires the assets of the subsidiary and assumes its liabilities.

Using the purchase method the acquisition value of the shares of the subsidiary is compared to the acquired equity in the subsidiary.

In determining the net assets of an acquired company, any recorded untaxed reserves, net of deferred taxes, must be included. This is the only situation in which deferred taxes are accounted for in Sweden.

The difference between the acquisition value of the shares and acquired equity obtained through this comparison is analysed through itemization into one or more items on the group balance sheet (goodwill or negative goodwill). The group acquired equity is, thus, unaffected by the difference on consolidation. In the purchase method, the group acquired equity is defined as the acquired equity of the parent company, including the equity in untaxed reserves and the profits earned by the subsidiary after the takeover.

The *pooling-of-interests method* differs from the purchase method. Using this method the book value of each company is retained and each company then declares its own net assets and liabilities on the balance sheet.

In retaining the book value of the company it is possible to avoid overestimations, typical of group companies, which are also the basis for write-offs. At the same time there is less capital left to yield interest.

Using this method, consolidated financial statements should meet the following conditions:

1. A new capital stock issue of the officially acquired company constitutes compensation for the shares in the subsidiary.
2. All the consolidated companies should be about the same size. One should not dominate the others by virtue of its size.
3. The combined enterprises of the companies should be run as before even after the consolidation.

The most essential reason for using the pooling method is not to be able to assess which company is buying which, when and if necessary.

Treatment of certain accounting items

In estimating the difference between the acquisition value of an acquired subsidiary and the acquired equity (purchase method), there is either a positive difference (goodwill) or a negative one (negative goodwill). The difference is either based on over or underestimations of the company net assets and liabilities at the takeover, or it is based on the forecast of the earnings trend and whether or not it is estimated as favourable. Acquired *goodwill* is declared as a fixed asset which does not need to be specified on the balance sheet. According to the Accounting Act (*bokföringslagen*, art. 17), goodwill may be amortized at a minimum rate of 10 per cent per annum. Good accounting practices, however, normally means much quicker write-offs.

FAR recommends that *negative goodwill* be seen as a provision by the group for expected losses or limited profits on the part of the subsidiary. Therefore, this item can be declared under the long-term liabilities of the group. The resolution should, normally, take place over a period of several years. Intangible assets should, normally, be set up as an asset if they are acquired through the purchase of shares in the subsidiary. Expenditures for research and development, pilot runs, market research or similar organizational costs should be set up as fixed assets, if they will be of significant future value. In this way legislation provides a write-off for capitalized costs, at a reasonable amount of at least 20 per cent per year, unless there are special circumstances. Write-offs of less than 20 per cent must always be in accordance with good accounting practices.

Group contribution (Koncernbidrag)

Transfer of income between different companies in a group, or *group contribution*, can be either overt or covert. An example of group contribution is the transfer of income through pricing between different companies. Since the group is not an object of taxation, covert transfers of income cannot be accepted as a matter of principle. In those situations where overt group contributions are declared without any fiscal consequences, any covert transfers are also normally accepted. Some general prerequisites for declaring overt transfers are:

1. The group must be qualified, i.e. the parent company must own more than 90 per cent of the shares in the subsidiary.
2. The group must have been in existence for the entire fiscal year.

A transfer of income to another country by means of a covert group contribution is an evasion of Swedish tax law, which does not permit transfers of this type. For this reason, an agreement between two companies with common financial interests, whether they are affiliated companies, or have any other type of common financial interest, must be assessed on the arm's-length principle.

Comparison with international accounting standards

The Swedish Institute (FAR) is a member of the International Accounting Standards Committee (IASC) and is thus involved in the international standards programme. The Institute's membership in IASC represents a commitment to use its best endeavours to promote local acceptance and observance of international accounting standards. At the present time, there is a tendency not to accept the IASC standards to the extent that they conflict with Swedish law. However, some public Swedish companies have disclosed the effects of applying the IASC standards to their financial statements as prepared in accordance with accounting principles generally accepted in Sweden.

Table 11.6 shows the more significant differences between Swedish accounting practices and the IASC standards summarized though in general, adherence to Swedish requirements ensures compliance with most of the IASC standards issued to date.

Audit requirements

The Companies Act requires that the annual reports of all AB's be audited by an appropriately qualified auditor. A qualified auditor may be either authorized or approved. An authorized public accountant is

Table 11.6 Comparison of Swedish accounting practices with international standards

IAS 1 – Disclosure of accounting policies	As indicated in the text, Swedish accounting tends to be more concerned with legal form than with economic substance, and is shaped to a considerable extent by tax requirements. Disclosure of accounting policies is required, but such disclosure falls short of what is contemplated in the international standard
IAS 2 – Valuation and presentation of inventories in the context of the historical-cost system	Disclosure of the main categories of inventory (e.g. materials, work in process, finished goods, merchandise, production supplies) is not required in Sweden
IAS 3 – Consolidated financial statements	The equity method of accounting for investments in unconsolidated subsidiaries and in associated companies is not used, since it is considered to be in conflict with Swedish law. Financial data on any subsidiaries that are excluded from consolidation is disclosed if material
IAS 5 – Information to be disclosed in financial statements	Security given in respect of liabilities (e.g. guarantees, pledged assets) is disclosed by category of security and not related to each liability. Amounts committed for future capital expenditures are not disclosed. Summaries of interest rates, repayment terms, etc. on long-term debt are generally not provided. Assets acquired on instalment purchase plans are not disclosed unless the seller retains title to such an asset until full payment is made. Deferred income is included in accrued liabilities. Intercompany transactions are not disclosed
IAS 7 – Statement of changes in financial position	A statement of changes in financial position is required for all but smaller companies, as defined in the Companies Act
IAS 8 – Unusual and prior-period items and changes in accounting principles	Prior-period adjustments and changes in accounting principles, if material, are normally quantified and disclosed

– *Continued*

Table 11.6 Continued

	as extraordinary items. However, this is an area requiring further clarification, and the Swedish Institute (FAR) has recently issued an exposure draft that should result in a much greater degree of conformity with the requirements of this international standard
IAS 12 – Accounting for income tax	Since Swedish tax law generally requires tax and book income to be the same, there are normally no material timing differences to account for. One exception is depreciation on buildings, which may be accelerated for tax purposes without any provision for such deferred taxes being made in the financial statements The potential tax savings from a loss carryforward must not be included in determining net income for the period of the loss. Taxes are not accrued on undistributed earnings from subsidiaries even if such earnings are deemed to be distributed. However, some companies disclose the existence of reductions in transfers of earnings from subsidiaries, indicating in a note to the consolidated financial statements, for example, that 'Repatriation of undistributed earnings would be subject to withholding taxes ranging from X per cent to Y per cent' The existence of loss carryforwards is not disclosed unless material, nor is there any reconciliation of the effective tax rate with the actual tax rate
IAS 14 – Reporting financial information by segment	The Companies Act requires that companies with significantly independent business segments shall report the operating result of each such segment separately. In many respects IAS 14 goes further and

– *Continued*

Table 11.6 Continued

	requires that listed companies shall disclose the following information for each business segment and for each geographical area in which the company operates: 1. sales, distinguishing between sales to outside customers and sales to other business segments/ geographical areas; 2. segment result; 3. capital employed (either in absolute amounts or percentually); 4. the basis of internal transfer pricing In addition a reconciliation should be given between the sum of the information by individual segment and the aggregate information presented in the financial statements
IAS 15 – Information reflecting the effects of changing prices	Swedish companies do not generally provide such information. The Swedish Institute (FAR) has issued an exposure draft on the subject
IAS 16 – Accounting for property. plant and equipment	The major part of the contents of IAS 16 has been incorporated in FAR's recommendation covering tangible fixed assets and compliance with FAR's recommendation will also ensure fulfilment of the related parts of IAS 16 Under certain circumstances, the Accounting Act permits gains resulting from the revaluation of non-current assets to be recorded as an offset against a permanent decline in the value of other non-current assets
IAS 17 – Accounting for leases	FAR's Recommendation No. 7 dealing with leasing departs from IAS 17 in that FAR requires a definite obligation to assume ownership of the leased object, even though this may be at a later point in time. As this is FAR's criterion for classification as a finance lease it results in a smaller number of finance leases being reported than if IAS 17 were applied

– Continued

Table 11.6 Continued

	The rules governing sale and leaseback transactions are broadly similar. Regarding disclosure of leasing commitments IAS 17 requires inter alia that commitments for future lease payments by year shall be separately disclosed for both finance leases and operating leases. FAR has taken another approach and recommends that disclosure is made of the estimated cost of the leased assets as well as of the rental charge for the year. FAR's Accounting Committee is presently considering whether its leasing recommendation should be harmonized with IAS 17
IAS 19 – Accounting for retirement benefits in the financial statements of employers	BFL does not require that the capital value of pension commitments is recorded as a liability nor that the accrued pension cost for the year is charged to the income statement. FAR's Recommendation No. 4 dealing with pension liabilities and pension expense states, however, that, the pension expense for the year should be recorded in the income statement even if the pension liability is only reported as a commitment (in which case the expense would be reversed under the heading 'transfer to/from untaxed reserves') but FAR does strongly recommend that the entire pension liability is recorded. As pension commitments under the PRI system have to be recorded as a liability pension commitments which are not shown as liabilities should be limited to older commitments and newer ones which are not included in the PRI system
IAS 20 – Accounting for government grants and disclosure of government assistance	In broad terms BFN regulation No. 11 dealing with government assistance satisfies the disclosure requirements in this standard while the accounting for such assistance is based more on tax regulations than on a strict matching

– Continued

Table 11.6 Continued

	with the costs which the which the assistance is intended to compensate
IAS 21 – Accounting for the effects of changes in foreign exchange rates	Since the promulgation of IAS 21 (which in broad terms follows the American standard) the international attitude to this problem has been clarified. FAR has now revised its recommendation regarding consolidated financial statements so that it now also covers the translation of subsidiaries financial statements. This recommendation now conforms with IAS 21 in all essential respects. BFN has undertaken to produce a regulation regarding the treatment of foreign currency items in an individual entity's accounts. A problem to be overcome is that the Accounting Act is considered to prohibit the income recognition of unrealized exchange gains
IAS 23 – Capitalization of borrowing costs	Neither the Companies Act nor the Accounting Act contain any rules regarding the capitalization of borrowing costs, nor has FAR issued any separate recommendation regarding the capitalization of borrowing costs. FAR's recommendations regarding tangible fixed assets and inventory pricing do, however, indicate that interest on borrowed capital may be capitalized
IAS 24 – Related party disclosures	The Companies Act stipulates that claims and liabilities attributable to related parties must be disclosed. In addition, information regarding the salaries and remuneration paid to the Managing Director and the Board of Directors must also be released. In 1986, the Stock Exchange Council issued a Code of Ethics which should be regarded as a recommendation to companies listed on the Stock Exchange. The Code of Ethics follows IAS 24 closely

considered to be the same as an authorized public accounting firm and an approved public accountant the same as an approved public accounting firm. The question of authorization or approval is decided by the Board of Commerce. Of the two, authorization is subject to the strictest requirements. Consequently, it is not sufficient to have only approved public accountants in the very largest companies. Such companies must have at least one authorized public accountant.

At least one of the public accountants appointed by the annual general meeting must thus be authorized if:

1. the net value of the assets reported in the adopted balance sheets for the two most recent financial years exceeds a figure equivalent to 1000 times the basic amount stipulated by the National Insurance Act for the last month of each financial year (the figure for the financial year 1986 was SEK 25.2 million);
2. the average number of employees in the company during the two most recent financial years exceeded 200; or
3. the company's shares or promissory notes are listed on the Stockholm Stock Exchange.

The auditor is usually appointed annually by a general meeting of company shareholders and addresses his report to them. The Companies Act and the ethics rules of Sweden's professional accounting bodies require the auditor to be independent of his client. In addition, he is required to carry out his work in accordance with professionally approved auditing standards.

The auditor is often appointed as an individual. In larger companies, it is common to appoint more than one auditor, and they are often selected from different accounting firms. However, the auditor's opinion is usually signed with his own name, and not the name of the firm with which he is associated.

The auditor is required to examine not only the annual financial statements and the underlying accounting records but the board of directors' report on the administration of the company as well.

In his report, the auditor is required to state that he has carried out his audit in accordance with generally accepted auditing standards and to indicate whether the annual report has been prepared in accordance with the Companies Act. The auditor is also required to give his recommendations to the company's shareholders on the following matters:

1. approval of the balance sheet and income statement, including, if applicable, the consolidated financial statements;
2. approval of the board's proposed allocation of earnings available for distribution as dividends;
3. granting of discharge of responsibility for the members of the board with respect to their administration of the company during the past year.

If the annual report has not been prepared in accordance with the Companies Act, or if the auditor has not been given all of the information or explanations he requested, he has a statutory duty to so indicate in his report. He is also expected to indicate in his report whether he has found any grounds for criticism of the board's conduct (in which event, the board could be liable for damages to the company).

Since 1981, business conducted in forms other than the AB, including partnerships, must have annual audits if they exceed a certain size.

6. EXCHANGE CONTROL AND FOREIGN INVESTMENT REGULATIONS

In principle, Swedish nationals and foreigners enjoy equal freedom and equal rights to form and operate corporations, make investments and acquire shares. The few exceptions are interpreted liberally. The law on foreign direct investment provides for an initial authorization, but no special restrictions apply to foreign operations after start-up.

Foreign investment

A new foreign investment or an expansion of an existing venture that needs imported capital requires *Riksbank approval* to bring in funds. The bank normally gives such approval in about a week if an applicant supplies complete information and if share capital and loans bear a reasonable relationship to the size of the enterprise. (At least 50 per cent of the share capital or purchase amount for a new investment must be supplied from abroad.) The state exerts nominal control over the location, start-up time, etc. of new factories under a voluntary agreement between the Federation of Swedish Industries and the Ministry of Labour.

Many Swedish companies have an *alien-ownership clause* in their by-laws stipulating that at least 60 per cent of their share capital and 80 per cent of voting rights *must be owned by Swedish nationals*. This clause cannot be changed except with the approval of the government and the consent of the company's shareholders at their annual meeting. If its by-laws do not include such a clause, a company is considered foreign and is barred from owning Swedish natural wealth, such as mines, oil deposits, farms, forests and waterfalls, and may not even own more than 20 per cent of the voting shares in another company holding such property. Foreigners are also prohibited from owning Swedish-registered vessels, holding bank shares (a government committee is investigating possible liberalization of this rule), manufacturing munitions, engaging in domestic air transport, or owning any enterprise that distributes credit information on Swedish companies and individuals.

No overall limits have been placed on the amount of equity a foreign company may hold in a Swedish company, and most foreign companies wholly own their Swedish operations. However, foreign equity in companies that own Swedish natural resources is limited to 20 per cent.

Acquisition of real estate by companies with more than 20 per cent foreign ownership requires permission from the county authorities. Approval is readily given unless the authorities believe that speculation is involved.

In addition to following the general rules on investment from abroad, foreign companies that wish to acquire Swedish subsidiaries must comply with *the Foreign Takeovers of Swedish Enterprises Act*, enacted in mid-1982. The new law applies to acquisitions by foreign companies as well as those by Swedish companies that do not have alien-ownership clauses (i.e. those in which foreigners could already have large shareholdings). Effective 1 January 1983, prior government permission is needed for any acquisition that pushes a foreign stake in a Swedish company over thresholds of 10, 20, 40 or 50 per cent. Such permission is likely to be forthcoming, unless the acquisition appears to be contrary to an essential national interest.

Companies must also consult trade unions to secure labour's consent when a merger or takeover is planned. Employees are particularly desirous of safeguarding their jobs if a foreign-owned company decides to shut down its Swedish operation and of achieving full implementation of the Codetermination Law. If labour approves a proposed merger, it will normally proceed smoothly. Otherwise, the Ministry of Industry is likely to be called in and asked to appoint a state representative to the board in addition to the two employee representatives.

Investment in Sweden and repatriation of funds require Riksbank approval unless a Swedish subsidiary of a non-Swedish company issues new shares and the parent company wishes to buy such shares up to the percentage of its ownership. When approval is required, it is normally given, and profits from such investments may then be remitted freely.

Transfers of *profits and dividends are free* and without limit, provided a company has met its legal reserve requirements and paid its taxes. However, companies domiciled in Sweden are sometimes obliged to set aside part of their profits in tax-deductible interest-free investment reserves with the Riksbank.

No restrictions apply to current commercial transactions either into or out of the country, including payments for imports and exports and *royalties* or other *licensing payment*. The payment of reimbursements for *management services, research expenditure* and similar expenses to the parent company by the Swedish subsidiary may also be made without a licence. However, the Riksbank may intervene against advance payments on imports (depending upon the amount and the relation between the advance and the amount of the total invoice) and on royalties, where the method used to calculate the royalties is contrary to established business practices and may involve currency speculation. Wages can be freely paid by a Swedish company to employees temporarily working abroad, but a permit is always required for payment of wages from abroad into Sweden.

Borrowing abroad is encouraged, and permits are issued to companies with the proviso that the foreign loans must help Sweden's balance of payments. Loans must normally exceed SEK 10 million and run for at least five years. The Riksbank has authorized banks to borrow abroad (up to a maximum determined for each bank) for on-lending primarily to small and medium-sized companies investing in productive facilities. Such loans should also have an average life of five years but may not exceed SEK 10 million.

Repayment of principal on foreign private loans requires Riksbank permission, which is normally granted unless a loan is repaid ahead of maturity. The Riksbank may then demand that an amount equal to the early repayment be borrowed in another currency. Transfer of interest is free and without limit.

Since the relaxation of the rules limiting foreigner's *trading of Swedish shares*, overseas interest in such shares has increased because of their low prices and good earnings record. As a result, many large companies are applying for permission from the Riksbank's Exchange Control Board to sell a greater number of shares abroad. Foreign portfolio investment in eight major Swedish companies has been made easier and less costly. Foreigners no longer need to purchase such shares with 'switch currency' derived from selling other Swedish shares at a 15 per cent premium over the normal purchase price for local currency. However, such restrictions still apply to purchases of shares in other companies. The Riksbank continues to limit the use of foreign shares in acquiring Swedish companies to one-third of the acquired company's total share value in most cases.

Import control

Import controls are few and are applied liberally, except on some agricultural products. Import freedom applies to practically all imports from the less-developed countries. Sweden is firmly committed to free trade; it has even permitted the virtual demise of its footwear and leather industry and a significant decline in its textile and clothing industry rather than reverse this commitment.

Sweden uses the Customs Co-operation Council Nomenclature. Its tariffs, which average 3 per cent ad valorem on all imports, are among the world's lowest.

While Sweden has no non-tariff barriers intended to restrain imports, some safety and other regulations effectively bar certain merchandise. Exporters to Sweden should be prepared to meet the following requirements:

Standards and regulations for electrical equipment, building and construction materials, weapons, explosives and precious metals are often troublesome, as are those for pharmaceuticals, medicines and poisons.

Sanitary certificates of origin testifying to the good condition of both the product and its packaging at the time of export are required for certain foods and plants. Foods must meet the comprehensive regulations of the National Food Administration (Livsmedelsvserket), which requires a detailed listing of the ingredients (including any additives) on the package, and a last date for consumption for most products. Packaging regulations are standard, except that straw and hay may not be used (for sanitary reasons). Anti-dumping legislation exists but is rarely invoked.

To meet specific social or political needs, state-owned companies may 'buy Swedish' with grants matching any export credit subsidies that foreign competitors receive. Local labour and management can encourage a government agency to award a particular order to a domestic company despite lower foreign bids.

SUMMARY

A foreign investor must obtain permission for the acquisition of a company from the county administration – and in cases of special importance from the government. Approval must also be obtained from the Central Bank regarding the transfer of funds.

In Sweden, an acquisition takes place, almost without exception, through the purchase of shares in the selling company. Purchase of assets is very rare because it is unfavourable to the seller with regard to taxation. The mode of payment, cash or shares etc, is not subject to taxation and has no other significance for the selling company.

From 1969 to 1983, 9025 acquisitions affecting over 800,000 employees in the purchased companies have been registered. The majoriy (6727 or 74 per cent) were companies with fewer than 50 employees.

To date, over 2000 companies have foreign ownership, however, account for over 7 per cent of the total number of companies in Sweden. Companies with foreign ownership, however, account for over 7 per cent of the total number of employees in Swedish industry. The US clearly dominates, with the largest number of foreign-owned businesses in Sweden, followed by the UK.

Takeovers and mergers are legally controlled by:

1. The Competition Act 1982, formerly the Restrictive Trade Practices Act.
2. The Foreign Takeovers of Swedish Enterprises Act.

The implementation of takeovers and mergers is also affected by the Law on Co-Determination at Work and the Stock Exchange Council's regulations. In comparison with the conditions in the US, the Competition Act in Sweden is considered to be relatively liberal.

As in many other countries, corporations are taxed in traditional manner. Corporate income is first *levied* on the corporation and subsequently, taxes are levied on the shareholders when dividends are paid.

Dividends paid to foreign citizens not domiciled in Sweden are subject to a 30 per cent withholding tax. The Swedish double taxation treaties, however, usually provide for tax relief of not less than 5 per cent of the withholding tax.

The basic principle governing the tax regulations applying to mergers and acquisitions is that the purchasing company's taxable initial values of the assets taken over from the company acquired must be the same as the taxable values of the assets in the subsidiary at the time of the acquisition or merger.

In determining the net assets of an acquired company, any recorded untaxed reserves, net of deferred taxes, must be included. This is the only situation in which deferred taxes are accounted for in Sweden.

Accounting principles and reporting requirements in Sweden derive essentially from three sources: The Companies Act of 1975, The Accounting Act of 1976, and The 1981 on Annual Reports of Certain Companies.

The *Companies Act* requires a joint stock company to prepare an annual report to be submitted to its shareholders and made available to the public by filing with a governmental agency. The Accounting Act 1976 is the main source of guidance on financial accounting and reporting requirements in Sweden.

Since 1964 The Swedish Institute of Authorized Public Accountants (FAR) has contributed to the development of generally accepted accounting principles in Sweden by issuing recommendations on accounting matters.

In accordance with chapter 11, sections 10 and 11 of the Companies Act, each parent company shall present a consolidated income statement and balance sheet. Increasing importance is being attached to consolidated financial statements. Companies are required to consolidate all entities (including partnerships) in which, directly or indirectly, they control more than *50 per cent* of the votes. New subsidiaries are generally accounted for by the purchase method.

In general, adherence to Swedish accounting requirements ensures compliance with most of the IASC standards issued to date.

The Companies Act requires that the annual reports of all ABs be audited by an appropriately qualified auditor. The auditor is usually appointed annually by a general meeting of company shareholders and addresses his report to them.

The law on foreign direct investment provides for an initial authorisation, but no special restrictions apply to foreign operations after start up. However, foreign companies that wish to acquire Swedish subsidiaries must comply with the *Foreign Takeovers* of Swedish Enterprises Act, enacted in mid-1982.

Transfers of profits and dividends are free, provided a company has met its legal reserve requirements and paid its taxes. The payment of reimbursements for management services, research expenditure and similar expenses to the parent company by the Swedish subsidiary may also be made without a licence.

Borrowing abroad is encouraged, and permits are issued to companies with the proviso that the foreign loans must help Sweden's balance of payments. Loans must normally exceed SEK 10 million and run for at least five years.

Import controls in Sweden are few and liberally applied, except with respect to some agricultural products.

12

United Kingdom

1. BUSINESS ORGANIZATIONS AND COMBINATIONS

Business organizations

The principal types of business organization in the UK are companies, branches of foreign corporations, partnerships and sole traders. Most foreign investors will be interested in trading as a branch or a company. Whilst the word *company* has no legal significance and is often used in names of partnerships, the term corporation refers to entities capable of perpetual succession and are often used by state-owned organizations.

Companies in Great Britain are regulated by Companies Act 1985 which consolidated the Acts of 1948, 1967, 1976, 1980 and 1981. In Northern Ireland, companies are incorporated under Companies Act (Northern Ireland) 1960 and as amended by the Companies (Amendment) Act (Northern Ireland) 1963, the Companies (Northern Ireland) Order 1978, the Companies (Northern Ireland) Order 1981 and the Companies (Northern Ireland) order 1982. Generally legislation in Northern Ireland follows that in Great Britain.

Companies may be limited or unlimited. A limited incorporated business entity has the advantage that the liability of its shareholders is limited to the extent of their investment in share capital including uncalled capital. Not surprisingly there is a cost to this advantage inasmuch as a limited liability company must comply with more formalities, regulations and disclosure requirements than an unincorporated entity which does not have limited liability.

A company not fulfilling the following requirements for a public company is designated a private company (section 1, CA 1985):

1. Two or more persons associated for lawful purposes subscribe their names to a memorandum of association.
2. The memorandum limits the liability of its members.
3. The memorandum states that it is a public company.
4. It is a registered public company.
5. It has a minimum share capital of £50,000 of which at least 25 per

cent plus the whole of the share premium account is paid up.
6. The name of the company must end in 'public limited company' or 'plc'.

Both private and public companies must have a minimum of two shareholders. The following are some of the main differences between the two types of companies:

1. A public company may issue shares or debentures to the public but a private company cannot.
2. A public company must have at least two directors whereas a private company needs only one.
3. A public company must have a trading certificate whereas a private company may commence trading immediately after registration.
4. Certain small and medium-sized companies may file modified accounts with the Registrar of Companies whereas a public company must file full accounts.
5. A public company is subject to stricter rules in a number of areas, e.g. purchase by a company of its own shares; financial assistance by a company for acquisition of its own shares; loans to directors.

Sometimes an overseas investor will initially decide to set up a branch in the UK with the view that if it is successful it would be transferred to a subsidiary. Parts I–III of Schedule 14, Companies Act 1985 provide details of the countries and territories in which an overseas branch register may be kept, general provisions with respect to overseas branch registers, and provisions for branch registers of overseas companies to be kept in Great Britain. An oversea company is one that establishes a place of business but is not incorporated in Great Britain. Within one month of establishing a place of business the following documents should be delivered to the registrar of companies (section 691):

1. a certified copy of the charter, statutes or memorandum and articles of the company in English;
2. a list of the company's directors and secretary;
3. a list of names and address of a resident(s) authorized to accept notices served on the company;
4. a statutory declaration stating the date on which the company's place of business was established in Great Britain.

An oversea company must deliver annual accounts including group accounts where applicable within 13 months of the end of the period.

Types of business combination

The way in which an acquisition may be effected is not prescribed by law, but a variety of regulations have influenced the development of these types of transactions. The following cover the majority of transactions:

1. a privately negotiated agreement with members of the company being taken over;
2. the purchase of new shares by private treaty;
3. the acquisition of the assets of the target company;
4. the purchase of shares on the Stock Exchange;
5. an offer to all shareholders for all or part of the offeree's share capital;
6. a scheme of arrangement, reconstruction or amalgamation.

The first three types of takeover usually involve private companies where it is possible to negotiate with a limited number of shareholders. Naturally changes in share ownership and the officers of the company must be registered at Companies House. The acquisition of a listed company by the purchase of shares on the Stock Exchange is not now common in the UK because of legal requirements and the City Code, which specify the disclosure of purchases and places an obligation for a compulsory offer once 30 per cent of the shares are obtained. Listed companies are normally taken over by the acquisition of shares as a result of an offer to shareholders. The offer document must be forwarded to all shareholders and also to the Stock Exchange and Quotations Department for examination and approval.

A takeover of a company may be undertaken for cash, loan capital, shares or valuable consideration or a combination of these.

Other types of mergers may occur as a result of a scheme of arrangement, reconstruction or amalgamation. Under section 425 of the Companies Act 1985 a company has the power to compromise with creditors and members provided court approval is obtained. If 75 per cent in value of the creditors or members or class of members vote in favour of an arrangement which has court approval, the decision is binding on the other 25 per cent. The Court will grant approval where a scheme of reconstruction, or amalgamation of two or more companies, involves the transfer of the whole or part of the undertaking and of its property and liabilities.

Section 582 of the Companies Act 1985 applies where a company is proposed to be wound up voluntarily and the whole or part of its business or property is to be transferred or sold to another company. The liquidator may accept shares as consideration for the sale of a company provided it is approved by a special resolution. Once the transfer has been completed the selling company is then dissolved.

2. TRENDS IN TAKEOVER ACTIVITY

There is little doubt that concentration in UK industry has increased considerably this century, at both the aggregate and market levels. At the aggregate level it has been estimated that the share of the 100 largest enterprises in UK manufacturing net output increased from 16 per cent in 1909 to 41 per cent in 1968 (Prais, 1981). During the period 1968–76 differences in the method of compilation of the statistics make comparisons difficult.

Measures of aggregate concentration hide the fact that certain UK industries have become highly concentrated. One way of assessing concentration at a market level is to compare over time the proportion of sales by the top five companies (CR5) in that sector. Based on the 1972 Census of Production, out of 158 industries within the standard industrial classification (SIC) 15 had CR5s in excess of 90 per cent; and in 39 per cent of the Census Industries the CR5 was greater than 60 per cent of the sales within the SIC category. High concentration was particularly acute in mining and quarrying; food, drink and tobacco; coal and petrol products; chemicals and allied industries; electrical engineering; and vehicle sectors. It is difficult to compare the figures with those in previous Censuses because of differences in the method of compilation. Furthermore, SIC numbers changed in 1980 in an attempt to align the UK classification with that used by the Statistical Office of the European Communities. The new SIC classification is by activity and not by commodity.

Another measure of concentration is that based on employment in the 100 largest enterprises. These data show a high and increasing level of concentration in UK industry comparable with that in the US. Much lower levels of concentration, based on employment, exist in the Federal Republic of Germany, France and Italy.

Concentration in industry may arise out of internal growth or external growth resulting from mergers and acquisitions. Prais (1976) estimates that approximately 50 per cent of the change in concentration in the UK is directly attributable to merger activity.

Statistics on acquisitions and mergers are compiled by the government and published in Business Monitor MQ7. Table 12.1 summarizes the statistics for the period 1969–85. The data are compiled from reports in the financial press and is supplemented by special enquiries into companies. Acquisitions and mergers in the financial sector including banking and insurance are not included in the figures in MQ7. Before 1980, statistics in the financial sector were prepared by the Bank of England and published in *Financial Statistics* but this practice has now been discontinued.

It is noticeable that there was a high level of merger activity in the periods 1972–3 and 1982 onwards. In the period 1972–3, the number of transactions was extremely high and has not yet been exceeded. The average value of transactions was also relatively high in 1972 and was not exceeded until 1979, despite the effects of high rates of inflation on asset values.

In contrast, the period 1982 onwards consists of high-value transactions, since the value of assets acquired is high, but the number of transactions is low. For example, the average value of an acquisition in 1981 was £2.53 million, whereas in 1984 it had reached £9.6 million representing nearly a fourfold increase. This trend to high-value acquisitions, which

Table 12.1 Acquisitions and mergers within the UK

Year	*Number acquired*	*Percentage change*	*Value (£m)*	*Percentage change*
1969	846		1069	
1970	793	− 6.3	1122	+ 5.0
1971	884	+11.5	911	− 18.8
1972	1210	+36.9	2532	+178.0
1973	1205	− 0.4	1304	− 48.5
1974	504	−58.2	508	− 61.0
1975	315	−37.5	291	− 42.7
1976	353	+12.1	448	+ 54.0
1977	481	+36.3	824	+ 83.9
1978	567	+17.9	1140	+ 38.3
1979	534	− 5.8	1656	+ 45.3
1980	469	−12.2	1475	− 10.9
1981	452	− 3.6	1144	− 22.4
1982	463	+ 2.4	2206	+ 92.8
1983	447	− 3.5	2343	+ 6.2
1984	568	+27.1	5474	+133.6
1985	474	−16.6	7090	+ 29.5
1986	695	+46.6	13,535	+ 90.9

Source: Business Monitor MQ7

also occurred in the US, continued to an even greater extent in 1985 with the average value of each transaction exceeding £14.95 million.

Table 12.2 shows expenditure on acquisitions of independent companies and mergers within the UK in 1985 by industry group of acquiring company. Acquiring companies came principally from the industrial and retailing sectors of the economy.

Another feature of recent takeover activity is that equity as a percentage of total expenditure on UK acquisitions exceeded cash payments in 1983. This is the first time that this has occurred since 1972, when UK industry was suffering a cash crisis (see table 12.3). It is interesting to note that in most years acquisition currency moves in line with the All-Share Index. For example, in 1973–4 the index fell, so intuitively one would expect the number of paper transactions to fall and the number of cash deals to increase. This is exactly what happened. In fact, the only exceptions to this occurred in 1981 and 1984, when the index went up and equity transactions fell. In 1985 equity transactions succeeded cash transactions reflecting a few very high-value share acquisitions.

Expenditure on acquisitions of UK companies by foreign companies is shown in table 12.4. It is noticeable that the number of transactions and value of transactions has been at a higher level in the 1980s than in the 1970s with much of the investment emanating from the US.

Table 12.2 Expenditure on acquisitions of independent companies and mergers within the UK in 1985.

Industry group of acquiring company	*Number acquired*	*£m*	*%*
Manufacturing industries	309	8708.2	71.8
Energy industries	6	79.8	0.7
Retailing	34	1155.3	9.5
Services	79	445.2	3.7
Mixed activities (mainly non-manufacturing)	18	700.8	5.8
Other industries	91	1035.8	8.5
	340	12,125.1	100.0

Table 12.3 UK acquisition currency (% total expenditure)

Year	*Cash*	*Equity*	*Fixed-interest securities*
1969	27.7	51.6	20.7
1970	22.4	53.1	24.5
1971	31.3	48.0	20.7
1972	19.5	57.6	22.9
1973	53.0	35.7	11.3
1974	68.3	22.4	9.3
1975	59.4	32.0	8.6
1976	71.7	26.8	1.5
1977	62.1	36.9	1.0
1978	57.4	40.6	2.0
1979	56.3	31.1	12.6
1980	51.5	45.4	3.1
1981	67.7	29.6	2.7
1982	58.1	31.8	10.1
1983	43.8	53.8	2.4
1984	53.8	33.6	12.6
1985	40.3	52.3	7.4
1986	17.9	63.8	18.3

Source: Business Monitor MQ7

Table 12.4 Expenditure on acquisitions of UK companies by foreign companies

Year	*Number acquired*	*Percentage change*	*Value (£m)*	*Percentage change*
1969	27		58.2	
1970	23	− 14.8	57.2	− 1.7
1971	21	− 8.7	32.7	− 42.8
1972	18	− 14.3	41.4	+ 26.6
1973	8	− 55.6	58.0	+ 40.1
1974	9	+ 12.5	184.9	+218.8
1975	9	0.0	53.5	− 71.1
1976	10	+ 11.1	72.8	+ 36.1
1977	12	+ 20.0	79.5	+ 21.6
1978	13	+ 8.3	38.6	− 51.4
1979	6	− 53.8	47.1	+ 22.0
1980	23	+283.3	169.7	+259.7
1981	75	+226.1	493.4	+190.7
1982	29	− 61.3	229.6	− 53.5
1983	24	− 17.2	198.4	− 13.6
1984	28	+ 16.7	512.2	+158.2
1985	21	− 25.0	223.6	− 56.4
1986	22	+ 4.8	485.9	+117.3

Source: Business Monitor MQ7

3. MERGER CONTROL

Regulation of mergers in the UK consists of both legal controls and self-regulatory controls administered by the Stock Exchange through the Panel on Takeovers and Mergers. In addition, as the UK is a member of the EEC it is also subject to the Treaty of Rome and specifically to competition policy based on Articles 85 and 86. These provisions have been discussed in chapter 1. The following controls apply equally to UK companies and overseas companies.

Legal controls

Fair Trading Act 1973

Section 1 of the Fair Trading Act empowers the Secretary of State for Trade and Industry to appoint a Director General of Fair Trading whose duty it is (section 2) to keep the commercial activities relating to goods and services under constant review. It is one of the responsibilities of the Director General that he should be aware of any circumstances that might adversely affect the economic interests of consumers.

The role of the Director General is to advise the Secretary of State as to whether a merger should be investigated by the Monopolies Commission.

It is important to note that reference decisions are made by the Secretary of State and not the Director General. For enterprises other than newspapers, the minimum criteria originally laid down in the Act for a reference were:

1. where at least one-quarter of all goods of a particular description are supplied by an enterprise; or
2. the value of the assets taken over exceeds £5 million.

The horizontal test of one-quarter of a market is fairly flexible, since it refers both to a product market and to geographical area, as the Act extends to local regional monopolies.

Section 64(7) of the Act provides authority for the Secretary of State to raise the asset threshold by order of a statutory instrument. This procedure has been adopted twice since 1973. In April 1980 the threshold was increased to £15 million and on 26 July 1984 was raised further to £30 million. On 5 July 1984 the Secretary of State announced that '. . .it's estimated that the change will initially reduce the number of mergers qualifying for investigation under the Fair Trading Act from some 200 a year to some 150 a year.'

Special provisions of the Act apply to newspaper mergers which require approval by the Secretary of State after obtaining a report from the Monopolies Commission. In certain circumstances, such as when a decision is urgent, the Secretary of State may grant approval without a referral and in practice this has usually been the case.

Table 12.5 shows the number of mergers meeting the criteria of the Fair Trading Act since 1973, together with the number of references to the Commission and their outcome. Since 1973, 89 cases have been referred to the Commission out of a total of 2840 mergers falling within the scope of the Act, representing a 1.5 per cent referral rate. The overwhelming probability is that even if a merger meets the criteria laid down in the Act, in 98.5 out of 100 cases there will be no referral. In those cases where a proposal is not abandoned, there is roughly an even chance of the case being found against as being cleared.

There is no requirement for companies to pre-notify the Office of Fair Trading although in practice many companies voluntarily inform the Office of their intention to make a bid. The Office collects information on mergers from the financial press and from companies. All mergers meeting the criteria laid down in the Act are examined by the Mergers Secretariat of the office to establish whether there are any public interest considerations. Its role here is one of sifting and not investigating. Relevant parties are consulted and if there are no public interest questions arising, the Director General will recommend to the Secretary of State that the merger should be cleared. The Secretary of State is not obliged to accept his recommendation, although in nearly all cases he does.

In more difficult cases, the Director General will have a meeting with the Mergers Panel, which consists of officials from government departments and other public authorities with special knowledge of a particular area.

Table 12.5 Scrutiny of mergers between 1973 and 1986

Mergers scope	*Within scope of FIA*	*Horizontal (%)*	*Vertical (%)*	*Diversified (%)*	*Mergers referred to* MMC	*Outcome of reference*		
						Proposal abandoned	*Found against*	*Cleared*
1973	134	70	4	26	6	4	1	1
1974	141	68	5	27	7	2	1	4
1975	160	71	5	24	4	1	2	1
1976	163	70	8	22	4	—	3	1
1977	194	64	11	25	8	5	2	1
1978	299	53	13	34	3	1	—	2
1979	257	51	7	42	3	—	—	3
1980	182	65	4	31	5	1	1	3
1981	164	62	6	32	8	1	5	2
1982	190	65	5	30	10	2	4[a]	4
1983	192	71	4	25	8	2	3	3
1984	259	63	4	33	4	1	—	3
1985	192	58	4	38	6	3	—	3
1986	313	69	2	29	13	7	3	3
Total	2840				89*	30	25	34

[a]The Charter Consolidated/Anderson Strathclyde merger was allowed to go ahead, despite an adverse MMC finding.
*The outcome of one case is still awaited.
Source: Office of Fair Trading.

The meeting will discuss all relevant issues of the case, based on a discussion paper prepared by the Mergers Secretariat. Decisions are normally taken quickly although where a preliminary examination is undertaken it may take three to four weeks.

A feature of the UK system of controlling monopolies is the confidential guidance system which enables companies to seek advice from the Office of Fair Trading as to the possibility of a referral, often before a bid is made.

Section 5(1) of the Fair Trading Act places a duty on the Commission to report on monopoly or possible monopoly situations; to report on the transfer of newspapers; and to report on qualifying mergers. The initial role of the Commission therefore is to determine whether a merger situation exists. If the Commission considers that the reference is within the terms of the Act its subsequent investigation is designed to establish whether the merger 'may be expected to operate against the public interest'.

In determining the public interest the Commission will consider, in particular, the following factors:

1. the maintenance or promotion of effective competition;
2. the promotion of the interests of consumers, purchasers and users of goods and services in the UK in respect of price, quality and variety;
3. the desirability of promoting the reduction of costs, the development and use of new techniques and new products and the entry of new competitors;
4. the maintenance and promotion of a balanced distribution of industry and employment in the UK; and
5. the maintenance and promotion of competitive activity in markets outside the UK on the part of the UK producers of goods and suppliers of goods and services.

Although the Commission is not technically a court, it has the authority to require people to attend and give evidence and may require persons carrying on any business to provide any information considered relevant. The Commission may take evidence on oath, but no one may be compelled to give evidence or produce information 'which he could not be compelled to give or produce in civil proceedings before the court'.

The report produced by the Commission finds either that the merger operates or may be expected to operate against the public interest or that it does not. If the merger is deemed not to be against the public interest, then no one has the power to stop the merger. If, however, the merger is deemed to be against the public interest, the Secretary of State has the power, although he is not so obliged, to follow the recommendation of the Commission and ban the merger.

Competition Act 1980

The Competition Act 1980 introduced provisions to prevent anti-competitive practices which complement the functions and powers of the

Director General as provided by the Fair Trading Act 1973. The Act defines a monopoly situation as where one person, company or group of interconnected companies, supplies or acquires at least one-quarter of any specified goods or services in the UK, or where two or more unconnected persons do so and so conduct their affairs in any way to prevent, restrict or distort competition.

Whereas an investigation under the Fair Trading Act applies to all firms in a complete market sector supplying the goods or services referred, an investigation under the Competition Act relates to individual firms which restrict, distort or prevent competition. An investigation into specific practices is more flexible and less time-consuming than a full investigation by the Commission, particularly as such references are based on their effects on competition.

Where an anti-competitive practice is established, either an undertaking may be accepted or the case may be referred to the Commission. The role of the Commission is to establish whether an anti-competitive practice is being pursued which is against the public interest.

The Financial Services Act 1986

The aim of the Act is to provide a comprehensive system for the regulation of all investment business in the UK. It replaces the Prevention of Fraud (Investments) Act 1958 which provided some protection to investors by making it illegal to induce others to buy or sell securities by making misleading, dishonest or reckless statements. Furthermore, the 1958 Act placed restrictions on the distribution of circulars. The Financial Services Act 1986 also incorporates some of the non-statutory rules of organizations such as the Stock Exchange.

The underlying principle of the 1986 Act is that it is an offence to carry on an investment business without proper authorization. In an attempt to provide a statutory regulatory system and yet be responsive to changes in the market place, it was considered appropriate to develop an overall framework for regulation with the detailed supervision being delegated, via the Securities and Investments Board (SIB), to five Self-Regulatory Organizations (SROs). These SROs will be run by practitioners who are specialists in a particular aspect of the investment business, viz.:

1. The Securities Association – firms dealing with and broking in securities, forward agreements and related futures and options etc.
2. The Association of Futures Brokers and Dealers – firms dealing in futures and options etc.
3. The Financial Intermediaries, Managers and Brokers Regulatory Association – firms dealing and broking in securities and collective investment products etc.
4. The Investment Management Regulatory Organization – investment managers and advisers and pension fund managers etc.
5. The Life Assurance and Unit Trust Regulatory Organization – life companies and unit trust managers and trustees etc.

Flexibility will be assisted by the provision that the legislation can be fairly quickly amended by Statutory Instrument.

After 1988 it will be illegal to carry on an investment business without authorization. Authorization can be obtained by application to the SIB or appropriate SRO. Details of key personnel, financial information and insurance arrangements will need to be provided together with a business plan. The aim is to ensure that only fit and proper persons may carry out an investment business and every authorized firm must have an adequate capital base. In addition, detailed rules will be provided on the conduct of the business records which need to be kept, and on financial reporting. Every authorized business must set up procedures to ensure that the rules are complied with and an independent annual review will be undertaken to assess the level of compliance. Non-compliance with the Act can lead to disciplinary measures and criminal and civil penalties. Every authorized business must have its accounts audited, regardless of the type of business organization.

At the time of writing the Act is gradually being implemented.

Self-regulatory controls

The UK Stock Exchange based in London and the provinces is a highly sophisticated exchange and provides facilities for the issue of commercial and government securities and operates a large secondary market in existing securities. Over 8000 securities are listed on the London Stock Exchange.

Control over the securities markets is undertaken by a self-regulatory body, the Council of the Stock Exchange which is controlled by another self-regulatory body, the Securities and Investments Board as introduced by the Financial Services Act 1986. Under the Stock Exchange (Listing) Regulations 1984, the Council became the 'competent authority' for EEC directives dealing with admissions, listing particulars, and interim reports. Controls affecting merger activity are imposed by the Stock Exchange and the Panel on Takeovers and Mergers.

The Stock Exchange

Although the Stock Exchange imposes self-regulatory controls on its members, most of the contents of the revised Yellow Book, *Admission of Securities to Listing*, effective from 1 January 1985, have statutory backing. These regulations apply to offerors or offerees, or their parent companies that are listed on the Stock Exchange or dealt with on the Unlisted Securities Market.

Once a company has a security listed on the Stock Exchange, there is a continuing obligation to keep shareholders adequately informed. The minimum listing requirements, which are normally considerably exceeded, are as follows:

1. The initial market capitalization must be at least £0.5 million.
2. At least 25 per cent of each class of issued equity capital must be held by the public.

3. The company must have a trading record of at least five years.
4. Companies with assets which consist mainly of cash or short-term investments will not normally be accepted.
5. There is a continuing obligation to give the Exchange immediate notification of dividends, profit and loss announcements, capital changes and other relevant information.

For listed companies the information to be disclosed and procedures to be followed depends upon the type of transaction. There are four classes of transaction with the first three having a size criteria based upon the following:

1. the value of assets acquired or disposed of compared with those of the acquirer (divesting company);
2. pre-tax profits from ordinary activities attributable to the assets acquired or disposed of compared with those of the acquirer/divesting company;
3. the total consideration given or received compared with the assets of the acquiring or disposing company;
4. equity capital issued as consideration compared with equity previously in issue.

Where the relative figure is 15 per cent or more the transaction is class I with the exception that where only test (4) shows a figure of 15 per cent or more and the consideration is calculated with reference to the market value of equity capital, the Committee on Quotations will normally accept such a transaction as class 2. Where the relative figure falls between 5 per cent and 15 per cent it will normally constitute a class 2 transaction and where less than 5 per cent it will normally be a class 3 transaction.

Where a transaction is deemed to be class 1, details should be given as soon as possible to the Quotations Department, together with a draft of the circular for approval; the announcement should be made simultaneously to the press. The circular contains information similar to that contained in the announcement together with the last five years' financial statements of the target company, and details of indebtedness and directors' interests. An accountant's report is not required where the target company is a listed company because of readily available information such as that published on Extel cards. However, a working capital letter is required where cash is a substantial part of the consideration of an acquisition. An accountant's report is required where the target company is an unlisted company.

For class 1 and class 2 transactions the announcement should contain the following information:

1. details and value of the assets acquired or disposed of;
2. a description and name of the business;
3. the total consideration and payment plans;
4. the net profits attributable to the assets being acquired or disposed of;

5. the benefits which are likely to accrue as a result of the company.

For class 3 transactions there is no requirement for an announcement although brief details should be given if shares of the listed company are issued as consideration.

A class 4 transaction is one which involves a director, a past director, a substantial shareholder, a past substantial shareholder or their associates, regardless of whether the transaction falls within any other class. Such transactions may not be entered into without prior approval from the Quotations Department. Often the Quotations Department will insist that a circular is sent to shareholders and the transaction be approved by shareholders in general meeting.

The City Code on takeovers and mergers

The City Code is issued on the authority of the Council for the Securities Industry and represents good business practice in the field of takeovers and mergers. The Code is administered by the Panel on Takeovers and Mergers and applies to takeovers involving public companies, listed or unlisted, but not private companies, unless they were involved publicly within ten years preceding the offer. The Code is not backed by law, and indeed many of its provisions could not be converted easily into statute. Instead the Code is backed by an understanding that if it is not observed, the facilities of the securities market in the UK may be withdrawn.

The Code is divided into two elements. First there are ten general principles of conduct some of which are based on the concept of equity between one shareholder and another. Secondly, there are 37 rules which represent the practical application of general principles to specific areas. The rules are made by the executive, although if a party, aggrieved shareholder or adviser wishes to contest a ruling, the full Panel may be called at short notice to consider the case. Where particularly difficult issues are raised, the executive may decide to ask the Panel for a decision rather than make a ruling itself which may be appealed against.

The rules covering bids in the UK are summarized below.

1. The offeror makes an offer to the board of the offeree or its advisers. Absolute secrecy is imperative.
2. After the first announcement of an offer, press details are circulated by the offeree company to its shareholders. The offer may not be withdrawn without permission from the Panel.
3. The offer document should be posted within 28 days of the announcement. Information should be prepared as if it were a prospectus within the meaning of the Companies Act 1948.
4. Information provided to a preferred suitor should be provided equally to all bona fide potential offerors requesting it.
5. Shareholders must be put in possession of all the facts, which should be presented accurately and fairly.
6. The offer documentation should include the following:
   intentions regarding continuation of the business;

intentions regarding the redeployment of assets;
the long-term commercial justification for the offer;
intentions with regard to continued employment;
existing shareholdings in the offeree and terms of the offer.

7. No offer may be declared unconditional until the offeror acquires more than 50 per cent of the voting rights.
8. The offer should remain open for at least 21 days after posting and for a further 14 days after posting any revised offer.
9. No offer may be declared unconditional after 60 days without the consent of the Panel.
10. Once the offer is declared unconditional, it must remain open for at least a further 14 days.
11. The offeror shall notify the Stock Exchange as to the outcome of the bid within certain time-limits.
12. The Panel's consent is required where a partial offer is made.
13. Persons privy to price-sensitive information may not deal in the shares.
14. Where the offeror pays more than the current offer for any shares, it must increase the value of the offer.
15. Where 15 per cent or more of the voting rights have been acquired during the twelve months prior to the offer, the offer shall be in cash or cash alternative.
16. Once a company owns 30 per cent of the voting rights of another company, it must make an offer for the remaining shares. The offer should be at a price not less than the highest price paid in the last twelve months and must include a cash alternative.

4. TAXATION

Background

The UK taxation system is complex. The principal taxes include income tax, corporation tax, capital gains tax, inheritance tax, and value added tax all of which are levied by central government. Administration of these taxes is undertaken by the Commissioners of Inland Revenue with authority being delegated to local tax inspectors. In addition, taxes levied on real estate, called rates, are levied and collected by local and municipal authorities.

The tax legislation was consolidated in 1970 as one Taxes Act and with annual subsequent Finance Acts a further consolidation is planned for 1987/8. The UK system for taxing corporations is an imputation in which distributions are not subject to deduction of income tax and instead the company pays advance corporation tax (ACT) which is then set against the company's gross corporation tax liability for the period in which the distribution is made. For companies with taxable profits the imputation system is largely neutral with respect to distributions, since the ACT paid acts as payment on account of the corporation tax liability on these profits.

The imputation system is linked with the income tax system, which is applicable to individuals and unincorporated businesses, to the extent that shareholders in total receive tax credits equal to the ACT paid by the company. This tax credit is added to the net dividend received by the individual to establish the gross dividend income. The tax credit thereby satisfies a shareholder's liability to basic rate income but not to higher rates of tax.

Another noticeable feature of the imputation system is that income which is received under deduction of income tax (e.g. certain interest and royalties) must still be included in the corporation tax computation of chargeable profits. However, dividends received from UK resident companies are not included, as the profits from which they have been paid have already been assessed for corporation tax in the hands of the paying company. Dividend income received in this way is referred to as franked investment income (FII), as it has been franked for corporation tax purposes where income is received under deduction of income tax, it is referred to as unfranked investment income (UFII) to distinguish it from dividend income. The income to be assessed for corporation tax purposes is dependent upon whether the company is resident or non-resident. A company is deemed to be resident if its central management and operational control is located in the UK regardless of where the business is incorporated. The location of the board of directors is often crucial in determining residency although the Revenue inspect the facts very carefully where there are significant tax benefits involved. Following such a rule it is possible for a corporation to be resident in several countries in which case double tax agreements usually deem residency to be located where its 'vital interests' are to be found.

A non-resident company only pays corporation tax if it operates a branch or agency in the UK. If a branch undertakes contracts in the UK that lead ultimately to profits then it will be subject to corporation tax on its branch income other than dividends received from resident companies. Income derived from royalties, rent or interest is subject to income tax at the basic rate (29 per cent in 1986/7) except where a tax treaty prescribes a lower rate. If a non-resident company does not carry on a trade in the UK it will not be subject to capital gains tax either.

Section 482 of the Taxes Act 1970 specifies that the following transactions require consent from the Treasury:

1. For a resident company to become non-resident.
2. For the whole or a part of a resident company's business to be transferred to a non-resident.
3. For a resident company to allow a non-resident company that it controls either to create or to issue any shares or debentures.
4. Except for the purposes of enabling a person to be qualified to act as a director, for a resident company to transfer any shares as debentures in a non-resident company that it controls.

Failure to comply with the above provision can result in a term of imprisonment.

The rate of corporation tax applicable to companies is 35 per cent from 1 April 1986 although a lower 'small companies rate' of 30 per cent applies to the income of a resident company with profits which do not exceed £100,000. In addition, there is marginal relief on profits between £100,000 and the £500,000 figure which is the point at which the full rate applies.

A further distinction between companies is made to distinguish between closely-held companies and other companies. In order to prevent individuals from sheltering income in companies and thereby avoiding higher rates of personal tax, section 282 of the Income and Corporation Tax Act 1970 introduces the term close company which applies to resident companies only. A close company is one controlled by five or fewer participants and in determining a participant's holding the shares of his spouse and children are aggregated with his own.

The provisions of section 282 apply mainly to companies whose main source of income is investment or income derived from real estate. From March 1980 the retention of income derived from trading activities is no longer penalized. Where a company constitutes a close company the tax authorities may require that 'relevant income' in excess of actual distributions be either distributed or apportioned to participants in accordance with their respective shareholding. If a company decides not to distribute the surplus the Inland Revenue has authority to levy ACT on the deemed distribution. Where an individual refuses to pay the high rates of tax levied the Revenue can, where necessary, collect the sum due from the company.

'Relevant income' consists of all the company's investment income plus one-half of its income from real estate, after charges on income, management expenses, and corporation tax. Where the company is a trading company its net income from real estate before the one-half reduction can be reduced by up to £25,000 depending on the ratio of real estate income to trading income. In addition to apportionment problems the close company may encounter difficulties in the areas of deductible expenses to participants, tax deductibility of interest and loans to participants.

As far as the foreign investor is concerned a UK subsidiary cannot be a close company where either the overseas parent company or the ultimate parent would not be a close company if resident in the UK. In practice where non-residents own at least 90 per cent of ordinary share capital, the Revenue will not impose the minimum distribution rules.

Unlike the US and the Federal Republic of Germany the UK does not have sophisticated regulations with respect to intercompany pricing. Section 485 of the Taxes Act 1970 does provide the Revenue with authority to adjust the price of property which is transacted at other than arm's length. However, the Revenue may not allocate profits between companies as is permissible in the US.

Another important area of legislation was introduced in 1984 and refers to UK resident companies with an interest in a controlled foreign company (CFC). The aim of such legislation is to prevent companies from accumulating profits in subsidiaries with low tax rates. The Revenue may impose an additional charge based on the apportionment of income to the UK company unless it qualifies for the publicly quoted exemption. To qualify the following conditions must be satisfied:

1. Within the 12 months before the end of the accounting period, the CFC's shares have been dealt in on a recognized stock exchange in the CFC's country of residence.
2. Within the same period, the shares have been quoted in the official list of such a stock exchange.
3. Throughout the accounting period, 35 per cent of the CFC's voting equity shares have been beneficially held by the public.
4. The total percentage of the voting power in the CFC held by persons who own more than five per cent of that power does not exceed 85 per cent at any time in the accounting period.

Business income for tax purposes is based on the financial statements prepared on an accruals basis but is subject to a number of modifications. Expenditure incurred should be on an arm's length basis and should be wholly and exclusively but not necessarily incurred for the purpose of the trade.

In calculating assessable income the following common deductions are permitted:

1. Capital allowances – depreciation on assets is not allowable against tax although the Revenue do permit capital allowances to be deducted based on the type of asset acquired. From 1 April 1986 there are no first-year allowances for plant and machinery or industrial buildings. However, there is a writing-down allowance on plant and machinery of 25 per cent based on a reducing balance basis. The allowance is applicable to both new and second hand capital expenditure. Proceeds from the sale of plant are deducted from expenditure before calculating the writing-down allowance. If the proceeds exceed the tax written-down value of all plant the excess is taxable as a balancing charge up to the original cost of the asset. Whilst plant and machinery is not defined by any taxing act, there is sufficient case law to establish that it includes machinery, furniture, fixtures and fittings, motor vehicles and computers. Whilst commercial vehicles are treated in the normal way there is a restriction on private vehicles, such as cars, to a maximum of £2000 allowance per annum.

   Qualifying expenditure on industrial buildings is subject to a 4 per cent allowance calculated on a straight-line basis. The allowances apply to factories, warehouses and other industrial budilings but specifically excludes office buildings. When such an asset is sold a balancing charge may arise where the proceeds exceed the tax written-down value. However, no balancing charge can arise where the building is sold after 25 years, if purchased after 6 November 1962, or 50 years where purchased before that date.

   New agricultural buildings are also eligible to a 4 per cent writing-down allowance on a straight-line basis and no balancing charge or allowance arises in the year of sale.

2. Investment allowances – in addition to capital allowances there is a range of incentives such as grants etc. applicable to certain regions. For example, all commercial buildings located in enterprise zones are eligible for a 100 per cent initial allowance.
3. Interest – is normally deductible on a paid basis rather than an accruable basis. Section 38, Finance Act 1976 restricted relief on interest payments to counter tax avoidance schemes involving the pre-payment of interest. Although UK law does not recognize the concept of 'thin capitalization' Revenue practice is to try to ensure that such transactions are on an arm's length basis. *Prima facie* all interest paid to foreign affiliates (75 per cent) is not deductible against tax unless it can be shown that the transaction is at arm's length. Where thin capitalization is established interest in excess of debt/equity limits is not deductible against tax and additionally ACT is levied on it as if it represents a distribution.
4. Losses – trading losses are eligible for a number of reliefs. Losses can be offset against other income including capital gains provided the losses arise from a trade in pursuit of profit. This relief is not available for losses derived from overseas trading. Where losses arise from first year allowances, which were given before 1986, they may be carried back up to three years before the accounting period in which the loss is incurred. Any losses not thereby relieved may be offset against any surplus FII in the current and immediately preceding year and the related tax credit reclaimed. Losses remaining unrelieved may be carried forward and offset against future profits without any time-limit.

   Any losses arising from capital transactions may be offset against capital profits in the year in which they occur or carried forward. Capital losses may not be carried back.
5. Scientific research – of a revenue nature is deductible against income in the year in which it is incurred. Any capital expenditure incurred on scientific research for trading purposes is also deductible in the year in which it is incurred with the exception of expenditure on land and houses.

Foreign subsidiaries and branches

Companies resident in the UK are normally allowed to offset taxes paid overseas against UK corporation tax. For non-resident companies operating in the UK the liability to taxation is normally limited to the extent of profits earned in the UK from its permanent establishment here. In both cases the terms of any double tax treaty should be scrutinized.

If the overseas investor forms a branch in the UK it will be taxed on its trading income and capital profits arising from its UK operations. There are no special provisions applicable to overseas investors in calculating its income other than the Revenue practice with respect to thin capitalization. Expenses incurred abroad wholly and exclusively in connection with a UK branch may be offset against income including a reasonable proportion of head office expenses. Any UFII received by the UK branch from a UK source may be offset against corporation tax in the year in which it is received.

Distributions made by a branch are not subject to restrictions and are not subject to ACT or withholding taxes. However, profits derived from a UK branch are subject to corporation tax at the full rate and not the small companies rate unless there is a nondiscrimination clause in the relevant double taxation treaty. A non-resident company cannot be a close company so the disadvantages of such an organization are not relevant.

ACT on any distributions. Under some double taxation treaties – for example, UK/US – part of the ACT paid by a UK subsidiary may be repaid to the overseas parent leading to a reduction in the overall UK tax burden. As previously mentioned, interest paid to foreign affiliates (75 per cent) is not deductible against tax and may be treated as a distribution unless a double taxation treaty is in force.

Another factor to be taken into consideration is the profitability of the UK enterprise. If the UK operation is likely to incur losses in the early years it may be beneficial to trade initially as a branch rather than a subsidiary so that relief can be achieved more quickly.

Whilst tax considerations are important in making a decision on the type of corporate structure other factors are also important. For example, the liability of a branch in the UK is not limited to the assets of the branch whereas a corporate structure does limit liability. In contrast, there are less legal formalities attached to a UK branch. For example, a UK company must have its accounts audited annually and these must be filed with the Companies Registrar. A branch located in the UK must be registered but need only file the accounts of the foreign company which may, or may not, be audited. An important difference between the two organizations is that a corporate structure provides a better profile than a branch.

Consolidated tax returns

In any discussion of the tax consequences of mergers and acquisitions it is important to consider groups of companies, since any acquisition may create a group or change an existing relationship. There are three main types of groups of companies depending on the proportion of shares held in the subsidiary and these shareholdings may be either direct or indirect.

The advance corporation tax group requires more than 50 per cent ownership of the voting shares of the subsidiary. Where such a relationship exists the parent company may surrender ACT paid by it to its subsidiaries for offsetting against their corporation tax liabilities. Companies within such a group may also elect to pay dividends and payments subject to deduction of income tax at source, for example, royalties, without respectively accounting for ACT or deducting and accounting for income tax.

The main advantage of not paying intra-group ACT is that dividends can be paid without bringing forward tax payment dates. In addition, the election saves on administration, since the ACT withheld by the subsidiary is exactly matched by the tax credit received by the parent. A further advantage is that it avoids the possibility of having unrelieved surplus ACT and unrelieved surplus FII on the group.

A second type of group structure is the group relief group. This occurs where 75 per cent of the shares are held in the subsidiary and allows trading losses to be surrendered between companies in a group. The loss may have arisen out of trading, an excess of charges paid in a period, or excess management expenses in an investment company. The loss so occasioned may be transferred by the parent to the subsidiary or vice versa, or between subsidiaries, provided that the parent owns the shares as an investment rather than a trading asset.

A capital gains tax group requires the parent to own 75 per cent of the shares in the subsidiary. Where assets are transferred within the group, capital gains or losses do not arise. Instead, the cost to the group is transferred and the gain or loss is not recognized until the asset is transferred outside the group.

Capital gains tax

Resident companies are liable to corporation tax on chargeable net capital gains based on capital gains tax principles. A number of assets such as cars, wasting assets and government securities held for more than one year are exempt. A gain is the difference between the sale proceeds of an asset and cost taking into consideration the cost of acquisition and sale. Since 1 April 1982 cost is indexed by the retail price index so that the indexation process may eliminate a gain but may not create a loss.

Where qualifying assets which have been used for trade purposes are sold and the proceeds are used to purchase a qualifying asset, a claim may be made so that the gain arising is used to reduce the cost of the new asset. This relief is termed 'rollover relief' and is only available where the new asset is purchased not more than one year before or three years after the sale of the old asset. The gains are effectively taxed at 30 per cent by exempting a fraction of the capital gain from corporation tax. However, the Finance Act 1987 introduced a change so that gains on disposal on or after 17 March 1987 will be charged at the normal or small companies corporation tax rate.

Taxation implications of mergers and acquisitions

Implications for the acquiring company

There are essentially two approaches a foreign investor can adopt to acquire a business in the UK. The foreign investor may have, or set up, a branch or subsidiary in the UK with a view to acquiring the business assets of a resident company. Alternatively a foreign subsidiary may be used to acquire the shares of a resident company.

The decision as to whether the acquiring company should purchase assets or shares depends to some extent on its own tax position. A taxpaying acquiring company may prefer to purchase assets rather than shares in as much as it is able to obtain writing-down allowances on qualifying assets based on purchase cost rather than original cost. This rules does not apply to industrial or agricultural buildings where the original cost of construction is the relevant cost. This means that by acquiring assets rather than shares writing-down allowances will be higher initially and also reduces the potential liability on capital gains tax.

A non-taxpaying acquiring company may prefer to purchase shares rather than assets to obtain a reduced purchase price to reflect tax avoided by the seller on balancing charges or chargeable gains. For example, the vendor may defer a capital gains liability on the sale of assets where the purchaser uses the rollover relief provisions for items such as goodwill, building land and fixed plant.

A further advantage accruing to the purchase of assets rather than shares is that only the assets worth taking need be acquired leaving less attractive assets and outstanding tax liabilities behind.

A number of advantages arise on the acquisition of a company rather than acquiring assets. For example, if the acquiree comany is part of a group prior to sale, then it ceases to be entitled to group relief and ACT surrenders from the date in the accounting period in which the arrangements come into existence. Once acquired, the company becomes part of a new tax group and may surrender/receive group relief in respect of the post-acquisition part of its accounting period.

It is probable that by purchasing a company any tax losses in the acquiree company may be offset against future trading income, provided there is no major change in the nature or conduct of the company's business for at least three years. In addition, it is possible that losses in the acquiree may be eligible for group relief.

The Taxes Act 1970 introduced two further conditions for eligibility of purchased tax losses in addition to the continuity of business test. First, there should not be a change of ownership of the company or a change in the nature and conduct of the trade and second the trading activities of the company should not have become small or negligible and there is a change in ownership before they have been revived.

A similar situation arises when acquiring companies with surplus ACT. The Revenue became concerned that such companies might become useful if taken over and so the conditions outlined above were also applied to companies with surplus ACT. However, any surplus ACT can be carried forward and relieved in the future, if the trade or business is continued without a major change for at least three years.

Where problems occur such as those outlined above it may be appropriate if part of the purchase price is deferred until the position is clarified with the Revenue.

Should the acquiring company ever decide to dispose of the acquiree, then the allowable expenditure is added to the consideration to establish the cost base for capital gains tax purposes. The allowable costs constitute incidental costs of acquisitions to the acquiring company and any expenditure wholly or exclusively incurred to enhance the value of the company, together with any incidental costs of making the disposal.

The provisions permitting the rolling over of gains on the sale of one chargeable asset into the tax cost of assets acquired for a sum equal to the disposal proceeds of the original asset can lead to the acquiring company finding hidden tax liabilities in the acquiree company. If the acquiree company sells a chargeable asset following acquisition at above original cost, the actual capital gain arising may be higher than expected, if the tax cost was below original cost due to a previous rollover claim. It should, however, be noted that all the trades carried on by the members of a group of companies are considered for rollover relief to be a single trade and consequently gains arising in the acquiree or acquiring company may be rolled over into new assets of, respectively, the acquiring and acquiree companies.

Implications for the shareholders of the acquiring corporation

There should be no signficant taxation implications for the shareholders of the acquiring company.

Implications for the acquiree company

Where the acquiree company sells assets it may have to pay capital gains tax on any excess of sales proceeds over indexed cost. However, it is possible that a higher price may be obtained by selling assets rather than shares where the company has tax losses.

Where the vendor corporation is a taxpaying company it may be more advantageous to sell shares rather than assets as it avoids capital gains tax liability on asset sales. Where shares are sold and the acquiree is part of a group prior to sale, then it ceases to be entitled to group relief and ACT surrenders from the date in the accounting period in which the arrangements came into existence.

As CGT group assets may be transferred within a group without a charge to taxation a tax avoidance scheme, known as the envelope scheme, was developed to transfer assets pregnant with capital gains to a new owner free of any tax liability. The scheme involved transferring the assets to a subsidiary, the shares in which were then sold to the new owner, who would then transfer the assets out of the subsidiary into his own company. This scheme was effectively neutralized by the Inland Revenue's introduction of a provision whereby assets transferred within a group will be deemed to have been sold and immediately reacquired at their market value on the transfer date, if the subsidiary acquiring the assets leaves the group within six years. This section does not apply if:

1. the asset was acquired by the subsidiary before 6 April 1965;
2. the asset owned by the subsidiary constitutes trading stock at the time it leaves the group.

Implications for the shareholders of the acquiree

A disposal of shares or debentures by a shareholder (either a person or a holding company) represents a chargeable event for capital gains purposes, except where the shares or debentures are held as a current asset or where the disposal is part of a reorganization. A disposal will be considered to be part of a reorganization under the following circumstances:

1. the shares or debentures in company A are exchanged for shares or debentures in another company B;
2. where the original holding in the company is cancelled, in return for new shares or debentures issued in proportion to the original holdings.

In both instances, the reorganization must be for *bona fide* commercial reasons and must not be part of a scheme or arrangement whose main purpose is the avoidance of tax. In addition, for an exchange of shares two further conditions must be met:

1. company A must hold, or in consequence of the exchange will hold, more than one-quarter of the ordinary share capital of company B;
2. the issue of shares or debentures must be made by company A as a result of a general offer to the members of company B, or any class of them and on condition in the first instance that company A will have control of company B.

Where these conditions are fulfilled, company A and company B are treated as if they were the same company and represent a reorganization of the single company's share capital. The effect of this is that the shareholder is considered not to have disposed of his original holding for capital gains purposes at the time of the exchange, and that on the subsequent sale of his new holding any gain or loss or disposal will be calculated by reference to the original holding's cost and date of acquisition. If the acquisition is part shares or debentures and part other consideration, the transaction is treated as if it were a part disposal.

There are also provisions in the capital gains legislation to prevent the creation of allowable losses by a 'depreciatory transaction'. The appropriate section applies where the depreciatory transaction occurred after 6 April 1965 and materially affected the value of the shares on disposal. A depreciatory transaction means:

1. any disposal of assets at other than market value by one member of a group of companies to another; or
2. unless the ultimate disposal occurred before 30 April 1969, any other transaction where the company whose shares are the subject of the ultimate disposal of any 75 per cent subsidiary of that company was a party with one or more members of the same group of companies at that time.

The two major examples of depreciatory transactions concern assets and dividends. A reorganization might involve transferring assets at less than market value by a subsidiary to its parent company; this would constitute a potential depreciatory transaction. The second situation concerns dividend strips, whereby the subsidiary pays an abnormal dividend to its parent, thereby potentially affecting the value of the shares in a material way. The general view is that these events could constitute depreciatory transactions, whereas the payment for outstanding group relief or ACT surrenders may not be, although this is not at all clear-cut.

It is important to emphasize that the price placed on the shares of the acquirer should be on the basis of commercial considerations and not for tax reasons. Naturally, a transaction of this nature will have fiscal implications and shareholders will wish the sale to be conducted in a tax-efficient manner. However, there are many anti-avoidance provisions to ensure that the main reason for the transaction is not tax avoidance and, where possible, the Inland Revenue's advance clearance that it considers the transaction to be *bona fide* commercial should be obtained. Some of the avoidance measures are specific to such transactions, but others are general provisions which may be applied to such transactions.

Finally there may be implications for former shareholders of a close company who may be liable for higher rate tax on undistributed income, especially where the sale realizes substantial liquid funds.

Tax planning

It would not be appropriate to discuss the taxation implications of mergers and acquisitions in the UK without a mention of some recent tax cases which affect tax planning. Since 1936 the principle has stood that 'every man is entitled if he can to order his affairs so that the tax attaching under the appropriate Acts is less than it otherwise would be'. However, in 1985 the case of *Ramsay* v. *CIR* took the first step towards taxing transactions on the basis of economic substance rather than legal form. Further clarification of this new principle was provided in *CIR* v. *Burmah Oil Co. Ltd* and *Furniss* v. *Dawson*. On 9 February 1984 the House of Lords effectively confirmed that schemes developed solely with the purpose of avoiding taxation will not succeed. At present there is no firm indication as to how the new principle will affect international operations.

5. ACCOUNTING IMPLICATIONS OF BUSINESS COMBINATIONS

Company disclosure in the UK is influenced by the following:

1. professional accounting bodies in the UK;
2. Companies Act 1985 in Britain and the equivalent legislation in Northern Ireland;

3. the EEC;
4. the listing requirements of the London Stock Exchange;
5. international recommendations such as those issued by the International Accounting Standards Committee.

There are six accountancy bodies in the UK including three Institutes of Chartered Accountants (England and Wales; Ireland; and Scotland), who undertake most of the auditing work. Members of the Chartered Association of Certified Accountants also undertake company audit work but members of the Chartered Institute of Management Accountants cannot. The six accountancy bodies are members of the Consultative Committee of Accountancy Bodies (CCAB).

In 1970 the Institute of Chartered Accountants in England and Wales (ICAEW) established the Accounting Standards Steering Committee to promulgate statements of standard accounting practice. Subsequent to its formation the other five accountancy bodies joined the CCAB in developing accounting standards. Members of accountancy bodies who assume responsibilities in respect of financial accounts are expected to observe accounting standards and may be investigated by the Professional Standards Committee where they do not.

Companies Act 1985 requires directors of companies to present annual accounts to shareholders which show a true and fair view of the company's state of affairs and profit or loss for the year and comply with the requirements of the Companies Act. Companies should maintain records of all transactions so that accounts may be prepared which show a true and fair view. The Companies Act also contains detailed rules of disclosure and valuation and prescribes formats in which accounts can be presented.

The EEC has had an impact on accounting in the UK, particularly the Fourth Directive which introduced formats for company accounts. Whilst statements of standard accounting practices (SSAPs) do not have legal force they are considered to be strongly persuasive. The statements deal with particular accounting problems including measurement problems, concepts and disclosure. Many of the basic concepts originally introduced into SSAPs have now been incorporated into company law.

The listing requirements of the Stock Exchange, which apply to public listed companies, attempt to increase the disclosure of information to investors and make relevant information more timely. For example all listed companies are required to publish unaudited statements of results for the first half of their financial year and make a preliminary announcement of the year-end results before publication of the accounts. Furthermore, there are additional disclosure requirements in the Directors' Report and other requirements such as disclosure of items of major financial significance such as material acquisitions or disposals.

International Accounting Standards also have an impact on UK accounting principles. The UK is a full voting member of the International Accounting Standards Committee (IASC) and undertakes to support the standards promulgated by the Committee. Furthermore, UK accounting standards are written in the context of any standard issued in the area by the IASC. Each UK standard contains a paragraph stating the extent to which compliance with its recommendations concur with international standards.

Whilst a foreign investor may initially trade in the UK as a branch a better profile together with limitation on liability means that in practice most foreign companies organize themselves as incorporated businesses. Often a foreign investor will set up a holding company in the UK which acquires subsidiaries on behalf of the ultimate parent company. Such a corporate formation necessitates the preparation of consolidated accounts.

Accounting for groups, acquisitions and mergers

The major influences on group accounts in the UK are the Companies Acts and SSAPs. The UK has a long history of preparing consolidated accounts stretching back as far as 1910 although it was not until 1947 that group accounts were required by law. Section 229 Companies Act 1985 places an obligation on a company to produce group accounts for the parent company and its subsidiaries. The requirement is for group accounts to be prepared and not consolidated accounts although in practice the latter are normally prepared and will become compulsory on implementation of the Seventh Directive. Where a parent company is the wholly-owned subsidiary of another company incorporated in Great Britain group accounts need only be prepared by the ultimate parent company (section 229(2)). However, where a subsidiary is not wholly owned and when the ultimate parent company is an overseas company the obligation to produce group accounts remains.

Section 736(1) states that one company is a subsidiary of another if:

1. the other company is a member of it and controls the composition of its board of directories; or
2. the other company holds more than half in nominal value of its issued equity share capital whether directly, indirectly or by nominees; or
3. where it is a subsidiary which is itself a subsidiary of the other company.

These legal definitions are also adopted in SSAP14, Group Accounts. Section 229(3) of the Companies Act permits directors to exclude a subsidiary from group accounts if:

1. its activities are so dissimilar that they cannot be considered to be a single undertaking; or
2. it would be harmful to the business of the company or any of its subsidiaries; or
3. it is impracticable; or
4. it would be of no real value to members as the amounts involved are not material; or
5. it would involve undue expense or delay out of proportion to the value of members of the company; or
6. it would be misleading.

Where a subsidiary is omitted from group accounts, for reasons (1) and (2) stated above, approval is required from the Secretary of State. Where a subsidiary is not included in group accounts the following additional information must be given in the notes to the accounts (Sch 4: 69):

1. the reasons why the subsidiaries are not included in the group accounts;
2. a statement, showing any audit qualifications on the accounts of the excluded subsidiary, which are material to members of the holding company;
3. the aggregate of the total investment in the excluded subsidiary determined using the equity method of valuation. This is not required where a wholly-owned subsidiary is excluded from group accounts.

Whilst section 229 stipulates that group accounts should be prepared consisting of a consolidated profit and loss account and a consolidated balance sheet, it is possible for there to be other forms of group accounts. Schedule 4: 68 requires that where other forms of group accounts are prepared they must give the same or equivalent information. Section 229(6) specifically permits the following alternative forms:

1. more than one set of consolidated accounts;
2. separate financial statements for each subsidiary and holding company;
3. statements expanding the information about the subsidiaries in the holding company's own financial statements;
4. any combination of the foregoing.

Where consolidated accounts are prepared, they should combine the financial information of the separate financial statements as if they were the accounts of an actual company (Sch 4: 61, 62). A holding company preparing consolidated accounts must also prepare its own balance sheet but does not have to publish its own profit and loss account provided that the consolidated accounts show how much of the consolidated profit or loss is dealt with in the accounts of the holding company (section 228(7)).

SSAP1 Accounting for the results of associated companies

SSAP1 was originally issued in January 1971, amended in August 1974, and revised in April 1982. The reasons why a standard was originally considered to be necessary was:

1. the growing practice of business ventures involving consortium or joint venture companies in which there was substantial but not actual controlling interest; and
2. the interest of the investing group or company is for the long-term and is substantial and having regard to the disposition of the other shareholdings, the investing group or company is in a position to exercise a significant influence over the company in which the investment is made.

Significant influence involves participation, but not necessarily control, in the financial and operating policy decisions of that company including its dividend policy. An indication of such participation is representation on the Board of Directors but this is not conclusive evidence. Where an investment amounts to 20 per cent or more of the equity voting rights it should be presumed that significant influence exists unless demonstrated otherwise. Where an investment is less than 20 per cent it should be presumed that significant influence does not exist unless demonstrated otherwise.

The bases for accounting for associated companies is that dividends received and receivable should be brought into the investing company's own financial statements. Included in the investing group's consolidated financial statements should be the investing group's share of profits less losses of associated companies. In the investing company's balance sheet, the amount at which the investing company's interests in associated companies should be shown is the cost of the investment less amounts written off. In the consolidated balance sheet, the associated company should be shown as the aggregate of:

1. the investing group's share of the net assets other than goodwill, after attributing fair values to the net assets at the time of acquisition of the interest;
2. the investing group's share of any goodwill in the associated companies' own financial statements;
3. the premium paid (or discount) on the acquisition of the interests in the associated companies in so far as it has not already been written off or amortized.

The first item should be disclosed separately, whereas the second and third may be shown as one aggregate account.

SSAP14 Group accounts

SSAP14 was issued in September 1978 in response to IAS 3, Consolidated Financial Statements, which differed in some respects to the law and practice in the UK and Ireland. The definition of a subsidiary in SSAP14 is identical with section 736(1), Companies Act 1985 as previously outlined.

Group accounts should be produced which include consolidated balance sheets, profit and loss accounts, and source and application of funds. The latter is not required by law. SSAP14 states that a holding company should prepare group accounts in the form of a single set of consolidated financial statements covering the holding company and its subsidiary companies, at home and overseas. If group accounts are prepared in a form other than consolidated accounts, the onus is on the directors to justify and state the reasons for reaching their conclusion.

Group accounts should be prepared on the basis of uniform accounting policies and wherever practicable to the same accounting date. A subsidiary should be excluded from consolidation if:

1. its activities are so dissimilar that consolidated financial statements would be misleading; or
2. the holding company owns directly or indirectly more than half of the equity share capital but not more than half of the votes; or
3. the subsidiary operates under severe conditions which significantly impair control; or
4. control is intended to be temporary.

Where a subsidiary is excluded from consolidation for reason (1) the separate financial statements should include the following information:

(a) a note of the holding company's interest;
(b) particulars of intra-group balances;
(c) a reconciliation with the amount included in the consolidated financial statements for the group's investment in the subsidiary which should be stated under the equity method of accounting.

Where a subsidiary is excluded from consolidation for reason (2), the investment should be dealt with either:

(a) under the equity method if in all other respects it satisfies the criteria for treatment as an associated company under SSAP1; or where the conditions are not met,
(b) as an investment at cost or valuation less any provision required.

In either of the above situations separate financial information should be included which meet the requirements of the Companies Acts.

Where a subsidiary is excluded for reason (3) the investment should be stated in the consolidated balance sheet at the amount applicable under the equity method at the date the restrictions came into force or a lower amount where there has been a decline in value. The following information should be disclosed in the group accounts:

(a) its net assets;
(b) its profits or losses for the period;
(c) any amounts included in the consolidated profit and loss account in respect of:
    (i) dividends received;
    (ii) write down of investment.

Where a subsidiary is excluded for reason (4) the temporary investment should be stated at the lower of cost and not realisable value in the balance sheet.

SSAP22 Accounting for goodwill

Goodwill arises because the value of a business as a whole differs from the value of its separable net assets. As such, this intangible asset cannot be realized except when the business as a whole is sold. Most businesses possess goodwill through the development of relations between suppliers and customers, although occasionally badwill or negative goodwill might occur.

Since it is extremely difficult to quantify internal or what is called inherent goodwill, it is unusual not to account for it except on the realization of the business as a whole. Consequently the treatment of purchased goodwill is important in relation to mergers and acquisitions both at the individual level and on consolidation. SSAP22 does not permit the capitalization of inherent goodwill.

SSAP22 specifies that goodwill should not be carried as a permanent balance sheet asset, but should be eliminated either by immediate write-off to reserves on acquisition or by amortization over its useful life through the profit and loss account. Although either method of treating goodwill is permissible, the standard recommends that the immediate write-off option should be used in normal circumstances. However, in practice there may be circumstances when an unusually large acquisition would have a significant effect on reserves, and in such cases it is reasonable to adopt the amortization option. Where the amortization option is adopted, goodwill should be written off over its useful life, although no maximum period of write-off is stipulated.

In practice, it is allowable under the standard for goodwill on one acquisition to be immediately written off and in the next transaction goodwill can be amortized.

Where goodwill is immediately written off, the question arises as to whether it should be against realized profits or unrealized profits. The distinctions is relevant for an individual company, but not in the consolidated accounts, because the distribution of dividends is made from the profits of individual companies and not from groups.

At the individual company level, goodwill should be eliminated against realized reserves where it is considered to have suffered a decrease in value. Where goodwill is written off on acquisition as a matter of accounting policy, realized profits should not be reduced immediately. In such a case, goodwill can be eliminated against unrealized profits and transferred to realized profits over its useful life.

Where negative goodwill arises in an individual company's accounts, it should be credited to an unrealized reserve initially and transferred to realized reserves over the period of depreciation or realization of the acquired assets.

SSAP22 is to be regarded as standard with respect to accounting periods commencing on or after 1 January 1985. Any goodwill existing on that date should be either written off directly against reserves or amortized. If the amortization policy is adopted, it may be written off to profit and loss account partly as a prior year adjustment, to represent amortization to date, and the balance amortized over the remaining useful economic life without a prior year adjustment.

It is a requirement of SSAP22 to disclose the accounting policy adopted and, where different, the policy existing on the introduction of the standard. In addition, the amount of material goodwill recognized in respect of each acquisition during the year should also be disclosed. Where goodwill is amortized, the net book value, cost and amortization movements should be disclosed, together with the period over which goodwill is being written off.

SSAP23 Accounting for acquisitions and mergers

The path to this standard started in the 1960s and early 1970s when a few companies, for example British Leyland Motor Corporation and Trust House Group Ltd used merger accounting to account for an acquisition rather than the traditional approach; the purchase method. In January 1971 the Accounting Standards Steering Committee (ASSC), now the Accounting Standards Committee, issued Exposure Draft 3 (ED3) which attempted to make a distinction between an acquisition and a merger. However, the ASSC never converted the exposure draft into a standard as doubts lay as to the legality of merger accounting. The problem surrounded section 56(1) of the Companies Act 1948, which provided that where shares were issued at a premium, for cash or otherwise, the premium should be recorded in a share premium account. Such a provision appeared to preclude merger accounting and was confirmed in the High Court in *Shearer* v. *Bercain*. Relief by sections 36–41 of the Companies Act 1985, thereby made merger accounting legally acceptable. These sections were incorporated as section 131 of the Companies Act 1985 and made merger accounting legal provided the issuing company has secured at least a 90 per cent equity holding by a share issue.

SSAP23 Accounting for acquisitions and mergers was issued in April 1985 and is to be regarded as affecting business combinations which are accounted for in accounting periods commencing on or after 1 April 1985. The standard deals with accounting for business combinations that arise when a company becomes a subsidiary of another company. The standard deals only with accounting in group accounts and not with an individual company's accounts.

A business combination may be accounted for as a merger if all of the following conditions are met:

1. the business combination results from an offer to the holders of all equity shares and the holders of all voting shares which are not already held by the offeror;
2. the offeror has secured, as a result of the offer, a holding of:
    (a) at least 90 per cent of all equity shares (taking each class of equity separately); and
    (b) the shares carrying at least 90 per cent of the votes of the offeree;
3. Immediately prior to the offer, the offeror does not hold:
    (a) 20 per cent or more of all equity shares of the offeree (taking each class of equity separately); or
    (b) shares carrying 20 per cent or more of the votes of the offeree;
4. not less than 90 per cent of the fair value of the total consideration given for the equity share capital (including that given for shares

Table 12.6 Comparison of UK accounting practices with international standards

International accounting standards	*UK standards*
IAS 3 – Consolidated financial statements	
Permits consolidation where the majority of equity shares but not voting shares are owned	SSAP14 does not permit this
Permits consolidation where the parent has the power to control the financial and operating policies	SSAP14 requires consolidation where the majority of the board is controlled
Requires an analysis of amounts under each significant balance sheet and income statement heading which are exposed to exceptional risks of operation in foreign countries, including the risk of foreign currency exchange fluctuations	No equivalent requirement
IAS 4 – Depreciation accounting	
All depreciable assets should be depreciated	SSAP12 states that exempt investment properties should be included at open market value at the balance sheet date and changes in value should go to reserves
IAS 5 – Information to be disclosed in the financial statements	
Methods of providing for pension and retirement plans should be disclosed.	No equivalent requirement
IAS 9 – Accounting for research and development	
Requires disclosure of the total research and development costs charged as an expense	No equivalent requirement
IAS 11 – Accounting for construction contracts	
Requires disclosure of construction work-in-progress, analysed between work accounted for under the percentage-of-completion and completed-contract methods	No equivalent requirement
IAS 12 – Accounting for taxes on income	
Disclose tax losses used to relieve current or future tax expense. Accrue	No equivalent requirement

– *Continued*

Table 12.6 Continued

International accounting standards	*UK standards*
tax on undistributed profits of subsidiaries or associated companies unless the liability will not arise	
IAS 14 – Reporting financial information by segment	
Requires public companies and other economically significant entities to provide segment information for each class of business and each geographic area	No equivalent requirement
Required information includes revenues, results, assets employed and basis of inter-segment pricing	
IAS 15 – Information reflecting the effects of changing prices	
Requires disclosure of such information on a supplementary basis	Not required at present as SSAP16 has been withdrawn
IAS 16 – Accounting for property, plant and equipment	
When property, plant and equipment is revalued the entire class of assets should be included	Not required by SSAP12
IAS 19 – Accounting for retirement benefits in the financial statements of employers	
Determine costs on a consistent basis either on an accrued benefit valuation approach or a projected benefit valuation method	A statement of intent has been issued which recommends that companies should match the cost of pensions with the benefit derived by charging the cost against profits on a systematic basis over the employees' service lives. There is no standard as yet
Disclose accounting policies, other significant matters and differences in funding since the inception of the plan and amounts charged to income	
IAS 20 – Accounting for government grants and disclosure of government assistance	

– *Continued*

Table 12.6 Continued

International accounting standards	*UK standards*
Requires disclosure of the nature and extent of government grants	No equivalent requirement
IAS 23 – Capitalization of borrowing costs The standard stipulates provisions which should be followed where a policy of capitalization is adopted. There is no requirement to capitalize borrowing costs	No equivalent requirement
IAS 24 – Related party disclosures Disclosure of the nature and type of related party transaction	No equivalent requirement

already held) is in the form of equity share capital; not less than 90 per cent of the fair value of the consideration given for voting non-equity share capital (including that given for shares already held) is in the form of equity and/or voting non-equity share capital.

It is important to note that if all the above conditions are fulfilled, the business combination may be, rather than must be, accounted for as a merger. Equally, the transaction may be accounted for as an acquisition.

Where all the above conditions are not met, it should be accounted for as an acquisition. Where merger accounting is adopted, it is not necessary to adjust assets and liability to reflect their fair value, although appropriate adjustments should be made to achieve uniformity of accounting policies within the group.

With respect to the disclosure of material business combinations, the following information should be provided in the financial statements of the acquiring company in the year in which the combination takes place:

1. the names of the combining companies;
2. the number and class of the securities issued in respect of the combination, and details of any other consideration given;
3. whether the transaction is accounted for as an acquisition or a merger;
4. the nature and amount of significant accounting adjustments in the year in which the business combination takes place.

International accounting standards (IAS)

A summary of the more important differences between UK standards and international accounting standards is provided in table 12.6. In general, compliance with the requirements of UK standards automatically ensures compliance with IAS.

6. EXCHANGE CONTROL/FOREIGN INVESTMENT REGULATIONS

There are no exchange controls in the UK and no limitation on the repatriation of capital, dividends, interest, royalties and fees. There are no specific limitations on overseas investors who may freely issue securities and borrow in the UK, subject to the rules which apply to all companies. Furthermore, there are no procedural formalities which apply specifically to foreign investors setting up a business in the UK.

The attitude of governments has been to encourage foreign investment in the UK. The only limitation placed on overseas investors is that, like UK companies, they may not invest in industries which are effectively closed to private enterprise, e.g. railway transportation, bulk crude steel manufacturers, coal mining other than open cast, etc. The UK government operates a liberal policy not only to foreign investment but to imports and exports generally.

SUMMARY

Takeover activity has increased considerably over the period 1985 to 1987 in terms of the average value of transactions. However, in terms of numbers of transactions activity is low relative to the period 1971–3. There is no doubt that takeover activity has contributed greatly to increased concentration in business in the UK although whether this is harmful to the UK economy is debatable.

In 1986 the Secretary of State for Trade and Industry announced that competition policy including merger control would be reviewed. At present the most important law affecting mergers and acquisitions is the Fair Trading Act 1973. The Act empowers the Secretary of State to appoint a Director General of Fair Trading whose responsibility it is to keep the commercial activities relating to goods and services under constant review. A merger may be referred to the Monopolies Commission if the enterprises which cease to be distinct will together supply or receive at least one-quarter of the goods or services in the UK or a substantial part of it or the value of worldwide assets taken over exceeds £30 million. Where these criteria are satisfied the Office of Fair Trading tries to establish the likely effects of the acquisition on competition and on other matters of concern to the public interest. The concept of the 'public interest' is rather vague which covers social and economic effects which extend beyond the interests of shareholders. It is to be hoped that the current review of competition policy will make a referral more certain, will take into consideration the international dimension of business, but will be sufficiently rigorous to ensure that domestic consumers are not exploited. This would undoubtedly mean a tougher regime.

The City Code on Takeovers and Mergers controls the behaviour of bidders for quoted companies. The Code does not have statutory backing and, whilst it proved successful before 'Big-Bang', it has shown itself to be inadequate at controlling participants involving business conglomerates. Statutory backing is required to strengthen its effectiveness.

The accounting profession in the UK has shown itself to be lacking in its will to improve comparability of financial reports in the UK. The standards on goodwill and on mergers and acquisitions represent little more than a codification of creative practices. Such an approach does not show professional leadership to countries who look to others for guidance. Hopefully, the review of the standards, in the light of the proposed implementation of the Seventh Directive, will generate something more worthwhile.

13

United States

1. BUSINESS ORGANIZATIONS AND COMBINATIONS

Business organizations

The major forms of business organizations in the US are corporations, branches of foreign corporations, partnerships, joint ventures and sole traders. All of these business organizations are recognized by national laws although control is exercised by laws of individual states. Prospective foreign investors will be interested mainly in corporations and to a much lesser extent the formation of branches of foreign corporations.

A corporation is formed by the issue of stock to shareholders whose liability is normally limited to the extent of their investment in the company. The requirements to form a corporation vary from state to state but a minimum of three founders is normally required. Some states have residency or citizenship qualifications for founders, but any such requirement is an organizational formality rather than a real problem.

The formation of corporations is inexpensive and can be completed within a matter of days. The incorporation documents must be filed with the Secretary of State in which the enterprise is formed and the documents are available for scrutiny by the public. In addition, each corporation must file an annual return in the state of incorporation, and pay franchise taxes in the states in which it operates.

Each state controls the capital structure of corporations but regulations are extremely liberal with the proviso that the rights of different classes of securities are clearly set out. However, debt–equity ratios are imposed by the federal tax system to avoid excessive debt. The Internal Revenue Service (IRS), in conjunction with the Treasury, prescribes regulations to determine whether an interest in a corporation is to be treated as stock or debt. The IRS issued section 385 of the Internal Revenue Code in 1980 which sets out factors which will be considered in determining whether a debtor–creditor relationship exists. The IRS tried to introduce amending regulations in 1982 but these proposals were withdrawn in November 1983.

Section 385 covers the following factors:

1. whether there is a written unconditional promise to pay on demand or on a specified date a sum certain in money in return for an adequate consideration in money or money's worth, and to pay a fixed rate of interest;
2. whether there is subordination to or preference over any indebtedness of the corporation;
3. the ratio of debt to equity of the corporation;
4. whether there is convertibility into the stock of the corporation; and
5. the relationship between holdings of stock in the corporation and holdings of the interest in question.

The penalty for exceeding specified debt–equity ratios is that the total interest payment together with the debt repayment will constitute appropriations rather than tax deductible expenses and capital repayments respectively.

An alternative to the incorporation of a subsidiary is to operate the enterprise as a division or branch of the foreign parent. Whilst there are more formalities to comply with as a subsidiary, for tax and legal reasons it is normally more convenient to operate as a corporation. In addition, the parent company is not liabile for the debts of its subsidiary and a better profile is obtained in US markets by operating as a US corporation rather than as an overseas branch.

Types of business combination

A US corporation may be acquired by a foreign company by the purchase of assets or shares. The foreign company can issue shares, debt or cash or a combination of the three as consideration for the acquiree. Where an asset acquisition is undertaken the acquirer will obtain most of the assets and liabilities of the acquiree. The acquiree, in agreement with its shareholders, is usually liquidated as part of the transaction. In contrast, a share acquisition may or may not lead to the liquidation of the acquiree. Approval is given for a takeover by the acquiree's shareholders agreeing to sell their shares whereas with an asset acquisition a formal vote must be undertaken.

A third form of acquisition is the statutory or reorganizational type of merger (section 368(a)(1)(A)). This, so-called 'triangular merger', is possible where a US subsidiary of a foreign parent acquires a US corporation by the issuance of stock in the foreign parent company.

The type of transaction undertaken and form of consideration will naturally depend on the requirements of buyer and seller who should have due regard to the important differing tax consequences – these are dealt with in section 4. Whereas the acquisition of public companies is primarily by the issuance of cash, the purchase of private companies is predominantly by share exchange. This may be because with private companies, the owners are few in number so that the receipt of cash would lead to the payment of capital gains tax whereas an exchange of stock leads to a deferment of the tax. In contrast, holders of shares in public companies may often have diversified portfolios in which their investment in one security is not so crucial. The receipt of cash to diversified shareholders may lead to a capital gain which may be offset against realized capital losses.

A further incentive for foreign companies to pay cash rather than shares for a US corporation is that if shares are issued it may become necessary to have them registered to comply with the securities laws. This depends on the number of shares issued and whether the US subsidiary of a foreign parent can issue its own shares.

2. TRENDS IN TAKEOVER ACTIVITY

Concentration in business may be measured at the market level or at the aggregate level. At the market level the share of a given number of firms, e.g. the top five or largest 100, in terms of a variable such as employment in a particular market, may be compared over time. In contrast, aggregate concentration, as measured by say assets or employment, which are controlled by the largest companies can also be measured over time. Unfortunately in nearly every country the available statistics are limited in some respect and the US is no exception to this. Furthermore, it is even more difficult to deduce the contribution of acquisition activity to trends in concentration.

Lawrence White (1982) discusses the problems of measuring aggregate concentration and the evidence for the US. He argues that based on census employment data and census value-added data there is no evidence of an increase in aggregate concentration in the 1960s and 1970s. However, based on the manufacturing sector alone there appears *prima facie* evidence that aggregage concentration has increased over that period. White argues that these measures are fundamentally flawed since they include overseas operations. By eliminating overseas operations he concludes that there was no increase in aggregate concentration in the US in the 1960s and 1970s. This view, however, is not shared by all economists, see for example, Mueller (1982).

Available merger data are summarized in table 13.1. Column 1 is the data published by the Federal Trade Commission (FTC) which, up to 1979, published information on an annual basis. Whilst continuing to monitor acquisition activity the FTC has discontinued the publication of its data. Column 2 is a second series of merger data prepared by W. T. Grimm, a private sector research body, and is based on more comprehensive data. Column 3 shows a merger series produced by the US journal *Mergers and Acquisitions*.

An appreciation of merger trends since 1895 may be obtained by considering the works of Nelson (1959) and Thorp (1941) which was continued by the FTC up until 1979. Some historians have categorized US merger activity into five movements. The first wave of activity occurred between 1898 and 1903 and was prompted by the outlawing of collusion introduced by the Sherman Act 1893.

The second wave of activity occurred between 1926 and 1929 and was marked by the extension of market control by horizontal acquisitions. The attempt to form oligopolies in a number of product markets ended with the great crash of 1929. The third upsurge in takeovers materialized between 1940 and 1949. The Harvard economist, J. K. Butters, maintains that this was a period when a substantial number of smaller firms wanted to sell their businesses in order to avoid death duties.

The fourth movement in merger activity took place between 1955 and 1968 and was distinguished by the growth in conglomerates which occurred for a number of specific reasons. First, horizontal acquisitions were not achieving the returns initially anticipated and control over such activity, along with control of vertical integration, had been substantially increased.

Table 13.1 Mergers and acquisitions: number of completed transactions

Year	*FTC*	*W.T. Grimm*	*Mergers and Acquisitions (Journal)*
1960	1345		
1961	1724		
1962	1667		
1963	1479	1361	
1964	1797	1950	
1965	1893	2125	
1966	1746	2377	
1967	2384	2975	1354
1968	3932	4462	1829
1969	4542	6107	1712
1970	3089	5152	1318
1971	2633	4608	1269
1972	2839	4801	1263
1973	2359	4040	1064
1974	1474	2861	926
1975	1047	2297	981
1976	1171	2276	1145
1977	1183	2224	1209
1978	1245	2106	1452
1979		2128	1529
1980		1889	1565
1981		2395	2326
1982		2346	2297
1983		2533	2385
1984		2543	3194
1985		3001	3397
1986		3336	4024

Sources: FTC, *Statistical Report on Mergers and Acquisitions*, various years; W.T. Grimm, various years; *Mergers and Acquisitions Journal*, various years

Table 13.2 Average and median purchase price in the USA, 1969–84

Year	Value ($m)	Base[a]	Number of transactions valued ≥ $100m	Average price ($m)	Median price ($m)
1969	23711	2300	NA	10.3	NA
1970	16415	1671	NA	9.8	NA
1971	12619	1707	NA	7.4	NA
1972	16681	1930	15	8.6	2.8
1973	16665	1574	28	10.6	3.4
1974	12466	995	15	12.5	3.6
1975	11796	848	14	13.9	4.3
1976	20030	998	39	20.1	5.1
1977	21937	1032	41	21.3	6.6
1978	34180	1071	80	31.9	8.1
1979	43535	1047	83	41.6	8.5
1980	44346	890	94	49.8	9.3
1981	82618	1126	113	73.4	9.0
1982	53755	930	116	57.8	10.50
1983	73081	1077	138	67.9	16.5
1984	122224	1084	200	112.8	20.1
1985	179768	1320	270	136.2	21.1
1986	173137	1468	346	117.9	24.9

[a] The number of transactions which disclosed a purchase price.
Source: W. T. Grimm and Co.

Secondly, acceptance of the theory of diversification had become widespread, in the sense that businessmen accepted the idea of reducing the risk of business cycles by diversification. Thirdly, the accounting practice known as pooling of interests, as opposed to acquisition accounting, became more acceptable and led to the growth of such giants as ITT.

Whilst there is some agreement about the first four waves of merger activity there is some debate as to whether a fifth movement has indeed happened. The evidence in terms of numbers of companies acquired does not support the view that there has been a considerable upsurge in activity although there has been a modest increase. However, in terms of dollars paid there has been a dramatic upswing since 1979 (table 13.2). The number of transactions with a consideration of at least $100 million has increased dramatically since 1977 and both average and median prices have increased substantially particularly in 1984 and 1985. This change in acquisition trends occurred first in 1981 when healthy companies with good stock-market ratings began to be acquired by similar companies.

W. T. Grimm believe that the high level of transactions over $100 million is the result of three scenarios:

1. major strategic purchases to provide access to needed technology or to broaden product lines and expand markets;
2. aggressive investors who acquire shares in undervalued and vulnerable companies, forcing managements to seek merger partners or to repurchase shares at a premium (greenmail);
3. managements who form investor groups with the aid of leverage buyout specialists with the aim of making their corporations private.

In terms of merger currency, 1983 was the first year since 1973 in which stock exceeded cash as the main payment source. Also in 1983 payments constituting a mixture of instruments were at an all-time high. However, in both the USA and UK cash again became the major source of payment in 1984 and 1985.

Foreign acquisitions of US companies regained momentum in 1984 (table 13.3) with the total dollar value paid increasing from $5.9 billion in 1983 to $15.1 billion in 1984. The table includes both foreign purchases of domestic companies and purchases of foreign-based subsidiaries of US corporations. In terms of numbers of transactions, the UK and Canada were the major purchasers in 1984, although the Royal Dutch–Shell's (Netherlands) tender offer for the remaining shares in Shell was the highest dollar value acquisition. Over time it is apparent that the UK and Canada are respectively first and second in acquiring companies in the US and the same ranking applies to purchases of foreign companies by US corporations.

Table 13.3 Foreign buyers in the US, by country, 1979–86

Country of purchaser	*Number of acquisitions* 1979	1980	1981	1982	1983	1984	1985	1986	*Cumulative 1976–86*
UK	60	50	81	55	42	49	78	89	633
Canada	50	57	62	36	28	36	25	64	508
France	18	20	14	12	7	7	4	6	112
Switzerland	16	7	6	7	7	7	10	6	85
Netherlands	11	6	8	5	7	5	17	9	86
Japan	11	9	9	4	6	6	9	16	93
Australia	5	2	7	2	6	5	10	12	58
Sweden	4	8	7	4	7	8	7	11	61
FRG	37	14	14	6	2	4	12	19	162
Other	24	14	26	23	17	24	25	32	289
Total foreign buyers	236	187	234	154	125	151	197	264	2087

Source: W.T. Grimm & Co.

The level of US acquisitions by foreign investors has not exceeded the levels of activity in 1979 and 1981, and probably reflects the weakness of the dollar in those years. With the dollar strengthening in 1983 the number of foreign purchases dropped considerably from the 1981 peak. The most noticeable decrease was by the Federal Republic of Germany with only two acquisitions in 1983 compared with 37 in 1979. Perhaps difficulties encountered by some FRG companies, such as Volkswagen, helped to discourage such activity. However, it would appear that currency fluctuation is no longer a major factor in foreign investment, since the dollar continued to be strong throughout 1984. The achievement of growth and ready access to a large homogeneous market may have become more important factors in decision-making. Historically foreign acquirers try to buy market share quickly which means that the medium purchase price paid is higher than for all acquisitions in the US since bigger companies are being acquired. For example, in the fourth quarter of 1983 the Huhtamaki Group of Finland made three significant acquisitions in a few days in order to take a sizeable market share of the US confectionary market.

Another noticeable feature is that foreign acquirers often acquire companies with strong management teams and retain them. This has had the effect that the takeover must generally be agreed rather than be hostile. The consequence of this is that foreigners normally pay an excess when compared with the average for US acquisitions.

To put merger and acquisition activity into some perspective foreign direct investment in the US grew 11 per cent in 1985 to \$183 billion according to statistics issued by the Department of Commerce. In contrast aggregate direct investment overseas in 1985 by the US increased 9 per cent to \$233 billion.

These statistics include investments in holdings of 10 per cent or more by foreign investors and exclude other portfolio and asset investment. In terms of aggregate assets at the end of 1984, investment in the US by foreigners totalled \$800 billion whereas investment abroad by the US reached \$900 billion.

3. MERGER CONTROL

Anti-trust laws

The US has a large body of measures aimed at maintaining a competitive environment. The first important anti-trust statute was the Sherman Act 1890 which effectively outlawed monopoly. A uniform federal law was imposed concerning the unenforceability of contracts in restraint of trade and monopoly, attempts to monopolize and conspiracy to monopolize, which were all made illegal.

One of the weaknesses of the Sherman Act was that some of the sections were too general to be enforced. In an attempt to make the Act more specific section 7 of the Clayton Act 1914 prohibited companies from acquiring other companies 'where in any line of commerce in any section of the country, the effect of such acquisitions may be substantially to lessen competition, or to tend to create a monopoly'. A further development in 1914 was the creation of the Federal Trade Commission (FTC), by an Act of that name, with the purpose of overseeing the competitive environment and prohibiting anti-competitive behaviour.

Further weaknesses became apparent and in 1936 the Robinson–Patman Act was passed dealing with price discrimination. Section 7 of the Clayton Act was found to be largely ineffective as it applied only to the acquisition of shares and not of assets. In an attempt to close this loophole the Celler–Kefauver Act 1950 extended the provisions to the acquisition of assets and also specified that a merger would be assessed on both a product line and a geographic basis. Since then a considerable amount of time has been spent in defining the terms 'relevant products' and 'geographic markets'.

Criminal prosecution for breaches of the Sherman Act are instigated by the Department of Justice and the FTC has the power to start investigations, to rule on questions of law and to issue orders to prevent actions in restraint of trade. It is important to point out however, that the guidelines offered by the Department of Justice outline the likelihood of a challenge in the courts. The decision as to whether to undertake an acquisition should be made in the context that the legality of a merger is ultimately determined by judges and not by the Department of Justice. Nevertheless for a foreign investor to attempt to acquire a US corporation which would lead to a breach of the Department of Justice's guidelines is likely to encounter substantial delays and litigation costs.

Department of Justice 1968 merger guidelines

In 1968 the department issued merger guidelines, which made it very difficult for horizontal and vertical mergers in adjacent stages of production and distribution to take place. This had the effect of encouraging conglomerate acquisitions. FTC statistics show that in the late 1940s and early 1950s conglomerates accounted for only 3 per cent of all assets acquired, but by the mid-1970s this had risen to 49 per cent. In the past the Justice Department has brought cases against conglomerates, but all have failed. Under the Reagan administration, no conglomerate mergers have been challenged by the department.

The 1968 guidelines specified the following thresholds which, if exceeded, would normally lead to a challenge by the Department:

1. Horizontal mergers – if the four-firm concentration ratio is less than 75 per cent a merger will normally be challenged where the acquirer's market is at least 25 per cent and the acquiree is 1 per cent or more; if the four-firm concentration ratio exceeds 75 per cent the percentages fall to 15 per cent and 1 per cent respectively.
2. Vertical mergers – where a supplying firm has at least 10 per cent of the sales in its market and the purchasing firm at least 6 per cent of the total purchases in that market, the merger will ordinarily be challenged.
3. Conglomerate mergers – where reciprocal buying or market dominance occurs.

Williams Act 1968

A further development in 1968 was the passing of the country's first tender offer statute, the Williams Act. Trends had changed so much in the 1960s that there was substantial lobbying for controls of tender offers. For example, in 1960 there were only eight cash tender offers for listed companies but by 1967 this had risen to 107. Vulnerable managements obtained the support of Senator Harrison Williams but his original Bill was amended so much that the Act reflected a balance of the interests of the tender offeror and target enterprise. The Act provided for increased disclosure, a minimum tender period and some anti-fraud measures. Those demanding legislation were very disappointed and their attention was then turned to state legislatures – by 1981 36 states had adopted tended offer regulations.

Hart–Scott–Rodino Anti-Trust Improvements Act 1976

This Act introduced the requirement that the Justice Department and Federal Trade Commission be informed of and supplied with information on a merger, if it meets either of two criteria. The first is if either party has worldwide assets of sales of $100 million or more and the other participating enterprise has sales or assets of $10 million or more. The second criterion relates to the size of transaction and is satisfied if a participant holds more than 15 per cent of the voting shares or assets of the other participant.

If a merger meets either criterion, the merger participants are required to notify the FTC and the acquisition is then deferred for 30 days to allow the Department of Justice or the FTC to make a decision as to whether a reference should be made to the Federal District Court. The time-period may be extended a further ten days, if additional information is required. A decision is then made by the inter-agency liaison committee of the Justice Department and FTC.

Department of Justice 1982 merger guidelines

These guidelines attempted to provide a set of objective criteria that would enable businessmen to decide whether the Department of Justice would challenge a merger. In particular, the guidelines took a different attitude to some mergers, on the grounds that most 'do not threaten competition and that many are in fact pro-competitive and benefit consumers'. The department became less interested in both conglomerate and vertical mergers. Instead the guidelines focused on horizontal mergers, although they are marginally more lenient than the 1968 guidelines.

The guidelines deal with the problems of defining product and geographic markets. Product markets are determined by asking how many buyers would shift to other products and how many sellers would enter the market if a 5 per cent price rise was instituted by the merger participants. A final product market is determined when a small price rise would be profitable to the sellers, but would not induce a significant number of buyers to leave or sellers to enter. The objective of this exercise is to ascertain whether a merger will lead to an oligopoly with the possibility of increased collusion.

A geographic market is determined when firms located elsewhere would not be able to sell sufficient quantities of the product within the market to make a small increase in price unprofitable within a period of one year. Sellers would therefore be able to increase profits by increasing price.

The guidelines also contain a discussion about the possibility of extending geographic markets beyond the boundaries of the USA. However, the guidelines note that effective international competition may not occur because of restraints in trade such as tariffs, exchange rates and political constraints.

An important change in these guidelines is the introduction of new techniques to assess competitive effects and to determine markets. The Herfindahl–Hirschman Index (HHI) is preferred to the four-firm concentration ratio (CR4) as the appropriate measure of concentration within a market. The four-firm concentration ratio measures the extent to which the top four firms monopolize a market whereas the HHI gives weight to the importance of each of the firms engaged in a market. The HHI does this by summing the squares of each individual market share. For example, if there are eight firms in a market X with market shares as follows:

A	30%	E	12%
B	16%	F	6%
C	14%	G	5%
D	13%	H	4%

CR4 = 30+16+14+13 = 73%

HHI = $30^2+16^2+14^2+13^2+12^2+6^2+5^2+4^2 = 1742$

If firms F and G merge, the new CR4 and HHI would be:

CR4 = 30+16+14+13 = 73%

HHI = $30^2+16^2+14^2+13^2+12^2+11^2+4^2 = 1802$

It is noticeable that whilst the CR4 has remained the same the HHI has increased by 60 points. Mathematicians will quickly realise that the increase in HHI may be calculated by doubling the product of the market shares of the merging firms,
i.e. $2 \times 6 \times 5 = 60$

The HHI may range from a maximum of 10,000 when the market is controlled by one firm, towards zero, where there are many equal sized firms. The advantage of the HHI is that relative weights are attached to each company, with greater emphasis being given to larger firms.

In addition to the introduction of the HHI measure, the guidelines distinguish three categories of market:

1. unconcentrated markets where HHI is less than 1000;
2. moderately concentrated markets with the HHI between 1000 and 1800;
3. highly concentrated markets where HHI exceeds 1800.

Figure 13.1 shows the National Economic Research Associates' flow chart of enforcement policies, which neatly summarizes the factors that the Department of Justice will consider in deciding whether to challenge a merger. In the example given above of a horizontal merger between companies F and G, the merger would lead to the HHI exceeding 1800 with an increase in excess of 50 points but less than 100 points. The Department of Justice would then consider the case carefully and their decision whether to challenge the merger would be dependent upon additional factors (see figure 13.1).

Department of Justice 1984 merger guidelines

On 14 June 1984 the Department of Justice published a 51-page document revising its anti-trust merger guidelines. The main revisions are in five key areas: market definition and measurement; factors affecting the significance of concentration and market-share data; treatment of foreign competition; efficiencies; and failing divisions of healthy firms. The major points are summarized below:

Market definition and measurement. The so-called '5 per cent test' is not an inflexible standard which is used in all cases, but is an analytical tool with which to analyse some types of evidence. In certain cases the test will define a market too broadly or too narrowly.

Factors affecting the significance of concentration and market-share data. The department does not merely collect data and come to a decision based on a mathematical formula; other factors are also relevant. However except in extraordinary circumstances, the department will not challenge a horizontal merger where the post-merger HHI does not exceed 1000 points. Where a merger results in a HHI of between 1000 and 1800 points, a challenge will normally be made if the merger results in an increase of at least 100 points. For mergers which exceed an HHI of 1800, a challenge will not be made if the increase in HHI does not exceeed 50 points.

Treatment of foreign competition. For the first time, foreign producers selling into US markets will be assigned market shares in the same way as indigenous firms.

Efficiencies. The 1982 guidelines gave the impression that efficiencies would only be considered in 'extraordinary cases'. The new guidelines emphasize that efficiencies will be given their appropriate weight in all cases.

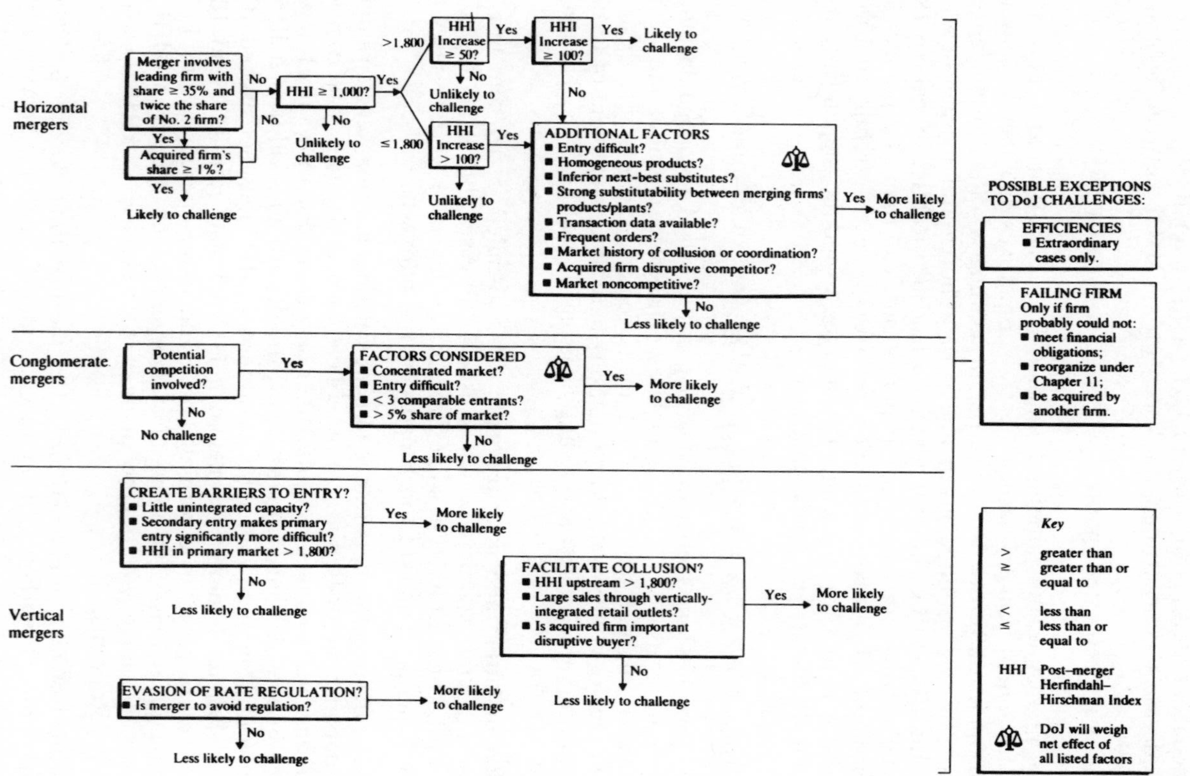

Figure 13.1 Department of Justice Merger guidelines

Failing divisions of healthy firms. The department emphasizes that it will consider the financial condition of firms in evaluating the competitive significance of their market shares. In addition, if the acquisition of a failing firm significantly increased efficiency, that fact will be considered.

Interest in the new guidelines has centred on foreign-company shares in US markets, especially since there are difficulties surrounding quantitative data on import penetration. However, import penetration appears to be particularly acute in radios and televisions, semi conductors, clothing, women's footwear, and pulp mill products. In addition, concern has been expressed about import penetration in traditional industries, such as cars and steel.

Securities laws

In addition to the anti-trust laws, there are federal securities laws which are administered by the Securities and Exchange Commission (SEC). The SEC seeks to ensure full and fair disclosure to investors through the Securities Exchange Acts of 1933 and 1934. One of the implications for acquirers occurs where a foreign investor intends to acquire a US corporation by issuing securities since it will be necessary to file a share listing application with the stock exchange on which a listing is required. A listing is only required where a market is required for trading subsequent to the initial offer since the offer is made to the public and not through the exchange. The listing application and registration requirements are unique to each exchange.In order to register with the SEC, duplicates of the listing application together with a completed registration statement must be submitted. All information that is required to be filed with the SEC is available for public inspection.

The first stage of the registration process for new issues is normally to appoint an investment banker (underwriter) who, amongst other things, will assist in preparing the registration forms which will have to be filed with the SEC before a public offering is made. Where problems arise, it is possible to have a pre-filing conference with the SEC. Once the problems are resolved and the audited financial statements for the last three years are available, the issuing company's team of experts will prepare and submit the registration document to its board of directors and subsequently to the SEC. The financial community is alerted to a forthcoming offer by a 'tombstone ad' which can be placed in a number of periodicals such as *Business Week* and the *Wall Street Journal*. At this point the advertisement does not constitute an offer to subscribe for securities. Immediately before approval by the SEC becomes effective, a 'due diligence meeting' is held so that underwriters, accountants and the company's counsel have all the necessary information. This is essential as participants are liable for breaches of the securities laws.

To comply with SEC regulations, foreign investors must be prepared to restate their accounts in accordance with US generally accepted accounting principles or, alternatively, to reconcile the differences. In practice, most companies reconcile the differences on a footnote to the accounts.

Where no securities are issued in a takeover it may still be necessary for Form 8-K Current Report to be completed where the transaction is material. Nevertheless, a cash tender offer is usually the form of consideration used by foreign investors to acquire US corporations since there are considerably less formalities to comply with and the merger may be completed in far less time. However, there are dangers to cash offers since thorough prebid analysis of the offeree is even more crucial than with a share exchange. For example, with a cash offer the offeror will normally acquire a foothold in a listed company by purchasing securities in the market place. If a bid is then made for the rest of the securities and it fails, say because of a successful counter-bid by another party, the original offeror still has his foothold within the company.

Where more than 5 per cent of a class of securities of a US 'registered' company is acquired for cash, it will be necessary to comply with the tender offer rules as laid out in Schedule 14D-1. The information which must be filed with the SEC includes the purpose of the tender offer, the source of funds used in the tender, the number of shares already owned in the offeree and transactions therein in the last 60 days.

4. TAXATION

Background

Taxes in the US are raised at the federal, state and local levels. The US income tax system is a classical system of taxation in contrast to the imputation system which is more common in EEC countries. The US system has been in operation since 1913 and is now based on the Internal Revenue Code of 1954 and its subsequent amendments and the Tax Reform Act (TRA) 1986. The code is administered by the Internal Revenue Service (IRS) which is an agency of the Treasury Department.

At the time of writing fundamental changes to the Tax Code are being implemented which involve cutting rates of taxation, increasing personal exemptions and creating a minimum rate of tax.

All corporations organized in the US are subject to income tax with the exception of nontaxable or special types of companies. Companies not subject to income tax include possession corporations, real estate investment trusts, regulated investment companies, small business corporations and tax-exempt organizations.

One of the tax problems faced by foreign corporations is the existence of unitary tax which existed in 23 states in 1985, e.g. California. The basis of such a tax system is that it ignores group relationships as well as national and state boundaries. An assessment for tax is based on worldwide earnings which is apportioned on some basis such as sales, payroll or property, regardless of the actual earnings of the corporation. This system of taxation is very controversial, so much so, that pressure from foreign corporations together with the threat of retaliation by overseas governments had led the federal government into appointing a review of the unitary tax system. Nevertheless the Supreme Court has upheld the constitutionality of unitary tax. Lobbying from governments and MNEs became so intense in 1986 that pressure was applied by the federal government on certain states. The effect of this was that on 5 September 1986 the state governor of California signed a bill which permits MNEs in California to be able to elect to be taxed on a water's-edge basis rather than on a unitary basis. The bill is effective from 1 January 1988 and leaves only Alaska, Montana and North Dakota still raising tax on a unitary basis. However, in California, tax may only be based on a water's-edge basis on payment of a levy of 0.03 per cent of a company's sales, payroll and property in California and once the election is made it must remain in force for at least 10 years.

A feature of the US tax system is that in some instances an IRS ruling can be obtained before a transaction is undertaken. However, the ruling may take several months to obtain and once given, the decision constitutes public information with the proviso that the names and identity of the parties involved are deleted. Access by the public to the deleted information is provided under the Freedom of Information Act.

Federal income tax was normally charged at 46 per cent regardless of whether income is retained or distributed. However, under TRA the maximum corporate tax rate will be 34 per cent from 1988 and a corporation distributing dividends to its shareholders will receive a deduction equal to 10 per cent of such an amount. In 1986, lower rates of tax applied to the first $100,000 on taxable income as follows:

Taxable income		
Over	*Not over*	*Rate on excess*
$	$	%
0	25,000	15
25,000	50,000	18
50,000	75,000	30
75,000	100,00	40
100,000		46

In 1987 the transitional top marginal corporate tax rate is reduced to 40 per cent and under the TRA the following rates apply from 1988:

Taxable income		
Over	*Not over*	*Rate on excess*
$	$	%
0	50,000	15
50,000	75,000	22
75,000	100,000	34
100,000		lesser of 5 per cent or $13,250

Since corporations are allowed to elect certain methods of deducting expenses which may affect the timing of earnings, known as tax preferences, the US imposes a minimum tax. The minimum tax of 15 per cent is equal to the total of the tax preference items which exceed the greater of $10,000 or the corporation's current year regular tax liability. Under TRA, the minimum rate of tax is 20 per cent of the excess 'alternative minimum taxable income' exceeding $40,000. At present, federal income taxes contain provisions which produce permanent tax savings which has the effect of lowering the statutory tax rate. The effective tax rate may be lower because of incentives introduced such as the investment tax credit which permits a credit against federal tax equal to 10 per cent of the purchase cost of certain depreciable property. However, under TRA, the investment tax credit would be repealed for property placed in service after 31 December 1985. Other incentives include tax-exempt interest on state and municipal bonds and accelerated depreciation in excess of book depreciation.

In calculating federal taxable income the following common deductions are permitted:

1. *Business expenses* – provided that transactions are at arm's-length nearly all business expenses incurred are deductible regardless of where paid, provided they are not capital expenditures. However, under TRA only 80 per cent of business meals and entertainment expenses will be allowable against tax.
2. *Depreciation* – in order to stimulate investment, the Accelerated Cost Recovery System (ACRS) was introduced in 1981 which permits recovery of capital costs when property is purchased. There are few restrictions with respect to the type of asset which this system applies except that land, inventory and goodwill are all excluded. The ACRS applies to all types of business. Provided property is used in a trade or business, all new or used tangible property placed in service after 31 December 1980 is eligible to be included in the ACRS. This system classifies tangible property into five categories which are referred to as three-year, five-year, ten-year, 15-year or 18-year assets. These classifications refer to the period over which the capital cost may be recovered although the period may be extended but not shortened. For example, personal property which includes plant and machinery and fixtures and fittings would fall into the five-year category whereas vehicles including light trucks are classified as three-year property.

   Under TRA, ACRS will be replaced with IDS which groups assets into ten classes requiring depreciation over periods from five to 36 years. IDS classes 1–9 allow the double declining balance method with a switch to the straight-line method at a time to maximize the depreciation allowance.

   For assets purchased before 1981 the ACRS does not apply but a variety of methods of allocation existed which included straight-line, declining balance or sum-of-years-digits. Anti-avoidance provisions exist to prevent assets which were purchased before 1961 from being brought into ACRS.

Since intangible assets, such as goodwill do not have determinable useful lives they are not eligible for ACRS. Previously trademarks and tradename expenditures could, at the election of the taxpayer, be deducted ratably over 60 months or more but TRA has repealed this rule. Another important point is that the depreciation methods used for tax purposes need not be the same as those used for financial statement purposes.

3. *Interest* – is normally deductible on either a cash or accrual basis depending upon whether the undertaking is a cash-basis corporation or accrual-basis corporation. Interest on a debt used to purchase or to continue to hold tax-exempt securities is not deductible.
4. *Inventory* – stock may be valued on a first in, first out basis (FIFO), on a last in, first out basis (LIFO) or by using an average cost method depending upon what is used in the annual financial statements and for credit purposes. It is permissible for a US subsidiary of a foreign corporation to adopt LIFO even though the method is not used by the parent undertaking.
5. *Trading losses* – such losses are called net operating losses for US tax purposes. Previously any losses incurred could be carried back three years to offset against available taxable income or carried forward for a period up to 15 years. A taxpayer could irrevocably elect to carry forward the loss rather than to carry back the loss. This could be an advantage if rates of tax before the loss was incurred were relatively low compared with those anticipated in the future. However, TRA stipulates that deductions for net operating losses are to be limited to the pre-acquisition equity of the corporation although there will be an unlimited carry forward period.
6. *Research and development expenditure* – such costs may be either capitalized or deducted against income regardless of where the expenses were incurred. A taxpayer may elect to amortize any research and development costs which have been capitalized on an equitable basis over 60 or more months.
7. *Taxes* – for federal tax purposes, state and local income taxes, employment taxes, and real property personal property taxes are all deductible.

As far as income is concerned, all income regardless of where earned is liable to federal corporation tax. However, all foreign income taxes are offset against the US liability regardless of whether a double tax relief treaty exists. The rules relating to the circumstances under which a foreign tax is allowed are very complex. Gross income for tax purposes includes rents, royalties, interest received and dividends. With respect to dividends received the general rule is that they are all taxable. Previously, a domestic corporation however, could deduct 85 per cent of dividends received from other taxable domestic companies from gross income. However, under

TRA the dividends received deduction has been reduced from 85 to 80 per cent. Dividends received from a wholly owned corporation are not subject to taxation.

Foreign subsidiaries and branches

Income earned by a foreign subsidiary is normally not taxable in the US until distributed to its US parent company. For taxation purposes a foreign corporation is one that is not organized under the laws of the US. However there is a complex set of rules that apply to some foreign corporations whereby the corporation's income may be deemed to be distributed even though it actually has not been. Such income is referred to as Subpart F and is apportioned to shareholders at the end of the corporation's tax year.

In contrast, the income of a branch of a foreign corporation is allocated as either active business income or passive investment income. Income which is effectively connected with the conduct of a trade or business within the US is taxed at the ordinary corporate tax rate whereas income not effectively connected with the conduct of a trade or business in the US, e.g. some interest and dividend income earned in the US, is taxed at 30 per cent. Provided that the foreign corporation files a tax return in the US its US branch may deduct allowable expenses from its income. The deductions may include apportionments such as a reasonable proportion of foreign head office expenses.

Another important difference between a foreign subsidiary and foreign branch is that dividends repatriated to head office are normally subject to withholding taxes in the former cases whereas they are not in the latter case. TRA adds a second level branch tax equal to 30 per cent of the foreign corporation's effectively connected income plus interest deducted by the branch against the effectively connected income. This provision is subject to any treaties in force. At present, however, when the foreign corporation pays a dividend its US branch is liable to a withholding tax called 'second dividend' tax. This arises where at least 50 per cent of the income of the foreign corporation is earned by its US branch. One way of avoiding the imposition of withholding taxes is to establish a separate corporation in a country which has a tax treaty with the US whereby withholding taxes are not imposed by the US to do business in the US, sometimes referred to as 'treaty shopping'. In the past such arrangements included the Netherlands and Netherland Antilles although this particular agreement was terminated in 1987. The advantage of such an arrangement is that the US branch of the tax treaty corporation would be subject to US tax at 46 per cent rather than 62.2 per cent where there is no treaty arrangement. The 62.2 per cent rate can occur because the income of the branch is subject to 46 per cent corporation tax and the residual income of 54 per cent becomes liable to a further withholding tax on repatriated earnings where there is no treaty arrangement.

Control

An important distinction needs to be made between legal control and control for tax purposes. Whereas corporate control is achieved when more than 50 per cent of the voting shares are acquired, control for tax purposes generally refers to ownership of at least 80 per cent of the voting power or value of the stock of the acquired corporation [IRC Section 1563 (a)(1)]. A further distinction is that a 'corporate merger' refers to the acquisition of a company followed by the liquidation of either the acquiree or acquirer company.

Consolidated tax returns

Provided the 80 per cent control condition is met, US corporations may file a consolidated tax return for an affiliated group. The advantage of being able to file such a return is that operating and capital profits may be offset against losses within the group and intercompany dividends and interest paid are tax free because of the aggregation process. However, some further clarification of the concept of an affiliated group is required since a foreign corporation cannot be a member of an affiliated group. If a foreign parent company directly owns two US subsidiaries A and B, companies A and B do not constitute an affiliated group since there is no direct domestic common ownership (control) between them. However, if the foreign parent transfers A to B so that A is now the subsidiary of B, then A and B can constitute an affiliated group. Alternatively, if the foreign parent creates a US holding company C which owns A and B, then A, B and C can constitute an affiliated group. Consequently a foreign investor in the US will normally own a subsidiary which acts as a holding company for its other US subsidiaries.

Capital gains tax

A capital gain is calculated by deducting cost less depreciation from the sale proceeds of an asset. Unlike the UK there is no index-linking for the effects of inflation. Capital gains may be offset against capital losses for the year in which they occurred or a loss may be carried back three years with any unrelieved amount being eligible to be carried forward for a period up to five years. In 1986 the rate of tax is 28 per cent for assets held for more than 12 months or six months where the asset is acquired after 22 June 1984 but before 1 January 1988. However, TRA has repealed use of the capital gains rate for corporations. Thus, capital gains would be subject to the new 34 per cent corporate tax rate.

Special rules apply where mergers and acquisitions involve US real estate. These rules are of particular importance to many US and some foreign corporations that constitute US real property holding companies

(USRPHC). In most cases where a US corporation liquidates into its foreign parent the transaction is not taxable. However, section 897 IRC stipulates that when a substantial part of the assets consists of real estate then liquidation into a foreign parent constitutes a taxable transaction on the realised gain. Additional provisions on real estate are provided in section 1445 of the Foreign Investment in Real Property Act (FIRPTA). This Act specifies that a foreign person selling US real property investments (USRPIs) is liable for tax on the capital gain. A USRPI is one with a direct interest in US real estate or an interest in a US company in which at least one-half of its assets constitutes US real property. Since the Tax Reform Act of 1984 the sale of USRPIs is subject, in most circumstances, to withholding tax of 10 per cent of the gross proceeds.

Taxation implications of mergers and acquisitions

Implications for the acquiring company

An acquisition of shares or assets in the US is treated as a taxable transaction to the seller if it does not constitute a reorganization as defined by section 308 of the Internal Revenue Code. An essential feature of a reorganization is that the acquirer either continues the acquired company's historic business or uses a significant part of the acquiree's assets in the business. Where the acquirer and acquiree are in the same business, it is normally presumed that the business continues. Provided that the transaction represents an exchange of voting stock or assets solely or substantially for stock the acquisition would normally be deemed to be tax-free. No capital gain or loss would accrue and the tax basis of the assets would be carried forward. The assets of a business constitute its historic business assets including intangibles as well as tangibles.

Not only is the transaction deemed to be tax-free in the above case but provided certain strict conditions are fulfilled it may be possible to utilize tax losses of the acquiree. However, as previously mentioned, TRA will limit deductions for net operating losses, in any tax year, to the pre-acquisition equity of the corporation. The carryforward period will be unlimited. Where the transaction constitutes a reorganization, with the exception that a de minimis amount of the consideration is in a form other than qualifying securities e.g. cash, the transaction may be deemed to be partly taxable and partly non-taxable. If the transaction fails to comply with the conditions specified in section 368 the reorganization will be taxable to the seller but not to the buyer. Provided a transaction qualifies as tax-free, it must be treated as such with no election available for taxable treatment. It is essential therefore that the regulations are complied with to ensure that the desired outcome is achieved. If however, the transaction is designated as a taxable asset acquisition or an acquisition of shares followed by a section 3 election, then the asset value used is its fair market value, which leads to higher depreciation, lower taxable income and increased cash flow. This is known in the US as the step-up in tax basis.

Before the passing of the Tax Equity and Fiscal Responsibility Act 1982 (TEFRA), an acquirer who purchased an acquiree with shares could only obtain a step-up in asset value if the acquiree was liquidated. TEFRA introduced a new section 338 to the IRC whereby a purchase by shares may be treated as a purchase of assets if an election is made. This election ensures that the step-up basis is applied and may be made within 75 days of the time in which at least 80 per cent of the voting shares are secured and 80 per cent of all other securities purchased.

A taxable transaction can lead to problems of allocation between assets and conflict between the acquirer and acquiree. Since depreciation is allowed on tangible assets but not on intangible assets the purchaser will wish to allocate as much of the consideration to tangible assets. In contrast, the seller will wish for the converse to occur in order to subject his gain to gains tax rather than ordinary income tax. Consequently an election by the purchaser under section 338 may lead to higher taxes being paid by the seller. Such problems need to be addressed at the negotiation stage.

Implications for the acquirer's shareholders

There are no significant taxation implications affecting the acquirer's shareholders.

Implications for the acquiree company

The implications for the acquiree's company depend upon whether a transaction is deemed to be taxable or non-taxable. Where an acquisition is for cash the amount received is the cash amount and the difference between that and the cost represents the capital gain or loss. Cost represents the original purchase price less depreciation benefits.

A capital gain is recognized to the selling shareholders in the year in which acquisition takes place unless part of the consideration is delayed in which case the transaction may qualify as an installment sale under IRC section 453. In such a case the gain is recognized as the seller receives the cash.

A problem may also arise when allocating the consideration among the purchased assets. Where stock is purchased the purchase price may be allocated *pro rata* to form the new tax basis. Normally the IRS will accept the allocation of the consideration between tangibles and intangibles on the basis of the contract. However, where the IRS is not satisfied that the allocation is fair and represents an arm's-length transaction a new allocation may be imposed. The acquiree will be taxed on realised capital gains which will be allocated for tax purposes as either ordinary income or capital gains. However, if the acquiree is liquidated within 12 months of the transaction and the assets are distributed to shareholders, no gain or loss to such a corporation is recognized and clawback of depreciation and investment credits may take place if the corporation is not at least 80 per cent owned.

Where the transaction constitutes a tax-free reorganization the acquiree company will not suffer any tax liability. The same is true for a 'statutory merger'.

Implications for the acquiree's shareholders

Where the transaction represents solely an exchange of stock no tax will become due to the acquiree's shareholders as an interest in his original investment is retained whereas if the exchange is for cash a realised capital gain or loss will accrue for tax purposes. Where a capital gain arises 60 per cent of the long-term gain may be excluded so that the maximum marginal rate of tax becomes 20 per cent, i.e. 40 per cent of the highest marginal rate of tax for individuals of 50 per cent (1986 rates).

Tax planning

If an acquisition is to be partially financed by borrowings and at least 80 per cent of the voting shares of a US corporation are to be acquired it will normally be better to borrow as much as possible in the US. This is because the interest is tax deductible although it is important that thin capitalization should not arise. The most usual arrangement is for a foreign corporation to set up a subsidiary in the US which acts as a holding company for future acquisitions. A further advantage of such an arrangement is that the group would be able to submit a consolidated US tax return.

An alternative arrangement is for the US holding company to borrow outside the US although there are two disadvantages to such an approach. First, the thin capitalization restrictions still apply, and secondly a withholding tax of 30 per cent may be levied on the interest. Provided that US rates of interest are not unduly high it is more likely for borrowings to be cheaper and also more convenient when raised in the US. Furthermore, one of the advantages of investing in the US is access to sophisticated financial markets.

As mentioned previously the withholding tax on interest may be reduced by forming a finance company in say the Netherlands. One of the essential requirements of such a scheme is that the foreign subsidiary must be able to service the debt and repay capital without recourse to its parent company. One of the aims of such an operation is to shift profits from the US subsidiary to the offshore finance company in order to reduce the tax burden. However, the IRS has many rulings which deal with transactions which have 'no business purpose' or which constitute 'sham transactions'. Furthermore, the IRS may adopt a 'substance over form' approach. Such rulings mean that transactions undertaken solely to avoid or reduce taxation may be challenged in the Courts.

A further factor to take into consideration is that if less than 80 per cent of shares are to be acquired a consolidated tax return cannot be submitted. Consequently the interest costs borne by the holding company formed in the US may not be offset against the income of the newly acquired company. An additional point to make is that whilst there are no capital taxes or stamp duties imposed at the federal level they may be imposed by individual states.

With regard to cross-border acquisitions there is no discrimination between foreign corporations with US subsidiaries and US corporations. However, the comments concerning transactions with no commercial substance should be borne in mind in tax planning.

5. ACCOUNTING

Background

Since 1973, the Financial Accounting Standards Board (FASB) has had the responsibility of establishing generally acccepted accounting principles (GAAP) for US-registered corporations. The FASB is a private-sector organization independent of the institute of Certified Public Accountants. The predecessor to the FASB was the Accounting Princples Board (APB), which issued opinions and interpretations on contentious accounting mergers. The SEC is a government-sponsored regulatory organization which seeks to administer the Securities Acts. The Securities Act 1933 provides for full disclosure of all material facts affecting securities which are offered for sale to the public and also to prevent fraudulent acts. The Securities Act 1934 imposed further detailed requirements to ensure full and fair disclosure of financial information and sought to further regulate securities market activities and to control credit in purchasing securities.

The SEC is an extremely important regulatory body which, in 1984, increased its enforcement activities in an attempt to reduce corporate accounting 'misdemeanours'. 'Misdemeanours' include euphemisms such as 'cute' or 'creative' accounting as well as the obvious, 'cooked books'.

Accounting for groups, acquisitions and mergers

The SEC, acting under the authority of Section 19 of the Securities Act 1933, has issued Regulation S-X which is the authoritative statement on form, content and disclosure in financial statements. Since the objective of SEC accounting requirements is to ensure fair disclosure of information, Article 3A of Regulation S-X specifies that consolidated accounts should be prepared. However, subsidiaries whose accounting year-end is not coterminous with the registrant should not be included where the difference exceeds 93 days. In addition, if the registrant possesses foreign subsidiaries which operate under political or economic restrictions the subsidiary should not be included in the consolidation. The 93-day rule does not apply to companies which are less than 50 per cent owned since the equity method should be adopted to account for affiliates.

Rule 3–16(a) of Regulation S-X requires disclosure of the underlying consolidation principles and rule 4–04 specifies the details which should be provided. As well as the underlying principles for inclusion or exclusion of subsidiaries, a list of companies involved should be provided including any changes during the year.

The underlying objective of such statements is that stated in Accounting Series Release No. 3: 'the purpose of a consolidated balance sheet is to reflect the financial condition of a parent company and its subsidiaries as if they were a single organization.' Further accounting recommendations come from Accounting Research Bulletins (ARB) which form part of GAAP. Essentially ARB 51 and ARB 43, ch. 12 specify that normally consolidated accounts should be prepared for groups of companies. However, where subsidiaries are involved in activities which are completely diverse from the parent or where control is temporarily restricted in any way, the relevant subsidiary may be exluded from the consolidation process. In such circumstances a summary of assets and liabilities, income or loss and the parent's equity should be provided.

Where consolidated accounts are produced there is no requirement for the parent company to disclose the income statement or balance sheet of the holding company (ARB 51.23). In addition, there is no requirement for the accounting policies of subsidiaries to be the same although they must comply with GAAP.

The method of accounting for business combinations in the US is provided by APB Opinions 16 and 17. APB Opinion 18 deals with accounting for the acquisition of a minority interest in a company using the equity method.

APBO 16 (1970) – Business combinations

It is important to note that business combinations in the US are accounted for either as purchases (acquisition accounting) or pooling-of-interests (merger accounting). Unlike some countries, e.g. the UK, the methods are not alternatives, so that provided 12 specific conditions are met the pooling-of-interests approach must be used (APBO 16.43–48). These conditions are summarized below:

1. Each of the combining companies should be autonomous for at least two years before they plan to combine. This precludes subsidiaries or divisions of another company, since they are not autonomous.
2. The companies should be independent of each other, so that not more than 10 per cent of the voting ordinary shares may be held by one of the participants in the company.
3. The combination should result from one transaction or one plan implemented within a year, to avoid significant changes in the ownership interests of the participants which might result if the transaction was completed over an extended period of time.
4. The transaction should result from an offer with identical rights to the majority of the existing voting shares. At least 90 per cent of the ordinary shares of the combining companies should be exchanged.
5. Neither of the combining companies may change the equity interest of its ordinary shareholders in anticipation of the combination.

6. The purchase of treasury stock to accomplish the combination is prohibited.
7. Individual shareholders should retain their proportionate share ownership *vis-à-vis* one another.
8. The voting rights of shareholders must not be restricted or deprived as a result of the combination.
9. The total consideration involved should be completed at the time of the merger.
10. Ownership of the participants should be continued. As such there should be no agreement for the retirement or reacquisition of shares involved in the combination.
11. All shareholders involved in the combination should be treated equally.
12. There should be no agreement to sell a significant part of the business within two years of the combination.

Since the conditions of APBO16 with respect to merger accounting are fairly stringent, it is not surprising that the number of qualifying transactions is low. In the majority of cases acquisition accounting is applied. However, prior to the issuance of APBO16 the trend had been to account for business combinations using the pooling-of-interests approach presumably to maximize reported income.

APBO16 defines a purchase as a 'business combination of two or more corporations in which an important part of the ownership interest in the acquired corporation or corporations is eliminated'. For a pooling approach to be valid both continuity of ownership and continuity of the existing business are necessary conditions.

APBO17 (1970) – Intangible assets

The recognition of goodwill is important in relation to mergers and acquisitions for taxation and accounting reasons. We have already discussed the taxation implications of the allocation of the consideration between tangible and intangible assets. Goodwill is important from an accounting viewpoint because it may be an intangible asset purchased on the acquisition of an unincorporated business but also because it will normally arise on consolidation when using the purchase method of accounting for business combinations. Goodwill will not arise using the pooling-of-interests approach as it is apparent that accounting for goodwill is intrinsically linked with accounting for business combinations.

APBO17 deals with intangible assets generally, including goodwill. Both inherent goodwill and purchased goodwill are considered, although inherent goodwill should not be capitalized as it does not comply with the necessary conditions. In order for costs to be capitalized as an intangible asset it is necessary for three conditions to be met. First,the costs must be related to an intangible asset that can be separately identified; secondly, the asset should have a determined life; and thirdly, the intangible asset should not be one inherent in a going concern and related to the enterprise as a whole. It is clear that inherent goodwill fails to meet any of these three conditions.

Intangible assets may be purchased individually or as part of a group of assets. However, goodwill arises only as a result of the latter, and in such circumstances it is necessary to value both tangible and intangible assets that can be separately identified at fair value. The difference between the consideration and total fair value of the separate assets is designated as goodwill and should be amortized over its useful life, which may not exceed forty years. Negative goodwill should be accounted for by *pro rata* allocation against the fair values of property and other non-monetary assets. Once these assets are written down to zero, a deferred credit is established for the remaining balance.

APBO18 (1971) – The equity method of accounting for investments in common stock

Where an investor owns more than 20 per cent but less than 50 per cent of the stock in an investee, the investment should be accounted for using the equity method (APBO18.17). Where less than 20 per cent of the common stock of the investee is owned the investment may still be accounted for using the equity method provided 'significant influence' is exercised over the investee's policies. Significant influence may be exercised by membership on the board of directors and/or participation in decision-making. In practice, the 20 per cent rule is virtually always applied.

When the equity method is used, the investor will recognize income in its accounts as it is earned by the investee which leads to an adjustment in the carrying value of the investment. The amount recognized in the investor's accounts is the proportionate share of reported net income after eliminating intercompany profits and cumulative preferred dividends even when not declared. The recognition of losses is similar to that for profits provided they do not exceed the carrying value of the investment. Once the carrying value has been reduced to nil the equity accounting method should be discontinued unless the investor guarantees future financial support. As far as the income statement is concerned there are no specific disclosure rules (APBO18.19(e)).

Where the cost of the investment exceeds its book value the difference should be designated as goodwill and accounted for as such (APBO18.19(b)). The investment should be included in the balance sheet at cost plus a share of post-acquisition retained profits (ABPO18.19(c)).

Where investees are material to the financial position of the group it is necessary to summarize details of assets, liabilities and also the results of operations should be disclosed in the notes to the accounts (APBO19.20(d)). An additional disclosure requirement is that dividends received from an investee should be stated in accordance with SEC regulation S-X 5.03.13.

International accounting standards

As a member of the International Accounting Standards Committee (IASC), the American Institute of Certified Public Accountants (AICPA) adopts a policy of 'best endeavour' towards harmonization of accounting standards. However, since the AICPA does not issue accounting standards its only influence is to encourage the FASB to consider significant differences between US GAAP and international standards with a view to international harmonization. A summary of the more important differences is provided in table 13.4.

Branches of foreign corporations

Branches of foreign corporations do not need to comply with SEC regulations although state laws must be observed. State laws normally require certain information to be filed and undertakings to be accepted in order to obtain the necessary certificate which enables it to operate.

Audit requirements

The SEC requires all registered companies to be audited each year. The audit should be undertaken by a certified public accountant (CPA) or a firm of CPAs which is independent of the corporation. The auditor expresses an opinion as to the fairness of presentation of the corporation's financial statements which must be prepared in accordance with GAAP. The work undertaken by the auditor should be that recommended in generally accepted auditing standards (GAAS).

If the auditor expresses a qualified opinion the consequences can be serious, particularly for listed companies, unless the qualification arises from inconsistencies in applying accounting principles. Certain types of qualified audit reports may not be acceptable to either the SEC or stock exchange. However, 'subject to' opinions are normally acceptable.

6. EXCHANGE CONTROL/FOREIGN INVESTMENT REGULATIONS

The general policy of the US government is to accept and treat foreign investment in the same manner as domestic investment. However, freedom of operation may be curtailed to foreigners by federal law in certain industries. In 1986 these sensitive industries included air transport, atomic energy, coastal and freshwater shipping, communications, defence contracting, fishing, hydroelectric power, and mining on government property. Furthermore, the International Investment Survey Act 1976

Table 13.4 Comparison of US accounting practices with international standards

International accounting standards	*GAAP in US*
IAS 1 – Disclosure of accounting policies	
Requires that financial statements should contain corresponding figures for the preceding period	Required for all SEC registered companies only (APBO 22)
IAS 2 – Valuation and presentation of inventories in the context of the historical cost system	
Valuation at the lower of cost and net realizable value	Valuation at the lower of current replacement cost and cost. The current replacement cost may not exceed net realisable value or be less than net realisable value reduced by the company's normal profit margin (ARB 43).
Inventories may not be valued at cost	In rare instances such as when valuing precious metals valuation may be at market value rather than cost (ARB 43)
IAS 3 – Consolidated financial statements	
Permits consolidation (a) where the parent company owns more than 50 per cent of equity capital but does not have voting control and (b) where there is less than 50 per cent control but exercises control by agreement or statute	Consolidation is not allowed in these circumstances (ARB 43 and 51)
Where uniform accounting policies are not followed the different policies should be disclosed together with details of the proportion of assets and liabilities affected in a single balance sheet classification	This information is not required although US GAAP must be followed (ARB 43 and 51)
IAS 4 – Depreciation accounting	
Requires detailed disclosure of the major classes of depreciable assets, depreciation rates, depreciation for the period and accumulated depreciation	This information is not required
IAS 9 – Research and development activities	
Some development costs may be capitalized provided certain conditions are met. Such deferrals must be amortized	All costs are charged as an expense in the year in which it is incurred (FAS 2). Exceptions to this rule include research and development performed for others and certain computer software development costs

– *Continued*

Table 13.4 Continued

International accounting standards	*GAAP in US*
IAS 12 – Accounting for taxes on income Permits the partial approach to deferred taxes provided conditions are fulfilled	Full deferral is required (APBO 11)
IAS 14 – Reporting financial information by segment Requires disclosure of revenue, results, assets employed for each reported industry and geographical segment; also disclose inter-segment pricing policies	Required for corporations registered with the SEC (FAS 14)
IAS 15 – Information reflecting the effects of changing prices Requires disclosure, where material, of adjustments for changing prices on depreciation, cost of sales, monetary items and on overall effects of such adjustments. Such information is regarded as supplementary	Current cost information is required for corporations with inventories and property which exceeds $125 million gross cost or where total assets exceed $1 billion (FAS 33)
IAS 16 – Accounting for property plant and equipment May be valued at or above cost	May not be valued above cost (APB 06.17)
IAS 19 – Accounting for retirement benefits in the financial statements of employers Requires entities to charge past and prior service costs to expenses over a period which does not exceed the expected remaining working lives of the participating employees	Unrecognized prior service costs must be assigned to each future period of service of each active employee in the scheme as at the date of the change in the plan
IAS 20 – Accounting for government grants Requires (a) an enterprise should recognize a government grant in income only when there is reasonable assurance that the grant will be received and comply with the conditions attached to it (b) grants should be included in income in the same period as the relevant costs accrue (c) grants related to assets should be accounted for either as deferred income or as deductions from related assets	There is no equivalent

– *Continued*

Table 13.4 Comparison of US accounting practices with international standards

International accounting standards	*GAAP in US*
IAS 21 – Accounting for the effects of changes in foreign exchange rates	
Permits exchange gains and losses on long-term foreign currency monetary items to be deferred and amortized over the remaining lives of the related monetary items, unless recurring exchange losses on the items can reasonably be expected to arise in the future	Not permitted under FAS 52
IAS 22 – Accounting for business combinations	
Negative goodwill may not be allocated to non-depreciable assets or to monetary assets	Required under APBO 16
Permits immediate write-off of goodwill against shareholders' equity	Not permitted under APBO 17
IAS 23 – Capitalization of borrowing costs	
It is not essential for borrowing costs to be capitalized as long as a consistent policy is adopted	Capitalization is required under FAS 34
IAS 25 – Accounting for investments	
Where investments are periodically revalued, a policy should be adopted with respect to the frequency of revaluations and that policy should apply to all long-term investments which should be revalued at the same time	Long-term investments may not be revalued

places an obligation on all US business undertakings, including real estate companies, to inform the Department of Commerce of direct or indirect investments by foreigners.

In addition to federal laws, a number of states prohibit foreign control of insurance companies, banks, real estate and even liquor companies. State laws may also apply to foreigners from particular countries as part of reciprocal action. Another form of control is that exercised by licence which effectively prohibits China, Cuba, Democratic Kampuchea, North Korea and Vietnam from investing in the US.

Other than the above restrictions, there are no other significant controls which limit the inflow or outflow of capital. US currency is freely converted although if a person physically transports, mails or ships monetary instruments which exceed $5000 either into or out of the country it is necessary for a form to be filed with the Commissioner of Customs. There are therefore no restrictions on the payment of dividends, interest, royalties and other fees to foreigners with the exception of withholding taxes.

Whilst foreign investments do not need to be registered or approved it is still necessary for federal reporting requirements to be adhered to. For example, the Treasury Department collects data on foreign investments in US corporations, the Department of Commerce monitors foreign direct investment, and the Agriculture Department monitors investment by foreigners in agricultural land in accordance with the Agricultural Foreign Investment Disclosure Act 1976. This Act requires foreigners transferring an interest in land to inform the Secretary of Agriculture within 90 days of the transfer.

In summary, the US does not impose exchange controls as applied by many foreign countries and in addition the general policy is one of neutrality between domestic and foreign capital and this is unlikely to change in the near future. Similarly foreign corporations, like domestic companies, must comply with the rules and regulations imposed by federal and state laws. For example, stringent regulations are imposed on all new pharmaceutical and cosmetic products and considerable product liability exists for these and also all food products.

Whilst controls are not generally exercised to prevent foreign investors from participating in US industry, several strategic industries have been identified which curtail potential foreign investment. However, the US does operate a liberal policy not only to foreign investment but to imports and exports generally. The US is a member of the General Agreement on Tariffs and Trade (GATT) and adopts a policy of low import tariffs. However, the administrative burden of exporting to the US is considerable because of the complicated tariff schedules. Tariffs are of two types. Tariff rate quotas are imposed on certain commodities up to a specified level of importation. Once the level is reached the duty increases. In contrast, absolute quotas are sometimes imposed which prevent further imports once a certain level has been attained.

One incentive to trade with the US is the existence of over 70 free trade or foreign trade zones which permit the importation of goods for assembly and manufacture and their subsequent export without incurring US customs charges. These zones are controlled by the Department of Commerce in Washington.

A second incentive permits developing countries preferential treatment by duty-free imports to the US provided at least 35 per cent of value is added by the developing country.

7. OTHER FACTORS

There are no other significant factors which are peculiar to takeovers by foreigners since the US adopts a policy of not discriminating between indigenous and foreign owned corporations.

SUMMARY

It is relatively easy to form a corporation in the US, a process that can be completed within a matter of days. Each state has its own requirements to form a corporation and ensure that companies file annual returns and pay franchise taxes. The capital structure of corporations is also controlled by each state although to a certain extent the debt–equity ratios imposed by the federal tax system are equally important.

Acquisitions may be undertaken by acquiring shares or assets and a statutory merger is also recognized. However, in the case of a statutory merger a foreign parent may acquire a US corporation by the issue of shares only if the transaction is undertaken through a US subsidiary of the foreign parent.

There is some dispute as to the extent of increased concentration in industry since the 1960s and the contribution that mergers have played in this process. However, whilst the number of mergers is just as high as in the late 1960s, it is clear that the average value of transactions has increased substantially and some massive takeovers have occurred over the last three years. One of the most important reasons is strategic, as corporations try to gain access to needed technology or to broaden product lines and expand markets. For historical reasons the UK is the largest single investor in the US, and vice versa.

In moving into any new market a foreign investor normally tries to buy market share by acquiring an existing US corporation. Normally an agreed bid is preferred with the effect that foreigners usually pay an excess when compared with the average for US acquisitions. Furthermore, foreign investors often prefer to acquire companies with strong management teams since they perceive themselves ill-equipped to undertake such a task. However, if such an approach is adopted it is essential that adequate monitoring is undertaken at a very high level. Since the US market is so large it is important that a senior executive, or preferably director reports frequently to head office.

Competition policy in the US is rigorously enforced and breaches of the Sherman Act may be investigated by the Department of Justice. In addition, the Federal Trade Commission (FTC) has the authority to commence investigations, to rule on questions of law and to issue orders to prevent actions in restraint of trade. The Department of Justice provides guidelines on the likelihood of a challenge in the courts although the legality of any merger can only be determined by the courts. However, any foreign investor who attempts to make an acquisition which would breach the Department of Justice's guidelines is likely to encounter substantial delays and litigation costs.

An important change in merger guidelines occurred in 1982 when the Department of Justice introduced the Herfindahl–Hirschman Index (HHI) to assess competitive effects and to determine markets. HHI was considered to be preferable to the four-firm concentration (CR4) ratio on the grounds that it gives weight to the importance of each of the firms engaged in a market whereas the CR4 ratio merely measures the extent to which the top four firms monopolize a market.

The 1984 merger guidelines issued by the Department of Justice considered, for the first time, the impact of foreign producers selling into US markets. Thus, whilst a market might seem highly concentrated in terms of US producers, competition may be effective as a result of foreign intervention. The guidelines also made it explicit that efficiency gains would be given adequate weight in all cases.

The important point is that anti-trust laws are administered by the FTC and Department of Justice with the objective of maintaining a competitive environment. Opposition to a bid may lead to the objector complaining to the FTC with the purpose of initiating an investigation. Furthermore, problems may arise after completion of an acquisition. For example, action may be taken in the courts by a complainant who has suffered damage as a result of an anti-competitive practice. It is also possible that the Department of Justice will challenge a takeover after the deal has been completed which may lead to a subsequent divestment. It is important, therefore, that competition within a market is carefully studied before a bid is made.

It is more common for foreign investors to acquire US corporations by using cash but where securities are issued with the view to subsequent trading in the US it is essential that SEC regulations are complied with. One of these requirements is that financial statements should be prepared in accordance with US generally accepted accounting principles although in practice, this is achieved by a reconciliation statement in a note to the accounts.

With respect to taxation in the US two major changes occurred in 1986. First, the number of states imposing unitary taxation fell from 23 in 1985 to three in 1986. One of the main protagonists of unitary taxation has been the state of California but on 5 September 1986 the state governor signed a bill which permits companies to elect to be taxed on a water's-edge basis. The bill is effective from 1 January 1988 but in order to avoid unitary law a levy is imposed of 0.03 per cent on a company's sales, payroll and property in California and once the election is made it must remain in force for at least ten years.

Secondly, the amendments contained in the Tax Reform Act 1986 constitute the most comprehensive review of US tax laws for the last 40 years and are designed to overhaul a tax system that has sometimes been considered unfair and unmanageable. However, no one appears to know what the aggregate impact will be of the Reform Act but it is characterized by a substantial shift in taxation from the individual to the corporate sector with the net overall effect being neutral. Whilst the rates of taxation to both companies and individuals are reduced the company sector will suffer from a reduction in reliefs against tax. The impact on industry will vary from sector to sector although in the end changes in taxation on the corporate sector do affect individuals as prices and dividends alter to reflect the changed circumstances.

The tax rate reductions for corporations appear significant but when considered alongside the repeal of the investment tax credit and tightening of depreciation allowances the real burden on companies will increase. Indeed, it has been estimated that these effects plus changes in minimum taxation should generate an aggregate $143 billion in revenue over the next five years. If the investment tax credits and accelerated cost recovery system were successful in encouraging capital formation, their repeal must depress capital spending. Consequently, real costs in the manufacturing sector will rise as the benefits are eliminated. This may seem somewhat ironic since recent history in US manufacturing is that jobs have been moving out of the country as manufactured products have swept in from the Pacific Basin, Europe and Latin America. In order for US multinational enterprises to compete effectively with manufactured imports some companies have shifted production in order to compete with the lower labour rates of foreign firms. The Tax Reform Act is likely to provide an added impetus to this trend.

In contrast to capital-intensive industries, some sectors such as service industries, retailers and high-technology companies should actually see the real burden of taxation decrease. The net effect will be an encouragement to such industries to the detriment of capital-intensive industries.

At present some profitable companies have managed to avoid federal tax as a result of tax preferences but the new minimum tax regulations will ensure that such corporations do pay the alternative minimum tax. Indeed the complexities of the minimum tax proposals are certain to cause problems in the future as more and more companies are required to calculate both their regular tax liabilities and their minimum tax liabilities. An additional requirement is that, in assessing their minimum tax liability, corporations must also calculate 50 per cent of the excess of pretax book income over taxable income thereby ensuring that federal tax is at least 10 per cent of earnings reported to shareholders. The complexities of these minimum tax proposals should ensure a full and prosperous future for accountants and revenue lawyers.

The Tax Reform Act should also prove to be the demise of dual resident companies. At present there is a difference between the UK and US definitions of residency so that it has been possible to be incorporated in the US but be resident in the UK. Dual residence enables the US corporation to borrow money for acquisitions and the interest can be offset against income in both the UK and US thereby deriving a benefit twice. These reliefs could then be allocated to the group via group relief provisions in the UK and consolidated income tax returns in the US. However, the Tax Reform Act will allow losses on dual resident companies to be eligible for UK group relief but would not be eligible for US tax relief.

When considering whether to operate as a branch or as a subsidiary in the US, there have been disadvantages to operating as a subsidiary where a tax treaty is not in force. Although the same rate of tax has been applicable there is a difference in treatment when earnings are repatriated to the foreign parent. Dividends repatriated by a US corporation are subject to withholding taxes whereas this tax is not applicable to branch repatriations. The important point here is whether relief for withholding taxes is obtained as a result of a double tax treaty. The new Tax Reform Act aims to eliminate this distinction by introducing a branch tax equal to 30 per cent on earnings of the US branch. This second level branch tax should severely curtail the activities of those with whom the US does not have a tax treaty. In practice, withholding taxes have been avoided by many overseas companies by operating through a tax-treaty intermediary, particularly the Netherlands Antilles.

A further effect on branches will be the provisions relating to the deductibility of interest. At present there are complicated rules whereby the interest expense deducted by a US branch may not be the same as the actual interest paid. The new Act stipulates that where interest is deducted by a branch which exceeds actual interest paid to third parties, the excess will be subject to withholding tax at the rate applicable in the appropriate treaty.

For the acquiring company two other provisions of the Tax Reform Act should prove to be important. Under the Tax Equity and Fiscal Responsibility Act 1982 an acquirer was allowed to purchase the shares of a company and be able to elect to obtain a step-up in asset value. The advantage to an acquirer of such an arrangement was to purchase assets at fair value, upon which depreciation allowances were calculated, and without any recognition of a gain being made. However, under the Reform Act a gain would be recognized on the difference between fair value and book value of the acquired assets. This provision does not apply to a stock purchase made before 1 January 1987 or for a further year provided a written binding contract was signed before 1 August 1986. A further consideration is that the new Act will limit deductions for net operating losses to the pre-acquisition equity of the corporation.

Finally from a taxation point of view acquisitions of US companies by foreigners may result in extensive informational reporting to the Internal Revenue Service. The Tax Reform Act will extend these requirements by including transactions with foreign-related individuals and partnerships.

From a regulatory point of view foreign investors who are registered with the Securities and Exchange Commission (SEC) will find the US more tightly controlled with more exacting accounting standards than any other country in the world. The SEC has the statutory authority to establish financial accounting and reporting standards. However, in practice, the SEC has delegated its responsibility to the Financial Accounting Standards Board (FASB) although the SEC does supplement FASB standards by additional rules specified in Regulation S-X. For companies that are privately owned there is no obligation to have the accounts audited or indeed to make available financial information to the public. In certain cases, however, creditors may demand that they have audited financial statements and there are also regulations for specific industries ranging from banking, hospitals, television to oil and gas companies.

The general policy of the US government has been to accept and treat foreign investment in the same manner as domestic investment. Over the last two years there have been many demands to indulge in trade wars, particularly against Japan, but many of these demands constitute rhetoric with the aim of deregulating foreign markets. There is considerable interest in investing in the US from foreigners keen to gain a share of the vast and relatively homogeneous consumer market. It is difficult, if not impossible, for any multinational enterprise to ignore the potential of the US, and those who do are unlikely to obtain the scale advantages necessary to compete on a global basis.

14

Other Countries

Argentina

1. BUSINESS ORGANIZATIONS AND COMBINATIONS

Businesses may be established as sole proprietorships, general or limited partnerships, co-operatives, branches, corporations (*sociedades anonimas* – SAs), or limited liability companies (*sociedades de responsabilidad limitada* – SRLs). Most foreign companies are organized as SAs, a few are SRLs, or as they are commonly called, *limitadas* (Ltdas).

The SA is the only entity that may issue shares to the public, and problems with sale of all or part of the company are minimal. The Ltda is, in effect, a partnership, but the liability of the individual partners is limited to the amount of their subscribed capital.

The *sociedad anonima* is the most commonly used form of business organization and is therefore the most important. The statute provides for either a publicly or privately held SA. Although some of the organizational formalities are different, the concept of an SA is similar to that of a US corporation. In general, the articles of incorporation detail the capital structure (that is, authorized and issued stock) and provide for the election of a board of directors responsible for managing the corporation.

The SA must have a minimum of two shareholders, either individuals or companies, with full legal rights to acquire or dispose of assets or enter into contractual agreements. The administration and supervision of an SA is carried out by a board of directors and a syndic or *comisión fiscalizadora* (control council). The syndic must be a registered public accountant or lawyer.

The board of directors is made up of one or more members appointed at a meeting of stockholders. For a *sociedad anonima* that is subject to permanent government control, the board must include a minimum of three directors, who need not necessarily be shareholders. The directors may be re-elected but their responsibilities may not be delegated. The board must meet at least once a month to discuss current activities of the company and discussions during those meetings must be recorded in corporate minutes.

In contrast, the branch form of business organization is used mainly for sales operations. Liability is unlimited as far as a foreign company is concerned and all earnings are taxed at a 45 per cent rate (approximately equal to the normal 33 per cent income tax plus the 17.5 per cent dividend tax on the remaining 67 per cent of the company's taxable income), whether or not profits are distributed.

Application for branch registration must be in Spanish, notarized and filed locally, and must include the following information: the parent company's charter and by-laws, the resolution setting up the Argentine branch, assigned capital, the credentials of the directors and the local representative's power of attorney. Before any business can be transacted, the parent's statutes must be inscribed in the Commercial Register.

There is no minimum capital requirement for branches. The branch must have a duly empowered representative, usually resident in Argentina. An annual income statement and balance sheet must be filed with the *Inspeccion de Justicia* and recorded in the Commercial Register. Changes in the capital of the parent and increases in branch capital must also be recorded in the Commercial Register.

The following is a summary of types of business combination allowed by law:

1. Transformation. A regular commercial company can be transformed, without dissolution, into a new company limited by shares, or any other type of company.
2. Merger. When two companies are dissolved, without liquidation and establish a new one or when one company incorporates another one to itself.
3. Excision. When a company uses part of its capital to merge with other companies or to participate with them for the organization of a new company.
4. When a company designates part of its capital, without dissolution to organize one or more new companies.
5. When a company is dissolved without liquidation to organize a new company or companies with all the capital.

2. TRENDS IN TAKEOVER ACTIVITY

With the new government there is a tendency to turn existing government companies into private ones. Three companies have already been privatized and the steel and petrochemical companies may be in the future.

There are no government statistics about takeover activity, but at present a number of small and medium-sized companies are being merged to reduce costs and obtain improved market share. In addition, a number of overseas companies have been buying Argentine companies but the level of activity is not significant.

3. MERGER CONTROL

Controlling, controlled and related companies

Controlling corporations are those that hold sufficient participation directly or through another controlled corporation, which entitles them to the necessary voting rights and enables them to make decisions in a controlled corporation. Related corporations are those where one holds more than 10 per cent of the capital of the other. Controlling corporations are required to file consolidated annual financial statements.

There are rules which forbid corporations from maintaining investments in others in excess of the free reserves and 50 per cent of the capital plus legal reserves. If this occurs their voting rights may be forfeited.

Foreign investment regulations

In 1980 the regulations were simplified in order to speed up the formalities connected with the approval and registration of investments. Capital investments must be registered with the Foreign Investments Under-Secretariat. Once they have been registered foreign investments have the same rights and are subject to the same obligations as national investments. Certain types of foreign capital investments require the prior approval of the Executive to be legally valid. These include: proposed investments in national defence and security, education, banking, insurance and financing, certain public utilities, broadcasting and publishing. In addition, approval is required from the Executive in the following circumstances:

1. When the capital contribution, made to an existing local firm whose net worth exceeds US$ 10 million, entails converting it into a local foreign capital company.
2. Investments that have special or promotional benefits of a national nature, or those exceeding US$ 20 million or those made by foreign states or public foreign judicial persons.
3. Investments to acquire the shares of an existing local company, not previously owned by foreign investors.

No approval is required to purchase Argentine companies listed on local stock exchanges where the investment is under US$ 2 million or less than 2 per cent of the investee's capital, and when the aggregate foreign capital investment in the investee is under 20 per cent of its capital.

Stock Exchange and Central Bank requirements

Companies whose shares are listed on one of the country's stock exchanges must file additional information, including details of accounts receivable, receivables from company directors, etc. Quarterly financial statements must be prepared and subjected to a limited review by an Argentine CP (such a limited review is not an examination in accordance with generally accepted auditing standards). The report of the CP must indicate that the quarterly statements have been prepared on a basis consistent with the company's annual financial statements. In general, the accountant will disclaim his opinion on the statements taken as a whole.

Since 1982, Central Bank regulations provide that quarterly financial statements must be prepared and subjected to a limited review by an Argentine CP.

4. TAXATION

The Argentine tax law has specific regulations about reorganizations in order to assist the optimization of productive factors. In such cases it considers the objectives and social purposes of the enterprises and proposals with respect to capital preservation.

A reorganization may be one of the following:

1. A merger of existing companies when two or more companies are dissolved without liquidation, or when an existing company merges with another which is dissolved without liquidation. In the first case at least 80 per cent of the capital of the new company should belong to the owner of the predecessor and, in the second case, the owner's participation in the absorbed company should represent less than the 80 per cent of the capital of the absorbed company.
2. Excision or division of enterprises: when a company designates part of its capital to a new enterprise or participates with the new one. In this case at least 80 per cent of the capital of the new enterprise, taken as a whole, should belong to the owners of the predecessor company.
3. Economic group: when 80 per cent or more of the capital of a new company belongs to the owner, partners or shareholders of the reorganized company. In this case, they must hold individually at least 80 per cent of the capital they had at the date of the reorganization in the predecessor company.

In the first two cases the new company must continue with the activities of the former enterprise for a period (not less than two years) to avoid losing the benefits. Once the enterprises are reorganized, the outcome will not be subject to income tax, capital tax, value-added tax or tax on transferred values. There are no direct benefits for the owners of the predecessor company of new companies.

There is an Argentine law for foreign investors in the case of the constitution of new companies and in the total or partial acquisition of predecessor companies. Where more than 49 per cent of a new or existing company is acquired by a foreign investor it is necessary to obtain prior government approval when the business is viewed as crucial to the economy.

5. ACCOUNTING

Argentine law stipulates that, where an investor holds more than 50 per cent of the shares and the majority of the votes, it is necessary to prepare consolidated financial statements. Where control is not exercised by a voting majority the equity method of accounting for the investment should be applied. There are a dearth of regulations in this area so that Argentina looks to the US for guidance.

6. EXCHANGE CONTROL/FOREIGN INVESTMENT REGULATIONS

Government controls and regulations

Exchange controls

Since April 1982, when the Argentine military seized the UK-held Malvinas/Falkland Islands and enacted Decrees 786 and 787, the government has exercised tight control over the exchange market to protect the country's foreign exchange reserves. These decrees were supplemented by Decree 387 in 1983, and other amendments in 1984. Current regulations governing foreign exchange outflows include the following:

1. All foreign-exchange transactions must receive Central Bank clearance.
2. Foreign companies may make royalty and technology transfer payments only with Bonex (external US dollar-denominated bonds).
3. Foreign companies' external debts may be paid only with Bonex.
4. Local companies' external debts that were previously payable in Argentine pesos may be paid only with Bonex.

Capital repatriation and profit or dividend remittances in hard currency are currently suspended. Instead, companies exchange their pesos for US dollar-denominated bonds (Bonex) at the official exchange rate and sell them at a discount (currently 12–15 per cent) in New York, London or Zurich. The discount reflects the gap between the official and parallel peso rates.

These tight restrictions may be loosened somewhat when the foreign exchange shortage subsides. However, given Argentina's limited foreign exchange availability, it is anticipated that the current exchange controls will continue to operate well into the foreseeable future.

On 3 October 1983, the Central Bank suspended all foreign exchange transactions for travel purposes and for any other purpose not explicitly mentioned in the previous decrees, except with the Central Bank's express approval. Also, all transactions authorized before 30 September 1983 have to be revalidated by the Central Bank. This measure applies to both the public and private sectors.

The 1976 foreign investment law eliminated all remittance ceilings. In their place it applied an excess-profits tax on non-reinvested net earnings above 12 per cent of registered capital. Under normal circumstances, profit remittances and repatriation of capital may be made in cash without limit. In case of a balance-of-payments crisis, however, the government reserves the right to sanction dividend and capital transfers only through external US dollar denominated government bonds. The government moved to exercise this right, effective 21 April 1982, because of the threat posed to Argentina's reserves. Because of the current balance-of-payments problems, all remittances are carried out through the purchase and sale of Bonex bonds.

Repatriation under the dollar-bond method is guaranteed for investors listed with the Registry of Foreign Capital. Outstanding external bonds have ten-year terms; interest is payable semiannually based on LIBOR for 180-day US dollar deposits. The bonds may be bought (with pesos) from the government or on the stock exchange, and they may be imported or exported freely.

Must multinational companies operating in Argentina are familiar with the dollar-bond option, which was previously in effect from 1971 to 1977 and has since been popular as a hedging technique. Companies considering buying should weigh the costs of this remittance method against the risk of waiting to make transfers as usual. Converting bonds to US dollars may involve a steep discount and companies that do not need cash immediately should avoid this alternative.

Argentina imposes no restrictions on the transfer of interest payable on loans that are contracted between non-related entities and duly authorized by the Central Bank. However, the interest must be paid in Bonex. Annual interest may not be more than two points above the prime rate in the financial market of the country of origin. Loans between a parent company and a subsidiary are normally treated in the same way as loans between independent entities. However, if the Central Bank objects to a loan because the subsidiary's indebtedness exceeds desirable levels (i.e. those typical under normal business circumstances), it could require that the loan be treated as a capital contribution. Repayment of the loan would then be considered a transfer of profits and would therefore be subject to the above-mentioned rules on profit remittances.

The transfer-of-technology law places some limitations on royalty and fee rates. Ordinarily, there are no exchange controls on allowable payments. At present, however, because of Argentina's depleted international reserves, royalty and technical-assistance payments may be made only through the purchase (in pesos) of Bonex.

Owing to an acute shortage of foreign exchange, capital may not be repatriated except in Bonex. However, the Central Bank can reinstate the old mechanism, under which capital would be repatriated three years after the investment was made, unless the original investment authorization specified a longer period. For tax purposes, the amount repatriated under this system takes into account the initial capital plus additional investments and reinvestments less repatriations already realized. If the sale price on repatriation exceeds the registered amount companies have to pay a tax on excess profits.

To obtain authorization for capital repatriation, a company has to submit an application to the Registrar of Foreign Investments along with a voucher signed by a public accountant indicating it did not have any outstanding debts. When a company sought repatriation as a result of the total or partial sale of stock participation, the application had to include the actual amount of the sale, verified by a copy of the transaction. If the sum to be repatriated was only partially registered, only the amount registered could qualify for transfer.

Repatriations that do not involve the use of foreign currency are not subject to prior authorization but have to be filed with the Registrar within 60 days. If the original terms of the investment permit, the Registrar could authorize the repatriation of capital goods.

Argentina imposes no restrictions on the remittance of principal on loans between unrelated entities, provided that the original contract was approved by and registered with the Central Bank. At present, however, these payments may be made only in Bonex.

7. OTHER FACTORS

Argentina has a well-trained workforce that includes skilled workers, technicians and executives. Government service provides jobs for a significant portion of the Argentine workforce. However, companies find some difficulty in recruiting skilled machinists, mechanics and electricians, since many of these have gone into business for themselves.

Under the military government the general practice was to grant wage increases in line with inflation. Although the Alfonsin administration reinstituted collective bargaining for wages, it also issued a resolution limiting wage increase. The normal workweek in Argentina is officially eight hours per day, 48 hours per week. Overtime is paid at time and half for weekdays and Saturday mornings, and at double time after 1pm on Saturdays, for Sundays and for holidays.

Brazil

1. BUSINESS ORGANIZATIONS AND COMBINATIONS

The most common types of business entities in Brazil are the limited liability company (*Sociedade por Quotas de Responsabilidade Limitada*) and the corporation (*Sociedade Anônima*), however, our comments will be restricted to the *Limitada*.

A *Limitada* is similar to a limited liability company in the UK and, according to the US concepts, the Brazilian *Limitada* is a cross between a partnership and a corporation. The formation of a *Limitada* requires a minimum of two investors (so-called quota-holders) which may be either companies or individuals. There is no minimum capital requirement for a *Limitada* and no deposit is necessary for its formation. The capital is divided in quotas of equal or unequal value as specified in the formation deed. Usually, however, the capital is divided into quotas of equal par value. Furthermore, ownership and the amounts thereof must be clearly stated in the formation and/or alteration deed.

Non-resident quota-holders must give a Power of Attorney to representative residents in Brazil to act on their behalf (at meetings, changes in the company's deed etc.).

The formation deed (*Contrato Social*), which is equivalent to a corporation's bylaws, should contain clear provisions on voting rights, distribution of management responsibilities and transferability of quotas, which may be subject to a first refusal right clause. Quotas of a *Limitada* capital cannot be pledged.

As compared to a *Sociedade Anônima*, a *Limitada* has some advantages: the quota-holders' liability for debts and losses is limited individually to their share of capital, quota-holders are jointly liable to the extent of any capital not paid in by other quota-holders.

Another advantage is that a *Limitada* is not required to publish its financial statements and meetings minutes, the only obligation in this respect is that the *Limitada* formation deed (and any changes thereafter) must be filed with the Commercial Registry.

There are no specific legal provisions on profit distributions, although dividends may only be paid out of book profits legally available for distribution (obviously after absorbing all prior year's losses).

Business transfers can be made as a normal sale at fair market value or as a contribution of capital to another company. Takeovers or share acquisition can be made if allowed by the deed. Merger is possible if approved by the entirety of quota-holders.

2. TRENDS IN TAKEOVER ACTIVITY

An economics or financial crisis often gives rise to business reorganizations, which includes mergers, consolidations and spin-offs. The Brazilian economy is presently facing such changes, mainly in the industrial and services area.

Despite the fact that there are no official statistics available on this subject, a great part of the Brazilian economy, such as petroleum (monopoly), mining and power plants is planned or conducted through governmental entities. Specialists say that 70 per cent of the whole economy is managed by government authorities or by companies owned by the government. Presently there is a great pressure towards privatization of most of these entities.

3. MERGER CONTROL

The main rules dealing with mergers are established by the Federal Constitution and other Federal Laws, such as the Corporation Law (Law no. 6404/76), the Foreign Capital Law (Law no. 4595/64), the Stock Exchange Law (Law no. 4728/65), the Securities Commission Law (Law no. 6385/76), the Industrial Property Code (Law no. 5772/71), the Anti-Trust Law (Law no. 4137/62), and those designed for some specific sectors like banking, insurance, telecommunications, aeronautics, hardware and software, etc.

Merger, consolidation and spin-off proposals should be submitted to a general meeting of the interested companies' management boards which shall discuss the reason or objectives of the operation; the shares which the preferred shareholders shall receive; and, if any changes in their rights are provided, the reasons therefore. In addition, the composition of capital after the operation, according to types and classes of shares to be issued by the companies in substitution for those to be extinguished and the refund value of the shares to which dissenting shareholders shall be entitled should also be discussed.

Merger, consolidation and spin-off operations may only be carried out under approved conditions and, if appointed, expert valuers determine that the total net value to be transferred equals the amount of capital to be paid up.

Any shareholder dissenting from a decision which approves the merger of a company into another (or its consolidation or spin-off) has the right to withdraw from the company and obtain a refund of his shares or quotas.

In some circumstances the law may impose conditions which involves the appointment of an individual to an administrative position in the company; in other cases previous approval from a government agency – such as the Central Bank, SUSEP (for the insurance industry), etc. –

might be necessary. Also, a general meeting may suspend the rights of any shareholder who fails to fulfil any obligation imposed by law or by the bylaws until the obligation is fulfilled.

An officer of a company is obliged to consider the best interests of the company whilst taking into consideration obligations to the public and the social role of the company. An officer is prohibited from performing any act of generosity to the detriment of the company, borrowing money or property from the company, or using its property or services for his benefit; lastly, he may not use his position for personal gain.

Government agencies

Foreign capital invested in Brazil must be registered with the Central Bank of Brazil, which controls, amongst other things the licensing of any banking institution. Prior approval from Central Bank is required before such an institution may establish or transfer its head office or any of its branches (whether in Brazil or abroad), or perform any corporate reorganization such as a merger or consolidation.

In order to operate an insurance company prior authorization from SUSEP (Insurance Companies Authority) is required. Foreign investments in insurance companies or insurance brokerage may not exceed one third of the capital, either directly or indirectly.

CVM – Commissão de Valores Mobiliários (the Securities Commission) is attached to the Ministry of Finance and controls the Stock Exchange and the over-the-counter market. The control of a publicly-owned company may be acquired through a public offer authorized by CVM. To transform a closely held company into a publicly held one (or vice versa), the *Sociedade Anônima* must comply with certain rules and obtain previous authorization from the CVM.

DNPM – Departamento Nacional da Produção Mineral (the Mining Industry Authority) – is responsible for controlling every entity engaged in mining activities. Its previous approval is required in several circumstances, including company reorganization operations.

4. TAXATION

There are no tax implications in Brazil when quotas of a Brazilian *Limitada* owned by a foreign investor are transferred to third parties resident or domiciled abroad. However, foreign shareholders of Brazilian companies being acquired by entities or individuals resident or domiciled in Brazil are subject to a flat 25 per cent withholding tax on the capital gain realized upon the total or partial sale of the registered investment. Furthermore, if the owner of the investment is an individual resident in Brazil, the capital gain realized on the sale of quotas held for less than five years is subject to income tax at progressive rates. Nevertheless the taxpayer may opt to tax the gain at a flat rate of 25 per cent. Should the owner of the investment be a legal entity resident or domiciled in Brazil, the capital gain realized is treated as ordinary taxable income.

Merger, consolidation and spin-off

A merger occurs when one or more companies are absorbed by another. A consolidation occurs when two or more companies unite to form a new company. In both cases, the surviving company succeeds its predecessors to all established rights and obligations. Mergers and consolidations require that a detailed reorganization plan be approved by the administrative bodies or partners of the companies involved and submitted to their quota-holders.

A spin-off is defined as the transfer by a corporation of all or part of its net assets to one or more companies set up for that purpose or already in existence. The split corporation is extinguished if all of its net assets are transferred. If the transfer is partial its capital is proportionately divided.

Companies consolidating or merging into other legal entities and split companies are required to file an income tax return by the end of the month and following the one in which the transaction took place. The related tax liability is payable in up to six monthly instalments.

In the case of a merger where one of the parties holds an investment in the other party, and that investment is to be substituted by the assets and liabilities of the investee, the taxable gain or tax-deductible loss will be computed as follows:

1. Taxable gains – is the value of the net assets received that exceeds the investment book value. To the extent that such a gain relates to permanent assets, taxation may be deferred based on the assets realized.
2. A tax deductible loss – is the difference between the investment book value and the fair market value of the investee's net assets. This loss may be deferred for amortization over a maximum of ten years.

Furthermore, if the investee's assets and/or liabilities are revalued as part of the transaction, the resulting surplus will not be immediately taxed, provided it is maintained in a revaluation reserve. Taxation of this surplus will occur upon its realization through disposal, depreciation, amortization or depletion of the underlying assets.

5. ACCOUNTING

Goodwill

Goodwill is recognized in Brazil and is defined as the excess cost of the acquired net worth based on book values at the date of acquisition. There is also recognition of negative goodwill (when the acquisition cost is less than the book value of the acquired net worth). Generally accepted accounting principles require that goodwill be split based on its source and nature as follows.

1. the market value of acquired non-monetary assets;
2. projected future profits;
3. intangibles and other economic reasons.

In fact, there are two categories of goodwill for accounting purposes; the first described above, which has to be allocated to the specific assets, and another described in the second and third above, which is to be treated as an asset subject to amortization.

The goodwill defined above should be amortized based on its category, as follows:

category (1) proportionally to the depreciation, amortization, withdrawal or realization of the related assets;
category (2) or (3) based on the estimated utilization and/or time of existence of the condition that originated the goodwill.

The amounts of goodwill and amortization for the year and accumulated values included in the financial statements as well as the policies for amortization are to be disclosed in the financial statements and/or their footnotes.

The sources of accounting requirements referred to above are Law no. 6.404/76 and Instruction no. 1 of CVM.

Accounting for mergers and acquisitions

The equity method of accounting is the main treatment for acquisitions. Any difference between acquisition cost and book value of acquired net assets is treated as goodwill. In contrast, mergers may either be accounted for based on the book values of the companies being merged or using appraisals to determine market value of the net assets. As a result of the merger, the merged company's net worth will correspond to a capital increase on the merging companies.

6. EXCHANGE CONTROL/FOREIGN INVESTMENT REGULATIONS

In the case of reorganizations resulting from consolidation, merger or spin-off where the investment ownership must be transferred, the Central Bank of Brazil compares the amount in foreign currency of the stockholders' equity at current exchange rates with the amount of the Registered Foreign Capital Certificate. Should the amount of the Certificate be larger than the amount of the stockholders' equity the Central Bank is likely to make a reduction in the registered capital amount. On the other hand, transfers of investment ownership between foreign investors directly carried out abroad, do not cause any changes in the registered foreign capital. The transfer of the Certificate to the new owner's name must be registered with the Central Bank, which will merely issue a new Certificate to the new investor.

The foreign investor can repatriate the premium (capital gain) realized on the total or partial sale of his registered investment, provided the corresponding withholding tax has been paid. However, the remittance must be approved by the Central Bank. To grant its approval, the Central Bank requires a sale price justification by means of an independent auditor's report supporting the price on the basis of the company's stockholders equity and the prospects of future profitability of the company.

Cultural and labour aspects

The general climate today is to encourage foreign investment in areas that have high priority for the economic development of Brazil, like agriculture, heavy industries, exports, tourism, etc. Also, expatriate executives are normally welcome within the local business community.

As previously mentioned, on corporate reorganizations, the surviving entity succeeds its predecessors in all of its obligations, including employee rights and pension obligations. Employment and labour practices in Brazil are governed by the Consolidated Labour Laws, which determine a minimum monthly salary (presently it is US$60). Social charges and employees' benefits increase a company's payroll by an average of 60 per cent. Some of the benefits and social charges are:

1. Employees get one month as a paid vacation after working a full year.
2. Employers must provide sick pay for the first 15 days of sick leave.
3. A 'thirteen month' bonus is mandatory.
4. Social Security Tax to be borne by employers corresponds to 10 per cent of gross payroll per month.
5. Employers must make monthly deposits of 8 per cent of each employee's gross salary in a blocked bank account as funding for the payment of severance rights.

As a general trend, labour laws are likely to act to the employees' benefit. Unions are becoming increasingly active and important in labour relationships.

Hong Kong

Hong Kong is not a country. By 1997 it is to revert to China and is expected to become a Special Administrative Region (SAR) to be administered with the intention of preserving its institutions including its financial and business environments. Presently, Hong Kong is, as its official name clearly indicates – British Crown Colony of Hong Kong – a territory administered by Britain until 30 June 1997.

Its laws, financial customs and practices, accounting standards and business structures are very much in the English mould. However, today's Hong Kong is for all intents and purposes a Chinese community and it is important, in any merger and acquisition exercise, to take the Chinese viewpoint with its own set of subtleties fully into account.

To the Chinese, all non-Chinese are foreigners. A Hong Kong fourth generation Indian or Englishman (by race) would still be a foreigner regardless of passport or identity card. This cultural set is, apropos, to make a point: 'foreigners' are just as welcome or unwelcome as anyone when buying up local companies. To a Hong Kong businessman, a buyer is simply that.

1. BUSINESS ORGANIZATIONS AND COMBINATIONS

Business organizations limited by shares

Two forms of business organization limited by shares are defined by the Hong Kong Companies Ordinance; namely, a private company and an incorporated company. Both types of organization can be formed by two or more persons, associated for any lawful purpose, by subscribing their names to a memorandum of association. The liability of its members is limited by the memorandum to the amount, if any, paid on the shares respectively held by them.

A private limited company, generally, has the right to transfer shares restricted such that the number of members of the company is limited to 52 or more persons holding one share counting as one; any invitation to the public to subscribe for any shares or debentures of the company is prohibited; and the company shall not have the power to issue warrants to bearer. The directors may, in their absolute discretion and without assigning any reason therefore, decline to register any transfer of any share, whether or not it is a fully paid share.

An incorporated company is not subject to the restrictions aforementioned. Both organizations limited by shares are subject to the regulations for management covered in the Companies Ordinance, chapter 32.

Business combinations permitted by law

Except for the limitations on the transfer of shares in the case of a private company limited by shares, there are no legal restrictions as to the types or forms of business combinations permitted in Hong Kong. Of course, business combinations for illegal purposes are not permitted by law. Mergers and takeovers involving the acquisition of shares of minority shareholders or by formation of holding companies are the most visible forms of business combination.

Although not prohibited by law, business transfers involving the transfer of a company's assets to a third party are not very common.

TRENDS IN TAKEOVER ACTIVITY

The Hong Kong Registry of Companies has annual financial reports of all companies registered in Hong Kong and these are available to the public. Statistics on business takeovers are not published by the government although records of share transfers are available at the Registry. Information on business combinations are matters of public record, but statistics are not readily available.

The South China Morning Post, a leading English language daily, published in 1986 a summary of corporate finance transactions on mergers and takeovers which we extract below:

Corporate Finance Activities, 1980–5

Merchant banks	*Takeovers and mergers*		*Rights issues*		*New issues*	
	No.	*HK$m*	*No.*	*HK$m*	*No.*	*HK$m*
1985	26	5293.0	9	2217.6	5	749.4
1984	5	11,751.5	6	1096.2	8	989.6
1983	6	370.7	4	1099.2	4	419.6
1982	15	1507.7	7	590.5	2	76.1
1981	21	7077.4	21	5410.0	7	2001.0
1980	12	4981.8	24	6023.8	6	1035.5
Total	85	30,982.1	71	16,436.7	32	5271.2

Notes:

1. HK$7.80 = US$1.00 as of February 1986
2. The above transactions relate to publicly-listed companies in Hong Kong.
3. Takeovers and mergers – the transactions relate to announced deals in the respective years, the amounts relate to money required to acquire the shares from minority shareholders in a takeover or mergers transaction.
4. Rights issues and new issues – the transactions relate to the prospectuses date in the respective years. Amounts relate to the money raised through the issue.

No published statistics are generally available on local company acquisitions abroad. As specialized mergers and acquisitions advisory companies are not visibly active in Honk Kong, it is safe to assume that the bulk of merger and takeover activity stems from those recorded by the merchant banks.

3. MERGER CONTROL

Hong Kong has a Committee on Takeovers and Mergers chaired by the Commissioner for Securities. Members include two other members of the Securities Commission, a representative from the Hong Kong Unified Stock Exchange, four representatives from financial institutions (together with three alternates), and a person nominated by the Committee on Unit Trusts. The Chairman has a deliberative and casting vote.

The Committee on Takeovers and Mergers is the implementing body for the Hong Kong Code on Takeovers and Mergers, last revised and approved by the Securities Commission on 1 October 1981. The Code does not have the force of law, but rather is regarded as representative of opinion on business standards of those concerned professionally in the field of business and takeovers. It is in the Securities Ordinance, however, where the law applies to mergers and acquisitions of listed companies on the Unified Exchange.

General principles of the Hong Kong Code on Takeovers and Mergers

The general principles of the Hong Kong Code on Takeovers and Mergers are as follows:

1. When control of a company changes hands there is an obligation upon the new controlling shareholder(s) to inform the general body of shareholders as soon as possible.
2. The new controlling shareholders should extend to other shareholders of the same class an offer in terms no less attractive than the highest price paid for shares purchased by the new controlling shareholders. If a general offer is not made, this action must be justified to the satisfaction of the Committee.
3. Shareholders must be given all the facts and opinions necessary for them to make a reasonably informed judgement of an offer.
4. Once a *bona fide* offer has been communicated to the board of an offeree company, or should the offeree company board believe an offer to be imminent, no action which could frustrate the *bona fide* offer, or deny the offeree company's shareholders an opportunity to decide on its merits shall be taken by the offeree company's board without the approval in a general meeting of its shareholders.
5. The boards of an offeror and offeree company (and their respective

advisers) have a primary duty to act in the best interests of their respective shareholders as a whole.

6. All parties in a takeover or merger transaction must endeavour to prevent the creation of a false market in the shares of an offeror or offeree company.
7. A board which receives an offer, or is approached with a view to an offer being made should, in the interests of its shareholders, seek competent independent advice. The names of the financial advisors to each company in an offer should be made public.
8. Rights of control must be received in good faith and never abused.
9. When an offeror intends to bid for only a proportion of any securities of a company, then an announcement must clearly state that the takeover is subject to the approval of the Committee on Mergers and Takeovers; the Committee expecting to have been previously consulted.

Hong Kong Securities Ordinance

The Securities Ordinance was approved by the Governor of Hong Kong on 16 January 1986. Its rules prescribe the requirements of the Securities Commission for the listing of securities on Hong Kong stock exchanges. They supplement the domestic requirements of these exchanges.

The Securities Ordinance endows the Commissioner of Securities with the power to act when, in his opinion, actions by boards and/or shareholders may be detrimental to an orderly market in Hong Kong. Powers of the Commission include de-listing, suspension of trading, and waiving of requirements of the rules. As Chairman of the Committee on Takeovers and Mergers, the Securities Commissioner uses appropriate rules in the Securities Ordinance to ensure compliance with the principles and rules of the Hong Kong Code on Mergers and Takeovers.

Undertakings prescribed under the securities rules

When a company enters into an undertaking with the Unified Exchange, it agrees to conform to obligations, disclosure and reporting requirements of particular relevance to mergers and takeovers.

Generally, companies are to keep the Exchange, the Commissioner, members of the company and holders of its listed securities informed as soon as reasonbly practicable of any information:

1. necessary to enable them and the public to appraise the financial position of the company and its subsidiaries;
2. necessary to avoid establishment of a false market in its securities; or
3. which would be likely to bring about material change in the price of its securities.

Notifiable transaction notices are sent in both English and Chinese within 40 days of the day on which the notifiable transaction is entered.

A notifiable transaction notice is sent in any acquisition or disposal of assets by a company or any of its subsidiaries, where the assets involved in the transaction are in excess of 15 per cent of the value of the company's assets or consolidated assets, or where assets represent 15 per cent of the company's consolidated pre-tax operating profit as disclosed in the last audited reports. A notice is sent if the assets acquired or disposed involve the company's or its subsidiaries' directors or chief executive or any subsidiary or any associate of such director or chief executive. The Securities Ordinance also requires transmittal of a transaction notice to the proper parties should a company enter into a transaction resulting in a company becoming or ceasing to be a subsidiary. Other notifiable transactions include loans and financial assistance granted to other companies, security or guaranty provided and any transaction by a listed company not in the ordinary course of its business.

The reporting requirements for a transactions notice are detailed in the rules, and would be of interest to those in mergers and acquisitions as the great majority of transactions in this field would be notifiable. Although the wording of the Ordinance (para. 6) does specify publication but not in any particular newspaper, media or language, it is common practice to publish notifiable transactions in both English and Chinese newspapers of wide circulation.

Control over mergers and takeovers, to recap, is primarily in the hands of the Commissioner of Securities, whose broad powers to take punitive action are backed by both law and codified common practice. The publication, to all who could be concerned, of transactions deemed notifiable provide the basic feedback opportunity for those objecting.

The rules and requirements for listing are, as previously mentioned, prescribed in the rules of the Securities Ordinance. The Unified Exchange of Hong Kong using the Ordinance as a guideline exercise the normal levels of self-policing and prudence in its control of operations.

Hong Kong has no formal and direct governmental control mechanism for its unlisted securities markets. However, it must be noted that the Securities Ordinance has disclosure requirements for any business organization, listed or otherwise, e.g. a holding company, a subsidiary, where the organization is linked with a listed company. Thus, albeit indirectly, some form of control of unlisted companies, and thus their securities, is exercised by the Hong Kong Government; punitive action may be taken, however indirectly.

4. TAXATION

The transfer of shares or businesses gives rise to the application of various provisions in the Hong Kong Inland Revene Ordinance and Stamp Duty Ordinance. Consideration should be given to taxation in arriving at an appropriate valuation for the shares or businesses transferred.

Implications of the transfer of shares

On the companies being acquired: Unless the acquisition of shares is for the sole or dominant purpose of utilizing available tax losses, if any (this is generally not the case for the majority of business acquisitions or mergers) the tax losses may be carried forward indefinitely to offset against the companies' own future profits.

On the acquiring companies/shareholders: Stamp duty of 0.3 per cent is payable on the value of the shares acquired.

On the shareholders of the companies being acquired. Unless the shares represent the shareholders' trading stock, profits or losses from disposal have no tax effect. There is no capital gains tax in Hong Kong. Stamp duty of 0.3 per cent is payable on the value of the shares sold.

Implications of the transfer of the business

On the companies being acquired: The value of trading stock transferred is that specified in the agreements, otherwise, it is the open market value on the day of transfer. The value of the depreciable plant transferred is that specified in the agreement, otherwise the Commissioner of Inland Revenue determines its value. Any profit on disposal above tax written-down value is assessable and any loss on disposal below such value is deductible. When trade debts are transferred, subsequent bad debts are not tax deductible. Therefore, it is suggested that writing off deductible bad debts or making deductible specific doubtful debt provisions be made before transferring.

Tax losses cannot be transferred and capital gains or losses have no effect. Stamp duty of 0.3 per cent is payable on the disposal of shares in Hong Kong to incorporated companies.

Closing-down expenses such as redundancy payments, penalty for early termination of contracts, etc. are not tax deductible. Profits on the sale of intellectual property rights (patent, trademark and design) are tax-free unless the costs of purchase have previously been allowed as tax deductions (only taxable to the extent of the deductible amount).

On the Acquiring Companies: The price paid for acquiring trading stock; depreciable plant (by claiming tax depreciation allowances); cost of patents, trademark and design used to produce Hong Kong assessable profits are tax deductible. Stamp duty of 0.3 per cent is payable on the acquisition of shares of Hong Kong incorporated companies and a maximum of 2.75 per cent on Hong Kong real estate.

On the shareholders of acquiring companies and on companies being acquired: All distributions received by shareholders either as dividends or return of capital are tax-free.

5. ACCOUNTING

Goodwill

Goodwill is the excess of the purchase consideration over the fair value of the accountable net identifiable assets acquired. The Hong Kong Society of Accountants (Statement 2.204, Accounting Standards and Guidelines) does not differentiate between goodwill specifically purchased and goodwill arising as part of a purchase of a company. The direct opposite of goodwill – negative goodwill – is recognized.

Recognized by the Society is 'impairment in value of goodwill', which is a reduction in the underlying value supporting the book amount of goodwill, e.g. where a significant reduction in trading results without a foreseeable prospect of recovery to the level of trading, envisaged at the time of acquisition. Permanent impairment in the value of goodwill may be written off as an extraordinary item in the profit and loss account.

Goodwill may be retained as a permanent intangible asset, i.e. treated as a fixed asset and not amortized, if it is considered to be consistently retained by the normal operations of the business. When goodwill is considered no different from any capital asset, it may be amortized over its estimated useful life.

When goodwill is considered to be of doubtful value especially on disposal, or that goodwill is not really an asset at all, it is recommended to be written off at the time of acquisition. The amount written off may be charged directly to reserves, or, where reserves are insufficient, to the profit and loss account as an extraordinary item. When the goodwill account balance is deducted from reserves before arriving at shareholder's funds, this is considered a direct write-off against reserves and it is not acceptable to reverse the goodwill in the future (the effect would be reinstating shareholder's funds).

Negative and positive goodwill are to be offset against each other in the balance sheet. The accounting policy adopted in the treatment of goodwill should always be disclosed, in view of the different treatments possible, to ensure compliance to the Hong Kong Society's Standards and Guidelines (statement 2.101). Statement 2.101 states that accounting policies which are judged to be material or critical in determining profits or losses for the year and in stating the financial position of the company should be disclosed by way of a note(s) to the accounts.

Accounting for mergers and acquisitions

The Hong Kong Society of Accountants does not provide standards and guidelines specifically for the accounting of mergers and acquisitions. Statement of Standard Accounting Practices 14 and 23 of the Accounting Standards Committee in the UK are used by the accounting profession in Hong Kong.

All business combinations are required to disclose, in the financial statements of the acquiring or issuing company in the year the combination takes place, sufficient information to enable shareholders to appreciate the effect of the combination on the consolidated results, and the dates from which major acquisitions are brought into the accounts.

The Hong Kong Society of Accountants does not treat cross-border mergers and acquisitions specifically in its standards and guidelines. However, this does not imply that reporting and disclosure requirements differ from those of the local variety. In practice, adjustments in accounting policy are usually made where another country imposes some limit, e.g. US recommendations on the amortization of goodwill.

6. EXCHANGE CONTROL/FOREIGN INVESTMENT REGULATIONS

For all intents and purposes, Hong Kong has no border in the context of mergers and takeovers. Nowhere is there, in law or codified practice, any mention of nationality, currency or political affiliation, either as a restriction or as a qualification. The words 'foreign-owned' or 'local ownership' are not in the lexicon.

Hong Kong exercises no foreign/local currency controls; thus, funds can and do flow freely in and out of the Territory.

7. OTHER FACTORS

Employee rights

The Hong Kong Employment Ordinance covers matters connected with employment in the Territory. Section 31J deals with changes in the ownership of a business and provides for two conditions: (a) when the employee agrees to a renewal of contract is re-engaged under a new contract by the new owner, the Ordinance would treat the case as if the new owner was the old owner, i.e. as if no change in ownership took place (section 31D/2 of the Employment Ordinance); (b) when an employee refuses to accept an offer of re-employment or a new contract by the new owner, the new owner may dismiss the employee without severance pay provided the new owner's offer is identical to or more favourable than that under which the employee was employed by the previous owner. The thrust of the Employment Ordinance in the case of a change of ownership is towards the continuation of business operations and maintenance of the status quo.

There are no specific provisions for the transfer of pension rights in the Ordinance. Pension obligations would be part of the employment contract and would fall under the same provisions aforementioned (section 31J).

Malaysia

1. BUSINESS ORGANIZATIONS AND COMBINATIONS

In Malaysia, there are three main types of companies limited by shares:

1. Private limited company, incorporated as *Sendirian Berhad* (Sdn Bhd) with a minimum of two shareholders and a maximum of 50 shareholders. The minimum paid-up capital is two shares. The Malaysian Companies Act has no restriction on the value of paid-up capital; i.e. these could be 50 sen shares.
2. Non-listed public company, incorporated as *Berhad* (Bhd) with a minimum of two shareholders.
3. Listed public company, incorporated as *Berhad* (Bhd) with a minimum paid-up capital of 5,000,000 ringgit, out of which 25 per cent or 1,250,000 ringgit, whichever is greater, must be in the hands of more than 500 shareholders.

A private company has the following characteristics which distinguish it from a non-listed private company.

1. There is a restriction on the right to transfer its shares.
2. The number of shareholders is limited to 50.
3. It is prohibited to invite the public to subscribe its shares or to deposit money.

The major types of business combination permitted by law are:

1. Takeovers – payment to shareholders of cash, shares or combinations of cash and shares.
2. Share acquisitions – a transfer by a private sale agreement by a small number of shareholders in an unlisted company.
3. Business transfers – a transfer by a company of its assets to a third party.
4. Mergers – of two or more similar sized organizations, often by the formation of a new holding company.

2. TRENDS IN TAKEOVER ACTIVITY

There are no published government statistics on takeover activity. Furthermore the Foreign Investment Committee (FIC) has information on takeover activities but does not make it available to the public. Furthermore the Kuala Lumpur Stock Exchange (KLSE) does not compile statistics on takeover activities. Their monthly publication, *Investors Digest*, only provides information on Malaysian incorporated listed companies' new issues of shares for the purpose of acquisition. The Capital Issues Committee (CIC) which monitors listing on the KLSE does not have information on takeovers either.

The only information available is a summary of acquisition activities published in the *Business Times* newspapers. Below is a summary of takeover activities in Malaysia for 1985: (acquisition of more than 33 per cent of the voting rights of a company constitutes a takeover in the Companies Act 1965, section 179).

Summary of takeovers, 1985

	No. of companies
Public listed company acquiring public company	9
Public company acquiring private limited company	54
Private limited company acquiring public company	18
Private limited company acquiring private limited company	6
	87

Business information on companies available to the public can be obtained from the directory, *Kompass – Buku Merah* (Red Book).

3. MERGER CONTROL

The Malaysian Companies Act lays down rules for takeovers. Pursuant to Section 179(3) of the Panel on Takeovers and Mergers (appointed under Section 179(2)) the Minister of Trade and Industry has formulated the Malaysian Code on Takeovers and Mergers containing general principles and rules to be complied with by all parties concerned in a takeover and merger situation.

A takeover results when a person acquires more than 33 per cent control of the company and any person seeking to effect a takeover has to extend an offer to other shareholders. This is in line with the New Economic Policy (NEP).

The Malaysian Code applies to all public companies (both listed and non-listed) and as well as to certain private companies.

The FIC assists the government in implementing the objectives of the NEP. The FIC's guidelines apply to the following:

1. any proposed acquisition by foreign interests of any substantial fixed assets in Malaysia;
2. any proposed acquisition of assets or any interests, mergers and takeovers of companies and businesses in Malaysia by any means, which will result in ownership or control passing to foreign interests;
3. any proposed acquisition of 15 per cent or more of the voting power by any one foreign interest or associated group, or by foreign interests in the aggregate of 30 per cent or more of the voting power of a Malaysian company;
4. control of Malaysian companies and businesses through any form of joint-venture agreement, management agreement, technical assistance agreement, or other arrangements;
5. any merger or takeover of any company or business in Malaysia whether by Malaysian or foreign interests;
6. any other proposed acquisition of assets or interests exceeding 5 million ringgit in value whether by Malaysian or foreign interests.

Acquisition of assets or mergers and takeovers by public limited companies, may be satisfied by way of cash, exchange of securities, or a combination of the two. The CIC, which examines all proposals, may approve the scheme subject to the company being suspended from trading on the KLSE. Companies suspended can re-apply for a lifting of the suspension after completion of the acquisition or merger transaction.

Acquisition by cash

Where the consideration for the acquisition, merger or takeover is entirely by cash, the approval of FIC is required. CIC approval is also required if the approval by the FIC is conditional upon the valuation of the assets or shares to be acquired.

Acquisition by share exchange

As regards takeovers and mergers which involve an issue of shares by public limited companies, the approval of the CIC is required. This approval must be obtained prior to the issue of the proposal document.

In addition to complying with the provisions of the Code on Takeovers and Mergers, the boards of the offeror or the offeree companies are bound to comply with section 179 of the Companies Act 1965 as well as the Listing Requirements of the Stock Exchange in every takeover and merger transaction.

A stock exchange for unlisted securities is not available in Malaysia.

4. TAXATION

Implications for the acquiree company

For the company being acquired there is merely a change in ownership. However, there are a number of tax implications:

1. The tax resident status may change. If a non-resident company acquires control of a local resident company and subsequently exercises management and control from outside Malaysia, the company being acquired loses its resident status. The main implications are that certain kinds of income (interest, royalties, technical and management fees, rental of moveable equipment) become subject to withholding taxes and there may be a withdrawal of certain tax incentives which are only made available to resident companies.
2. Unabsorbed capital allowances (tax depreciation) available to be carried forward may be lost if the company being acquired switches its principal business activities to an entirely new line.
3. The status of any tax carry forward losses is unaffected in a situation where ownership of a company changes hands although there may be a change in its business activity. There is no provision with regard to the maintenance of a base percentage in unchanged shareholdings. There is, however, a risk of application of S140, the Malaysian anti-avoidance provisions if the tax authorities believe that the acquisition is purely to obtain the benefit of tax losses of the company being acquired.

Implications for the acquiree's shareholders

1. Where the shares being disposed of are shares in a 'land-based company' (company owning land in Malaysia as the main asset or as one of the assets at the time of disposal of shares or a company that holds 20 per cent voting shares in a company which owns land in Malaysia) and the disposal is by value one million ringgit or more or where the disposals within a period of 12 months of each other aggregate by value one million ringgit or more and where such shares are not listed on any stock exchange, the disposer is liable to share transfer tax at a rate of 2 per cent on the *gross market value of the disposal*.
2. Shareholders disposing their shares in the companies being acquired are not subject to tax on any *gains on disposals* except for those shareholders who are in the business of dealing in shares.

Implications for the acquiring company

1. The cost of borrowing which is attributable to the acquisition is not allowable as a deduction in Malaysia unless it is an income-producing

investment in which case interest paid may be taken as a deduction against dividends received.
2. A bonus issue (stock dividend) received from the acquired company is not subject to tax as there are no provisions in the Malaysian Tax Act to deem these as dividends.
3. As there are no provisions for 'group relief' in the Malaysian Act, any unabsorbed tax losses in the acquired company are unavailable for setting-off purposes against the income of any members of a group.
4. In the event of a requirement for terminal payouts (e.g. compensation for loss of employment), the expenditure must not be accounted for in the books of the acquiring company as it will not be deductible for tax purposes. The company being acquired is to bear the expenses.

Implications for the acquirer's shareholders

There is no taxation impact on the shareholders of an acquiring company.

5. ACCOUNTING

Goodwill

Companies Act 1965 specifies that the amount of goodwill on consolidation should be disclosed as follows:

1. The accounting policy on the treatment of goodwill arising on acquisition is to be disclosed in accordance to IAS 1 and 3.
2. The method and period of amortization or write off of goodwill should be disclosed in accordance with IAS 5.

Accounting for mergers and acquisitions

Business combinations may be accounted for by two methods: acquisition accounting and merger accounting.

In acquisition accounting (purchase method) the results of the acquired company are brought into the group accounts only from the date of acquisition. Assets acquired are restated at cost to the acquiring group in the consolidated accounts. In merger accounting (pooling of interests method), the financial statements are aggregated and presented as if the combining entities had always been operating together as a single unit.

A business combination should be accounted for under the purchase method except in the rare circumstances when it is deemed to be a pooling of interests.

In the past, pooling of interests was disallowed under the Companies Act 1965 and business combinations had to be accounted for under the purchase method. With effect from 1 February 1986, section 60 of the Companies Act, 1965 has been amended to allow for pooling of interests under the following circumstances:

1. where an issuing company has secured at least 90 per cent equity holding in another company
2. in group reconstruction where the issuing company (a) is a wholly-owned subsidiary of another company (the holding company) and allots shares to the holding company or (b) to another wholly-owned subsidiary of the holding company in consideration for the transfer to it of shares in another subsidiary.

On the acquisition of companies, including those with landed properties held for property development purposes, the Capital Issues Committee (CIC) will value the shares of the company to be acquired, based on the net tangible asset value after taking into consideration the valuation by the government valuer and the deferred tax liability arising from the revaluation of the landed properties.

While the CIC allows for revaluation of investments and landed properties, the revaluation in the financial statements should not result in the net carrying amount being greater than the recoverable amount of the assets concerned. An increase in net carrying amount arising on revaluation of assets should be credited directly to shareholders' interests under the heading of revaluation surplus.

6. EXCHANGE CONTROL/FOREIGN INVESTMENT REGULATIONS

There are no restrictions imposed on remittances or transfers abroad subject to completion of exchange control forms for sums in excess of $10,000 (ringgit). Commercial banks in Malaysia are authorized to approve without prior reference to the Central Bank (Bank Negara).

In the case of payment for purchase of shares or immovable property, there are no restrictions provided the payments are not financed with funds borrowed in ringgit in Malaysia.

Present exchange control is very liberal and applies uniformly to all countries except South Africa and Israel. There are no restrictions on repatriation of capital, dividends, royalties, or service fees. Interest and loan repayment in respect of loans abroad must be made in accordance with terms and conditions approved by Bank Negara.

7. OTHER FACTORS

The Malaysian government encourages foreign investment through equity participation. The Industrial Coordination Act recently has been amended to attract more foreign investment. Emphasis is placed on the need for greater technology transfer. It is believed this can only be achieved through greater foreign participation.

Nigeria

1. BUSINESS ORGANIZATIONS AND COMBINATIONS

Many of the companies operating in Nigeria are registered under the Companies Act 1968 which is very similar to the UK Companies Act 1948. Although almost all registered companies in Nigeria are private or public limited liability companies (possessing the same characteristics as similar companies in the UK of 1948–67) only 95 of over 70,000 registered companies are quoted on the Nigerian Stock Exchange. In 1985, a Second-Tier stock market was created although only four companies have so far taken advantage of these new provisions.

Many of the big companies in Nigeria originate from international partnerships between the Nigerian government, institutional and/or individual investors on the one hand and foreign governments, multinational enterprises and/or foreign investors on the other. All companies operating in Nigeria are expected to be registered as Nigerian companies; there is, therefore, technically no 'subsidiaries' of multinational enterprises operating in the country. The shares held by governments (Nigerian and foreign), foreign investors and institutional investors are usually not available for trading on the stock market for strategic reasons. Only the few shares held by Nigerian investors are available for trading. These few shares are usually not brought into the market for speculative reasons because most Nigerians hold dear to the idea that share certificates are assets similar to family silver which should pass from one generation to the next and need to be kept as fixed deposits.

2. TRENDS IN TAKEOVER ACTIVITY

A major activity relating to takeovers – i.e. the transfer of shares by an offer to Nigerian shareholders – has been entirely nurtured by government action. In 1974, the government passed a law (amended in 1977), which made it mandatory for Nigerians to have interests in the equities of enterprises operating in the country. Equities as defined by law do not include fixed interest or dividend-bearing contributions into a company.

Enterprises are classified under the Nigerian Enterprises Promotion Act [NEP] 1977 into three schedules:

Schedule 1 enterprises are reserved exclusively for Nigerian citizens and associations and foreigners are not allowed to engage in business falling under this category which includes distributive trades, services and department stores with less than ₦2 million annual turnover;

Schedule 2 enterprises, predominantly manufacturing, are those with a maximum of 40% foreign participation in their equities;

Schedule 3 enterprises, mostly high-technology such as iron and steel, are those with up to 60 per cent foreign participation.

Enterprises with foreign interests are referred to as 'alien' regardless of the Nigerian interests in them and these enterprises cannot acquire 100 per cent ownership in any enterprise unless such an acquisition is approved by the regulatory authorities specified below. If a Nigerian company has a subsidiary, both the company and its subsidiary must comply with the provisions of the NEP Act except where the parent or holding company is a non-trading company and its subsidiary has complied with the NEP Act on or before 30 June 1977.

3. MERGER CONTROL

The structure of industries in Nigeria is characteristically monopolistic (if, at times, oligopolistic). Little or no competition exists and so merger activities can hardly be said to have arisen because of a desire to suppress competition. There are no takeover codes and no specific stock exchange control rules with respect to mergers.

There are no statutory rules specifically regulating merger activities in Nigeria. It is, however, expected that enterprises quoted on the Nigerian Stock Exchange would conduct any merger arrangements within the code of conduct of that organization. All merger proposals are subject to the approval of the Nigerian Enterprises Promotion Board and the acquisition prices and/or share exchange ratio have to be approved by the Nigerian Securities and Exchange Commission.

An interesting feature of merger and takeover activities in Nigeria is that they normally involve companies listed on the Stock Exchange taking over unlisted companies. Many mergers in Nigeria have been between companies with common connections with a foreign multinational.

There are not many takeovers in Nigeria. For example, in 1984 and 1985 only four such transactions were approved:

1984

1. Lever Brothers (Nigeria) Ltd, a Nigerian quoted company, took over Lipton of Nigeria Ltd an unlisted company.
2. Nigerian Bottling Company Ltd acquired the interests in Leventis Technical Co. Ltd. Both companies were listed on the Nigerian Stock Exchange.

1985

1. John Holts Ltd, a quoted company, took over Bauchi Bottling Company Ltd, an unlisted and a Schedule 1 company.
2. SCOA, a quoted company, took over the assets of Automotive Components Ltd a private unlisted company.

There is no activity in respect of the acquisition of overseas interests in companies registered in Nigeria by any Nigerian company. In fact, there is no 'foreign company' in Nigeria. All companies are registered under the Nigerian Companies Act 1968.

4. TAXATION

Ordinarily, there is no tax advantage to companies and their shareholders in a merger arrangement. Indeed the arrangement could be a disadvantage because transactions between such related enterprises are treated by the tax authorities as real rather than artificial. As a result, profits arising to one company from sales to another are fully taxable, despite the fact that the profits have not been fully realized by the group.

If a company sells all its assets and liabilities to another company, the business of the vendor company is treated for tax purposes as wound up and those of the acquiring company, in respect of the business purchased as commencing. Cessation and commencement provisions would apply to both companies respectively. The tax authorities are, however, prepared to waive the application of the cessation and commencement rules but they must be satisfied that the transfer is made in order to facilitiate better management of the business or to transfer the management to Nigeria. However, the waiver which the tax authorities would allow, would not include the transfer to the acquiring company of the 'unused' portion of tax allowances arising from the trading losses of the vendor company in previous years. The transferred fixed assets are treated as having been sold for an amount equal to the residue of expenditures incurred by the vendor company for purposes of capital allowances.

The companies may, of course, opt to be treated under the cessation and commencement provisions respectively. In this case, the major tax effect on the vendor company is that the difference between the selling price or the original cost (whichever is the lower) of each asset and its written-down value would be subject to a balancing charge (if positive) or a balancing allowance (if negative). If the selling price of an asset is higher than the original cost the difference will be subject to capital gains tax. The shareholders of the vendor company would be subject to capital gains tax on the excess of the value of the new shares acquired in replacement of the old, or the proceeds of the sale of their shares over the cost of the shares previously held.

The acquiring company will be able to claim capital allowances on what was paid for the assets of the company acquired. The shareholders of the acquiring company are not affected.

5. ACCOUNTING

Accounting implications of business combinations

The Nigerian Accounting Standards Board (NASB) has not issued any standard on accounting for mergers and acquisitions. However, there is no void in this area. This is because the Institute of Chartered Accountants of Nigeria (ICAN), a board member of the International Accounting Standards Committee (IASC), has requested all its members to apply International Accounting Standards (IASs) on topics and transactions for which there are no local standards. The provisions of the IAS 22 – Accounting for business combinations – in respect of goodwill and mergers and acquisitions apply in the country.

6. EXCHANGE CONTROL/FOREIGN INVESTMENT REGULATIONS

Foreign exchange is a scarce commodity in Nigeria and there are stringent controls for its transfer. All foreign companies seeking to invest in Nigeria must secure approval (known as Approved Status) for such an investment from the Federal Ministry of Finance if the desire is to repatriate the proceeds of the sale of such investments in the future or any dividends accruing from such investments. Proceeds from sales of foreign investors' interests in equities have recently been subjected to piecemeal repatriation with each tranche not greater than ₦300,000 every six months.

It is, however, possible to repatriate proceeds of such a sale under the recently created 'Second-Tier Foreign Exchange Market'. The Central Bank of Nigeria releases, on a fortnight basis, a fixed sum of foreign exchange for sale, on a tender basis, and allocates foreign exchange to banks which are prepared to offer higher local currency in exchange for the foreign currency released. The prevailing second-tier market price has been higher than the official rate, although the overall goal is to gradually depreciate the value of the Naira until the official rate is at par with the second-tier rate.

7. OTHER FACTORS

Cultural

The entrepreneurial skills of Nigerians are channelled to buying and selling activities rather than industrial activities. There are, therefore, not many industrial enterprises owned by Nigerians. Foreigners are not used to buying up local companies; they either establish new industrial enterprises or sell equity interests in these businesses to Nigerians. Culturally, Nigerians welcome foreign investors, although the NEP Act restricts the scope of foreigners' activities to Schedules 2 and 3 businesses. Foreign investment and technology are welcome in agriculture and high technology industrial (e.g. iron and steel and petrochemicals) sectors of the economy.

Employee rights

Employee rights are well protected. There is a legal provision for every company to create a trust for Nigerian employees whereby they can acquire up to 10 per cent interests in the equity of the company.

Foreign employees can repatriate no more than 25 per cent of their net earnings per annum or 100 per cent of their net earnings whilst on vacation. They are also allowed to repatriate their gratuities at the end of their contract, if they have fully paid their tax liabilities.

Pension obligations

There are no legal requirements for a company to make provisions for the pensions of its employees. Where this exists, the obligations of the company depends on negotiations with the unions.

South Africa

1. BUSINESS ORGANIZATIONS AND TYPES OF BUSINESS COMBINATIONS

The main types of business organizations limited by shares are companies incorporated under the Companies Act 1973. These are of two main kinds: public companies and private companies. Public companies are required to have the word 'limited' at the end of their names and private companies have the words '(proprietary) limited'. The main distinctions between public and private companies are that private companies may not have more than 50 shareholders and must have provisions in their Articles of Association restricting the right of shareholders to transfer shares.

A more recent type of corporate body is the close corporation which has limited liability but which is designed specifically for small business and which is limited to ten members.

The remainder of this section will deal with companies incorporated under the Companies Act 1973.

The types of business combinations permitted by law in South Africa include:

1. Business transfer – the sale by a company of its business or a portion of its business as a going concern to a third party. This would entail the transfer of the assets and/or liabilities of the business to the third party.
2. Takeover – the purchase of a majority of shares in a company by a third party who makes an offer to shareholders.
3. Share acquisition – the transfer by a private agreement of sale between a relatively small number of shareholders in a private or unlisted public ompany.
4. Merger – of two or more companies by one of the procedures permitted under the Companies Act. A merger may be achieved in a number of different ways, of which the most common is the formation of a new holding company or the reconstruction of one of the parties to the merger.

2. TRENDS IN TAKEOVER ACTIVITY

No government statistics are available on takeover activity in South Africa. The only authoritative survey of merger activity was produced by the Merger Research Bureau at the Department of Accounting of the

University of the Witwatersrand. Two publications were produced by this bureau covering the period 1976–80. There have, however, been a number of articles in the financial press on this subject over the years.

Two main trends in takeover activity have been noticeable in South Africa over the last decade:

1. a trend towards a small number of immensely powerful business organizations which control a large portion of business activity in the economy,
2. more recently, a trend to the purchase of subsidiaries of foreign companies by local management and businessmen. This trend has been exacerbated by the political stigma attached in many countries to investment in South Africa.

The extent of acquisitions of foreign companies by South African companies is not insignificant. However, because of the sensitivity of such acquisitions they are frequently disguised and no published statistics are available.

3. MERGER CONTROL

Merger control in South Africa takes three forms:

1. the Companies Act 1973, as amended;
2. Rules of the Johannesburg Stock Exchange; and
3. Actions of the Competition Board in terms of the Maintenance and Promotion of Competition Act 1979.

There are no self-regulatory controls such as a takeover code, although the Competition Board has followed the example of the British City Code in a number of respects. There are no separate controls in regard to mergers over the second-tier official listed market (known in South Africa as the Development Capital Market).

The three forms of merger control will be dealt with in order.

The Companies Act

The Companies Act permits the takeover or merger of a company in four main ways:

1. a takeover offer;
2. a scheme of arrangement;
3. a reduction of capital; and
4. the conversion of the minority's shares to redeemable preference shares and their subsequent redemption.

The takeover offer is the most appropriate method to use where less than 100 per cent of the purchased company is desired. It is also the only available method when the target company is unwilling or unlikely to cooperate in the merger.

The following protections are offered to minority shareholders:

1. 90 per cent of all shareholders in a class must accept the offer before a shareholder may be compelled to accept against his will;
2. disgruntled minority shareholders have access to the courts;
3. full disclosure from the offeror of the terms of the offer and other information;
4. compulsory disclosure by the present directors of the company of their opinion of the offer, an update of the company's recent performance and details of directors' interests;
5. provisions to ensure fairness to all and sanctions against misrepresentation.

A scheme of arrangement is appropriate for an offeror which wishes to acquire 100 per cent control of the offeree and where the controlling shareholders of the two companies have already agreed in principle to a merger. A scheme of arrangement affords less protection to minorities as only 75 per cent of each class of shareholders present and voting at a meeting of shareholders has to agree to the merger.

The reduction of capital and redeemable preference share routes were conceived primarily in order to save stamp duty on transfer of shares (currently $1\frac{1}{2}$ per cent of the consideration). There is some legal controversy over the validity of these methods of achieving mergers.

In recent years relatively few mergers have been effected in South Africa by the takeover route. Most have been carried out under schemes of arrangement or by reduction of capital.

Proposals to amend the Companies Act were published in 1986. These proposals provide for a panel on takeover and mergers to be established. The panel will have power to inquire into mergers and takeovers and to formulate rules which will have the force of the law.

Rules of the Johannesburg Stock Exchange

The purpose of the Johannesburg Stock Exchange Rules regarding mergers and takeovers is to ensure that shareholders are fairly treated. Normally, where a change in control of a listed company occurs as a result of transactions outside the Stock Exchange, the offeror is required to extend its offer to all shareholders at the highest price paid in acquiring control. Disclosure of the consideration paid must be made to all shareholders together with information of earnings and dividend yields and net assets per share. Changes in proportionate holdings between members of a controlling consortium or family may not be regarded as changes in control.

There have been a number of occasions in which the rule that offers should be extended to minorities has been waived by the Stock Exchange Committee. These failures to enforce the rule have been criticized in the financial press. One of the problems facing the committee is that its ultimate sanction is to delist the company and this is seldom in the interests of minority shareholders. The proposed new panel on takeovers referred to above, is likely to improve the safeguards available to minorities.

Reverse takeovers occur when a listed company acquires assets or shares simultaneously with a change in control in the listed company. In such cases the Johannesburg Stock Exchange requires a transmuted listing statement setting out full details of the company in its new form. This statement is similar to a prospectus required under the Companies Act.

The Competition Board

In 1981 the Competition Board issued policy guidelines on acquisition and control. The Board has power to investigate and recommend that an acquisition be prohibited. It also provides a consultative service to would-be acquisitors. There appear to have been few, if any, cases where these powers have been exercised to prevent or influence acquisitions.

4. TAXATION

Taxation implications of mergers and acquisitions

Taxation of companies

In general, the tax consequences of any reorganization to the companies concerned would depend on whether a business is transferred from one company to another or whether the companies continue to operate as separate entities.

The concept of group taxation is not applied in South Africa. Consequently each company in a group is taxable as a separate entity and the losses of one cannot be offset against the profits of another. A change in the shareholding of a company has no effect on the basis of computation of the taxable income of the company.

Where there is a purchase of the underlying assets and liabilities of a company as opposed to the shares then:

1. the seller is regarded as having disposed of its business and is taxed on any profits to the date of transfer, including any recouping of depreciation. Any loss on the sale of inventory is allowable, but a loss on the sale of debtors will be disallowed. If a tax loss was incurred prior to transfer it may be set off against the seller's other income in the year of disposal or carried forward if the company continues to trade. Such a loss is not transferable to the new corporation. The conditions under which such losses may be absorbed are limited by the anti-tax avoidance measures in the Income Tax Act.
2. the buyer's profits are taxable from the date of transfer without regard to any allowance granted to the seller. Depreciation may usually be claimed on the full acquisition cost of qualifying assets, but the

enhanced allowances will not be allowed. No bad debt deduction will be allowed on debts acquired from the seller. The tax value of inventory will be the purchase consideration (special rules apply when there is no ascertainable consideration or the consideration is less than market value). LIFO is no longer an acceptable method of valuing stock for tax purposes. However, companies that used this basis in the past may have a material LIFO reserve which in effect qualifies as a permanent deduction from stock and will only be reduced in limited circumstances. This reserve is in a scheme of group rationalization with the prior approval of the Revenue authorities.

If a business is sold without allocating the sale price between the various assets, the Revenue authorities may place reasonable values on the items transferred.

Other taxes which are significant in mergers, acquisitions and similar transactions are detailed below:

Marketable securities tax (on shares in companies) is payable as follows:

	Rate
An increase in authorized share capital	R5 per R1000
An issue of share capital	5c per R20 including share premium
The sale of shares	1.5% of price

All transfers of ownership of real estate to a company are subject to a transfer duty of 5 per cent of the purchase consideration.

Taxation of shareholders

South African tax law contains certain provisions relating to the 'reconstruction' of a company, but the term is not defined and has no precise legal meaning. The following rules apply to shareholders which depend upon the type of business transfer.

An amalgamation (which usually involves the merger of two companies to form a third entity or the absorption of one company by another) must be distinguished from a reconstruction, because the receipt of any cash or other asset in the event of an amalgamation has no tax consequences to any shareholder who is not a dealer in shares.

A reconstruction, on the other hand, usually involves the business of one company being transferred to another company, having substantially the same shareholders, with the intention that the business will thereafter be carried on by the transferee company. In this case if the sum of any cash and the value of any asset given to the shareholder exceeds the par value of the shares held by him prior to the reconstruction, the excess is regarded as a dividend for tax purposes. In addition, if any earnings (whether capital or revenue) had previously been capitalized and such transfer had not been regarded as a dividend distribution, then any part of the cash or assets given to the shareholder that represents a distribution of such profits is regarded as a dividend distribution.

In the event of a liquidation, distribution made to shareholders out of capital profits are not regarded as dividends for tax purposes (except in the case where liquidation takes place in the course of a reconstruction). Distributions made to shareholders out of revenue profits, whether or not capitalized, are regarded as dividends. If liquidation is part of a dividend-stripping operation, distributions may be taxable in full.

Interest payable on a loan raised to acquire shares is deductible from dividend income. However, since companies are exempt from tax on dividends the interest would not be deductible. Neither can the interest be offset against the earnings of the acquired company.

If a shareholder disposes of a dormant company with undistributed profits, the selling price received (limited to the distributable reserves of the company) may, in terms of the dividend-stripping legislation, be regarded as a dividend.

Any dividend or deemed dividend received by a shareholder would be subject to withholding tax if the shareholder were a non-resident individual or company, or would be included in the gross income of a resident individual taxpayer and would form part of the total net profits of a company liable to undistributed profits tax.

Cross-border tax implications

All corporations, whether domestic of foreign, are taxable on income arising from sources within or deemed to be within South Africa, subject to the provisions of any Double Tax Treaty which might apply. The deeming provisions generally encompass contracts of sale, know-how payments, interest, royalties and the use of patents, copyrights and similar rights. Dividends, interest, royalties and know-how payments (which may cover management fees) made to any foreign resident are subject to deduction of a withholding tax. No withholding tax is applied in respect of the transfer of current profits of local branches of foreign operations.

5. ACCOUNTING

At the national level there is no accounting standard in South Africa which deals exclusively or exhaustively with goodwill. It has been treated in a discussion paper issued by the South African Institute of Chartered Accountants but no definitive statement has been issued.

Current practice followed by the majority of public companies is to write off goodwill on acquisition. This write off is often disclosed as an extraordinary item. In a minority of cases, goodwill is amortized as an expense before arriving at net income.

The Companies Act requires disclosure in the balance sheet of the amount of goodwill, patents and trademarks not written off.

A provision in the Companies Act has the effect of requiring mergers to be accounted for as purchases rather than as poolings of interest. This provision requires that all profits earned by an acquired company prior to acquisition are not available for distribution by the acquiring company.

At an international level foreign subsidiaries acquired by South African companies will be accounted for under South African accounting rules.

6. EXCHANGE CONTROL/FOREIGN INVESTMENT REGULATIONS

Exchange control is rigorously enforced over cross-border financial transactions. It is enforced by the South African Reserve Bank acting through the commercial banks. Non-residents may invest and disinvest in equity investments through normal banking channels without approval. Such transactions must be made through the medium of the financial rand which is normally quoted at a discount to the commercial rand. Investment and disinvestment through loan capital requires exchange control approval. Dividends may not be remitted overseas out of profits earned prior to 1984. As exchange control regulations alter frequently and without warning, enquiries should be made regarding the current rules before any transactions are planned or set in motion.

Except in the insurance and banking sectors there has been no significant government regulation against foreign investment.

7. OTHER FACTORS

South Africa is a developing country and needs continual injections of foreign capital to maintain its economic growth targets. The country also has a long history of foreign investment, largely from Britain. Recently, because of economic uncertainty and distaste for its political policies there have been pressures on multinational companies to disinvest from South Africa.

Since the early 1980s there has been a rapid growth in the size and influence of black trade unions. Although employee rights in industry are not as extensive as those in Western Europe, this aspect of business is changing rapidly and a would-be acquisitor would do well to take the trade union movement into account.

Pension obligations are separately funded in South Africa under the Pension Fund Act which safeguards the rights of employees.

Appendix

Acquiring an Overseas Company – An Information Checklist

BACKGROUND AND ORGANIZATION OF THE BUSINESS

History and business

1. The nature, history and organizational structure of the business.
2. Business strengths and weaknesses including factors limiting growth.
3. Location of operations including branches and subsidiaries in the home country and abroad.
4. Details of factors peculiar to the industry including legislation and special trade agreements.
5. Overall business strategy including acquisitions and disposals of substantial investments or assets.
6. Industrial relations record.
7. Sources of finance and form of that finance.

Officers and managers

8. Identify senior management and directors and their responsibilities within the organizational structure.
9. Establish curriculum vitae's for key personnel and ascertain their service contracts.
10. Is there adequate succession within the management structure?
11. Is the company dominated by any one individual? Is there adequate life insurance cover for a key inidividual and can the company operate in his absence?
12. Are any changes in management planned?

Products and marketplace

13. What are the main products, their lifecycles and obsolescence?
14. Are products protected by patents, trademarks, registered designs or are they made under licence?
15. Analysis of turnover by product and geographical area.
16. Principal markets, customers, competitors and market leaders.

17. Customer range – reliance on a small number?
18. The extent of reliance on a limited number of suppliers.
19. Size of the market and company's share – is it growing or declining?
20. Review the order book and past order cancellation record.
21. Details of sales methods, exports, franchising and long-term contracts.
22. Details of terms of trade, marketing policy and current sales performance.
23. Marketing and advertising methods.

Costs and expenses

24. Major suppliers, sources of raw materials and possible restrictions on future supplies.
25. Are there any retention of title clauses in suppliers' contracts?
26. Number and age of employees, distribution of skills, and extent of trade union organization.
27. Labour relations including history of redundancies and short time working.
28. Conditions of employment including wage agreements, benefits, bonuses and share incentive schemes.
29. Details of any pension schemes in operation including the level of funding.
30. Description of processes and production control.
31. Does the company design and engineer its own products?
32. How much is spent annually on research and does the business rely on such expenditure?
33. If the know-how is marketable in its own right is it protected by patents?

HISTORICAL FINANCIAL INFORMATION

The following information is often required for at least the last three years and probably five years.

34. Have the accounts received an unqualified opinion each year?
35. Review the principal accounting policies and appropriateness in relation to accountings standards, law and industry practice.
36. Any material changes in accounting policies or fundamental accounting errors.
37. Any acquisition or disposals during the period?
38. Differences from UK GAAP which could have a significant effect on the accounts.

Trading results

39. Turnover – analysis by product and market, seasonality, commissions offered and discounts given.
40. Cost of sales – analysis of costs (see also stock).
41. Gross profits – by product, market, division, branch etc. Trends of margins.
42. Depreciation and amortization – rates, treatment of grants.
43. Leasing and hire charges.
44. Remuneration of the directors and auditors.
45. Details of extraordinary and exceptional items. Ensure adequately disclosed and correctly treated.
46. Interest payable and received and other investment income. Income gearing ratios and the effect of conversion rights.

47. Taxation including deferred and overseas tax.
48. Earnings per share if a public limited company or equivalent or seeking a listing/USM quotation.
49. Minority interests.
50. Overheads – analysis and trends including treatment of holiday pay and pension costs.
51. Rates of dividends.
52. Obtain explanation for unusual variations in any revenue or expense items.

Capital employed

Fixed assets – property

53. Location, accessibility and size of factories and offices.
54. Potential for expansion.
55. Basis of ownership, rateable values and annual rates.
56. Book value, existing use value, alternative use value, insurance value, and replacement cost. What is the revaluation policy of this company?
57. Age, condition and depreciation policy in relation to buildings.
58. Are there any restrictions on the use of buildings by terms of leases or planning restrictions?
59. Is the property used to capacity or are there surplus assets with the possibility of rationalization?
60. Are there any securities held over the land and buildings?

Fixed assets – plant and equipment

61. Summary of main items of plant and equipment include age, condition and whether purchased or leased under a finance lease.
62. What is the replacement and depreciation policy of the company?
63. Is the equipment specifically designed for its present use?
64. Details of leased assets together with outstanding lease commitments.
65. Are any assets subject to hire purchase or deferred terms?
66. Availability of grant assistance.
67. Does the company operate a plant register?
68. Capital expenditure approved by the board; contracted for; not yet contracted for.
69. Is insurance cover adequate?

Fixed assets – investments

70. Range of investments and reason for holdings.
71. Cost, market value and liquidity.
72. Consider any taxation liability on disposal.

Fixed assets – intangibles

73. Details of goodwill, patents, copyrights and other rights.
74. The extent of capitalized development expenditure.
75. Review depreciation amortization and capitalization of intangible assets.

Share capital

76. Authorized and issued share capital and rights attached with respect to dividends, votes and repayment of capital.
77. Principal shareholders and details of share option schemes.
78. Distribution policy including a history of dividends and dividend cover.
79. Details of material contracts with shareholders.

Stocks and work in progress

80. Analysis of stocks including the basis of arriving at physical quantities.
81. Valuation of stocks and review provision for obsolete and slow-moving stock and assess its adequacy.
82. Review work in progress including its labour and material content.
83. Review system for allocating costs including overheads to contracts and ensure consistence with standard accounting practice
84. Review payments on account and profit recognition procedures on long term contracts.
85. Are losses adequately provided for?

Debtors

86. Review trade debtors listing and identify major customers.
87. Discuss with company officials the degree of reliance on particular customers.
88. Review listing of bad and doubtful debts and consider other debtors which may be doubtful.
89. Assess adequacy of credit control and debt collection procedures.
90. Review other debtors and prepayments and consider any claims for regional development grants and VAT.

Trade creditors

91. Identify major suppliers and review listing generally.
92. Discuss with officials reliance upon particular suppliers.
93. Do major suppliers have trading conditions including reservation of title?
94. Review availability of discounts and advantage taken of them.

Other creditors

95. Review listing including PAYE, NI, VAT, etc.
96. Summarize hire purchase creditors and capitalized leases.
97. Review accruals and potential major items not included e.g. rates, rents, wages, holiday pay, telephone etc.

Group and associate company balances

98. Review basis of valuation of investments in subsidiaries and associates.
99. Are intercompany balances agreed?
100. Consider need for provisions against amounts due by subsidiaries or associates and consequent effect on future distributions.

Bank and cash

101. Review all bank balances, reconcile to the cash book and explain large reconciling items.
102. Where bank balances are in overdraft, ensure the overdraft is within the bank facilities available at the time.
103. Consider any restrictions on withdrawals.

Borrowings

104. Borrowing powers contained in the Memorandum and Articles.
105. Main sources of finance including debentures and other entries in the register of charges.
106. Borrowing arrangements including facilities available, terms of facilities including security guarantees etc. Are the arrangements temporary or semi-permanent?
107. Ensure conditions attached to loans are not breached.
108. Discuss with officials the company's ability to meet repayments and identify necessity for rescheduling of loans if one exists.

Financial policy

109. What financial or capital commitments does the company have?
110. Does the company have a policy of renting property?
111. Have assets been sold and leased back? If so, is the rental in excess of normal market rental?
112. Details of equipment leased or bought on HP rather than being bought outright.
113. What are the relative amounts of credit allowed to customers and taken from suppliers?
114. Is maximum use made of government grants?

Share price

115. If quoted, range of share prices.
116. If unquoted, prices at which recent transactions have occurred.

Other matters

117. Discuss with company officials the existence of any contingent liabilities, capital or other commitments affecting the company (e.g. outstanding litigation).
118. Are there any post-balance sheet events which are material to an understanding of the company's accounts?
119. Carry out an analytical review and commentary on historical financial information.

Taxation

120. Review tax charges and extent of agreement with the authorities.
121. Consider any matters in dispute with the authorities.

122. To what extent has relief been obtained for leases.
123. Is the company affected by special provisions e.g. close company and assess the implications?
124. Consider group relief provisions, e.g. in the context of CGT or ACT.
125. Review potential liabilities, tax planning and tax avoidance.

REVIEW OF PROFIT FORECASTS

126. Consider the purpose of the forecast. Is it realistic or a goal?
127. Evaluate the reliability of the systems producing the forecasts.
128. Consider cost of sales, overheads, provisions. How are they accounted for?
129. Compare the accuracy of previous management accounts with actual results.
130. Is forecasting or long range planning a normal procedure for the company? If so is this forecast prepared on the usual basis?
131. Consider the involvement of senior executives in preparing the forecasts.
132. What are the principal limiting factors governing its preparation, e.g. sales, production, technology, working capital?
133. How sensitive is the forecast?
134. Are there any inherent risks in forecasting in the industry?
135. What are the assumptions underlying the forecast? Are these assumptions reasonable?
136. Compare the sales mix forecasted to that achieved in previous periods.
137. Review sales price in the current forecast and compare with present, past, and competitor's levels.
138. Review gross margins by product line.
139. Compare forecasted turnover per employee to previous period and similar companies.
140. Review external sources for future trend of prices of major raw materials in use.
141. Consider other costs such as discounts payable, warehousing costs, interest costs, rectification costs and other guarantee/warranty type costs.
142. Review inter-company trading and extent of any invested profits/losses.
143. Review the assumptions underlying any working capital forecast and in relation to past trading experience.
144. Are accounting policies used consistently?

COUNTRY RISK ANALYSIS

The investment climate

145. The geographical location of the country and its climatic conditions.
146. The geographical location of neighbours and their political stability.
147. The location of major markets.
148. The condition of the infrastructure and its future development including transport and communications.
149. Resources of the country including major minerals.
150. Extent of export of primary commodities and the impact of this on currency fluctuations.
151. Major energy sources for the country.
152. Rate of growth and number of the population.

153. What is the main language of the country and what proportion of the population speak the main language?
154. What proportion of the population is literate?
155. What type of government prevails e.g. federal, democratic, military?
156. Stability of the government and probability of a radical change.
157. Extent of significant powerful opposition groups.
158. Potential for civil unrest and/or terrorism.
159. What is the likelihood that the present or future government might expropriate or nationalize foreign assets?
160. What is the attitude towards foreign capital?
161. What alliances does the government have with other groups and countries?

The economy

162. What is the extent of government regulation and control?
163. To what extent is it likely that there will be a shift in government policies?
164. What is the rate of growth of GDP, the levels of GDP and GDP per capita, and the extent to which growth is centrally planned?
165. To what extent does the economy rely on aid support?
166. What has been the growth in capital formation, its current level and projected levels?
167. What is the rate of inflation and that anticipated in the future?
168. What is the rate of interest and projected rates?

Labour

169. What is the system for determining pay levels: free negotiation or collective bargaining?
170. To what extent are arbitration facilities available?
171. Levels of unemployment, labour costs, payroll costs, redundancy costs.
172. Availability of a social security system.
173. Availability of local skilled labour.
174. Extent of unionization.
175. Availability of profit sharing schemes.
176. Benefits to employees including holidays.
177. Attitude towards foreign owners and managers and to the training of local people.

International trade and transactions

178. Extent of trade, trading partners, membership of trading blocs, and protectionism.
179. Contribution of exports to GDP and the balance of payments.
180. Unit of currency and whether floating or fixed.
181. Extent of present, past and future currency fluctuations.
182. To what extent is there a ready market for the currency?
183. What is the normal currency for export invoicing?
184. Policy towards the repatriation of profits, dividends, capital, royalties, and interest.

The business environment

185. Extent of regulation and controls imposed by the state and self-regulatory organizations.
186. Level and availability of investment incentives to foreigners.
187. Extent of supervision imposed by the government on the banking system.
188. What is the structure and stability of the banking system?
189. Should finance be raised locally or offshore?
190. Extent of local and regional capital markets.
191. Extent of regulation imposed by company law on business enterprises.
192. What are the principal forms of enterprise and requirements for formation?
193. What books and records are required by the principal forms of enterprises?
194. What are the commercial trading practices of enterprises including attitudes towards payments and willingness and ability to pay?
195. What are the main audit and accounting requirements laid down by government, by law and by self-regulatory bodies.
196. Who imposes taxes, what are they, where are they taxed, and at what rates?
197. To what extent are deductions allowable against tax?
198. Is it possible to allocate any head office expenses to overseas subsidiaries?
199. Are there investment allowances, special industry allowances, and special tax legislation for specific industries?
200. What is the treatment of interest for tax purposes?
201. How are distributions, royalties, service fees and intercompany dividends dealt with for tax purposes?
202. Is loss relief available for tax purposes?
203. What is the treatment of tax havens?
204. Extent of tax treaties, international agreements including international transfer pricing.
205. Extent of withholding taxes and tax avoidance legislation.
206. Are there any branch taxes or is a subsidiary more favourably treated for tax purposes?
207. Is it possible to submit consolidated tax returns?
208. Are there any special tax provisions for closely-held companies?
209. Do the authorities undertake tax audits?

Cultural factors

210. What is the general attitude towards foreign managers and owners?
211. Attitude towards training by foreigners.
212. Extent of corruption, repression etc., prevalent in the country.
213. Class structure and extent of urbanization.

Selected References

GENERAL

Aharoni, Y. (1966) *The Foreign Investment Decision Process*, Boston, Mass.: Graduate School of Business Administration, Harvard University.

Armentano, D. T. (1987) 'Battling the real sources of monopoly power', *Financial Times*, 4 March.

Baird, J. (1983) 'Where Did Country Risk Analysts Go Wrong?', *Institutional Investor*, May.

Baumol, W. J. (1968) 'Entrepreneurship in Economic Theory', *American Economic Review (Papers and Proceedings)*, vol. 58, pp. 64–71.

Baxter, G. C. and Spinney, J. C. (1975) 'A Closer Look at Consolidated Financial Statement Theory', *CA Magazine*, January and February.

Bird, G. (1986) 'New Approaches to Country Risk', *Lloyds Bank Review*, October.

Blair, R. D. and Kaserman, D. L. (1985) *Antitrust Economics*, Homewood, Illinois: Richard D. Irwin.

Briloff, A. J. (1976) *Of Pools and Fools*, New York: Harper & Rowe.

Brozen, Y. (1982) *Concentration, Mergers, and Public Policy*, New York: Macmillan.

Buckley, P. J. (1981) 'The Entry Strategy of Recent European Direct Investors in the USA', *Journal of Comparative Corporate Law and Securities Regulation*, vol. 3, pp. 169–91.

Buckley, P. J. and Casson, M. (1976) *The Future of the Multinational Enterprise*, London: Macmillan and New York: Holmes-Meier.

Burton, F. N. and Inone, H. (1983) 'Country Risk Evaluation Methods: A Survey of Systems in Use', *The Banker*, January.

Calverley, J. (1985) *Country Risk Analysis*. London: Butterworths.

Casson, M. C. (1979) *Alternatives to the Multinational Enterprise*, London: Macmillan.

Catlett, G. R. and Olson, N. O. (1968) 'Accounting for Goodwill', *Accounting Research Study No. 10*, New York: AICPA.

Caves, R. E. (1971) 'International Corporations: The Industrial Economics of Foreign Investment', *Economica* (New Series) vol. 38, pp. 1–27.

Chiplin, B. and Wright, M. (1987) *The Logic of Mergers*, London: IEA.

Clark, J. J. (1985) *Business Merger and Acquisition Strategies*, Englewood Cliffs, New Jersey: Prentice-Hall.

Cooke, T. E. (1986) *Mergers and Acquisitions*, Oxford: Basil Blackwell.

Dale, R. S. (1983) 'Country Risk and Bank Regulation', *The Banker*, March.

Dunning, J. H. (1977) 'Trade, Location of Economic Activity and the Multinational Enterprise: A Search for an Eclectic Approach', in B. Ohlin et al. (eds), *The International Allocation of Economic Activity*, London: Macmillan.

Dunning, J. H. (1980) 'Towards an Eclectic Theory of International Production', *Journal of International Business Studies*, vol. 11, pp. 9–31.

Dunning, J. H. (1981) *International Production and the Multinational Enterprise*, London: George Allen & Unwin.

Dunning, J. H. (1983) 'Changes in the Structure of International Production: the Last 100 Years', in M. C. Casson (ed.), *The Growth of International Business*, London: George Allen & Unwin.

Dunning, J. H. (1985) *Multinational Enterprises, Economic Structure and International Competitiveness*, Chichester: John Wiley.

Eiteman, D. K. and Stonehill, A. I. (1986) *Multinational Business Finance Reading*, Massachusetts: Addison-Wesley.

Ensor, R. (1981)*Assessing Country Risk*, London: Euromoney.

Evans, T. G., Taylor, M. E. and Holzmann, O. (1985) *International Accounting and Reporting*, New York: Macmillan.

Feros, J. and Pengilley, W. (1984) *Business Appraisals*, Melbourne: Australian Society of Accountants.

Galbraith, J. K. (1967) *The New Industrial State*, London: Hamish Hamilton.

Giddy, Ian H. (1978) 'The Demise of the Product Cycle Model in International Business Theory', *Columbia Journal of World Business*, vol. 13, pp. 90–7.

Giddy, I. H. and Young, S. (1982) 'Conventional Theory and Unconventional Multinationals: Do New Forms of Multinational Enterprise Require New Theories?', in A. M. Rugman (ed.), *New Theories of the Multinational Enterprise*, Beckenham, Kent: Croom Helm, pp. 55–78.

Goldberg, W. H. (1983) *Mergers – Motives, Modes, Methods*. Aldershot: Gower.

Gutmann, P. (1980) 'Assessing Country Risk', *National Westminster Bank Quarterly Review*, May.

Hagg, C. (1984) 'The OECD Guidelines for Multinational Enterprises. A Critical Analysis', *Journal of Business Ethics*.

Hogue, W. D. (1967) 'The Foreign Investment Decision-Making Process', *Association for Education in International Business Proceedings*, 29 December.

Holzer, H. P. et al. (1984) *International Accounting*, New York: Harper & Rowe.

Hopt, K. J. (ed.) (1982) *European Merger Control*, Berlin: Walter de Gruyter.

Hoog, H., Kaplan, R. S. and Mandelker, G. (1978) 'Pooling *vs* Purchase. The Effects of Accounting for Mergers on Stock Prices', *The Accounting Review*, January.

Hymer, S. H. (1976) *The International Operations of National Firms*. Lexington, Mass: Lexington Books.

Keenan, M. and White, L. J. (1982) *Mergers and Acquisitions*, Lexington: Lexington Books.

Kindleberger, C. P. (1969) *American Business Abroad*, New Haven: Yale University Press.

Krayenbuehl, T. E. (1983) 'How Country Risk Should be Monitored', *The Banker*, May.

Krayenbuehl, T. E. (1985) *Country Risk*, Cambridge: Woodhead-Faulkner.

Lamers, E. A. A. M. (1976) *Joint Venture between Yugoslav and Foreign Enterprises*, Tilburg: Tilburg University Press.

Layton, C. (1971) *Cross Frontier Mergers in Europe*. Bath: Bath University Press.

Lindgren, U. (1982) *Foreign Acquisitions. Management of the Integration Process*. Stockholm: IBB/EFI.

Marris, R. (1964) *The Economic Theory of Managerial Capitalism*, London: Macmillan.

Morris, J. M. (1984) *Acquisitions, Divestitives and Corporate Joint Ventures*. New York: John Wiley.

Mueller, D. (ed.) (1980) *The Determinants and Effects of Mergers – An International Comparison*. Cambridge, Massachusetts/Oelgeschlager, Gunn and Hain.

Newbould, G. D. and Luffman, G. A. (1978) *Successful Business Policies*, Farnborough: Gower.

Nobes, C. W. and Parker, R. H. (1985) *Comparative International Accounting*, Oxford: Philip Allan.

OECD (1984) *Merger Policies and Recent Trends in Mergers*, Paris: OECD.

O'Brien, D. P. and Swann, D. (1968) *Information Agreements, Competition and Efficiency*, London: Macmillan.

Oldham, K. M. (1987) *Accounting Systems and Practice in Europe*, Aldershot: Gower.

Overholt, W. H. (1983) *Political Risk, How to Assess, Quantify and Monitor it*, London: Euromoney.

Prais, S. J. (1981) *The Evolution of Giant Firms in Britain*, Cambridge: Cambridge University Press.

Rodriguez, R. M. and Carter, E. E. (1984) *International Financial Management*, Engelwood Cliffs, New Jersey: Prentice-Hall.

Rowe, F. M. (1980) 'Antitrust Aspects of European Acquisitions', *Law and Policy in International Business*.

Rugman, A. M. (1976) 'Risk Reduction by International Diversification', *Journal of International Business Studies*, vol. 7, pp. 75–80.

Rugman, A. M. (1977) 'International Diversification by Financial and Direct Investment', *Journal of Economics and Business*, vol. 30.

Rugman, A. M. (1981) *Inside the Multinationals*, London: Croom Helm.

Rugman, A. M. (ed.) (1982) *New Theories of the Multinational Enterprise*, London: Croom Helm.

Rummel, R. J. and Heenan, D. A. (1978) 'How Multinational Analyse Political Risk', *Harvard Business Review*, January/February.

Shapiro, A. C. (1986) *'Multinational Financial Management'*, Boston: Allyn & Bacon.

Stopford, J. M. and Dunning, J. H. (1983) *Multinationals: Company Performance and Global Trends*, London: Macmillan.

Stopford, J. M. and Turner, L. (1985) *Britain and the Multinationals*. Chichester: John Wiley.

Vernon, R. (1966) 'International Investment and International Trade in the Product Cycle', *Quarterly Journal of Economics*, vol. 80, pp. 190–207.

Vernon, R. (1974) 'The Location of Economic Activity', in J. H. Dunning (ed.), *Economic Analysis and the Multinational Enterprise*, London: George Allen and Unwin.

Vernon, R. (1977) *Storm over the Multinationals: The Real Issue*, London: Macmillan.

Vernon, R. (1979) 'The Product Cycle Hypothesis in a New International Environment', *Oxford Bulletin of Economics and Statistics*, vol. 41, pp. 255–67.

Webb, M. (1971) *How to Acquire a Company*, Farnborough: Gower.

Wine, H. (1983) *Buying and Selling Private Companies and Businesses*, London: Butterworths.

AUSTRALIA

Bannerman, R. H. (1984) 'The Debate on the Exposure Draft Bill to amend the Trade Practices Act', Unpublished paper given at Monash University, 29 March.

Baxt, R. (1983) 'Reform of the Takeover Code?', *Companies and Securities Law Journal*, November.

Bruce, R., McKern, B. and Pollard, I. (1986) *Handbook of Australian Corporate Finance*, Sydney: Butterworths.

CCH (1986) *Australian Master Tax Guide*, Sydney: CCH.

Department of the Treasury (1986) *Australia's Foreign Investment Policy. A Guide for Investors*, Canberra: Australian Government Publishing Service.

Deutsch, R. L. (1983) 'Takeovers and the Scope of the Companies (Acquisition of Shares) (NSW) Code, *Australian Business Law Review*, June.

Dodd, P. R. (1976) 'Company Takeovers and the Australian Equity Market', *Australian Journal of Management*.

Foreign Investment Review Board (1986) *Annual Report 1984–5*, Canberra: Australian Government Publishing Service.

Fox, L. (1981) *Multinationals Take Over Australia*, Sydney: APCOL.

Gorr, L. (1982) 'Taxation Implications of Amalgamations, Takeovers and Reorganizations', *Australian Accountant*, March.

Harrison, F. L. (1975) 'Joint Ventures and the Trade Practices Act 1974: The American Approach and The Applicability to Australia', *Australian Business Law Review*.

Hoggett, J. R. and Leo, K. J. (1984) *Company Accounting in Australia*, Brisbane: John Wiley.

Hone, G. W. (1983) 'Income Taxation Implications of Corporate Takeovers', *Australian Law Review*.

Leo, K. (1983) 'The Need to Distinguish Requisitions and Mergers', *Chartered Accountant in Australia*.

Ma, R. and Parker, R. H. (1983) *Consolidation Accounting in Australia*, Melbourne: Longman Cheshire.

McGregor, W. J. (1985) 'New ASRB Approved Accounting Standards – Legal Backing for the Profession's Standards', *Australian Accountant,* December.

Parker, R. H. (1986) '*Australian Standards and the Law: An Australian Experiment*', Paper presented to the annual conference of the British Accounting Association.

Pengilley, W. (1980) 'Building an Australian enterprise based on overseas technology – antitrust considerations', *The Antitrust Bulletin*, Winter.

Renton, N. E. (1984) 'Company takeovers: some reforms needed', *National Australia Bank Monthly Survey*, Parts I and II.

Reserve Bank of Australia (1985) 'Company Finance', *Bulletin Supplement*, March.

Standish, P. E. M. (1972) *Australian Financial Reporting*, Accountancy Research Study No. 2, Canberra: Accounting and Auditing Research Committee.

CANADA

CICA (1986) *Financial Reporting in Canada*, Toronto: The Canadian Institute of Chartered Accountants.

CICA (updated) The Canadian Institute of Chartered Accountants, Toronto: CICA.

Iacobucci, F., Pilkington, M. L. and Prichard, J. R. S. (1977) *Canadian Business Corporations*, Agincourt, Ontario: Canada Law Book.

Nagy, P. and Scott, D. (1982) 'What economic forces have led to the recent takeover binge?', *Business Quarterly*.

Ontario Securities Commission (1983) Report of the Committee to Review the Provisions and the Securities Act (Ontario) Relating to Take-Over Bids and Issuer Bids.

Royal Bank of Canada (1986) *Canadian Business Basics*.

Royal Bank of Canada (1986) *Investment Canada*.

Securities Industry Committee (1983) *The Regulation of Take-over Bids in Canada: Premium Private Agreement Transactions*.

Toronto Stock Exchange (1979) *Memorandum, Current Procedure in Take-over Bids, Issuer Bids and Insider Bids Through the Facilities of the Stock Exchange*.

FEDERAL REPUBLIC OF GERMANY

Arthur Young International (updated) *World Business Report – FRG*.

Bechtold (1982) *Das neue Kartellrecht*, München: C. H.Becksche Verlagsbuchhandlung.

Beeny, J. H. (1975) *European Financial Reporting: West Germany*, London: ICAEW.

Forrester, Goren and Ilgen (1975) *The German Civil Code*, New York: Elsevier–North-Holland Publishing.

Green and Forrester (1978) *The German Commercial Code*, New York: Elsevier–North-Holland Publishing.

Immenga and Mestmäcker (1981) *GWB, Gesetz gegen Wettbewerbsbeschränkungen*, München: C. H. Becksche Verlagsbuchhandlung.

Langen, Niederleithinger, Ritter and Schmidt (1982) *Kommentar zum Kartellgesetz*, Nenwied, Darmstadt: Hermann Luchterhand Verlag.

Mueller, R. and Galbraith, E. G. (1976) *The German Stock Corporation Law*, Frankfurt: Fritz Knapp Berlag.

Mueller, R. and Schneider (1981) *The German Antitrust Law*, Frankfurt: Frtiz Knapp Verlag.

Mueller, R., Miester and Heidenhain (1981) *The German Gmbh Law*, Frankfurt: Fritz Knapp Verlag.

Schmidt and Ludwig (1986) *Einkommentenergesetz Kommentar*, München: C. H. Becksche Verlagsbuchhandlung.

Schneider and Kingsman (1976) *The German Codetermination Act of 1976*, Frankfurt: Fritz Knapp Verlag.

Schneider, Hellwig and Kingsman (1978) *The German Banking System*, Frankfurt: Fritz Knapp Verlag.

Widmann, S. and Mayer, R. (1986) *Unwandlungsrecht*, Bonn: Stollfuss Verlag.

Wysock, K. von (1984) 'The Fourth Directive and Germany', in S. J. Gray and A. G. Coenenberg (eds) (1984), *EEC Accounting Harmonisation. Implementation and Impact of the Fourth Directive*, Amsterdam: North-Holland Publishing.

FRANCE

Arthur Young International (updated) *World Business Report – France*.

BDA–CCAS–HSD (Arthur Young International), (1987) *L'Information financière en 1987*, Paris: Clet.

Beeny, J. (1976) *European Financial Reporting II: France*, London: ICAEW.
Berger, P. and Laxtagne, J. A. (1986) *La transmission des entreprises*, Nouvelles Editions Fiduciaries.
Bied-Charreton, F. and Raffegeau, J. (1987) *Guide pratique du financement des entreprises*, Francis Lefebvre.
Calmes-Meille, D., Charveriat, A. and Meille, B. (1986) *Le Redressement Judiciarie*, Francis Lefebvre.
INSEE et CEPME (1987) *Statistiques mensuelles de créations d'entreprises*.
Pham, D. (1984) 'A true and fair view: a French perspective', in S. J. Gray and A. G. Coenenberg, eds. (1984) *EEC Accounting Harmonisation: Implementation and Impact of the Fourth Directive*, Amsterdam: North-Holland.

ITALY

Arthur Young (1981) *Establishing a Business in Italy*.
Arthur Young International (updated) *World Business Report – Italy*.
Banca Nazionale del Lavoro (annual) *A Guide for Foreign Investors in Italy*.
Beltramo, M., Longo, G. E. and Merryman, J. H. (1978) *The Italian Civil Code*, translated, New York: Oceana Publications.
Caratozzolo, M. (1984) *I bilanci di fusione della società incorporante e incorporata: Aspetti technici & giuridici*.
Consiglio Nazionale dei Dottori Commercialisti (updated) *Principi & Raccomandazioni per la redazione, revisione & certificazione dei bilanci*.
Credito Italiano (annual) *Review of Economic Conditions in Italy*. Milan: Credito Italiano.
IASM (periodic updates) *Regulations Governing Investments and Incentives in the Mezzogiorno*, Rome: IASM.
Templeman, D. C. (1981) *The Italian Economy*, Rome.

JAPAN

Allen, A. C. (1981) *The Japanese Economy*, London: Weidenfeld and Nicolson.
Arthur Young International (1982) *World Business Reports: Japan*, January.
Ballon, R. J., Tomita, I. and Usami, H. (1976) *Financial Reporting in Japan*, Tokyo: Kodansha International.
Campbell, L. (1983) 'Current Accounting Practices in Japan', *Accountant's Magazine*, August.
Campbell, L. (1985) 'Financial Reporting in Japan', in C. W. Nobes and R. H. Parker (eds) *Comparative International Accounting*, London: Philip Allan Publishers.
Fujita, Y. (1986) 'Accounting and Reporting in Japan', *Harmonisation of Accounting Standards: Achievements and Prospects*, OECD.
Fujita, Y. (1966) 'The Evolution of Financial Reporting in Japan', *The International Journal of Accounting and Research*, Fall.
Gomi, Y. (1981) *Guide to Japanese Taxes 1981–82*. Zaikei Shoho Sha.
Iino, T. (1967) 'Accounting Principles and Contemporary Legal Action in Japan', *The International Journal of Accounting Education and Research*, Spring.
Iino, T. and Inouye, R. (1984) 'Financial Accounting and Reporting in Japan', in H. Peter Holzer (ed.) *International Accounting*, New York: Harper and Row.
The Economic Research Institution of Daiwa Securities Ltd (1986) Keiei Senryaku to Shiteno Gappei. [Merger as Business Strategy], Shoji Homu, Kenkyukai.

The Japanese Institute of Certififed Public Accounts (1982) *Corporate Disclosure in Japan: Overview*, July.
The Japanese Institute of Certified Public Accounts (1984) *Corporation Disclosure in Japan: Reporting*, July.
Vogel, E. F. (1979) *Japan as Number One: Lessons for America*, Harvard University Press.
Watson, T. S. (1982) 'Accounting in Japan: Regulation and Practice', *Journal of Accountancy*, August.

NETHERLANDS

Ashton, R. K. (1981) *Use and Extent of Replacement Value Accounting in the Netherlands*, London: ICAEW.
Beeny, J. and Chastney, J. (1978) *European Financial Reporting: The Netherlands*, London: ICAEW.
Bindenga, A. J. (1981) 'Het rapporteren over vermogen en resultaat van een economishe eenheid na een fusie of overname?', *Maandblad voor Accountancy en Bedrijfsuishoudkunde*, November.
Council for Annual Reporting (1985) *Netherlands Accounting Guidelines*, Amsterdam.
Klassen, J. (1980) 'An accounting court: the impact of the Enterprise Chamber of financial reporting in the Netherlands', *Accounting Review*, April.
Krekel, N. R. A., van der Woerd, T. G. and Wouterse, J. J. (1967) *Ontwikkeling, Samenherking, fusie*, Brussels: Samson, Alphen ald Rija.
Lorenz, C. (1986) 'Overnames: 50% Kans op succes', *Financial Economisch Magazine*, January.
Ministerie van Economische Zaken (1986) *Vaststellingbegroting van de uitgaven voor Let jaar*.
Moret, and Limperg (1984) *New Dutch Legislation on Annual Reports*, Rotterdam.
Muis, J. (1975) 'Current value accounting in the Netherlands: Fact or Fiction?', *Accountant's Magazine*, November.
Schuurman and Jorelens, (1984) *Wet Financiete Betrekkingen Buitenland Zwolle: Tjeenk Willink*.
Von der Heijden, Z. J. J. and van der Grinten, W. C. L. (1984) *Handboek voor de Naamloze en Busloten Vennootschap*, Zwolle: Tjeenk Willink.

SWEDEN

Boman, R. (1986) *Securities Markets in Europe*, Stockholm: EAAP/EFFAS.
Cooke, T. E. (1985) 'A Survey of the Accounts of Some Major Swedish International Companies', *The Investment Analyst*, April.
Cooke, T. E. (forthcoming) *Financial Reporting in Sweden*, London: ICAEW.
Dahlman, F. (1976) 'Business Operations and Repatriation of Earnings', *Tax Management International Journal*.
FAR (1977; 1978; 1979; 1981; 1984) *Survey of Accounting Practices*, Stockholm: FAR.
FAR (1983) *Swedish Accounting and Auditing. The Main Laws and Standards*, Stockholm: FAR.
FAR (1985) *Samlings-Volym*, Stockholm: FAR.
FAR/Swedish Business Report (1987) *Key to Understanding Swedish Financial Statements*. Stockholm: *Affärsvarldon*.

Fridman, B. (1986) 'Goal Conflicts in Developing Accounting Standards in Small Countries – The Swedish Case'. *EAA Newsletter*.
Grosstopf, G. (1985) *The Swedish Tax System*, Stockholm: Hagström and Sillen.
Johansson, S. E. and Ostman, L. (1985) 'Atervandsgraud for nya redurisnings – standards', *Balans*, 4.
Lindgren, U. (1982) *Foreign Acquisitions – Management of the Integration Process*,
Rundfelt, R. (1986) 'Standard Setting the Swedish Way', *International Accounting Bulletin*.
SASP (1985–7) *The Swedish Stock Market Newsletter*, Stockholm: SASP.
Stockholm Stock Exchange (1984) *Report on the Activities of the Stockholm Stock Exchange*, Stockholm: Stockholm Stock Exchange.
Zeff, S. A. and Johansson, S.-E. (1984) 'The Curious Accounting Treatment of the Swedish Government Loan to Uddeholm', *The Accounting Review*, Vol. LIX, No. 2.

UNITED KINGDOM

Barnes, P. (1978) 'The effect of a merger on the share price of the attacker', *Accounting and Business Research*, Summer.
Biggadike, R. (1979) 'The risk business of diversification', *Harvard Business Review*, May–June.
Buckley, A. (1972) 'A profile of industrial acquisitions in 1971', *Accounting and Business Research*, Autumn.
Chiplin, B. and Wright, M. (1987) 'The Logic of Mergers', *Hobart Paper 107*, London: IEA.
Coffee, J., Lowenstein, L. and Rose-Ackerman, S. (eds) (1987) *Takeovers and Contests for Corporate Control*, Oxford: Oxford University Press.
Cooke, T. E. (1984) 'The Seventh Directive – an accountant's perspective?', *European Law Review*, June.
Cooke, T. E. (1986) *Mergers and Acquisitions*, Oxford: Basil Blackwell.
Cooke, T.E. and Whittaker, J. (1984) 'Extraordinary items, deferred taxation and earnings per share', *Investment Analyst*, July.
Cowling, K. et al. (1980) *Mergers and Economic Performance*, Cambridge: Cambridge University Press.
Coyne, J. and Wright, M. (eds) (1986) *Divestment and Strategic Change*, Oxford: Philip Allan.
Dodd, P. (1980) 'Company takeovers and the Australian equity market', *Australian Journal of Management*.
Firth, M. (1976) *Share Prices and Mergers*, Aldershot: Gower.
Firth, M. (1980) 'Takeovers, Shareholder Returns and the Theory of the Firm', *Quarterly Journal of Economics, No. 2*, March.
Franks, J. R. and Harris, R. S. (1986) 'Shareholder Wealth Effects of Corporate Takeovers: the UK Experience 1955–85', *LBS Working Paper*, June.
Franks, J. R., Broyles, J. E. and Hecht, M. J. (1977) 'An Industry Study of the Profitability of Mergers in the United Kingdom', *Journal of Finance, No. 5*, December.
Jensen, M. C. and Ruback, R. S. (1983) 'The Market for Corporate Control: The Evidence', *Journal of Financial Economics*.
Keown, A. J. and Pinkerton, J. M. (1981) 'Merger Announcements and Insider Trading Activity: An Empirical Investigation', *Journal of Finance*, September.

Kitching, J. (1967) 'Why do Mergers Miscarry?', *Harvard Business Review*, November–December.

Kitching, J. (1974) 'Why acquisitions are abortive?', *Management Today*, November.

Knoeber, C. R. (1986) 'Golden Parachutes, Shark Repellants and Hostile Tender Offers', *American Economic Review*, March.

Lofthouse, S. (1983) 'UK Merger Policy Should be made Tougher', *Journal of General Management*, Spring.

Marris, R. (1964) *The Economic Theory of Managerial Capitalism*, London: Macmillan.

Meeks, G. (1977) *Disappointing Marriage: A Study of the Gains from Merger*, Cambridge: Cambridge University Press.

Newbould, G. D. (1970) *Management and Merger Activity*, Liverpool: Guthstead.

Pickering, J. F. (1980) 'The Implementation of British Competition Policy on Mergers', *European Competition Law Review*.

Prais, S. J. (1976) *The Evolution of Giant Firms in Britain* (rev. edn. 1981), Cambridge: Cambridge University Press.

Prais, S. J. (1981) *The Evolution of Giant Firms in Britain*, Cambridge: Cambridge University Press.

Singh, A. (1971) *Takeovers: Their Relevance to the Stock Market and the Theory of the Firm*, Cambridge: Cambridge University Press.

Steiner, P. O. (1975) *Mergers: Motives, Effects, Control*, Ann Arbor: University of Michigan Press.

Utton, M. A. (1974) 'On Measuring the Effects of Industrial Mergers', *Scottish Journal of Political Economy*, February.

Wright, M. and Coyne, J. (1986) *Management Buy-outs*, Oxford: Philip Allan.

UNITED STATES

Arthur Young International (updated) *World Business Reports – US*.

Baker, H. K., Miller, T. O. and Ramsperger, B. J. (1981) 'An Inside Look at Corporate Mergers and Acquisitions', *MSU Business Topics*, Winter.

Bobchick, R. (1982) 'The Case for Facilitating Competing Tender Offers?', 95 *Harvard Law Review* 1028.

Booker, J. A. and Jarnagin, W. D. (1979) *Financial Accounting Standards – Explanation and Analysis*, Chicago: CCH.

Buckley, J. W., Buckley, M. H. and Plank, T. M. (1980) *SEC Accounting*, New York: John Wiley.

CCH (1986) *US Master Tax Guide*, Chicago: CCH.

De Angelo, H. and Rice, E. M. (1983) 'Anti-takeover Charter Amendments and Stockholder Wealth', *Journal of Financial Economics*, No. 11.

Ginsburg, M. D. (1983) 'Taxing Corporate Acquisitions', *Tax Law Review*.

Glennie, J. R. (1984) 'New Guidelines for Mergers', *Business* (Atlanta) January/March.

Neale, A. D. and Goyder, D. G. (1980) *The Antitrust Laws of the USA*, Cambridge: Cambridge University Press.

Previts, G. J. (1981) *The Development of SEC Accounting*. Reading, Massachusetts: Addison-Wesley.

ARGENTINA

Bomchil, M. (1983) 'Foreign Investment Regime in Argentina', *Brooklyn Journal of International Law*, 27.

Cabanellas, G. and Etzrodt, M. (1983) 'The New Argentina Antitrust Law', 17 *Journal of World Trade*, 34.

Dahl, E. (1982) 'Argentina's System of Foreign Investments', 6 *Fordham International Law Journal*, 33.

McKinnis, G. L. (1978) 'The Argentina Foreign Investment Law of 1976', 17 *Columbia Journal of International Law*, 357.

BRAZIL

Pinheiro, J. H. (1980) 'Defensive measures against company take-overs – Brazil', 8 *International Business Lawyer*, 135.

Index